Enterprise Web Development

Yakov Fain, Victor Rasputnis, Anatole Tartakovsky, and Viktor Gamov

Beijing · Cambridge · Farnham · Köln · Sebastopol · Tokyo

Enterprise Web Development

by Yakov Fain, Victor Rasputnis, Anatole Tartakovsky, and Viktor Gamov

Printed in the United States of America.

Published by O'Reilly Media, Inc., 1005 Gravenstein Highway North, Sebastopol, CA 95472.

O'Reilly books may be purchased for educational, business, or sales promotional use. Online editions are also available for most titles (*http://my.safaribooksonline.com*). For more information, contact our corporate/institutional sales department: 800-998-9938 or *corporate@oreilly.com*.

Editors: Mary Treseler and Brian Anderson
Production Editor: Melanie Yarbrough
Copyeditor: Sharon Wilkey
Proofreader: Kim Cofer

Indexer: Judith McConville
Cover Designer: Karen Montgomery
Interior Designer: David Futato
Illustrator: Rebecca Demarest

June 2014:   First Edition

Revision History for the First Edition:

2014-06-30:   First release

See *http://oreilly.com/catalog/errata.csp?isbn=9781449356811* for release details.

Nutshell Handbook, the Nutshell Handbook logo, and the O'Reilly logo are registered trademarks of O'Reilly Media, Inc. *Enterprise Web Development*, the cover image of a Roseate Spoonbill, and related trade dress are trademarks of O'Reilly Media, Inc.

Many of the designations used by manufacturers and sellers to distinguish their products are claimed as trademarks. Where those designations appear in this book, and O'Reilly Media, Inc. was aware of a trademark claim, the designations have been printed in caps or initial caps.

While every precaution has been taken in the preparation of this book, the publisher and authors assume no responsibility for errors or omissions, or for damages resulting from the use of the information contained herein.

ISBN: 978-1-449-35681-1

[LSI]

Preface

This book will help web application developers and software architects pick the right strategy for developing cross-platform applications that run on a variety of desktop computers as well as mobile devices. The primary audience is developers from a large organization who need to learn how to develop web applications using the HTML5 stack.

What's an Enterprise Application?

This book has the word *enterprise* in its title, and we'll explain what we consider to be *enterprise applications* by giving you some examples. Creating a web application that processes orders is not the same as creating a website to publish blogs. Enterprise applications require company-specific workflows, which usually need to be integrated with various internal systems, data sources, and processes.

Google Docs is not an enterprise web application. But Google Search Appliance, which integrates search operations with company documents, databases, processes, and tickets, and provides collaboration is: it integrates the consumer-workforce front office with what the company does (back office).

Google Maps is not an enterprise application. But Google Maps integrated with a company site used by insurance agents to plan their daily route, create scheduling, perform address verification, and use geocoding is.

Just using a web application in a business doesn't make it an enterprise web application. If you take Gmail as is, it won't be an enterprise application until you integrate it into another process of your business.

Is an online game an enterprise application? It depends on the game. A multiplayer online roulette game hooked up to a payment system and maintaining users' accounts is an enterprise web application. But playing Sudoku online doesn't feel too enterprisey.

How about a dating website? If the site just offers an ability to display singles, it's just a publishing site because there is not much of a business there. Can you turn a dating website into an enterprise application? It's possible.

Some people will argue that an enterprise application must support multiple users and a high data load, include data grids and dashboards, be scalable, have business and persistence layers, offer professional support, and more. This is correct, but we don't believe that a web application should do all this to qualify for the adjective *enterprise*.

Let's create a simple definition of an enterprise web application:

An enterprise web application is one that helps an organization run its business online.

Why the Authors Wrote This Book

The authors of this book have 90 years of combined experience in developing enterprise applications. During all these years, we've been facing the same challenges regardless of which programming language we use:

- How to make the application code base maintainable
- How to make the application responsive by modularizing its code base
- How to minimize the number of production issues by applying proper testing at earlier stages of the project life cycle
- How to design a UI that looks good and is convenient for users
- Which frameworks or libraries to pick
- Which design patterns to apply in coding

This list can be easily extended. Ten years ago, we were developing UIs mainly in Java; five years ago, we used Adobe Flex; today, we use HTML5-related technologies. This book shares with you our understanding of how to approach these challenges in HTML5.

Who This Book Is For

Web application development with HTML5 includes HTML, JavaScript, CSS, and dozens of JavaScript frameworks. The main goal of this book is to give you a hands-on overview of developing web applications that can be run on a variety of devices—desktops, tablets, and smartphones. We expect you to have some experience with any programming language. Knowledge of basic HTML is also required. Understanding the principles of object-oriented programming would be helpful, too.

This book is intended for software developers, team leaders, and web application architects who want to learn the following:

- The interactive live pie chart is something that many modern enterprise dashboards include.
- Clicking the Table tab (right next to the Chart tab) shows the same donation stats in a grid (that one is grayish).
- Integration with the mapping API allows you to visually present the locations of important events for this business or nonprofit organization.
- Under the hood, this pretty window will use the high-speed, full-duplex communication protocol WebSocket.

As a matter of fact, the company that employs the authors of this book has a customer that is a nonprofit organization that is in the business of helping people fighting a certain disease. That application has two parts: consumer-facing and back-office. The former looks more colorful, whereas the latter has more gray grids indeed. Both parts process the same data, and this organization can't operate if you remove either of these parts.

Would these features make Save The Child an enterprise web application? Yes, because it can help our imaginary nonprofit organization run its business: collecting donations for sick kids. Would you rather see a fully functioning Wall Street trading system? Maybe. But this book and our sample application incorporate all software components that you'd need to use for developing a financial application.

How We Are Going to Build This App

Instead of presenting unrelated code samples, we decided to develop multiple versions of the same web application, built with different libraries, frameworks, and techniques. This approach allows you to compare apples to apples and to make an educated decision about which approach best fits your needs.

First, we'll show how to build this application in pure HTML/JavaScript. Then, we'll rewrite it using the jQuery library, and then with the Ext JS framework. Users will be able to see where different charity events are being run (via Google Maps integration). The page will integrate a video player and display a chart with stats on donors by geographical location. One of the versions shows how to modularize the application; this is a must for any enterprise system. Another version shows how to use WebSocket technology to illustrate the server-side data push while adding an auction to this web application. The final chapters of the book show various ways of building different versions of the same Save The Child application to run on mobile devices (responsive design, jQuery Mobile, Sencha Touch, and PhoneGap). We believe that this application will help you to compare all these approaches and select those that fit your objectives.

The Goals of the Book

First, we want to say what's not the goal of this book: we are not planning to convince you that developing a cross-platform web application is the right strategy for you. Don't be surprised if, after reading this book, you decide that developing applications in HTML5 is not the right approach for the tasks you have at hand. This book should help decision makers pick the right strategy for developing cross-platform applications that run on a variety of desktop computers as well as mobile devices.

Technologies Used in This Book

This is an HTML5 book, and the main programming language used here is JavaScript. We use HTML and CSS, too. Most JavaScript development is done using various libraries and frameworks. The difference between a *library* and a *framework* is that the former does not dictate how to structure the code of your application; a library simply offers a set of components that will spare you from writing lots of manual code. The goal of some frameworks is to help developers test their applications. The goal of other frameworks is just to split the application into separate modules. There are tools just for building, packaging, and running JavaScript applications. Although many of the frameworks and tools are mentioned in this book, the main technologies/libraries/tools/techniques/protocols used in this book are listed here:

- Balsamiq Mockups
- Modernizr
- jQuery
- jQuery Mobile
- Ext JS
- Sencha Touch
- RequireJS
- Jasmine
- Clear Data Builder
- WebSocket
- PhoneGap
- Grunt
- Bower
- WebStorm IDE
- Eclipse IDE

Although you can write your programs in any text editor, using specialized integrated development environments (IDEs) is more productive, and we'll use the Aptana Studio IDE by Appcelerator and the WebStorm IDE by JetBrains.

How the Book Is Organized

Even though you may decide not to read some of the chapters, we still recommend that you to skim through them. If you're not familiar with JavaScript, start from the online bonus chapter (*http://bit.ly/1iJO41S*).

Chapters 1 and 2 are must reads; if you can't read JavaScript code or are not familiar with CSS, Ajax, or JSON, the rest of the book will be difficult to understand. On the other hand, if you're not planning to use, say, the Ext JS framework, you can just skim through Chapter 4. Following is a brief book outline.

The Preface includes a brief discussion of the difference between enterprise web applications and websites. It also touches on the evolution of HTML.

Chapter 1 describes the process of mocking up the application Save The Child, which will solicit donations to children, embed a video player, integrate with Google Maps, and eventually feature an online auction. We show you how to gradually build all the functionality of this web application while explaining each step of the way. By the end of this chapter, we'll have the web design and the first prototype of the Save The Child application written using just HTML, JavaScript, and CSS.

Chapter 2 is about bringing external data to web browsers by making asynchronous calls to a server. The code from the previous chapter uses only hardcoded data. Now it's time to learn how to make asynchronous server calls by using Ajax techniques and consume the data in JSON format. The Save The Child application will start requesting the data from the external sources and sending them the JSON-formatted data.

Chapter 3 shows how to use a popular jQuery library to lower the amount of manual coding in the Save The Child application. First, we introduce the jQuery Core library, and then rebuild our Save The Child application with it. In the real world, developers often increase their productivity by using JavaScript libraries and frameworks.

Chapter 4 is a mini tutorial of a comprehensive JavaScript framework called Ext JS. This is one of the most feature-complete frameworks available on the market. Sencha, the company behind Ext JS, has managed to extend JavaScript to make its syntax closer to classical object-oriented languages. Sencha also developed an extensive library of the UI components. Expect to see another rewrite of the Save The Child application here.

Chapter 5 is a review of productivity tools (including npm, Grunt, Bower, Yeoman, and CDB) used by enterprise developers. It's about using build tools, working with code generators, and managing dependencies (a typical enterprise application uses various software that needs to work in harmony).

Chapter 6 explains how to modularize large applications. Reducing startup latency and implementing lazy loading of certain parts of the application are the main reasons for modularization. We give you an example of how to build modularized web applications that won't bring large, monolithic code to the client's machine, but rather loads the code on an as-needed basis. You'll also see how to organize the data exchange between programming modules in a loosely coupled fashion. The Save The Child application is rewritten with the RequireJS framework, which will load modules on demand rather than the entire application.

Chapter 7 is dedicated to test-driven development with JavaScript. To shorten the development cycle of your web application, you need to start testing it in the early stages of the project. It seems obvious, but many enterprise IT organizations haven't adopted agile testing methodologies, which costs them dearly. JavaScript is dynamically typed interpreted language—there is no compiler to help identify errors as it's done in compiled languages like Java. This means that a lot more time should be allocated for testing JavaScript web applications. We cover the basics of testing and introduce you to some of the popular testing frameworks for JavaScript applications. Finally, you'll see how to test the Save The Child application with the Jasmine framework.

Chapter 8 shows how to substantially speed up interactions between the client and the server by using the WebSocket protocol introduced in HTML5. HTTP adds a lot of overhead for every request and response object that serve as wrappers for the data. You'll see how to introduce a WebSocket-based online auction to the new version of our Save The Child application. This is what Ian Hickson, the HTML5 spec editor from Google, said about why the WebSocket protocol is important:

> Reducing kilobytes of data to 2 bytes is more than a little more byte efficient, and reducing latency from 150 ms (TCP round-trip to set up the connection plus a packet for the message) to 50 ms (just the packet for the message) is far more than marginal. In fact, these two factors alone are enough to make WebSocket seriously interesting to Google.

Chapter 9 is a brief introduction to web application security. You'll learn about vulnerabilities of web applications and will get references to recommendations on how to protect your application from attackers. This chapter concludes with some of the application-specific security considerations (like regulatory compliance) that your business customers can't ignore.

Chapter 10 opens up a discussion of how to approach creating web applications that should run not only on desktops, but also on mobile devices. In this chapter, you become familiar with the principles of responsive design, which allow you to have a single code base that will be flexible enough to render a UI that looks good on large and small screens. You'll see the power of CSS *media queries* that automatically reallocate UI components based on screen width of the device on which the website is being viewed. The new version of the Save The Child application will demonstrate how to go about responsive design.

Chapter 11 introduces you to jQuery Mobile—a library that was specifically created for developing mobile web applications. But main principles implemented in the larger jQuery library remain in place, and studying the materials from Chapter 3 is a prerequisite for understanding this chapter. Then you'll create the mobile version of the Save The Child application with jQuery Mobile.

Chapter 12 is about a little brother of Ext JS—Sencha Touch. This framework was developed for mobile devices, and you'll need to read Chapter 6 in order to understand the materials from this one. As usual, we develop another variation of the mobile version of the Save The Child application with Sencha Touch.

Chapter 13 shows how you can create hybrid mobile applications, which are written with HTML/JavaScript/CSS but can use the native API of the mobile devices. Hybrids are packaged as native mobile applications and can be submitted to popular online app stores or marketplaces the same way as if they were written in the programming language native for the mobile platform in question. This chapter illustrates how to access the camera of a mobile device by using the PhoneGap framework.

The bonus online chapter is an introduction to programming with JavaScript. In about 60 pages, we cover the main aspects of this language. No matter what framework you choose, a working knowledge of JavaScript is required.

Appendix A is a brief overview of selected APIs from the HTML5 specification. They are supported by all modern web browsers. We find these APIs important and useful for many web applications. The following APIs are reviewed:

- Web Messaging
- Web Workers
- Application Cache
- Local Storage
- Indexed Database
- History API

Appendix B is a brief discussion of the IDEs that are being used for HTML5 development in general and in this book in particular.

Conventions Used in This Book

The following typographical conventions are used in this book:

Italic
> Indicates new terms, URLs, email addresses, filenames, and file extensions.

`Constant width`
> Used for program listings, as well as within paragraphs to refer to program elements such as variable or function names, databases, data types, environment variables, statements, and keywords.

`Constant width bold`
> Shows commands or other text that should be typed literally by the user.

`Constant width italic`
> Shows text that should be replaced with user-supplied values or by values determined by context.

This element signifies a tip or suggestion.

This element signifies a general note.

This element indicates a warning or caution.

The Source Code for the Examples

The source code for all versions of the Save The Child application are available for download from O'Reilly at the book's catalog page (*http://bit.ly/enterprise-web-development*). There is also a GitHub repository (*http://bit.ly/1uFXI5u*) where the authors keep the source code of the book examples.

The authors also maintain the website (*http://savesickchild.org*), where various versions of the sample Save The Child application are deployed so you can see them in action.

This book is here to help you get your job done. In general, if example code is offered with this book, you may use it in your programs and documentation. You do not need to contact us for permission unless you're reproducing a significant portion of the code. For example, writing a program that uses several chunks of code from this book does not require permission. Selling or distributing a CD-ROM of examples from O'Reilly books does require permission. Answering a question by citing this book and quoting example code does not require permission. Incorporating a significant amount of example code from this book into your product's documentation does require permission.

We appreciate, but do not require, attribution. An attribution usually includes the title, author, publisher, and ISBN. For example: "*Enterprise Web Development* by Yakov Fain, Victor Rasputnis, Anatole Tartakovsky, and Viktor Gamov (O'Reilly). Copyright 2014 Yakov Fain, Victor Rasputnis, Anatole Tartakovsky, and Viktor Gamov, 978-1-449-35681-1."

If you feel your use of code examples falls outside fair use or the permission given above, feel free to contact us at *permissions@oreilly.com*.

Safari® Books Online

 *Safari Books Online* is an on-demand digital library that delivers expert content in both book and video form from the world's leading authors in technology and business.

Technology professionals, software developers, web designers, and business and creative professionals use Safari Books Online as their primary resource for research, problem solving, learning, and certification training.

Safari Books Online offers a range of product mixes and pricing programs for organizations, government agencies, and individuals. Subscribers have access to thousands of books, training videos, and prepublication manuscripts in one fully searchable database from publishers such as O'Reilly Media, Prentice Hall Professional, Addison-Wesley Professional, Microsoft Press, Sams, Que, Peachpit Press, Focal Press, Cisco Press, John Wiley & Sons, Syngress, Morgan Kaufmann, IBM Redbooks, Packt, Adobe Press, FT Press, Apress, Manning, New Riders, McGraw-Hill, Jones & Bartlett, Course Technology, and dozens more. For more information about Safari Books Online, please visit us online.

How to Contact Us

Please address comments and questions concerning this book to the publisher:

O'Reilly Media, Inc.
1005 Gravenstein Highway North
Sebastopol, CA 95472
800-998-9938 (in the United States or Canada)
707-829-0515 (international or local)
707-829-0104 (fax)

We have a web page for this book, where we list errata, examples, and any additional information. You can access this page at *http://bit.ly/enterprise-web-development*.

To comment or ask technical questions about this book, send email to *bookques tions@oreilly.com*.

For more information about our books, courses, conferences, and news, see our website at *http://www.oreilly.com*.

Find us on Facebook: *http://facebook.com/oreilly*

Follow us on Twitter: *http://twitter.com/oreillymedia*

Watch us on YouTube: *http://www.youtube.com/oreillymedia*

Acknowledgments

You see four names on this book cover. But this book is a product of more than four people. It's a product of our company, Farata Systems.

In particular, we'd like to thank Alex Maltsev, who plays the a role of Jerry-the-Designer from Chapter 1 onward. Alex created all the UI prototypes for the sample web application Save The Child that is designed, redesigned, developed, and redeveloped several times in this book. He also developed code samples for the book and all CSS files.

Our big thanks to Anton Moiseev, who developed the Ext JS and Sencha Touch versions of our sample application.

Our hats off to the creators of the Asciidoc text format (*http://asciidoc.org/*). The drafts of this book were prepared in this format, with the subsequent generation of PDF, EPUB, MOBI, and HTML documents.

Our sample application uses two images from the iStockPhoto (*http://www.istockpho to.com/*) collection: the smiling boy by the user *jessicaphoto* and the logo by the user *khalus*. Thank you, guys!

Finally, our thanks to the O'Reilly editors for being so patient while we were trying to hit lots of moving and evolving targets that together represent the universe known as HTML5.

Introduction

During the last decade, the authors of this book worked on many enterprise web applications using a variety of programming languages and frameworks: HTML, JavaScript, Java, and Flex, to name a few. Apache Flex and Java produce compiled code that runs in a well-known and predictable virtual machine (JVM and Flash Player, respectively).

This book is about developing software by using what's known as the HTML5 stack. But only the second chapter of this book offers you an overview of the selected HTML5 tags and APIs. The first chapter is an advanced introduction to JavaScript. The rest of the chapters are about designing, redesigning, developing, and redeveloping a sample website for Save The Child. You'll be learning whatever is required for building this web application on the go.

You'll be using dynamic HTML (DHTML), which is HTML5, JavaScript, and Cascading Style Sheets (CSS). We'll add to the mix the `XMLHttpRequest` object that lives in a web browser and communicates with the server without the need to refresh the entire web page (a.k.a. Ajax). JSON will be our data format of choice for data exchange between the web browser and the server.

Moving from DHTML to HTML5

DHTML stands for *Dynamic HTML*. Back in 1999, Microsoft introduced the `XMLHttpRe quest` object to allow the web version of its mail client, Outlook, to update the browser's window without the need to refresh the entire web page. Several years later, it was substituted with a more popular acronym, AJAX (which stood for Asynchronous JavaScript and XML); today we refer to it simply as a name, "Ajax." The market share of Internet Explorer 5 was about 90 percent at the time, and in enterprises it was literally the only approved browser.

Many years passed by, and today's Internet ecosystems have changed quite a bit. Web browsers are a lot smarter, and the performance of JavaScript has improved substantially.

The browsers support multiple simultaneous connections per domain (as opposed to 2 five years ago), which gave a performance boost to all Ajax applications. At least one-third of all web requests are being made from smartphones or tablets. Apple started its war against all browser plug-ins; hence using embedded Java VM or Flash Player is not an option there. The growing need to support a huge variety of mobile devices gave another boost for the HTML5 stack, which is supported by all devices.

But choosing HTML5 as the least common denominator that works in various devices and browsers means lowering requirements for your enterprise project. The UI might not be pixel-perfect on any particular device, but it will be made somewhat simpler (compared to developing for one specific VM, device, or OS) and will have the ability to adapt to different screen sizes and densities. Instead of implementing features that are specific to a particular device, the functional specification will include requirements to test under several web browsers, in many screen sizes and resolutions. HTML5 developers spend a lot more time in the debugger than people who develop for a known VM. You'll have to be ready to solve problems such as a drop-down not showing any data in one browser while working fine in others. Can you imagine a situation when the click event is not always generated while working in Java, Flex, or Silverlight? Get ready for such surprises while testing your HTML5 application.

You'll save some time because there is no need to compile JavaScript, but you'll spend more time testing the running application during development and Quality Assurance (QA) phases. The final deliverable of an HTML5 project might have as low as half of the functionality compared to the same project developed for a VM. But you'll gain a little better web adaptability, easier implementation of full-text search, and the ability to create mashups (*http://en.wikipedia.org/wiki/Mashup_(web_application_hybrid)*). Integration with other technologies will also become easier with HTML/JavaScript. If all these advantages are important to your applications, choose HTML5.

JavaScript will enforce its language and tooling limitations on any serious and complex enterprise project. You can develop a number of fairly independent windows, but creating well-tested and reliable HTML5 applications takes time. It can be significantly easier with the use of libraries or a framework.

In this book, we use some JavaScript frameworks; there are dozens on the market. Several of them promise to cover all the needs of your web application. Overall, there are two main categories of frameworks:

- Those that allow you to take an existing HTML5 website and easily add new attributes to all or some page elements so they would start shining, blinking, or do some other fun stuff. Such frameworks don't promote component-based development. They may not include navigation components, grids, or trees, which are pretty typical for any UI of the corporate tasks. JQuery is probably the best representative of this group; it's light (30 Kb), extendable, and easy to learn.

- Another group of frameworks offers rich libraries of high-level components and allow you to extend them. But overall, such components are supposed to be used together, becoming a platform for your web UI. These components process some events, offer support of the Model-View-Controller paradigm (or an offshoot of that), have a proprietary way of laying out elements on the web page, organize navigation, and more. Ext JS from Sencha belongs to this group.

Dividing all frameworks into only two categories is an oversimplification, of course. Frameworks such as Backbone.js, AngularJS, and Ember.js have no "components" in terms of the UI sense, and some don't even quite dictate how you build your application (as in, they are not full-stack like Sencha). Some of the frameworks are less intrusive, whereas others are more so. But our goal is not to compare and contrast all HTML5 frameworks, but rather to show you some selected ones.

We'll use both jQuery and Ext JS and show you how to develop web applications with each of them. jQuery is good for improving an existing JavaScript site and can be used to program about 80 percent of a website's functionality. However, for the UI components, you'll need to use another framework (for example, jQuery UI). You should use jQuery for the look-and-feel support, which is what it's meant for. But you can't use it for building your application component model. The component model of Ext JS becomes a fabric of the website, which includes an application piece rather than just being a set of web pages. Besides, Ext JS comes with a library of the UI components.

 JavaScript frameworks are hiding from software developers all incompatibilities and take care of the cases when a web browser doesn't support some HTML5, CSS3, or JavaScript features yet.

High-level UI components and workflow support are needed for a typical enterprise application in which the user needs to perform several steps to complete the business process. And 20 percent of an application's code will require 80 percent of the project time of complex development. So choosing a framework is not the most difficult task. The main problem with DHTML projects is not how to pick the best JavaScript framework for development, but finding the right software developers. A lack of qualified developers increases the importance of using specialized frameworks for code testing. The entire code base must be thoroughly tested over and over again. We discuss this subject in Chapter 5, which is dedicated to test-driven development.

A JavaScript developer has to remember all unfinished pieces of code. Many things that we take for granted with compiled languages simply don't exist in JavaScript. For example, in Java or C#, just by looking at the method signature, you know the data types of the method's parameters. In JavaScript, you can only guess if the parameter names are self-descriptive. Take the Google framework, GWT, which allows developers to write code in Java by auto-generating the JavaScript code. Writing code in one language with further conversion and deployment in another one is a controversial idea unless the source and generated languages are very similar. We're not big fans of GWT, because after writing the code, you'll need to be able to debug it. This is when a Java developer meets a foreign language: JavaScript.The ideology and psychology of programming in JavaScript and Java are different. A person who writes in Java/GWT has to know how to read and interpret deployed JavaScript code. On the other hand, using TypeScript or CoffeeScript to produce JavaScript code can be a time-saver.

The Ext JS framework creators decided to extend JavaScript by introducing their version of classes and a more familiar syntax for object-oriented languages. Technically, they are extending or replacing the constructs of JavaScript itself by extending the alphabet. Ext JS recommends creating objects by using `ext.create` instead of the operator `new`. But Ext JS is still a JavaScript framework.

The jQuery framework substantially simplifies working with a browser's Document Object Model (DOM) elements, and there are millions of small components that know how to do one thing well; for example, sliding effects (*http://api.jquery.com/category/effects/sliding/*). But it's still JavaScript and requires developers to understand the power of JavaScript functions, callbacks, and closures.

Developing in HTML5

Should we develop in HTML5, given that this standard has not been finalized yet? The short answer is yes. If you are planning to develop mainly for the mobile market, it's well equipped with the latest web browsers, so if you run into issues there, they won't be caused by a lack of HTML5 support. In the market of enterprise web applications, the aging Internet Explorer 8 is still being widely used, and it doesn't support some of the HTML5-specific features. But it's not a show-stopper either. If you are using one of the JavaScript frameworks that offers cross-browser compatibility, most likely it takes care of Internet Explorer 8 issues.

Remember that, even if you rely on a framework that claims to offer cross-browser compatibility, you will still need to test your application in the browsers that you expect to support to ensure that it functions as intended. The chances are that you may need to fix the framework's code here and there. Maintaining compatibility is a huge challenge for any framework's vendor, which in some cases can consist of just one developer. Spend some time working with the framework, and then work on your application code. If you can, submit your fixes back to the framework's code base—most frameworks are open source.

If you are planning to write pure JavaScript, add the tiny framework Modernizr (see Chapter 1) to your code base, which will detect whether a certain feature is supported by the user's web browser, and if not, provide an alternative solution. We like the analogy of TV sets. People with the latest 3D HDTV sets and those who have 50-year-old black-and-white televisions can watch the same movie, even though the quality of the picture will be drastically different.

Challenges of the Enterprise Developer

If you are an enterprise developer starting work on your first HTML5 enterprise project, get ready to solve the same tasks that all UI software developers face, regardless of what programming language they use:

- Reliability of network communications. What if the data never arrives from/to the server? Is it possible to recover the lost data? Where did it get lost? Can we resend the lost data? What to do with duplicates?

- Modularization of your application. If your application has certain rarely used menus, don't even load the code that handles them.

- Perceived performance. How quickly is the main window of your application loaded into the user's computer? How heavy is the framework's code base?

- Should you store the application state on the server or on the client?

- Does the framework offer a rich library of components?

- Does the framework support creation of loosely coupled application components? Is the event model well designed?

- Does the framework of your choice cover most of the needs of your application, or will you need to use several frameworks?

- Is well-written documentation available?

- Does the framework of your choice lock you in? Does it restrict your choices? Can you easily replace this framework with another one if need be?

- Is there an active community to ask for help with technical questions?

- What is the right set of tools to increase your productivity (debugging, code generation, build automation, dependency management)?

- What are the security risks that need to be addressed to prevent exposing sensitive information to malicious attackers?

We could continue adding items to this list. But our main message is that developing HTML5 applications is not just about adding <video> and <canvas> tags to a web page. It's about serious JavaScript programming. In this book, we discuss all of these challenges.

Summary

HTML5 is ready for prime time. There is no need to wait for the official release of its final standard. All modern web browsers have supported most HTML5 features and APIs for a couple of years now. To be productive, you'll need to use not just HTML, JavaScript, and CSS, but third-party libraries, frameworks, and tools. In this book, we introduce you to a number of them, which will help you make the final choice of the right set of productivity tools that work best for your project.

Building Your Application

This book has three parts. In Part I, we start building web applications. We'll be building and rebuilding a sample application titled Save The Child.

 We assume that you know how to write programs in JavaScript. If you are not familiar with this language, study the materials in the bonus online chapter first. You'll find a fast-paced introduction to Java-Script there.

In Chapter 1 we'll start working with a web designer. We'll create a mockup, and will start development in pure JavaScript. By the end of this chapter, the first version of this application will be working, using hardcoded data.

Chapter 2 shows you how to use Ajax techniques to allow web pages to communicate with external data sources, without the need to refresh the page. We also cover JavaScript Object Notation (JSON)—a de facto standard data format when it comes to communication between web browsers and servers.

Chapter 3 shows how to minimize the amount of manually written JavaScript by introducing the popular jQuery library. You'll rebuild the Save The Child application with jQuery.

After reading this part, you'll be ready to immerse yourself into more heavy-duty tools and frameworks that are being used by enterprise developers.

## CHAPTER 1

Mocking Up the Save The Child Application

Let's start working on our web application, Save The Child. This web application will contain a form for donations to sick children and an embedded video player, will integrate with Google Maps, will have charts, and more. The goal is for you to gradually build all the functionality of this web application while we explain each step so that you can understand why we are building it the way we do. By the end of this chapter, you'll have the web design and the first prototype of Save The Child.

The proliferation of mobile devices and web applications requires new skills for development of what used to be boring-looking enterprise applications. In the past, design of the user interface (UI) of most enterprise applications was done by developers to the best of their artistic abilities: a couple of buttons here, and a grid there, on a gray background. Business users were happy because they did not know any better. The application allowed users to process business data—what else was there to wish for? Enterprise business users used to be happy with any UI, as long as the application helped them to take care of their business.

But today's business users are spoiled by nice-looking consumer-facing applications, and more often than not, new development starts by inviting a web designer to create a prototype of the future application. For example, we've seen some excellent (from the UI perspective) functional specifications for boring financial applications made by professional designers. Business users are slowly but surely becoming more demanding in the area of UI design solutions. The trend is clear: a developer's art does not cut it anymore.

In enterprise IT shops, web design is usually done by a professional web designer. Software developers are not overly familiar with the tools that web designers are using. But to make this book useful even for smaller shops that can't afford professional web design, we illustrate the process of design and prototyping of the UI of a web application.

Our web designer—let's call him Jerry—is ready to start working on the *mockup* (a.k.a. *wireframes*); this is a set of images depicting various views of the future Save The Child application. We expect him to deliver images with comments that briefly explain what should change in a view if a user takes certain actions (for example, clicks a button). You can also think of an application's UI as a set of states, and the user's action results in your application transitioning from one state to another. As nerds and mathematicians say, the UI of your application is a finite state machine (*http://bit.ly/1nYG1f4*), which at any given point in time is in one of a finite number of states (for example, in the view state Donate Form or Auction).

Considering Mobile First

While starting work on the design of a new web application, keep in mind that some users likely will access it from mobile devices. Will the proposed UI look good on mobile devices with smaller screens? Some people suggest using a so-called Mobile First approach, which means that from the very early stages of web application development, you should do the following:

- Ensure that your web application (design and layout) looks good on smaller screens.
- Differentiate the content to be shown on large versus small screens (start with small screens and enhance for the larger ones).
- Test your application on slow (3G-like) networks and minimize the "weight" of the landing page.
- Decide on an approach: should you use responsive web design (see Chapter 10), HTML5 mobile frameworks, native, or hybrid (see Chapter 13)?
- If you are planning to use geographical location services, decide on the API to be used for mobile devices, but don't forget about desktops, too.

 Users of iOS and Android devices are used to being able to find the closest restaurant or gas station based on their current location. Did you know that this location feature can be available on desktops, too? Google Maps is just one of the services that can find the location of a user's desktop based on its IP address, WiFi router's ID, or proximity to cell towers. Zeroing in on your device might not be as precise as with a smartphone's GPS, but it might be good enough. So, why not plan on adding this feature to all versions of your web application? Finding the closest charity event or a local child in need can be done by knowing an approximate location of your desktop computer.

Let's consider pointing devices. At the time of this writing, the vast majority of desktop users work with pixel-perfect mouse pointers or track pads. Smartphone or tablet users work with their fingers. One finger touch can cover a square comprising roughly 100 pixels. CNN's site, for example, shows lots of news links located very close to one another on the screen. A finger might cover more than one link, and Android devices offer you a larger pop-up, allowing you to select the link you really wanted to touch. Having a Mobile First state of mind doesn't mean that CNN needs to keep a larger distance between links for all the users. However, it does mean that CNN should foresee the issues or innovate using the features offered by modern mobile devices.

Chapter 10 covers the *responsive web design* techniques that allow us to create UIs for web applications that automatically re-allocate screen content based on the size of the display on the user's device. Although this chapter is about the desktop version of the Save The Child web application, its screen will consist of several rectangular areas that can be allocated differently (or even hidden) on smartphones or tablets.

Before writing this book, we discussed how our application should look and work on mobile devices. But strictly speaking, because the work on multiple chapters was done in parallel, this was not a Mobile First approach.

Consider reading Chapter 12 now to better understand what you will need to deal with when developing web applications that look good on desktop monitors as well as on mobile screens. Understanding responsive design principles will help you in communications with your web designer.

One of the constraints that mobile users have is the relatively slow speed of the mobile Internet. This means that even though your desktop users will use fast LAN connection lines, your web application has to be modularized so that only a minimal number of modules has to be loaded initially. Often, mobile providers charge users based on the amount of consumed data, too.

The chances are slim that desktop users will lose an Internet connection for a long period of time. On the other hand, mobile users might stay in an area with no connection or a spotty one. In this case, the Mobile First thinking can lead to introducing an offline mode with limited functionality.

Thinking up front of the minimal content to be displayed on small mobile screens might force you to change the design of desktop web pages, too. In our sample Save The Child application, we need to make sure that there is enough space for the Donate Now button even on the smallest devices.

Introducing Balsamiq Mockups

Visualize a project owner talking to our web designer, Jerry, in a cafeteria, and Jerry is drawing sketches of the future website on a napkin. Well, in the 21st century, he's using an electronic napkin, so to speak—an excellent prototyping tool called Balsamiq Mockups (*http://balsamiq.com*). This easy-to-use program gives you a working area where you create a mockup of your future web application by dragging and dropping the required UI components from the toolbar onto the image of the web page (see Figure 1-1).

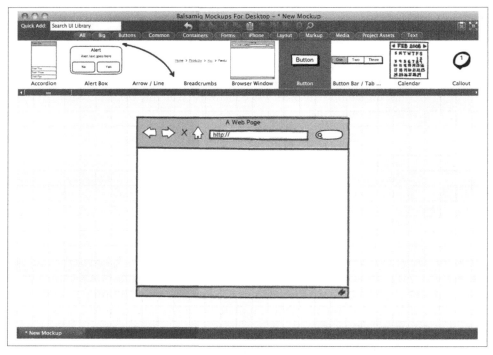

Figure 1-1. The working area of Balsamiq Mockups

If you can't find the required image in Balsamiq's library, add your own by dragging and dropping it onto the top toolbar. For example, the mockup in Chapter 10 uses our images of the iPhone that we've added to Balsamiq assets.

 If you prefer using free tools, consider using MockFlow (*http://mockflow.com*).

When the prototype is done, it can be saved as an image and sent to the project owner. Another option is to export the Balsamiq project into XML, and if both the project owner and web designer have Balsamiq installed, they can work on the prototype in collaboration. For example, the designer exports the current state of the project, the owner imports it and makes corrections or comments, and then exports it again and sends it back to the designer.

The Project Owner Talks to a Web Designer

During the first meeting, Jerry talks to the project owner about the required functionality and then creates the UI to be implemented by web developers. The artifacts produced by a designer vary depending on the qualifications of that designer. For instance, a set of images might represent different states of the UI with little *callouts* explaining the navigation of the application. If the web designer is familiar with HTML and CSS, developers might get a working prototype in the form of HTML and CSS files, and this is exactly what Jerry will create by the end of this chapter.

Our project owner says to Jerry: *"The Save The Child web application should allow people to make donations to the children. Users should be able to find these children by specifying a geographical area on the map. The application should include a video player and display statistics about donors and recipients. The application should include an online auction, with proceeds going to the charity. We'll start working on the desktop version first, but your future mockup should include three versions of the UI, supporting desktops, tablets, and smartphones."*

After the meeting, Jerry launches Balsamiq and begins to work. He decides that the main window will consist of four areas laid out vertically:

- The header with the logo and several navigation buttons
- The main area with the Donate section plus the video player
- The area with statistics, and charts
- The footer with several housekeeping links plus the icons for Twitter and Facebook

Creating First Mockups

The first deliverable of our web designer (see Figures 1-2 and 1-3) depicts two states of the UI: before and after clicking the Donate Now button. The web designer suggests that on the button click, the video player turn into a small button revealing the donation form.

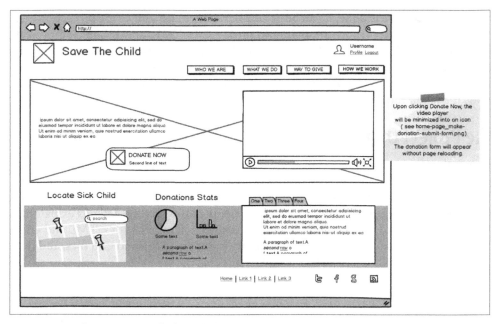

Figure 1-2. The main view before clicking Donate Now

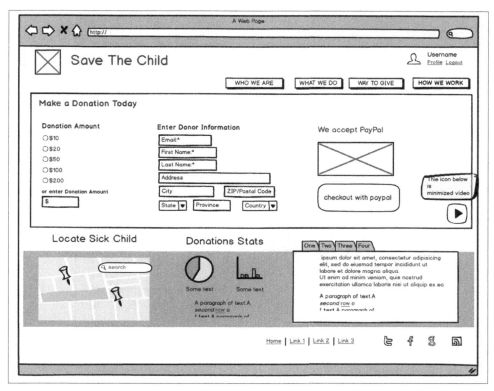

Figure 1-3. The main view after clicking Donate Now

The project owner suggests that turning the video into a Donate Now button might not be the best idea. We shouldn't forget that the main goal of this application is collecting donations, so they decide to keep the user's attention on the Donate area and move the video player to the lower portion of the window.

Next, they review the mockups of the authorization routine. The view states in this process can be:

1. Not Logged On
2. The Login Form
3. Wrong ID/Password
4. Forgot Password
5. Successfully Logged On

The web designer's mockups of some of these states are shown in Figures 1-4 and 1-5.

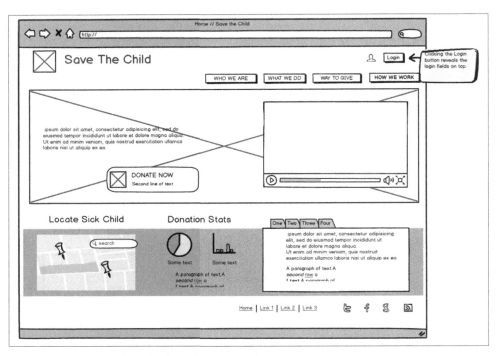

Figure 1-4. The user hasn't clicked the Login button

The latter shows different UI states should the user decide to log in. The project owner reviews the mockups and returns them to Jerry with some comments. The project owner wants to make sure that the user doesn't have to log on to the application to access the website. The process of making donations has to be as easy as possible, and forcing the donor to log on might scare some people away, so the project owner leaves the comment shown in Figure 1-5.

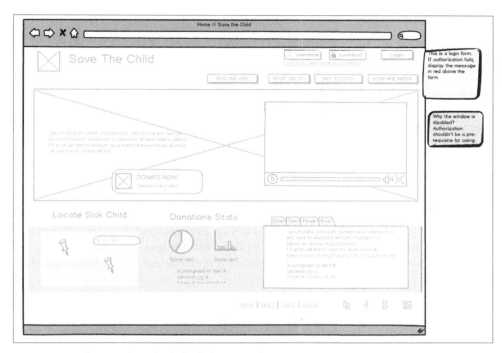

Figure 1-5. The user hasn't clicked the Login button

This is enough of a design for us to build a working prototype of the app and start getting feedback from business users. In the real world, when a prospective client (including business users from your enterprise) approaches you, asking for a project estimate, provide a document with a detailed work breakdown and screenshots made by Balsamiq or a similar tool.

Turning Mockups into a Prototype

We are lucky, because Jerry knows HTML and CSS. He's ready to turn the still mock-ups into the first working prototype. It will use only hardcoded data, but the layout of the site will be done in CSS and will use HTML5 markup. He'll design this application as a single-page application (SPA).

Single-Page Applications

An SPA is an architectural approach that doesn't require the user to go through multiple pages to navigate a site. The user enters the URL in the browser, which brings up the web page that remains open on the screen until the user stops working with that application. A portion of the user's screen might change as the user navigates the application, new data might come in via Ajax techniques (see Chapter 2), or new DOM elements might need to be created during runtime, but the main page itself isn't reloaded. This allows building so-called *fat client applications* that can remember the state. Besides, most likely your HTML5 application will use a JavaScript framework, which in SPA is loaded only once, when the home page is created by the browser.

Have you ever seen a monitor of a trader working for a Wall Street firm? Traders usually have three or four large monitors, but let's look at just one of them. Imagine a busy screen with lots and lots of fluctuating data grouped in dedicated areas of the window. This screen shows the constantly changing prices from financial markets, orders placed by the trader to buy or sell products, and notifications on completed trades. If this were a web application, it would live on the same web page. There would be no menus to open other windows.

The price of an Apple share was $590.45 just a second ago, and now it's $590.60. How can this be done technically? Here's one possibility: Every second, an Ajax call is made to the remote server providing current stock prices, and the JavaScript code finds in the DOM the HTML element responsible for rendering the price and then modifies its value with the latest price.

Have you seen a web page showing the content of a Google Gmail input box? It looks like a table with rows representing the sender, subject, and date of each email's arrival. Suddenly, you see a new row in bold on top of the list—a new email came in. How was this done technically? A new object(s) was created and inserted into a DOM tree. No page changes, no need for the user to refresh the browser's page. An undercover Ajax call gets the data, and JavaScript changes the DOM. The content of DOM changed, and the user sees an updated value.

Running Code Examples from WebStorm

The authors of this book use WebStorm IDE 7 from JetBrains for developing real-world projects. Appendix B explains how to run code samples in WebStorm.

This chapter includes lots of code samples illustrating how the UI is gradually being built. We've created a number of small web applications. Each of them can be run independently. Just download and open in the WebStorm (or any other) IDE the directory containing samples from Chapter 1. After that, you'll be able to run each of these examples by right-clicking *index.html* in WebStorm and choosing Open in Browser.

We assume that the users of our Save The Child application work with modern versions of web browsers (two years old or newer). Real-world web developers need to find workarounds to the unsupported CSS or HTML5 features in old browsers, but modern IDEs generate HTML5 boilerplate code that include large CSS files providing different solutions to older browsers.

JavaScript frameworks implement workarounds (a.k.a., polyfills) for features unsupported by old browsers, too, so we don't want to clutter the text by providing several versions of the code just to make book samples work in outdated browsers. This is especially important when developing enterprise apps for situations in which the majority of users are locked in a particular version of an older web browser.

Our First Prototype

In this section, you'll see several projects that show how the static mockup will turn into a working prototype with the help of HTML, CSS, and JavaScript. Because Jerry, the designer, decided to have four separate areas on the page, he created the HTML file *index.html* that has the tag <header> with the navigation tag <nav>, two <div> tags for the middle sections of the page, and a <footer>, as shown in Example 1-1.

Example 1-1. The first version of the home page

```
<!DOCTYPE html>
<html lang="en">
 <head>
        <meta charset="utf-8">
        <title>Save The Child | Home Page</title>
        <link rel="stylesheet" href="css/styles.css">
 </head>
 <body>
        <div id="main-container">
                <header>
                 <h1>Save The Child</h1>
                 <nav>
                 <ul>
                        <li>
                          <a href="javascript:void(0)">Who we are</a>
                        </li>
                        <li>
                          <a href="javascript:void(0)">What we do</a>
                        </li>
                        <li>
                          <a href="javascript:void(0)">Way to give</a>
                        </li>
                        <li>
                          <a href="javascript:void(0)">How we work</a>
                        </li>
                 </ul>
```

```
            </nav>
        </header>
        <div id="main" role="main">
                <section>
                  Donate section and Video Player go here
                </section>
                <section>
                  Locate The Child, stats and tab folder go here
                </section>
        </div>
        <footer>
                <section id="temp-project-name-container">
                        <b>project 01</b>: This is the page footer
                </section>
        </footer>
    </div>
 </body>
</html>
```

Note that this HTML file uses the `<link>` tag to include the CSS file shown in Example 1-2. Because there is no content yet for the navigation links to open, we use the syntax `href="javascript:void(0)` to create a live link that doesn't load any page, which is fine in prototyping stage.

Example 1-2. The file styles.css

```
/* Navigation menu */
nav {
        float: right
}
nav ul li {
        list-style: none;
        float: left;
}
nav ul li a {
        display: block;
        padding: 7px 12px;
}

/* Main content
 #main-container is a wrapper for all page content
 */
#main-container {
        width: 980px;
        margin: 0 auto;
}
div#main {
        clear: both;
}

/* Footer */
footer {
```

```
        /* Set background color just to make the footer standout*/
        background: #eee;
        height: 20px;
}
footer #temp-project-name-container {
        float: left;
}
```

This CSS controls not only the styles of the page content, but also the page layout. The `<nav>` section should be pushed to the right. If an unordered list is placed inside the `<nav>` section, it should be left-aligned. The width of the HTML container with the ID `main-container` should be 980 pixels, and it has to be automatically centered. The footer will be 20 pixels high and should have a gray background. The first version of our web page is shown in Figure 1-6. Run *index.html* from *project-01-get-started*.

In Chapter 10, you'll see how to create web pages with more flexible layouts that don't require specifying absolute sizes in pixels.

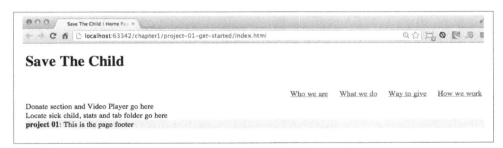

Figure 1-6. Working prototype, take 1: Getting Started

The next version of our prototype is more interesting and contains a lot more code. The CSS file will become fancier, and the layout of the four page sections will properly divide the screen real estate. We'll add a logo and a nicely styled Login button to the top of the page. This version of the code will also introduce some JavaScript that supports user authorization. Run *project-02-login*, and you'll see a window similar to Figure 1-7.

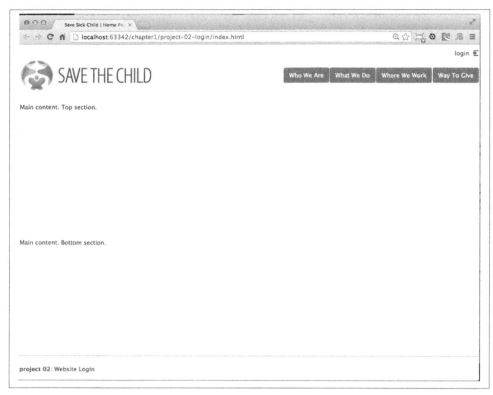

Figure 1-7. Working prototype, take 2: Login

This project has several directories to keep JavaScript, images, CSS, and fonts separate. We'll talk about special icon fonts later in this section, but first things first: let's take a close look at the HTML code in Example 1-3.

Example 1-3. The second version of the home page

```
<!DOCTYPE html>
<html lang="en">
 <head>
        <meta charset="utf-8">
        <meta http-equiv="X-UA-Compatible" content="IE=edge,chrome=1">
        <title>Save The Child | Home Page</title>
        <link rel="stylesheet" href="assets/css/styles.css">

 </head>
  <body>
        <div id="main-container">
         <header>

          <h1 id="logo"><a href="javascript:void(0)">Save The Child</a></h1>
```

```
<nav id="top-nav">
    <ul>
      <li id="login">
       <div id="authorized">
        <span class="icon-user authorized-icon"></span>
        <span id="user-authorized">admin</span>
        <br/>
        <a id="profile-link" href="javascript:void(0);">profile</a> |
        <a id="logout-link" href="javascript:void(0);">logout</a>
       </div>

        <form id="login-form">
         <span class="icon-user login-form-icons"></span>
         <input id="username" name="username" type="text"
                    placeholder="username" autocomplete="off" />
           <span class="icon-locked login-form-icons"></span>
         <input id="password" name="password"
                    type="password" placeholder="password"/>
        </form>
        <a id="login-submit" href="javascript:void(0)">login  
                    <span class="icon-enter"></span> </a>

            <div id="login-link" class="show-form">login
                          <span class="icon-enter"></span></div>

            <div class="clearfix"></div>
      </li>
      <li id="top-menu-items">
            <ul>
                <li>
                        <a href="javascript:void(0)">Who We Are</a>
                </li>
                <li>
                        <a href="javascript:void(0)">What We Do</a>
                </li>
                <li>
                        <a href="javascript:void(0)">Where We Work</a>
                </li>
                <li>
                        <a href="javascript:void(0)">Way To Give</a>
                </li>
            </ul>
      </li>
      </ul>
  </nav>
</header>

<div id="main" role="main">
    <section id="main-top-section">
            <br/>
            Main content. Top section.
```

```
                </section>
                <section id="main-bottom-section">
                        Main content. Bottom section.
                </section>
        </div>
        <footer>
                <section id="temp-project-name-container">
                        <b>This is the footer</b>
                </section>
        </footer>
        </div>
        <script src="assets/js/main.js"></script>
 </body>
</html>
```

Usually, the logos on multipage websites are clickable—they bring up the home page.
That's why Jerry placed the anchor tag in the logo section. But we are planning to build
a single-page application, so having a clickable logo won't be needed.

Run this project in WebStorm and click the Login button; you'll see that it reacts. But
looking at the login-related <a> tags in the <header> section, you'll find nothing but
href="javascript:void(0)". So why does the button react? Read the code in *main.js*
shown in Example 1-4, and you'll find the line loginLink.addEventListen
er('click', showLoginForm, false); that invokes the callback showLoginForm().
That's why the Login button reacts. This seems confusing because the anchor component was used here just for styling purposes. In this example, a better solution would
be to replace the anchor tag <a id="login-link" class="show-form" href="java
script:void(0)"> with another component that doesn't make the code confusing—
for example, <div id="login-link" class="show-form">.

 We do not want to build web applications the old way wherein a
server-side program prepares and sends UI fragments to the client.
The server and the client send each other only the data. If the server
is not available, we can use the local storage (the offline mode) or
mock up data on the client.

Our Main Page JavaScript

Now let's examine the JavaScript code located in *main.js*. This code self-invokes the
anonymous function, which creates an object-encapsulated namespace stc (short for
Save The Child). This avoids polluting the global namespace. If we wanted to expose
anything from this closure to the global namespace, we could have done this via the
variable stc, as described in the section "Closures" in the bonus online chapter. See
Example 1-4.

Example 1-4. The JavaScript code of the home page

```javascript
// global namespace ssc
var stc = (function() {
    // Encapsulated variables

    // Find login section elements                         ❶
    // You can use document.getQuerySelector() here
    // instead of getElementByID ()
        var loginLink = document.getElementById("login-link");
        var loginForm = document.getElementById("login-form");
        var loginSubmit = document.getElementById('login-submit');
        var logoutLink = document.getElementById('logout-link');
        var profileLink = document.getElementById('profile-link');
        var authorizedSection = document.getElementById("authorized");

        var userName = document.getElementById('username');
        var userPassword = document.getElementById('password');

        // Register event listeners                         ❷

        loginLink.addEventListener('click', showLoginForm, false);
        loginSubmit.addEventListener('click', logIn, false);
        logoutLink.addEventListener('click', logOut, false);
        profileLink.addEventListener('click', getProfile, false);

        function showLoginForm() {
                loginLink.style.display = "none";            ❸
                loginForm.style.display = "block";
                loginSubmit.style.display = "block";
        }

        function showAuthorizedSection() {
                authorizedSection.style.display = "block";
                loginForm.style.display = "none";
                loginSubmit.style.display = "none";
        }

        function logIn() {
                //check credentials
                var userNameValue = userName.value;
                var userNameValueLength = userName.value.length;
                var userPasswordValue = userPassword.value;
                var userPasswordLength = userPassword.value.length;

                if (userNameValueLength == 0 || userPasswordLength == 0) {
                        if (userNameValueLength == 0) {
                                console.log("username can't be empty");
                        }
                        if (userPasswordLength == 0) {
                                console.log("password can't be empty");
                        }
                } else if (userNameValue != 'admin' ||
```

```
                              userPasswordValue != '1234') {
                   console.log('username or password is invalid');

              } else if (userNameValue == 'admin' &&
                                   userPasswordValue == '1234') {

                   showAuthorizedSection();                        ❹
              }
        }

        function logOut() {
              userName.value = '';
              userPassword.value = '';
              authorizedSection.style.display = "none";
              loginLink.style.display = "block";
        }

        function getProfile() {
              console.log('Profile link clicked');
        }

})();
```

❶   Query the DOM to get references to login-related HTML elements.

❷   Register event listeners for the clickable login elements.

❸   To make a DOM element invisible, set its `style.display="none"`. Hide the
     Login button and show the login form having two input fields for entering the
     user ID and the password.

❹   If the user is *admin* and the password is *1234*, hide the `loginForm` and make the
     top corner of the page look as in Figure 1-8.

 We keep the user ID and password in this code just for illustration
purposes. Never do this in your applications. Authentication has to
be done in a secure way on the server side.

Figure 1-8. After successful login

Where to put JavaScript

We recommend placing the `<script>` tag with your JavaScript at the end of your HTML file as in our *index.html* shown previously. If you move the line `<script src="js/main.js"></script>` to the top of the `<body>` section and rerun *index.html*, the screen will look like Figure 1-7, but clicking Login won't display the login form as it should. Why? Registering of the event listeners in the script *main.js* failed because the DOM components (`login-link`, `login-form`, and others) were not created by the time this script was running. Open Firebug, Chrome Developer Tools, or any other debugging tool, and you'll see an error on the console that will look similar to the following:

```
__TypeError: loginLink is null
loginLink.addEventListener('click', showLoginForm, false);__
```

Of course, in many cases, your JavaScript code could have tested whether the DOM elements exist before using them, but in this particular sample, it's just easier to put the script at the end of the HTML file. Another solution is to load the JavaScript code located in *main.js* in a separate handler function that would run only when the window's `load` event, which is dispatched by the browser, indicates that the DOM is ready: `window.addEventListener('load', function() {...}`. You'll see how to do this in the next version of *main.js*.

The CSS of our main page

Now that we have reviewed the HTML and JavaScript code, let's spend a little more time with the CSS that supports the page shown in Figure 1-7. The difference between the screenshots shown in Figure 1-6 and Figure 1-7 is substantial. First, the upper-left image is nowhere to be found in *index.html*. Open the *styles.css* file and you'll see the line `background: url(../img/logo.png) no-repeat;` in the header `h1#logo` section.

The page layout is also specified in the file *styles.css*. In this version, the size of each section is specified in pixels (px), which won't make your page fluid and easily resizable. For example, the HTML element with `id="main-top-section"` is styled like this:

```
#main-top-section {
        width: 100%;
        height: 320px;
        margin-top: 18px;
}
```

Jerry styled the main section to take the entire width of the browser's window and to be 320 pixels tall. If you keep in mind the Mobile First mantra, this might not be the best approach because 320 pixels means a different size (in inches) on the displays with different screen density. For example, 320 pixels on the iPhone 5 with Retina display will look a lot smaller than 320 pixels on the iPhone 4. You might want to consider switching from px to em units: 1 em is equal to the current font height, 2 em means twice the size, and so forth. You can read more about creating scalable style sheets with *em* units at link:http://bit.ly/1lJnSUL.

What looks like a Login button in Figure 1-7 is not a button, but a styled `div` element. Initially, it was a clickable anchor `<a>`, and we've explained this change right after Example 1-2. The CSS fragment supporting the Login button looks like this:

```
li#login input {
        width: 122px;
        padding: 4px;
        border: 1px solid #ddd;
        border-radius: 2px;
        -moz-border-radius: 2px;
        -webkit-border-radius: 2px;
}
```

The `border-radius` element rounds the corners of the HTML element to which it's applied. But why do we repeat it three times with the additional prefixes `-moz-` and `-webkit-`? These are *CSS vendor prefixes*, which allow web browser vendors to implement experimental CSS properties that haven't been standardized yet. For example, `-webkit-` is the prefix for all WebKit-based browsers: Chrome, Safari, Android, and iOS. Microsoft uses `-ms-` for Internet Explorer, and Opera uses `-o-`. These prefixes are temporary measures, which make the CSS files heavier than they need to be. The time will come when the CSS3 standard properties will be implemented by all browser vendors, and you won't need to use these prefixes.

As a matter of fact, unless you want this code to work in the very old versions of Firefox, you can remove the line `-moz-border-radius: 2px;` from our *styles.css* because Mozilla has implemented the property `border-radius` in most of its browsers. You can find a list of CSS properties with the corresponding vendor prefixes in this list (*http://bit.ly/1pSuBMl*) maintained by Peter Beverloo.

The Footer Section

The footer section comes next. Run the project called *project-03-footer* and you'll see a new version of the Save The Child page with the bottom portion that looks like Figure 1-9. The footer section shows several icons linking to Facebook, Google Plus, Twitter, RSS feed, and email.

project 03: Footer Section | Using Icon Fonts

Figure 1-9. The footer section

The HTML section of our first prototype is shown in Example 1-5. At this point, it has a number of `<a>` tags, which have the dummy references `href="java script:void(0)"` that don't redirect the user to any of these social sites.

Example 1-5. The footer section's HTML

```
<footer>
 <section id="temp-project-name-container">
       <b>project 03</b>: Footer Section | Using Icon Fonts
 </section>
 <section id="social-icons">
       <a href="javascript:void(0)" title="Our Facebook page">
           <span aria-hidden="true" class="icon-facebook"></span></a>
       <a href="javascript:void(0)" title="Our Google Plus page">
           <span aria-hidden="true" class="icon-gplus"></span></a>
       <a href="javascript:void(0)" title="Our Twitter">
           <span aria-hidden="true" class="icon-twitter"></span></a>  
       <a href="javascript:void(0)" title="RSS feed">
           <span aria-hidden="true" class="icon-feed"></span></a>
       <a href="javascript:void(0)" title="Email us">
           <span aria-hidden="true" class="icon-mail"></span></a>
 </section>
</footer>
```

Each of the preceding anchors is styled using vector graphics icon fonts that we've selected and downloaded from link:http://icomoon.io/app. Vector graphics images are being redrawn using vectors (strokes)—as opposed to raster graphics, which are predrawn in certain resolution images. Raster graphics can give you boxy, pixelated images if the size of the image needs to be increased. We use vector images for our footer section that are treated as fonts. They will look as good as the originals on any screen size, and you can change their properties (for example, color) as easily as you would with any other font. The images that you see in Figure 1-9 are located in the *fonts* directory of *project-03-footer*. The IcoMoon web application will generate the fonts for you based on your selection and you'll get a sample HTML file, fonts, and CSS to be used with your application. Our icon fonts section in *styles.css* will look like Example 1-6.

Example 1-6. Icon fonts in CSS

```
/* Icon Fonts */
@font-face {
      font-family: 'icomoon';
      src:url('../fonts/icomoon.eot');
      src:url('../fonts/icomoon.eot?#iefix') format('embedded-opentype'),
          url('../fonts/icomoon.svg#icomoon') format('svg'),
          url('../fonts/icomoon.woff') format('woff'),
          url('../fonts/icomoon.ttf') format('truetype');
      font-weight: normal;
      font-style: normal;
}
```

The Donate Section

The section with the Donate Now button and the donation form will be located in the top portion of the page, directly below the navigation area. Initially, the page opens with the background image of a sick but smiley boy on the right and a large Donate Now button on the left. The image shown in Figure 1-10 is taken from a large collection of photos at the iStockphoto (*http://www.istockphoto.com*) website. We're also using two more background images here: one with the flowers, and the other with the sun and clouds. You can find the references to these images in the *styles.css* file. Run *project-04-donation* and you'll see the new version of our Save The Child page that will look like Figure 1-10.

Figure 1-10. The initial view of the Donate section

Lorem Ipsum is a dummy text widely used in printing, typesetting, and web design. It's used as a placeholder to indicate the text areas that should be filled with real content later. You can read about it at Lipsum (*http://www.lipsum.com*). Example 1-7 shows what the HTML fragment supporting Figure 1-10 looks like (no CSS is shown for brevity).

Example 1-7. The donate section before clicking Donate Now

```
<div id="donation-address">
     <p class="donation-address">
             Lorem ipsum dolor sit amet, consectetur e magna aliqua.
             Nostrud exercitation ullamco laboris nisi ut aliquip ex
             ea commodo consequat.
             Duis aute irure dolor in reprehenderit in voluptate velit
             esse cillum dolore eu fugiat nulla pariatur.
             Excepteur sint occaecat cupidatat non proident.
     </p>
     <button class="donate-button" id="donate-btn">
             <span class="donate-button-header">Donate Now</span>
             <br/>
             <span class="donate-2nd-line">Children can't wait</span>
     </button>

</div>
```

Clicking the Donate Now button should reveal the form where the user can enter a name, address, and donation amount. Instead of opening a pop-up window, we'll just change the content on the left revealing the form, and move the Donate Now button to the right. Figure 1-11 shows how the top portion of our page will look after the user clicks the Donate Now button.

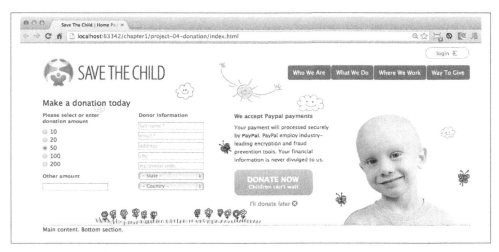

Figure 1-11. After clicking the Donate Now button

The HTML of this donation is shown in Example 1-8. When the user clicks the Donate Now button, the content of the form should be sent to PayPal or any other payment processing system.

Example 1-8. The donate section after clicking the Donate Now button

```
<div id="donate-form-container">
 <h3>Make a donation today</h3>
 <form name="_xclick" action="https://www.paypal.com/cgi-bin/webscr" method="post">
  <div class="donation-form-section">
      <label class="donation-heading">Please select or enter
              <br/> donation amount</label>
      <input type="radio" name = "amount" id= "d10" value = "10"/>
      <label for = "d10">10</label>
      <br/>
      <input type="radio" name = "amount" id = "d20" value="20" />
      <label for = "d20">20</label>
      <br/>
      <input type="radio" name = "amount" id="d50" checked="checked" value="50" />
      <label for="d50">50</label>
      <br/>
      <input type="radio" name = "amount" id="d100" value="100" />
      <label for="d100">100</label>
      <br/>
      <input type="radio" name = "amount" id="d200" value="200" />
      <label for="d200">200</label>
      <label class="donation-heading">Other amount</label>
      <input id="customAmount" name="amount" value=""
              type="text"  autocomplete="off" />
  </div>
  <div class="donation-form-section">
      <label class="donation-heading">Donor information</label>
      <input type="text" id="full_name" name="full_name"
              placeholder="full name *" required>
      <input type="email" id="email_addr" name="email_addr"
              placeholder="email *" required>
      <input type="text" id="street_address" name="street_address"
              placeholder="address">
      <input type="text" id="city" name="scty" placeholder="city">
      <input type="text" id="zip" name="zip" placeholder="zip/postal code">
      <select name="state">
              <option value="" selected="selected"> - State - </option>
              <option value="AL">Alabama</option>
              <option value="WY">Wyoming</option>
      </select>
      <select name="country">
              <option value="" selected="selected"> - Country - </option>
              <option value="United States">United States</option>
              <option value="Zimbabwe">Zimbabwe</option>
      </select>
  </div>
```

```
<div class="donation-form-section make-payment">
    <h4>We accept Paypal payments</h4>
    <p>
            Your payment will processed securely by <b>PayPal</b>.
            PayPal employ industry-leading encryption and fraud prevention tools.
            Your financial information is never divulged to us.
    </p>

    <button  type="submit" class="donate-button donate-button-submit">
            <span class="donate-button-header">Donate Now</span>
            <br/>
            <span class="donate-2nd-line">Children can't wait</span>
    </button>
    <a id="donate-later-link" href="javascript:void(0);">I'll donate later
    <span class="icon-cancel"></span></a>
  </div>
 </form>
</div>
```

The JavaScript code supporting the UI transformations related to the Donate Now button is shown next. It's the code snippet from *main.js* from *project-04-donation*. Clicking the Donate Now button invokes the event handler showDonationForm(), which simply hides <div id="donation-address"> with *Lorem Ipsum* and displays the donation form:

```
<form name="_xclick" action="https://www.paypal.com/cgi-bin/webscr"
  method="post">">.
```

When the form field loses focus or after the user clicks the Submit button, the data from the form _xclick must be validated and sent to PayPal. If the user clicks "I'll donate later," the code hides the form and shows the Lorem Ipsum from the <div id="donation-address"> again.

Not including proper form validation is a sign of a rookie developer. This can easily irritate users. Instead of showing error messages like "Please include only numbers in the phone number field," use regular expressions to programmatically strip nondigits away (read more about these in *Regular Expressions*.

Two select drop-downs in the preceding code contain hardcoded values of all states and countries. For brevity, we've listed just a couple of entries in each. In Chapter 2, we'll populate these drop-downs by using external data in JavaScript Object Notation (JSON) format.

Don't show all the countries in the drop-down unless your application is global. If the majority of users live in France, display France at the top of the list, and not Afghanistan (the first country in alphabetical order).

Assigning function handlers: take 1

Example 1-9 is an extract of the JavaScript file *main.js* provided by Jerry. This code contains function handlers that process user clicks in the Donate section.

Example 1-9. The first version of event handlers

```
(function() {
        var donateBotton = document.getElementById('donate-button');
        var donationAddress = document.getElementById('donation-address');
        var customAmount = document.getElementById('customAmount');
        var donateForm = document.forms['_xclick'];
        var donateLaterLink = document.getElementById('donate-later-link');
        var checkedInd = 2;

        function showDonationForm() {
                donationAddress.style.display = "none";
                donateFormContainer.style.display = "block";
        }

    // Register the event listeners
        donateBotton.addEventListener('click', showDonationForm, false);
        customAmount.addEventListener('focus', onCustomAmountFocus, false);
        donateLaterLink.addEventListener('click', donateLater, false);
        customAmount.addEventListener('blur', onCustomAmountBlur, false);

        // Uncheck selected radio buttons if the custom amount was chosen
        function onCustomAmountFocus() {
                for (var i = 0; i < donateForm.length; i++) {
                        if (donateForm[i].type == 'radio') {
                                donateForm[i].onclick = function() {
                                        customAmount.value = '';
                                }
                        }
                        if (donateForm[i].type == 'radio' && donateForm[i].checked) {
                                checkedInd = i;
                                donateForm[i].checked = false;
                        }
                }
        }

        function onCustomAmountBlur() {

                if (isNan(customAmount.value)) {
                    // The user haven't entered valid number for other amount
```

```
                    donateForm[checkedInd].checked = true;
            }
    }

    function donateLater(){
            donationAddress.style.display = "block";
            donateFormContainer.style.display = "none";
    }

})();
```

This code contains an example of an inefficient loop that assigns a click event handler to each radio button should the user click any radio button after visiting the Other Amount field. This reflects Jerry's understanding of how to reset the value of the customAmount variable. Jerry was not familiar with the capture phase of the events that can intercept the click event on the level of the radio buttons and simply reset the value of customAmount regardless of which specific radio button is clicked.

Assigning function handlers: take 2

Let's improve the code from the previous section. The idea, as shown in Example 1-10, is to intercept the click event during the capture phase (see the section "DOM Events" in the bonus online chapter) and if the Event.target is any radio button, perform customAmount.value = '';.

Example 1-10. The event handler for the Reset button

```
var donateFormContainer = document.getElementById('donate-form-container');

// Intercept any click on the donate form in a capturing phase
donateFormContainer.addEventListener("click", resetCustomAmount, true);
function resetCustomAmount(event){

    // reset the customAmount
        if (event.target.type=="radio"){
                customAmount.value = '';
        }
}
```

The code of onCustomAmountFocus() doesn't need to assign function handlers to the radio buttons any longer, as shown in Example 1-11.

Example 1-11. The Custom Amount field gets focus

```
function onCustomAmountFocus() {
        for (var i = 0; i < donateForm.length; i++) {
                if (donateForm[i].type == 'radio' && donateForm[i].checked) {
                        checkedInd = i;
                        donateForm[i].checked = false;
                }
```

```
        }
}
```

In the Donate section, we started working with event handlers. You'll see many more examples of event processing throughout the book.

Adding Video

In this section, we'll add a video player to our Save The Child application. The goal is to play a short animation encouraging kids to fight the disease. We've hired a professional animation artist, Yuri, who has started working on the animation. Meanwhile, let's take care of embedding the video player showing any sample video file.

Adding the HTML5 Video Element

Let's run the project called *project-05-html5-video* to see the video playing, and after that, we'll review the code. The new version of the Save The Child app should look like Figure 1-12. Users will see an embedded video player on the right that can play the video located in the *assets/media* folder of the project *project-05-html5-video*.

Figure 1-12. The video player is embedded

Let's see how *index.html* has changed since its previous version. The bottom part of the main section includes the `<video>` tag. In the past, videos in web pages were played predominantly by the browser's Flash Player plug-in (even older popular plug-ins included RealPlayer, Media Player, and QuickTime). For example, you could have used the HTML tag `<embed src="myvideo.swf" height="300" width="300">`, and if the user's browser supports Flash Player, that's all you need for basic video play. Although there were plenty of open source video players, creation of the enterprise-grade video player for Flash videos became an important skill for some software developers. For example, HBO, an American cable network, offers an advanced multifeatured video player embedded into link:http://www.hbogo.com for its subscribers.

In today's world, most modern mobile web browsers don't support Flash Player, and video content providers prefer broadcasting videos in formats that are supported by all browsers and can be embedded into web pages by using the standard HTML5 element `<video>` (see its current working draft (*http://bit.ly/1hTqKPd*)).

Example 1-12 illustrates how we've embedded the video into the bottom portion of our web page (*index.html*). It includes two <source> elements, which allows us to provide alternative media resources. If the web browser supports playing video specified in the first <source> element, it'll ignore the other versions of the media. For example, the following code offers two versions of the video file: *intro.mp4* (in H.264/MPEG-4 format natively supported by Safari and Internet Explorer) and *intro.webm* (WebM format for Firefox, Chrome, and Opera).

Example 1-12. The HTML container for the video element

```
<section id="main-bottom-section">
 <div id="video-container">
        <video controls poster="assets/media/intro.jpg"
                width="390px" height="240" preload="metadata">

                <source src="assets/media/intro.mp4" type="video/mp4">
                <source src="assets/media/intro.webm" type="video/webm">
                <p>Sorry, your browser doesn't support video</p>
        </video>

                <h3>Video header goes here</h3>
                <h5><a href="javascript:void(0);">More videos</a></h5>
 </div>
</section>
```

The Boolean property `controls` asks the web browser to display the video player with controls (the Play/Pause buttons, the full-screen mode, and so forth). You can also control the playback programmatically in JavaScript. The `poster` property of the <video> tag specifies the image to display as a placeholder for the video—this is the image you see in Figure 1-12. In our case, `preload=metadata` instructs the web browser to preload just the first frame of the video and its metadata. Should we use `preload="auto"`, the video would start loading in the background as soon as the web page was loaded, unless the user's browser doesn't allow it (for example, Safari on iOS) in order to save bandwidth.

All major web browsers released in 2011 and later (including Internet Explorer 9) come with their own embedded video players that support the <video> element. It's great that your code doesn't depend on the support of Flash Player, but browsers' video players look different.

If neither *.mp4* nor *.webm* files can be played, the content in the <p> tag displays the fallback message "Sorry, your browser doesn't support video." If you need to support older web browsers that don't support HTML5 video, but support Flash Player, you can replace this <p> tag with the <object> and <embed> tags that embed another media file that Flash Player understands. Finally, if you believe that some users might have browsers that support neither the <video> tag nor Flash Player, just add links to the files listed in the <source> tags right after the closing </video> tag.

Embedding YouTube Videos

Another way to include videos in your web application is by uploading them to YouTube first and then embedding them into your web page. This provides several benefits:

- The videos are hosted on Google's servers and use their bandwidth.

- The users either can watch the video as a part of your application's web page or, by clicking the YouTube logo on the status bar of the video player, can continue watching the video from its original YouTube URL.

- YouTube streams videos in compressed form, and the user can watch as the bytes come in. The video doesn't have to be fully preloaded to the user's device.

- YouTube stores videos in several formats and automatically selects the best one based on the user's web browser (user agent).

- The HTML code to embed a YouTube video is generated for you by clicking the Share and then the Embed link under the video itself.

- You can enrich your web application by incorporating extensive video libraries via the YouTube Data API (*http://bit.ly/1mdF1Hp*). You can create fine-tuned searches to retrieve channels, playlists, and videos; manage subscriptions; and authorize user requests.

- Your users can save the YouTube videos on their local drive by using free web browser add-ons such as the DownloadHelper extension for Firefox or RealDownloader.

Embedding a YouTube video into your HTML page is simple. Find the page with the video on YouTube and click the links Share and Embed located right under the video. Then select the size of your video player and HTTPS encryption if needed (see Chapter 9 on web security for reasoning). When this is done, copy the generated iFrame section into your page.

Open the file *index.html* in *project-06-YouTube-video* and you'll see the code that replaces the <video> tag of the previous project. It should look like Example 1-13.

Example 1-13. The HTML container for the YouTube video

```
<section id="main-bottom-section">
 <div id="video-container">
  <div id="video-container">
  <iframe
   src="http://www.youtube.com/embed/VGZcerOhCuo?wmode=transparent&hd=1&vq=hd720"
   frameborder="0" width="390" height="240"></iframe>

  <h3>Video header goes here</h3>
  <h5><a href="javascript:void(0);">More videos</a></h5>
  </div>
```

Figure 1-13. The YouTube player is embedded

```
  </div>
</section>
```

Note that the initial size of our video player is 390×240 pixels. The `<iframe>` wraps the URL of the video, which in this example ends with parameters `hd=1` and `vq=hd720`. This is how you can force YouTube to load video in HD quality. Run *project-06-YouTube-video* and you will see a web page that looks like Figure 1-13.

Now let's do yet another experiment. Enter the URL of our video directly in your web browser and then turn on Firebug or Chrome Developer Tools as explained in the bonus online chapter. We used Firebug under the Mac OS and selected the Net tab. Then, the HTML Response looks like Figure 1-14. YouTube recognizes that this web browser is capable of playing Flash content (`FLASH_UPGRADE`) and picks QuickTime as a fallback (`QUICKTIME_FALLBACK`).

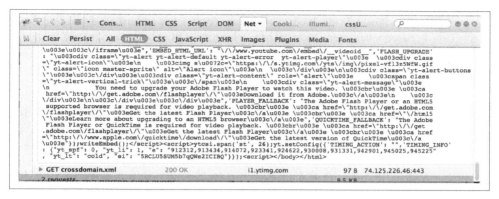

\u003e\u003c\/iframe\u003e", 'EMBED_HTML_URL': "\/\/www.youtube.com\/embed\/__videoid__", 'FLASH_UPGRADE'
: "\u003cdiv class=\"yt-alert yt-alert-default yt-alert-error yt-alert-player\"\u003e \u003cdiv class
=\"yt-alert-icon\"\u003e\n   \u003cimg s\u0072c=\"https:\/\/s.ytimg.com\/yts\/img\/pixel-vfl3z5WfW.gif
\" class=\"icon master-sprite\" alt=\"Alert icon\"\u003e\n \u003c\/div\u003e\n\u003cdiv class=\"yt-alert-buttons
\"\u003e\u003c\/div\u003e\u003cdiv class=\"yt-alert-content\" role=\"alert\"\u003e   \u003cspan class
=\"yt-alert-vertical-trick\"\u003e\u003c\/span\u003e\n   \u003cdiv class=\"yt-alert-message\"\u003e
\n   You need to upgrade your Adobe Flash Player to watch this video. \u003cbr\u003e \u003ca
 href=\"http:\/\/get.adobe.com\/flashplayer\/\"\u003eDownload it from Adobe.\u003c\/a\u003e\n   \u003c
\/div\u003e\n\u003c\/div\u003e\u003c\/div\u003e", 'PLAYER_FALLBACK': "The Adobe Flash Player or an HTML5
 supported browser is required for video playback. \u003cbr\u003e \u003ca href=\"http:\/\/get.adobe.com
\/flashplayer\/\"\u003eGet the latest Flash Player\u003c\/a\u003e \u003cbr\u003e \u003ca href=\"\/html5
\"\u003eLearn more about upgrading to an HTML5 browser\u003c\/a\u003e", 'QUICKTIME_FALLBACK': "The Adobe
 Flash Player or QuickTime is required for video playback. \u003cbr\u003e \u003ca href=\"http:\/\/get
.adobe.com\/flashplayer\/\"\u003eGet the latest Flash Player\u003c\/a\u003e \u003cbr\u003e \u003ca href
=\"http:\/\/www.apple.com\/quicktime\/download\/\"\u003eGet the latest version of QuickTime\u003c\/a
\u003e"});writeEmbed();}\/script\u003e\u003cscript\u003eytcsi.span('st', 26);yt.setConfig({'TIMING_ACTION': "", 'TIMING_INFO'
: {'yt_spf': 0, 'yt_li': 1, "e": "912312,913434,914072,923341,924622,930008,931331,942901,945025,945225"
, "yt_lt": "cold", "ei": "5RCLU5SUM5b7qQWs2ICIBQ"}});\u003cscript\u003e\u003c/body\u003e\u003c/html\u003e

| ▶ GET crossdomain.xml | 200 OK | i1.ytimg.com | 97 B | 74.125.226.46:443 |

Figure 1-14. HTTP Response object from YouTube

YouTube offers an Opt-In Trial of HTML5 video (*https://www.youtube.com/html5*), which allows the users to request playing most of the videos using HTML 5 video (even those recorded for Flash Player). Try to experiment on your own and see if YouTube streams HTML5 videos in your browser.

Our brief introduction to embedding videos in HTML is over. Let's keep adding new features to the Save The Child web application. This time, we'll become familiar with the HTML5 Geolocation API.

Adding Geolocation Support

HTML5 includes a Geolocation API that allows you to programmatically determine the latitude and longitude of a user's device. Most people are accustomed to the non-Web GPS applications in cars or mobile devices that display maps and calculate distances based on the current coordinates of the user's device or motor vehicle. But why do we need a Geolocation API in a desktop web application?

The goal of this section is to demonstrate a very practical feature: finding registered Save The Child events based on the user's location. This way, users of this application not only can donate, but can participate in such an event or even find children in need of assistance in a particular geographical area. In this chapter, you'll just learn the basics of the HTML5 Geolocation API, but we'll continue improving the location feature of the Save The Child application in the next chapter.

The World Wide Web Consortium (W3C) has published a proposed recommendation of the Geolocation API Specification (*http://bit.ly/Twpgyv*), which can become a part of the HTML5 spec soon.

Does your old desktop computer have GPS hardware? Most likely it doesn't. But its location can be calculated with varying degrees of accuracy. If your desktop computer is connected to a network, it has an IP address or your local WiFi router might have a Service Set Identifier (SSID) given by the router vendor or your Internet provider. Therefore, the location of your desktop computer is not a secret, unless you change the SSID of your WiFi router. Highly populated areas have more WiFi routers and cell towers, so the accuracy increases. In any case, properly designed applications must always ask the user's permission to use the current location of a computer or other connected device.

GPS signals are not always available. However, various location services can help identify the position of a device. For example, Google, Apple, Microsoft, Skyhook, and other companies use publicly broadcast WiFi data from a wireless access point. Google Location Server uses a Media Access Control (MAC) address to identify any device connected to a network.

Every web browser has a global object `window`, which includes the `navigator` object containing information about the user's browser. If the browser's `navigator` object includes the property `geolocation`, geolocation services are available. Although the Geolocation API allows you to get just a coordinate of your device and report the accuracy of this location, most applications use this information with some user-friendly UI; for example, mapping software. In this section, our goal is to demonstrate the following:

1. How to use the Geolocation API
2. How to integrate the Geolocation API with Google Maps
3. How to detect whether the web browser supports geolocation services

To respect people's privacy, web browsers will always ask for permission to use the Geolocation API unless the user changes the settings on the browser to always allow it.

Geolocation Basics

The next version of our application is called *project-07-basic-geolocation*, where we simply assume that the web browser supports geolocation. The Save The Child page will get a new container in the middle of the bottom main section, where we are planning to display the map of the current user's location. But for now, we'll show just the coordinates: latitude, longitude, and the accuracy. Initially, the map container is empty, but we'll populate it from the JavaScript code as soon as the position of the computer is located:

```
<div id="map-container">

</div>
```

Example 1-14 from *main.js* makes a call to the `navigator.geolocation` object to get the current position of the user's computer. In many code samples, we'll use `console.log()` (*http://mzl.la/VzUx5l*) to print debug data in the web browser's console.

Example 1-14. Finding coordinates with navigator.geolocation

```
var mapContainer = document.getElementById('map-container');              ❶

function successGeoData(position) {
        var successMessage = "We found your position!";                    ❷
        successMessage += '\n Latitude = ' + position.coords.latitude;
        successMessage += '\n Longitude = ' + position.coords.longitude;
        successMessage += '\n Accuracy = ' + position.coords.accuracy +
        console.log(successMessage);

        var successMessageHTML = successMessage.replace(/\n/g, '<br />');
        var currentContent = mapContainer.innerHTML;
        mapContainer.innerHTML = currentContent + "<br />"
                                        + successMessageHTML;             ❸

}

function failGeoData(error) {                                              ❹
        console.log('error code = ' + error.code);

        switch(error.code) {
                case error.POSITION_UNAVALABLE:
                        errorMessage = "Can't get the location";
                        break;
                case error.PERMISSION_DENIED:
                        errorMessage = "The user doesn't want to share location";
                        break;
                case error.TIMEOUT:
                        errorMessage = "Timeout - Finding location takes too long";
                        break;
                case error.UNKNOWN_ERROR:
                        errorMessage = "Unknown error: " + error.code;
```

```
                break;
        }
        console.log(errorMessage);
        mapContainer.innerHTML = errorMessage;
}

if (navigator.geolocation) {
        var startMessage = 'Your browser supports geolocation API :)';
        console.log(startMessage);
        mapContainer.innerHTML = startMessage;
        console.log('Checking your position...');
        mapContainer.innerHTML = startMessage + '<br />Checking your position...';

        navigator.geolocation.getCurrentPosition(successGeoData,
            failGeoData,                                          ❺
            {maximumAge : 60000,
                enableHighAccuracy : true,                        ❻
                timeout : 5000
            }
        );

} else {
        mapContainer.innerHTML ='Your browser does not support geolocation';
}
```

❶   Get a reference to the DOM element map-container to be used for showing the results.

❷   The function handler to be called in case of the successful discovery of the computer's coordinates. If this function is called, it will get a position object as an argument.

❸   Display the retrieved data on the web page (see Figure 1-15).

❹   This is the error-handler callback.

❺   Invoke the method getCurrentPosition(), passing it two callback functions as arguments (for success and failure) and an object with optional parameters for this invocation.

❻   Optional parameters: accept the cached value if not older than 60 seconds, retrieve the best possible results, and don't wait for results for more than 5 seconds. You might not always want the best possible results, to lower the response time and the power consumption.

If you run *project-07-basic-geolocation*, the browser will show a pop-up (it can be located under the toolbar) asking a question similar to "Would you like to share your location with 127.0.01?" Allow this sharing and you'll see a web page, which will include the information about your computer's location, similar to Figure 1-15.

If you don't see the question asking permission to share your location, check the privacy settings of your web browser; most likely you've allowed using your location at some time in the past.

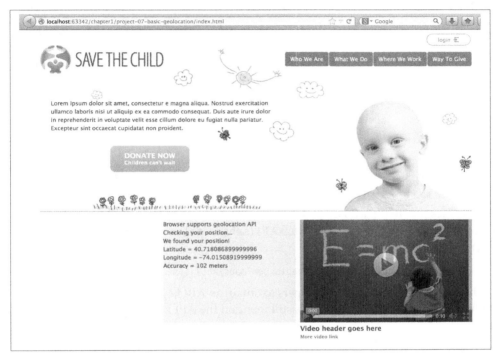

Figure 1-15. The latitude and longitude are displayed

 If you want to monitor the position as it changes (the device is moving), use `geolocation.watchPosition()`, which implements an internal timer and checks the position. To stop monitoring the position, use `geolocation.clearWatch()`.

Integration with Google Maps

Knowing the device coordinates is important, but let's make the location information more presentable by feeding the device coordinates to the Google Maps API (*http://bit.ly/1k61pfX*). In this version of Save The Child, we'll replace the gray rectangle from Figure 1-15 with the Google Maps container. We want to show a familiar map fragment with a pin pointing at the location of the user's web browser. To follow our show-and-tell style, let's see it working first. Run *project-08-geolocation-maps*, and you'll see a map with your current location, as shown in Figure 1-16.

Figure 1-16. Showing your current location

Now comes the "tell" part. First, take a look at the bottom of the *index.html* file. It loads Google's JavaScript library with its Map API (`sensor=false` means that we are not using a sensor-like GPS locator):

```
<script src="http://maps.googleapis.com/maps/api/js?sensor=false"></script>
```

In the past, Google required developers to obtain an API key and include it in the URL. Although some of Google's tutorials still mention the API key, it's no longer a must.

 An alternative way of adding the `<script>` section to an HTML page is by creating a `<script>` element. This gives you the flexibility of postponing the decision about which JavaScript to load. For example:

```
var myScript=document.createElement("script");
myScript.src="http://......somelibrary.js";
document.body.appendChild(myScript);
```

Our *main.js* will invoke the function for Google's library as needed. The code that finds the location of your device is almost the same as in "Geolocation Basics" on page 37. We've replaced the call to `geolocation.watchPosition()` so that this program can modify the position if your computer, tablet, or a mobile phone is moving. We store the returned value of `watchPosition()` in the variable `watcherID` in case you decide to stop watching the position of the device by calling `clearWatch(watcherID)`. Also, we lower the value of the `maximumAge` option so the program will update the UI more frequently, which is important if you are running this program while in motion (Example 1-15).

Example 1-15. Integrating geolocation with the mapping software

```
(function() {

  var locationUI = document.getElementById('location-ui');
  var locationMap = document.getElementById('location-map');
  var watcherID;

  function successGeoData(position) {
    var successMessage = "We found your position!";
    var latitude = position.coords.latitude;

    var longitude = position.coords.longitude;
    successMessage += '\n Latitude = ' + latitude;
    successMessage += '\n Longitude = ' + longitude;
    successMessage += '\n Accuracy = ' + position.coords.accuracy
                                       + ' meters';
    console.log(successMessage);

    // Turn the geolocation position into a LatLng object.
    var locationCoordinates =
          new google.maps.LatLng(latitude, longitude);          ❶

    var mapOptions = {
        center : locationCoordinates,
        zoom : 12,
        mapTypeId : google.maps.MapTypeId.ROADMAP,              ❷
        mapTypeControlOptions : {
          style : google.maps.MapTypeControlStyle.DROPDOWN_MENU,
          position : google.maps.ControlPosition.TOP_RIGHT
        }
    };

    // Create the map
    var map = new google.maps.Map(locationMap, mapOptions);    ❸

    // set the marker and info window
    var contentString = '<div id="info-window-content">' +
        'We have located you using HTML5 Geolocation.</div>';

    var infowindow = new google.maps.InfoWindow({              ❹
        content : contentString,
        maxWidth : 160
    });

    var marker = new google.maps.Marker({                      ❺
        position : locationCoordinates,
        map : map,
        title : "Your current location"

    });

        google.maps.event.addListener(marker, 'click',        ❻
```

```
                function() {
                    infowindow.open(map, marker);
                }
            );

            // When the map is loaded show the message and
            // remove event handler after the first "idle" event
            google.maps.event.addListenerOnce(map, 'idle', function(){
              locationUI.innerHTML = "Your current location";
        })

    }

    // error handler
    function failGeoData(error) {
          clearWatch(watcherID);
          //the error processing code is omitted for brevity
    }

    if (navigator.geolocation) {
          var startMessage =
              'Browser supports geolocation API. Checking your location...';
          console.log(startMessage);

          var currentContent = locationUI.innerHTML;
          locationUI.innerHTML = currentContent +' '+startMessage;

          watcherID = navigator.geolocation.watchPosition(successGeoData,  ❼
              failGeoData, {
                  maximumAge : 1000,
                  enableHighAccuracy : true,
                  timeout : 5000
          });

    } else {
          console.log('browser does not support geolocation :(');
    }
})();
```

❶   The Google API represents a point in geographical coordinates (latitude and longitude) as a LatLng object, which we instantiate here.

❷   The object google.maps.MapOptions is an object that allows you to specify various parameters of the map to be created. In particular, the map type can be one of the following: HYBRID, ROADMAP, SATELLITE, TERRAIN. We've chosen ROAD MAP, which displays a normal street map.

❸   The function constructor google.maps.Map takes two arguments: the HTML container where the map has to be rendered and the MapOption as parameters of the map.

❹　Create an overlay box that will show the content describing the location (for example, a restaurant name) on the map. You can do it programmatically by calling `InfoWindow.open()`.

❺　Place a marker on the specified position on the map.

❻　Show the overlay box when the user clicks the marker on the map.

❼　Invoke the method `watchPosition()` to find the current position of the user's computer.

This is a pretty basic example of integrating geolocation with the mapping software. The Google Maps API consists of dozens JavaScript objects and supports various events that allow you to build interactive and engaging web pages that include maps. Refer to the Google Maps JavaScript API Reference (*http://bit.ly/TwpjtZ*) for the complete list of available parameters (properties) of all objects used in *project-08-geolocation-maps* and more. Chapter 2 presents a more advanced example of using Google Maps; we'll read the JSON data stream containing coordinates of the children so the donors can find them based on the specified postal code.

 For a great illustration of using Google Maps, look at the PadMapper (*https://www.padmapper.com*) web application. We use it for finding rental apartments in Manhattan.

Browser Feature Detection with Modernizr

Now we'll learn how to use the detection features offered by a JavaScript library called Modernizr (*http://modernizr.com*). This is a must-have feature-detection library that helps your application figure out whether the user's browser supports certain HTML5/CSS3 features. Review the code of *index.html* from *project-08-1-modernizr-geolocation-maps*. Note that *index.html* includes two `<script>` sections. The Modernizr's JavaScript is loaded first, whereas our own *main.js* is loaded at the end of the `<body>` section:

```
<!DOCTYPE html>

<html class="no-js" lang="en">
    <head>
            <meta charset="utf-8">

            <title>Save The Child | Home Page</title>
            <link rel="stylesheet" href="assets/css/styles.css">

            <script src="js/libs/modernizr-2.5.3.min.js"></script>

    </head>
    <body>
```

```
!-- Most of the HTML markup is omitted for brevity --!

        <script src="js/main.js"></script>
    </body>
</html>
```

Modernizr is an open source JavaScript library that helps your script to determine whether the required HTML or CSS features are supported by the user's browser. Instead of maintaining a complex cross-browser feature matrix to see if, say, border-radius is supported in the user's version of Firefox, the Modernizer queries the <html> elements to see what's supported and what's not.

Note the fragment at the top of *index.html*: <html class="no-js" lang="en">. For Modernizr to work, your HTML root element has to include the class named no-js. On page load, Modernizr replaces the no-js class with its extended version that lists all detected features; those that are not supported are labeled with the prefix no-. Run *index.html* from *project-08-1-modernizr-geolocation-maps* in Chrome and you'll see in the Developer Tools panel that the values of the class property of the html element are different now. You can see in Figure 1-17 that our version of Chrome doesn't support touch events (no-touch) or flexbox (no-flexbox).

Figure 1-17. Modernizr changed the HTML's class property

For example, there is a new way to do page layouts, using the so-called CSS Flexible Box Layout module. This feature is not widely supported yet, and as you can see in Figure 1-17, our web browser doesn't support it at the time of this writing. If the CSS file of your application implements two class selectors, .flexbox and .no-flexbox, the browsers that support flexible boxes will use the former, and the older browsers will use the latter.

When Modernizr loads, it creates a new JavaScript object `window.Modernizr` with lots of Boolean properties indicating whether a certain feature is supported. Add the `Mod ernizr` object as a watch expression in the Chrome Developer Tools panel and see which properties have the `false` value (see Figure 1-18).

Figure 1-18. window.Modernizr object

Hence, your JavaScript code can test whether certain features are supported.

What if Modernizer detects that a certain feature is not supported by a user's older browser? You can include polyfills in your code that replicate the required functionality.

You can write such a polyfill on your own or pick one from the collection at Modernizr's GitHub repository (*http://bit.ly/mod-list*).

Addy Osmani published The Developer's Guide To Writing Cross-Browser JavaScript Polyfills (*http://bit.ly/1sRn30Y*).

The Development version of Modernizr is only 42 KB in size and can detect lots of features. But you can make it even smaller by configuring the detection of only selected features. Just visit Modernizr (*http://modernizr.com/*) and click the red Production button that enables you to configure the build specifically for your application. For example, if you're interested in just detecting the HTML5 video support, the size of the generated Modernizr library will be reduced to under 2 KB.

Let's review the relevant code from *project-08-1-modernizr-geolocation-maps* that illustrates the use of Modernizr (see Example 1-16). In particular, Modernizr allows you to load one or the other JavaScript code block based on the result of some tests.

Actually, the Modernizr loader internally utilizes a tiny (under 2 KB) resource loader library, yepnope.js (*http://yepnopejs.com*), which can load both JavaScript and CSS. This library is integrated in Modernizr, but we just wanted to give proper recognition to *yepnope.js*, which you can use as an independent resource loader, too.

Example 1-16. Using the Modernizr loader

```
(function() {

  Modernizr.load({

      test: Modernizr.geolocation,

      yep: ['js/get-native-geo-data.js','https://www.google.com/jsapi'],

      nope: ['js/get-geo-data-by-ip.js','https://www.google.com/jsapi'],

      complete : function () {
            google.load("maps", "3",
                      {other_params: "sensor=false", 'callback':init});
      }
  });
})();
```

The preceding code invokes the function `load()`, which can take different arguments. In our example, the argument is a specially prepared object with four properties: `test`, yep, nope, and complete. The load() function will test the value of Modernizr.geolo cation and if it's true, it'll load the scripts listed in the yep property. Otherwise, it will load the code listed in the nope array. The code in *get-native-geo-data.js* gets the user's location the same way as was done earlier in "Integration with Google Maps" on page 39.

Now let's consider the nope case. The code of *get-geo-data-by-ip.js* has to offer an alternative way of getting the location of browsers that don't support the HTML5 Geolocation API. We found the GeoIP JavaScript API offered by MaxMind (*http:// www.maxmind.com*). Its service returns country, region, city, latitude, and longitude, which can serve as a good illustration of how a workaround of a nonsupported feature can be implemented. The code in *get-geo-data-by-ip.js* (see Example 1-17) is simple for now.

Example 1-17. Reporting nonimplemented features

```
function init(){

    var locationMap = document.getElementById('location-map');
    locationMap.innerHTML="Your browser does not support HTML5 geolocation API.";

    // The code to get the location by IP from http://j.maxmind.com/app/geoip.js
    // will go here. Then we'll pass the latitude and longitude values to
    // Google Maps API for drawing the map.

}
```

Most likely your browser supports the HTML5 Geolocation API, and you'll see the map created by the script *get-native-geo-data.js*. But if you want to test nonsupported geolocation (the nope branch), either try this code in the older browser or change the test condition to look like this: Modernizr.fakegeolocation,.

Google has several JavaScript APIs—for example, Maps, Search, Feed, and Earth. Any of these APIs can be loaded by the Google AJAX Loader (*http://bit.ly/1x51AAc*) goo gle.load(). This is a more generic way of loading any APIs compared to loading maps from maps.googleapis.com/maps/api (*http://bit.ly/1lJoF80*), as shown in the previous section on integrating geolocation and maps. The process of loading the Google code with the Google Ajax loader consists of two steps:

1. Load Google's common loader script (*https://www.google.com/jsapi*).
2. Load the concrete module API, specifying its name, version, and optional parameters. In our example, we are loading the Maps API of version 3, passing an object with two properties: sensor=false and the name of the callback function to invoke right after the mapping API completes loading, 'callback':init.

If you want to test your web page in a specific older version of a particular web browser, you can find distributions at oldapps.com (*https://www.oldapps.com*). For example, you can find all the old versions of Firefox for Mac OS (*http://bit.ly/1mN5RVz*) and for Windows (*http://www.oldapps.com/firefox.php*).

Search and Multimarkers with Google Maps

We've prepared a couple of more examples to showcase the features of Google Maps. The working examples are included in the code accompanying this book, and we provide brief explanations in this section.

The chapter's code samples include the *project-09-map-and-search* Webstorm project, which is an example of an address search using Google Maps. Figure 1-19 shows a fragment of the Save The Child page after we've entered the address **26 Broadway ny ny** in the search field. You can do a search by city or zip code, too. This can be a useful feature if you want to allow users to search for children living in a particular geographical area so their donations could be directed to specific people.

Figure 1-19. Searching by address

Our implementation of the search is shown in Example 1-18, a code fragment from *main.js*. It uses *geocoding*, which is the process of converting an address into geographic coordinates (latitude and longitude). If the address is found, the code places a marker on the map.

Example 1-18. Finding map location by address

```javascript
var geocoder = new google.maps.Geocoder();

function getMapByAddress() {
 var newaddress = document.getElementById('newaddress').value;

 geocoder.geocode(                                          ❶
  {'address' : newaddress,
  'country' : 'USA'
  },

  function(results, status) {                               ❷
   console.log('status = ' + status);

   if (status == google.maps.GeocoderStatus.OK) {

        var latitude = results[0].geometry.location.lat();  ❸
        var longitude = results[0].geometry.location.lng();

        var formattedAddress = results[0].formatted_address;
        console.log('latitude = ' + latitude +
                    ' longitude = ' +  longitude);
        console.log('formatted_address = ' + formattedAddress);

        var message = '<b>Address</b>: ' + formattedAddress;
        foundInfo.innerHTML = message;

        var locationCoordinates =
              new google.maps.LatLng(latitude, longitude);  ❹
        showMap(locationCoordinates, locationMap);

   } else if (status == google.maps.GeocoderStatus.ZERO_RESULTS) { ❺
        console.log('geocode was successful but returned no results. ' +
          'This may occur if the geocode was passed a nonexistent ' +
          'address or a latlng in a remote location.');

   } else if (status == google.maps.GeocoderStatus.OVER_QUERY_LIMIT) {
        console.log('You are over our quota of requests.');

   } else if (status == google.maps.GeocoderStatus.REQUEST_DENIED) {
        console.log('Your request was denied, ' +
          'generally because of lack of a sensor parameter.');

   } else if (status == google.maps.GeocoderStatus.INVALID_REQUEST) {
        console.log('Invalid request. ' +
            'The query (address or latlng) is missing.');
   }
 });
}
```

❶ Initiate request to the `Gecoder` object, providing the `GeocodeRequest` object with the address and a function to process the results. Because the request to the Google server is asynchronous, the function is a callback.

❷ When the callback is invoked, it will get an array with results.

❸ Get the latitude and longitude from the result.

❹ Prepare the `LatLng` object and give it to the mapping API for rendering.

❺ Process errors.

The Geocoding API is simple and free to use until your application reaches a certain number of requests. Refer to the Google Geocoding API documentation (*http://bit.ly/1jCIGsw*) for more details. If your application is getting the status code `OVER_QUERY_LIM IT`, you need to contact the Google Maps API for Business sales team for information on licensing options.

Adding multiple markers on the map

Our designer, Jerry, has yet another idea: show multiple markers on the map to reflect several donation campaigns and charity events that are going on at various locations. If we display this information on the Save The Child page, more people might donate or participate in other ways. We've just learned how to do an address search on the map, and if the application has access to data about charity events, we can display them as the markers on the map. Run *project-10-maps-multi-markers* and you'll see a map with multiple markers, as shown in Figure 1-20.

Figure 1-20. Multiple markers on the map

The JavaScript fragment in Example 1-19 displays the map with multiple markers. In this example, the data is hardcoded in the array charityEvents. In Chapter 2, we modify this example to get the data from a file in JSON form. The for loop creates a marker for each of the events listed in the array charityEvents. Each element of this array is also an array containing the name of the city and state, the latitude and longitude, and the title of the charity event. You can have any other attributes stored in such an array and display them when the user clicks a particular marker in an overlay by calling Info Window.open().

Example 1-19. Displaying a map with multiple markers

```
(function() {

  var locationUI = document.getElementById('location-ui');
  var locationMap = document.getElementById('location-map');

  var charityEvents = [['Chicago, Il', 41.87, -87.62, 'Giving Hand'],
    ['New York, NY', 40.71, -74.00, 'Lawyers for Children'],
    ['Dallas, TX', 32.80, -96.76, 'Mothers of Asthmatics '],
    ['Miami, FL', 25.78, -80.22, 'Friends of Blind Kids'],
    ['Miami, FL', 25.78, -80.22, 'A Place Called Home'],
    ['Fargo, ND', 46.87, -96.78, 'Marathon for Survivors']
  ];

  var mapOptions = {
              center : new google.maps.LatLng(46.87, -96.78),
              zoom : 3,
              mapTypeId : google.maps.MapTypeId.ROADMAP,
              mapTypeControlOptions : {
                      style : google.maps.MapTypeControlStyle.DROPDOWN_MENU,
                      position : google.maps.ControlPosition.TOP_RIGHT
              }
        };

  var map = new google.maps.Map(locationMap, mapOptions);

  var infowindow = new google.maps.InfoWindow();

  var marker, i;

  // JavaScript forEach() function is deprecated,
  // hence using a regular for loop
  for ( i = 0; i < charityEvents.length; i++) {
        marker = new google.maps.Marker({
                position : new google.maps.LatLng(charityEvents[i][1],
                                                  charityEvents[i][2]),
                map : map
        });

        google.maps.event.addListener(marker, 'click', (function(marker, i) {
                return function() {
```

```
                    var content = charityEvents[i][0] + '<br/>' + charityEvents[i][3];
                    infowindow.setContent(content);
                    infowindow.open(map, marker);
                }
        })(marker, i));

        google.maps.event.addListenerOnce(map, 'idle', function(){
                locationUI.innerHTML = "Donation campaigns and charity events.";
        })
    }

})();
```

Summary

This chapter described the process of mocking up our future website by our web designer, Jerry, who went a lot further than creating images with short descriptions. Jerry created a working prototype of the Save The Child page. Keep in mind that Jerry and his fellow web designers like creating good-looking web pages.

But we web developers need to worry about other things, like making web pages responsive and lightweight. The first thing you need to do after receiving the prototype from Jerry is run it through Google Developer Tools or Firebug (see the section "Debugging JavaScript in Web Browsers" in the online bonus chapter (*http://bit.ly/ 1iJO41S*) for details) and measure the total size of the resources being downloaded from the server. If your application loads 1 MB or more worth of images, ask Jerry to review the images and minimize their size.

The chances are that you don't need to download all the JavaScript code at once. We discuss modularization of large applications in Chapter 6.

The next phase of improving this prototype is to remove the hardcoded data from the code and place it into external files. The next chapter covers the JSON data format and how to fill our single-page application with this data by using a set of techniques called Ajax.

## CHAPTER 2

Using Ajax and JSON

This chapter is about bringing external data to our HTML web pages. In Chapter 1, we used only hardcoded data because our goal was to show how to lay out the web page and how to change that layout in response to certain events (for example, the user clicking a menu button). Now we'll make sure that our single-page application, Save The Child, can request data from external sources and send data, too. This comes down to two questions:

- How does an HTML web page exchange data with web servers?
- What format do we use to present the application data?

Even though there could be different answers to these questions, we'll be using Ajax techniques as an answer to the first question and JavaScript Object Notation (JSON) data format as an answer to the second one. We'll start this chapter by explaining why Ajax and JSON are appropriate choices for the Save The Child web application and many others.

Understanding Ajax

In the early days of the Internet, every new page, whether it was hosted on the same or separate website, required a new request and response to the web server. This, in turn, would re-render the entire contents of the new page. If a user points her web browser to one URL and then changes it to another, the new request will be sent to the new URL, and the new page will arrive and will be rendered by the browser. The URL might have been changed not because the user decided to go to visit a different website, but simply because the user selected a menu item that resulted in bringing a new web page from the same domain. This was pretty much the only way to design websites in the '90s.

Back in 1999, Microsoft decided to create a web version of Outlook, its popular email application. Microsoft's goal was to be able to modify the Input folder as new emails arrived, but without refreshing the entire content of the web page. It created an ActiveX control called `XMLHTTP` that lived inside Internet Explorer 5 and could make requests to the remote servers to receive data without needing to refresh the entire web page. Such a Web Outlook client would make periodic requests to the mail server, and if the new mail arrived, the application would insert a new row on top of the Inbox by directly changing the DOM object from JavaScript.

In the early 2000s, other web browsers implemented their own versions of `XMLHTTPRe` `quest`. Its Working Draft 6 is published by W3C (*http://bit.ly/1qJZqmF*). Google created its famous email client, Gmail, and its Maps web application. In 2005, Jesse James Garrett wrote an article titled "AJAX: A New Approach to Web Applications." The web developer community liked the term AJAX, which stands for Asynchronous JavaScript and XML (it was originally presented as an acronym; today, it's considered as a name, hence the now more common spelling, "Ajax"), and this gave birth to a new breed of web applications that could update the content of just a portion of a web page without re-retrieving the entire page. Interestingly enough, the last letter in the AJAX acronym stands for XML, although presenting the data in XML form is not required, and currently is seldom used as a data format in client-server exchanges. JSON is used a lot more often to represent data, but apparently AJAJ didn't sound as good as AJAX.

Visit the Google Finance (*http://www.google.com/finance*) or Yahoo! Finance (*http://finance.yahoo.com/*) web pages when the stock market is open, and you'll see how price quotes or other financial indicators change while most of the content remains the same. This gives an illusion of the server pushing the data to your web client. But most likely, it is not a data push but rather periodic *polling* of the server's data using Ajax. In modern web applications, we expect to see more of real server-side data push using the HTML5 WebSocket API, which is described in detail in Chapter 8.

Understanding JSON

JSON (*http://bit.ly/1iN2TkH*) stands for JavaScript Object Notation. Compared to XML, it's a more compact way to represent data. Besides, all modern web browsers understand and can parse JSON data. Now that you've learned about JavaScript object literals in Chapter 1, you'll see that presenting data in JSON format is almost the same as writing JavaScript object literals.

Figure 2-1 depicts a high-level view of a typical web application. All of the code samples from Chapter 1 (and the online bonus chapter (*http://bit.ly/1iJO41S*), Appendix A, and Appendix B) were written in HTML, JavaScript, and CSS. In this chapter, we add to the mix the `XMLHttpRequest` object that will send and receive the JSON content wrapped into `HTTPRequest` and `HTTPResponse` objects.

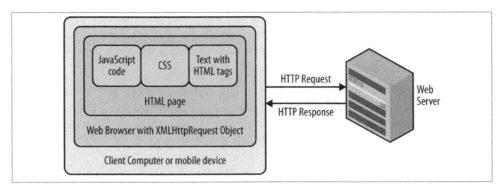

Figure 2-1. Anatomy of a web application

When a web page is loaded, the user doesn't know (and doesn't have to know) that the page content was brought from several servers that could be located thousands of miles apart. More often than not, when the user enters the URL requesting an HTML document, the server-side code can engage several servers to bring all the data requested by the user. Some data is retrieved by making calls to one or more web services. The legacy web services were built using SOAP + XML, but the majority of today's web services are built using lighter *RESTful architecture* (*http://bit.ly/1a1pDEq*) (REST standing for Representational State Transfer), and JSON has become a de facto standard data exchange format for REST web services.

Working with Ajax

Imagine a single-page application that needs some data refreshed in real time. For example, our Save The Child application includes an online auction where people can bid and purchase goods as a part of a charity event. If John from New York places a bid on a certain auction item, and some time later Mary from Chicago places a higher bid on the same item, we want to make sure that John knows about it immediately, in real time. This means that the server-side software that received Mary's bid has to push this data to all users who expressed their interest in the same item.

But the server has to send, and the browser has to modify, only the new price while the rest of the content of the web page should remain the same. You can implement this behavior by using Ajax. First, however, the bad news: you can't implement real-time server-side push with Ajax. You can only emulate this behavior by using polling techniques, whereby the XMLHttpRequest object sits inside your JavaScript code and periodically sends HTTP requests to the server asking whether any changes in bids occurred since the last request.

If, for instance, the last request was made at 10:20:00A.M., the new bid was placed at 10:20:02A.M., and the application makes a new request (and updates the browser's window) at 10:20:25 A.M., this means that the user will be notified about the price change with a 3-second delay. Ajax is still a request-response–based way of getting the server's data, and strictly speaking, doesn't offer true real-time updates. Some people use the term *near real-time* notifications.

Other bad news is that Ajax uses HTTP for data communication, which means that substantial overhead in the form of an `HTTPResponse` header will be added to the new price, and it can be as large as several hundred bytes. This is still better than sending the entire page to the web browser, but HTTP adds a hefty overhead.

 We implement such an auction in Chapter 8 by using a much more efficient protocol called WebSocket, which supports a real-time data push and adds only several extra bytes to the data load.

Retrieving Data from the Server

Let's try to implement Ajax techniques for data retrieval. The process of making an Ajax request is well defined and consists of the following steps:

1. Create an instance of the `XMLHttpRequest` object.

2. Initialize the request to your data source by invoking the method `open()`.

3. Assign a handler to the `onreadystatechange` attribute to process the server's response.

4. Make a nonblocking request to the data source by calling `send()`.

5. In your handler function, process the response when it arrives from the server. This is where *asynchronous* comes from: the handler can be invoked at any time, whenever the server prepares the response.

6. Modify the DOM elements based on the received data, if need be.

 Most likely you are going to be using one of the popular JavaScript frameworks, which will spare you from knowing all these details, but knowing how Ajax works under the hood can be beneficial.

In most books on Ajax, you'll see browser-specific ways of instantiating the `XMLHttpRe quest` object (a.k.a. XHR). Most likely you'll be developing your application by using a JavaScript library or framework, and all browser specifics in instantiating `XMLHttpRe`

quest will be hidden from you. Chapter 3 and Chapter 4 include such examples, but let's stick to the standard JavaScript way implemented by all modern browsers:

```
var xhr = new XMLHttpRequest();
```

The next step is to initialize a request by invoking the method open(). You need to provide the HTTP method (for example, GET or POST) *and* the URL of the data source. Optionally, you can provide three more arguments: a Boolean variable indicating whether you want this request to be processed asynchronously (which is the default), and the user ID and password if the authentication is required. Keep in mind that the following method does not request the data yet:

```
xhr.open('GET', dataUrl);
```

> Always use HTTPS if you need to send the user ID and password. Using secure HTTP should be your preferred protocol in general (read more in Chapter 9).

XHR has an attribute called readyState, and as soon as it changes, the callback function assigned to onreadystatechange will be invoked. This callback should contain your application-specific code to analyze the response and process it accordingly. Assigning such a callback is pretty simple:

```
xhr.onreadystatechange = function(){...}
```

Inside such a callback function, you'll be analyzing the value of the XHR's attribute readyState, which can have one of the values listed in Table 2-1.

Table 2-1. States of the request

Value	State	Description
0	UNSENT	The XHR has been constructed.
1	OPENED	open() was successfully invoked.
2	HEADERS_RECEIVED	All HTTP headers have been received.
3	LOADING	The response body is being received.
4	DONE	The data transfer has been completed.

Finally, send the Ajax request for data. The method send() can be called with or without parameters, depending on whether you need to send the data to the server. In its simplest form, the method send() can be invoked as follows:

```
xhr.send();
```

The complete cycle of the readyState transitions is depicted in Figure 2-2.

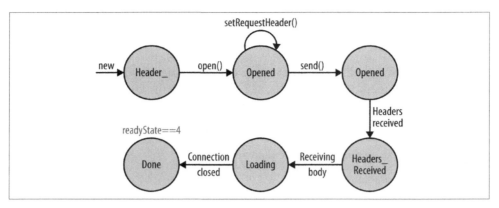

Figure 2-2. Transitions of the readyState attribute

Let's spend a bit more time discussing the completion of this cycle when the server's response is received and the XHR's `readyState` is equal to 4. This means that we've received something, which can be either the data we've expected or an error message. We need to handle both scenarios in the function assigned to the `onreadystate change` attribute (see Example 2-1). This is a common way to do it in JavaScript without using frameworks.

Example 2-1. Processing an Ajax response

```
xhr.onreadystatechange = function(){

 if (xhr.readyState == 4) {

   if((xhr.status >=200 && xhr.status <300) || xhr.status===304) {

      // We got the data. Get the value from one of the response attributes
      // e.g. xhr.responseText and process the data accordingly.

   } else {
      // We got an error. Process the error code and
      // display the content of the statusText attribute.
   }

 }
};
```

One note about the third line of this code. Here we're checking the HTTP status code (*http://bit.ly/1dkzBVq*) received from the server. W3C splits the HTTP codes into groups. The codes numbered 1*xx* are informational, 2*xx* are successful codes, 3*xx* are about redirections, 4*xx* represent bad requests (such as the infamous 404 for Not Found), and 5xx indicate server errors. That's why the preceding code fragment checks for all 2*xx* codes and for 304: the data was not modified and taken from cache.

If your application needs to post the data to the server, you need to open the connection to the server with the POST parameter. You'll also need to set the HTTP header attribute Content-type to either multipart/form-data for large-size binary data or to application/x-www-form-urlencoded (for forms and small-size alphanumeric data). Then prepare the data object and invoke the method send():

```
var data="This is some data";
xhr.open('POST', dataUrl, true);
xhr.setRequestHeader('Content-type', 'application/x-www-form-urlencoded');

...
xhr.send(data);
```

XMLHttpRequest Level 2 (*http://bit.ly/1m2szbI*) adds new functionality including FormData objects, timeouts, ArrayBuffers, and more. It's supported by most (*http://caniuse.com/xhr2*) web browsers.

Ajax: Good and Bad

Ajax techniques have their pros and cons. You saw how easy it is to create a web page that doesn't have to refresh itself but can provide users with a means of communicating with the server. This certainly improves the user experience. The fact that Ajax allows you to reduce the amount of data that goes over the wire is important, too. Another important advantage of Ajax is that it works in a standard HTML/JavaScript environment and is supported by all web browsers. The JavaScript frameworks hide all the differences in instantiating XMLHttpRequest and simplify making HTTP requests and processing responses. Because the entire page is not reloaded, you can create *fat clients* that keep certain data preloaded so that it can be reused in your JavaScript in different use cases. With Ajax, you can lazy-load content as needed rather than loading everything at once. Finally, the autocompletion feature, which is often taken for granted, would not be possible in an HTML/JavaScript application without Ajax.

On the bad side, with Ajax, the user loses the functionality of the browser's Back button, which reloads the previous web page in a way that enables the user to see the previous state of that page.

Because Ajax brings most content dynamically, search engines might not rank your web pages as high as if the content were statically embedded in the HTML. If discoverability of your web application is important, extra steps should be taken to make it more Search Engine Optimization (SEO)–friendly (for example, using an SEO Server (*http://bit.ly/1vnVl7Q*)).

Increasing the number of Ajax interactions means that your application will have to send more JavaScript code to the web browser, which increases the complexity of programming and decreases the scalability of your application.

 Using the HTML5 History API (see Chapter 1) will help you teach the old dog (the browser's Back button) new tricks.

Ajax applications are subject to *the same origin policy (http://mzl.la/1r5U8Eq)* (the same protocol, hostname, and port), which allows `XMLHttpRequest` to make HTTP requests only to the domains where the web application was loaded from. It's a security measure to limit the ability of JavaScript code to interact with resources that arrive to the web browser from a different web server.

 W3C has published a working draft of Cross-Origin Resource Sharing (*http://mzl.la/1iN36En*) (CORS), a mechanism to enable client-side cross-origin requests.

Populating States and Countries from HTML Files

To see the first example for which we use Ajax in our Save The Child application, run *project-01-donation-ajax-html*. In this example, we've removed the hardcoded data about countries and states from HTML and saved it in two separate files: *data/us-states.html* and *data/countries.html*. In this project, the file *index.html* has two empty combo boxes (`<select>` elements), as shown in Example 2-2.

Example 2-2. State and Country drop-downs

```
<select name="state" id="state">
  <option value="" selected="selected"> - State - </option>
  <!-- AJAX will load the rest of content -->
</select>
<select name="country" id="counriesList">
  <option value="" selected="selected"> - Country - </option>
  <!-- AJAX will load the rest of content -->
</select>
```

The resulting Save The Child page will look the same as the last sample from the previous chapter, but the Country and State drop-downs are now populated by the data located in these files (later in this chapter, in the section on JSON, we replace this HTML file with its JSON version). Example 2-3 presents the first three lines (out of 241) from the file *countries.html*.

Example 2-3. A fragment from the file countries.html

```
<option value="United States">United States</option>
<option value="United Kingdom">United Kingdom</option>
<option value="Afghanistan">Afghanistan</option>
```

The JavaScript code that reads countries and states from files (text and HTML markup) and populates the drop-downs comes next. Example 2-4 demonstrates that the content of these files is assigned to the innerHTML attribute of the given HTML <select> element.

Example 2-4. Loading HTML content into the Country and State drop-downs

```
function loadData(dataUrl, target) {
  var xhr = new XMLHttpRequest();
  xhr.open('GET', dataUrl, true);
  xhr.onreadystatechange = function() {
        if (xhr.readyState == 4) {
           if((xhr.status >=200 && xhr.status <300) ||
                              xhr.status===304){

                    target.innerHTML += xhr.responseText;
        } else {

                    console.log(xhr.statusText);
        }
      }
  }
  xhr.send();
}

// Load the countries and states using XHR
loadData('data/us-states.html', statesList);
loadData('data/countries.html', counriesList);
```

 The preceding code has an issue, which might not be so obvious, but can irritate users. The problem is that it doesn't handle errors. Yes, we print the error message on the developer's console, but the end user will never see it. If for some reason the data about countries or states doesn't arrive, the drop-downs will be empty, the donation form won't be valid, and the users will become angry that they can't make a donation and don't know why. Proper error handling and reports are important for any application, so never ignore it. You should display a user-friendly error message on the web page. For example, the else statement in the preceding example can display the received message in the page footer, as demonstrated in Example 2-5.

Example 2-5. Displaying the Ajax error in the page footer

```
else {
        console.log(xhr.statusText);

        // Show the error message on the Web page
        footerContainer.innerHTML += '<p class="error">Error getting ' +
                    target.name + ": "+ xhr.statusText + ",code: "+
                    xhr.status + "</p>";
}
```

This code uses the CSS selector error (see Example 2-6) that will show the error message on the red background. You can find it in the file *styles.css* in *project-02-donation-error-ajax-html*.

Example 2-6. Styling an error message with CSS

```
footer p.error {
        background:#d53630;
        text-align:left;
        padding: 0.9em;
        color: #fff;
}
```

Example 2-7 shows how to add the received data to a certain area on the web page. This code creates an HTML paragraph <p> with the text returned by the server and then adds this paragraph to the <div> with the ID main.

Example 2-7. Styling a paragraph

```
if (xhr.readyState == 4) {

  // All status codes between 200 and 300 mean success
  // and 304 means Not Modified
  if((xhr.status >=200 && xhr.status <300) || xhr.status===304){
      var p = document.createElement("p");

      p.appendChild(document.createTextNode(myRequest.responseText));

      document.getElementById("main").appendChild(p);
  }
}
```

Using JSON

In any client-server application, one of the important decisions to be made is about the format of the data that goes over the network. We are talking about application-specific data. Someone has to decide how to represent the data about an auction item, customer, donation, and so forth. The easiest way to represent text data is by using the comma-separated value (CSV) format, but it's not easily readable by humans, is hard to validate, and re-creation of JavaScript objects from a CSV feed would require additional information about the headers of the data.

Sending the data in XML form addresses the readability and validation issues, but it's very verbose. Every data element has to be surrounded by an opening and closing tag describing the data. Converting the XML data to/from JavaScript objects requires special parsers, and you'd need to use one of the JavaScript libraries for cross-browser compatibility.

Douglas Crockford popularized a new data format called JavaScript Object Notation, or JSON, which has become the most popular data format on the Web today. It's not as verbose as XML, and JSON's notation is almost the same as JavaScript object literals. It's easily readable by humans, and every ECMAScript 5–compliant browser includes a native JSON object: window.JSON. Even though JSON-formatted data looks like JavaScript object literals, JSON is language independent. Example 2-8 illustrates some JSON-formatted data.

Example 2-8. Sample JSON-formatted data

```
{
 "fname":"Alex",
 "lname":"Smith",
 "age":30,
 "address": {
     "street":"123 Main St.",
     "city": "New York"}
}
```

Anyone who knows JavaScript understands that this is an object that represents a person, which has a nested object that represents an address. Note the difference with JavaScript literals: the names of the properties are always strings, and every string must be represented in quotation marks. Representing the same object in XML would need a lot more characters (for example, <fname>Alex</fname>).

There are some other important differences between JSON and XML. The structure of an XML document can be defined by using Document Type Definitions (DTDs) or XML Schema, which simplifies data validation, but requires additional programming and schema maintenance. On the other hand, JSON data has data types—for example, the age attribute in the preceding example is not only a Number, but will be further evaluated by the JavaScript engine and will be stored as an integer. JSON also supports arrays, whereas XML doesn't.

For parsing JSON in JavaScript, you use the method JSON.parse(), which takes a string and returns a JavaScript object. For example:

```
var customer=JSON.parse('{"fname":"Alex","lname":"Smith"}');

console.log("Your name is " + customer.fname + " " + customer.lname);
```

For a reverse operation—turning an object into a JSON string—use `JSON.stringi` `fy(customer)`. The older browsers didn't have the `JSON` object, and an alternative way of parsing JSON is with the help of the script *json2.js*, which creates the JSON property on the global object. This script is freely available on GitHub (*http://bit.ly/aUMLnL*). In Chapter 1, you learned about feature detection with Modernizr, and you can automate the loading of this script if needed:

```
Modernizr.load({
    test: window.JSON,
    nope: 'json2.js',
    complete: function () {
        var customer = JSON.parse('{"fname":"Alex","lname":"Smith"}');
    }
});
```

Usually, JSON-related articles and blogs are quick to remind you about the evil nature of the JavaScript function `eval()`, which can take arbitrary JavaScript code and execute it. The `JSON.parse()` method is pictured as a protection against the malicious JavaScript that can be injected into your application's code and then executed by `eval()` via the web browser. The main argument is that `JSON.parse()` will not process the incoming code unless it contains valid JSON data.

Protecting your application code from being infected by means of `eval()` can be done outside your application code. Replacing HTTP with secure HTTPS helps a lot in this regard. Some web applications eliminate the possibility of cross-origin scripting by routing all requests to third-party data sources via proxying such requests through your trusted servers. But proxying all requests through your server may present scalability issues—imagine if thousands of concurrent users are routed through your server—so do some serious load testing before making this architectural decision.

 There are several JSON tools useful for developers. To make sure that your JSON data is valid and properly formatted, use JSONLint (*http://jsonlint.com*). If you paste ugly one-line JSON data, JSONLint will reformat it into a readable form. The add-on JSONView is also available both for Firefox (*http://mzl.la/VzV33h*) and Chrome (*http://bit.ly/1vnVyIm*) browsers. With JSONView, the JSON objects are displayed in a pretty, formatted, collapsible format. If errors exist in the JSON document, they will be reported. At the time of this writing, Chrome's version of JSONView does a better job of reporting errors.

Populating States and Countries from JSON Files

Earlier in this chapter, you saw an example of populating states and countries in the donate form from HTML files. Now you'll see how to retrieve JSON data by making an Ajax call. In the web browser, open *project-04-2-donation-ajax-json*, which reads the countries and states from the files *countries.json* and *us_states.json*, respectively. The beginning of the file *countries.json* is shown here:

```
{
"countrieslist": [
        {
                "name": "Afghanistan",
                "code": "AF"
        }, {
                "name": "Åland Islands",
                "code": "AX"
        }, {
                "name": "Albania",
                "code": "AL"
        },
```

The JavaScript code that populates the countries and states combo boxes comes next. Note the difference in creating the <option> tags from JSON versus HTML. In case of HTML, the received data is added to the <select> element as is: `target.innerHTML += xhr.responseText;`. In JSON files, the data is not wrapped into the <option> tags, so it's done programmatically, as shown in Example 2-9.

Example 2-9. Loading JSON-formatted countries and states

```
function loadData(dataUrl, rootElement, target) {
  var xhr = new XMLHttpRequest();
  xhr.overrideMimeType("application/json");
  xhr.open('GET', dataUrl, true);

  xhr.onreadystatechange = function() {
    if (xhr.readyState == 4) {
      if (xhr.status == 200) {

        //parse jsoon data
        var jsonData = JSON.parse(xhr.responseText);

        var optionsHTML = ''
        for(var i= 0; i < jsonData[rootElement].length; i++){
          optionsHTML+='<option value="'+jsonData[rootElement][i].code+'">'
                    + jsonData[rootElement][i].name+'</option>'
        }

        var targetCurrentHtml = target.innerHTML;
        target.innerHTML = targetCurrentHtml + optionsHTML;

      } else {
        console.log(xhr.statusText);

        // Show the error on the Web page
        tempContainer.innerHTML += '<p class="error">Error getting ' +
          target.name + ": "+ xhr.statusText + ",code: "+ xhr.status + "</p>";
      }
```

```
      }
    }
    xhr.send();
}

loadData('data/us-states.json', 'usstateslist', statesList);
loadData('data/countries.json', 'countrieslist', counriesList);
```

As shown in Example 2-9, we call the method `XMLHttpRequest.overrideMimeType()`
to ensure that the data will be treated by the browser as JSON even if the server won't
report it as such.

Using Arrays in JSON

JSON supports arrays, and Example 2-10 shows you how the information about a customer can be presented in JSON format. A customer can have more than one phone,
which can be stored in an array.

Example 2-10. Accessing an array of phones in JSON data

```
<script >
    var customerJson = '{"fname":"Alex",
                         "lname":"Smith",
                         "phones":[
                             "212-555-1212",
                             "565-493-0909"
                         ]
                         }';

    var customer=JSON.parse(customerJson);

    console.log("Parsed customer data: fname=" + customer.fname +
                " lname=" + customer.lname +
                " home phone=" + customer.phones[0] +
                " cell phone=" + customer.phones[1]);
</script>
```

This code creates an instance of the JavaScript object referenced by the variable `custom
er`. In this example, the `phones` array holds just two strings. But you can store objects
in a JSON array the same way as you would in a JavaScript object literal—just don't
forget to put every property name in quotes:

```
    var customerJson = '{"fname":"Alex",
                         "lname":"Smith",
                         "phones":[
                             {"type":"home", "number":"212-555-1212"},
                             {"type":"work","number":"565-493-0909"}]
                         }';
```

Loading Charity Events by Using Ajax and JSON

The last example in Chapter 1 displays various charity events by using the Google Maps API. But the data about these events is hardcoded in HTML files. After becoming familiar with Ajax and JSON, it should not be too difficult to create a separate file with the information about charities in JSON format and load them by using the XMLHTTPRe quest object

The next version of Save The Child displays the charity events via Google Maps by using the information about the events that's stored in the file *campaigndata.json*, which is shown in Example 2-11.

Example 2-11. The events information in campaignsdata.json

```
{
  "campaigns": {
    "header": "Nationwide Charity Events",
    "timestamp":"10/04/2014",
    "items": [
      {
        "title": "Lawyers for Children",
        "description":"Lawyers offering free services for the children",
        "location":"New York,NY"
      },
      {
        "title": "Mothers of Asthmatics",
        "description":"Mothers of Asthmatics - nationwide asthma network",
        "location": "Dallas,TX"
      },
      {
        "title": "Friends of Blind Kids",
        "description":"Semi-annual charity events for blind kids",
        "location":"Miami,FL"
      },
      {
        "title": "A Place Called Home",
        "description":"Adoption of the children",
        "location":"Miami,FL"
      },
      {
        "title": "Marathon for Survivors",
        "description":"Annual marathon for cancer survivors",
        "location":"Fargo, ND"
      }
    ]
  }
}
```

Run *project-03-maps-json-data* and you'll see the map with the markers for each of the events loaded from the file *campaigndata.json* (see Figure 2-3). Click a marker to see an overlay with the event details.

Figure 2-3. Markers built from JSON data

Note that this JSON file contains the object `campaigns`, which includes the array of objects representing charity events. Example 2-12 shows that the `XMLHttpRequest` object loads the data and the JSON parses it, assigning the `campaigns` object to the variable `campaignsData` that is used in `showCampaignsInfo()` with the Google Maps API (we've omitted the mapping part for brevity).

Example 2-12. Displaying campaigns data

```
function showCampaignsInfo(campaigns) {

        campaignsCount = campaigns.items.length;

        var message = "<h3>" + campaigns.header + "</h3>" +
                            "On " + campaigns.timestamp +
                      " we'll run " + campaignsCount + " campaigns.";

    locationUI.innerHTML = message + locationUI.innerHTML;
        resizeMapLink.style.visibility = "visible";

        createCampaignsMap(campaigns);
}

function loadCampaignsData(dataUrl) {
 var xhr = new XMLHttpRequest();
 xhr.open('GET', dataUrl);

 xhr.onreadystatechange = function() {
        if (xhr.readyState == 4) {
          if ((xhr.status >= 200 && xhr.status < 300) ||
```

```
                              xhr.status === 304) {
            var jsonData = xhr.responseText;

            var campaignsData = JSON.parse(jsonData).campaigns;
            showCampaignsInfo(campaignsData);
        } else {
            console.log(xhr.statusText);

          tempContainer.innerHTML += '<p class="error">Error getting ' +
              target.name + ": "+ xhr.statusText +
              ",code: "+ xhr.status + "</p>";
        }
      }
  }
  xhr.send();
}

var dataUrl = 'data/campaignsdata.json';
loadCampaignsData(dataUrl);
```

Some older web browsers may bring up a File Download pop-up window when the content type of the server's response is set to `application/json`. Try to use the MIME type `text/html`, instead, if you run into this issue.

For simplicity, in this section we've been loading JSON-formatted data from files, but in real-world applications, the JSON data is created on the server dynamically. For example, a browser makes a RESTful call to a Java-based server, which queries a database, generates a JSON-formatted result, and then sends it back to the web server.

Using JSON in CMS

Large-scale web applications could be integrated with content management systems (CMSs), which could supply content such as charity events and sales promotions. CMS servers can be introduced into the architecture of a web application to separate the work of preparing the content from the application, delivering it as shown in Figure 2-4, which depicts a web application integrated with the CMS server.

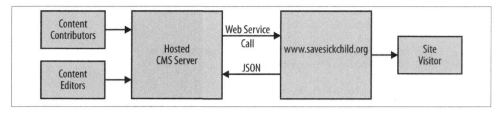

Figure 2-4. CMS in the picture

The content contributors and editors prepare the information on the charities and donation campaigns by using a separate application, not the Save The Child page. The CMS server and the web application server *www.savesickchild.org* may be located in the same or separate data centers. The server-side code of Save The Child makes a call to a CMS server whenever the site visitor requests information about charity events. If you get to pick a CMS for your future web application, make sure it offers a data feed in JSON format.

Some time ago, one of the authors of this book was helping Mercedes Benz USA develop its consumer-facing web application, with which users could search for, review, and configure their next car. Figure 2-5 shows a snapshot taken from *mbusa.com*. Three rectangular areas at the bottom were created by web designers to display the deals and promotions of the day. The up-to-date content for these areas (in JSON format) is retrieved from a CMS server when the user visits *mbusa.com*.

Figure 2-5. Current Mercedes deals from CMS

There's a side benefit of learning JSON: it's used as the data format in NoSQL databases such as MongoDB (*http://www.mongodb.com/*).

Handling JSON in Java

If a web browser receives a JSON stream from the server, the application needs to turn it into JavaScript objects. If a web client needs to send JavaScript objects to the server, they can be converted into JSON strings. Similar tasks have to be performed on the server side. Our Save The Child application uses a Java application server. Various third-party Java libraries can consume and generate JSON content.

Java Enterprise Edition 7 includes Java API for JSON Processing (*http://bit.ly/1pPKnGB*). Also, Several Java libraries can convert Java objects into their JSON representation and back—for example, Google's Gson (*http://code.google.com/p/google-gson*), Jackson (*http://jackson.codehaus.org*), and json-simple (*http://bit.ly/1qr1qTc*).

Google's Gson is probably the simplest one to use. It provides the methods `toJson()` and `fromJson()` to convert Java objects to JSON and back. Gson allows pre-existing unmodifiable objects to be converted to and from JSON and supports Java Generics. Gson works well with complex objects with deep inheritance hierarchies.

Let's say JavaScript sends to Java the following JSON string:

```
{"fname": "Alex", "lname":"Smith","skillLevel": 11}
```

The Java code can turn it into an instance of the `Customer` object by calling the method `Gson.fromJson()`. Similarly, Java code can create a JSON string from an object instance. Both of these operations are illustrated here:

```java
public Customer createCustomerFromJson(String jsonString){

    Gson myGson = new Gson();
    Customer cust = myGson.fromJson(jsonString, Customer.class);
    return cust;
}

public String createJsonFromCustomer(Customer cust){

    Gson gson = new Gson();

    return gson.toJson(cust, Customer.class);
}
```

Of course, the declaration of the Java class `Customer` must exist in the classpath, and don't forget to include *gson.jar* in your Java project.

The JSON data format is often used in non-JavaScript applications. For example, a Java server can exchange JSON-formatted data with a .NET server.

 The Java EE 7 specification includes JSR 353, which defines a standardized way for parsing and generating JSON. JSR 353 defines the Java API from JSON Processing (JSON-P) that shouldn't be confused with another acronym, JSONP or JSON-P (*http://json-p.org*), which is JSON with Padding (we'll discuss it at the end of this chapter).

Compressing JSON

JSON format is more compact than XML and is readable by human beings. But when you are ready to deploy your application in production, you still want to compress the data so fewer bytes will travel over the wire to the user's browser. Server-side libraries that generate JSON will make the data sent to the client compact by removing the tab and the newline characters.

If you want to turn the pretty-print JSON into a more compact one-line format, just use such websites as JavaScript Compressor (*http://bit.ly/1olD9Od*) or JSON Formatter (*http://bit.ly/ST5rRP*). For example, after running the 12 KB file *countries.json* through this compressor, its size was decreased to 9 KB. JSONLint can also compress JSON if you provide this URL: *http://jsonlint.com?reformat=compress*.

Like most content that is sent to browsers by web servers, JSON data should be compressed. Gzip (*http://bit.ly/1q9QeIY*) and Deflate (*http://bit.ly/1n8WH36*) are the two main compression methods used today. Both use the same compression algorithm *Deflate*, but whereas with Deflate the compressed data is being streamed to the client, Gzip first compresses the entire file, calculates the size, and adds some additional headers to the compressed data. So Gzip might need some extra time and memory, but you are more protected from getting incomplete JSON, JavaScript, or other content. Both Gzip and Deflate are easily configurable by major web servers, but it's hard to say which one is better for your application. Set up some tests with each of them and decide which one works faster or takes less system resources, but don't compromise on reliability of the compressed content.

We prefer using Gzip, which stands for GNU zip compression. On the server side, you'd need to configure the Gzip filters on your web server. You need to refer to your web server's documentation for instructions on the configuration, which is done by the MIME type. For example, you can request to Gzip everything except images (you might want to do this if you're not sure whether all browsers can properly uncompress certain MIME types).

For example, applying the Gzip filter to the 9 KB *countries.json* file will reduce its size to 3 KB, which means serious bandwidth savings, especially for web applications with lots of concurrent users. This is even more important for mobile web clients, which might be operating in areas with slower connections. Web clients usually set the HTTP request attribute `Accept-Encoding: gzip`, inviting the server to return Gzipped content, and the web server may compress the response if it does support it or unzipped content otherwise. If the server supports Gzip, the HTTP response will have the attribute `Content-Encoding: gzip`, and the browser will know to unzip the response data before use.

Gzip is being used for compressing all types of content: HTML, CSS, JavaScript, and more. If your server sends JSON content to the client by setting the content type to `application/json`, don't forget to include this MIME type in your server configuration for Gzip.

Web browsers support Gzipping, too, and your application can set `Content-Ecoding: gzip` in the HTTP request while sending the data from the web client to the server. But web clients usually don't send massive amounts of data to the server, so the benefits of the compression on the client side might not be as big.

Adding Charts to Save The Child

Let's consider yet another use case for JSON in Save The Child. We want to display charts with statistics about donations. By now, our application doesn't look exactly like the original mockup from Figure 1-2, but it's pretty close. There is an empty space to the left of the maps, and the charts showing donation statistics can fit right in. Now we need to decide how to draw the charts by using nothing but HTML5 elements. Note that we are not talking about displaying static images by using the `<img>` element. The goal is to draw the images dynamically in the client's code. You can accomplish this by using the HTML5 elements `<canvas>` or `<svg>`.

The `<canvas>` (*http://bit.ly/VzV9Ig*) element provides a bitmap canvas, where your scripts can draw graphs, game graphics, or other visual images on the fly without using any plug-ins such as Flash Player or Silverlight. To put it simply, `<canvas>` defines a rectangular area that consists of pixels, where you can draw. Keep in mind that the DOM object can't peek inside the canvas and access specific pixels. So if you are planning to create an area with dynamically changing graphics, you might want to consider using `<svg>`.

The `<svg>` element supports Scalable Vector Graphics (SVG) (*http://www.w3.org/TR/SVG11*), the XML-based language for describing two-dimensional graphics. Your code has to provide commands to draw the lines, text, images, and so forth.

Adding a Chart with the Canvas Element

Let's review some code fragments from *project-04-canvas-pie-chart-json*. The HTML section defines <canvas> as 260 x 240 pixels. If the user's browser doesn't support <canvas>, the user won't see the chart, but will see the text "Your browser does not support HTML5 Canvas" instead. You need to give an ID to your <canvas> element so your JavaScript code can access it:

```
<div id="charts-container">
    <canvas id="canvas" width="260" height="240">
        Your browser does not support HTML5 Canvas
    </canvas>
    <h3>Donation Stats</h3>
    <p> Lorem ipsum dolor sit amet, consectetur</p>
</div>
```

Run *project-04-canvas-pie-chart-json*, and you'll see the chart with donation statistics by city, as shown in Figure 2-6. We haven't styled our <canvas> element, but we could add a background color, border, or other bells and whistles if required.

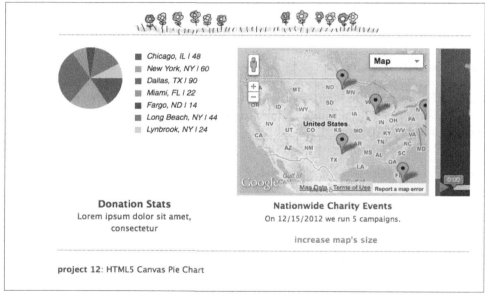

Figure 2-6. Adding a chart

The data to be used for drawing a pie chart in our canvas is stored in the file *data/chartdata.json*, but in the real world, the server-side code could generate it based on the up-to-the-second donation data and send it to the client. For example, you could do it as explained previously in "Handling JSON in Java" on page 71. Example 2-13 presents the contents of our *chartdata.json* file.

Example 2-13. The contents of chartdata.json

```
{
  "ChartData": {
    "items": [
      {
        "donors": 48,
        "location":"Chicago, IL"
      },
      {
        "donors": 60,
        "location": "New York, NY"
      },
      {
        "donors": 90,
        "location":"Dallas, TX"
      },
      {
        "donors": 22,
        "location":"Miami, FL"
      },
      {
        "donors": 14,
        "location":"Fargo, ND"
      },
      {
        "donors": 44,
        "location":"Long Beach, NY"
      },
      {
        "donors": 24,
        "location":"Lynbrook, NY"
      }
    ]
  }
}
```

Loading *chartdata.json* is done by using Ajax techniques as explained earlier. Although in our example we're loading the chart immediately when the Save The Child page loads, the code in Example 2-14 could be invoked only when the user requests to see the chart by clicking a menu item on the page.

Example 2-14. Loading chartdata.json

```
function getChartData(dataUrl, canvas) {
  var xhr = new XMLHttpRequest();
  xhr.open('GET', dataUrl, true);

  xhr.onreadystatechange = function() {
```

```
              if (xhr.readyState == 4) {
                  if ((xhr.status >= 200 && xhr.status < 300) ||
                                      xhr.status === 304) {
                          var jsonData = xhr.responseText;

                          var chartData = JSON.parse(jsonData).ChartData;        ❶


                          drawPieChart(canvas, chartData, 50, 50, 49);           ❷

                  } else {
                          console.log(xhr.statusText);
                          tempContainer.innerHTML += '<p class="error">Error getting '
                              + target.name + ": "+ xhr.statusText +
                              ",code: "+ xhr.status + "</p>";
                  }
              }
      }
      xhr.send();
}

loadData('data/chartdata.json', document.getElementById("canvas"));
```

❶   Parse JSON and create the `ChartData` JavaScript object.

❷   Pass the data to the `drawPieChart()` function that will draw the pie in the
     `<canvas>` element with the center coordinates x=50 and y=50 pixels. The upper-
     left corner of the canvas has coordinates (0,0). The radius of the pie will be 49
     pixels. The code of the function that draws the pie on the canvas goes next (see
     Example 2-15).

Example 2-15. Drawing the pie chart in `<canvas>`

```
function drawPieChart (canvas, chartData, centerX, centerY, pieRadius) {
      var ctx;   // The context of canvas
      var previousStop = 0;   // The end position of the slice
      var totalDonors = 0;

      var totalCities = chartData.items.length;

  // Count total donors
      for (var i = 0; i < totalCities; i++) {
                  totalDonors += chartData.items[i].donors;        ❶
      }

      ctx = canvas.getContext("2d");                               ❷
      ctx.clearRect(0, 0, canvas.width, canvas.heigh);

  var colorScheme = ["#2F69BF", "#A2BF2F", "#BF5A2F",        ❸
          "#BFA22F", "#772FBF", "#2F94BF", "#c3d4db"];
```

```
for (var i = 0; i < totalCities; i++) {                        ❹

    //draw the sector
    ctx.fillStyle = colorScheme[i];
    ctx.beginPath();
    ctx.moveTo(centerX, centerY);
    ctx.arc(centerX, centerY, pieRadius, previousStop, previousStop +
            (Math.PI * 2 * (chartData.items[i].donors/totalDonors))
,false);
    ctx.lineTo(centerX, centerY);
    ctx.fill();

    // label's bullet
    var labelY = 20 * i + 10;
    var labelX = pieRadius*2 + 20;

    ctx.rect(labelX, labelY, 10, 10);
    ctx.fillStyle = colorScheme[i];
    ctx.fill();

    // label's text
    ctx.font = "italic 12px sans-serif";
    ctx.fillStyle = "#222";
    var txt = chartData.items[i].location + " | " +
                                chartData.items[i].donors;
    ctx.fillText (txt, labelX + 18, labelY + 8);

    previousStop += Math.PI * 2 *
    (chartData.items[i].donors/totalDonors);
  }
}
```

❶ Count the total number of donors.

❷ Get the 2D context of the <canvas> element. This is the most crucial element to know for drawing on a canvas.

❸ The color scheme is the set of colors used to paint each slice (sector) of the pie.

❹ The for loop paints one sector on each iteration. This code draws lines, arcs, and rectangles, and adds text to the canvas. Describing the details of each method of the context object is out of the scope of this book, but you can find the details of the context API in the W3C documentation (*http://www.w3.org/TR/2dcon text*) available online.

To minimize the amount of manual coding, consider using one of the JavaScript libraries that helps with visualization (for example, D3.js (*http://d3js.org*)).

Adding a Chart by Using SVG

What if we want to make this chart dynamic and reflect the changes in donations every five minutes? If you're using <canvas>, you'll need to redraw each and every pixel of our canvas with the pie. With SVG, each element of the drawing would be the DOM element so we would have to redraw only those elements that have changed. If with <canvas> your script draws using pixels, the SVG drawings are done with vectors.

To implement the same donation statistics pie with the <svg> element, you'd need to replace the <canvas> element with the following markup:

```
<div id="charts-container">
        <svg id="svg-container" xmlns="http://www.w3.org/2000/svg">

        </svg>
        <h3>Donation Stats</h3>
        <p>
                Lorem ipsum dolor sit amet, consectetur
        </p>
</div>
```

Running *project-05-svg-pie-chart-json* would show you pretty much the same pie, because it uses the file *chartdata.json* with the same content, but the pie was produced differently. The code for the new version of drawPieChart() is shown in Example 2-16. We won't discuss all the details of the drawing with SVG but will highlight a couple of important lines of code that illustrate the difference between drawing on <canvas> versus <svg>.

Example 2-16. Drawing the pie chart in <svg>

```
function drawPieChart(chartContainer, chartData, centerX, centerY,
                      pieRadius, chartLegendX, chartLegendY) {
    // the XML namespace for svg elements
    var namespace = "http://www.w3.org/2000/svg";
    var colorScheme = ["#2F69BF", "#A2BF2F", "#BF5A2F", "#BFA22F",
                "#772FBF", "#2F94BF", "#c3d4db"];

    var totalCities = chartData.items.length;
    var totalDonors = 0;

    // Count total donors
    for (var i = 0; i < totalCities; i++) {
            totalDonors += chartData.items[i].donors;
    }

    // Draw pie sectors
    startAngle = 0;
    for (var i = 0; i < totalCities; i++) {
            // End of the sector = starting angle + sector size
            var endAngle = startAngle + chartData.items[i].donors
                / totalDonors * Math.PI * 2;
```

```
                    var x1 = centerX + pieRadius * Math.sin(startAngle);
                    var y1 = centerY - pieRadius * Math.cos(startAngle);
                    var x2 = centerX + pieRadius * Math.sin(endAngle);
                    var y2 = centerY - pieRadius * Math.cos(endAngle);

                    // This is a flag for angles larger than than a half circle
                    // It is required by the SVG arc drawing component
                    var big = 0;
                    if (endAngle - startAngle > Math.PI) {
                            big = 1;
                    }

                    //Create the <svg:path> element
                    var path = document.createElementNS(namespace, "path");    ❶

        // Start at circle center
                    var pathDetails = "M " + centerX + "," + centerY +         ❷
                    // Draw line to (x1,y1)
                    " L " + x1 + "," + y1 +
                    // Draw an arc of radius
                    " A " + pieRadius + "," + pieRadius +
                    // Arc's details
                    " 0 " + big + " 1 " +
                    // Arc goes to (x2,y2)
                    x2 + "," + y2 +
                    " Z";
                    // Close the path at (centerX, centerY)

                    // Attributes for the <svg:path> element
                    path.setAttribute("d", pathDetails);
                    // Sector fill color
                    path.setAttribute("fill", colorScheme[i]);

                    chartContainer.appendChild(path);    ❸

                    // The next sector begins where this one ends
                    startAngle = endAngle;

                    // label's bullet
                    var labelBullet = document.createElementNS(namespace, "rect");
                    // Bullet's position
                    labelBullet.setAttribute("x", chartLegendX);
                    labelBullet.setAttribute("y", chartLegendY + 20 * i);

    // Bullet's size
                    labelBullet.setAttribute("width", 10);
                    labelBullet.setAttribute("height", 10);
                    labelBullet.setAttribute("fill", colorScheme[i]);

                    chartContainer.appendChild(labelBullet);    ❹

                    // Add the label text
```

```
                  var labelText = document.createElementNS(namespace, "text");

    // label position = bullet's width(10px) + padding(8px)
                  labelText.setAttribute("x", chartLegendX + 18);
                  labelText.setAttribute("y", chartLegendY + 20 * i + 10);
                  var txt = document.createTextNode(chartData.items[i].location +
                  " | "+chartData.items[i].donors);

                  labelText.appendChild(txt);
                  chartContainer.appendChild(labelText);        ❺
        }

    }

❶   Create the <svg:path> HTML element, which is the most important SVG
    element for drawing basic shapes. It includes a series of commands that produce
    the required drawing. For example, *M 10 10* means *move to the coordinate 10,10*
    and *L 20 30* means *draw the line to the coordinate 20,30*.

❷   Fill the details of the <svg:path> element to draw the pie sector. Run *project-05-
    svg-pie-chart-json* to see the Save The Child page, and then right-click the pie
    chart and select Inspect Element (this is the name of the menu item in Firefox).
    Figure 2-7 shows the resulting content of our <svg> element. As you can see, it's
    not pixel based but a set of XML-like commands that drew the content of the
    chart. If you run the previous version of our application (*project-04-canvas-pie-
    chart-json*) and right-click the chart, you will be able to save it as an image, but
    won't see the internals of the <canvas> element.

❸   Add the internal elements of the chart container to the DOM: path, bullets, and
    text. These elements can be modified if needed without redrawing the entire
    content of the container.
```

In our code example, we have written the path commands manually
to process the data dynamically. But web designers often use tools
(Adobe Illustrator (*http://adobe.ly/1ls92x2*) or Inkscape (*http://
inkscape.org*)) to draw and then export images into SVG format. In
this case all paths will be encoded as <svg:path> automatically.

Because the SVG is XML-based, it's easy to generate the code shown in Figure 4-7 on
the server, and lots of web applications send ready-to-display SVG graphics to the users'
web browsers. But in our example, we are generating the SVG output in the JavaScript
from JSON received from the server, which provides a cleaner separation between the
client and the server-side code. The final decision on what to send to the web browser
(ready-to-render SVG or raw JSON) has to be made after considering various factors
such as available bandwidth, and the size of data, the number of users, and the existing
load on server resources.

```
000
                                                                Firebug – Save Sick Chil
           ≡  ▾    Console  HTML ▾  CSS  Script  DOM  Net  Cookies  Illuminations  cssUpdater
  ⫶⫶  Edit  Sync now  ◂  path  <  svg#svg-container  <  div#charts-container  <  section#...-section  <  div#main  ◂
           ▼ <div id="charts-container">
              ▼ <svg id="svg-container" xmlns="http://www.w3.org/2000/svg">
                   <path d="M 50,52 L 50,3 A 49,49 0 0 1 91.19635194393138,25.469628979003286
                   Z" fill="#2F69BF">
                   <rect x="115" y="10" width="10" height="10" fill="#2F69BF">
                   <text x="133" y="20">Chicago, IL | 48</text>
                   <path d="M 50,52 L 91.19635194393138,25.469628979003286 A 49,49 0 0 1
                   88.21877053797101,82.66472857479614 Z" fill="#A2BF2F">
                   <rect x="115" y="30" width="10" height="10" fill="#A2BF2F">
                   <text x="133" y="40">New York, NY | 60</text>
                   <path d="M 50,52 L 88.21877053797101,82.66472857479614 A 49,49 0 0 1
                   9.36449499269846,79.3816678235927 Z" fill="#BF5A2F">
                   <rect x="115" y="50" width="10" height="10" fill="#BF5A2F">
                   <text x="133" y="60">Dallas, TX | 90</text>
                   <path d="M 50,52 L 9.36449499269846,79.3816678235927 A 49,49 0 0 1
                   1.447380111154402,58.606292600943014 Z" fill="#BFA22F">
                   <rect x="115" y="70" width="10" height="10" fill="#BFA22F">
                   <text x="133" y="80">Miami, FL | 22</text>
                   <path d="M 50,52 L 1.447380111154402,58.606292600943014 A 49,49 0 0 1
                   1.5953235862052395,44.385060651861934 Z" fill="#772FBF">
                   <rect x="115" y="90" width="10" height="10" fill="#772FBF">
                   <text x="133" y="100">Fargo, ND | 14</text>
                   <path d="M 50,52 L 1.5953235862052395,44.385060651861934 A 49,49 0 0 1
                   26.53713764295629,8.982630368484621 Z" fill="#2F94BF">
                   <rect x="115" y="110" width="10" height="10" fill="#2F94BF">
                   <text x="133" y="120">Long Beach, NY | 44</text>
                   <path d="M 50,52 L 26.53713764295629,8.982630368484621 A 49,49 0 0 1
                   50.00000000000003,3 Z" fill="#c3d4db">
                   <rect x="115" y="130" width="10" height="10" fill="#c3d4db">
                   <text x="133" y="140">Lynbrook, NY | 24</text>
                </svg>
                <h3>Donation Stats</h3>
                <p> Lorem ipsum dolor sit amet, consectetur </p>
             </div>
          </section>
       </div>
```

Figure 2-7. The chart content in SVG

SVG supports animations and transformation effects, whereas canvas doesn't.

Loading Data from Other Servers by Using JSONP

Imagine that a web page was loaded from the domain *abc.com*, and it needs JSON-formatted data from another domain (*xyz.com*). As mentioned earlier, Ajax has cross-origin restrictions, which prevent this. JSONP is a technique used to relax the cross-origin restrictions. With JSONP, instead of sending plain JSON data, the server wraps it up into a JavaScript function and then sends it to the web browser for execution as a callback. The web page that was originated from *abc.com* might send the request *http://xyz.com?callback=myDataHandler*, technically requesting the server *xyz.com* to invoke the JavaScript callback named myDataHandler. This URL is a regular HTTP GET request, which may have other parameters so that you can send some data to the server, too.

The server then sends to the browser the JavaScript function that might look as follows:

```
function myDataHandler({"fname": "Alex", "lname":"Smith","skillLevel":
11});
```

The web browser invokes the callback myDataHandler(), which must exist in the web page. The web browser passes the received JSON object as an argument to this callback:

```
function myDataHandler(data){
  // process the content of the argument data - the JSON object
  // received from xyz.com
}
```

If all you need is to retrieve data from a different domain on the page, just add the following tag to your HTML page:

```
<script src="http://xyz.com?callback=myDataHandler">
```

But what if you need to dynamically make such requests periodically (for example, get all tweets with a hashtag #savesickchild by sending an HTTP GET using the Twitter API at *http://search.twitter.com/search.json?q=savesickchild&rpp=5&include_entities=true&with_twitter_user_id=true&result_type=mixed*)? You add a change handler to the option that is called and passes or grabs the value needed.

You can dynamically add a <script> tag to the DOM object from your JavaScript code. Whenever the browser sees the new <script> element, it executes it. The script injection can be done like this:

```
var myScriptTag = document.createElement("script");
myScriptTag.src = "http://xyz.com?callback=myDataHandler";
document.getElementsByTagName("body").appendChild(myScriptTag);
```

Your JavaScript can build the URL for the myScriptTag.src dynamically and pass parameters to the server based on a user's actions.

Of course, this technique presents a danger if there is a chance that the JavaScript code sent by *xyz.com* is intercepted and replaced by a malicious code (similarly to the JavaScript eval() danger). But it's not more dangerous than receiving any JavaScript from a nontrusted server. Besides, your handler function could always make sure that the received data is a valid object with expected properties, and only after that handle the data.

If you decide to use JSONP, don't forget about error handling. Most likely you'll use one of the JavaScript frameworks, which usually offer a standard mechanism for JSONP error handling, dealing with poorly formatted JSON responses, and recovery in cases of network failure. One such library is called jQuery-JSONP (*https://github.com/jaubourg/jquery-jsonp*).

Beer and JSONP

In this section, you'll see a small code example illustrating the data retrieval from the publicly available Open Beer DataBase (*http://openbeerdatabase.com*), which exists to help software developers test code that makes RESTful web service calls and works with JSON and JSONP data. Our Save The Child page won't display beer bottles, but we want to show that in addition to the retrieval of the donations and charts data from one domain, we can get the data from a third-party domain *openbeerdatabase.com*.

First, enter the URL **http://api.openbeerdatabase.com/v1/breweries.json** in the address bar of your web browser; it will return the following JSON data (only two out of seven breweries are shown for brevity):

```
{
    "page": 1,
    "pages": 1,
    "total": 7,
    "breweries": [
        {
            "id": 1,
            "name": "(512) Brewing Company",
            "url": "http://512brewing.com",
            "created_at": "2010-12-07T02:53:38Z",
            "updated_at": "2010-12-07T02:53:38Z"
        },
        {
            "id": 2,
            "name": "21st Amendment Brewing",
            "url": "http://21st-amendment.com",
            "created_at": "2010-12-07T02:53:38Z",
            "updated_at": "2010-12-07T02:53:38Z"
        }
    ]
}
```

Now let's request the same data, but in a JSONP format, by adding to the URL a parameter with a callback name myDataHandler. Entering **http://api.openbeerdata base.com/v1/breweries.json?callback=processBeer** in the browser returns the following (it's a short version):

```
processBeer({"page":1,"pages":1,"total":7,"breweries":[{"id":1,"name":"(512)
Brewing Company","url":"http://512brewing.com","created_at":
"2010-12-07T02:53:38Z", "updated_at":"2010-12-07T02:53:38Z"},
```

```
{"id":2,"name":"21st Amendment Brewing","url":"http://21st-amendment.com",
"created_at":"2010-12-07T02:53:38Z","updated_at":"2010-12-07T02:53:38Z"}]})
```

Because we haven't declared the function `processBeer()` yet, it won't be invoked. Let's fix that now. The function first checks whether the received data contains information about the breweries. If it does, the name of the first brewery prints on the JavaScript console. Otherwise, the console output will read, "Retrieved data has no breweries info."

```
var processBeer=function (data){

    // Uncomment the next line to emulate malicious data
    // data="function evilFunction(){alert(' Bad function');}";

      if (data.breweries == undefined){
       console.log("Retrieved data has no breweries info.");
      } else{
       console.log("In the processBeer callback. The first brewery is "
                  + data.breweries[0].name);
      }
  }

var myScriptTag = document.createElement("script");
  myScriptTag.src =
     "http://api.openbeerdatabase.com/v1/breweries.json?callback=processBeer";

var bd = document.getElementsByTagName('body')[0];
bd.appendChild(myScriptTag);
```

Figure 2-8 is a screen snapshot taken in Firebug when it reached the breakpoint placed inside the `processBeer` callback on the `console.log(in the processBeer call back")`. You can see the content of the `data` argument: the beer has arrived.

As a training exercise, try to replace the data retrieval from the beer web service with the data feed from Twitter based on certain hash tags. See if you can find a place in the Save The Child web page to display (and periodically update) this Twitter stream.

 json-generator.com is a handy website that can generate a file with JSON or JSONP content based on your template. You can use this service to test Ajax queries—the generated JSON can be saved on this server to help test your web application.

```
▶ this                          Window index_beer.html
▼ data                          Object { page=1, pages=1, total=7, more... }
  ▼ breweries                   [ Object { id=1, name="(512) Brewing Company",
                                url="http://512brewing.com", more... }, Object { id=2, name="21st
                                Amendment Brewing", url="http://21st-amendment.com", more... }, Object
                                { id=3, name="Abbaye de Leffe", url="http://www.abbaye-
                                de-leffe.be", more... }, 4 more... ]
    ▼ 0                         Object { id=1, name="(512) Brewing Company",
                                url="http://512brewing.com", more... }
        created_at              "2010-12-07T02:53:38Z"
        id                      1
        name                    "(512) Brewing Company"
        updated_at              "2010-12-07T02:53:38Z"
        url                     "http://512brewing.com"
    ▶ 1                         Object { id=2, name="21st Amendment Brewing", url="http://21st-
                                amendment.com", more... }
    ▶ 2                         Object { id=3, name="Abbaye de Leffe", url="http://www.abbaye-
                                de-leffe.be", more... }
    ▶ 3                         Object { id=4, name="Abita Brewing Company", url="http://abita.com",
                                more... }
    ▶ 4                         Object { id=5, name="Alaskan Brewing Company",
                                url="http://alaskanbeer.com", more... }
    ▶ 5                         Object { id=6, name="Ale Asylum", url="http://aleasylum.com", more... }
    ▶ 6                         Object { id=7, name="AleSmith", url="http://alesmith.com", more... }
    page                        1
    pages                       1
    total                       7
▶ arguments                     [ Object { page=1, pages=1, total=7, more... } ]
▶ Closure Scope                 Closure Scope { toString=function() }
▶ Window                        Window index_beer.html
```

Figure 2-8. The beer has arrived

Summary

In this chapter, you learned about using Ajax as a means of providing communication between your web browser and servers. Ajax also deserves credit for making the Java-Script language popular again by showing a practical way of creating single-page web applications. Over the years, JSON became the standard way of exchanging data on the Web. The current version of the Save The Child application cleanly separates the code from the data, and you know how to update the content of the web page without needing to re-retrieve the entire page from the server. In the next chapter, you'll learn a more productive way of developing web applications by using a library called jQuery.

## CHAPTER 3

Introducing the jQuery Library

Until now, we've been using HTML, plain JavaScript, and CSS to create the Save The Child web application. In the real world, developers try to be more productive by using JavaScript libraries.

Libraries such as jQuery Core (*http://jqueryui.com*) substantially minimize the amount of manual coding while programming the core functionality of a web application. The jQuery UI library offers widgets, animations, and advanced effects. The RequireJS (*http://requirejs.org*) library is a module loader that allows you to modularize HTML5 applications. Hundreds of micro libraries are also available that can do just one thing and can be used à la carte (visit MicroJS (*http://microjs.com*) for details).

Libraries are different from frameworks, which we discuss in Chapter 4. Whereas frameworks force you to organize your code in a certain way, a library simply offers components that allow you to write less code.

This chapter presents the JavaScript library jQuery (*http://jquery.com*), or to be more precise, JQuery Core. About half of the top websites use jQuery (visit Built With (*http://bit.ly/1uYqUF0*) for the current statistics). jQuery is simple to use and doesn't require you to dramatically change the way you program for the Web. jQuery offers a helping hand with the tasks that most web developers need to deal with—for example, finding and manipulating DOM elements, processing browser events, and dealing with browser incompatibility, which makes your code more maintainable. Because jQuery is an extensible library, lots and lots of plug-ins have been created by developers from around the world, and all of them are available for free. If you can't find the plug-in that fits your need, you can create one yourself.

The jQuery UI library is a close relative of jQuery Core. It's a set of user interface interactions, effects, widgets, and themes built on top of jQuery. You can find such widgets as Datepicker, Accordion, Slider, Tabs, and Autocomplete. jQuery UI will also help you add various interactions (for example, drag-and-drop) and effects (for example, adding CSS classes or animations) to your web pages. (jQuery Core also has some effects.) jQuery UI is built on top of jQuery Core and can't be used independently. jQuery UI is covered in the *jQuery UI* by Eric Sarrion (O'Reilly).

jQuery Mobile is yet another library built on top of jQuery Core. But this one is geared toward creating mobile applications. Chapter 11 covers jQuery Mobile in detail.

This chapter is not a detailed jQuery Core primer; jQuery books and the online API documentation (*http://api.jquery.com/*) provide a comprehensive explanation of jQuery. But we'll give you just enough information to understand how jQuery can be used. In "Programming Save The Child by Using jQuery" on page 100, we'll review the code of several versions of this application highlighting the benefits of using the jQuery library.

Getting Started with jQuery

At the time of this writing, you can download either jQuery version 1.9 or jQuery 2.0 (the latter doesn't support Internet Explorer 6, 7, or 8). You can download one of two distributions of jQuery. The Gzipped minified version of jQuery is 33 KB in size (it's 93 KB if unzipped), and this is all you need unless you are planning to develop jQuery plug-ins, in which case get the larger development version (it's about 270 KB). We've downloaded jQuery from jquery.com and included it in the `<script>` tag in our HTML code samples so you can run them even if an Internet connection is not available.

But instead of deploying the jQuery framework on your servers as a part of your application, you should use a common content delivery network (CDN) URL in your HTML, as shown in the code that follows. Because jQuery is an extremely popular library, many websites use it. If more than one web page were to get it from the same CDN, the web browser would cache it locally and reuse it rather than downloading a separate copy from different servers for every web application that uses jQuery. The download page of jquery.com (*http://jquery.com/download*) offers three CDNs: Google, Microsoft, and Media Temple. For example, if you don't need to use HTTPS with your application, Media Temple's CDN will suffice:

```
<script src="http://code.jquery.com/jquery-1.9.1.min.js"></script>
```

Using a CDN can have another advantage: the content (jQuery, in this case) is distributed around the globe and might be served to the user from servers located in the same city/country, thus reducing the latency.

You can provide a fallback URL by adding one extra line that will load jQuery from an alternative location if your CDN fails:

```
<script> window.jQuery || document.write('<script
    src="http://code.jquery.com/jquery-1.9.1.min.js"></script>')
</script>
```

You may find code samples that use the URL *http://code.jquery.com/ jquery-latest.min.js* to download the latest version of jQuery. But keep in mind that by doing this, you might run into a situation in which some of the API of jQuery has been changed or deprecated. For example, jQuery 2.0 stopped supporting (*http://bit.ly/ 1x53fWz*) Internet Explorer 6, 7, and 8 and automatically switching to the latest version may result in malfunctioning of your application. We recommend using the specific version that has been tested with your application.

After covering the basics of jQuery Core, we are going to continue reviewing the code of a series of projects representing the same Save The Child application, but this time using jQuery. Other than adding validation to the Donate form and using an image slider, this application remains the same as in Chapter 2; we just want to show that developers can be more productive in achieving the same result.

Some say that anyone who knows HTML can easily learn jQuery, but this is not so. Understanding JavaScript is required (see the bonus online chapter for reference). Programming with jQuery components starts with invoking the jQuery constructor jQuery(). But people use the shorter version of this constructor that's represented by a $ sign: $(). This $ property is the only object that jQuery will create in the global namespace. Everything else will be encapsulated inside the $ object.

Although it's easier to write `$()` than `jQuery()`, keep in mind that if you decide to use another library in your application in addition to jQuery, the chances are higher that you will run into a conflict with having another `$` than another `jQuery` in the global namespace. To make sure you won't find yourself in the "Another day, another $" position, put your code inside a closure, passing it `jQuery`. The following code allows you to safely use the `$` object:

```
(function($){
    // Your code goes here
})(jQuery);
```

As you remember, JavaScript functions do not require you to invoke them with exactly the same number of parameters as they were declared with. Hence, when you invoke the jQuery constructor, you can pass different things to it. You can pass a string as an argument or another function, and the jQuery constructor will invoke different code based on the argument type. For example, if you pass it a string, jQuery will assume that it's a CSS selector, and the caller wants to find element(s) in the DOM that match this selector. Basically, you can think of it this way: whenever you want jQuery do something for you, invoke `$()` passing it your request.

You'll need to get used to yet another feature of jQuery: method chaining. Each function returns an object, and you don't have to declare a variable to hold this object. You can just write something like `funcA().funcB();`. This means that the method `funcB()` will be called on the object, returned by the `funcA()`.

Although method chaining is often presented as a great feature that allows you to do more with less typing, it can complicate the debugging of your code. Imagine that `funcA()` returns null for whatever reason. The entire chain (`funcB()` in our example) attached to `funcA()` won't work properly, and you might need to unchain these methods to find the problem.

Also, if you need to access a DOM object more than once, save the reference in a variable and reuse it rather than invoking the same selector method in several chains. This can improve the performance of your web page.

Hello World

The Hello World program is always a good start when learning any new software, and we'll go this route, too. Example 3-1 uses jQuery to display a web page that reads, "Hello World!" Note the functions that start with the `$` sign—they are all from the jQuery library.

Example 3-1. Hello World with jQuery

```html
<!DOCTYPE html>
<html lang="en">
  <head>
        <meta charset="utf-8">

        <title>Hello jQuery</title>
  </head>
  <body>
        <script src="js/libs/jquery-1.9.1.min.js"></script>
        <script>
                $(function(){                                      ❶
                        $("body").append("<h1>Hello World!</h1>");   ❷

                });
        </script>
  </body>
</html>
```

❶ If the script passes a function as an argument to jQuery, this function is called when the DOM object is ready: the jQuery's `ready()` function is invoked. Keep in mind that it's not the same as invoking a function handler `window.onload`, which is called after all window resources (not just the DOM object) are completely loaded (read more in "Handling Events" on page 94).

❷ If the script passes a string to jQuery, this string is treated as a CSS selector, and jQuery tries to find the matching collection of HTML elements (it will return the reference to just one `<body>` in the Hello World script). This line also demonstrates method chaining: the `append()` method is called on the object returned by `$("body")`.

Using Selectors and Filters

Probably the most frequently used routine in JavaScript code that's part of an HTML page is finding DOM elements and manipulating them, and this is where jQuery's power is. Finding HTML elements based on CSS selectors (*http://mzl.la/V2udjX*) is easy and concise. You can specify one or more selectors in the same query. Example 3-2 presents a snippet of code that contains random samples of selectors. Going through this code and reading the comments will help you understand how to use jQuery selectors (*http:// bit.ly/1lJq3aP*). (Note that with jQuery, you can write one selector for multiple IDs, which is not allowed in the pure JavaScript's `getElementById()`.)

Example 3-2. Sample jQuery selectors

```javascript
$(".donate-button"); // find the elements with the class donate-button

$("#login-link")  // find the elements with id=login-link
```

```
// find elements with id=map-container or id=video-container
$("#map-container, #video-container");

// Find an HTML input element that has a value attribute of 200
$('input[value="200"]');

// Find all <p> elements that are nested somewhere inside <div>
$('div p');

// Find all <p> elements that are direct children (located directly inside) <div>
$('div>p');

// Find all <label> elements that are styled with the class donation-heading
$('label.donation-heading');

// Find an HTML input element that has a value attribute of 200
// and change the text of its next sibling to "two hundred"
$('input[value="200"]').next().text("two hundred");
```

 If jQuery returns a set of elements that match the selector's expression, you can access its elements by using array notation: `var theSecondDiv = $('div')[1]`. If you want to iterate through the entire set, use the jQuery method `$(selector).each()` (*http://api.jquery.com/each*). For example, if you want to perform a function on each paragraph of an HTML document, you can do so as follows: `$("p").each(function(){...})`.

Testing jQuery Code with JSFiddle

The handy online site JSFiddle (*http://jsfiddle.net*) can help you perform quick testing of code fragments of HTML, CSS, JavaScript, and other popular frameworks. This web page has a sidebar on the left and four large panels on the right. Three of these panels are for entering or copying and pasting HTML, CSS, and JavaScript, respectively, and the fourth panel is for showing the results of applying this code (see Figure 3-1).

Copy and paste fragments from the HTML and CSS written for the Donate section of the Save The Child page into the top panels, and click the Run button on JSFiddle's toolbar. You'll see our donate form, where each radio button has a label in the form of digits (10, 20, 50, 100, 200). Now select jQuery 1.9.0 from the drop-down at the upper left and copy and paste the jQuery code fragment you'd like to test into the JavaScript panel located under the HTML one. As you see in Figure 3-1, we've pasted `$('input[value="200"]').next().text("two hundred");`. After clicking the Run button, the jQuery script executes and the label of the last radio button changes from 200 to two hundred (test this fiddle here (*http://bit.ly/1mzUwU5*)). Also check out JSFiddle's tutorial (*http://bit.ly/1rPH2c3*).

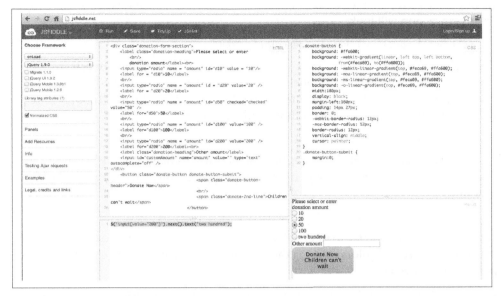

Figure 3-1. Testing jQuery by using JSFiddle

If you chained a method (for example, an event handler) to the HTML element returned by a selector, you can use $(this) from inside this handler to get a reference to this HTML element.

Filtering Elements

If the jQuery selector returns a number of HTML elements, you can further narrow this collection by applying filters. jQuery has such filters as eq(), has(), first(), and more.

For example, applying the selector $('label'); to the Donate section of the HTML fragment shown in Figure 3-1 would return a set of HTML elements called <label>. Say we want to change the background of the label 20 to be red. This is the third label in the HTML from Figure 3-1, and the eq(n) filter selects the element at the zero-based index n within the matched set.

You can apply this filter by using the following syntax: $('label:eq(2)');. But jQuery documentation suggests using the syntax $('label').eq(2); for better performance (*http://api.jquery.com/eq-selector*).

Using method chaining, we'll apply the filter eq(2) to the set of labels returned by the selector $('label') and then change the styling of the remaining HTML element(s) by using the `css()` method that can perform all CSS manipulations. This is how the entire expression will look:

```
$('label').eq(2).css('background-color', 'red');
```

Test this script in JSFiddle or in the code of one of the Save The Child projects from this chapter. The background of the label 20 will become red. If you wanted to change the CSS of the first label in this set, the filter expressions would look like `$('label:first')` or, for the better performance, you should do it like this:

```
$('label').filter(":first").css('background-color', 'red');
```

If you display data in an HTML table, you might want to change the background color of every even or odd row `<tr>`, and jQuery offers you the filters `even()` and `odd()`. For example:

```
$('tr').filter(":even").css('background-color', 'grey');
```

Usually, you'd be doing this to interactively change the background colors. You can also alternate background colors by using the straight CSS selectors `p:nth-child(odd)` and `p:nth-child(even)`.

Check out jQuery API documentation for the complete list of selectors (*http://bit.ly/1IJq3aP*) and traversing filters (*http://bit.ly/TJs1gf*).

 If you need to display data in a grid-like form, consider using a Java-Script grid called SlickGrid (*http://bit.ly/V2uYJH*).

Handling Events

Adding events processing with jQuery is simple. Your code will follow the same pattern: find the element in DOM by using a selector or filter, and then attach the appropriate function that handles the event. We'll show you a handful of examples, but you can find a description of all methods that deal with events in the jQuery API documentation (*http://bit.ly/1mzV6Br*).

There are a couple of ways of passing the handler function to be executed as a callback when a particular event is dispatched. For example, our Hello World code passes a handler function to the `ready` event:

```
$(function());
```

This is the same as using the following syntax:

```
$(document).ready(function());
```

For the Hello World example, this was all that mattered; we just needed the DOM object to be able to append the <h1> element to it. But this would not be the right solution if the code needed to be executed only after all page resources have been loaded. In this case, the code could be written to utilize the DOM's window.load event, which in jQuery looks as follows:

```
$(window).load(function(){
            $("body").append("<h1>Hello World!</h1>");
});
```

If the user interacts with your web page by using a mouse, the event handlers can be added by using a similar procedure. For example, if you want the header in our Hello World example to process click events, find the reference to this header and attach the click() handler to it. Adding the following to the <script> section of Hello World will append the text each time the user clicks the header:

```
$("h1").click(function(event){
    $("body").append("Hey, you clicked on the header!");
})
```

If you'd like to process double-clicks, replace the click() invocation with dblclick(). jQuery has handlers for about a dozen mouse events, which are wrapper methods to the corresponding JavaScript events that are dispatched when a mouse enters or leaves the area, the mouse pointer goes up/down, or the focus moves in or out of an input field. The shorthand methods click() and dblclick() (and several others) internally use the method on(), which you can and should use in your code, too (it works during the bubbling phase of the event, as described in the section "DOM Events" in the bonus online chapter).

Attaching Event Handlers and Elements by Using the Method on()

Event methods can be attached just by passing a handler function, as in the preceding examples. You can also process the event by using the on() method, which allows you to specify the native event name and the event handler as its arguments. In "Programming Save The Child by Using jQuery" on page 100, you'll see lots of examples that use the on() method. The following one-liner assigns the function handler named showLo ginForm to the click event of the element with the id login-link. Example 3-3 includes the commented-out pure-JavaScript version of the code (see *project-02-login* in Chapter 1) that has the same functionality.

Example 3-3. Handling the click on login link

```
// var loginLink = document.getElementById("login-link");
// loginLink.addEventListener('click', showLoginForm, false);

    $('#login-link').on('click', showLoginForm);
```

The on() method allows you to assign the same handler function to more than one event. For example, to invoke the showLoginForm function when the user clicks or moves the mouse over the HTML element, you could write on('click mouseover', showLoginForm).

The method off() is used for removing the event handler so that the event won't be processed anymore. For example, if you want to turn off the login link's ability to process the click event, simply write this:

```
$('#login-link').off('click', showLoginForm);
```

Delegating Events

The method on() can be called by passing an optional selector as an argument. Because we haven't used selectors in this example, the event was triggered only when it reached the element with the ID login-link. Now imagine an HTML container that has child elements—for example, a calculator implemented as <div id="calculator"> containing buttons. The following code assigns a click handler *to each* button styled with the class .digitButton:

```
$("div#calculator .digitButton").on("click", function(){...});
```

But instead of assigning an event handler to each button, you can assign an event handler to the container and specify an additional selector that can find child elements. The following code assigns the event handler function *to only one* object—the div#calculator instructing this container to invoke the event handler when any of its children matching .digitButton is clicked:

```
$("div#calculator").on("click", ".digitButton",function(){...});
```

When the button is clicked, the event bubbles up and reaches the container's level, whose click handler will do the processing (jQuery doesn't support the capturing phase of events). The work on processing clicks for digit buttons is delegated to the container.

Another good use case for delegating event processing to a container is a financial application that displays the data in an HTML table containing hundreds of rows. Instead of assigning hundreds of event handlers (one per table row), assign one to the table. There is one extra benefit to using delegation in this case: if the application can dynamically add new rows to this table (say, the order execution data), there is no need to explicitly assign event handlers to them; the container will do the processing for both old and new rows.

Starting from jQuery 1.7, the method on() is a recommended replacement of the methods bind(), unbind(), delegate(), and unde legate() that are still being used in earlier versions of jQuery. If you decide to develop your application with jQuery and its mobile version with jQuery Mobile, you need to be aware that the latter may not implement the latest code of the core jQuery. Using on() is safe, though, because at the time of this writing jQuery Mobile 1.2 supports all the features of jQuery 1.8.2. Chapter 10 shows you how using responsive design principles can help you reuse the same code on both desktop and mobile devices.

The method on() allows passing the data to the function handler (see the jQuery documentation (*http://api.jquery.com/on/*) for details).

You are also allowed to assign different handlers to different events in one invocation of on(). The following code snippet from *project-11-jQuery-canvas-pie-chart-json* assigns handlers to focus and blur events:

```
$('#customAmount').on({
        focus : onCustomAmountFocus,
        blur : onCustomAmountBlur
});
```

Using Ajax with jQuery

Making Ajax requests to the server is also easier with jQuery than with pure JavaScript. All the complexity of dealing with various flavors of XMLHttpRequest is hidden from the developers. The method $.ajax() (*http://bit.ly/1m2tDfK*) spares JavaScript developers from writing the code with multiple browser-specific ways of instantiating the XMLHttpRequest object. By invoking ajax(), you can exchange data with the server and load the JavaScript code. In its simplest form, this method takes just the URL of the remote resource to which the request is sent. This invocation uses global defaults that must be set in advance by invoking the method ajaxSetup() (*http://bit.ly/1ohVFUA*).

But you can combine specifying parameters of the Ajax call and making the ajax() call. Just provide as an argument a configuration object that defines the URL, the function handlers for success and failures, and other parameters such as a function to call right before the Ajax request (beforeSend) or caching instructions for the browser (cache).

Spend some time becoming familiar with all the configuration parameters that you can use with the jQuery method ajax(). Here's a sample template for calling jQuery ajax():

```
$.ajax({
        url: 'myData.json',
        type: 'GET',
        dataType: 'json'
```

```
    }).done(function (data) {...})
        .fail(function (jqXHR, textStatus) {...});
```

This example takes a JavaScript object that defines three properties: the URL, the type of the request, and the expected data type. Using chaining, you can attach the methods `done()` and `fail()`, which have to specify the function handlers to be invoked in case of success and failure, respectively. jqXHR (*http://bit.ly/jq-ajax*) is a jQuery wrapper for the browser's `XMLHttpRequest` object.

Don't forget about the asynchronous nature of Ajax calls, which means that the `ajax()` method will be finished before the `done()` or `fail()` callbacks will be invoked. You can attach another *promised callback* method called `always()` that will be invoked regardless of whether the `ajax()` call succeeds or fails.

 An alternative to having a `fail()` handler for each Ajax request is setting the global error-handling routine by using `ajaxSetup()`. Consider doing this for some serious HTTP failures such as 403 (access forbidden) or errors with codes 5*xx*. For example:

```
$(function() {
    $.ajaxSetup({
        error: function(jqXHR, exception) {
            if (jqXHR.status == 404) {
                alert('Requested resource not found. [404]');
            } else if (jqXHR.status == 500) {
                alert('Internal Server Error [500].');
            } else if (exception === 'parsererror') {
                alert('JSON parsing failed.');
            } else {
                alert('Got This Error:\n' + jqXHR.responseText);
            }
        }
    });
});
```

If you need to chain asynchronous callbacks (`done()`, `fail()`, `always()`) that don't need to be called right away (they wait for the result), the method `ajax()` returns the `De ferred` (*http://bit.ly/1nWLxxN*) object. It places these callbacks in a queue to be called later. As a matter of fact, the callback `fail()` might never be called if no errors occur.

If you specify JSON as a value of the `dataType` property, the result will be parsed automatically by jQuery; there is no need to call `JSON.parse()` as was done in Chapter 2. Even though the jQuery object has a utility method called `parseJSON()`, you don't have to invoke it to process a return of the `ajax()` call.

In the preceding example, the type of Ajax request was `GET`. But you can use `POST`, too. In this case, you need to prepare valid JSON data to be sent to the server, and the configuration object that you provide as an argument to the method `ajax()` has to include the property `data` containing valid JSON.

Handy Shorthand Methods

jQuery has several shorthand methods that allow making Ajax calls with a simpler syntax, which we'll consider next.

The method `load()` (*http://bit.ly/1x54CUZ*) makes an Ajax call from an HTML element(s) to the specified URL (the first argument) and populates the HTML element with the returned data. You can pass optional second and third arguments: HTTP request parameters and the callback function to process the results. If the second argument is an object, the `load()` method will make a POST request; otherwise, GET. You'll see the code that uses `load()` to populate states and countries from remote HTML files later in this chapter, in the section "Loading HTML States and Countries by Using jQuery Ajax" on page 104. But the next line shows an example of calling `load()` with two parameters, the URL and the callback:

```
$('#counriesList').load('data/countries.html', function(response, status, xhr)
{...});
```

The global method `get()` (*http://bit.ly/1nYK3nJ*) allows you to specifically issue an HTTP GET request. Similarly to the `ajax()` invocation, you can chain the `done()`, `fail()`, and `always()` methods to `get()`. For example:

```
$.get('ssc/getDonors?city=Miami', function(){alert("Got the donors");})
  .done(function(){alert("I'm called after the donors retrieved");}
  .fail(function(){alert("Request for donors failed");});
;
```

The global method `post()` makes an HTTP POST request to the server. You must specify at least one argument—the URL on the server—and, optionally, the data to be passed, the callback to be invoked on the request completion, and the type of data expected from the server. Similarly to the `ajax()` invocation, you can chain the `done()`, `fail()`, and `always()` methods to `post()`. The following example makes a POST request to the server, passing an object with the new donor information:

```
$.post('ssc/addDonor', {id:123, name:"John Smith"});
;
```

The global method `getJSON()` (*http://bit.ly/1iSQ4oF*) retrieves and parses the JSON data from the specified URL and passes the JavaScript object to the specified callback. If need be, you can send the data to the server with the request. Calling `getJSON()` is like calling `ajax()` with the parameter `dataType: "json"`, as shown in Example 3-4.

Example 3-4. Getting JSON data using an Ajax call

```
$.getJSON('data/us-states-list.json', function (data) {
            // code to populate states combo goes here})
        .fail(function(){alert("Request for us states failed");});});
```

The method `serialize()` (*http://bit.ly/1qK1n2B*) is used when you need to submit to the server a filled-out HTML `<form>`. This method presents the form data as a text string in a standard URL-encoded notation. Typically, the code finds a required form by using a jQuery selector and then calls `serialize()` on this object. You can invoke `serial ize()` not only on the entire form, but also on selected form elements. The following is sample code that finds the form and serializes it:

```
$('form').submit(function() {
  alert($(this).serialize());
  return false;
});
```

Returning `false` from a jQuery event handler is the same as calling either `preventDefault()` or `stopPropagation()` on the `jQuery.Event` object. In pure JavaScript, returning `false` doesn't stop propagation (try to run this fiddle (*http://jsfiddle.net/APQk6/*)).

Later in this chapter, in "Submitting the Donate Form" on page 108, you'll see code that uses the `serialize()` method.

Programming Save The Child by Using jQuery

In this section, we'll review code samples from several small projects (see Appendix B for running instructions) that are jQuery rewrites of the corresponding pure-JavaScript projects from Chapter 1 and Chapter 2. We are not going to add any new functionality —the goal is to demonstrate how jQuery allows you to achieve the same results while writing less code. You'll also see how it can save you time by handling browser incompatibility for common uses (like Ajax).

Login and Donate

The file *main.js* from *project-02-jQuery-Login* is 33 percent smaller than *project-02-login* written in pure JavaScript. jQuery allows your programs to be brief. For example, the following code shows how six lines of JavaScript can be replaced with one: the jQuery function `toggle()` toggles the visibility of `login-link`, `login-form`, and `login-submit`:

The total size of your jQuery application is not necessarily smaller than the pure JavaScript one, because it includes the code of the jQuery library.

```
function showLoginForm() {

// The JavaScript way
// var loginLink = document.getElementById("login-link");
// var loginForm = document.getElementById("login-form");
// var loginSubmit = document.getElementById('login-submit');
// loginLink.style.display = "none";
// loginForm.style.display = "block";
// loginSubmit.style.display = "block";


// The jQuery way
$('#login-link, #login-form, #login-submit').toggle();
}
```

The code of the Donate section also becomes slimmer with jQuery. For example, the following section from the JavaScript version of the application is removed:

```
var donateBotton = document.getElementById('donate-button');
var donationAddress = document.getElementById('donation-address');
var donateFormContainer = document.getElementById('donate-form-container');
var customAmount = document.getElementById('customAmount');
var donateForm = document.forms['_xclick'];
var donateLaterLink = document.getElementById('donate-later-link');
```

The jQuery method chaining allows you to combine (in one line) finding DOM objects and acting upon them. Example 3-5 presents the entire code of *main.js* from *project-01-jQuery-make-donation*, which includes the initial version of the code of the Login and Donate sections of Save The Child.

Example 3-5. The entire jQuery script from main.js

```
/* --------- login section -------------- */

$(function() {

  function showLoginForm() {
      $('#login-link, #login-form, #login-submit').toggle();
  }

  $('#login-link').on('click', showLoginForm);

  function showAuthorizedSection() {
      $('#authorized, #login-form, #login-submit').toggle();
  }
```

```
    function logIn() {
        var userNameValue = $('#username').val();
        var userNameValueLength = userNameValue.length;
        var userPasswordValue = $('#password').val();
        var userPasswordLength = userPasswordValue.length;

        //check credentials
        if (userNameValueLength == 0 || userPasswordLength == 0) {
            if (userNameValueLength == 0) {
                console.log('username is empty');
            }
            if (userPasswordLength == 0) {
                console.log('password is empty');
            }
        } else if (userNameValue != 'admin' || userPasswordValue != '1234') {
            console.log('username or password is invalid');
        } else if (userNameValue == 'admin' && userPasswordValue == '1234') {
            showAuthorizedSection();
        }
    }

    $('#login-submit').on('click', logIn);

    function logOut() {
        $('#username, #password').val('')
        $('#authorized, #login-link').toggle();
    }

    $('#logout-link').on('click', logOut);

    $('#profile-link').on('click', function() {
        console.log('Profile link was clicked');
    });
});
/* --------- make donation module start ------------- */
$(function() {
  var checkedInd = 2;  // initially checked radiobutton


  // Show/hide the donation form if the user clicks
  // the button Donate Now or the link I'll Donate Later
  function showHideDonationForm() {
      $('#donation-address, #donate-form-container').toggle();
  }
  $('#donate-button').on('click', showHideDonationForm);
  $('#donate-later-link').on('click', showHideDonationForm);
  // End of show/hide section

  $('#donate-form-container').on('click', resetOtherAmount);

  function resetOtherAmount(event) {
```

```
                    if (event.target.type == "radio") {
                            $('#otherAmount').val('');
                    }
        }

        //uncheck selected radio buttons if other amount was chosen
        function onOtherAmountFocus() {
                var radioButtons = $('form[name="_xclick"] input:radio');
                if ($('#otherAmount').val() == '') {
                        checkedInd = radioButtons.index(radioButtons.filter(':checked'));
                }
                $('form[name="_xclick"] input:radio').prop('checked', false);    ❶
        }

        function onOtherAmountBlur() {
                if ($('#otherAmount').val() == '') {
                        $('form[name="_xclick"] input:radio:eq(' + checkedInd + ')')
                                            .prop("checked", true);    ❷
                }
        }
        $('#otherAmount')
            .on({focus:onOtherAmountFocus, blur:onOtherAmountBlur});    ❸

});
```

❶   This one-liner finds all elements of the form named _xclick, and immediately applies the jQuery filter to remove from this collection any elements except radio buttons. Then, it deselects all of them by setting the property checked to false. This has to be done if the user places the focus inside the Other Amount field.

❷   If the user leaves the Other Amount field, return the check to the previously selected radio button again. The eq filter picks the radio button whose number is equal to the value of the variable checkedInd.

❸   A single invocation of the on() method registers two event handlers: one for the focus and one for the blur event.

jQuery includes a number of effects (*http://bit.ly/1pPMdHN*) that make the user experience more engaging. Let's use one of them, called fadeToggle(). In the preceding code, a section that toggles visibility of the Donate form. If the user clicks the Donate Now button, the form becomes visible (see Figure 1-11). If the user clicks the link "I'll donate later," the form becomes hidden, as in Figure 1-10. The jQuery method toggle() does its job, but the change happens abruptly. The fadeToggle() effect allows us to introduce slower fading, which improves the user experience, at least to our taste.

If you wanted to hide/show just one component, the code change would be trivial—replacing toggle() with fadeToggle('slow') would do the trick. But in our case, the toggle changes visibility of two <div>s: donation-address and donation-form-container, which should happen in a certain order. The following code is a replacement of the show/hide section of *main.js* to introduce the fading effect:

```
function showHideDonationForm(first, next) {
        first.fadeToggle('slow', function() {
                next.fadeToggle('slow');
        });
}

var donAddress = $('#donation-address');
var donForm = $('#donate-form-container');

$('#donate-button').on('click', function() {
        showHideDonationForm(donAddress, donForm)});

$('#donate-later-link').on('click', function() {
        showHideDonationForm(donForm, donAddress)});
```

If you want to see the difference, first run *project-01-jQuery-make-donation* and click the Donate Now button (no effects), and then run *project-04-jQuery-donation-ajax-json*, which has the fading effect.

Loading HTML States and Countries by Using jQuery Ajax

The *project-03-jQuery-donation-ajax-html* project illustrates retrieving HTML data about the states and countries by using the jQuery method load(). Example 3-6 shows the fragment from *main.js* that makes two load() calls. The second call purposely misspells the name of the file to generate an error.

Example 3-6. Loading data and processing errors

```
function loadData(dataUrl, target, selectionPrompt) {
  target.load(dataUrl,
            function(response, status, xhr) {              ❶
        if (status != "error") {
            target.prepend(selectionPrompt);               ❷
        } else {
            console.log('Status: ' + status + ' ' + xhr.statusText);

            // Show the error message on the Web page
            var tempContainerHTML = '<p class="error">Error getting ' + dataUrl +
            ": "+ xhr.statusText + ", code: "+ xhr.status + "</p>";

        $('#temp-project-name-container').append(tempContainerHTML); ❸
         }
  });
}

var statePrompt =
        '<option value="" selected="selected"> - State - </option>';
loadData('data/us-states.html', $('#state'), statePrompt);
```

```
var countryPrompt =
        '<option value="" selected="selected"> - Country - </option>';

// Pass the wrong data URL on purpose
loadData('da----ta/countries.html', $('#counriesList'), countryPrompt); ❹
```

❶ The callback to be invoked right after the load() completes the request.

❷ Using the jQuery method prepend(), insert the first element into the HTML
    element <select> to prompt the user to select a state or a country.

❸ Display an error message at the bottom of the web page in the <div> section
    with the ID temp-project-name-container.

❹ Pass the misspelled data URL to generate an error message.

Loading JSON States and Countries by Using jQuery Ajax

The project named *project-04-jQuery-donation-ajax-json* demonstrates how to make a
jQuery ajax() call to retrieve the JSON data about countries and states and populate
the respective combo boxes in the donation form. The function loadData() in
Example 3-7 takes three arguments: the data URL, the name of the root element in the
JSON file, and the target HTML element to be populated with the data retrieved from
the Ajax call.

Example 3-7. Loading countries and states with ajax()

```
function loadData(dataUrl, rootElement, target) {
  $.ajax({
      url: dataUrl,
      type: 'GET',
      cache: false,
      timeout: 5000,                                              ❶
      dataType: 'json'
  }).done(function (data) {                                       ❷
      var optionsHTML = '';
      $.each(data[rootElement], function(index) {
              optionsHTML+='<option value="'+data[rootElement][index].code+'">' +
                                  data[rootElement][index].name+'</option>'
      });

      var targetCurrentHTML = target.html();                      ❸
      var targetNewHTML = targetCurrentHTML + optionsHTML;
      target.html(targetNewHTML);
  }).fail(function (jqXHR, textStatus, error) {          ❹

      console.log('AJAX request failed: ' + error +
                      ". Code: " + jqXHR.status);

      // The code to display the error in the
```

```
        // browser's window goes here
  });
}

// Load the State and Country comboboxes
loadData('data/us-states-list.json',                              ❺
                          'usstateslist', $('#state'));
loadData('data/counries-list.json',                               ❻
                          'countrieslist', $('#counriesList'));
```

❶ Set the timeout. If the result of the `ajax()` call won't return within 5 seconds, the method `fail()` will be invoked.

❷ The handler function to process the successfully retrieved data.

❸ Get the content of the HTML `<select>` element to populate with states or countries. The jQuery method `html()` uses the browser's `innerHTML` property.

❹ The handler function to process errors, if any.

❺ Calling `loadData()` to retrieve states and populate the `#state` combo box. The `usstatelist` is the name of the root element in the JSON file *us-states-list.json*.

❻ Calling `loadData()` to retrieve countries and populate the `#countriesList` combo box.

Compare this code with the pure JavaScript version from Chapter 2 that populates states and countries. If the jQuery code doesn't seem to be shorter, keep in mind that writing a cross-browser version in pure JavaScript would require more than a dozen additional lines of code that deal with the instantiation of `XMLHttpRequest`.

Run *project-04-jQuery-donation-ajax-json*. Open Google Developer Tools and click the Network tab. In Figure 3-2, you can see that jQuery made two successful calls, retrieving two JSON files with the data on states and countries.

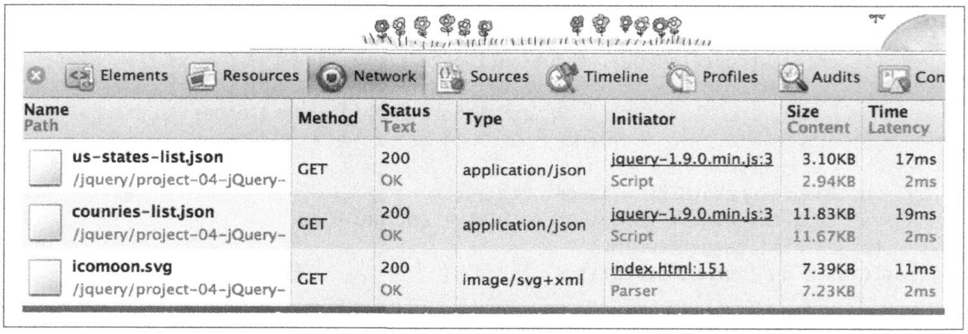

Elements
Resources
Network
Sources
Timeline
Profiles
Audits
Con
Name Path
Method
Status Text
Type
Initiator
Size Content
Time Latency
us-states-list.json
/jquery/project-04-jQuery-
GET
200 OK
application/json
jquery-1.9.0.min.js:3
Script
3.10KB
2.94KB
17ms
2ms
counries-list.json
/jquery/project-04-jQuery-
GET
200 OK
application/json
jquery-1.9.0.min.js:3
Script
11.83KB
11.67KB
19ms
2ms
icomoon.svg
/jquery/project-04-jQuery-
GET
200 OK
image/svg+xml
index.html:151
Parser
7.39KB
7.23KB
11ms
2ms

Figure 3-2. Calling ajax() to retrieve states and countries

Click *countries-list* on the left (see Figure 3-3) and you'll see the JSON data in the response object.

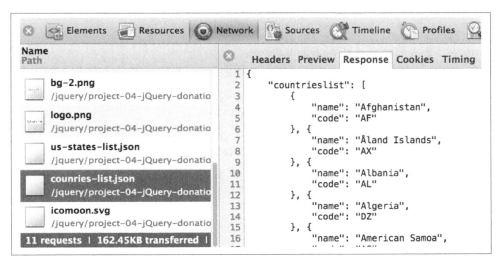

Figure 3-3. The JSON with countries is successfully retrieved

Now let's create an error situation to test the `$.ajax().fail()` chain. Just change the name of the first parameter to `data/counries.json` in the `loadData()` invocation. There is no such file, and the Ajax call will return the error 404. The watch expressions in Figure 3-4 depict the moment when the script execution stopped at the breakpoint in the `fail()` method.

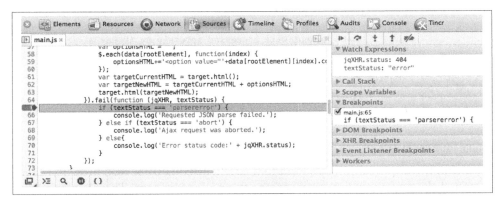

Figure 3-4. The file counries.json is not found: 404

Submitting the Donate Form

Our Save The Child application should be able to submit the donation form to PayPal. The file *index.html* from *project-04-jQuery-donation-ajax-json* contains the form with id="donate-form". The fragment of this form is shown in Example 3-8.

Example 3-8. A fragment of the Donate form

```
<form id="donate-form" name="_xclick" action="https://www.paypal.com/cgi-bin/webscr"
  method="post">
        <input type="hidden" name="cmd" value="_xclick">
        <input type="hidden" name="paypal_email"
         value="email-registered-in-paypal@site-url.com">
        <input type="hidden" name="item_name" value="Donation">
        <input type="hidden" name="currency_code" value="USD">
        <div class="donation-form-section">
                <label class="donation-heading">Please select or enter
                        <br/>
                        donation amount</label>
                <input type="radio" name = "amount" id="d10" value = "10"/>
                <label for = "d10">10</label>
        ...

        </div>
        <div class="donation-form-section">
                <label class="donation-heading">Donor information</label>
                <input type="text" id="full_name" name="full_name"
                                        placeholder="full name *" required>
                <input type="email" id="email_addr" name="email_addr"
                                        placeholder="email *" required>
        ...
        </div>
        <div class="donation-form-section make-payment">
                <h4>We accept Paypal payments</h4>
                <p>
                        Your payment will processed securely by <b>PayPal</b>.
                </p>
        ...
                <button class="donate-button donate-button-submit"></button>
        ...
    </div>
</form>
```

Manual form serialization

If you simply want to submit this form to the URL listed in its action property when the user clicks the Submit button, there is nothing else to be done. This already works, and PayPal's login page opens in the browser. But if you want to seamlessly integrate your page with PayPal or any other third-party service, a preferred way is not to send the user to the third-party website but do it without leaving your web application. We won't be implementing such integration with PayPal here, but technically it would be possible to pass the user's credentials and bank information to charge the donor of Save The Child without even opening the PayPal web page in the browser. To do this, you'd need to submit the form by using Ajax, and the PayPal API would process the results of this transaction by using standard Ajax techniques.

To post the form to a specified URL by using jQuery Ajax, we'll serialize the data from the form on the submit event. The code fragment from *main.js* finds the form with the ID donate-form and chains to it the submit() method, passing to it a callback that will prepare the data and make an Ajax call. You can use the method submit() instead of attaching an event handler to process clicks of the Donate Now button; the method submit() will be invoked not only on the Submit button click event, but when the user presses the Enter key while the cursor is in one of the form's input fields:

```
$('#donate-form').submit(function() {
  var formData = $(this).serialize();
  console.log("The Donation form is serialized:" + formData);
  // Make an AJAX call here and pass the data to the server

  return false;  // stop event propagation and default action
});
```

Run *project-04-jQuery-donation-ajax-json* and open Chrome Developer Tools or Firebug. Then, fill out the donation form as shown in Figure 3-5.

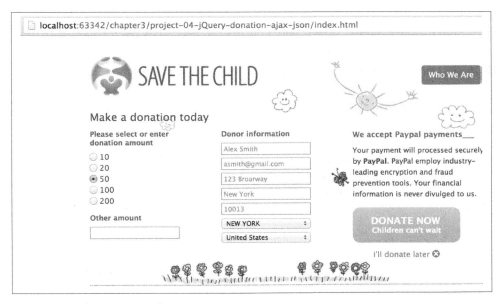

Figure 3-5. The Donation form

Now press the Enter key, and you'll see the output in the console with serialized form data that looks like this:

```
The Donation form is serialized: cmd=_xclick&business=email-registered-in-
paypal%40site-url.com&item_name=Donation&currency_code=USD&amount=50&amount=
&full_name=Alex+Smith&email_addr=asmith%40gmail.com&street_address=
123+Broadway&scty=New+York&zip=10013&state=NY&country=US
```

Manual form serialization has other advantages, too. For example, you don't have to pass the entire form to the server, but select only some of the input fields to be submitted. Example 3-9 shows several ways of sending the partial form content.

Example 3-9. Samples of sending partial form content

```
var queryString;

queryString = $('form[name="_xclick"]')                          ❶
             .find(':input[name=full_name],:input[name=email_addr]')
             .serialize();

queryString = $('form[name="_xclick"]')                          ❷
             .find(':input[type=text]')
             .serialize();

queryString = $('form[name="_xclick"]')                          ❸
             .find(':input[type=hidden]')
             .serialize();
```

❶   Find the form named *_xclick*, apply the filter to select only the full name and the email address, and serialize only these two fields.

❷   Find the form named *_xclick*, apply the filter to select only the input fields of type text, and serialize them.

❸   Find the form named *_xclick*, apply the filter to select only the hidden input fields, and serialize them.

We've prepared for you one more project illustrating manual serialization of the Donation form: *project-15-jQuery-serialize-form*. The *main.js* file in this project suppresses the default processing of the form submit event and sends the form to a server-side PHP script.

We decided to show you a PHP example, because Java is not the only language for developing server-side code in enterprise applications. Running JavaScript on the server with Node.JS or using one of the JavaScript engines such as Google's V8 or Oracle's Nashorn can be considered too.

For the purposes of our example, we will use a common technique of creating a server-side echo script that simply returns the data received from the server. Typically, in enterprise IT shops, server-side development is done by a separate team, and having a dummy server will allow frontend developers lower dependency on the readiness of the server with the real data feed. The file *demo.php* is shown in Example 3-10. It's located in the same directory as *index.html*.

Example 3-10. The server-side script demo.php

```php
<?php
if (isset($_POST['paypal_email'])) {
        $paypal_email = $_POST['paypal_email'];
        $item_name = $_POST['item_name'];
        $currency_code = $_POST['currency_code'];
        $amount = $_POST['amount'];
        $full_name = $_POST['full_name'];
        $email_addr = $_POST['email_addr'];

        echo('Got from the client and will send to PayPal: ' .
            $paypal_email . '    Payment type: ' . $item_name .
        '   amount: ' . $amount .' '. $currency_code .
                        '      Thank you ' . $full_name
        . '     The confirmation will be sent to ' . $email_addr);

} else {
        echo('Error getting data');
}
exit();
?>
```

The process of integration with the payment system using the PayPal API (*http://bit.ly/1pEnI4x*) is out of this book's scope, but at least we can identify the place to do it; it's typically done on the server side. In this chapter's example, it's a server-side PHP script, but it can be a Java, .NET, Python, or any other server. You need to replace the echo statement with the code making requests to PayPal or any other payment system. Example 3-11 is the fragment from *main.js* that shows how to make a request to *demo.php*.

Example 3-11. Submitting the Donate form to demo.php

```javascript
$('.donate-button-submit').on('click', submitSerializedData);

function submitSerializedData(event) {

  // disable the button to prevent more than one click
  onOffButton($('.donate-button-submit'), true, 'submitDisabled');

  event.preventDefault();                        ❶

  var queryString;
```

```
queryString = $('form[name="_xclick"]')        ❷
    .find(':input[type=hidden][name!=cmd], :input[name=amount][value!=""],
    :input[name=full_name], :input[name=email_addr]')
    .serialize();

console.log('-------- get the form inputs data  -----------');
console.log("Submitting to the server: " + queryString);

    $.ajax({
        type : 'POST',
        url : 'demo.php',                        ❸
        data : queryString
    }).done(function(response) {
            console.log('-------- response from demo.php  -----------');
            console.log("Got the response from the ajax() call to demo.php: " +
                                                              response);
            // enable the donate button again
            onOffButton($('.donate-button-submit'), false, 'submitDisabled');
    }).fail(function (jqXHR, textStatus, error) {

    console.log('AJAX request failed: ' + error + ". Code: "
                                + jqXHR.status);

    // The code to display the error in the
    // browser's window goes here
    });
}
```

❶ Prevent the default processing of the submit event. We don't want to simply send the form to the URL listed in the form's `action` property.

❷ Serialize the form fields, excluding the empty amounts and the hidden field with the name `cmd`.

❸ The serialized data from `queryString` will be submitted to the server-side script *demo.php*.

Installing the XAMPP Server with PHP Support

The preceding example uses a server-side PHP script to echo data sent to it. If you'd like to see this script in action so you can test that the client and server can communicate, deploy this script in any web server that supports PHP. For example, you can install on your computer the XAMPP package from the Apache Friends website (*http://bit.ly/1x55auj*), which includes Apache Web Server that supports PHP, FTP, and comes with a preconfigured MySQL database server (we are not going to use it). The installation process is simple: just go through the short instructions on the website that are applicable to your OS. Start the XAMPP Control application and click the Start button next to the

---

label Apache. By default, Apache Web Server starts on port 80, so entering **http://local-host** opens the XAMPP welcome page.

 If you use Mac OS X, you might need to kill the preinstalled Apache server by using the `sudo apachectl stop` command.

The directory *xampp/htdocs* is the document root of the Apache Web Server, so you can place the *index.html* of your project there or in one of its subdirectories. To test that a PHP is supported, save the following code in *helloworld.php* in the *htdocs* directory:

```php
<?php
  echo('Hello World!');
?>
```

After entering the URL *http://localhost/helloworld.php* in your web browser, you should see a greeting from this simple PHP program. The home web page of the XAMPP server contains the link `phpinfo()` on the left panel that shows the current configuration of your PHP server.

The easiest way to test *project-15-jQuery-serialize-form* that uses *demo.php* is to copy this folder into the *htdocs* directory of your XAMPP installation. Then, enter the URL *http://localhost/project-15-jquery-serialize-form/* in your web browser, and you'll see the Save The Child application. Fill out the form and click the Donate Now button. The form will be serialized and submitted to *demo.php* as explained previously. If you open Google Developers Tools in the Network tab, you'll see that *demo.php* has received the Ajax request and the console will show output similar to the following (for Alex Smith, *alex@gmail.com*):

```
-------- get the form inputs data ----------- main.js:138
Submitting to the server: paypal_email=email-registered-in-paypal%40
site-url.com&item_name=Donation+to+the+Save+Sick+Child&currency_code
=USD&amount=50&full_name=Alex+Smith&email_addr=alex%40gmail.com main.js:139

-------- response from demo.php ----------- main.js:146
Got the response from the ajax() call to demo.php: Got from the client
and will send to PayPal: email-registered-in-paypal@site-url.com
Payment type: Donation to the Save The Child   amount: 50 USD
Thank you Alex Smith
The confirmation will be sent to alex@gmail.com main.js:147
```

Using jQuery Plug-ins

jQuery plug-ins are reusable components that know how to do a certain thing—for example, validate a form or display images as a slide show. Thousands of third-party jQuery plug-ins are available in the jQuery Plugin Registry (*http://plugins.jquery.com*). The following are some useful plug-ins:

jTable (http://www.jtable.org)
> Ajax-based tables (grids) for CRUD applications

jQuery Form (http://bit.ly/1nxfjds)
> An HTML form that supports Ajax

HorizontalNav (http://bit.ly/1m6y1pA)
> A navigational bar with tabs that uses the full width of its container

EGrappler (http://bit.ly/1l4eHJA)
> A stylish Akordeon (collapsible panel)

Credit Card Validator (http://bit.ly/1jJNhce)
> Detects and validates credit card numbers

Responsive Carousel (http://bit.ly/1pFbRRi)
> A slider to display images in a carousel fashion

morris.js (http://bit.ly/1yGbPN1)
> A plug-in for charting

Map Marker (http://bit.ly/1pbqmi0)
> Puts multiple markers on maps using Google Maps API V3

The Lazy Load plug-in (http://bit.ly/1qFc88x)
> Delays loading of images, which are outside viewports

The chances are that you will be able to find a plug-in that fits your needs. jQuery plug-ins are usually freely available and their source code is plain JavaScript, so you can tweak it a little if need be.

Validating the Donate Form by Using a Plug-in

The *project-14-jQuery-validate* project illustrates the use of the jQuery Validator (*http://bit.ly/1q1UprG*) plug-in, which allows you to specify the rules to be checked when the user tries to submit the form. If the value is not valid, your custom message is displayed. We've included this plug-in in *index.html* of *project-14-jQuery-validate*:

```
<script src="js/plugins/jquery.validate.min.js"></script>
```

To validate a form with this plug-in, you need to invoke a jQuery selector that finds the form and then call the method **validate()** on this object; this is the simplest way of using this plug-in. But to have more control over the validation process, you need to pass the object with validation options:

```
$("#myform").validate({// validation options go here});
```

The file *main.js* includes the code to validate the Donation form. The validation routine can include many options, which are described in plug-in documentation. Our code sample uses the following options:

- The highlight and unhighlight callbacks
- The HTML element to be used for displaying errors
- The name of the CSS class to style the error messages
- The validation rules

 Validating data only on the client side is not sufficient. It's a good idea to warn the user about data issues without sending the data to the server. But to ensure that the data was not corrupted/modified while traveling to the server, revalidate them on the server side too. Besides, a malicious user can access your server without using your web application. Performing server-side validation is a must.

Example 3-12 displays error messages in the HTML element <div id="validation Summary"></div> that's placed above the form in *index.html*. The Validator plug-in provides the number of invalid form entries by invoking validator.numberOfInval ids(), and our code displays this number unless it's equal to zero.

Example 3-12. Displaying validation errors

```
var validator = $('form[name="_xclick"]').validate({

  highlight : function(target, errorClass) {                   ❶
      $(target).addClass("invalidElement");
      $("#validationSummary").text(validator.numberOfInvalids() +
                                        " field(s) are invalid");
      $("#validationSummary").show();
  },

  unhighlight : function(target, errorClass) {                 ❷
      $(target).removeClass("invalidElement");

      var errors = validator.numberOfInvalids();
      $("#validationSummary").text( errors + " field(s) are invalid");

      if(errors == 0) {
            $("#validationSummary").hide();
      }
```

```
        },

    rules : {                                                    ❸
        full_name : {
                required : true,
                minlength : 2
        },
        email_addr : {
                required : true,
                email : true
        },
        zip : {
                digits:true
        }
    },

    messages : {                                                 ❹
            full_name: {
        required: "Name is required",
        minlength: "Name should have at least 2 letters"
       },
            email_addr : {
                    required : "Email is required",
            }
        }
});
```

❶   When an invalid field is highlighted, this function is invoked. It changes the styling of the input field and updates the error count to display in the validation summary <div> on top of the form.

❷   When the error is fixed, the highlighting on the corrected field is removed, and this function is invoked. It revokes the error styling of the input field and updates the error count. If the error count is zero, the validation summary <div> becomes hidden.

❸   Set the custom validation rules for selected form fields.

❹   Set the custom error messages to be displayed if the user enters invalid data.

Figure 3-6 shows the preceding code in action. After entering a one-character name and an improper email address, the user will see the corresponding error messages. Each message is shown when the user leaves the corresponding field. But as soon as the user fixes any of them (for example, enters one more letter in the name), the form is immediately revalidated and the error messages are removed.

Figure 3-6. *The Validator plug-in's error messages*

Before including a jQuery plug-in in your application, spend some time testing it. Check its size and compare its performance with competing plug-ins.

Adding an Image Slider

Often, you need to add a feature to cycle through the images on a web page. The Save The Child page, for example, could display sequential images of the kids saved by the donors. To give you yet another demonstration of using a jQuery plug-in, we've created the project *project-16-jQuery-slider* and integrated the jQuery plug-in called Responsive Carousel (*http://bit.ly/1pFbRRi*). The file *index.html* of this project includes the CSS styles and the JavaScript code plug-in, as follows:

```
<link rel="stylesheet" href="assets/css/responsive-carousel.css" />
<link rel="stylesheet" href="assets/css/responsive-carousel.slide.css" />
<link rel="stylesheet" href="assets/css/responsive-carousel.fade.css" />
<link rel="stylesheet" href="assets/css/responsive-carousel.flip.css" />
...
<script src="js/plugins/responsive-carousel/responsive-carousel.min.js">
</script>
<script src="js/plugins/responsive-carousel/responsive-carousel.flip.js">
</script>
```

Run *project-16-jQuery-slider*, and you'll see how three plain slides display in succession, as shown in Figure 3-7. The HTML part of the container includes the three slides as follows:

```
<div id="image-carousel" class="carousel carousel-flip"
                                data-transition="flip">
        <div>
                <img src="assets/img/slides/slide-1.jpg" />
        </div>
        <div>
                <img src="assets/img/slides/slide-2.jpg" />
        </div>
        <div>
                <img src="assets/img/slides/slide-3.jpg" />
        </div>
</div>
```

Figure 3-7. Using the Responsive Carousel plug-in

With this plug-in, the JavaScript code that the application developer has to write to implement several types of rotation is minimal. When the user clicks one of the radio buttons (Fade, Slide, or Flip Transitions) the following code just changes the CSS class name to be used with the carousel:

```
$(function() {
        $("input:radio[name=transitions]").click(function() {
                var transition = $(this).val();
                var newClassName = 'carousel carousel-' + transition;
                $('#image-carousel').attr('class', '');
                $('#image-carousel').addClass(newClassName);
                $('#image-carousel').attr('data-transition', transition);
        });
});
```

To see code samples of using the Responsive Carousel plugin (including popular autoplaying slide shows), check out the Responsive Carousel variations (*http://bit.ly/1prR6tB*).

The Validator and Responsive Carousel plugins clearly demonstrate that jQuery plugins can save you some serious time writing code to implement commonly required features. It's great that the members of the jQuery community from around the world share their creations with other developers. If you can't find a plug-in that fits your needs or have specific custom logic that needs to be used or reused in your application, you can write your own plugin. Should you decide to write a plug-in of your own, refer to the Plugins/Authoring (*http://bit.ly/1hQJcYr*) document.

Summary

In this chapter, you became familiar with the jQuery Core library, which is the de facto standard library in millions of web applications. Its simplicity and extensibility via the mechanism of plug-ins make it a must-have in almost every web page. Even if your organization decides on a more complex and feature-rich JavaScript framework, the chances are that you might find a handy jQuery plug-in that will complement "the main" framework and make it into the code of your application. There is nothing wrong with this, and you shouldn't be in the position of "either jQuery or XYZ"—most likely they can coexist.

We can recommend one of the small frameworks that will complement your jQuery code: Twitter's Bootstrap (*http://twitter.github.io/bootstrap*). Bootstrap can quickly make the UI of your desktop or mobile application look stylish. Bootstrap is the most popular framework (*http://bit.ly/1ohWjBI*) on GitHub.

Chapter 7 shows you how to test jQuery applications. In this chapter, we rewrote a pure JavaScript application for illustration purposes. But if this were a real-world project to convert the Save The Child application from JavaScript to jQuery, having tests even for the JavaScript version of the application would have helped to verify that everything transitioned to jQuery successfully.

In Chapter 11 you'll learn how to use the jQuery Mobile library—an API on top of jQuery code that allows building UIs for mobile devices.

Now that we've covered JavaScript, HTML5 APIs, Ajax, JSON, and the jQuery library, we're going to the meat of the book: frameworks, productivity tools, and strategies for making your application enterprise-ready.

Enterprise Considerations

The content of this part justifies having the word *enterprise* on this book's cover.

In Chapter 4, you'll learn how to use a rich and feature-complete framework: Ext JS from Sencha. Even though using this framework might be overkill for a small website, it's pretty popular in the enterprise world, where a rich-looking UI is required. Besides learning how to work with this framework, you'll build a new version of the Save The Child application in Ext JS. In this version (*http://bit.ly/1ohJZRR*), we introduce an interactive chart (a popular feature for enterprise dashboards) and a data grid (any enterprise application uses grids).

Chapter 5 is a review of productivity tools used by enterprise developers (such as npm, Grunt, Bower, Yeoman, and CDB). It's about build tools, code generators, and managing dependencies. (A typical enterprise application uses various software that needs to work in harmony.)

Chapter 6 is dedicated to dealing with issues that any mid-to-large enterprise web application is facing: how to modularize the application to reduce the load time and make it more responsive. Our sample application, Save The Child, will be divided into modules with the help of the RequireJS framework.

Chapter 7 is a review of test-driven development (TDD), which is a way of writing less-buggy applications. TDD originated in large projects written in such languages as Java, C++, or C#, and now it's adopted by the HTML5 community. After reviewing how to do TDD in JavaScript, we'll show how to introduce testing into the Save The Child application.

Chapter 8 is about WebSocket, a new HTML5 API that can be a game changer for enterprise web applications that need to communicate with servers as fast as possible (think financial trading applications or online auctions). We'll show how to add an auction to our sample charity application.

Chapter 9 is a brief overview of various web application security issues. Although small websites often forget about dealing with security vulnerabilities, this subject can't be ignored in the enterprise world.

## CHAPTER 4

Developing Web Applications in the Ext JS Framework

In Chapter 3, you became familiar with the JavaScript library jQuery. Now we'll introduce you to a more complex product: the JavaScript framework Ext JS (*http://www.sencha.com/products/extjs*) from Sencha (*http://www.sencha.com*). This is one of the most feature-complete frameworks available on the market, and you should give it serious consideration while deciding on the tooling for your next enterprise HTML5 application.

Exploring JavaScript Frameworks

The word *framework* implies that there is some precreated "software frame," and application developers need to fit their business-specific code inside such a frame. Why would you want to do this, as opposed to having full freedom in developing your application code the way you want? The reason is that most enterprise projects are developed by teams of software engineers, and having an agreed-upon structure of the application, with clear separation of software layers, can make the entire process of development more productive.

Some JavaScript frameworks are mainly forcing developers to organize application code in layers by implementing the Model-View-Controller (MVC) design pattern. More than a dozen MVC JavaScript frameworks are being used by professional developers: Backbone.js (*http://backbonejs.org*), ExtJS (*http://www.sencha.com/products/extjs*), AngularJS (*http://angularjs.org/*), Ember.js (*http://emberjs.com*), and Knockout (*http://knockoutjs.com*), just to name a few.

Ext JS also supports MVC, and you can read about it later in this chapter in "Best Practice: MVC" on page 139.

An excellent website called TodoMVC (*http://todomvc.com*) shows examples of implementing one application (a Todo list) by using various popular frameworks. Studying the source code of this application implemented in several frameworks can help you select one for your project.

To keep the size of this book manageable, we were not able to review more JavaScript frameworks. But if you'd ask us to name one more great JavaScript framework that didn't make it into this book, we would recommend that you learn AngularJS from Google. There are lots of free online resources on AngularJS that Jeff Cunningham has collected all in one place on GitHub (*http://bit.ly/1qr3ieB*).

Besides splitting the code into tiers, frameworks might offer prefabricated UI components and build tools. Ext JS is one of those frameworks.

If you decide to develop your application with Ext JS, you don't need to use the jQuery library.

Choosing to Use Ext JS

After learning how the jQuery library can simplify development of HTML5 applications, you might be wondering what's so good about Ext JS that makes it worthwhile for studying. First, jQuery Core is just a library of utilities that simplify working with the Document Object Model (DOM), and you still need to write the web application by using HTML and JavaScript. In addition, there are lots and lots of jQuery plug-ins that include handy widgets to add to your manually created website. We just mentioned the frameworks that help with better organizing or modularizing your project, but enterprise applications might need more. So here comes the Ext JS sales pitch:

- Ext JS is an HTML5 framework that doesn't require you to write HTML. Your single HTML file (*index.html*) will include just three files in the <head> section: one with the Ext JS framework, one CSS file, and one *app.js*, but the <body> section will be empty.

- Ext JS includes a comprehensive library of JavaScript-based classes that can help you with pretty much everything you need to develop a web application (UI components, UI layouts, collections, networking, CSS compiler, packaging tool, and more).

- Ext JS offers a way to write object-oriented code (for those who like it), to define classes and inheritance in a way that's closer to classical inheritance and doesn't require the `prototype` property.

- Ext JS can jump-start your application development by generating the initial code layered according to the MVC design pattern.

- Ext JS is a cross-browser framework that promises to automatically take care of all differences in major web browsers.

If you just finished reading Chapter 3, you'll need to switch to a different state of mind. The jQuery Core library was light; it didn't drastically change the way of developing pure HTML/JavaScript applications. But working with Ext JS is a completely different ball game. It's not about improving an existing web page; it's about rewriting it from scratch without using HTML. Ext JS includes a rich library of UI components, a flexible class system, custom layouts, and code generators. But web browsers understand only HTML, DOM, CSS, and JavaScript. This means that the framework will have to do some extra work in converting the code written using the homemade Ext JS class system into the same old HTML objects. Such extra work requires additional processing time, and we'll discuss this in "Exploring a Component's Life Cycle" on page 146.

The title clearly states that this chapter is about the Ext JS framework. Providing detailed coverage of Ext JS in one chapter is almost mission impossible because of the vast variety of features this framework offers. Consider this chapter a hands-on overview of Ext JS. The material in this chapter is divided into two parts:

1. You'll get a high-level overview of the Ext JS framework.

2. We'll do a code review of a new version of the Save The Child application developed with Ext JS. This is where we want you to spend most of the time in this chapter. Learn while studying commented code. We've also provided multiple links to the relevant product documentation.

Downloading and Installing Ext JS

First, you need to know that Ext JS can be used for free only for noncommercial projects. To use Ext JS for enterprise web development, you or your firm has to purchase one of the Ext JS licenses (*http://bit.ly/TwrttK*). But for studying, you can download the complete commercial version of Ext JS for free for a 45-day evaluation period.

 The materials presented in this chapter were tested only with the current version of Ext JS, which at the time of this writing was 4.2.

After downloading the Ext JS framework, unzip it to any directory of your choice. Later the framework will be copied either into your project directory (see "Generating Applications with the Sencha CMD Tool" on page 129) or in the document root of your web server.

After unzipping the Ext JS distribution, you'll find some files and folders there. There are several JavaScript files containing various packages of the Ext JS framework. You'll need to pick just one of these files. The files that include the word *all* in their names contain the entire framework, and if you choose one of them, all the classes will be loaded to the user's browser even though your application may never use most of them.

ext-all.js
> Minimized version of the source code of Ext JS, which looks like one line of 1.4 million characters (it's still JavaScript, of course). Most likely you won't deploy this file on your production server.

ext-all-debug.js
> Human-readable source code of Ext JS with no comments. If you like to read comments, use *ext-all-debug-w-comments.js*.

ext-all-dev.js
> Human-readable source code of Ext JS that includes `console.log()` statements that generate and output debugging information in the browser's console.

Similarly, there are files that don't include *all* in their names: *ext.js*, *ext-debug.js*, and *ext-dev.js*. These are much smaller files that do not include the entire framework, but rather a minimum set of classes required to start the application. Later, the additional classes may be lazy-loaded on an as-needed basis.

 Typically, you shouldn't use the *all* files. We recommend that you use the file *ext.js* and the Sencha CMD tool to create a customized version of the Ext JS library to be included with your application. You can find more details in "Generating Applications with the Sencha CMD Tool" on page 129.

The *docs* folder contains extensive documentation; just open the file *index.html* in your browser and start reading and studying.

The *builds* folder includes sandboxed versions of Ext JS in case you need to use, say, Ext JS 4.2 along with older versions of this framework. Browsing the *builds* folder reveals that the Ext JS framework consists of three parts:

Ext Core
    A free-to-use JavaScript library (*http://bit.ly/1nWMdTy*) for enhancing websites. It supports DOM manipulation with CSS selectors, events, and Ajax requests. It also offers syntax to define and create classes that can extend from one another. The functionality of Ext Core is comparable to Core jQuery.

Ext JS
    A UI framework that includes a rich library of UI components.

The Foundation
    A set of useful utilities.

Such code separation allowed the creators of Ext JS to reuse a large portion of the framework's code in the mobile library Sencha Touch, which we cover in Chapter 12.

 The Ext JS framework is large, so be prepared for your application to be at least 1 MB in size. This is not an issue for enterprise applications that run on fast networks. But if you need to create a small consumer-oriented website, you might be better off using the lightweight, easy-to-learn, and free jQuery library or one of a dozen other JavaScript frameworks that either improve organizational structure of your project or offer a set of a la cart components to prettify your HTML5 application. On the other hand, if you have had a chance to develop or use rich Internet applications developed with such frameworks as Microsoft Silverlight or Apache Flex, you'll quickly realize that Ext JS is the closest in terms of functionality, with its rich set of components and tools.

Becoming Familiar with Ext JS and Tooling

This section is not an Ext JS tutorial that gradually explains each and every feature and API of Ext JS. For that, we'd need to write a fat Ext JS book. Sencha publishes detailed documentation, multiple online examples (*http://bit.ly/1o8xvtb*), and videos (*http://bit.ly/1z2dE7p*). In this chapter, you'll get an overview of the framework.

Creating the First Version of Hello World

Before we explain how things work in Ext JS, we'll develop a Hello World application. Later, you'll review the code of the Save The Child application as a hands-on way of learning the framework. You'll read the code fragments followed by brief explanations. You'll be able to run and debug this application on your own computer and see how various components and program layers work in practice. But first things first—let's create a couple of versions of Hello World.

Create a new directory (for example, *hello1*). Inside *hello1* create a subdirectory named *ext* and copy there the entire content of your Ext JS installation directory. Create yet another subdirectory named *app* inside *hello1*—this is where your application JavaScript files will go.

At a very minimum, every Ext JS application will contain one HTML and one JavaScript file—usually *index.html* and *app.js*. The file *index.html* will include the references to the CSS and JavaScript code of Ext JS and will include your *app.js* containing the code of the Hello World application:

```
<!DOCTYPE HTML>
<html>
<head>
    <meta charset="UTF-8">
    <title>HelloWorld</title>
      <link rel="stylesheet" href="ext/resources/ext-all-gray.css">
      <script src="ext/ext.js"></script>
      <script src="app/app.js"></script>
</head>
<body></body>
</html>
```

Next comes the content of *app.js* that you should place in the *app* directory of your project. This is what *app.js* might look like:

```
Ext.application({
    launch: function(){
      alert("Hello World");
    }
});
```

This `Ext.application()` method gets a *configuration object* as an argument—a JavaScript literal—with a configured `launch` method that's called automatically when the web page has completely loaded. In our case, this object literal mandates launching the anonymous function that displays the "Hello World" message. In Ext JS, you'll be using such configuration objects a lot.

Open the file *index.html* in your web browser and you'll see this greeting. But this was a plain vanilla Hello World. In the next section, we'll automate the process of creating a fancier Hello World (or the initial version of any other application) by using the Sencha CMD tool.

Configuration Options

In the versions of Ext JS prior to 4.0, you'd invoke the `Ext.onReady()` method instead of passing the configuration object with the `launch` *config option*.

Providing a function argument as a configuration object overrides configurable properties of the current instance of the class. This is different from class properties, which are defined at the prototype level, and changing the value of a property would apply to all instances of the class. When you read Ext JS online documentation for any class, you'll see three categories of class elements: configs, properties, and methods. For example, this is how you can create a panel passing configs:

```
Ext.create('Ext.panel.Panel', {
    title: 'Hello',
    width: 200,
    html: '<p>World!</p>',
});
```

In this example, we are creating an instance of the panel by using a configuration object with three config options: `title`, `width`, and `html`. The values of these properties will be assigned to the corresponding properties of this instance only. For example, the documentation for `Ext.panel.Panel` (*http://docs.sencha.com/extjs/4.2.0/#!/api/Ext.panel.Panel*) lists 116 available configs that you can set on the panel instance.

Ext JS classes are organized into packages. For example, the class `Panel` in the preceding example is located in the package `Ext.panel`. You'll be using packaging in your applications too. For example, in the next chapter you'll see classes from Save The Child and Clear frameworks named as `SSC.view.DonateForm` or `Clear.override.ExtJSOverrid er`. Such packages should be properly *namespaced*, and `SSC` and `Clear` are top-level namespaces here. The next fragment shows how to give a name to your application, and such a given name will serve as a top-level namespace:

```
Ext.application({
    name: 'SSC',
    // more config options can go here
});
```

In the next section, we'll automate the process of creating the Hello World application.

Generating Applications with the Sencha CMD Tool

Sencha CMD is a handy command-line tool that automates your work, from scaffolding your application to minimizing, packaging, and deploying it.

Download Sencha CMD (*http://bit.ly/senchacmd-install*). Run the installer, and when it's complete, open the terminal or command window and enter the command **sen-**

cha. You should see a prompt with all possible commands and options that CMD understands.

For example, to generate the initial project structure for the Hello World application, enter the following command, specifying the absolute path to your Ext JS SDK directory (we keep it in the */Library* directory) and to the output folder, where the generated project should reside:

```
sencha -sdk /Library/ext-4.2 generate app HelloWorld /Users/yfain11/hello
```

After the code generation is complete, you'll see the folder *hello* with the structure shown in Figure 4-1.

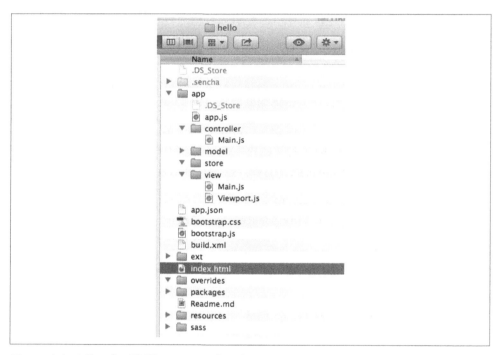

Figure 4-1. A Sencha CMD–generated project

The generated project is created with the assumption that your application will be built using the MVC paradigm discussed in "Best Practice: MVC" on page 139. The JavaScript is located in the *app* folder, which includes the *view* subfolder with the visual portion of your application, the *controller* folder with controller classes, and the *model* folder for data. The *ext* folder contains multiple distributions of the Ext JS framework. The *sass* folder contains your application's CSS files (see "SASS and CSS" on page 163).

The entry point to your application is *index.html*, which contains the references to the main application file *app.js*, the Ext JS framework *extdev-js*, the CSS file *bootstrap.css* (imports the classic theme), and the supporting script *bootstrap.js*, which contains the mapping of the long names of the framework and application classes to their shorter names (*xtypes*). Here's how the generated *index.html* file looks:

```
<!DOCTYPE HTML>
<html>
<head>
    <meta charset="UTF-8">
    <title>HelloWorld</title>
    <!-- <x-compile> -->
        <!-- <x-bootstrap> -->
            <link rel="stylesheet" href="bootstrap.css">
            <script src="ext/ext-dev.js"></script>
            <script src="bootstrap.js"></script>
        <!-- </x-bootstrap> -->
        <script src="app/app.js"></script>
    <!-- </x-compile> -->
</head>
<body></body>
</html>
```

The content of the generated *app.js* is shown next. This script just calls the method `Ext.application()`, passing as an argument a configuration object that specifies the application name, and the names of the classes that play roles of views and controller. We'll go into details a bit later, but at this point let's concentrate on the big picture:

```
Ext.application({
    name: 'HelloWorld',

    views: [
        'Main',
        'Viewport'
    ],

    controllers: [
        'Main'
    ],

    autoCreateViewport: true
});
```

Finally, if you open *index.html* in your web browser, you'll see our Hello World initial web page that looks like Figure 4-2. This view uses a so-called border layout and shows a panel on the west and a tabpanel in the central region of the view.

The total size of this version of the Hello World application is pretty large: 4 MB. The browser makes 173 requests to the server by the time the user sees the application shown in Figure 4-2. But Sencha CMD knows how to build the production version of the Ext

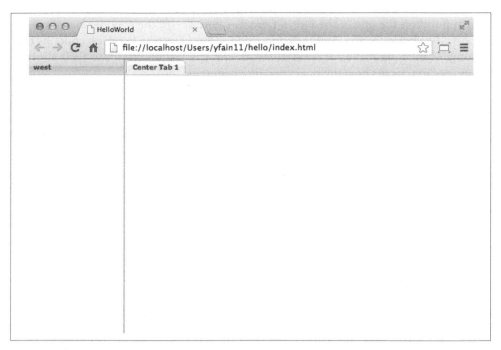

Figure 4-2. The UI of our Sencha CMD–generated application

JS application. It minimizes and merges the application's and required framework's JavaScript code into one file. The application's CSS file is also minimized, and the references to the image resources become relative, hence shorter. Besides, the images may be automatically sliced—cut into smaller rectangular pieces that can be downloaded by the browser simultaneously.

To create an optimized version of your application, go to the terminal or a command window and change to the root directory of your application (in our case, it's */Users/yfain11/hello*) and run the following command:

```
sencha app build
```

After the build is finished, you'll see a newly generated version of the application in the directory *build/HelloWorld/production*. Open the file *index.html* while running Chrome Developer Tools, and you'll see that the total size of the application is substantially lower (about 900 KB) and that the browser had to make only five requests to the server (see Figure 4-3). Using Gzip will reduce the size of this application to 600 KB, which is still a lot, but the Ext JS framework is not the right choice for writing Hello World types of applications or light websites.

Name Path		Method	Status Text	Type	Initiator	Size Content	Time Latency
index.html /Users/yfain11/hello/build/HelloWorld/production		GET	Success	text/html	Other	0 B 240 B	1 ms 0
default-scroll-right-top.gif /Users/yfain11/hello/build/HelloWorld/production/resources		GET	Success	image/...	all-classes.js:1 Script	0 B 347 B	23 ms 0
default-scroll-left-top.gif /Users/yfain11/hello/build/HelloWorld/production/resources		GET	Success	image/...	all-classes.js:1 Script	0 B 344 B	23 ms 0
all-classes.js /Users/yfain11/hello/build/HelloWorld/production		GET	Success	text/ja...	index.html:7 Parser	0 B 744 KB	15 ms 0
HelloWorld-all.css /Users/yfain11/hello/build/HelloWorld/production/resources		GET	Success	text/css	index.html:6 Parser	0 B 187 KB	1 ms 0

5 requests | 0 B transferred | 319 ms (onload: 187 ms, DOMContentLoaded: 187 ms)

Figure 4-3. Running a production version of HelloWorld

For more details about code generation, refer to the section Using Sencha Cmd with Ext JS (*http://bit.ly/1izOLL2*) in the product documentation.

Sencha Desktop Packager (*http://bit.ly/1rriI01*) allows you to take an existing Ext JS web application (or any other HTML5 application) and package it as a native desktop application for Windows and Mac OS X. Your application can also integrate with native menus and file dialog boxes and access the filesystem.

We'll use the Sencha CMD tool again in "Building a production version of Save The Child" on page 184 to create an optimized version of the Save The Child application.

Sencha CMD comes with an embedded web server (*http://bit.ly/1i414PQ*). To start the server on the default port 1841, open the terminal or command window in your application directory and run the command `sencha web start`. To serve your web application on another port (for example, 8080) and from any directory, run it as follows: `sencha fs web -port8080 start -map /path/to/app/docrootdir`.

If your organization is developing web applications with Ext JS without using Sencha CMD, it's a mistake. Sencha CMD is a useful code generator and optimizer that also enforces the MVC principles of application design.

Choosing Which Ext JS Distribution to Use

First, you need to select the packaging of the Ext JS framework that fits your needs. You can select its minimized version to be used in production or a larger and commented version with detailed comments and error messages. As we mentioned earlier in this chapter, you can select a version of Ext JS that includes either all or only the core classes. The third option is to create a custom build of Ext JS that includes only those framework classes that are used by your application.

The files with the minimized production version of Ext JS are called *ext-all.js* (all classes) and *ext.js* (just the core classes plus the loader of required classes). We usually pick *ext-all.js* for development, but for production use the distribution fine-tuned for our application, as described in "Generating Applications with the Sencha CMD Tool" on page 129.

If this application will be used on high-speed networks and size is not an issue, simply add it to your *index.html* from your local servers or see if Sencha offers the CDN for the Ext JS version you need, which might look similar to the following:

```
<link rel="http://cdn.sencha.io/ext-4.2.0-gpl/resources/css/ext-all.css" />

<script type="text/javascript" charset="utf-8"
        src="http://cdn.sencha.io/ext-4.2.0-gpl/ext.js"></script>
```

Declaring, Loading, and Instantiating Classes

Pure JavaScript doesn't have classes; constructor functions are the closest components it has to classes-language elements. Ext JS extends the JavaScript language and introduces classes and a special way to define and instantiate them with the functions `Ext.define()` and `Ext.create()`. Ext JS also allows us to extend one class from another by using the property `extend` and to define class constructors by using the property `constructor`. With `Ext.define()`, you declare a class declaration, and `Ext.create()` instantiates it. Basically, `define()` serves as a template for creating one or more instances.

Usually, the first argument you specify to `define()` is a fully qualified class name, and the second argument is an object literal that contains the class definition. If you use `null` as the first argument, Ext JS creates an anonymous class.

The next class `Header` has a 200-pixel height, uses the `hbox` layout, has a custom `config` property `logo`, and extends `Ext.panel.Panel`:

```
Ext.define("SSC.view.Header", {
  extend: 'Ext.panel.Panel',
```

```
      title: 'Test',
      height: 200,
      renderTo: 'content',        ❶

      config: {
         logo: 'sony_main.png'     ❷
      },

      layout: {
         type: 'hbox',
         align: 'middle'
      }
   });
```

❶   Render this panel to an HTML element with id=content.

❷   Define a custom config property logo.

You can optionally include a third argument for define(), which is a function to be called when the class definition is created. Now you can create one or more instances of the class. For example:

```
var myHeader = Ext.create("SSC.view.Header");
```

The values of custom config properties from the config{} section of the class can be reassigned during the class instantiation. For example, the next code snippet will print *sony.png* for the first instance of the header, and *sony_small.png* for the second one. Please note that Ext JS automatically generates getters and setters for all config properties, which allows us to use the method getLogo():

```
Ext.onReady(function () {
   var myHeader1 = Ext.create("SSC.view.Header");
   //
   var myHeader2 = Ext.create("SSC.view.Header",
                           { logo: 'sony_small.png' });

   console.log(myHeader1.getLogo());
   console.log(myHeader2.getLogo());
});
```

Don't forget about the online tool JSFiddle, which allows you to test and share JavaScript code snippets. JSFiddle knows about Ext JS 4.2 already. For example, you can run the preceding code snippet by following this JSFiddle link (*http://bit.ly/1ohWQDC*). If it doesn't render the styles properly, check the URL of *ext-all.css* in the section External Resources.

If a class has dependencies on other classes that must be preloaded, use the `requires` parameter. For example, the next code snippet shows that the class `SSC.view.View port` requires the `Panel` and the `Column` classes. So the Ext JS loader will check whether `Panel` and/or `Column` are loaded yet and will dynamically lazy-load them first (see Example 4-1).

Example 4-1. Loading dependencies with the keyword requires

```
Ext.define('SSC.view.Viewport', {
    extend: 'Ext.container.Viewport',
    requires: [
        'Ext.tab.Panel',
        'Ext.layout.container.Column'
    ]
    // the rest of the class definition is omitted
});
```

`Ext.create()` is a preferred way of instantiation because it does more than the `new` operator that is also allowed in Ext JS. But `Ext.create()` can perform additional functionality—for example, if `Ext.Loader` is enabled, `create()` will attempt to synchronously load dependencies (if you haven't used the option `require`). But with `re quires`, you preload all dependencies asynchronously in parallel, which is a preferred way of specifying dependencies. Besides, the async mode allows loading from different domains, whereas sync loading doesn't.

 Ed Spencer published some useful recommendations on improving performance of Ext JS applications in his blog titled SenchaCon 2013: Ext JS Performance Tips (*http://bit.ly/1nJEOtD*).

Dynamic Class Loading

The singleton Ext.Loader (*http://bit.ly/1ls3rMH*) offers a powerful mechanism for dynamic loading of any classes on demand. You have to explicitly enable the loader immediately after including the Ext JS framework in your HTML file, providing the paths where the loader should look for files. For example:

```
<script type="text/javascript">
    Ext.Loader.setConfig({
        enabled: true,
        disablrCaching: false,
        paths: {
            'SSC': 'my_app_path'
        }
    });
</script>
```

Then, the manual loading of a class can be done by using `Ext.require(SSC.Some Class)` or `Ext.syncRequire(SSC.SomeClass)`. You need to explicitly enable the loader (`enabled:true`) to support lazy-loading of the required classes.

For each class, Ext JS creates one instance of the special class `Ext.Class`, which will be shared by all objects instantiated from this class.

The instance of any object has access to its class via the special variable `self` (*http://bit.ly/1x56cX4*).

Prior to creating a class, Ext JS will run some preprocessors and some postprocessors based on the class definition. For example, the class `SSC.view.Viewport` from the preceding code sample uses `extend: 'Ext.container.Viewport'`, which will engage the *extend* preprocessor that will do some background work to properly build a subclass of extend: `Viewport`. If your class includes the `config` section, the *config* preprocessor will be engaged.

xtype: An efficient way to create class instances

One of the interesting preprocessors is *xtype*, which is an alternative to the invocation of the `create()` method for creating the instance of the class. Every Ext JS component has an assigned and documented `xtype`. For example, `Ext.panel.Panel` has an `xtype` of `panel`. Online documentation displays the name of the corresponding `xtype` in the header of each component, as shown in Figure 4-4.

Figure 4-4. Each component has an xtype

Using `xtype` instead of `create()` leads to more-efficient memory management. If the object is declared with the `xtype` attribute, it won't be instantiated until a container uses it. You are encouraged to assign `xtype` to your custom classes, and Ext JS will instantiate if for you without the need to call `create()`. You can find many examples of using the `xtype` property in "Developing Save The Child with Ext JS" on page 150 later in this chapter.

For example, the following class definition includes many components with the `xtype` property:

```
Ext.define("SSC.view.LoginBox", {
    extend: 'Ext.Container',
    xtype: 'loginbox',

    layout: 'hbox',

    items: [{
        xtype: 'container',
        flex: 1
    }, {
        xtype: 'textfield',
        emptyText: 'username',
        name: 'username',
        hidden: true
    }, {
        xtype: 'textfield',
        emptyText: 'password',
        inputType: 'password',
        name: 'password',
        hidden: true
    }, {
        xtype: 'button',
        text: 'Login',
        action: 'login'
    }]
});
```

Most of these components use the standard Ext JS `xtype` values, so the fact that you have included them in the class `SSC.view.LoginBox` is a command for Ext JS to instantiate all these buttons and text fields. But the class `SSC.view.LoginBox` also includes `xtype: 'loginbox'`—we decided to assign the value `loginbox` to serve as the `xtype` of our class. Now, you can use the statement `xtype: 'loginbox'` in any other container, and it will know how to instantiate it. For example, later in this chapter, you'll see the complete code of the main window `SSC.view.ViewPort`, which includes (and instantiates) our login box as shown in Example 4-2.

Example 4-2. Instantiating the custom component LoginBox with xtype

```
items: [{
    xtype: 'loginbox',
    margin: '10 0 0 0'
},
// more items go here
]
```

Supporting multiple inheritance by uisng mixins

The object-oriented languages Java and C# can be considered simpler versions of C++. One of the C++ features that didn't make it into Java and C# was support of multiple inheritance: in these languages, a class can extend only one other class. This was done for a good reason: debugging of the C++ programs that were written with multiple inheritance was difficult.

Ext JS supports multiple inheritance via JavaScript mixins. A class constructor can get any object as an argument, and Ext JS will use its property values to initialize the corresponding properties defined in the class, if they exist, and the rest of the properties will be created on the fly. The following code snippet shows how to define a classB that will have features defined in the classes classA, classC, and classD:

```
Ext.define("MyApp.classB",{
  extend: "MyApp.classA",
  mixins: {classC: "MyApp.classC"
           classD, "MyApp.classD"}

  }
  // The rest of the classB code goes here

});
```

 If more than one mixin has a method with the same name, the first method that was applied to the resulting class wins. To avoid collisions, Ext JS allows you to provide the fully qualified name of the method—for example, this.mixins.classC.conflictingName(); this.mixins.classD.conflictingName();.

Best Practice: MVC

Even though Ext JS doesn't force you to architect your application based on the MVC paradigm, it's a really good idea to do so. Earlier in "Generating Applications with the Sencha CMD Tool" on page 129, you saw how this tool generates a project, which separates model, views, controllers, and stores into separate directories (as shown earlier in Figure 4-1, which depicted the structure of the Hello World project). But later in this chapter, we'll build our Save The Child application the same way. Figure 4-5 presents a diagram illustrating the Ext JS application that contains all Model-View-Controller tiers.

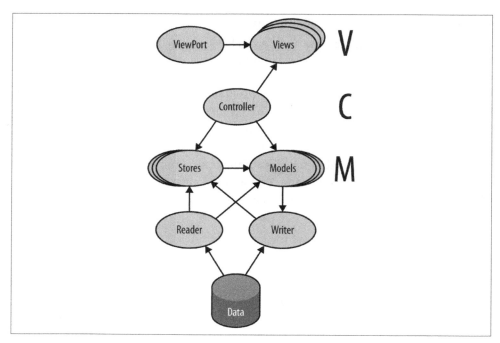

Figure 4-5. Model-View-Controller in Ext JS

The MVC tier comprises the following:

Controller

An object that serves as an intermediary between the data and the views. The data has arrived at your application, and the controller has to notify the appropriate view. The user changed the data on the view, and the controller should pass the changes to the model (or stores, in the Ext JS world). The controller is the place to write event listeners' reaction to some important events of your application (for example, a user clicked a button). In other words, the controller maps the events to actions to be performed on the data or the view.

View

A certain portion of the UI that the user sees. The view is populated with the data from the model (or stores).

Model

Represents some business entity (for example, Donor, Campaign, Customer, or Order). In Ext JS, models are accessed via stores.

Store

Contains one or more model instances. Typically, a model is a separate class that is instantiated by the store object, but in simple cases, a store can have the model data embedded in its own class. A store can use more than one model if need be. Both stores and model can communicate with the data feed that in a web application is usually provided by a server-side data feed.

The application object defines its controllers, views, models, and stores. When Save The Child is ready, the code of its *app.js* will look as follows:

```
Ext.application({
    name: 'SSC',

    views: [
        'CampaignsMap',
        'DonateForm',
        'DonorsPanel',
        'Header',
        'LoginBox',
        'VideoPanel',
        'Viewport'
    ],

    stores: [
        'Campaigns',
        'Donors'
    ],

    controllers: [
        'Donate'
    ]
});
```

This code is clean and simple to read/write and helps Ext JS to generate additional code required for wiring views, models, controllers, and stores together. There is no explicit models section, because in our implementation, the models were defined inside the stores. For better understanding of the rest of this chapter, you should read the MVC Architecture (*http://bit.ly/1lst0gD*) section from the Ext JS documentation. We don't want to repeat the content of the Sencha product documentation, but rather will be giving you brief descriptions while reviewing the Save The Child application.

Models and stores

When you create a class to be served as a model, it must be a subclass of Ext.data.Mod el. A model has the fields property. For example, you can represent a Donor entity by using just two fields—name and location:

```
Ext.define('HR.model.Donor',{
    extend: 'Ext.data.Model',
    requires: [
        'Ext.data.Types'
    ],
```

```
        fields: [
            { name: 'donors',   type: Ext.data.Types.INT },
            { name: 'location', type: Ext.data.Types.STRING}
        ]
});
```

Think of an instance of a model as one record representing a business entity—for example, Donor. Ext JS generates getters and setters for models, so if an instance of the model is represented by the variable sscDonor, you can set or get its value as follows:

```
sscDonor.set('name', 'Farata Systems');
var donorName= sscDonor.get('name');
```

A store in Ext JS holds a collection of instances of a model. For example, if your application has retrieved the information about 10 donors, it will be represented in Ext JS as a collection of 10 instances of the class Donor. A custom store in your application has to extend from the class Ext.data.Store.

If you need to quickly create a mock store for testing purposes, you can declare a store with inline data that you can specify using the config option data. The next code sample shows a declaration of the store for providing information about the donors as inline data:

```
Ext.define('SSC.store.Donors', {
    extend: 'Ext.data.Store',

    fields: [
        { name: 'donors',   type: 'int' },
        { name: 'location', type: 'string' }
    ],

    data: [
        { donors: 48, location: 'Chicago, IL' },
        { donors: 60, location: 'New York, NY' },
        { donors: 90, location: 'Dallas, TX' }
    ]
});
```

It's a good idea to have a mock store with the test data located right on your computer. This way, you won't depend on the readiness and availability of the server-side data. But usually, a store makes an Ajax call to a server and retrieves the data via the object Ext.data.reader.Reader or one of its descendants. For example:

```
Ext.define('SSC.store.Donors', {
    extend: 'Ext.data.Store',

    model: 'SSC.model.Donor',    ❶
    proxy: {                     ❷
        type: 'ajax',
        url: 'donors.json',      ❸
        reader: {                ❹
```

```
                  type: 'json'
            }
        }
    });
```

❶   The model `SSC.model.Donor` has to be described in your application as a separate class and contain only the fields defined, no data.

❷   Unless you need to load some raw data from a third-party server provider, wrap your reader into a Proxy object (*http://bit.ly/1qK2n6K*). Server proxies are used for implementing create, read, update, and destroy (CRUD) operations and include the corresponding methods `create()`, `read()`, `update()`, and `destroy()`.

❸   For the mockup mode, we use a JavaScript Object Notation (JSON)–formated file that contains an array of object literals (each object represents one donor). The *donors.json* file should look like the content of the `data` attribute in the code of `SSC.store.Donors`.

❹   The `Reader` object will consume JSON. Read the Ext JS documentation (*http://bit.ly/1vskrnY*) to decide how to properly configure your JSON reader. The reader knows how to convert the data into the model.

Populating a store with external data is usually done via a `Proxy` object, and Ext JS offers several server-side proxies: `Ajax`, `JsonP`, `Rest`, and `Direct`. To retrieve the data from the server, you call the method `load()` on your `Store` object. To send the data to the server, call the method `sync()`.

The most frequently used proxy is `Ajax`, which uses `XMLHttpRequest` to communicate with the server. The following code fragment shows another way of defining the store `Donors`. It specifies via the config `api` the server-side URIs responsible for the four CRUD operations. We've omitted the `reader` section here because the default data type is JSON anyway. Because we've specified the URIs for the CRUD operations, there is no need to specify the `url` attribute, as in the preceding code sample:

```
Ext.define('SSC.store.Donors', {
    extend: 'Ext.data.Store',

    model: 'SSC.model.Donor',
    proxy: {
        type: 'ajax',
        api: {
            create: '/create_donors',
            read: '/read_donors',
            update: '/update_donors',
            destroy: '/destroy_donors'
        }
    }
});
```

When you create an instance of the data store, you can specify the `autoload` parameter. If it's `true`, the store will be populated automatically. Otherwise, explicitly call the method `load()` whenever the data retrieval is needed. For example, you can call the method `myStore.load({callback:someCallback})`, passing it some callback to be executed.

 In Appendix A, we discuss the HTML5 local storage API. Ext JS has a class Ext.data.proxy.LocalStorage (*http://bit.ly/1qK2wHv*) that saves the model data locally if the web browser supports it.

Controllers and views

Your application controller is a liaison between the data and the views. This class has to extend `Ext.app.Controller`, and will include references to the views and, possibly, stores. The controller will automatically load every class mentioned in its code, create an instance of each store, and register each instance with the class `Ext.StoreManager`.

A controller class has the config properties `stores`, `models`, and `views`, where you can list stores, models, and views that the controller should know about. Example 4-3 shows that the controller `SSC.controller.Donate` includes the names of two stores: `SSC.store.Campaigns` and `SSC.store.Donors`.

Example 4-3. The Donate controller

```
Ext.define('SSC.controller.Donate', {
    extend: 'Ext.app.Controller',
    stores: ['SSC.store.Campaigns', 'SSC.store.Donors']    ❶

    refs: [{                                                ❷
        ref: 'donatePanel',
        selector: '[cls=donate-panel]'
    }
    // more views can go here
    ],

    init: function () {                                     ❸

        this.control({
            'button[action=showform]': {
                click: this.showDonateForm
            }
            // more event listeners go here
        });
    },

    showDonateForm: function () {                           ❹
        this.getDonatePanel().getLayout().setActiveItem(1);
```

```
      }
});
```

❶ List stores in your controller. Actually, in most cases, you'd list stores in the Ext.application singleton as we did earlier. But if you need to dynamically create controllers, you don't have a choice but to declare stores in such controllers.

❷ List one or more views of your application in the refs property, which simplifies the search of the component globally or within some container. The controller generates getters and setters for each object listed in the refs.

❸ Register event listeners in the function init(). In this case, we're registering the event handler function showDonateForm that will process clicks of the button, which has an attribute action=showform.

❹ The getter getDonatePanel() will be autogenerated by Ext JS because donate Panel was included in the refs section.

Ext.StoreManager provides a convenience method to look up the store by store ID. If stores were automatically injected into Ext.StoreManager by the controller, the default store ID is its name; for example, SSC.store.Donors:

```
var donorsStore = Ext.data.StoreManager.lookup('SSC.store.Donors');

// An alternative syntax to use StoreManager lookup
var donorsStore = Ext.getStore('SSC.store.Donors');
```

The preceding SSC.controller.Donate doesn't use the config property views, but if it did, Ext JS would generate getters and setters for every view (the same is true for stores and models). It uses refs instead to reference components, and getters and setters will be generated for each component listed in refs; for example, getDonatePanel(). Lookup of such components is done based on the value in selector using the syntax compatible with ComponentQuery (*http://bit.ly/1jCMwSw*). The difference between refs and the config property views is that the former generates references to instances of specific components from views, whereas the latter generates getters and setters only to the "class" (not the instance) of the entire view for further instance creation.

 You can view and test Ext JS components against bundled themes by browsing the Theme Viewer at the Ext JS 4.2 Examples (*http://bit.ly/1uxCg2O*) page.

Exploring a Component's Life Cycle

In previous versions of our Save The Child application, CSS was responsible for all layouts of the UI components. In Chapter 10, you'll learn about *responsive web design* techniques and CSS media queries, which allow you to create fluid layouts that automatically adjust to the size of the viewport. But this section is about the Ext JS proprietary way of creating and adding UI components to web pages. Before the user will see a component, Ext JS will go through the following phases for each component:

Load
> Load the required (or all) Ext JS classes and their dependencies.

Initialization
> Initialize components when the DOM is ready.

Layout
> Measure and assign sizes.

Rendering
> Convert components to HTML elements.

Destruction
> Remove the reference from the DOM, remove event listeners, and unregister from the component manager.

Rendering and layout are the most time-consuming phases. The rendering does a lot of preparation to give the browser's rendering engine HTML elements and not Ext JS classes. The layout phase is slow because the calculation of sizes and positions (unless they are in absolute coordinates) and applying of cascading stylesheets takes time.

There's also the issue of *reflows*, which happen when the code reads-measures-writes to the DOM and makes dynamic style modifications. Fortunately, Ext JS 4.1 was redesigned to minimize the number of reflows; now a large portion of recalculations is done in a batch before modifying the DOM.

Components as containers

If a component can contain other components, it's a container (for example, `Ext.pan el.Panel`) and will have `Ext.container.Container` (*http://bit.ly/13QH0TG*) as one of its ancestors. In the Ext JS class hierarchy, `Container` is a subclass of `Component`, so all methods and properties defined for a component are available for a container, too. Each web page consists of one or more containers, which include some children components (in Ext JS, they are subclasses of `Ext.Component` (*http://bit.ly/Zy3iZU*)), for example, `Ext.button.Button`.

You'll be defining your container class as a subclass of a container by including `extend: Ext.container.Container`. The child elements of a container are accessible via its property `items`. In the `Ext.define()` statement of the container, you may specify the code that will loop through this `items` array and, say, style the components, but actual instances of the children will be provided during the `Ext.create()` call via the configuration object.

The process of adding a component to a container will typically consist of invoking `Ext.create()` and specifying in a configuration object where to render the component to; for example, `renderTo: Ext.getBody()`.

But under the hood, Ext JS will do a lot more work. The framework will autogenerate a unique ID for the component, assign some event listeners, instantiate component plugins if specified, invoke the `initComponent()`, and add the component to `Ext.Compo nentManager`.

 Even though you can manually assign an ID to the component via a configuration object, it's not recommended because it could result in duplicate IDs.

Working with Events

Events in Ext JS are defined in the mixin `Ext.util.Observable`. Components interested in receiving events can subscribe to them by using one of the following methods:

- By calling the method `addListener()`
- By using the method `on()`
- Declaratively

The next code snippet shows two ways by which a combo box can subscribe to the event `change`. The handler function is a callback that will be invoked if the event `change` is dispatched on this combo box:

```
combobox.addListener('change', myEventHandlerFunction);

combobox.on('change', myEventHandlerFunction);
```

To unsubscribe from the event, call the method `removeListener()` or its shorter version, `un()`:

```
combobox.removeListener('change', myEventHandlerFunction);
combobox.un('change', myEventHandlerFunction);
```

You can also declaratively subscribe to events by using the `listeners` config property of the component:

```
Ext.create('Ext.button.Button', {
    listeners: {
        click: function() { // handle event here }
    }
}
```

JavaScript supports event bubbling (see the online bonus chapter (*http://bit.ly/ 1iJO41S*)). In Ext JS, an event-bubbling mechanism enables events dispatched by components that include `Ext.util.Observable` to bubble up through all enclosing containers. For components, it means that you can handle a component's event on the container level. It can be handy to subscribe and handle multiple similar events in one place. To enable bubbling for selected events, use the `enableBubble()` method. For example:

```
this.enableBubble(['textchange', 'validitychange']);
```

To define custom events, use the method `addEvents()`, where you can provide one or more of the custom event names:

```
this.addEvents('messagesent', 'updatecompleted');
```

For components, you have to define custom events inside the `initComponent()` method. For controllers—inside `init()`, and for any other class—inside its constructor.

Specifying Layouts

The container's `layout` property controls how its children are laid out. It does so by referring to the container's `items` property, which lists all of the child components. If you don't explicitly set the `layout` property, its default value is `Auto`, which places components inside the container, top to bottom, regardless of the component size.

Usually, you explicitly specify the layout. For example, the `hbox` layout arranges all components inside the container horizontally next to each other, but the `vbox` layout arranges them vertically. The `card` layout places the components one under another, but only the top component is visible (think of a tabbed folder, for which the content of only one tab is visible at any given time).

The `border` layout is often used to arrange components in the main viewport (a.k.a. home page) of your application. This layout allows you to split the container's real estate into five imaginary regions: `north`, `east`, `west`, `south`, and `center`. If you need to allocate the top menu items, place them into the region `north`. The footer of the page is in the `south`, as shown in the following code sample:

```
Ext.define('MyApp.view.Viewport', {
    extend: 'Ext.container.Viewport',

    layout: 'border',

    items: [{
```

```
    width: 980,
    height: 200,
    title: "Top Menu",
    region: "north",
    xtype:  "panel"},
  {
    width: 980,
    height: 600,
    title: "Page Content",
    region: "center",
    xtype:  "panel"},
  },
  {
    width: 980,
    height: 100,
    title: "The footer",
    region: "south",
    xtype:  "panel"},
  }]
});
```

Setting proportional layouts by using the flex property

Ext JS has a flex property that allows you to make your layout more flexible. Instead of specifying the width or height of a child component in absolute values, you can split the available space proportionally. For example, if the space has to be divided between two components having the flex values 2 and 1, this means that 2/3 of the container's space will be allocated to the first component, and 1/3 to the second one, as illustrated in the following code snippet:

```
layout: 'vbox',

items: [{
  xtype: 'component',
  html: 'Lorem ipsum dolor',
  flex: 2
  },
  {
  xtype: 'button',
  action: 'showform',
  text: 'DONATE NOW',
  flex: 1
}]
```

 The format of this book doesn't allow us to include detailed descriptions of major Ext JS components. If you plan to use Ext JS to develop enterprise web applications, allocate some extra time to learn the data grid Ext.grid.Panel that's used to render tabular data. You should also master working with forms with Ext.form.Panel.

In the next section, you'll see Ext JS layouts in action while working on the Save The Child application.

Developing Save The Child with Ext JS

In this section, we'll do a code walk-through of the Ext JS version of our Save The Child application. Ext JS is often used in enterprise applications that communicate with the Java-based server side. The most popular IDE among Java enterprise developers is called Eclipse. That's why we decided to switch from WebStorm to Eclipse. Apache Tomcat is one of the most popular servers among Java developers.

We've prepared two separate Eclipse projects:

- *SSC_Top_ExJS* contains the code required to render the top portion of the UI.
- *SSC_Complete_ExtJS* contains the complete version.

To test these applications in Eclipse, you need to install it and configure it with Apache Tomcat, as described next.

If you are not planning to work with Java servers, you can continue using WebStorm. Just open in WebStorm the *WebContent* directory from the preceding project (as you did in the previous chapters) and open the *index.html* file in the browser. WebStorm will run the web application by using its internal web server.

To make WebStorm work faster, exclude the directories *ext*, *packages*, *build*, and *WEB-INF* from the project (click the wrench icon on the toolbar and then select Directories→Excluded). This way, WebStorm won't index these directories.

Setting Up the Eclipse IDE and Apache Tomcat

Eclipse is the most popular IDE among Java developers. You can use it for developing JavaScript, too, although this would not be the best choice. But we'll need it to demonstrate the HTML/Java application generation in the next chapter, so let's set it up.

Sencha offers an Eclipse plug-in (not covered in this book) for those who purchase a license for Sencha Complete.

We'll use the Eclipse IDE for Java EE Developers version, which is available free of charge at the Eclipse Downloads site (*http://bit.ly/V2y9Rx*). The installation comes down to unzipping the downloaded archive. Then, double-click the Eclipse executable to start this IDE.

Apache Tomcat

In Chapter 3, we used an XAMPP server that was running PHP scripts. Because this chapter includes server-side code written in Java, we'll use Apache Tomcat (*http://tomcat.apache.org*), which is one of the popular (*http://bit.ly/1pAsNda*) servers used by Java developers for deploying web applications. Besides being a web server, Tomcat also contains a Java Servlet container that will be used in "Generating a CRUD Application" on page 203. But for most examples, we'll use Tomcat as a web server where Ext JS code will be deployed.

Get the latest version of Apache Tomcat from the Download section at Apache website (*http://tomcat.apache.org*). At the time of this writing, Tomcat 7 is the latest production-quality build, so download the ZIP file with Tomcat's Binary Distributions (Core). Unzip the file in the directory of your choice.

Even though you can start Tomcat from a separate command window, the more productive way is to configure Tomcat right in the Eclipse IDE. This will allow you to deploy your applications and start/stop Tomcat without the need to leave Eclipse. To add a server to Eclipse, open the Eclipse Java EE perspective (by choosing Window→Open Perspective), choose File→New→Other→Server→Server→Apache→Tomcat v7.0 Server, select your Tomcat installation directory, and then click Finish. If you don't see Tomcat 7 in the list of Apache servers, click "Download additional server adapters."

You'll see the Tomcat entry in the Eclipse Project Explorer. From the Eclipse menu, choose Windows→Show View and open the Servers view. Start Tomcat by using the right-click menu.

 By default, the Eclipse IDE keeps all required server configuration and deployment files in its own hidden directory. To see where exactly they are located in your computer, just double-click Tomcat in the Server view. The server path field contains the path. Keep in mind that whereas Tomcat documentation defines *webapps* as a default deployment directory, Eclipse uses the *wtpwebapps* directory instead. If you prefer to deploy your Eclipse projects under your original Tomcat installation path, select the option Use Tomcat Installation.

In the next section, you'll learn how to create dynamic web projects in Eclipse for which you'll need to specify the target runtime for deployment of your web applications. This newly installed and configured Tomcat server will serve as a deployment target for our sample projects.

Dynamic web projects and Ext JS

Eclipse for Java EE developers comes with a Web Tools Platform (*http://bit.ly/ Twf4pH*) that simplifies development of web applications by allowing you to create a so-called dynamic web project. This is an Eclipse preconfigured project that already knows where its Java server is located, and deployment to the server is greatly simplified. Sample projects from this chapter will be specifically created for deployment under the Apache Tomcat server.

To create such a project, from the Eclipse menu, choose File→New→Other→Web→Dynamic Web Project. It will pop up a window similar to Figure 4-6. Note that the target runtime is Apache Tomcat v7.0 that we configured in the previous section.

Upon creation, this project will include several directories, including one called *Web-Content*. This directory serves as a document root of the web server in Eclipse dymamic web projects. This is the place to put your *index.html* and one possible place to keep the Ext JS framework. Create a subdirectory named *ext* under *WebContent* and copy there all files from the Ext JS distribution. The *app* directory should also go under *WebContent*.

Unfortunately, the Eclipse IDE is infamous for slow indexing of JavaScript files, and given the fact that Ext JS has hundreds of JavaScript files, your work may be interrupted by Eclipse trying to unnecessarily revalidate these files. Developers of the Sencha Eclipse plug-in decided to solve this problem by creating a special type of library file (*ext.ser*) supporting code assistance in Eclipse. This solution will work until some of the Ext JS API changes; after that, Sencha should update the type library file.

If you don't have the Sencha Eclipse plug-in, there are a couple of solutions to this problem (we'll use the first one):

- Exclude from the Eclipse build the following Ext JS directories: *ext*, *build*, and *packages*.
- Don't copy the Ext JS framework into your Eclipse project. Keep it in the place known for Tomcat, and configure as a loadable module.

To implement the first solution, right-click the properties of your project and choose JavaScript→Include Path. Then, switch to the Source tab, expand the project's web content, click the Edit button, and then click Add. One by one, add *ext*, *build*, and *packages* directories as exclusion patterns (add the slash at the end), as shown in Figure 4-7.

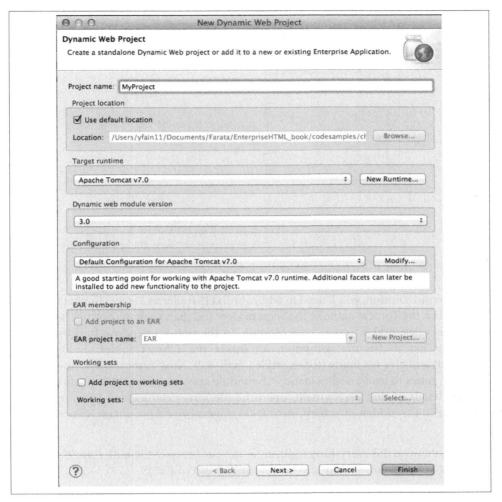

Figure 4-6. Creating a dynamic web project in Eclipse

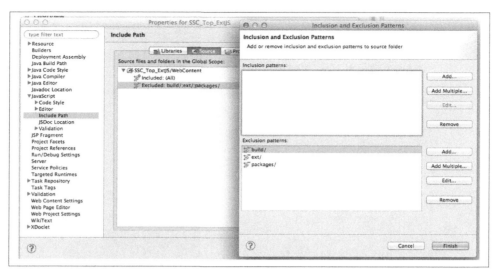

Figure 4-7. Solution 1: Excluding folders in Eclipse

For the second solution, you'll need to add your Ext JS folder as a static Tomcat module. Double-click the Tomcat name in the Servers view and then click the bottom tab, Modules. Then, click Add External Web Module. In the pop-up window, find the folder containing Ext JS (in my computer, it's inside the *Library* folder, as shown in Figure 4-8) and give it a name (for example, */extjs-4.2*). Now Tomcat will know that on each start, it has to load another static web module known as */extjs-4.2*. If you're interested in details of that deployment, open the file *server.xml* located in your Eclipse workspace in the hidden directory *.metadata/.plugins/org.eclipse.wst.server.core/tmp0/conf*.

To ensure that you did everything right, enter in your browser the URL *http://localhost:8080/extjs-4.2*, and you should see the welcome screen of Ext JS.

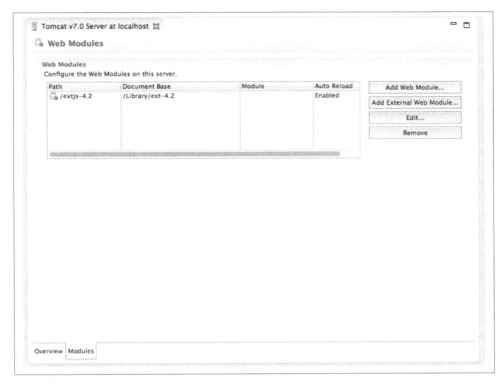

Figure 4-8. Solution 2: Adding Ext JS to Tomcat as a static module

In both of these solutions, you'll lose the Ext JS context-sensitive help, but at least you will eliminate the long pauses caused by Eclipse's internal indexing processes. Developing with ExtJS in the WebStorm or IntelliJ IDEA IDEs would spare you from all these issues because these IDEs are smart enough to produce context-sensitive help from an external JavaScript library.

 If you decide to stick with WebStorm, you can skip the Eclipse-related instructions that follow and just open in your browser *index.html* located in the *WebContent* directory of the *SSC_Top_ExtJS* project. In any case, the browser will render the page that looks like Figure 4-10.

In this section, we brought together three pieces of software: the Eclipse IDE, Apache Tomcat server, and Ext JS framework. Let's bring one more program to the mix: Sencha CMD. We already went through the initial code generation of Ext JS applications. If you already have a dynamic web project in the Eclipse workspace, run Sencha CMD, specifying the *WebContent* directory of your project as the output folder, where the generated project will reside. For example, if the name of your dynamic web project is hello2, the Sencha CMD command will look as follows:

```
sencha -sdk /Library/ext-4.2 generate app HelloWorld /Users/yfain11/
myEclipseWorkspace/hello2/WebContent
```

Running the Top Portion of the Save The Child UI

To run the top portion of the UI, from the Eclipse menu, choose File→Import→General→Existing Projects into Workspace and click the Next button. Then select the option "Select root directory" and click Browse to find *SSC_Top_ExtJS* on your disk. This will import the entire dynamic web project, and most likely you'll see one error in the Problems view indicating that the target runtime with so-and-so name is not defined. This may happen because the name of the Tomcat configuration in your Eclipse project is different from the one in the directory *SSC_Top_ExtJS*.

To fix this issue, right-click the project name and choose Properties→Targeted runtimes. Then, deselect the Tomcat name that was imported from our archive and select the name of your Tomcat configuration. This action makes the *SSC_Top_ExtJS* project deployable under your Tomcat server. Right-click the server name in the Servers view and choose Add and Remove. You'll see a pop-up window similar to Figure 4-9, which depicts a state when the *SSC_Top_ExtJS* project is configured (deployed), but *SSC_Complete_ExtJS* isn't yet.

Right-click the project name *SSC_Top_ExtJS*, and choose Run as→Run on server. Eclipse may offer to restart the server; accept it, and you'll see the top portion of the Save The Child application running in the internal browser of Eclipse that will look as shown in Figure 4-10. You can either configure Eclipse to use your system browser or enter the URL *http://localhost:8080/SSC_Top_ExtJS/* in the browser of your choice. The web page will look the same.

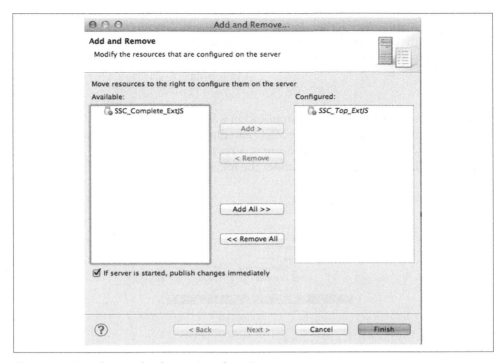

Figure 4-9. Deploying the dynamic web project

Figure 4-10. Running SSC_Top_ExtJS

Apache Tomcat runs on port 8080 by default. If you want to change the port number, double-click the Tomcat name in the Servers view and change the port there.

It's time for a code review. The initial application was generated by Sencha CMD, so the directory structure complies with the MVC paradigm. This version has one controller (*Donate.js*) and three views (*DonateForm.js*, *Viewport.js*, and *Header.js*), as shown in Figure 4-11. The images are located under the folder resources.

Figure 4-11. Controller, views, and images of SSC_Top_ExtJS

The *app.js* file is pretty short—it just declares SSC as the application name, views, and controllers. By adding the property `autoCreateViewport: true`, we requested the application to automatically load the main window, which must be called *Viewport.js* and be located in the *view* directory:

```
Ext.application({
    name: 'SSC',

    views: [
        'DonateForm',
        'Header',
        'Viewport'
    ],

    controllers: [
        'Donate'
```

```
    ],

    autoCreateViewport: true
  });
```

In this version of the application, the *Donate.js* controller is listening to the events from the view `DonateForm`. It's responsible just for showing and hiding the `Donate` form panel. We've implemented the same behavior as in the previous version of the Save The Child application—clicking the Donate Now button reveals the donation form. If the application needs to make Ajax calls to the server, such code would also be placed in the controller. The code of the `Donate` controller is shown in Example 4-4.

Example 4-4. The Donate controller of Save The Child

```
Ext.define('SSC.controller.Donate', {
  extend: 'Ext.app.Controller',

  refs: [{
    ref: 'donatePanel',
    selector: '[cls=donate-panel]'
  }],

  init: function () {                        ❶

    this.control({
      'button[action=showform]': {           ❷
        click: this.showDonateForm
      },

      'button[action=hideform]': {
        click: this.hideDonateForm
      },

      'button[action=donate]': {
        click: this.submitDonateForm
      }
    });
  },

  showDonateForm: function () {              ❸
    this.getDonatePanel().getLayout().setActiveItem(1);  ❹
  },

  hideDonateForm: function () {
    this.getDonatePanel().getLayout().setActiveItem(0);
  },

  submitDonateForm: function () {
    var form = this.getDonatePanel().down('form');  ❺
    form.isValid();
  }
});
```

❶ The init() method is invoked only once on instantiation of the controller.

❷ The control() method of the controller takes selectors as arguments to find components with the corresponding event listeners to be added. For example, *button[action=showform]* means "find a button that has a property action with the value showform"—it has the same meaning as in CSS selectors.

❸ Event handler functions to process show, hide, and submit events.

❹ In containers with a card layout, you can make one of the components visible (the top one in the card deck) by passing its index to the method setActiveItem(). *Viewport.js* includes a container with the card layout (see cls: 'donate-panel' in the next code sample).

❺ Finding the children of the container can be done by using the down() method. In this case, we are finding the child <form> element of a donate panel. If you need to find the parents of the component, use up().

 Because the MVC paradigm splits the code into separate layers, you can unit-test them separately—for example, test your controllers separately from the views. Chapter 7 is dedicated to JavaScript testing; it contains the sections "Testing the Models" on page 285 and "Testing the Controllers" on page 286 that illustrate how to arrange for separate testing of the models and controllers in the Ext JS version of the Save The Child application.

The top-level window is SSC.view.Viewport, which contains the Header and the Donate form views, as shown in Example 4-5.

Example 4-5. The viewport for Header and Donate

```
Ext.define('SSC.view.Viewport', {
  extend: 'Ext.container.Viewport',
  requires: [
    'Ext.tab.Panel',
    'Ext.layout.container.Column'
  ],

  cls: 'app-viewport',
  layout: 'column',            ❶
  defaults: {
    xtype: 'container'
  },

  items: [{
    columnWidth: 0.5,
    html: ' ' // Otherwise column collapses
  }, {
    width: 980,
```

```
      cls: 'main-content',
      layout: {
        type: 'vbox',              ❷
        align: 'stretch'
      },

      items: [
        {
        xtype: 'appheader'
        },
        {
        xtype: 'container',
        minHeight: 350,
        flex: 1,

        cls: 'donate-panel',       ❸
        layout: 'card',

        items: [{
          xtype: 'container',
          layout: 'vbox',

          items: [{
            xtype: 'component',
            html: 'Lorem ipsum dolor sit amet, consectetur elit. Praesent ...',

            maxWidth: 550,
            padding: '80 20 0'
          }, {
            xtype: 'button',
            action: 'showform',
            text: 'DONATE NOW',
            scale: 'large',
            margin: '30 230'
          }]
        }, {
          xtype: 'donateform',
          margin: '80 0 0 0'
        }]
      }, {
        xtype: 'container',
        flex: 1
      }]
    }, {
      columnWidth: 0.5,
      html: ' '
    }]

});
```

❶ Our viewport has a column layout, which is explained after Figure 4-12.

❷ The vertical box layout displays components from the items array one under another, the `appheader` and the `container`, which is explained next.

❸ The container with the class selector `donate-panel` includes two components, but because they are laid out as `card`, only one of them is shown at a time: either the one with the "Lorem ipsum" text, or `donateform`. Which one to show is mandated by the `Donate` controller, by invoking the method `setActiveItem()` with the appropriate index.

Figure 4-12 shows a snapshot from WebStorm, with a collapsed code section just so that you can see the big picture of the columns in the column layout—they are marked with arrows.

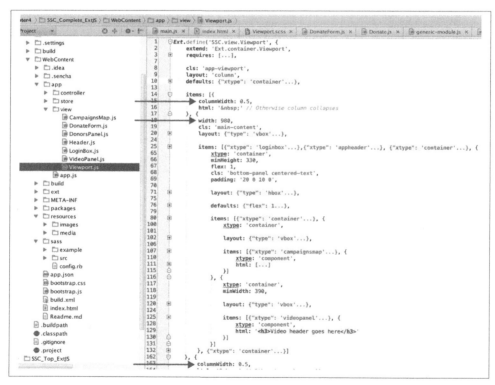

Figure 4-12. Collapsed code of Viewport.js

Choose Preferences→JavaScript→Libraries and add the file *ext-all-debug-w-comments.js* as a global library. Press F1 to display available comments about a selected Ext JS element. Configuring Ext JS as an external library allows you to remove Ext JS files from a Web-Storm project without losing context-sensitive help.

In Ext JS, the column layout is used when you are planning to present the information in columns, as explained in the product documentation (*http://bit.ly/T0QxsG*). Even though there are three columns in this layout, the entire content on this page is located in the middle column having the width of 980. The column on the left and the column on the right just hold one nonbreakable space each to provide centering of the middle column in monitors with high resolutions wider than 980 pixels (plus the browser's chrome).

The width of *0.5, 980, 0.5* means to give the middle column 980 pixels and share the remaining space equally between empty columns.

You also can lay out this screen by using the horizontal box (hbox) with the pack configuration property (*http://bit.ly/T0QywW*), but we decided to keep the column layout for illustration purposes.

Consider using Ext Designer (*http://bit.ly/1lHNHEd*) for creating layouts in WYSIWYG mode.

SASS and CSS

Take a look at the project structure shown in Figure 4-12. It has a *sass* directory, which contains several files with styles: *CampaignsMap.scss*, *DonateForm.scss*, *Header.scss*, and *Viewport.scss*. Note that the filename extension is not *css*, but *scss*—it's Syntactically Awesome Stylesheets (SASS). The content of *Viewport.scss* is shown in the code that follows. In particular, if you've been wondering where the images of the boy and the background flowers are located, they're right there:

```
.app-viewport {
  background: white;
}

.main-content {
  background: url("images/bg-1.png") no-repeat;
```

```
        }

        .donate-panel {
          background: url("images/child-1.jpg") no-repeat right bottom,
          url("images/bg-2.png") no-repeat 90px bottom;
          border-bottom: 1px dotted #555;
        }
```

SASS (*http://bit.ly/1ls6qVu*) is an extension of CSS3, which allows using variables, mixins, inline imports, inherit selectors, and more with CSS-compatible syntax. The simplest example of SASS syntax is to define a variable that stores a color code—for example, `$mypanel-color: #cf6cc2;`. Now if you need to change the color, you just change the value of the variable in one place rather than trying to find all places in a regular CSS file where this color was used. But because modern web browsers don't understand SASS styles, they have to be converted into regular CSS before deploying to your web applications.

Ext JS includes Compass (*http://compass-style.org*), which is an open source CSS authoring framework built on top of SASS. It includes modules and functions that will save you time when defining things such as border radius, gradients, transitions, and more in a cross-browser fashion. For example, you write one SASS line, `.simple { @include border-radius(4px, 4px); }`, but Compass will generate the following cross-browser CSS section:

```
        -webkit-border-radius: 4px 4px;
        -moz-border-radius: 4px / 4px;
        -khtml-border-radius: 4px / 4px;
        border-radius: 4px / 4px; }
```

See the Compass documentation (*http://bit.ly/1ls6nsI*) for more examples like this. To manually compile your SASS into CSS, you can use the command *compass compile* from the command or terminal window. This step is also performed automatically during the Sencha CMD application build. In the Save The Child application, the resulting CSS file is located in *build/SSC/production/resources/SSC-all.css*.

We are not using any extended CSS syntax in our Save The Child application, but because SASS is a superset of CSS, you can use your existing CSS as is—just save it in the *.scss* file. If you'd like to learn more about SASS syntax, visit the site sass-lang.com, which has tutorials and reference documentation.

In general, Ext JS substantially reduces the need for manual CSS writing by using predefined themes (*http://bit.ly/1pAupDC*). Sencha offers a tutorial (*http://bit.ly/1q3Q053*) explaining how to use SASS and Compass for theming.

Besides SASS, there is another dynamic CSS language called LESS (*http://lesscss.org*). It adds to CSS variables, mixins, operations, and functions. However, it's not used in Ext JS.

Now let's look at the child elements of SSC.view.Viewport. The SSC.view.Header is the simplest view. Because Save The Child does not include a bunch of forms and grids, we'll use the lightest top-level container class Container where possible. The class Container gives you the most freedom in what to put inside and how to lay out its child elements. Our SSC.view.Header view extends Ext.Container and contains child elements, some of which have the xtype: component, and others have container, as shown in Example 4-6.

Example 4-6. The Header view of Save The Child

```
Ext.define("SSC.view.Header", {
  extend: 'Ext.Container',
  xtype: 'appheader',          ❶

  cls: 'app-header',           ❷

  height: 85,

  layout: {                    ❸
    type: 'hbox',
    align: 'middle'
  },

  items: [{                    ❹
    xtype: 'component',
    cls: 'app-header-logo',
    width: 75,
    height: 75
  }, {
    xtype: 'component',
    cls: 'app-header-title',
    html: 'Save The Child',
    flex: 1
  }, {
    xtype: 'container',        ❺
    defaults: {
      scale: 'medium',
      margin: '0 0 0 5'
    },
    items: [{
      xtype: 'button',
      text: 'Who We Are'
    }, {
      xtype: 'button',
      text: 'What We Do'
    }, {
      xtype: 'button',
      text: 'Where We Work'
    }, {
      xtype: 'button',
      text: 'Way To Give'
```

```
    }]
  }]
});
```

❶ We assign appheader as the xtype value of this view, which will be used as a reference inside the SSC.view.Viewport.

❷ cls is a class attribute of a DOM element. In this case, it is the same as writing class=app-header in the HTML element.

❸ The header uses the hbox layout with center alignment.

❹ Child components of the top container are the logo image, the text "Save The Child," and another container with buttons.

❺ A container with button components.

Let's review the DonateForm view next, which is a subclass of Ext.form.Panel and contains the form with radio buttons, fields, and labels. This component named donate form will be placed under SSC.view.Header inside SSC.view.Viewport. We've removed some of the lines of code to make it more readable, but its full version is included in the source code samples accompanying this book. Example 4-7 shows first part of the SSC.view.DonateForm.

Example 4-7. The DonateForm view—Part 1

```
Ext.define('SSC.view.DonateForm', {
  extend: 'Ext.form.Panel',
  xtype: 'donateform',
  requires: [                        ❶
    'Ext.form.RadioGroup',
    'Ext.form.field.*',
    'Ext.form.Label'
  ],

  layout: {
    type: 'hbox'                     ❷
  },

  items:[{
    xtype: 'container',              ❸
    layout: 'vbox',

    items: [{
      xtype: 'container',

      items: [{
        xtype: 'radiogroup',
        fieldLabel: 'Please select or enter donation amount',
        labelCls: 'donate-form-label',
```

```
      vertical: true,
      columns: 1,

      defaults: {
        name: 'amount'
      },

      items: [
        { boxLabel: '10',  inputValue: '10'  },
        { boxLabel: '20',  inputValue: '20'  }
        // more choices 50, 100, 200 go here
      ]
    }]
  }, {
    xtype: 'textfield',
    fieldLabel: 'Other amount',
    labelCls: 'donate-form-label'
  }]
},
```

❶ DonateForm depends on several classes listed in the requires property. Ext JS checks to see whether these classes are present in memory, and if not, the loader loads all dependencies first, and only after the DonateForm class.

❷ Our DonateForm uses the horizontal box (hbox) layout, which means that certain components or containers will be laid out next to each other horizontally. But which ones? The children of the container located in the items[] arrays will be laid out horizontally in this case. But the preceding code contains several items[] arrays with different levels of nesting. How to identify those that belong to the topmost container DonateForm? This is a case that clearly demonstrates how having a good IDE can be of great help.

Figure 4-13 shows a snapshot from the WebStorm IDE illustrating how can you find matching elements in long listings. The top-level items[] arrays starts from line 23, and we see that the first element to be laid out in hbox has the xtype: container, which in turn has some children. If you move the blinking cursor of the WebStorm editor right after the first open curly brace in line 23, you'll see a thin, blue vertical line that goes down to line 60. This is where the first object literal ends.

Hence, the second object to be governed by the hbox layout starts on line 61. You can repeat the same trick with the cursor to see where that object ends and the fieldcontainer starts. This might seem like a not overly important tip, but it really saves a developer's time.

❸ The first element of the hbox is a container that is internally laid out as a vbox (see Figure 4-14). The radiogroup is on top, and the textfield for entering Other amount is at the bottom.

The second part of the SSC.view.DonateForm comes next, as shown in Example 4-8.

Example 4-8. The DonateForm view—Part 2

```
{
  xtype: 'fieldcontainer',          ❶
  fieldLabel: 'Donor information',
  labelCls: 'donate-form-label',

  items: [{
    xtype: 'textfield',
    name: 'donor',
    emptyText: 'full name'
  }, {
    xtype: 'textfield',
    emptyText: 'email'
  }
  // address,city,zip code,state and country go here
  ]
}, {
  xtype: 'container',               ❷
  layout: {
    type: 'vbox',
    align: 'center'
  },

  items: [{
    xtype: 'label',
    text: 'We accept PayPal payments',
    cls: 'donate-form-label'
  }, {
    xtype: 'component',
    html: 'Your payment will be processed securely by PayPal...'
  }, {
    xtype: 'button',
    action: 'donate',
    text: 'DONATE NOW'
  }, {
    xtype: 'button',
    action: 'hideform',
    text: 'I will donate later'
  }]
}]
});
```

❶ The `fieldcontainer` (*http://bit.ly/1uxE63D*) is a lightweight Ext JS container useful for grouping components—the donor information, in this case. It's the central element in the `hbox` container shown in Figure 4-14.

❷ The right side of the `hbox` is another container with the `vbox` internal layout to show the "We accept PayPal" message, Donate Now, and "I will donate later" buttons (see Figure 4-14). You can find event handlers for these buttons in the *Donate.js* controller.

```
 9
10      layout: {
11        type: 'hbox',
12        align: 'stretch'
13      },
14
15      bodyStyle: {
16        backgroundColor: 'transparent'
17      },
18
19      defaults: {
20        margin: '0 50 0 0'
21      },
22
23      items:[{
24        xtype: 'container',
25        layout: 'vbox',
26
27        items: [{
28          xtype: 'container',
29          width: 200,
30
31          items: [{
32            xtype: 'radiogroup',
33            fieldLabel: 'Please select or enter donation amount',
34            labelAlign: 'top',
35            labelSeparator: '',
36            labelCls: 'donate-form-label',
37
38            vertical: true,
39            columns: 1,
40
41            defaults: {
42              name: 'amount'
43            },
44
45            items: [
46              { boxLabel: '10',  inputValue: '10'  },
47              { boxLabel: '20',  inputValue: '20'  },
48              { boxLabel: '50',  inputValue: '50'  },
49              { boxLabel: '100', inputValue: '100' },
50              { boxLabel: '200', inputValue: '200' }
51            ]
52          }]
53        }, {
54          xtype: 'textfield',
55          fieldLabel: 'Other amount',
56          labelAlign: 'top',
57          labelSeparator: '',
58          labelCls: 'donate-form-label'
59        }]
60      }, {
61        xtype: 'fieldcontainer',
62        fieldLabel: 'Donor information',
63        labelAlign: 'top',
64        labelSeparator: '',
```

WebContent (~/Documents/Farata/Enterprise
- .sencha
- app
  - controller
    - Donate.js
  - model
  - view
    - DonateForm.js
    - Header.js
    - Viewport.js
  - app.js
- build
- ext
  - builds
  - cmd
  - locale
  - src
  - bootstrap.js
  - build.xml
  - ext.js
  - ext-all.js
  - ext-all-debug.js
  - ext-all-debug-w-comments.js
  - ext-all-dev.js
  - ext-all-rtl.js
  - ext-all-rtl-debug.js
  - ext-all-rtl-debug-w-comments.js
  - ext-all-rtl-dev.js
  - ext-debug.js
  - ext-debug-w-comments.js
  - ext-dev.js
  - ext-theme-access.js
  - ext-theme-classic.js
  - ext-theme-classic-sandbox.js
  - ext-theme-gray.js
  - ext-theme-neptune.js
  - file-header.js
  - license.txt
- META-INF
- overrides
- packages
- resources
  - images
    - bg-1.png
    - bg-2.png

Figure 4-13. Collapsed code of Viewport.js

Debugging frameworks that are extensions of JavaScript in web browsers can be difficult, because although you might be operating with, say, Ext JS classes, the browser will receive regular `<div>`, `<p>`, and other HTML tags and JavaScript. Illuminations (*http://bit.ly/1i46vy4*) is a Firebug add-on that allows you to inspect elements showing not just their HTML representations, but the corresponding Ext JS classes that were used to create them.

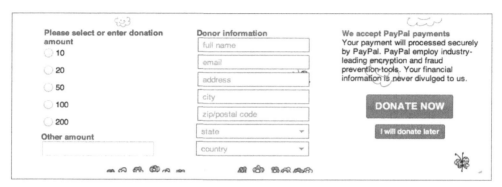

Figure 4-14. DonateForm.js: an hbox with three vbox containers

The code review of the top portion of the Save The Child application is finished. Run the *SSC_Top_ExtJS* project and turn on the Chrome Developer Tools. Scroll to the bottom of the Network tab, and you'll see that the browser made about 250 requests to the server and downloaded 4.5 MB in total. Not too exciting, is it?

On the next runs, these numbers will drop to about 30 requests and 1.7 MB transferred, as the browser's caching kicks in. These numbers would be better if instead of *ext-all.js* we'd link *ext.js*, and even better if we created a custom build (see "Generating Applications with the Sencha CMD Tool" on page 129) for the Save The Child application, merging the application code into one file to contain only those framework classes that are actually used.

Completing Save The Child

In this section, we'll review the code supporting the lower half of the Save The Child UI, which you should import into the Eclipse IDE from the directory *SSC_Complete_ExtJS*.

If you see the target runtime error, read the beginning of "Running the Top Portion of the Save The Child UI" on page 156 for the cure. Stop the Tomcat server if it's running, and deploy *SSC_Complete_ExtJS* under the Tomcat server in the Servers view (from the right-click menu, choose Add and Remove). Start Tomcat in Eclipse, right-click the project, and then run it on the server. It will open a web browser pointing at *http://localhost:8080/SSC_Complete_ExtJS* showing a window similar to the one depicted in Figure 4-15.

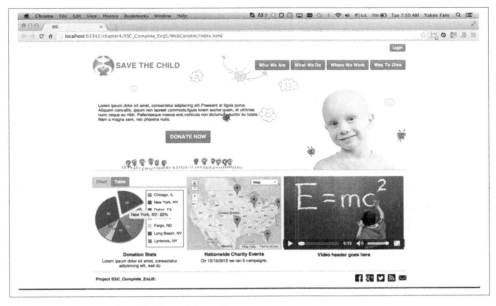

Figure 4-15. Save The Child with live charts

This version has some additions compared to the previous ones. Notice the lower-left panel with charts. First, the charts are placed inside the panel with the tabs Charts and Table. The same data can be rendered either as a chart or as a grid. Second, the charts became live thanks to Ext JS. We took a snapshot of the window shown in Figure 4-15 while hovering the mouse over the pie slice representing New York, and the slice has extended from the pie showing a tool tip.

SSC_Complete_ExtJS has more Ext JS classes than *SSC_Top_ExtJS*. You can see more views in Figure 4-16. Besides, we've added two classes, *Donors.js* and *Campaigns.js*, to serve as data stores for the panels with charts and maps.

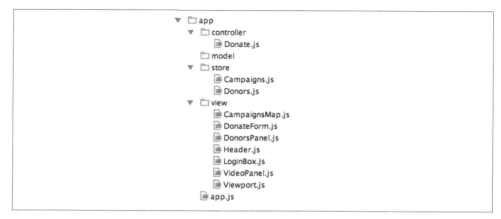

Figure 4-16. JavaScript classes of SSC_Complete_ExtJS

Adding the login box

The Login Box view is pretty small and self-explanatory:

```
Ext.define("SSC.view.LoginBox", {
    extend: 'Ext.Container',
    xtype: 'loginbox',

    layout: 'hbox',

    items: [{
        xtype: 'container',
        flex: 1
    }, {
        xtype: 'textfield',
        emptyText: 'username',
        name: 'username',
        hidden: true
    }, {
        xtype: 'textfield',
        emptyText: 'password',
        inputType: 'password',
        name: 'password',
        hidden: true
    }, {
        xtype: 'button',
        text: 'Login',
        action: 'login'
    }]
});
```

The code to process the user's logins is added to the *Donate.js* controller.

```
'button[action=login]': {
    click: this.showLoginFields
```

```
    }
    ...

    showLoginFields: function () {
        this.getUsernameBox().show();
        this.getPasswordBox().show();
    }
}
```

Adding the video

The bottom portion of the window includes several components. The video view simply reuses the HTML `<video>` tag we used in Chapter 4 and Chapter 5. Ext JS 4.2 doesn't offer any other solutions for embedding videos. On one hand, subclassing `Ext.Compo nent` is the lightest way of including any arbitrary HTML markup. On the other hand, turning HTML into an Ext JS component allows us to use it the same way as any other Ext JS component (for example, participate in layouts). Here's the code for *VideoPanel.js*:

```
Ext.define("SSC.view.VideoPanel", {
  extend: 'Ext.Component',
  xtype: 'videopanel',

  html: [
    '<video controls="controls" poster="resources/media/intro.jpg"
      width="390px" height="240px" preload="metadata">',
      '<source src="resources/media/intro.mp4" type="video/mp4"/>',
      '<source src="resources/media/intro.webm" type="video/webm"/>',
      '<p>Sorry, your browser doesn\'t support the video element</p>',
    '</video>'
  ]

});
```

 Ext JS has a wrapper for the HTML5 `<video>` tag. It's called `Ext.Vid eo`, and we use it in Chapter 12.

Adding the maps

Adding the map takes considerably more work on our part. The mapping part is located in the view *CampaignsMap.js*. Initially, we tried to use `Ext.ux.GMapPanel` (*http://bit.ly/1pEoMFz*), but it didn't work as expected. As a workaround, we've added the HTML `<div>` element to serve as a map container. The first part of the content of *CampaignsMap.js* is shown in Example 4-9.

Example 4-9. The CampaignsMap component—Part 1

```
Ext.define("SSC.view.CampaignsMap", {
  extend: 'Ext.Component',
```

```
xtype: 'campaignsmap',

html: ['<div class="gmap"></div>'],

renderSelectors: {                          ❶
    mapContainer: 'div'
},

listeners: {                                ❷
 afterrender: function (comp) {
    var map,
        mapDiv = comp.mapContainer.dom;     ❸

    if (navigator && navigator.onLine) {    ❹
        try {
            map = comp.initMap(mapDiv);
            comp.addCampaignsOnTheMap(map);
        } catch (e) {
            this.displayGoogleMapError();
        }
    } else {
        this.displayGoogleMapError();
    }
 }
},
```

❶ Because we've added the map container just by including the HTML `<div>`
component, Ext JS creates a generated ID for this `<div>`. It's just not a good way
to reference an element on the page, because the ID should be unique, and we
can easily run into conflicting situations. We didn't want to create an ID
manually, and so we used the property `renderSelectors` to map an arbitrary
name to a DOM selector. When we reference this element somewhere inside the
Ext JS code by using this `renderSelector`, for example, `this.mapContainer`
(`mapContainer` is an arbitrary name here), it returns an `Ext.dom.Element` object
—an abstraction over the plain HTML element—that eliminates cross-
browser API differences.

❷ Sencha documentation states that declaring `listeners` during `Ext.define()` is
a bad practice, and doing it during `Ext.create()` should be preferred. This is
an arguable statement. Yes, there is a possibility that the handler function will
be created during `define()` but never used during `create()`, which will lead to
unnecessary creation of the handler's instance in memory. But the chances are
slim. The other consideration is that if listeners are defined during `create()`,
each instance can handle the same event differently. We'll leave it up to you to
determine the right place for defining listeners. The good part about keeping
listeners in the class definition is that the entire code of the class is located in
one place.

❸ Query the DOM to find the `mapContainer` defined in the `renderSelectors` property. Note that we are getting the reference to this DOM element after the view is rendered in the event handler function `afterrender`. The object `comp` will be provided to this handler, and it points at the instance of the current component, which is `SSC.view.CampaignsMap`. Think of `comp` as `this` for the component.

❹ If Google Maps is not available, display an error message, as shown in Figure 4-17. This code was added after one of the authors was testing this code while sitting on a plane with no Internet connection. But checking the status of `navigator.onLine` (*http://mzl.la/1mdJ1HT*) may not be a reliable indicator of the offline status, so we've wrapped it into a `try/catch` block just to be sure.

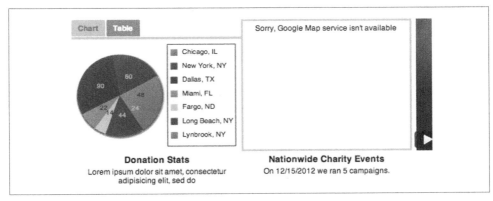

Figure 4-17. If Google Maps server is not responding

Next comes the second part of *CampaignsMap.js*, as shown in Example 4-10.

Example 4-10. The CampaignsMap component—Part 2

```
initMap: function (mapDiv) {                          ❶
    // latitude = 39.8097343 longitude = -98.55561990000001
    // Lebanon, KS 66952, USA Geographic center of the contiguous United States
    // the center point of the map
    var latMapCenter = 39.8097343,
        lonMapCenter = -98.55561990000001;

    var mapOptions = {
        zoom    : 3,
        center  : new google.maps.LatLng(latMapCenter, lonMapCenter),
        mapTypeId: google.maps.MapTypeId.ROADMAP,
        mapTypeControlOptions: {
            style   : google.maps.MapTypeControlStyle.DROPDOWN_MENU,
            position: google.maps.ControlPosition.TOP_RIGHT
        }
```

```
    };

    return new google.maps.Map(mapDiv, mapOptions);
},

addCampaignsOnTheMap: function (map) {
 var marker,
     infowindow = new google.maps.InfoWindow(),
     geocoder   = new google.maps.Geocoder(),
     campaigns  = Ext.StoreMgr.get('Campaigns');      ❷

 campaigns.each(function (campaign) {
     var title       = campaign.get('title'),        ❸
         location    = campaign.get('location'),
         description = campaign.get('description');

     geocoder.geocode({
         address: location,
         country: 'USA'
     }, function(results, status) {
         if (status == google.maps.GeocoderStatus.OK) {

             // getting coordinates
             var lat = results[0].geometry.location.lat(),
                 lon = results[0].geometry.location.lng();

             // create marker
             marker = new google.maps.Marker({
                 position: new google.maps.LatLng(lat, lon),
                 map      : map,
                 title    : location
             });

             // adding click event to the marker
             // to show info-bubble with data from json
             google.maps.event.addListener(marker, 'click', (function(marker) {
                 return function () {
                     var content = Ext.String.format(
                         '<p class="infowindow">
                           <b>{0}</b><br/>{1}<br/><i>{2}</i></p>',
                         title, description, location);

                     infowindow.setContent(content);
                     infowindow.open(map, marker);
                 };
             })(marker));
         } else {
             console.error(
              'Error getting location data for address: '
               + location);
         }
     });
 });
```

```
      });
   },

   displayGoogleMapError: function () {
      console.log('Error is successfully handled while rendering Google map');
      this.mapContainer.update('<p class="error">
        Sorry, Google Map service isn\'t available</p>');
   }
});
```

❶ The rest of the code in this class has the same mapping functionality as described in "Adding Geolocation Support" on page 35.

❷ The data for the campaign information is coming from the store *Campaigns.js* located in the folder *store*. The store manager can find the reference to the store either by assigned `storeId` (*http://bit.ly/1i473nV*) or by the name `Campaigns` listed in the `stores` array in *app.js*.

❸ We configure the mapping panel to get the information about the campaign title, location, and description from the fields with corresponding names from the store `SSC.store.Campaigns`, which is shown here in *app.js*:

```
Ext.application({
    name: 'SSC',

    views: [
        'CampaignsMap',
        'DonateForm',
        'DonorsPanel',
        'Header',
        'LoginBox',
        'VideoPanel',
        'Viewport'
    ],

    stores: [
        'Campaigns',
        'Donors'
    ],

    controllers: [
        'Donate'
    ],

    autoCreateViewport: true
});
```

In Chapter 2 the information about campaigns was taken from a file with JSON-formatted data. In this version, the data will be taken from the class `SSC.store.Cam paigns` that's shown next. This class extends `Ext.data.JsonStore` (*http://bit.ly/*

TwsxxL), which is a helper class for creating stores based on the JSON data. The class `JsonStore` is a subclass of the more generic `Ext.data.Store`, which implements client-side caching of model objects, can load the data via the `Proxy` object, and supports sorting and filtering.

Later, in Chapter 12, you'll see another version of our Save The Child application, in which all stores are inherited from `Ext.data.Store`. But in the version presented in Example 4-11, we are not reading the code from external JSON sources, and inheriting from `Ext.data.Store` would suffice.

Example 4-11. The Campaigns store

```
Ext.define('SSC.store.Campaigns', {
    extend: 'Ext.data.JsonStore',

    fields: [                                        ❶
        { name: 'title',       type: 'string' },
        { name: 'description', type: 'string' },
        { name: 'location',    type: 'string' }
    ],

    data: [{                                         ❷
        title:       'Lorem ipsum',
        description: 'Lorem ipsum dolor sit amet, consectetur adipiscing elit.',
        location:    'Chicago, IL'
    }, {
        title:       'Donors meeting',
        description: 'Morbi mollis ante at ante posuere tempor.',
        location:    'New York, NY'
    }, {
        title:       'Sed tincidunt magna',
        description: 'Donec ac ligula sit amet libero vehicula laoreet',
        location:    'Dallas, TX'
    }, {
        title:       'Fusce tellus dui',
        description: 'Sed accumsan nibh sapien, interdum ullamcorper velit.',
        location:    'Miami, FL'
    }, {
        title:       'Aenean lorem quam',
        description: 'Pellentesque habitant morbi tristique senectus',
        location:    'Fargo, ND'
    }]
});
```

❶ We have not created a separate model class for each campaign, because this information is used in only one place. The `fields` array defines our inline model, which consists of objects (`data`) containing the properties `title`, `description`, and `location`.

❷ Hardcoded data for the model.

Adding the chart and table panels

The lower-left area of the Save The Child window is occupied by a subclass of
Ext.tab.Panel. The name of our view is SSC.view.DonorsPanel, and it contains two
tabs: Chart and Table. Accordingly, the class definition starts by declaring dependencies
for the Ext JS classes that support charts and a data grid.

Charting is an important part of many enterprise applications, and Ext JS offers solid
chart-drawing capabilities without the need to install any plug-ins. We'd like to stress
that both Chart and Table panels use the same data—they just provide different views
of the data. Let's review the code in Example 4-12.

Example 4-12. The DonorsPanel includes charts and grids

```
Ext.define("SSC.view.DonorsPanel", {
 extend: 'Ext.tab.Panel',
 xtype: 'donorspanel',
 requires: [
    'Ext.chart.Chart',
    'Ext.chart.series.Pie',
    'Ext.grid.Panel',
    'Ext.grid.column.Number',
    'Ext.grid.plugin.CellEditing'
],

maxHeight: 240,
plain: true,                         ❶

items: [{
  title: 'Chart',                    ❷
  xtype: 'chart',
  store: 'Donors',
  animate: true,
  legend: {
     position: 'right'
  },
  theme: 'Base:gradients',
  series: [{
     type: 'pie',                    ❸
     angleField: 'donors',
     showInLegend: true,
     tips: {                                   ❹
        trackMouse: true,
        renderer: function (storeItem ) {

           var store = storeItem.store,
              total = 0;

           store.each(function(rec) {
              total += rec.get('donors');       ❺
           });
```

```
                    this.update(Ext.String.format('{0}: {1}%',
                        storeItem.get('location'),              ❻
                        Math.round(storeItem.get('donors') / total * 100)));
                }
            },
            highlight: {
                segment: {
                    margin: 20
                }
            },
            label: {                        ❼
                field: 'location',
                display: 'horizontal',
                contrast: true,
                renderer: function (label, item, storeItem) {
                    return storeItem.get('donors');
                }
            }
        }
    }]
}, {
    title: 'Table',                    ❽
    xtype: 'gridpanel',
    store: 'Donors',
    columns: [                          ❾
        { text: 'State',  dataIndex: 'location', flex: 1},
        { text: 'Donors', dataIndex: 'donors',
                xtype: 'numbercolumn', format: '0', editor: 'numberfield' }
    ],
    plugins: [{
        ptype: 'cellediting'
    }]
}]

});
```

❶ By default, the top portion of the tab panel shows a blue background, which we didn't like, so we turned this style off to give these tabs a little cleaner look.

❷ The first panel is an instance of the xtype: 'chart', which gets the data from the store object Donors.

❸ Configuring and creating a pie chart (*http://bit.ly/1rPJP52*). The width of each sector is controlled by the angleField property, which is mapped to the field donors defined in the store SSC.store.Donors (see the code listing that follows).

❹ We've overriden the config renderer (*http://bit.ly/16fgnO5*) to provide custom styling for each element. In particular, we've configured tips (*http://bit.ly/1i0LV1x*) to be displayed on mouse hover.

❺ Calculating total for proper display of the percentages on mouse hover.

❻   The label for each pie sector is retrieved from the field location defined in the store SSC.store.Donors shown in the code listing that follows.

❼   Displaying the chart legend on the right side. If the user moves the mouse over the legend, the pie sectors start to animate.

❽   The second tab contains an instance of xtype *gridpanel*. Note that the store object is the same as the Chart panel uses.

❾   The grid has two columns. One is simple text, but the other is rendered as a numbercolumn (*http://bit.ly/1lHKKDO*) that displays the data according to a format string.

The store Donors contains the hardcoded data for our pie chart as well as for the table. In the real world, the data would be retrieved from the server side. Because we were getting ready to consume JSON data (not implemented), our Donors class extends JsonStore:

```
Ext.define('SSC.store.Donors', {
    extend: 'Ext.data.JsonStore',

    fields: [
        { name: 'donors',   type: 'int' },        ❶
        { name: 'location', type: 'string' }
    ],

    data: [                                        ❷
        { donors: 48, location: 'Chicago, IL' },
        { donors: 60, location: 'New York, NY' },
        { donors: 90, location: 'Dallas, TX' },
        { donors: 22, location: 'Miami, FL' },
        { donors: 14, location: 'Fargo, ND' },
        { donors: 44, location: 'Long Beach, NY' },
        { donors: 24, location: 'Lynbrook, NY' }
    ]
});
```

❶   Defining inline model.

❷   Hardcoded data for the model.

The data located in the store SSC.store.Donors can be rendered not only as a chart, but in a tabular form as well. To switch to the table view shown in Figure 4-18, the user has to click the Table tab.

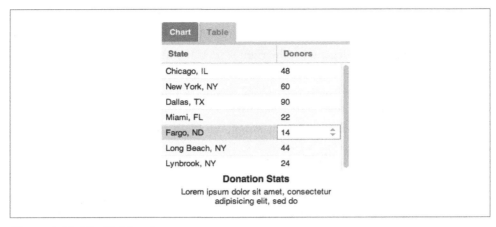

Figure 4-18. The Table tab

The following code fragment from DonorsPanel is all it takes to render the donors' data as a grid. The xtype of this component is gridpanel. For illustration purposes, we made the Donors column editable—double-click a cell with a number and it will turn this field into a numeric field, as shown in Figure 4-18 for the location Fargo, ND:

```
{
  title: 'Table',
  xtype: 'gridpanel',
  store: 'Donors',        ❶
  columns: [
      { text: 'City/State',  dataIndex: 'location', flex: 1},
      { text: 'Donors', dataIndex: 'donors', xtype: 'numbercolumn', format: '0',
        editor: 'numberfield' }
  ],
  plugins: [{
      ptype: 'cellediting'        ❷
  }
}
```

❶ Reusing the same store as in the Chart panel.

❷ We are using one of the existing Ext JS plug-ins here, namely, Ext.grid.plu
gin.CellEditing, to allow editing the cells of the Donors column. In this example, we are using an existing Ext JS editor numberfield in the Donors column. Because we don't work with decimal numbers here, the editor uses format:0. To make the entire row of the grid editable, use the plug-in Ext.grid.plugin.RowEditing. If you want to create a custom plug-in for a cell, you need to define it by the rules for writing Ext JS plug-ins.

Modify any value in the Donor's cell and switch to the Chart panel. You'll see that the size of the corresponding pie sector changes accordingly.

The total number of code lines in `DonorsPanel` and in the store `Donors` is under 100. Being able to create a tab panel with a chart and grid with almost no manual coding is quite impressive, isn't it?

Adding a footer

To complete the Save The Child code review, we need to mention the icons located at the bottom of *ViewPort.js*, shown in Figure 4-19. Usually, links at the bottom of the page statically refer to the corresponding social network's account. Integration with social networks is out of this book's scope. But you can study, say, the Twitter API and implement functionality to let donors tweet about their donations. The Facebook icon can either have a similar functionality or you might consider implementing automated login to the Save The Child application by using OAuth2, which is briefly discussed in Chapter 9.

Project SSC_Complete_ExtJS:

Figure 4-19. The Viewport footer

This footer is implemented in the following code snippet. We've implemented these little icons as regular images:

```
items: [{
    xtype: 'component',
    flex: 1,
    html: '<strong>Project SSC_Complete_ExtJS:</strong>'
}, {
    src: 'resources/images/facebook.png'
}, {
    src: 'resources/images/google_plus.png'
}, {
    src: 'resources/images/twitter.png'
}, {
    src: 'resources/images/rss.png'
}, {
    src: 'resources/images/email.png'
}]
```

A more efficient way to do this is by using a numeric character code that renders as an image (see the glyph config property (*http://bit.ly/1lHLzfS*)). The Pictos library (*http://pictos.cc*) offers more than 300 tiny images in both vector and PNG form. You'll see the example of using Pictos fonts in Chapter 12.

The Ext JS library contains lots of JavaScript code, but it allows developers to produce nice-looking applications with a fraction of the code compared to other frameworks. Also, even though this version of Save The Child offers more functionality than those from the previous chapters, we've had to write only a bare minimum of CSS code, thanks to Ext JS theming (*http://bit.ly/1pAupDC*).

Building a production version of Save The Child

Run the completed version of our application in a Chrome browser with Developer Tools turned on. Go to the Network tab and scroll to the bottom. You'll see a message reporting that the browser made 365 requests to the server and downloaded 6.4 MB of content, as shown in Figure 4-20.

Figure 4-20. The size of the development version of Save The Child

Now let's create a production version with all JavaScript merged into one file. Open the terminal or command window and change the directory to the Eclipse workspace directory where your project was created (for example, *.../SSC_Complete_ExtJS/WebContent*) and enter the command described in "Generating Applications with the Sencha CMD Tool" on page 129:

```
sencha app build
```

The production version of the Save The Child application generates in the directory *.../SSC_Complete_ExtJS/WebContent/build/SSC/production*. All your application Java-Script code merges with the required classes of the Ext JS framework into one file, *all-classes.js*, which in our case amounts to 1.2 MB. The generated CSS file *SSC-all.css* will be located in the directory *resources*. All images are there, too. This is what the production version of *index.html* looks like:

```
<!DOCTYPE HTML>
<html>
<head>
    <meta charset="UTF-8">
    <title>SSC</title>
```

```
        <script src="http://maps.googleapis.com/maps/api/js?sensor=false"></script>
<link rel="stylesheet" href="resources/SSC-all.css"/>
<script type="text/javascript" src="all-classes.js"></script>
</head>
<body></body>
</html>
```

Deploy the content of *production* under any web server and load this version of the application in Chrome with Developer Tools turned on. This time, the number of downloaded bytes is three times lower (2.3 MB). Ask your web server administrator to enable Gzip or Deflate, and the size of the JavaScript will go down from 1.2 MB to 365 KB. The size of other resources will decrease even more. Don't forget that we are loading a 500 KB video file *intro.mp4*. The number of server requests went down to 55, but more than 30 of them were Google Maps API calls.

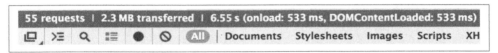

Figure 4-21. The size of the production version of Save The Child

Summary

Creating enterprise web applications involves many steps that need to be done by developers. But with the right set of tools, repetitive steps can be automated. Besides, the Ext JS class-rich component library and themes allow you to reduce the amount of manual programming.

Remember the DRY principle: don't repeat yourself. Try to do more with less effort. This rather long chapter will help you get started with Ext JS. It's an extensive framework, which doesn't allow an easy way out should you decide to switch to another one. But for the enterprise applications that require a rich UI, dashboards with fancy charts, and advanced data grids, Ext JS can be a good choice.

## CHAPTER 5

Selected Productivity Tools for Enterprise Developers

The toolbox of an enterprise HTML5 developer contains tools that can improve productivity. In this chapter, we share with you some of the tools that we use.

We'll start this chapter with a brief introduction of Node.js (or simply Node)—the server-side JavaScript framework and Node Package Manager (npm). Node and npm serve as a foundation for the tools covered in this chapter.

Next, we'll highlight a handful of productivity tools that we use in our consulting projects, namely:

Grunt
> A task-runner framework for JavaScript projects that allows you to automate repetitive operations such as running tests.

Bower
> A package manager for web projects that helps in maintaining application dependencies.

Yeoman
> A collection of code-generation tools and best practices.

In addition to these tools that can be used with various JavaScript frameworks, we'll introduce you to Clear Toolkit for Ext JS, which includes the code generator Clear Data Builder—this tool was created and open-sourced by our company, Farata Systems. With Clear Toolkit, you'll be able to quickly start a project that utilizes the Ext JS framework for frontend development and Java on the server side.

Using Node.js, V8, and npm

Node.js is a server-side JavaScript framework. Node uses *V8*, the JavaScript engine by Google (Chrome/Chromium also use it). Node provides the JavaScript API for accessing the filesystem, sockets, and running processes, which makes it great for general-purpose scripting runtime. You can find more information about Node at its website (*http://nodejs.org/about/*).

Many tools are built on top of Node JavaScript APIs. The Grunt (*http://gruntjs.com/*) tool is one of them. We will use Grunt later in this book to automate execution of repetitive development tasks.

npm is a utility that comes bundled with Node. npm provides a unified API and metadata model for managing dependencies in JavaScript projects. A *package.json* file is the project's dependencies descriptor. npm installs project dependencies using information from *package.json*. npm uses a community repository (*https://npmjs.org/*) for open source JavaScript projects to resolve dependencies. npm can also use private repositories.

Node and npm are cross-platform software and binaries available for Windows, Linux, and OS X operating systems.

To use this book's code samples, you need to download and install Node from its website (*http://nodejs.org/download*).

Automating Everything with Grunt

You should automate every aspect of the development workflow to reduce the cost of building, deploying, and maintaining your application. In this section, we introduce Grunt (*http://gruntjs.com/*)—a task runner framework for JavaScript projects that can help you automate repetitive operations such as running tests when the code changes. You can follow the instructions from Grunt's website (*http://bit.ly/1qr4ChO*) to install it on your machine.

Grunt can watch your code changes and automate the process of running tests when the code changes. Tests should help in assessing the quality of our code.

With the Grunt tool, you can have a script to run all your tests. If you come from the Java world, you know about Apache Ant, a general-purpose command-line tool to drive processes that describe *build files* as *targets* in the *build.xml* file. Grunt also runs the tasks described in scripts. A wide range of tasks are available today—starting with running automated unit tests and ending with JavaScript code minification. Grunt provides a separate layer of abstraction on which you can define tasks in a special domain-specific language (DSL) in a Gruntfile for execution.

Exploring the Simplest Gruntfile

Let's start with the simplest Grunt project setup, shown in Example 5-1. The following two files must be present in the project directory:

package.json
> This file is used by npm to store metadata and project dependencies.
>
> List Grunt and its plug-ins that your project needs as *devDependencies* in this file.

Gruntfile
> This file is named *Gruntfile.js* or *Gruntfile.coffee*; it is used to configure or define the tasks and load Grunt plug-ins.

Example 5-1. The simplest possible Gruntfile

```
module.exports = function (grunt) {
    'use strict';

    grunt.registerTask('hello', 'say hello', function(){      ❶
        grunt.log.writeln('Hello from grunt');                ❷
    });

    grunt.registerTask('default', 'hello');                   ❸
};
```

❶   Register a new task named hello.

❷   Print the greeting text by using grunt's log API (*http://bit.ly/TwsFgJ*).

❸   With grunt.registerTask, we define a default task to run when Grunt is called without any parameters.

Each task can be called separately from the command line by passing the task's name as a command-line parameter. For example, grunt hello would execute only the task named hello from the preceding script.

Let's run this hello task with the following command:

```
grunt --gruntfile Grunt_simple.js hello

Running "hello" task
Hello from grunt

Done, without errors.
```

Using Grunt to Run JSHint Checks

Now that we've covered the basics of Grunt tool, we can use it for something more interesting than just printing *hello world* on the screen. Because JavaScript is an interpreted language, there is no compiler to help catch syntax errors. But you can use JSHint (*http://www.jshint.com*), an open source tool, which helps identify errors in JavaScript code in lieu of a compiler. Consider the JavaScript code in Example 5-2.

Example 5-2. A JavaScript array with a couple typos

```
var bonds = [                    ❶
          'Sean Connery',
          'George Lazenby',
          'Roger Moore',
          'Timothy Dalton',
          'Pierce Brosnan',
          'Daniel Craig',        ❷
          //'Unknown yet actor'
     ]                           ❸
```

❶ We want to define an array that contains names of actors who played James Bond in the canonical series.

❷ Here is an example of a typo that may cause errors in some browsers. A developer commented-out the line containing an array element but kept the comma in the previous line.

❸ A missing semicolon is a typical typo. Although it is not an error (and many JavaScript developers do consider omitting semicolons a best practice), an automatic semicolon insertion (ASI) will get you covered in this case.

What Is an Automatic Semicolon Insertion?

In JavaScript, semicolons are optional, which means that you can omit a semicolon between two statements written on separate lines. Automatic semicolon insertion is a source code parsing procedure that infers omitted semicolons in certain contexts into your program. You can read more about optional semicolons in *JavaScript: The Definitive Guide* by David Flanagan (O'Reilly).

The preceding code snippet is a fairly simple example that can cause trouble and frustration if you don't have proper tools to check the code semantics and syntax. Let's see how JSHint can help in this situation.

JSHint can be installed via npm with the command `npm install jshint -g`. Now you can run JSHint against our code snippet:

```
> jshint jshint_example.js
jshint_example.js: line 7, col 27, Extra comma. (it breaks older versions of IE)
jshint_example.js: line 9, col 10, Missing semicolon. # ❶

2 errors            # ❷
```

❶ JSHint reports the location of the error and a short description of the problem.

❷ The total count of errors.

 The WebStorm IDE has built-in support (*http://bit.ly/1rpYtzz*) for the JSHint tool. There is a third-party plugiin for Eclipse: jshint-eclipse (*http://bit.ly/1j65aSg*).

Grunt also has a task to run JSHint against your JavaScript code base. Example 5-3 shows what a JSHint configuration in Grunt looks like.

Example 5-3. A Gruntfile with JSHint support

```
module.exports = function(grunt) {
  grunt.initConfig({
    jshint: {
      gruntfile: {             ❶
        src: ['Gruntfile_jshint.js']
      },
      app: {
        src: ['app/js/app.js']
      }
    }
  });

  grunt.loadNpmTasks('grunt-contrib-jshint');
  grunt.registerTask('default', ['jshint']);      ❷
};
```

❶ Because *Gruntfile* is a JavaScript file, JSHint can check it as well and identify the errors.

❷ grunt-contrib-jshint (*http://bit.ly/1lrDyGV*) has to be installed. When `grunt` is run without any parameters, the default task `jshint` is triggered:

```
> grunt

Running "jshint:gruntfile" (jshint) task
>> 1 file lint free.

Running "jshint:app" (jshint) task
>> 1 file lint free.

Done, without errors.
```

Watching for the File Changes

Another handy task to use in a developer's environment is the watch task. The purpose of this task is to monitor files in preconfigured locations. When the watcher detects any changes in those files, it will run the configured task. Example 5-4 shows what a watch task config looks like.

Example 5-4. A watch task config

```
module.exports = function(grunt) {
    grunt.initConfig({
        jshint: {
            // ... configuration code is omitted
        },
        watch: {              ❶
            reload: {
                files: ['app/*.html', 'app/data/**/*.json', 'app/assets/css/*.css',
                    'app/js/**/*.js', 'test/test/tests.js', 'test/spec/*.js'], ❷
                tasks: ['jshint']              ❸
            }
        }
    });
    grunt.loadNpmTasks('grunt-contrib-jshint');   ❹
    grunt.loadNpmTasks('grunt-contrib-watch');
    grunt.registerTask('default', ['jshint']);
};
```

❶ The watch task configuration starts here.

❷ The list of the files that need to be monitored for changes.

❸ An array of tasks to be triggered after a file change event occurs.

❹ The grunt-contrib-watch plug-in (*http://bit.ly/1vszKwX*) has to be installed.

You can run grunt watch from the command line (keep in mind that it never ends on its own):

```
> grunt watch

Running "watch" task
Waiting...OK
>> File "app/js/Player.js" changed.
Running "jshint:gruntfile" (jshint) task
>> 1 file lint free.

Running "jshint:app" (jshint) task
>> 1 file lint free.

Done, without errors.

Completed in 0.50s at Tue May 07 2013 00:41:42 GMT-0400 (EDT) - Waiting...
```

The article Grunt and Gulp Tasks for Performance Optimization (*http://bit.ly/1i0Pzse*) lists various useful Grunt tasks for optimizing loading of images and CSS.

Using Bower

Bower (*http://bit.ly/V2z3xA*) is a package manager for web projects. Twitter has donated it to the open source community. Bower is a utility and a community-driven repository of libraries that help download third-party software required for application code that will run in a web browser. Bower's purpose is similar to npm, but the latter is more suitable for server-side projects.

Bower can take care of transitive (dependency of a dependency) dependencies and download all required library components. Each Bower package has a *bower.json* file, which contains the package metadata for managing the package's transitive dependencies. Also, *bower.json* can contain information about the package repository, readme file, license, and so forth. You can find *bower.json* in the root directory of the package. For example, *components/requirejs/bower.json* is a path for the RequireJS metadata file. Bower can be installed via npm. The following line shows how to install Bower globally in your system:

```
npm install -g bower
```

Java developers use package managers like Gradle or Maven that have functionality similar to Bower's.

Let's begin using Bower now. For example, here is a Bower command to install the library RequireJS:

```
bower install requirejs --save
```

Bower installs RequireJS into the *components/requirejs* directory and saves information about dependencies in the *bower.json* configuration file.

Bower simplifies the delivery of dependencies into a target platform, which means that you don't need to store dependencies of your application in the source control system. Just keep your application code there and let Bower bring all other dependencies described in its configuration file.

There are pros and cons for storing dependencies in the source control repositories. Read the article by Addi Osmani (*http://bit.ly/1uxJW4U*) that covers this subject in more detail.

Your application will have its own *bower.json* file with the list of the dependencies (see Figure 5-1). At this point, Bower can install all required application dependencies with one command, bower install, which will deliver all your dependency files into the components directory. Here is the content of *bower.json* for our Save The Child application:

```
{
  "name": "ch7_dynamic_modules",
  "description": "Chapter 7: Save The Child, Dynamic Modules app",
  "dependencies": {
    "requirejs": "~2.1.5",
    "jquery": ">= 1.8.0",
    "qunit": "~1.11.0",
    "modernizr": "~2.6.2",
    "requirejs-google-maps": "latest"
  }
}
```

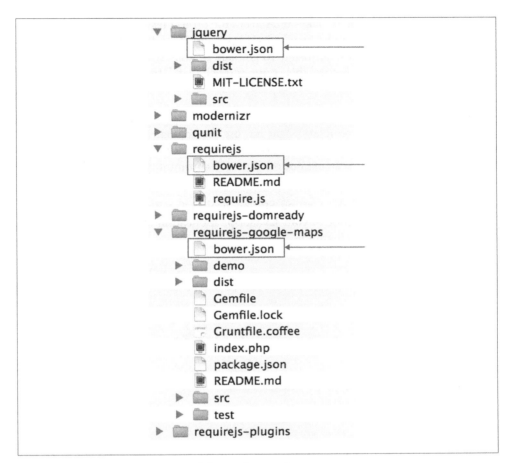

Figure 5-1. Directory structure of the application's components

Application dependencies are specified in the corresponding `dependencies` section. The >= sign indicates that the corresponding software cannot be older than the specified version.

Also, there is a Bower search tool (*http://bit.ly/1q1QH1g*) to find the desired component in its repository.

Using Yeoman

Yeoman (*http://yeoman.io/*) is a collection of tools and best practices that help bootstrap a new web project. Yeoman consists of three main parts: Grunt, Bower, and Yo. Grunt and Bower were explained earlier in this chapter.

Yo is a code-generation tool. It makes the start of the project faster by scaffolding a new JavaScript application. Yo can be installed via npm similar to the other tools. The following command shows how to install Yo globally in your system; if you didn't have Grunt and Bower installed before, this command will install them automatically:

```
npm install -g yo
```

For code generation, Yo relies on plug-ins called *generators*. A generator is a set of instructions to Yo and file templates. You can use the Yeoman Generators search tool (*http://bit.ly/1iSRyiy*) (see Figure 5-2) to discover community-developed generators. At the time of this writing, you can use one of about 430 community-developed generators to scaffold your project.

For example, let's scaffold the Getting Started project for RequreJS. RequireJS is a framework that helps dice code of your JavaScript application into modules. We cover this framework in detail in Chapter 6.

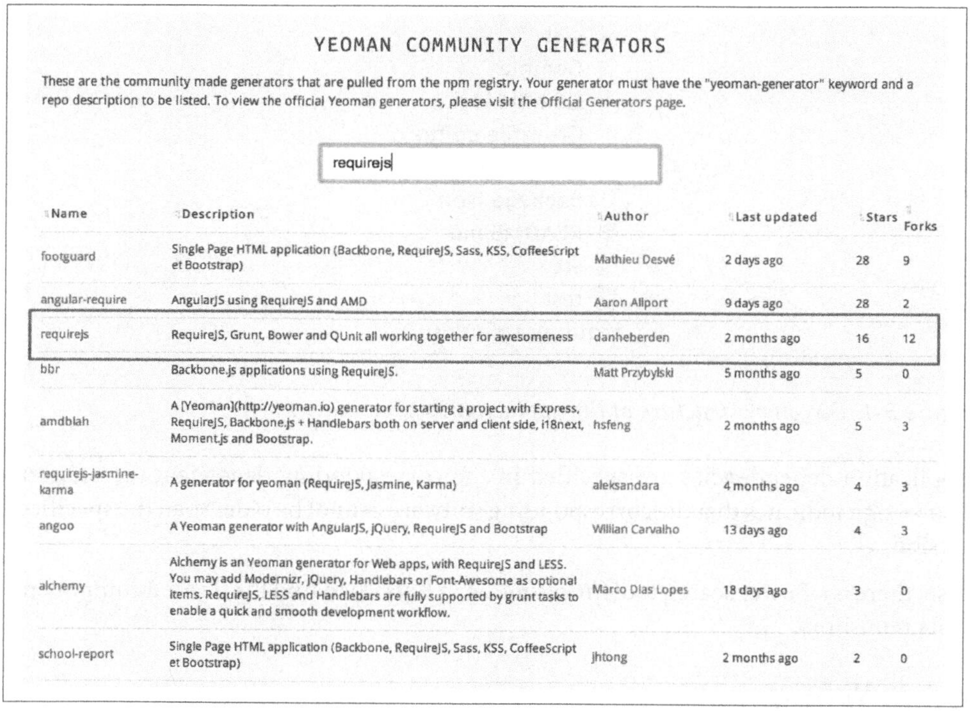

YEOMAN COMMUNITY GENERATORS

These are the community made generators that are pulled from the npm registry. Your generator must have the "yeoman-generator" keyword and a repo description to be listed. To view the official Yeoman generators, please visit the Official Generators page.

requirejs

Name	Description	Author	Last updated	Stars	Forks
footguard	Single Page HTML application (Backbone, RequireJS, Sass, KSS, CoffeeScript et Bootstrap)	Mathieu Desvé	2 days ago	28	9
angular-require	AngularJS using RequireJS and AMD	Aaron Allport	9 days ago	28	2
requirejs	RequireJS, Grunt, Bower and QUnit all working together for awesomeness	danheberden	2 months ago	16	12
bbr	Backbone.js applications using RequireJS.	Matt Przybylski	5 months ago	5	0
amdblah	A [Yeoman](http://yeoman.io) generator for starting a project with Express, RequireJS, Backbone.js + Handlebars both on server and client side, i18next, Moment.js and Bootstrap.	hsfeng	2 months ago	5	3
requirejs-jasmine-karma	A generator for yeoman (RequireJS, Jasmine, Karma)	aleksandara	4 months ago	4	3
angoo	A Yeoman generator with AngularJS, jQuery, RequireJS and Bootstrap	Willian Carvalho	13 days ago	4	3
alchemy	Alchemy is an Yeoman generator for Web apps, with RequireJS and LESS. You may add Modernizr, jQuery, Handlebars or Font-Awesome as optional items. RequireJS, LESS and Handlebars are fully supported by grunt tasks to enable a quick and smooth development workflow.	Marco Dias Lopes	18 days ago	3	0
school-report	Single Page HTML application (Backbone, RequireJS, Sass, KSS, CoffeeScript et Bootstrap)	jhtong	2 months ago	2	0

Figure 5-2. Yeoman Generators search tool

The search tool found a bunch of generators that have the keyword `requirejs` in their name or description. We're looking for a generator that's called "requirejs" (see Figure 5-2, highlighted with a red square). When we click the name link, the GitHub page of the RequireJS generator (*http://bit.ly/1q3Xkhf*) displays. Usually, the generator developers provide a reference of the generator's available tasks.

Next we need to install the generator on our local machine by using the following command:

```
npm install -g generator-requirejs
```

After installation, we can start the *yo* command and as a parameter, we need to specify the generator's name. To start scaffolding a RequireJS application, we can use the following command:

```
yo requirejs
```

We need to provide answers to the wizard's questions. A sample dialog with Yeoman is shown in Example 5-5.

Example 5-5. Yeoman prompt

```
      _-----_
     |       |
     |--(o)--|    .--------------------------.
    `---------´   |    Welcome to Yeoman,     |
     ( _´U`_ )    |   ladies and gentlemen!   |
     /___A___\    '_____'
      |  ~  |
    __'.___.'__
  ´   `  |° ´ Y `

This comes with requirejs, jquery, and grunt all ready to go
[?] What is the name of your app? requirejs yo
[?] Description: description of app for package.json
   create Gruntfile.js
   create package.json
   create bower.json
   create .gitignore
   create .jshintrc
   create .editorconfig
   create CONTRIBUTING.md
   create README.md
   create app/.jshintrc
   create app/config.js
   create app/main.js
   create test/.jshintrc
   create test/index.html
   create test/tests.js
   create index.htm

I'm all done. Running bower install & npm install for you to install the required
dependencies. If this fails, try running the command yourself.

.... npm install output is omitted
```

You will get all directories and files set up, and you can start writing your code immediately. The structure of your project will reflect common best practices from the JavaScript community (see Figure 5-3).

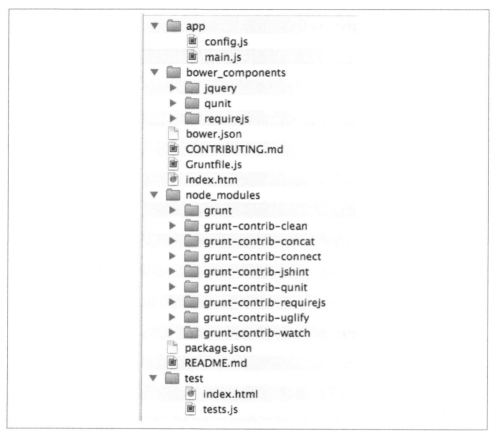

Figure 5-3. Scaffolded RequireJS application directory structure

After executing the *yo* command, you will get Grunt set up with following configured tasks:

clean
    Cleans files and folders.

concat
    Concatenates files.

uglify
    Minifies files with UglifyJS.

`qunit`
>   Runs QUnit unit tests in a headless PhantomJS instance.

`jshint`
>   Validates files with JSHint.

`watch`
>   Runs predefined tasks whenever watched files change.

`requirejs`
>   Builds a RequireJS project.

`connect`
>   Starts a connect web server.

`default`
>   An alias for `jshint`, `qunit`, `clean`, `requirejs`, `concat`, `uglify` tasks.

`preview`
>   An alias for `connect:development` tasks.

`preview-live`
>   An alias for `default`, `connect:production` tasks.

Yeoman also has a generator for generator scaffolding (*http://bit.ly/1rPKcwk*). It might be very useful if you want to introduce your own workflow for a web project.

The next code generator that we'll cover is a more specific one. It can generate the entire ExtJS-Java application.

Using Ext JS and CDB for Productive Enterprise Web Development

The authors of this book work for a company called Farata Systems, which has developed the open source, freely available software called Clear Toolkit for Ext JS, and the code generator and Eclipse IDE plug-in Clear Data Builder (CDB) comes with it. CDB is a productivity tool that was created specifically for enterprise applications that use Java on the server side and need to retrieve, manipulate, and save data in persistent storage.

Such enterprise applications are known as *CRUD applications* because they perform create, retrieve, update, and delete operations with data. If the server side of your web application is developed in Java, with CDB you can easily generate a CRUD application, wherein the Ext JS frontend communicates with the Java backend. In this section, you'll learn how to jump-start development of such CRUD web applications.

Familiarity with core Java concepts such as classes, constructors, getters and setters, and annotations is required for understanding the materials of this section.

The phrase *to be more productive* means to write less code while producing results faster. This is what CDB is for, and you'll see it helps you integrate the client side with the backend by using the remote procedure call (RPC) style and how to implement data pagination for your application. To be more productive, you need to have the proper tools installed. We'll cover this next.

Ext JS MVC Application Scaffolding

This section covers the following topics:

- Using Clear Toolkit for Ext JS
- Creating an Ext JS MVC frontend for a Java-based project
- Deploying and running your first Ext JS and Java application on an Apache Tomcat server

Clear Toolkit for Ext JS includes the following:

Clear Data Builder
An Eclipse plug-in that supports code generation of Ext JS MVC artifacts based on the code written in Java. CDB comes with wizards to start new project with plain Java or with popular frameworks including Hibernate, Spring, and MyBatis.

Clear JS
A set of JavaScript components that extends the Ext JS standard components. In particular, it includes a ChangeObject that traces the modifications of any item in a store.

Clear Runtime
Java components that implement the server-side part of ChangeObject, DirectOptions, and others.

CDB is distributed as a plug-in for Eclipse, a popular Java IDE. The current update site of CDB is located here (*http://bit.ly/UFxUfz*). As of this writing, the current version is 4.1.4. You can install this plug-in via the Install New Software menu in Eclipse. Figure 5-4 shows Clear Data Builder for Ext JS Feature in the list of Installed Software in your Eclipse IDE, which means that CDB is installed.

You have to work with the Eclipse IDE for Java EE Developers, which includes plug-ins for automating web application development.

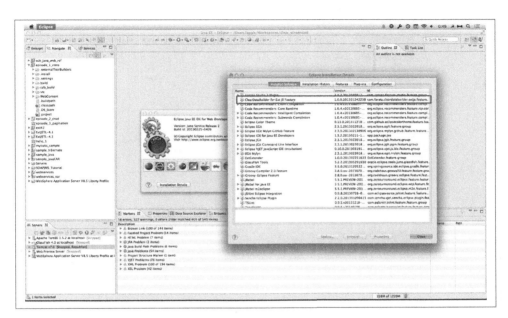

Figure 5-4. Verifying CDB installation

Clear Data Builder comes with a set of prepared examples that demonstrate its integration with the popular Java frameworks, MyBatis, Hibernate, and Spring. There is also a plain Java project example that doesn't use any persistence frameworks. Let's start with the creation of a new project: from the Eclipse menu, choose File → New → Other → Clear. You'll see a window similar to Figure 5-5.

Name the new project `episode_1_intro`. CDB supports different ways of linking the Ext JS framework to the application. CDB automatically copies the Ext JS framework under the web server (Apache Tomcat, in our case). We're going to use this local Ext JS URL, but you can specify any folder in your machine, and CDB will copy the Ext JS file from there into your project. You can also use Ext JS from the Sencha content delivery network (CDN), if you don't want to store these libraries inside your project. Besides, using a common CDN will allow web browsers to reuse the cached version of Ext JS.

For this project, we are not going to use any server-side persistence frameworks like MyBatis or Hibernate. Just click the Finish button, and you'll see some some initial CDB

Figure 5-5. New CDB Project Wizard

messages on the Eclipse console. When CDB runs for the first time, it creates in your project's *WebContent* folder the directory structure recommended by Sencha for Model-View-Controller (MVC) applications. It also generates *index.html* for this application, which contains the link to the entry point of our Ext JS application.

CDB generates an empty project with one sample controller and one view, *Viewport.js*. To run this application, you need to add the newly generated dynamic web project to Tomcat and start the server (right-click Tomcat in the Servers view of Eclipse). See Figure 5-6.

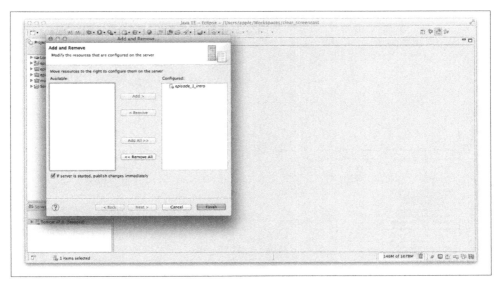

Figure 5-6. Adding the web project to Tomcat

Open this application in your web browser at *http://localhost:8080/episode_1_intro* . Voilà! In less than a couple of minutes, we've created a new dynamic web project with the Ext JS framework and one fancy button, as shown in Figure 5-7.

The next step is to make something useful out of this basic application.

Generating a CRUD Application

Part 2 of the CDB section covers the process of creating a simple CRUD application that uses Ext JS and Java. We'll go through the following steps:

- Create a plain old Java object (POJO) and the corresponding `Ext.data.Model`.
- Create a Java service and populate `Ext.data.Store` with data from that service.
- Use the autogenerated Ext JS application.
- Extend the autogenerated CRUD methods.
- Use `ChangeObject` to track the data changes.

Now let's use CDB to create a CRUD application. You'll learn how turn a POJO into an Ext JS model, namely:

- How to populate the Ext JS store from a remote service
- How to use an automatically generated UI for that application
- How to extend the UI

Figure 5-7. Running the scaffolded application

- What the `ChangeObject` class is for

First, we'll extend the application from Part 1—the CRUD application needs a Java POJO. To start, create a Java class `Person` in the package `dto`. Then add to this class the properties (as well as getters and setters) `firstName`, `lastName`, `address`, `ssn`, `phone`, and `id`. Add the class constructor that initializes these properties, as shown in Example 5-6.

Example 5-6. Person data transfer object

```
package dto;

import com.farata.dto2extjs.annotations.JSClass;
import com.farata.dto2extjs.annotations.JSGeneratedId;

@JSClass
public class Person {

  @JSGeneratedId
  private Integer id;
  private String firstName;
  private String lastName;
  private String phone;
  private String ssn;
```

```
  public Person(Integer id, String firstName, String lastName,
                             String phone, String ssn) {
    super();
    this.id = id;
    this.firstName = firstName;
    this.lastName = lastName;
    this.phone = phone;
    this.ssn = ssn;
  }

  // Getters and Setters are omitted for brevity
}
```

You may also add a `toString()` method to the class. Now you'll need the same corresponding Ext JS model for the Java class `Person`. Just annotate this Java class with the annotation `@JSClass`, and CDB generates the Ext JS model.

 CDB integrates into standard Eclipse a build lifecycle. You don't need to trigger a code generation procedure manually. If you have the Build Automatically option selected in the Project menu, code generation starts immediately after you've saved the file.

The next step is to annotate the `id` field with the CDB annotation `@JSGeneratedId`. This annotation instructs CDB to treat this field as an autogenerated ID. Let's examine the directory of the Ext JS MVC application to see what's inside the *model* folder. In the JavaScript section is the folder *dto*, which corresponds to the Java `dto` package where the `PersonModel` resides, as illustrated in Figure 5-8.

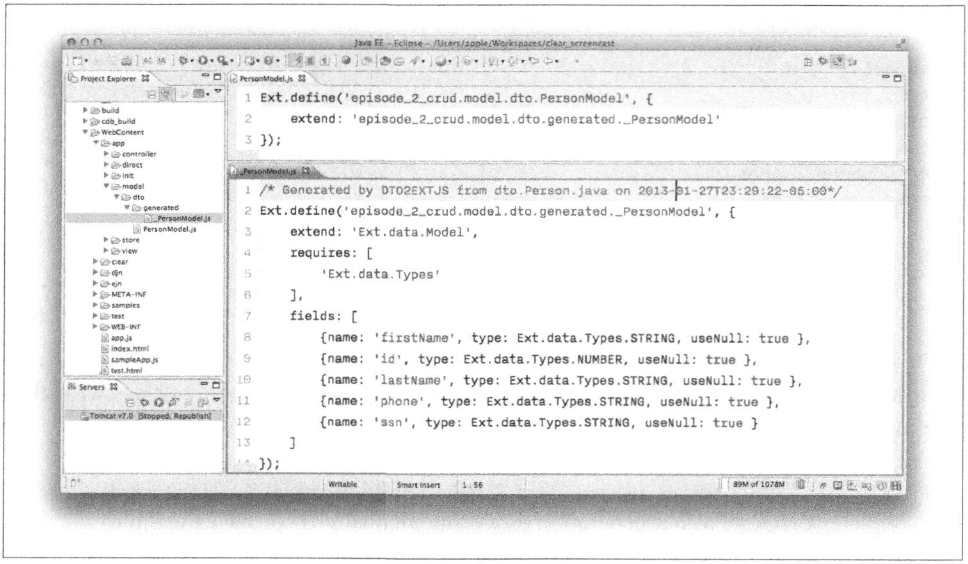

Figure 5-8. Generated from Java class Ext JS model

Clear Data Builder generates two files as recommended by the Generation Gap pattern (*http://bit.ly/VzXBhQ*), which is about keeping the generated and handwritten parts separate by putting them in different classes linked by inheritance. Let's open the person model. In our case, *PersonModel.js* is extended from the generated *PersonModel.js*. Should we need to customize this class, we'll do it inside *Person.js*, but this underscore-prefixed file will be regenerated each and every time when we change something in our model. CDB follows this pattern for all generated artifacts—Java services, Ext JS models, and stores. This model contains all the fields from our Person data transfer object (DTO).

Now we need to create a Java service to populate the Ext JS store with the data. Let's create the Java interface PersonService in the package service. This service will return the list of Person objects. This interface contains one method: List<Person> getPersons().

To have CDB expose this service as a remote object, we'll use the annotation called @JSService. Another annotation, @JSGenetareStore, will instruct CDB to generate the store. In this case, CDB will create the *destination-aware store*. This means that the store will know from where to populate its content. All configurations of the store's proxies will be handled by the code generator. With the @JSFillMethod annotation, we will identify our main read method (the *R* in CRUD).

Also it would be nice to have some sort of sample UI to test the service; the annotation @JSGenerateSample will help here. CDB will examine the interface PersonService, and based on these annotations, will generate all Ext JS MVC artifacts (models, views, controller) and the sample application. See Example 5-7.

Example 5-7. PersonService interface annotated with CDB annotations

```
@JSService
public interface PersonService {
    @JSGenerateStore
    @JSFillMethod
    @JSGenerateSample
    List<Person> getPersons();
}
```

When the code generation is complete, you'll get the implementation for the service: `PersonServiceImpl`. The *store* folder inside the application folder (*WebContent/app*) has the Ext JS store, which is bound to the previously generated `PersonModel` (see Figure 5-9). In this case, CDB generated the store that binds to the remote service.

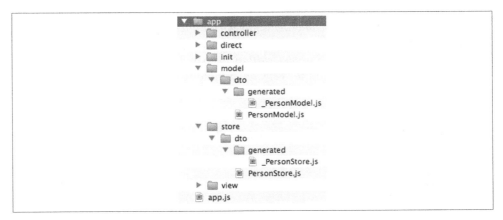

Figure 5-9. Structure of store and model folders

All this intermediate translation from JavaScript to Java, and from Java to JavaScript, is done by DirectJNgine, which is a server-side implementation of the Ext Direct protocol. You can read about this protocol in the Ext JS documentation (*http://bit.ly/1p9cPmG*).

CDB has generated a sample UI for us, too. Check out the *samples* directory shown in Figure 5-10.

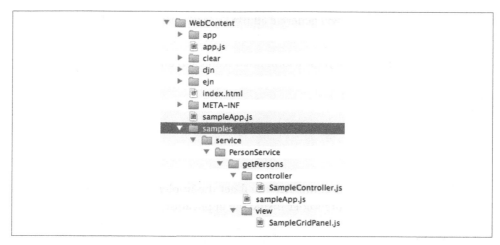

Figure 5-10. Folder with generated UI files

CDB has generated *SampleController.js*, *SampleGridPanel.js*, and the Ext JS application entry point *sampleApp.js*. To test this application, just copy the file *SampleController.js* into the *controller* folder, *SampleGridPanel.js* panel into the *view* folder, and the sample application in the root of the *WebContent* folder. Change the application entry point to be *sampleApp.js* in *index.html* of the Eclipse project, as shown here:

```
<script type="text/javascript" src="sampleApp.js"></script>
```

The generated UI of the sample application looks like Figure 5-11.

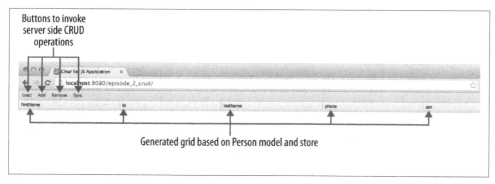

Figure 5-11. A scaffolded CRUD application template

On the server side, CDB also follows the *Generation Gap Pattern* and generates stubs for the service methods. Override these methods when you're ready to implement the CRUD functionality, similar to Example 5-8.

Example 5-8. Implementation of PersonService interface

```java
package service;
import java.util.ArrayList;
import java.util.List;

import clear.data.ChangeObject;
import dto.Person;
import service.generated.*;

public class PersonServiceImpl extends _PersonServiceImpl { ❶

  @Override
  public List<Person> getPersons() {                        ❷
      List<Person> result = new ArrayList<>();
      Integer id= 0;
      result.add(new Person(++id, "Joe", "Doe",
                    "555-55-55", "1111-11-1111"));
      result.add(new Person(++id, "Joe", "Doe",
                    "555-55-55", "1111-11-1111"));
      result.add(new Person(++id, "Joe", "Doe",
                    "555-55-55", "1111-11-1111"));
      result.add(new Person(++id, "Joe", "Doe",
                    "555-55-55", "1111-11-1111"));
      return result;                     ❸
  }

  @Override
  public void getPersons_doCreate(ChangeObject changeObject) { ❹
      Person dto = (Person) deserializeObject(
                    (Map<String, String>) changeObject.getNewVersion(),
                    Person.class);

      System.out.println(dto.toString());
  }

  @Override
  public void getPersons_doUpdate(ChangeObject changeObject) { ❺
      // TODO Auto-generated method stub
      super.getPersons_doUpdate(changeObject);
  }

  @Override
  public void getPersons_doDelete(ChangeObject changeObject) { ❻
      // TODO Auto-generated method stub
      super.getPersons_doDelete(changeObject);
  }
}
```

❶   Extend the generated class and provide the actual implementation.

❷   The getPerson() is our retrieve (fill) method (the *R* in CRUD).

❸   For this sample application, we can use the `java.util.ArrayList` class as in-memory server-side storage of the `Person` objects. In real-world applications, you'd use a database or other persistent storage.

❹   `fillMethodName +_doCreate()` is our create method (the *C* in CRUD).

❺   `fillMethodName +_doUpdate()` is our update method (the *U* in CRUD).

❻   `fillMethodName +_doDelete()` is our delete method (the *D* in CRUD).

Click the Load menu on the UI, and the application will retrieve four persons from our server.

To test the rest of the CRUD methods, we'll ask the user to insert one new row, modify three existing ones, and remove two rows by using the generated web client. The `Clear.data.DirectStore` object will automatically create a collection of six `ChangeOb jects`—one to represent a new row, three to represent the modified ones, and two for the removed rows.

When the user clicks the Sync UI menu, the changes will be sent to the corresponding `do...` remote method. When you `sync()` a standard `Ext.data.DirectStore`, Ext JS is POST-ing new, modified, and deleted items to the server. When the request is complete, the server's response data is applied to the store, expecting that some items can be modified by the server. In case of `Clear.data.DirectStore`, instead of passing around items, we pass the deltas, wrapped in `ChangeObject`.

Each instance of the `ChangeObject` contains the following:

newVersion
> This is an instance of the newly inserted or modified item. On the Java side, it's available via `getNewVersion()`.

prevVersion
> An instance of the deleted old version of the modified item. On the Java side it's available via `getPrevVersion()`.

array of changepropertyNames
> An array of `changepropertyNames` will exist with instances of `ChangeObject` if it's an update operation.

The rest of the `ChangeObject` details are described in the Clear Toolkit Wiki (*http://bit.ly/1vo1iS9*).

The corresponding Java implementation of `ChangeObject` is available on the server side, and Clear Toolkit passes `ChangeObject` instances to the appropriate do* method of the service class. Take a look at the `getPersons_doCreate()` method in Example 5-8. When the server needs to read the new or updated data arrived from the client, your Java class has to invoke the method `changeObject.getNewVersion()`. This method will return the JSON object that you need to deserialize into the object `Person`. This is done in Example 5-8 and looks like this:

```
Person dto = (Person) deserializeObject(
          (Map<String, String>) changeObject.getNewVersion(),Person.class);
```

When the new version of the `Person` object is extracted from `ChangeObject`, you can do with it whatever has to be done to persist it in the appropriate storage. In our example, we just print the new person information on the server-side Java console. This is why we said earlier that it might be a good idea to provide a pretty printing feature on the class `Person` by overriding the method `toString()`. Similarly, when you need to do a delete, `changeObject.getPrevVersion()` would give you a person to be deleted.

Data Pagination

The pagination feature is needed in almost every enterprise web application. Often you don't want to bring all the data to the client at once; a page-by-page feed brings the data to the user a lot faster. The user can navigate back and forth between the pages by using pagination UI components. To do that, we need to split our data on the server side into chunks, to send them page by page by the client request. Implementing pagination is the agenda for this section.

We'll add data pagination to our sample CRUD application by doing the following:

- Add the `Ext.toolbar.Paging` component.
- Bind both *grid* and *pagingtoolbar* to the same store.
- Use the `DirectOptions` class to read the pagination parameters.

We are going to improve our CRUD application by adding the paging toolbar component bound to the same store as the grid. The class `DirectOptions` will handle the pagination parameters on the server side.

So far, CDB has generated the UI from the Java backend service as well as the Ext JS store and model. We'll refactor the service code from the previous example to generate more data (a thousand objects) so we have something to paginate; see Example 5-9.

Example 5-9. Refactored implementation of PersonService interface

```
public class PersonServiceImpl extends _PersonServiceImpl {
  @Override
    public List<Person> getPersons() {
        List<Person> result = new ArrayList<>();
        for (int i=0; i<1000; i++){
            result.add(new Person(i, "Joe", "Doe", "555-55-55",
                                              "1111-11-1111"));
        }
        return result;
```

```
    }
}
```

If you rerun the application now, the Google Chrome console will show that `Person Store` is populated with 1,000 records. Now we'll add the Ext JS paging `toolbarpaging` UI component to the file *sampleApp.js*, as shown Example 5-10.

Example 5-10. Sample application entry

```
Ext.Loader.setConfig({
  disableCaching : false,
  enabled : true,
  paths : {
    episode_3_pagination : 'app',
    Clear : 'clear'
  }
});

Ext.syncRequire('episode_3_pagination.init.InitDirect');
// Define GridPanel
var myStore = Ext.create('episode_3_pagination.store.dto.PersonStore',{}); //❶
Ext.define('episode_3_pagination.view.SampleGridPanel', {
  extend : 'Ext.grid.Panel',
  store : myStore,
  alias : 'widget.samplegridpanel',
  autoscroll : true,
  plugins : [{
    ptype : 'cellediting'
  }],
  dockedItems: [
    {
      xtype: 'pagingtoolbar',    //❷
      displayInfo: true,
      dock: 'top',
      store: myStore         //❸
    }
  ],
  columns : [
    {header : 'firstName', dataIndex : 'firstName',
               editor : {xtype : 'textfield'}, flex : 1 },
    {header : 'id', dataIndex : 'id', flex : 1 },
    {header : 'lastName', dataIndex : 'lastName',
               editor : {xtype : 'textfield'}, flex : 1 },
    {header : 'phone', dataIndex : 'phone',
               editor : {xtype : 'textfield'}, flex : 1 },
    {header : 'ssn', dataIndex : 'ssn',
               editor : {xtype : 'textfield'}, flex : 1 }],
  tbar : [
    {text : 'Load', action : 'load'},
    {text : 'Add', action : 'add'},
    {text : 'Remove', action : 'remove'},
    {text : 'Sync', action : 'sync'}
```

```
    ]
  });
// Launch the application
Ext.application({
  name : 'episode_3_pagination',
  requires : ['Clear.override.ExtJSOverrider'],
  controllers : ['SampleController'],
  launch : function() {
    Ext.create('Ext.container.Viewport', {
      items : [{
        xtype : 'samplegridpanel'
      }]
    });
  }
});
```

❶ Manual store instantiation: create a separate variable myStore for this store with an empty config object.

❷ Add the xtype pagingtoolbar to this component's docked items property to display the information and dock this element at the top.

❸ Now the paging toolbar is also connected to the same store.

The next step is to fix the automatically generated controller to take care of loading data upon clicking the Load button, as shown in Example 5-11.

Example 5-11. Controller for sample application

```
Ext.define('episode_3_pagination.controller.SampleController', {
  extend: 'Ext.app.Controller',
  stores: ['episode_3_pagination.store.dto.PersonStore'],
  refs: [{                    //❶
    ref: 'ThePanel',
    selector: 'samplegridpanel'
  }],

  init: function() {
    this.control({
      'samplegridpanel button[action=load]': {
        click: this.onLoad
      }
    });
  },

  onLoad: function() {
    // returns instance of PersonStore
    var store = this.getThePanel().getStore();    //❷
    store.load();
  }
});
```

❶   Bind the store instance to our grid panel. In the controller's `refs` property, we're referencing our `simplegrid` panel with `ThePanel` alias.

❷   In this case, there is no need to explicitly retrieve the store instance by name. Instead, we can use the getters `getPanel()` and `getStore()`, which were automatically generated by the Ext JS framework.

When the user clicks the Next or Previous button, the method `loadPage` of the underlying store is called. Let's examine the `directprovider` URL—the server-side router of the remoting calls—to see what this direct request looks like. Open Google Chrome Developer Tools by choosing View → Developer, refresh the web page, and then go to the Network tab. You'll see that each time the user clicks the *next* or *previous* button on the pagination toolbar, the component sends `directOptions` as a part of the request.

The default Ext Direct request doesn't carry any information about the page size. Clear JS has the client-side extension of the Ext JS framework that adds some extra functionality to the `Ext.data.DirectStore` component to pass the page `start` and `limit` values to the server side. At this point, the `directOptions` request property (see Figure 5-12) can be extracted on the server side to get the information about the page boundaries. Let's add some code to *PersonServiceImpl.java*. At this point, the pagination doesn't work. The server sends the entire thousand records, because it doesn't know that the data has to be paginated. We'll fix it in Example 5-12.

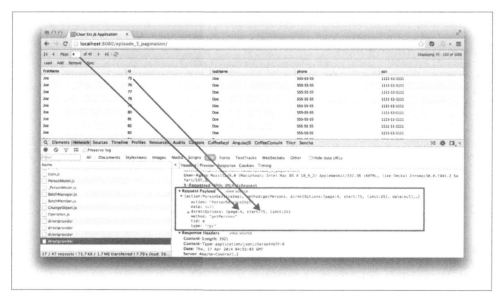

Figure 5-12. Request payload details

Example 5-12. Implementation of PersonService with pagination

```java
package service;
import java.util.ArrayList;
import java.util.List;

import clear.djn.DirectOptions;        //❶

import dto.Person;
import service.generated.*;

public class PersonServiceImpl extends _PersonServiceImpl {
  @Override
  public List<Person> getPersons() {
    List<Person> result = new ArrayList<>();
    for (int i=0; i<1000; i++){
      result.add(new Person(i, "Joe", "Doe", "555-55-55","1111-11-1111"));
    }
    //❷
    int start = ((Double)DirectOptions.getOption("start")).intValue();
    int limit = ((Double)DirectOptions.getOption("limit")).intValue();

    limit = Math.min(start+limit, result.size() );     //❸
    DirectOptions.setOption("total", result.size());   //❹
    result = result.subList(start, limit);        //❺

    return result;
  }
}
```

❶ On the server side, there is a special object called `DirectOptions`, which comes with Clear Toolkit.

❷ We want to monitor the `start` and `limit` values (see Figure 5-12).

❸ Calculate the actual limit. Assign the size of the data collection to the `limit` variable if it's less than the page size (`start+limit`).

❹ Notify the component about the total number of elements on the server side by using the `DirectOptions.setOption()` method with the `total` option.

❺ Before returning the result, create a subset, an actual page of data using the method `java.util.List.sublist()`, which produces the view of the portion of this list between indexes specified by the `start` and the `limit` parameters.

As you can see on the Network tab in Figure 5-12, we've limited the data load to 25 elements per page. Clicking the Next or Previous button will get you only a page worth of data. The Google Chrome Developer Tools Network tab shows that we are sending the `start` and `limit` values with every request, and the response contains the object with 25 elements.

If you'd like to repeat all of the preceding steps on you own, watch the screencasts (*http://bit.ly/1kGjzEh*) demonstrating all the actions described in the section on CDB. For current information about CDB, visit cleardb.io.

Summary

Writing enterprise web applications can be a tedious and time-consuming process. A developer needs to set up frameworks, boilerplates, abstractions, dependency management, and build processes, and the list of requirements for a frontend workflow appears to grow each year. In this chapter, we introduced several tools that can help you automate a lot of mundane tasks and make you more productive.

## CHAPTER 6

Modularizing Large-Scale JavaScript Projects

Reducing an application's startup latency and implementing lazy loading of certain parts of an application are the main reasons for modularization.

A good illustration of why you might want to consider modularization is the well-designed web application of Mercedes Benz USA (*http://www.mbusa.com*). This web application serves people who live in the United States and either own or are considering purchasing cars from this European car manufacturer.

One of the purchasing options is called European Delivery. An American resident who chooses this particular package can combine a vacation with her car purchase. She flies to the Mercedes Benz factory in Europe, picks up her car, and has a two-week vacation, driving her new vehicle throughout Europe. After the vacation is over, the car is shipped to her hometown in the US.

Needless to say, this program adds several thousand dollars to the price of the car. Of course, Mercedes Benz wants to ensure that visitors to its site view accurate vehicle prices. So, from an application design point of view, we don't want or need to include the code that supports the European Delivery to each and every user who decides to visit mbusa.com. *If* the user visits the menu Owners and clicks the European Delivery link, then *and only then* the required code and resources are pushed to the user's computer or mobile device.

The snapshot in Figure 6-1 was taken after clicking this link with the Chrome Developer Tools panel open.

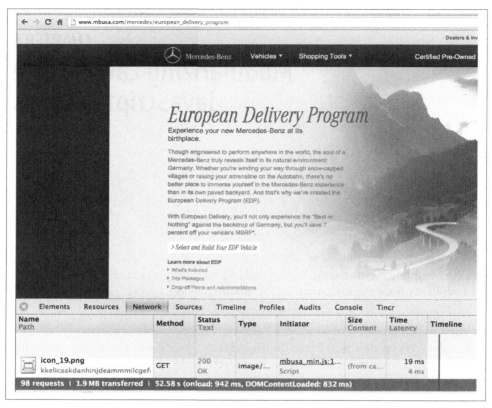

Figure 6-1. MB USA: European Delivery

In addition, as you can see, *1.9 MB* worth of code and other resources have been down-loaded as a result of this click. Were the application architects of MB USA to decide to bring this code to the user's device on the initial load of *http://mbusa.com*, the wait time would increase by another second or more. This additional latency is unnecessary be-cause only a tiny number of American drivers would be interested in exploring the European Delivery option. This example illustrates a use case for which modularization and lazy loading is needed.

Our Save The Child application is not as big as the one by Mercedes Benz. But we'll use it to give you an example of how to build modularized web applications that won't bring large blocks of monolithic code to the client's machine, but will load the code on an as-needed basis. We'll also give an example of how to organize the data exchange between different programming modules in a loosely coupled fashion.

Users consider a web application fast for one of two reasons: either it's actually fast or it gives an impression of being fast. Ideally, you should do your best to create a web application that's very responsive.

No matter how slow your web application is, it should never feel like it's being frozen.

This chapter covers modularization techniques that will enable quick rendering of the first page of your web application by the user's browser while loading the rest of the application in the background or on demand. We will continue refactoring the Save The Child application to illustrate using modules.

In this chapter, we're going to discuss the following frameworks for modularization of JavaScript projects:

- Browserify (*http://browserify.org*)
- RequireJS (*http://requirejs.org*) and RequireJS Optimizer (*r.js*)
- ECMASctipt 6 (ES6) Module Transpiler (*http://bit.ly/UGOVpm*)

Understanding Modularization Basics

Modules are code fragments that implement certain functionality and are written by using specific techniques. There is no out-of-the box modularization scheme in the JavaScript language. The upcoming ECMAScript 6 specification tends to resolve this by introducing the *module concept* in the JavaScript language itself. This is the future.

You might ask, "Aren't *.js* files modules already?" Of course, you can include and load each JavaScript file by using the `<script>` tag. But this approach is error prone and slow. Developers have to manually manage dependencies and file-loading order. Each `<script>` tag results in an additional HTTP call to the server. Moreover, the browser blocks rendering until it loads and executes JavaScript files.

As the application becomes larger, the number of script files grows accordingly, which is illustrated in Example 6-1.

Example 6-1. Multiple <script> tags complicate controlling application dependencies

```
<!DOCTYPE html>

<html lang="en">
<head>
    <meta charset="utf-8">

    <title>Save The Child | Home Page</title>
    <link rel="stylesheet" href="assets/css/styles.css">
</head>
```

```
<body>
<!-- page body -->

<!-- body content is omitted -->
    <script src="components/jquery.js"></script>        ❶
    <script type="text/javascript" src="app/modules/utils/load-html-content.js">
    </script>
    <script type="text/javascript" src="app/modules/utils/show-hide-div.js"></script>
    <script type="text/javascript" src="app/modules/svg-pie-chart.js"></script>
    <script type="text/javascript" src="app/modules/donation.js"></script>
    <script type="text/javascript" src="app/modules/login.js"></script>
    <script type="text/javascript" src="app/modules/utils/new-content-loader.js">
    </script>
    <script type="text/javascript" src="app/modules/generic-module.js"></script>
    <script type="text/javascript" src="app/modules/module1.js"></script>    ❷
    <script type="text/javascript" src="app/modules/module2.js"></script>
    <script type="text/javascript" src="app/config.js"></script>
    <script type="text/javascript" src="app/main.js"></script>    ❸
</body>    ❹
</html>
```

❶   Load the jQuery script first because all other modules depend on it.

❷   Other application components may also have internal dependencies on other scripts. Those scripts need to be loaded before the respective components. Having the proper order of these script tags is very important.

❸   The script for the main web page should be loaded after all dependencies have finished loading.

❹   We're putting script elements at the end of the document, as it blocks as little content as possible.

As you can see, we need a better way to modularize applications than simply adding <script> tags. As our first step, we can use the Module design pattern and use the so-called immediately invoked function expressions.

Next, we'll introduce and compare two popular JavaScript solutions and modularization patterns, CommonJS and Asynchronous Module Definition (AMD), which are alternative approaches to modularization. Both CommonJS and AMD are specifications defining sets of APIs.

You'll learn the pros and cons of both formats later in the chapter, but the AMD format plays nicely with the asynchronous nature of the Web. You'll see the use of the AMD format and RequireJS (*http://requirejs.org/*) framework to implement the modularized version of the Save The Child application.

Also, you'll see how to use the RequireJS APIs to implement on-demand (*lazy*) loading of the application components (for example, What We Do, Ways To Give, and so forth).

The upcoming ECMAScript 6 specification suggests how to handle modules, and how to start using ES6 module syntax today with the help of third-party tools such as transpiler (*http://bit.ly/1y8HR4a*). The ES6 module syntax can be compiled down to existing module solutions like CommonJS or AMD. You can find more details about CommonJS, AMD, and the ES6 module format in the corresponding sections of this chapter.

After application modules are asynchronously loaded, they need to communicate with one another. You can explicitly specify the component dependencies, which is fine as long as you have a handful of components. A more generic approach is to handle intermodule communications in a loosely coupled fashion by using the *Mediator* pattern, CommonJS, or AMD formats. By *loosely coupled*, we mean that components are not aware of one another's existence.

The next section reviews various approaches and patterns of modular JavaScript applications.

Exploring Roads to Modularization

Although JavaScript has no built-in language support of modules, the developers' community has managed to find a way for modularization by using existing syntax constructs, libraries, and conventions to emulate module-like behavior. In this section, we'll explore the following options for modularizing your application:

- The Module pattern
- CommonJS
- Asynchronous Module Definition (AMD)

Of these three, the *Module pattern* doesn't require any additional frameworks and works in any JavaScript environment. The *CommonJS* module format is widely adopted for server-side JavaScript, whereas the *AMD* format is popular in applications running in web browsers.

The Module Pattern

In software engineering, the Module pattern was originally defined as a way to implement encapsulation of reusable code. In JavaScript, the Module pattern is used to emulate the concept of classes. We're able to include both public and private methods as well as variables inside a single object, thus hiding the encapsulated code from other global scope objects. Such encapsulation lowers the likelihood of conflicting function names defined in different scripts that could be used in the same application's scope.

Ultimately, it's just some code in an immediately invoked function expression (IIFE) that creates a module object in the internal scope of a function and exposes this module to the global scope by using the JavaScript language syntax. Consider the following three code samples illustrating how the Module pattern could be implemented using IIFEs (see Examples 6-2, 6-3, and 6-4).

Example 6-2. Creating a closure that hides implementation of the login module

```
var loginModule = (function() {          ❶
    "use strict";

    var module = {};
    var privateVariable = 42;

    var privateLogin = function(userNameValue, userPasswordValue) {          ❷
        if (userNameValue === "admin" && userPasswordValue === "secret") {
            return privateVariable;
        }
    };

    module.myConstant = 1984;
    module.login = function(userNameValue, userPasswordValue) {
        privateLogin(userNameValue, userPasswordValue);
        console.log("login implementation omitted");
    };

    module.logout = function() {
        console.log("logout implementation omitted");
    };

    return module;
})();
```

❶   Assign the module object that was created in the closure to the variable logi nModule.

❷   Because of the JavaScript's function scoping, other parts of the code can't access the code inside the closure. With this approach, you can implement encapsulation and private members.

Example 6-3. Injecting the module into the global object

```
(function(global) {          ❶
    "use strict";
    var module = {};

    var privateVariable = 42;
    var privateLogin = function(userNameValue, userPasswordValue) {
        if (userNameValue === "admin" && userPasswordValue === "secret") {
            return privateVariable;
        }
    };

    module.myConstant = 1984;
    module.login = function(userNameValue, userPasswordValue) {
```

```
        privateLogin(userNameValue, userPasswordValue);
        console.log("rest of login implementation is omitted");
    };

    module.logout = function() {
        console.log("logout implementation omitted");
    };

    global.loginModule = module;
})(this);   ❷
```

❶   Instead of exporting the module to a variable as in the previous example, we're passing the global object as a parameter inside the closure.

❷   Attach the newly created object to the global object. After that, the `loginMod` `ule` object can be accessed from the external application code as `window.logi` `nModule` or just `loginModule`.

Example 6-4. Introducing namespaces in the global object

```
(function(global) {
    "use strict";

    var ssc = global.ssc;   ❶
    if (!ssc) {
        ssc = {};
        global.ssc = ssc;
    }

    var module = ssc.loginModule = {};   ❷

    module.myConstant = 1984;
    module.login = function(userNameValue, userPasswordValue) {
        console.log("login implementation for " + userNameValue + "and" +
                    userPasswordValue + "omitted");
    };

    module.logout = function() {
        console.log("logout implementation omitted");
    };
})(this);
```

❶   Here we have modification of the approach described in the previous snippet. To avoid name conflicts, create a namespace for our application called `ssc`. Note that we check for this object existence in the next line.

❷   Now we can logically structure application code using namespaces. The global `ssc` object will contain only the code related to the Save The Child application.

The Module pattern works well for implementing encapsulation in rather small applications. It's easy to implement and is framework-agnostic. However, this approach doesn't scale well because, when working with an application with the large number of modules, you might find yourself adding lots of boilerplate code, checking objects' existence in the global scope for each new module. Also, you need to be careful with managing namespaces: because you are the one who put an object into the global scope, you need to think about how to avoid accidental names conflicts.

The Module pattern has a serious drawback: you still need to deal with manual dependency management and manually arrange `<script>` tags in the HTML document.

CommonJS

CommonJS (*http://www.commonjs.org*) is an effort to standardize JavaScript APIs. People who work on CommonJS APIs have attempted to develop standards for various JavaScript APIs (similar to standard libraries in Java, Python, and so forth), including standards for modules and packages. The CommonJS module proposal specifies a simple API for declaring modules, but mainly on the server side. The CommonJS module format has been optimized for nonbrowser environments since the early days of server-side JavaScript.

On the web-browser side, you always need to consider potentially slow HTTP communications, which is not the case on the server. One solution suitable for browsers is to concatenate all scripts into a handful of bundles to decrease the number of HTTP calls, which is not a concern for server-side JavaScript engines because file access is nearly instantaneous. On the server side, separation of the code allows us to dedicate each file to exactly one module for ease of development, testing, and maintainability.

In brief, the CommonJS specification requires the environment to have three free variables (*http://bit.ly/1qr5q6m*): `require`, `exports`, and `module` (see Example 6-5). The syntax to define the module is called *authoring format*. To make the module loadable by a web browser, it has to be transformed into *transport format*.

Example 6-5. A CommonJS sample module

```
"use strict";
var loginModule = {};
var privateVariable = 42;

var ldapLogin = require("login/ldap");             ❶
var otherImportantDep = require("modules/util/strings"); ❷

var privateLogin = function(userNameValue, userPasswordValue) {
    if (userNameValue === "admin" && userPasswordValue === "secret") {
        ldapLogin.login(userNameValue, userPasswordValue);
        return privateVariable;
    }
};
```

```
loginModule.myConstant = 1984;
loginModule.login = function(userNameValue, userPasswordValue) {
    privateLogin(userNameValue, userPasswordValue);
    console.log("login implementation omitted");
};

loginModule.logout = function() {
    console.log("logout implementation omitted");
};

exports.login = loginModule;          ❸
// or
module.exports = loginModule;         ❹

loginModule.printMetadata = function(){
    console.log(module.id);           ❺
    console.log(module.uri);
};
```

❶ ❷ If a module requires other modules, declare references to those modules inside the current module's scope by using the `require` function. You need to call `require(id)` for each module it depends on. The module ID has slashes defining the file path or a URL to indicate namespaces for external modules. Modules are grouped into packages.

❸ The `exports` object exposes the public API of a module. All objects, functions, and constructors that your module exposes must be declared as properties of the `exports` object. The rest of the module's code won't be exposed.

❹ ❺ The `module` variable provides the metadata about the module. It holds such properties as `id` and a unique `uri` for each module. The `module.export` exposes the `exports` object as its property. Because objects in JavaScript are passed as references, the `exports` and `module.export` point at the same object.

The preceding snippet might give you the impression that the module's code is executed in the global scope, but it's not. Each module is executed in its own scope, which helps to isolate them. This works automatically when you write modules for a NodeJS environment running on the server. But to use the CommonJS module format in the web browser, you need to use an extra tool to generate transport format from *authoring format*. Browserify (*http://browserify.org*) takes all your scripts and concatenates them into one large file. Besides the module's code, the generated transport bundle will contain the boilerplate code that provides CommonJS modules runtime support in the browser environment. This build step complicates the development workflow. Usually, developers perform the *code/save/refresh browser* routine, but it doesn't work in this case and requires extra steps as you need to install the additional build tool and write build scripts.

The following are pros of using CommonJS:

- It's a simple API for writing and using modules.
- Such a pattern of organizing modules is widespread in server-side JavaScript, for example, NodeJS.

Cons to using CommonJS:

- Web browsers don't automatically create the scoped variables `require`, `exports`, and `module`, so the additional build step is required.
- The `require` method is synchronous, but there is no exact indication if a dependent module's values are fully loaded because of the asynchronous nature of web browsers. There is no event to notify the application that 100 percent of the required resources are loaded.
- The CommonJS API is suitable for loading *.js* files, but it can't load other assets such as CSS and HTML.

If you want to write modules in a format that can be used in both browser and server environments, read our suggestions in "Universal Module Definition" on page 230.

You can find additional materials on CommonJS by following these links:

- CommonJS Modules 1.1 specification (*http://bit.ly/1ohYoxk*)
- Node.js Modules Reference (*http://bit.ly/1x59eut*)
- Browserify (*http://browserify.org*)

Asynchronous Module Definition

The AMD format itself is a proposal for defining modules, whereby both the module and dependencies can be asynchronously loaded. The AMD API is based on this specification (*http://bit.ly/Yp9ozD*).

AMD began as a draft specification for module format in CommonJS, but because full agreement about its content was not reached, further work on the module's format moved to the amdjs GitHub page (*https://github.com/amdjs*).

The AMD API has the following main functions:

- define for defining the module
- require for loading the module and its dependencies

The define function takes three arguments, as shown in Example 6-6:

- The optional module ID
- An optional array of IDs of the dependencies
- A callback function (a.k.a., *factory function*), which will be invoked when dependencies are loaded

Example 6-6. The signature of the define function

```
define(
    module_id,          ❶
    [dependencies],     ❷
    function {}
);
```

❶   This string literal defines module_id, which will be used by the AMD loader to load this module.

❷   An optional array of the dependencies' IDs.

The preceding factory function{} will be executed only once.

For example, the Save The Child application has a Way To Give menu, which in turn depends on another module called otherContent. If the user clicks this menu, we can load the module that can be defined in the *wayToGive.js* file, as shown in Example 6-7.

Example 6-7. The definition of the wayToGive module

```
define(["otherContent"], function(otherContent) {     ❶
    var wayToGive;

    console.log("otherContent module is loaded");
    wayToGive = function() {
        return {
            render: function() {
                var dataUrl, newContainerID, whatWeDoButton;

                whatWeDoButton = "way-to-give";
                newContainerID = "way-to-give-container";
                dataUrl = "assets/html-includes/way-to-give.html";
                otherContent.getNewContent(whatWeDoButton, newContainerID,
                    dataUrl);     ❷
                return console.log("way-to-give module is rendered");
            },
            init: function() {
                return console.log("way-to-give init");
            }
        };
    };
    return wayToGive;     ❸
});
```

❶ This code doesn't have the optional module_id. The loader will use the filename without the *.js* extension as module_id. Our module has one dependency, called otherContent. The dependent module instance will be passed in the factory method as the variable otherContent.

❷ We can start using the dependency object immediately. The AMD loader has taken care of loading and instantiation of this dependency.

❸ The module returns a constructor function to be used for creation of new objects.

The require function takes two arguments:

- An array of module IDs to load. The module ID is a string literal.
- A callback to be executed after those modules are available. The modules loaded by IDs are passed into the callback in order. Example 6-8 shows the require function usage.

Example 6-8. An example of require function usage

```
require(["main"], function() {
    console.log("module main is loaded");
});
```

The following are pros of using AMD:

- It's a simple API that has only two functions: `require` and `define`.

- A wide variety of loaders is available. You'll find more coverage on loaders in "Dicing the Save The Child Application into Modules" on page 234.

- The CommonJS module authoring format is supported by the majority of loaders. You'll see an example of modules later in Example 6-23.

- Plug-ins offer an immense amount of flexibility.

- AMD is easy to debug.

  Consider the following error messages that the JavaScript interpreter may throw:

  *There was an error in `/modules/loginModule.js` on line **42***

  versus

  *There was an error in `/built-app.js` on line **1984***

  In modularized applications, you can more easily localize errors.

- Performance: Modules are loaded only when required; hence, the initial portion of the application's code become smaller.

The following are cons of using AMD:

- The dependency array can get rather large for complex modules:

  ```
  define(
          ["alpha", "beta", "gamma", "delta", "epsilon", "omega"],
          function(alpha, beta, gamma, delta, epsilon, omega){
              "use strict";
              // module's code omitted
      });
  ```

  In real-world enterprise applications, the array of dependency modules might be pretty large.

- Human errors can result in a mismatch between the dependency array and callback arguments:

  ```
  define(
          ["alpha", "beta", "gamma", "delta", "epsilon", "omega"],
          function(alpha, beta, gamma, delta, omega, epsilon){
              "use strict";
              // module's code omitted
      });
  ```

The mismatch of module IDs and factory function arguments will cause module usage problems.

Universal Module Definition

Universal Module Definition (UMD) is a series of patterns and code snippets that provide compatibility boilerplate to make modules environment-independent. These patterns can be used to support multiple module formats. UMD is not a specification or a standard. You need to pay attention to UMD patterns if your modules will run in more than one type of environment (for example, in a web browser and on the server-side engine running NodeJS). In most cases, it makes a lot of sense to use a single module format.

Example 6-9 shows a module definition in UMD notation. In this example, the module can be used with the AMD loader and as one of the variations of the Module pattern.

Example 6-9. The module in UMD notation

```
(function(root, factory) {
    "use strict";
    if (typeof define === "function" && define.amd) {     ❶
        define(["login"], factory);
    } else {
        root.ssc = factory(root.login);     ❷
    }
}(this, function(login) {     ❸
    "use strict";
    return {
        myConstant: 1984,
        login: function(userNameValue, userPasswordValue) {
            console.log("login for " + userNameValue + " and " + userPasswordValue);
        },
        logout: function() {
            console.log("logout implementation omitted");
        }
    };
}));
```

❶ If the AMD loader is available, proceed with defining the module according to the AMD specification.

❷ If the AMD loader isn't present, use the factory method to instantiate the object and attach it to the `window` object.

❸ Passing in the top-level context and providing an implementation of a factory function.

You can find more information about UMD and commented code snippets for different situations in the UMD project repository (*https://github.com/umdjs/umd*).

ECMAScript 6 Modules

The ECMAScript 6 (ES6) specification is an evolving draft outlining changes and features for the next version of the JavaScript language. This specification is not finalized yet, so browser support for anything defined in ES6 will be experimental at best. You cannot rely on ES6 for web applications that must be deployed in production mode in multiple browsers.

One of the most important features of the ES6 specification is *module syntax*. Example 6-10 provides a login module definition.

Example 6-10. Login module definition

```
export function login(userNameValue, userPasswordValue) {
    return userNameValue + "_" + userNameValue;
}
```

The keyword `export` specifies the function or object (a separate file) to be exposed as a module, which can be used from any other JavaScript code, as shown in Example 6-11.

Example 6-11. Main application module

```
import {login} from './login'
var result = login("admin", "password");
```

With the `import` keyword, we assign an instance of the `login()` function imported from the `login` module.

ES6 Module Transpiler

Although the ES6 standard is not implemented yet by most browsers, you can use third-party tools to get a taste of upcoming enhancements in the JavaScript language. The ES6 Module Transpiler (*http://bit.ly/1y8HR4a*) library developed by Square (*http://squareup.com/*) engineers helps use the module authoring syntax from ES6 and compile it down to the transport formats that you learned earlier in this chapter.

Consider the module *circle.js*, shown in Example 6-12.

Example 6-12. A circle.js module

```
function area(radius) {
    return Math.PI * radius * radius;
}

function circumference(radius) {
    return 2 * Math.PI * radius;
}

export {area, circumference};
```

This module exports two functions: `area()` and `circumference()`, as shown in Example 6-13.

Example 6-13. The main application's script main.js can use these functions

```
import { area, circumference } from './circle';     ❶

console.log("Area of the circle: " + area(2) + " meter squared");     ❷
console.log("Circumference of the circle: " + circumference(5) + " meters");
```

❶   The `import` keyword specifies the objects we want to use from the module.

❷   A sample use of the imported functions

The ES6 Module Transpiler's command `compile-module` can compile the module to be compliant with CommonJS, AMD, or the code that implements the Module pattern. With the `type` command-line option, you can specify that the output format will be *amd*, *cjs*, or *globals*:

```
compile-modules circle.js --type cjs --to ../js/
compile-modules main.js --type cjs --to ../js/
```

Example 6-14 shows the resulting *circle.js* module in CommonJS format.

Example 6-14. circle.js

```
"use strict";
function area(radius) {
    return Math.PI * radius * radius;
}

function circumference(radius) {
    return 2 * Math.PI * radius;
}

exports.area = area;
exports.circumference = circumference;
```

Example 6-15 shows the resulting *main.js* module in CommonJS format.

Example 6-15. main.js

```
"use strict";
var area = require("./circle").area;
var circumference = require("./circle").circumference;

console.log("Area of the circle: " + area(2) + " meter squared");
console.log("Circumference of the circle: " + circumference(5) + " meters");
```

If we compile the modules into AMD format by using the option *amd*, we would receive a different output in AMD format.

Example 6-16 shows the resulting *circle.js* module in AMD format. Example 6-17 shows the resulting *main.js* module in AMD format.

Example 6-16. circle.js

```
define("circle",
  ["exports"],
  function(__exports__) {
    "use strict";
    function area(radius) {
        return Math.PI * radius * radius;
    }

    function circumference(radius) {
        return 2 * Math.PI * radius;
    }

    __exports__.area = area;
    __exports__.circumference = circumference;
  });
```

Example 6-17. main.js

```
define("main",
  ["./circle"],
  function(__dependency1__) {
    "use strict";
    var area = __dependency1__.area;
    var circumference = __dependency1__.circumference;

    console.log("Area of the circle: " + area(2) + " meter squared");
    console.log("Circumference of the circle: " + circumference(5) + " meters");
  });
```

Using the `globals` option in the `compile-modules` command line produces the code that can be used as described in "The Module Pattern" on page 221.

In Example 6-18, the resulting *circle.js* module uses browser globals (the Module pattern) as its module format.

Example 6-18. circle.js

```
(function(exports) {
    "use strict";

    function area(radius) {
        return Math.PI * radius * radius;
    }

    function circumference(radius) {
        return 2 * Math.PI * radius;
    }
    exports.circle.area = area;
```

```
    exports.circle.circumference = circumference;
})(window);
```

In Example 6-19, the resulting *main.js* module uses browser globals (the Module pattern) as its module format.

Example 6-19. main.js

```
(function(circle) {
    "use strict";
    var area = circle.area;
    var circumference = circle.circumference;

    console.log("Area of the circle: " + area(2) + " meter squared");
    console.log("Circumference of the circle: " + circumference(5) + " meters");

})(window.circle);
```

For up-to-date information on ES6 browser support, visit the ECMAScript 6 compatibility table (*http://bit.ly/1iSSdAL*).

TypeScript (*http://www.typescriptlang.org*) is an open source language from Microsoft that compiles to JavaScript and brings object-oriented concepts such as classes and modules to JavaScript. It has a module syntax, which is similar to what the ES6 standard proposes. The TypeScript compiler can produce CommonJS and AMD formats. You can learn more about TypeScript from its language specification (*http://bit.ly/1mA0K6o*).

Dicing the Save The Child Application into Modules

Now that you know the basics of AMD and different modularization patterns, let's see how you can dice our Save The Child application into smaller pieces. In this section, we'll apply the AMD-compliant module loader from the framework RequireJS (*http://requirejs.org*).

curl.js (*http://github.com/cujojs/curl*) offers another AMD-compliant asynchronous resource loader. Both curl.js and RequireJS have similar functionality, and to learn how they differ, follow this thread on the RequireJS group (*http://bit.ly/U2rtCu*).

Let's start with a brief explanation of the directory structure of the modularized Save The Child application. Figure 6-2 shows this directory structure.

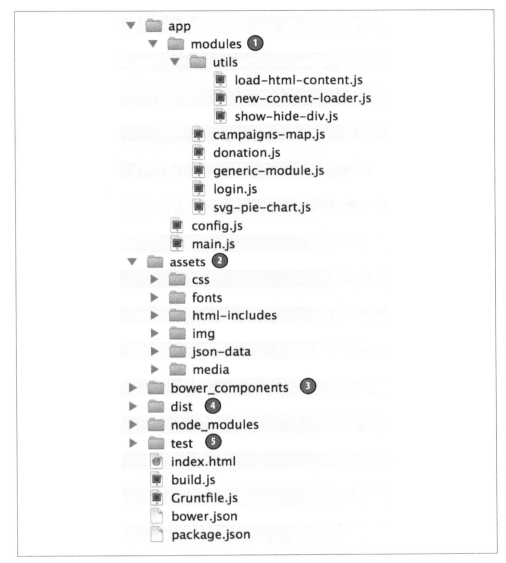

Figure 6-2. A directory structure of Save The Child

The content of the project folders is listed here:

1. All application JavaScript files reside in the *app/modules* directory. Inside the *modules* directory, you can have as many nested folders as you want (for example, *utils* folder).

2. The application assets remain the same as in previous chapters.

3. We keep all Bower-managed dependencies in the *bower_components* directory (such as RequireJS and jQuery).

4. The *dist* directory serves as the location for the optimized version of our application. We cover optimization with *r.js* in the section "Using RequireJS Optimizer" on page 242.

5. The QUnit/Jasmine tests reside in the *test* directory. Testing is covered in Chapter 7.

We are not going to dice the Save The Child application into multiple modules, but will show you how to start the process. Figure 6-3 illustrates the modules' dependencies. For example, the `main` module depends on `login`, `svg-pie-chart`, `campaigns-map`, `dona tion`, and `generic`. There is also a group of modules that will be loaded on demand: `whereWeWork`, `whatWeDo`, `wayToGive`, `whoWeAre`.

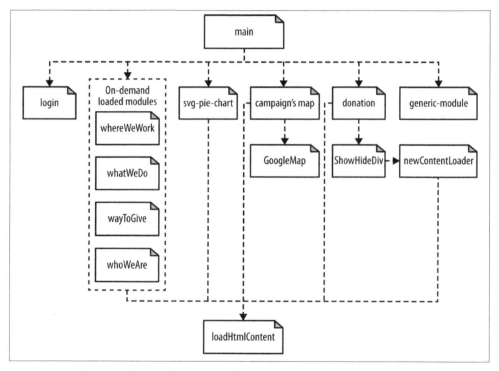

Figure 6-3. The modules graph of Save The Child

To dice the application into modules, you need the modularization framework RequireJS, which can either be downloaded from its GitHub repository or you can install it by using the package manager Bower that was explained in Chapter 5.

After RequireJS is downloaded and placed into the project directory, add it to the *index.html* file, as demonstrated in Example 6-20.

Example 6-20. Adding RequireJS to the web page

```html
<!DOCTYPE html>
<head>
    <!-- content omitted -->
</head>
<body>
<!-- page body -->

<script src="bower_components/requirejs/require.js"
        data-main="app/config"></script> ❶

</body>
</html>
```

❶   When the RequireJS library is loaded, it will look for the `data-main` attribute and attempt to load the *app/config.js* script asynchronously. The *app/config.js* script will become the entry point of our application.

Inside the RequireJS Configuration: config.js

RequireJS uses a configuration object that includes modules and dependencies that have to be managed by the framework, as shown in Example 6-21.

Example 6-21. The config.js file from the Save The Child app

```javascript
require.config({              ❶
    paths: {                  ❷
        'login': 'modules/login',
        'donation': 'modules/donation',
        'svg-pie-chart': 'modules/svg-pie-chart',
        'campaigns-map': 'modules/campaigns-map',
        'showHideDiv': 'modules/utils/show-hide-div',
        'loadHtmlContent': 'modules/utils/load-html-content',
        'newContentLoader': 'modules/utils/new-content-loader',
        'bower_components': "../bower_components",
        'jquery': '../bower_components/jquery/jquery',
        'main': 'main',
        'GoogleMap': '../bower_components/requirejs-google-maps/dist/GoogleMap',
        'async': '../bower_components/requirejs-plugins/src/async'
    }
});


require(['main'], function () {    ❸
});
```

❶   The RequireJS documentation (*http://bit.ly/TwttSM*) has a comprehensive overview of all configuration options. We've included some of them here.

❷   The `paths` configuration option defines the mapping for module names and their paths. The `paths` option is used for module names and shouldn't contain file extensions.

❸   After configuring the modules' paths, we're loading the *main* module. The navigation of our application flow starts there.

Writing AMD Modules

Example 6-22 provides a closer look at the module's internals that make it consumable by the RequireJS module loader.

Example 6-22. Generic module loader: generic-module.js

```
define(["newContentLoader"], function(contentLoader) {          ❶
    "use strict";
    var genericModule;

    genericModule = function(moduleId) {          ❷
        return {
            render: function(button, containerId, dataUrl) {
                contentLoader.getNewContent(button, containerId, dataUrl);          ❸
                console.log("Module " + moduleId + " is rendered...");
            }
        };
    };
    return genericModule;
});
```

❶   As we discussed in the section "Asynchronous Module Definition" on page 227, the code that you want to expose as a module should be wrapped in the de `fine()` function call. The first parameter is an array of dependencies. The location of dependency files is defined inside the config file. The dependency object doesn't have the same name as the dependency string ID. The order of arguments in the factory function should be the same as the order in the dependencies array.

❷   In this module, we export only the constructor function, which in turn returns the *render* function to draw the visual component on the screen.

❸   The `contentLoader` object loaded from *app/modules/util/new-content-loader.js* (see the `paths` property in the RequireJS config object), is instantiated by RequireJS and is ready to use.

RequireJS also supports the CommonJS module format with a slightly different signature for the `define()` function. This helps bridge the gap between AMD and Com-

---

monJS. If your factory function accepts parameters but no dependency array, the AMD environment assumes that you wish to emulate the CommonJS module environment. The standard `require`, `exports`, and `module` variables will be injected as parameters into the factory.

Example 6-23 shows the CommonJS module format with RequireJS.

Example 6-23. Using CommonJS module format in RequireJS

```
define(function(require, exports, module) {     ❶
    "use strict";
    module.exports = (function() {              ❷

        var dependency = require("dependencyId");      ❸

        function AuctionDTO(_arg) {
            this.auctionState = _arg.auctionState;
            this.item = _arg.item;
            this.bestBid = _arg.bestBid;
            this.auctionId = _arg.auctionId;
            dependency.doStuff();
        }

        AuctionDTO.prototype.toJson = function() {
            return JSON.stringify(this);
        };

        return AuctionDTO;
    })();
});
```

❶ The factory receives up to three arguments that emulate the CommonJS `require`, `exports`, and `module` variables.

❷ Export your module rather than return it. You can export an object in two ways: assign the module directly to `module.exports`, as shown in this snippet, or set the properties on the `exports` object.

❸ In CommonJS, dependencies are assigned to local variables by using the `require(id)` function.

Loading Modules On Demand

As per the Save The Child modules graph, some components shouldn't load when the application starts. Similar to the Mercedes Benz website example, some functionality of Save The Child can be loaded later, when the user needs it. The user might never want to visit the Where We Work section. Hence, this functionality is a good candidate for the *load on-demand* module. You might want to load such a module on demand when the user clicks a button or selects a menu item. Example 6-24 shows the code for loading a module on demand (on a button click).

At any given time, a module can be in one of three states:

- Not loaded (`module === null`)
- Loading is in progress (`module === 'loading'`)
- Fully loaded (`module !== null`)

Example 6-24. Loading the module on demand

```
var module;
var buttonClickHandler = function(event) {
    "use strict";
    if (module === "loading") {          ❶
      return;
    }
    if (module !== null) {               ❷
      module.render();
    } else {
      module = "loading";                ❸
      require(["modules/wereWeWork"], function(ModuleObject) {  ❹
        module = new ModuleObject();
        module.render();
      });
    }
};
```

❶ Checking whether module loading is in progress.

❷ Don't reload the same module. If the module was already loaded, just call the method to render the widget on the web page.

❸ Setting the module into the intermediate state until it's fully loaded.

❹ After the `whereWeWork` module is loaded, the callback will receive the reference to this module—instantiate `whereWeWork` and render it on the page.

Let's apply the technique demonstrated in Example 6-24 for the Save The Child application to lazy-load the Who We Are, What We Do, Where We Work, and What To Give modules only if the user clicks the corresponding top bar link. See Example 6-25.

Example 6-25. The main module

```
define(['login',
    'donation',
    'campaigns-map',
    'svg-pie-chart',
    'modules/generic-module'  ❶
], function() {
    var initComponent, onDemandLoadingClickHandlerFactory;
```

```
onDemandLoadingClickHandlerFactory = function(config) {
    return function(event) {  ❷
        if (config.amdInstance === 'loading') {
            return;
        }
        if (config.amdInstance != null) {
            config.amdInstance.render(event.target.id, config.containerId,
                                      config.viewUrl);
        } else {
            config.amdInstance = 'loading';
            require(['modules/generic-module'], function(GenericModule) {
                var moduleInstance;
                moduleInstance = new GenericModule(config.moduleId);
                moduleInstance.render(event.target.id, config.containerId,
                                      config.viewUrl);
                config.amdInstance = moduleInstance;
            });
        }
    };
};
initComponent = function(config) {
    config.button.addEventListener('click',
                                  onDemandLoadingClickHandlerFactory(config),  ❸
                                  false);
};
return (function() {
    var componentConfig,
        componentConfigArray,
        way_to_give, what_we_do,
        where_we_work,
        who_we_are, _i, _len;
    way_to_give = document.getElementById('way-to-give');
    what_we_do = document.getElementById('what-we-do');
    who_we_are = document.getElementById('who-we-are');
    where_we_work = document.getElementById('where-we-work');
    componentConfigArray = [{          ❹
        moduleId: 'whoWeAre',
        button: who_we_are,
        containerId: 'who-we-are-container',
        viewUrl: 'assets/html-includes/who-we-are.html'
    }, {
        moduleId: 'whatWeDo',
        button: what_we_do,
        containerId: 'what-we-do-container',
        viewUrl: 'assets/html-includes/what-we-do.html'
    }, {
        moduleId: 'whereWeWork',
        button: where_we_work,
        containerId: 'where-we-work-container',
        viewUrl: 'assets/html-includes/where-we-work.html'
    }, {
        moduleId: 'wayToGive',
```

```
            button: way_to_give,
            containerId: 'way-to-give-container',
            viewUrl: 'assets/html-includes/way-to-give.html'
        }];
        for (_i = 0, _len = componentConfigArray.length; _i < _len; _i++) {
            componentConfig = componentConfigArray[_i];
            initComponent(componentConfig); ❺
        }
        console.log('app is loaded');
    })();
});
```

❶   The first argument of the `define` function is an array of dependencies.

❷   Here, we're using the approach described in Example 6-24. This factory function
     produces the handler for the button click event. It uses the RequireJS API to load
     the module after the user clicks the button.

❸   Instantiate the click handler function by using `onDemandLoadingClickHandler`
     `Factory` and assign it to the button defined in the module config.

❹   An array of modules that can be loaded on demand.

❺   In the last step, we need to initialize each module button with the lazy-loading
     handler.

Using RequireJS Plug-ins

RequireJS plug-ins are special modules that implement a specific API. For example, the
text plug-in allows you to specify a text file as a dependency, and *cs!* translates *Coffee-
Script* files into JavaScript. The plug-in's module name comes before the *!* separator.
Plug-ins can extend the default loader's functionality.

In the Save The Child application, we use the *order.js* plug-in that allows us to specify
the exact order in which the dependencies should be loaded. You can find the full list
of available RequireJS plug-ins at the wiki page (*http://bit.ly/1pAGHvZ*).

Using RequireJS Optimizer

RequireJS comes with the optimization tool called *r.js* (*http://bit.ly/1qHiV1v*), which is
a utility that performs module optimization. Earlier in this chapter, we specified the
dependencies as an array of string literals that are passed to the top-level `require` and
`define` calls. The optimizer will combine modules and their dependencies into a single
file based on these dependencies.

Furthermore, *r.js* integrates with other optimization tools such as UglifyJS (*http://bit.ly/
1vo281q*) and Closure Compiler (*http://bit.ly/1lJvK8M*) to minify the content of script
files. We are going to use the JavaScript task runner Grunt (*http://gruntjs.com*) that you
learned about in Chapter 5.

Let's configure our Grunt project to enable the optimization task. Example 6-26 shows the command to install RequireJS, and Grunt's task packages clean, concat, and ugli fy, and save them as development dependencies in the file *package.json*.

Example 6-26. Adding dependencies to package.json

```
> npm install grunt-contrib-requirejs\
grunt-contrib-concat grunt-contrib-clean\
grunt-contrib-uglify --saveDev
```

Example 6-27 describes the script to set up the RequireJS optimizer and the related optimization tasks for Grunt. You'll need to run this script to generate an optimized version of the Save The Child application.

Example 6-27. Script to set up RequireJS optimizer

```
"use strict";

module.exports = function (grunt) {

    // Project configuration.
    grunt.initConfig({
        // Task configuration.
        clean: {
            files: ["dist"] ❶
        },
        requirejs: {              ❷
            compile: {
                options: {
                    name: "config",
                    mainConfigFile: "app/config.js",
                    out: "<%= concat.dist.dest %>",
                    optimize: "none"
                }
            }
        },
        concat: {            ❸
            dist: {
                src: ["components/requirejs/require.js",
                      "<%= concat.dist.dest %>"],
                dest: "dist/require.js"
            }
        },
        uglify: {            ❹
            dist: {
                src: "<%= concat.dist.dest %>",
                dest: "dist/require.min.js"
            }
        }
    });

    grunt.loadNpmTasks("grunt-contrib-clean");        ❺
```

```
grunt.loadNpmTasks("grunt-contrib-requirejs");
grunt.loadNpmTasks("grunt-contrib-concat");
grunt.loadNpmTasks("grunt-contrib-uglify");

grunt.registerTask("default", ["clean", "requirejs", "concat", "uglify"]); ❻
};
```

❶ The `clean` task cleans the output directory. In the `files` section of the task `config`, we specify folder that should be cleaned.

❷ The `requirejs` task. The configuration properties of the `requrejs` task are self-explanatory. `mainConfigFile` points at the same file as the `data-main` attribute of the RequireJS script tag. The `out` parameter specifies the output directory where the optimized script will be created.

❸ The `concat` task combines/concatenates optimized module code and RequireJS loader code.

❹ The `uglify` task minifies files using UglifyJS (*http://bit.ly/1sRs7SY*)—a compressor/minifier tool. Input and output of this task is configured with `src` and `dest` properties of `uglify` object.

❺ Loading plug-ins that provide necessary tasks.

❻ The default task to execute all tasks in order.

Run the Save The Child (*http://localhost:8080/ssc-requirejs*) application built with RequireJS and monitor the network traffic in Chrome Developer Tools. You'll see many HTTP requests that load modules asynchronously. As you can see in Figure 6-4, 12 out of 24 of the browser's requests are for loading all required modules. The modules that may be loaded on demand are not here.

Figure 6-5 shows the loading of the Save The Child application, optimized with the RequireJS optimizer. We've managed to pack all our modules, their dependencies, and the loader's code into a single file, which considerably decreases the number of server-side calls.

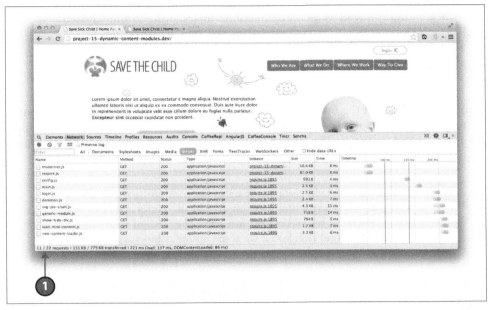

Figure 6-4. Unoptimized version of the Save The Child application

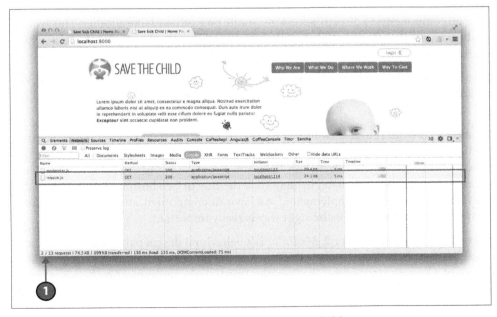

Figure 6-5. Loading the optimized version of Save The Child

You can read more on optimization topics at the RequireJS documentation site under Optimization (*http://bit.ly/1qHiV1v*).

RequireJS took care of the optimal module loading, but you should properly arrange the intermodule communication. The Save The Child application doesn't have modules that heed to exchange data, so we'll describe how to properly arrange intermodule communications in a separate application.

Google has created PageSpeed Insights (*http://bit.ly/1q9Xgxw*), a web tool that offers suggestions for improving the performance of your web application on all devices. Just enter the URL of your application and a second later you'll see some optimization suggestions.

Loosely Coupled InterModule Communications with Mediator

Almost any complex enterprise web application consists of various components and modules. A simple approach of arranging communication among components is to allow all components to directly access the public properties of one another. This would produce an application with tightly coupled components that know about one another, but removal of one component could lead to multiple code changes in the application.

A better approach is to create loosely coupled components that are self-contained, do not know about one another, and can communicate with the "outside world" by sending and receiving events.

Creating a UI from reusable components and applying messaging techniques requires creation of loosely coupled components. Say you've created a window for a financial trader. This window gets a data push from the server, showing the latest stock prices. When the trader likes the price, he may click the Buy or Sell button to initiate a trade. The trading engine can be implemented in a separate component, and establishing inter-component communications the right way is really important.

As you learned from Chapter 2, *Mediator* is a behavioral design pattern that allows you to unify communication of the application components. The Mediator pattern promotes the use of a single shared object that handles (mediates) communication between other objects. None of the components is aware of the others, but each of them knows about a single object—the mediator.

In Chapter 2 we introduced an example of a small fragment of a trader's desktop. Let's reuse the same example—this time not with `postMessage`, but with the Mediator object.

In Figure 6-6, the Price panel on the left gets the data feed about the current prices of IBM stock. When the user clicks the Bid or Ask button, the Price panel just sends the event with the relevant trade information (for example, a JSON-formatted string containing the stock symbol, price, buy or sell flag, or date).

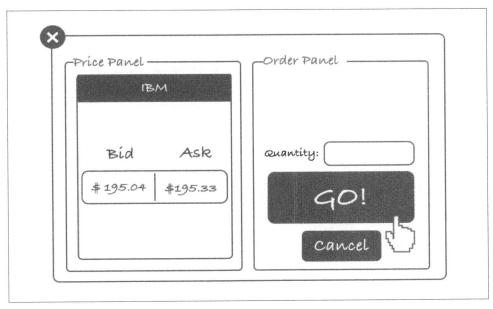

Figure 6-6. Before the trader clicks the Price panel

Figure 6-7 shows the wire after the user clicks the Price panel.

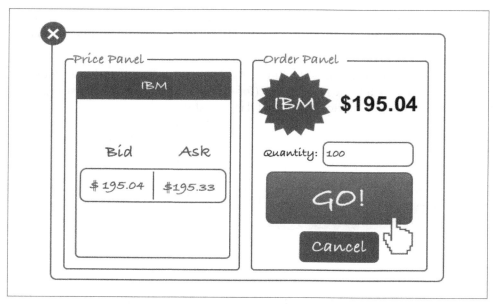

Figure 6-7. After the trader clicks the Price panel

Example 6-28 shows an HTML code snippet that implements this scenario.

Example 6-28. Implementation of Mediator Design Pattern

```html
<!DOCTYPE html>
<html>
<head>
    <meta charset="utf-8">
    <title>An example of Mediator Design Pattern</title>
    <script data-main="app/config" src="bower_components/requirejs/require.js">
    </script>
</head>
<body>
    <h1>mediator and RequireJS example</h1>

    <div id="pricePanel">          ❶
        <p>IBM</p>
        <label for="priceInput">Bid:</label>
        <input type="text" id="priceInput" placeholder="bid price"/>

        <label for="priceInput">Ask:</label>
        <input type="text" id="priceInput" placeholder="bid price"/>
    </div>
    <div id="orderPanel">          ❷
        <p id="priceText"></p>
        <label for="quantityInput">Quantity:</label>
        <input type="text" id="quantityInput" placeholder=""/>
        <button id="goButton">Go!</button>
```

```
                <button id="cancelButton">cancel</button>
        </div>

</body>
</html>
```

❶ This div element contains *Price Panel* with Bid and Ask controls.

❷ This div element contains *Order Panel* with Quantity, Go, and Cancel controls.

As we stated earlier, we need a mediator to handle communication among application components. The components need to register themselves with the mediator so that it knows about them and can route communications. Example 6-29 is a sample mediator implementation (we use define and require from RequireJS here).

Example 6-29. The implementation of the Mediator pattern

```
define(function() {
    "use strict";
    return (function() {          ❶
        var components = {};

        function Mediator() {}

        Mediator.registerComponent = function(name, component) {    ❷
            var cmp;
            for (cmp in components) {
                if (components[cmp] === component) {
                    break;
                }
            }
            component.setMediator(Mediator);                 ❸
            components[name] = component;                    ❹
        };

        Mediator.broadcast = function(event, args, source) {        ❺
            var cmp;
            if (!event) {
                return;
            }
            args = args || [];
            for (cmp in components) {
                if (typeof components[cmp]["on" + event] === "function") {       ❻
                    source = source || components[cmp];
                    components[cmp]["on" + event].apply(source, args);
                }
            }
        };
        return Mediator;
    })();
});
```

❶ Return the private object that stores registered components.

❷ With the `Mediator.register()` function, we can store components in the associative array. The mediator is a singleton object here.

❸ Assign the mediator instance to the component being registered.

❹ Register the component in the array by using the provided `name` as key.

❺ The component can invoke `Mediator.broadcast()` when it has some information to share with other application components.

❻ If a component has a function property with the name matching the pattern `"on" + event`-for example, `++onClickEvent++`-the mediator will in voke this function in the context of the `source object.

Example 6-30 shows the main entry point of the application that uses the mediator.

Example 6-30. The application entry point

```
define(["mediator", "pricePanel", "orderPanel"], function(Mediator, PricePanel,
                                                   OrderPanel) {   ❶
    "use strict";
    return (function() {
        Mediator.registerComponent("pricePanel", new PricePanel());    ❷
        Mediator.registerComponent("orderPanel", new OrderPanel());

        document.getElementById("priceInput").addEventListener("click",
                                                   function() {   ❸
            if ( !! this.value) {
                return Mediator.broadcast("BidClick", [this.value]);    ❹
            }
        });

    })();
});
```

❶ Required modules will be loaded by RequireJS.

❷ Register our components with the mediator.

❸ Add the `click` event listener for the Bid Price component.

❹ When the user clicks the bid price, the mediator will broadcast the `BidClick` event to all registered components. Only the component that has this specific event handler with the name matching the pattern `"on" + event` will receive this event.

Examples 6-31 and 6-32 show the code of the `PricePanel` and `OrderPanel` components, respectively.

Example 6-31. The PricePanel module

```
define(function() {
    "use strict";
    return (function() {
        var mediator;

        function PricePanel() {
        }

        PricePanel.prototype.setMediator = function(m) {        ❶
            mediator = m;
        };

        PricePanel.prototype.getMediator = function() {         ❷
            return mediator;
        };

        PricePanel.prototype.onBidClick = function(currentPrice) {       ❸
            console.log("Bid clicked on price " + currentPrice);
            this.getMediator().broadcast("PlaceBid", [currentPrice]);
        };

        PricePanel.prototype.onAskClick = function() {          ❹
            console.log("Ask clicked");
        };

        return PricePanel;
    })();
});
```

❶ The setter of the Mediator object. The mediator injects its instance during component registration (refer to Example 6-29).

❷ The getter of the Mediator object.

❸ The onBidClick event handler. The mediator will call this function when the BidClick event is broadcast. Using the getter getMediator, we can broadcast the PlaceBid event to all registered components.

❹ The onAskClick event handler. The mediator will call this function when the AskClick event is broadcast.

Example 6-32. The OrderPanel module

```
define(function () {
    "use strict";
    return (function () {
        var mediator;

        function OrderPanel() {
        }
```

```
OrderPanel.prototype.getMediator = function () {        ❶
    return mediator;
};

OrderPanel.prototype.setMediator = function (m) {
    mediator = m;
};

OrderPanel.prototype.onPlaceBid = function (price) {    ❷
    console.log("price updated to " + price);
    var priceTextElement = document.getElementById("priceText");
    priceTextElement.value = price;
};

return OrderPanel;

        })();
});
```

❶ The mediator's getter and setter have a purpose similar to that described in previous snippet.

❷ Defining the `PlaceBid` event handler, `onPlaceBid()`.

As you noticed, both `OrderPanel` and `PricePanel` don't know about the existence of each other, but nevertheless they can send and receive data with the help of an intermediary—the Mediator object.

The introduction of the mediator increases reusability of components by decoupling them from each other. The Mediator pattern simplifies the maintenance of any application by centralizing the navigational logic.

Summary

The size of any application tends to increase with time, and sooner or later you'll need to decide how to cut it into several loadable blocks of functionality. The sooner you start modularizing your application, the better.

In this chapter, we reviewed several options for writing modular JavaScript by using modern module formats. These formats have advantages over using just the classical Module pattern. These advantages include avoiding creating global variables for each module and better support for static and dynamic dependency management.

Understanding various technologies and frameworks available in JavaScript, combined with the knowledge of different ways of linking modules and libraries, is crucial for developers who want their JavaScript applications to be more responsive.

## CHAPTER 7

Test-Driven Development with JavaScript

To shorten the development cycle of your web application, you need to start testing it in the early stages of the project. It seems obvious, but many enterprise IT organizations haven't adopted agile testing methodologies, which costs them dearly. JavaScript is a dynamically typed interpreted language—there is no compiler to help identify errors as is done in compiled languages such as Java. This means that a lot more time should be allocated for testing JavaScript web applications. Moreover, a programmer who doesn't introduce testing techniques into his daily routine can't be 100 percent sure that his code works properly.

The static code analysis and code quality tools such as Esprima (*http://esprima.org*) and JSHint (*http://www.jshint.com*) will help reduce the number of syntax errors and improve the quality of your code.

 We demonstrate how to set up JSHint for your JavaScript project and automate the process of checking your code for syntax errors in Chapter 5.

To switch to a test-driven development mode, make testing part of your development process in its early stages rather than scheduling testing after the development cycle is complete. Introducing test-driven development can substantially improve your code quality. It is important to receive feedback about your code on a regular basis. That's why tests must be automated and should run as soon as you've changed the code.

There are many testing frameworks in the JavaScript world, but we'll give you a brief overview of two of them: QUnit (*http://qunitjs.com/*) and Jasmine (*http://bit.ly/1pPx7lo*). The main goal of each framework is to test small pieces of code, a.k.a. *units*.

We will go through basic testing techniques known as test-driven development and Test First. You'll learn how to automate the testing process in multiple browsers with Testem Runner (*http://bit.ly/1vnEqCj*) or by running tests in so-called *headless* mode with PhantomJS (*http://phantomjs.org*).

The second part of this chapter is dedicated to setting up a new Save The Child project in the IDE with selected test frameworks.

Why Test?

All software has bugs. But in interpreted languages such as JavaScript, you don't have the help of compilers that could point out potential issues in the early stages of development. You need to continue testing code over and over again to catch regression errors, to be able to add new features without breaking the existing ones. Code that is covered with tests is easy to refactor. Tests help prove the correctness of your code. Well-tested code leads to better overall design of your programs.

Testing Basics

This chapter covers the following types of testing:

- Unit testing
- Integration testing
- Functional testing
- Load (a.k.a. stress) testing

Quality Assurance versus User Acceptance Testing

Although *quality assurance* (QA) and *user acceptance testing* (UAT) are far beyond the scope of this chapter, you need to understand their differences.

Software QA (a.k.a., *quality control*, or QC) is a process that helps identify the correctness, completeness, security compliance, and quality of the software. QA testing *is performed by specialists* (testers, analysts). The goal of QA testing is to ensure that the application complies with a set of the predefined behavior requirements.

UAT *is performed by business users* or subject-area experts. UAT should result in an endorsement that the tested application/functionality/module meets the agreed-upon requirements. The results of UAT give the confidence to the end user that the system will perform in production according to specifications.

During the QA process, the specialist intends to perform all tests, trying to break the application. This approach helps find errors undiscovered by developers. On the con-

---

trary, during UAT the user runs business-as-usual scenarios and makes sure that business functions are implemented in the application.

Let's go over the strategies, approaches, and tools that will help you in test automation.

Unit Testing

A *unit test* is a piece of code that invokes a method being tested. It *asserts* some assumptions about the application logic and behavior of the method. Typically, you'll write such tests by using a unit-testing framework of your choice. Tests should run fast and be automated with clear output. For example, you can test that if a function is called with particular arguments, it should return an expected result. We take a closer look at unit-testing terminology and vocabulary in "Test-Driven Development" on page 259.

Integration Testing

Integration testing is a phase in which already tested units are combined into a module to test the interfaces between them. You might want to test the integration of your code with the code written by other developers; for example, a third-party framework. Integration tests ensure that any abstraction layers we build over the third-party code work as expected. Both unit and integration tests are written by application developers.

Functional Testing

Functional testing is aimed at finding out whether the application properly implements business logic. For example, if the user clicks a row in a grid with customers, the program should display a form view with specific details about the selected customer. In functional testing, business users should define what has to be tested, unlike unit or integration testing, for which tests are created by software developers.

Functional tests can be performed manually by a real person clicking through each and every view of the web application, confirming that it operates properly or reporting discrepancies with the functional specifications. But there are tools to automate the process of functional testing of web applications. Such tools allow you to record users' actions and replay them in automatic mode. The following are brief descriptions of two such tools—Selenium and CasperJS:

Selenium (http://docs.seleniumhq.org)
Selenium is an advanced browser automation tool suite that has capabilities to run and record user scenarios without requiring developers to learn any scripting languages. Also, Selenium has an API for integration with many programming languages such as Java, C#, and JavaScript. Selenium uses the WebDriver API to talk to browsers and receive running context information. WebDriver is becoming the

standard API for browser automation (*http://bit.ly/1kXX7vq*). Selenium supports a wide range of browsers and platforms (*http://bit.ly/1vnEsKr*).

Casper.js (http://bit.ly/1pEdhhr)

CasperJS is a scripting framework written in JavaScript. CasperJS allows you to create interaction scenarios such as defining and ordering navigation steps, filling and submitting forms, or even scrapping web content and making web page screenshots. CasperJS works on top of PhantomJS and SlimerJS browsers, which limits the testing runtime environment to WebKit-based and Gecko-based browsers. Still, it's a useful tool when you want to run tests in a continuous integration (CI) environment.

What Is PhantomJS and SlimerJS?

PhantomJS is a headless WebKit-based rendering engine and interpreter with a JavaScript API. Think of PhantomJS as a browser that doesn't have any graphical user interface. PhantomJS can execute HTML, CSS, and JavaScript code. Because PhantomJS is not required to render a browser's GUI, it can be used in display-less environments (for example, a CI server) to run tests. *SlimerJS* follows the same idea of a headless browser, similar to PhantomJS, but it uses the Gecko engine, instead.

PhantomJS is built on top of WebKit and JavaScriptCore (*http://bit.ly/1iSSuDw*) (like Safari), and SlimerJS is built on top of Gecko and SpiderMonkey (*http://mzl.la/1kXXRkc*) (like Firefox). You can find a comprehensive list of differences between PhantonJS and SlimerJS APIs in SlimerJS's documentation site (*http://bit.ly/1nfFoxq*).

In our case, Grunt automatically spawns the PhantomJS instance, executes the code of our tests, reads the execution results using the PhantomJS API, and prints them out in the console. If you're not familiar with Grunt tasks, refer to the online bonus chapter (*http://bit.ly/1iJO41S*) for additional information about using Grunt in our Save The Child project.

Load Testing

Load testing is a process that can help answer the following questions:

- How many concurrent users can work with your application without bringing your server to its knees?

- Even if your server is capable of serving a thousand users, is your application performance in compliance with the service-level agreement (SLA), if any?

It all comes down to two factors: availability and response time of your application. Ideally, these requirements should be well defined in the SLA document, which should clearly state what metrics are acceptable from the user's perspective. For example, the

SLA can include a clause stating that the initial download of your application shouldn't take longer than 10 seconds for users with a slow connection (under 1 Mbps). An SLA can also state that the query to display a list of customers shouldn't run for more than 5 seconds, and the application should be operational 99.9 percent of the time.

To avoid surprises after going live with your new mission-critical web application, don't forget to include in your project plan an item to create and run a set of heavy stress tests. Do this well in advance, before your project goes live. With load testing, you don't need to hire a thousand interns to play the roles of concurrent users to find out whether your application will meet the SLA.

Automated load-testing software allows you to emulate the required number of users, set up throttling to emulate a slower connection, and configure the ramp-up speed. For example, you can simulate a situation in which the number of users logged on to your system grows at the speed of 50 users every 10 seconds. Stress-testing software also allows you to prerecord user interactions, and then you can run these scripts emulating a heavy load.

Professional stress-testing software allows simulating the load close to real-world usage patterns. You should be able to create and run mixed scripts simulating a situation in which some users are logging on to your application, while others are retrieving the data and performing data modifications. The following are some tools worth considering for load testing.

Apache Benchmark

Apache Benchmark (*http://bit.ly/apacheparam*) is a simple-to-use command-line tool. For example, with the command ab -n 10 -c 10 -t 60 http://savesickchild.org:8080/ssc_extjs/, Apache Benchmark will open 10 concurrent connections with the server and will send 10 requests via each connection to simulate 10 visitors working with your web application for 60 seconds. The number of concurrent connections is the actual number of concurrent users. You can find an Apache Benchmark sample report in Example 7-1.

Example 7-1. A sample Apache Benchmark report

```
This is ApacheBench, Version 2.3 <$Revision: 655654 $>
Copyright 1996 Adam Twiss, Zeus Technology Ltd, http://www.zeustech.net/
Licensed to The Apache Software Foundation, http://www.apache.org/
Server Software:      GlassFish
Server Hostname:      savesickchild.org
Server Port:      8080
Document Path:    /ssc_extjs/
Document Length:     306 bytes
Concurrency Level:   10
Time taken for tests:    60.003 seconds
Complete requests:   17526
Failed requests:     0
```

```
Total transferred:   11988468 bytes
HTML transferred:    5363262 bytes
Requests per second:    292086.73
Transfer rate:  199798.72 kb/s received
Connnection Times (ms)
          min avg max
Connect:    10  13  1305
Processing: 11  14  12
Total:      21  27  1317
```

jMeter

Apache JMeter (*http://jmeter.apache.org*) is a tool with a graphical user interface (see Figure 7-1). You can use it to simulate heavy load on a server, a network, or an object to test its strength or to analyze overall performance under different load types. You can find more about testing web applications by using JMeter in the official documentation (*http://bit.ly/1pAIMbc*).

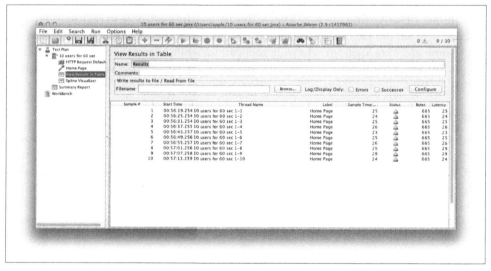

Figure 7-1. JMeter test results output example

PhantomJS

Refer to "What Is PhantomJS and SlimerJS?" on page 256 to familiarize yourself with PhantomJS (*http://phantomjs.org*). The slide deck titled "Browser Performance metering with PhantomJS" (*http://bit.ly/1vsVeK5*) is yet another good resource for seeing how you can use PhantomJS for performance testing.

Test-Driven Development

The methodology known as *test-driven development (TDD)* substantially changes the way traditional software development is done. This methodology wants you to write tests *even before* writing the application code. Instead of just using testing to verify your work *after it's done*, TDD moves testing into the earlier application design phase. You should use these tests to clarify your ideas about what you are about to program. Here is the fundamental mantra of TDD:

1. Write a test and make it fail.
2. Make the test pass.
3. Refactor.
4. Repeat.

This technique is also referred to as red-green-refactor because IDEs and test runners use red to indicate failed tests and green to indicate those that pass.

When you are about to start programming a class with business logic, ask yourself, "How can I ensure that this function works as expected?" After you know the answer, write a test JavaScript class that calls this function *to assert* that the business logic gives the expected result.

An *assertion* is a true-false statement that represents what a programmer assumes about program state. For example, `customerID >0` is an assertion. According to Martin Fowler (*http://bit.ly/UA6xDb*), assertion is a section of code that assumes something about the state of the program. Failure of an assertion results in test failure.

Run your test, and it will immediately fail because no application code is written yet! Only after the test is written, start programming the business logic of your application.

You should write the simplest possible piece of code to make the test pass. Don't try to find a generic solution at this step. For example, if you want to test a calculator that needs to return 4 as result of 2 + 2, write code that simply returns 4. Don't worry about the performance or optimization at this point. Just make the test pass. After you write it, you can refactor your application code to make it more efficient. Now you might want to introduce a real algorithm for implementing the application logic without worrying about breaking the contract with other components of your application.

A failed unit test indicates that your code change introduces *regression*, which is a new bug in previously working software. Automated testing and well-written test cases can reduce the likelihood of regression in your code.

TDD allows you to receive feedback from your code almost immediately. It's better to find that something is broken during development rather than in an application deployed in production.

Learn by heart the Golden Rule of TDD:

Never write new functionality without a failing test.

In addition to business logic, web applications should be tested for proper rendering of UI components, changing view states, dispatching, and handling events.

With any testing framework, your tests will follow the same basic pattern. First, you need to set up the test environment. Second, you run the production code and check that it works as it is supposed to. Finally, you need to clean up after the test runs—remove everything that your program has created during setup of the environment.

This pattern for authoring unit tests is called *arrange-act-assert-reset* (AAAR (*http:// bit.ly/TJiWUI*)).

- In the *Arrange* phase, you set up the unit of work to test. For example, create Java-Script objects and prepare dependencies.
- In the *Act* phase, you exercise the unit under test and capture the resulting state. You execute your production code in a unit-test context.
- In the *Assert* phase, you verify the behavior through assertions.
- In the *Reset* phase, you reset the environment to the initial state. For example, erase the DOM elements created in the Arrange phase. Most of the frameworks provide a "teardown" function that would be invoked after the test is done.

Later in this chapter, you'll see how different frameworks implement the *AAAR* pattern.

In next sections, we will dive into testing frameworks for JavaScript.

Implementing TDD by Using QUnit

We'll start our journey to JavaScript testing frameworks with QUnit (*http:// qunitjs.com*), which was originally developed by John Resig (*http://ejohn.org/about*) as part of jQuery. QUnit now runs completely as a standalone and doesn't have any jQuery dependencies. Although it's still being used by the jQuery project itself for testing jQuery, jQuery UI, and jQuery Mobile code, QUnit can be used to test any generic JavaScript code.

Setting up Grunt with QUnit

In this section, you're going learn how to automatically run QUnit tests using Grunt. Let's set up our project by adding the QUnit framework and test file. Begin by downloading the latest version by using Bower, as shown in Example 7-2.

Example 7-2. Installing QUnit with Bower

```
bower install qunit
```

You need to get only two files: *qunit.js* and *qunit.css*, as shown in Figure 7-2.

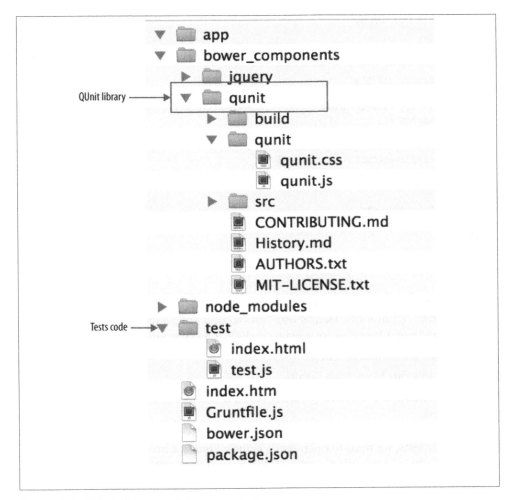

Figure 7-2. QUnit framework in our project

The code fragment shown in Example 7-3 demonstrates a simple test function.

Example 7-3. Our first QUnit test

```
'use strict';
test('my first qunit test', function() {
```

```
      ok(2 + 2 === 4, 'Passed!');
});
```

You'll also need a test runner for the test setup. A test runner is an HTML file that contains links to a QUnit framework JavaScript file, as shown in Example 7-4.

Example 7-4. A test runner

```
<!DOCTYPE html>
<html>
<head>
    <meta charset="utf-8">
    <title>Test Suite</title>
    <link rel="stylesheet" href="../bower_components/qunit/qunit/qunit.css"
     media="screen">
    <script src="../bower_components/qunit/qunit/qunit.js"></script>
    <script src="../bower_components/jquery/dist/jquery.min.js"
     type="text/javascript"></script> ❶
    <script src="test/tests.js" type="text/javascript" charset="utf-8"></script> ❷
</head>
<body>
<div id="qunit"></div>❸
<div id="qunit-fixture">
    ❹
</div>
</body>
</html>
```

❶ In this section, we continue working on the jQuery-based version of the Save The Child application. Hence, our "production environment" depends on the availability of jQuery, so we need to include jQuery in the test runner.

❷ Test files are included, too.

❸ QUnit fills this block with results.

❹ Any HTML you want to be present in each test is placed here. It will be reset for each test.

To run all our tests, we need to open *qunit-runner.html* in a browser. (See Figure 7-3.) Example 7-5 shows a sample Grunt task for executing the QUnit tests by using the provided HTML runner.

Example 7-5. Grunt config for QUnit test runner

```
module.exports = function(grunt) {
    'use strict';
    grunt.initConfig({
        qunit: {
            all: ['test/qunit-runner.html']
        }
    });
```

```
    grunt.registerTask('test', 'qunit');
    grunt.loadNpmTasks('grunt-contrib-qunit');    ❶
};
```

❶   Grunt loads the task from the local npm repository. To install this task in the
      node_modules directory, use the command npm install grunt-contrib-
      qunit.

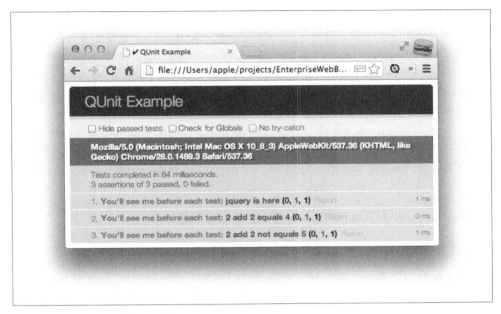

Figure 7-3. Test results in a browser

Now let's briefly review QUnit API components. Example 7-6 shows a typical QUnit
script.

Example 7-6. A sample QUnit test

```
(function($) {
    module('SaveSickChild: login component test', {    ❶
        setup: function() {    ❷
            // test setup code goes here
        },
        teardown: function() {    ❸
            // test cleanup code goes here
        }
    });
    test('jquery is here', function() {    ❹
        ok($, "yes, it's here");
    });
```

```
    test("2 add 2 equals 4", function() {
        ok(2 + 2 === 4, "Passed!");     ❺
    });
    test('2 add 2 not equals 5', function() {
        notEqual(2 + 2, 5, "failed");     ❻
    });
}(jQuery)); // ❼
```

❶   A module function allows you to combine related tests as a group.

❷   Here, we can run the Arrange phase. A setup function is called before each test.

❸   A teardown function is called after each test, respectively. This is our Reset phase.

❹   You need to place the code of your test in a corresponding test function.

❺   Typically, you need to use assertions to make sure the code being tested gives
     expected results. The function ok (*http://bit.ly/1r5x3Sn*) examines the first
     argument to be true.

❻   A pair of functions, equal and notEqual, check for the equivalence of the first
     and second arguments, which could be expressions, as well.

❼   A code of the test is wrapped in IIFE and passes the jQuery object as a $ variable.

You can find more details about QUnit in its product documentation (*http://
api.qunitjs.com*) and QUnit Cookbook (*http://bit.ly/1vnELF6*).

Behavior-Driven Development with Jasmine

The idea behind *behavior-driven development* (BDD) is to use the natural language
constructs to describe what you think your code should be doing, or more specifically,
what your functions should be returning.

Similarly to unit tests, with BDD you write short specifications that test one feature at
a time. Specifications should be sentences. For example, "Calculator adds two positive
numbers." Such sentences will help you easily identify the failed test by simply reading
this sentence in the resulting report.

Now we'll demonstrate this concept using Jasmine—the BDD framework for JavaScript.
Jasmine provides a nice way to group, execute, and report JavaScript unit tests.

Setting up Grunt with Jasmine

Now let's learn how to execute a Jasmine specification with Grunt. We cover Jasmine
basics in the next section, but for the moment think of Jasmine as a piece of code that
should be executed by Grunt.

Let's begin by downloading the latest version of Jasmine by using Bower:

```
bower install jasmine
```

Unzip *jasmine-standalone-2.0.0.zip* in the *dist* directory. Jasmine comes with an example spec (*spec* folder) and an HTML test runner, *SpecRunner.html*. Let's open this file in a browser, as shown in Figure 7-4.

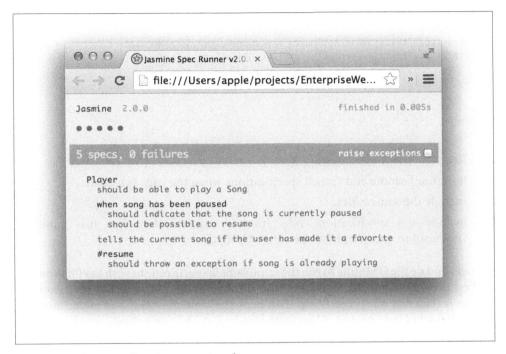

Figure 7-4. Running Jasmine specs in a browser

SpecRunner.html, shown in Example 7-7, is structured similarly to the QUnit HTML runner. You can run specifications by opening the runner file in a browser.

Example 7-7. The test runner SpecRunner.html

```
<!DOCTYPE HTML>
<html>
<head>
  <meta http-equiv="Content-Type" content="text/html; charset=UTF-8">
  <title>Jasmine Spec Runner v2.0.0</title>

  <link rel="shortcut icon" type="image/png"
   href="lib/jasmine-2.0.0/jasmine_favicon.png">
  <link rel="stylesheet" type="text/css" href="lib/jasmine-2.0.0/jasmine.css">

  <script type="text/javascript" src="lib/jasmine-2.0.0/jasmine.js"></script> ❶
  <script type="text/javascript" src="lib/jasmine-2.0.0/jasmine-html.js">
  </script>
```

```
<script type="text/javascript" src="lib/jasmine-2.0.0/boot.js"></script> ❷

❸
<script type="text/javascript" src="src/Player.js"></script>
<script type="text/javascript" src="src/Song.js"></script>

❹
<script type="text/javascript" src="spec/SpecHelper.js"></script>
<script type="text/javascript" src="spec/PlayerSpec.js"></script>

</head>

<body>
</body>
</html>
```

❶   Required Jasmine framework library.

❷   Initialize Jasmine and run all specifications when the page is loaded.

❸   Include the source files.

❹   Include the specification code. It's not required, but files that contain specification code can have the suffix *Spec.js*.

Now let's update the Gruntfile to run the same sample specifications with the PhantomJS headless browser. Copy the content of the *src* folder of your Jasmine distribution into the *app/js* folder of our project, and then copy the content of the *spec* folder into the *test/spec* folder of your project. Also create a folder *test/lib/jasmine* and copy the content of the Jasmine distribution *lib* folder there. (See Figure 7-5.)

Now you need to edit *Gruntfile_jasmine.js* to activate Jasmine support, as shown in Example 7-8.

Example 7-8. Gruntfile_jasmine.js with Jasmine running support

```
module.exports = function(grunt) {
    'use strict';

    grunt.initConfig({
        jasmine: {    ❶
            src: ['app/Player.js', 'app/Song.js'],    ❷
            options: {
                specs: 'test/spec/PlayerSpec.js',    ❸
                helpers: 'test/spec/SpecHelper.js'    ❹
            }
        }
    });

    // Alias the `test` task
    grunt.registerTask('test', 'jasmine');
    // loading jasmine grunt module
```

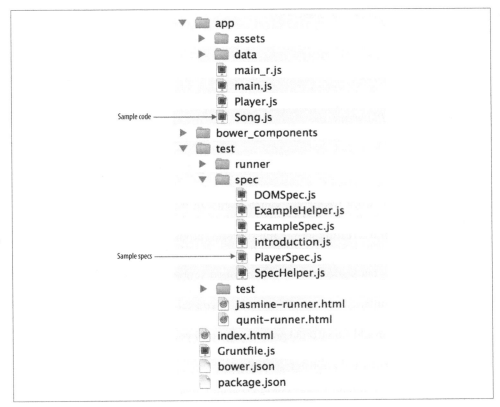

Figure 7-5. Jasmine specifications in our project

```
    grunt.loadNpmTasks('grunt-contrib-jasmine');   ❺
};
```

❶ Configuring the Jasmine task.

❷ Specifying the location of the source files.

❸ Specifying the location of Jasmine specs.

❹ Specifying the location of Jasmine helpers (Jasmine helpers are covered later in this chapter).

❺ Grunt loads the task from the local npm repository. To install this task in the *node_modules* directory, use the command npm install grunt-contrib-jasmine.

To execute tests, run the command grunt --gruntfile Gruntfile_jasmine.js jasmine, and you should see something like this:

```
Running "jasmine:src" (jasmine) task
Testing jasmine specs via phantom
.....
5 specs in 0.003s.
>> 0 failures

Done, without errors.
```

In this example, Grunt successfully executes the tests with PhantomJS of all five specifications defined in *PlayerSpec.js*.

What Is Continuous Integration?

Continuous integration (CI) is a software development practice whereby members of a team integrate their work frequently, which results in multiple integrations per day. Introduced by Martin Fowler and Matthew Foemmel, the theory of CI (*http://bit.ly/ 1e7nG9j*) recommends creating scripts and running automated builds (including tests) of your application at least once a day. This allows you to identify issues in the code early.

The authors of this book successfully use the open source framework called Jenkins (*http://jenkins-ci.org*), shown in Figure 7-6, for establishing a continuous build process. (There are other similar CI servers.) With Jenkins, you can have scripts that run either at a specified time interval or on each source code repository check-in of the new code. You may also force an additional build process whenever you like. The Grunt command-line tool should be installed and be available on a CI machine to allow the Jenkins server to invoke Grunt scripts and publish test results.

We use it to ensure continuous builds of internal and open source projects.

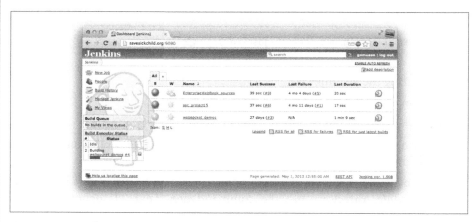

Figure 7-6. Jenkins CI server running at the savesickchild.org website and used to build the sample applications for this book

In the next section, you will learn how write your own specifications.

Exploring Jasmine basics

After we've set up the tools for running tests, let's begin developing tests and learn the Jasmine framework constructs. Every specification file has a set of *suites* defined in the `describe` function. Example 7-9 shows a specification file that describes two test suites.

Example 7-9. ExampleSpec.js

```
describe("My function under test should", function() {    ❶
    it("return on", function() {    ❷
        // place specification code here
        //
    });
    describe("another suite", function() {    ❸
        it("spec1", function() {

        });
    });
    it("my another spec", function() {    ❹
        var truth = true;
        expect(truth).toBeTruthy();
    });
    it("2+2 = 4", function() {
        expect(2 + 2).toEqual(4);    ❺
    });
});
```

❶ The function `describe()` accepts two parameters: the name of the test suite and the callback function. The function is a block of code that implements the suite. If for some reason you would like to skip the suite's execution, you can use the method `xdescribe()` and a whole suite will be excluded until you rename it back to `describe()`.

❷ The function `it()` also accepts similar parameters—the name of the test specification, and the function that implements this specification. As with suites, Jasmine has a corresponding `xit` method to exclude the specification from execution.

❸ Each suite can have any number of nested suites.

❹ Each suite can have any number of specifications.

❺ The code checks whether `2 + 2` equals 4. We used the function `toEqual()`, which is a *matcher*. Define expectations with the function `expect()`, which takes a value, called the *actual*. It's chained with a matcher function, which takes the expected value (in our case, it's 4) and checks whether it satisfies the criterion defined in the matcher.

Various flavors of matchers are shipped with the Jasmine framework, and we're going to review a couple of the frequently used matcher's functions:

Equality
> Function `toEqual()` check whether two things are equal.

True or False?
> Functions `toBeTruthy()` and `toBeFalsy()` checks whether something is true or false, respectively.

Identity
> Function `toBe()` checks whether two things are *the same object*.

Nullness
> Function `toBeNull()` checks whether something is `null`.

Is Element Present
> Function `toContain()` checks whether an actual value is an element of an array:
>
> ```
> expect(["James Bond", "Austin Powers", "Jack Reacher", "Duck"])
>         .toContain("Duck");
> ```

Negate Other Matchers
> This function is used to reverse matchers to ensure that they aren't `true`. To do that, simply prefix matchers with `.not`:
>
> ```
> expect(["James Bond", "Austin Powers", "Jack Reacher"])
>     .not.toContain("Duck");
> ```

Here, we've listed only some of the existing matchers. You can find the complete documentation with code examples at the official Jasmine website (*http://bit.ly/1mzA3if*) and wiki (*http://bit.ly/100yWTt*).

> A large set of jQuery-specific matchers are available at link:https://github.com/velesin/jasmine-jquery.

Specification setup

The Jasmine framework has an API to arrange your specification (based on the "Test-Driven Development" concept). It includes two methods, `beforeEach()` and `afterEach()`, which allow you to execute code before and after each spec, respectively. It's useful for instantiation of the shared objects or cleaning up after the tests complete. If you need to fulfill your test with some common dependencies or set up the environment, just place code inside the `beforeEach()` method. Such dependencies and environments are known as *fixtures*. Example 7-10 includes a `beforeEach` function that prepares a fixture.

What Is a Fixture?

A test *fixture* refers to the fixed state used as a baseline for running tests. The main purpose of a test fixture is to ensure that there is a well-known and fixed environment in which tests are run so that results are repeatable. Sometimes a fixture is referred to as a *test context*.

Example 7-10. Specification setup with beforeEach

```
(function($) {
    describe("DOM manipulation spec", function() {
        var usernameInput;
        var passwordInput;
        beforeEach(function() {      ❶
            usernameInput = document.createElement("input");      ❷
            usernameInput.setAttribute("type", "text");
            usernameInput.setAttribute("id", "username");
            usernameInput.setAttribute("name", "username");
            usernameInput.setAttribute("placeholder", "username");
            usernameInput.setAttribute("autocomplete", "off");

            passwordInput = document.createElement("input");
            passwordInput.setAttribute("type", "text");
            passwordInput.setAttribute("id", "password");
            passwordInput.setAttribute("name", "password");
            passwordInput.setAttribute("placeholder", "password");
            passwordInput.setAttribute("autocomplete", "off");
        });

        afterEach(function() {      ❸

        });

        it("jquey should be present", function() {
            expect($).not.toBeNull();
        });
        it("inputs should exist", function() {
            expect(usernameInput.id).toBe("username");
            expect(passwordInput.id).toBe("password");
        });
        it("should not allow login with empty username and password and return code
            equals 0", function() {
            var result = ssc.login(usernameInput, passwordInput);      ❹
            expect(result).toBe(0);
        });
        it("should allow login with user admin and password 1234 and return code
```

```
        equals 1", function() {
            usernameInput.value = "admin";    ❺
            passwordInput.value = "1234";
            var result = ssc.login(usernameInput, passwordInput);
            expect(result).toBe(1);
        });
    });
})(jQuery);
```

❶   This method will be called before each specification.

❷   In the `beforeEach()` method, we create two input fields. These two inputs will
    be available in all specifications of this suite.

❸   You can place additional cleanup code inside the `afterEach()` function.

❹   A `beforeEach()` function helps implement the *Don't Repeat Yourself* principle
    in our tests. You don't need to create the dependency elements inside each
    specification manually.

❺   You can change defaults inside each specification without worrying about
    affecting other specifications. Your test environment will be reset for each
    specification.

Custom matchers

The Jasmine framework is easily extensible, and it allows you to define your own
matchers if for some reason you're unable to find the appropriate matchers in the Jasmine distribution. In such cases, you'd need to write a custom matcher. Example 7-11
shows a sample custom matcher that checks whether a string contains the name of a
"secret agent" from the defined list of agents.

Example 7-11. Custom toBeSecretAgent matcher

```
beforeEach(function() {
    'use strict';
    var customMatcher = {
        toBeSecretAgent: function() {
            return {
                compare: function(actual, expected) {  ❶
                    if (expected === undefined) {
                        expected = '';
                    }
                    var result = {};  ❷
                    var agentList = [
                        'James Bond',
                        'Ethan Hunt',
                        'Jason Bourne',
                        'Aaron Cross',
                        'Jack Reacher'
                    ];
                    result.pass = agentList.indexOf(actual) !== -1;  ❸
```

```
                    if (result.pass) {     ❹
                        result.message = actual + ' is a super agent';     ❺
                    } else {
                        result.message = actual + ' is not a secret agent';
                    }
                    return result;
                }
            };
        }
    };

    jasmine.addMatchers(customMatcher);
});
```

❶   We need to implement the function `compare` that accepts two parameters from the `expect` call: actual and expected values.

❷   The function `compare` should return the `result` object.

❸   This function checks whether `agentsList` contains the actual value.

❹   The `pass` property of the `result` object indicates success or failure of matcher execution.

❺   We can customize an error message (a `message` property the of `result` object) if the test fails.

The invocation of this helper can look like this:

```
it("part of super agents", function () {
    expect("James Bond").toBeSecretAgent();          ❶
    expect("Jason Bourne").toBeSecretAgent();
    expect("Austin Powers").not.toBeSecretAgent();   ❷
    expect("Austin Powers").toBeSecretAgent();       ❸
});
```

❶   Calling the custom matcher.

❷   Custom matchers could be used together with the `.not` modifier.

❸   This expectation will fail because *Austin Powers* is not in the list of secret agents.

The following custom failure message displays on the console.

```
grunt --gruntfile Gruntfile_jasmine.js test
Running "jasmine:src" (jasmine) task
Testing jasmine specs via PhantomJS
 My function under test should
   ✓ return on
   another suite
     ✓ spec1
   ✓ my another spec
   ✓ 2+2 = 4
```

```
    X part of super agents
        Austin Powers is not a secret agent (1)

5 specs in 0.01s.
>> 1 failures
Warning: Task "jasmine:src" failed. Use --force to continue.

Aborted due to warnings.
```

"Austin Powers is not a secret agent (1)" is a custom failure message.

Spies

Test *spies* are objects that replace the actual functions with the code to record information about the function's usage through the systems being tested. Spies are useful when
determining a function's success is not easily accomplished by inspecting its return value
or changes to the state of objects with which it interacts.

Consider the login functionality shown in Example 7-12. A showAuthorizedSec
tion() function will be invoked within the login function after the user enters the
correct username and password. We need to test that the invocation of showAuthori
zedSection() is happening in this sequence.

Example 7-12. Production code of the login function

```
var ssc = {};
(function() {
    'use strict';
    ssc.showAuthorizedSection = function() {
        console.log("showAuthorizedSection");
    };
    ssc.login = function(usernameInput, passwordInput) {
        // username and password check logic is omitted
        this.showAuthorizedSection();
    };
})();
```

And here is how we can test it using Jasmine's spies:

```
describe("login module", function() {
    it("showAuthorizedSection has been called", function() {
        spyOn(ssc, "showAuthorizedSection"); ❶
        ssc.login("admin", "1234"); ❷
        expect(ssc.showAuthorizedSection).toHaveBeenCalled(); ❸
    });
});
```

❶ The spyOn function will replace the showAuthorizedSection() function with
   the corresponding spy.

❷ The `showAuthorizedSection()` function will be invoked within the `login()` function in case of successful login.

❸ The assertion `toHaveBeenCalled()` would be not possible without a spy.

Multibrowser Testing

The previous section was about executing your test and specification in headless mode by using Grunt and PhantomJS, which is useful for running tests in CI environments. Although PhantomJS uses the WebKit rendering engine, some browsers don't use WebKit. It's obvious that running tests manually in each browser is tedious and not productive. To automate testing in all web browsers, you can use the Testem runner. Testem executes your tests, analyzes their output, and then prints the results on the console. In this section, you'll learn how to install and configure Testem to run Jasmine tests.

Installation

Testem uses Node.js APIs and can be installed with npm:

```
npm: install testem -g
```

Testem configuration file

Testem will just pick any JavaScript file in your project directory. If Testem can identify any test among the *.js* files, it will run it. But Testem tasks can be customized by using a configuration file

You can configure Testem to specify which files should be included in testing. Testem starts by trying to find the configuration file *testem.json* in the project directory. A sample *testem.json* file is shown in Example 7-13.

Example 7-13. A Testem configuration file

```
{
    "framework": "jasmine2",        ❶
    "src_files": [                  ❷
        "ext/ext-all.js",
        "test.js"
    ]
}
```

❶ The `framework` directive is used to specify the test framework. Testem supports QUnit, Jasmine, and many more frameworks. You can find a full list of supported frameworks on the Testem GitHub page (*http://bit.ly/1mNbCTe*).

❷ The list of test and production code source files.

Running tests

Testem supports two running modes: test-driven development mode (*tdd-mode*) and continuous integration (*ci-mode*). (For more about continuous integration, see the note on CI). In tdd-mode, shown in Figure 7-7, Testem starts the development server.

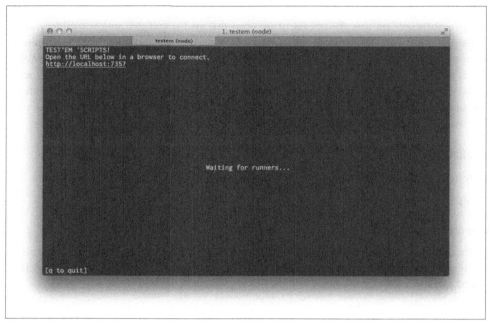

Figure 7-7. Testem tdd-mode

In tdd-mode, Testem doesn't spawn any browser automatically. On the contrary, you'd need to open a URL in the browser you want run a test against, to connect it to the Testem server. From this point, Testem executes tests in all connected browsers. In Figure 7-8, you can see we added different browsers, including a mobile version of Safari (running on an iOS simulator).

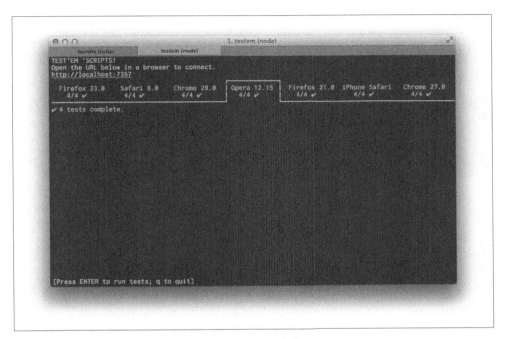

Figure 7-8. Testem is running the tests on multiple browsers

Because the Testem server itself is an HTTP server, you can connect remote browsers to it as well. For example, Figure 7-9 shows Internet Explorer 10 running on a Windows 7 virtual machine connected to the Testem server.

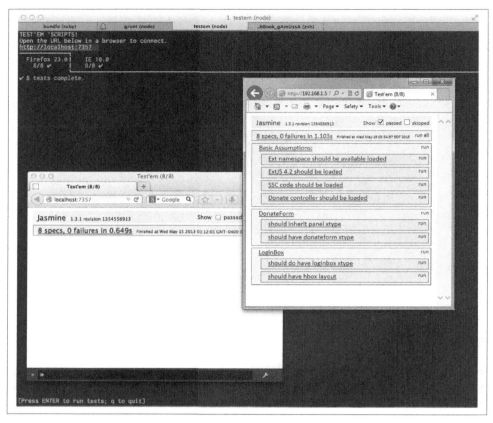

Figure 7-9. Using Testem to test code on remote Internet Explorer 10

You can combine running the tests with the Testem runner with the previously introduced Grunt tool. Figure 7-10 shows two tests in parallel: Testem runs tests on the real browsers, and Grunt runs tests on the headless PhantomJS.

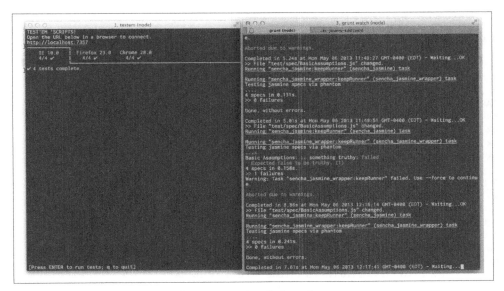

Figure 7-10. Using Testem and grunt watch side by side

Testem supports live reloading mode. This means that Testem will watch the filesystem for changes and will execute tests in all connected browsers automatically. You can force a test to run by switching to the console and pressing the Enter key.

In CI mode, Testem examines the system for all available browsers and executes tests on them. You can get a list of the browsers that Testem can use to run tests by using the `testem launchers` command. The following shows the sample output after running this command:

```
# testem launchers
Have 5 launchers available; auto-launch info displayed on the right.

Launcher      Type          CI  Dev
------------  ------------  --  ---
Chrome        browser       ✔
Firefox       browser       ✔
Safari        browser       ✔
Opera         browser       ✔
PhantomJS     browser       ✔
```

Now you can run our test simultaneously in all browsers installed in your computer—Google Chrome, Safari, Firefox, Opera, and PhantomJS—with one command:

```
testem ci
```

Sample output of the `testem ci` command is shown in Example 7-14.

Example 7-14. Output of the testem ci command

```
# Launching Chrome      # ❶
#

# Launching Firefox     # ❷
# ....
TAP version 13
ok 1 - Firefox Basic Assumptions:  Ext namespace should be available loaded.
ok 2 - Firefox Basic Assumptions:  ExtJS 4.2 should be loaded.
ok 3 - Firefox Basic Assumptions:  SSC code should be loaded.
ok 4 - Firefox Basic Assumptions:  something truthy.

# Launching Safari      # ❸
#

# Launching Opera       # ❹
# ....
ok 5 - Opera Basic Assumptions:  Ext namespace should be available loaded.
ok 6 - Opera Basic Assumptions:  ExtJS 4.2 should be loaded.
ok 7 - Opera Basic Assumptions:  SSC code should be loaded.
ok 8 - Opera Basic Assumptions:  something truthy.

# Launching PhantomJS     # ❺
#

1..8
# tests 8
# pass  8

# ok
....
```

❶   The tests are run on Chrome…

❷   … Firefox

❸   … Safari

❹   … Opera

❺   … and on headless WebKit—PhantomJS

Testem uses TAP (*http://bit.ly/V28HvG*) format to report test results.

Testing the DOM

As is discussed in Chapter 1, the Document Object Model (DOM) is a standard browser API that allows a developer to access and manipulate page elements. Often, your Java-Script code needs to access and manipulate the HTML page elements in some way. Testing the DOM is a crucial part of testing your client-side JavaScript. By design, the DOM standard defines a browser-agnostic API. But in the real world, if you want to make sure that your code works in a particular browser, you need to run the test inside this browser.

Earlier in this chapter, we introduced the Jasmine method `beforeEach()`, which is the right place for setting all required DOM elements and making them available in the specifications. Example 7-15 illustrates the programmatic creation of the required DOM element `<input>`.

Example 7-15. Using jQuery APIs to create DOM elements before running the spec

```
describe("spec", function() {
    var usernameInput;
    beforeEach(function() { ❶
        usernameInput = $(document.createElement("input")).attr({ ❷
            type: 'text',
            id: 'username',
            name: 'username'
        })[0];
    });
});
```

❶   Inside the `beforeEach()` method, we use the API to manipulate the DOM programmatically. Also, if you're using an HTML test runner, you can add the fixture by using HTML tags. But we don't recommend this approach, because soon you will find that the test runner will become unmaintainable and clogged with tons of fixture HTML code.

❷   Create an `<input>` element by using jQuery APIs, which will turn into the following HTML:

```
<input type="text" id="password" name="password" placeholder="password"
    autocomplete="off">
```

The jQuery selectors API is more convenient for working with the DOM than a standard JavaScript DOM API. But in future examples, we will use the jasmine-fixture (*http://bit.ly/1sRcgDK*) library for easier setup of the DOM fixture. Jasmine-fixture uses syntax that is similar to that of jQuery selectors for injecting HTML fixtures. With this library, you will significantly decrease the amount of repetitive code while creating the fixtures.

Example 7-16 shows how the example from the previous code snippet looks with the jasmine-fixture library.

Example 7-16. Using jasmine-fixture to set up the DOM before spec run

```
describe("spec", function() {
    var usernameInput;
    beforeEach(function() {
        usernameInput =
                affix('input[id="username"][type="text"][name="username]')[0]; ❶
    });
```

```
        it("should not allow login with empty username and password and return code
            equals 0", function() {
                var result = ssc.login(usernameInput, passwordInput); ❷
                expect(result).toBe(0);
        });
});
```

❶ By using the `affix()` function provided by the *jasmine-fixture* library and
    expressiveness of CSS selectors, we can easily set up required DOM elements.
    You can find more examples of possible selectors at the documentation page
    (*http://bit.ly/TJjeLl*) of jasmine-fixture.

❷ When all requirements for our production code (`login()` function) are satisfied,
    we can run it in the context of a test and assert the results.

As you can see, testing the DOM manipulation code is much like any other type of unit
testing. You need to prepare a fixture (a.k.a., the testing context), run the production
code, and assert the results.

Building Save The Child with TDD

We assume that you've read Chapter 6, and in this section you'll apply your newly
acquired Ext JS skills. As a reminder, the Ext JS framework encourages using MVC
architecture. The separation of responsibilities between models, views, and controllers
makes an Ext JS application a perfect candidate for unit testing. In this section you'll
learn how to test the Ext JS version of the Save The Child application from Chapter 6.

Harnessing the ExtJS Application

Let's create a skeleton application that can provide a familiar environment for our classes
that should be tested (see Example 7-17).

Example 7-17. An HTML runner for Jasmine and Ext JS application

```
<!doctype html>
<html lang="en">
<head>
    <meta charset="UTF-8">
    <title id="page-title">ExtJS Jasmine Tester</title>
    <link rel="stylesheet" type="text/css"
     href="test/bower_components/jasmine/lib/jasmine-core/jasmine.css"/>
    <script type="text/javascript" src=ext/ext-all.js></script>        ❶

    <script type="text/javascript"
     src="test/bower_components/jasmine/lib/jasmine-core/jasmine.js"></script>      ❷
    <script type="text/javascript"
     src="test/bower_components/jasmine/lib/jasmine-core/jasmine-html.js"></script>
```

```
<script type="text/javascript"
 src="test/bower_components/jasmine/lib/jasmine-core/boot.js"></script>

<script type="text/javascript"
 src="test/bower_components/jasmine-fixture/dist/jasmine-fixture.min.js">
</script>

<script type="text/javascript" src="test.js"></script>    ❸
```
```
</head>
<body>

</body>
</html>
```

❶   Adding Ext JS framework dependencies.

❷   Adding the Jasmine framework dependencies.

❸   This is our skeleton Ext JS application that will set up a "friendly" environment
     for components under the test. You can see the content of *test.js* in Example 7-18.

Example 7-18. An Ext JS testing endpoint

```
Ext.Loader.setConfig({
    disableCaching: false,
    enabled: true,
    paths: {
        Test: 'test',    ❶
        SSC: 'app'    ❷
    }
});

var application = null;

Ext.onReady(function() {
    application = Ext.create('Ext.app.Application', {
        name: 'SSC',    ❸
        requires: [
            'Test.spec.AllSpecs'    ❹
        ],
        controllers: [
            'Donate'    ❺
        ],
        launch: function() {
            Ext.create('Test.spec.AllSpecs');
        }
    });
});
```

❶   Ext JS loader needs to know the location of the testing classes...

❷   … and about the location of production code.

❸   Create a skeleton application in the namespace of the production code to provide the execution environment.

❹   The `AllSpec` class will be requesting loading of the rest of the specs. We show the code for the `AllSpec` class in Example 7-19.

❺   The skeleton application will test the controllers from the production application code.

By placing our spec names in a `requires` config property, we delegate the loading of specified specs to the Ext JS loader during a fixture application startup.

Example 7-19. The AllSpec class

```
Ext.define('Test.spec.AllSpecs', {
    requires: [          ❶
        'Test.spec.BasicAssumptions'
    ]
});
```

❶   The `requires` property includes an array of Jasmine suites. All further tests will be added to this array. Ext JS will be responsible for loading and instantiating all test classes.

Example 7-20 shows how our typical test suite will look.

Example 7-20. A BasicAssumptions class

```
Ext.define('Test.spec.BasicAssumptions', {}, function() {      ❶
    describe("Basic Assumptions: ", function() {               ❷
        it("Ext namespace should be available loaded", function() {
            expect(Ext).toBeDefined();
        });
        it("SSC code should be loaded", function() {
            expect(SSC).toBeDefined();
        });
    });
});
```

❶   Wrap the Jasmine suite into an Ext JS class.

❷   The rest of the code is similar to the Jasmine code sample shown earlier in this chapter.

After setting up the testing harness for the Save The Child application, we will suggest a testing strategy for Ext JS applications. Let's begin by testing the models and controllers, followed by testing the views.

Testing the Models

The *SaveSickChild.org* home page displays information about fundraising campaigns by using chart and table views backed by a collection of `Campaign` models. A `Campaign` model should have three properties: `title`, `description`, and `location`. The `title` property of the model should have a default value: `Default Campaign Title`. The `location` property of the model is a required field.

In the spirit of TDD, let's write a specification that will meet the requirements described, as shown in Example 7-21.

Example 7-21. CampaignModelAssumptions specification

```
Ext.define('Test.spec.CampaignModelAssumptions', {}, function() {
    'use strict';
    beforeEach(function() {

    });

    afterEach(function() {
        Ext.data.Model.cache = {};     ❶
    });

    describe('SSC.model.Campaign model', function() {
        it('exists', function() {     ❷
            var model = Ext.create('SSC.model.Campaign', {});
            expect(model.$className).toEqual('SSC.model.Campaign');
        });
        it('has properties', function() {     ❸
            var model = Ext.create('SSC.model.Campaign', {
                title: 'Donors meeting',
                description: 'Donors meeting agenda',
                location: 'New York City'
            });
            expect(model.get('title')).toEqual('Donors meeting');
            expect(model.get('description')).toEqual('Donors meeting agenda');
            expect(model.get('location')).toEqual('New York City');
        });
        it('property title has default values', function() {     ❹
            var model = Ext.create('SSC.model.Campaign');
            expect(model.get('title')).toEqual('Default Campaign Title');
        });
        it('requires campaign location', function() {     ❺
            var model = Ext.create('SSC.model.Campaign');
            var validationResult = model.validate();
            expect(validationResult.isValid()).toBeFalsy();
        });
    });

});
```

❶ By default, `Ext.data.Model` caches every model created by the application in a global in-memory array. We need to clean up the Ext JS model cache after each test run.

❷ Instantiate the `Campaign` model class to check that it exists.

❸ We need to check whether the model has all required properties.

❹ The property `title` has a default value.

❺ Validation will fail on the empty `location` property:

```
Ext.define('SSC.model.Campaign', {
    extend: 'Ext.data.Model',
    fields: [
        {
            name: 'title',
            type: 'string',
            defaultValue: 'Default Campaign Title'
        },
        {
            name: 'description',
            type: 'string'
        },
        {
            name: 'location',
            type: 'string'
        }
    ],
    validations: [
        {
            field: 'location',
            type: 'presence'
        }
    ]
});
```

Testing the Controllers

Controllers in Ext JS are classes like any others and should be tested the same way. In Example 7-22, we test the Donate Now functionality. When the user clicks the Donate Now button on the Donate panel, the controller's code should validate the user input and submit the data to the server. Because we are just testing the controller's behavior, we're not going to submit the actual data. We'll use Jasmine spies, instead.

Example 7-22. Donate controller specification

```
Ext.define("Test.spec.DonateControllerSpec", {}, function () {
    describe("Donate controller", function () {
        beforeEach(function () {
            // controller's setup code is omitted
        });
```

```
it('should exists', function () {                    ❶
    var controller = Ext.create('SSC.controller.Donate');
    expect(controller.$className).toEqual('SSC.controller.Donate');
});
describe('donateNow button', function () {
    it('calls donate on DonorInfo if form is valid', function () {
        var donorInfo = Ext.create('SSC.model.DonorInfo', {});
        var donateForm = Ext.create('SSC.view.DonateForm', {});
        var controller = Ext.create('SSC.controller.Donate');
        spyOn(donorInfo, 'donate');                    ❷
        spyOn(controller, 'getDonatePanel').and.callFake(function () { ❸
            donateForm.down = function () {
                return {
                    isValid: function () {
                        return true;
                    },
                    getValues: function () {
                        return {};
                    }
                };
            };
            return donateForm;
        });
        spyOn(controller, 'newDonorInfo').and.callFake(function () { ❹
            return donorInfo;
        });
        controller.submitDonateForm();
        expect(donorInfo.donate).toHaveBeenCalled();    ❺
    });
});
});
});
```

❶ First, you need to test whether the controller's class is available and can be instantiated.

❷ With the help of Jasmine's spyOn() function, substitute the DonorInfo model's donate() function.

❸ We're not interested in the view's interaction—only the contract should be tested. At this point, some methods can be substituted with the fake implementation to let the test pass. In this case, the specification tests the situation when the form is valid.

❹ You need to inject emulated controller dependencies. The function donate() was replaced by the spy.

❺ Finally, you can assert whether the function was called by the controller.

Example 7-23 shows what the function looks like under the test.

Example 7-23. The testable Donate controller

```
Ext.define('SSC.controller.Donate', {
    extend: 'Ext.app.Controller',
    refs: [{
            ref: 'donatePanel',
            selector: '[cls=donate-panel]'
        }
    ],
    init: function() {
        'use strict';
        this.control({
            'button[action=donate]': {
                click: this.submitDonateForm
            }
        });
    },
    newDonorInfo: function() {                    ❶
        return Ext.create('SSC.model.DonorInfo', {});
    },
    submitDonateForm: function() {
        var form = this.getDonatePanel().down('form');
        if (form.isValid()) {            ❷
            var donorInfo = this.newDonorInfo();
            Ext.iterate(form.getValues(), function(key, value) {  ❸
                donorInfo.set(key, value);
            }, this);
            donorInfo.donate();      ❹
        }
    }
});
```

❶ The factory method for creating a new instance of the SSC.model.DonorInfo class.

❷ If the form is valid, read data from the form fields…

❸ …and populate properties of corresponding objects.

❹ DonorInfo can be submitted by calling the donate() method.

Testing the Views

UI tests can be divided into two constituent parts: interaction tests and component tests. Interactions tests simulate real-world scenarios of application usage as if a user is using the application. It's better to delegate the interaction tests to functional testing tools such as Selenium or CasperJS.

Another UI testing tool is worth mentioning, especially in the context of testing Ext JS applications: Siesta (*http://bit.ly/1pEdDo5*). Siesta allows you to perform testing of the DOM and simulate user interactions. Written in JavaScript, Siesta uses unit and UI testing. There are two editions of Siesta: lite and professional.

Component tests isolate independent and reusable pieces of your application to verify their display, behavior, and contract with other components (see the section "Testing the Controllers" on page 286). Let's see how we can do that. Consider Example 7-24.

Example 7-24. Testing the view

```
Ext.define('Test.spec.ViewsAssumptions', {}, function () {
    function prepareDOM(obj) {          ❶
        Ext.DomHelper.append(Ext.getBody(), obj);
    }
    describe('DonateForm ', function () {
        var donateForm = null;          ❷
        beforeEach(function () {
            prepareDOM({tag: 'div', id: 'test-donate'});      ❸
            donateForm = Ext.create('SSC.view.DonateForm', {      ❹
                renderTo: 'test-donate'
            });
        });
        afterEach(function () {
            donateForm.destroy();          ❺
            donateForm = null;
        });
        it('should have donateform xtype', function () {
            expect(donateForm.isXType('donateform')).toEqual(true);  ❻
        });
    });
});
```

❶   A helper function for creating a fixture for DOM elements.

❷   A reusable scoped variable.

❸   Create a fixture for the div test element.

❹   Create a fresh form for every test to avoid test pollution.

❺   Destroy the form after every test so we don't pollute the environment.

❻   In this test, you need to make sure that the DonateForm component has the donateform xtype.

Setting Up the IDE for TDD

In this section, we will set up WebStorm to use the previously described tools inside this IDE. We will show how to integrate Grunt with WebStorm to run Grunt tasks from there.

Let's begin with the Grunt setup. Currently, the WebStorm IDE has no native support for the Grunt tool. Because Grunt is a command-line tool, you can use a general launching feature of the WebStorm IDE and configure it as an external tool. Open the WebStorm preferences and navigate to the External Tools section to access the external tools configuration, as shown in Figure 7-11.

Figure 7-11. The External Tools configuration window in WebStorm

Click the + button to create a new external tool configuration, and you'll see the window shown in Figure 7-12.

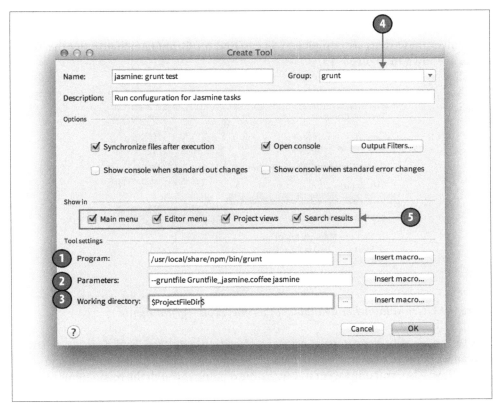

Figure 7-12. External tool configuration

To configure an external tool in WebStorm (Grunt, in this case), you need to do the following:

1. Specify the full path to the application executable.
2. Some tools require command-line parameters. In this example, we explicitly specify the task runner configuration file (with the `--gruntifle` command-line option) and the task to be executed.
3. Specify the Working Directory to run the Grunt tool. In our case, the Grunt configuration file is located in the root of our project. WebStorm allows you to use macros to avoid hardcoded paths. Most likely, you don't want to set up external tools for each new project, but to just create a universal setup. In our example, we use the `$ProjectFileDir$` macros that will be resolved as the current WebStorm project folder root.
4. WebStorm allows you to organize related tasks into logical groups.

5. You can configure how to access the external tool launcher.

When all of these steps are complete, you can find the Grunt launcher under the Tools menu, as shown in Figure 7-13.

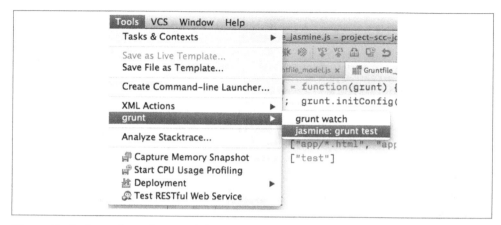

Figure 7-13. Grunt launcher available under the Tools→grunt menu

Unit tests are really important as a means of getting quick feedback from your code. You can work more efficiently if you manage to minimize context switching during your coding flow. Also, you don't want to waste time digging through the menu items of your IDE, so assigning a keyboard shortcut for launching external tools is a good idea.

Let's assign a keyboard shortcut for our newly configured external tool launcher. In WebStorm Preferences, go to the Keymap section. Use the filter to find our created launcher `jasmine: grunt test`. Specify either the Keyboard or the Mouse shortcut by double-clicking the appropriate list item, as shown in Figure 7-14.

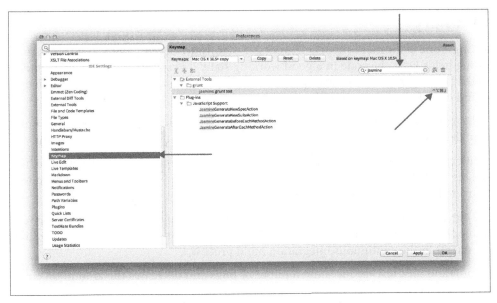

Figure 7-14. Setting up a keyboard shortcut for Grunt launcher

By pressing a combination of keys specified in the previous screen, you will be able to launch Grunt for Jasmine tests with one click of a button(s). WebStorm will redirect all the output from the Grunt tool into its Run window, as shown in Figure 7-15.

Figure 7-15. Grunt output in WebStorm

Summary

Testing is one of the most important processes of software development. Well-organized testing helps keep the code in a good working state. It's especially important in interpreted languages such as JavaScript, which has no compiler to provide a helping hand to find lots of errors in very early stages.

In this situation, static code analysis tools, such as JSHint (discussed in Chapter 5) could help identify typos and enforce best practices accepted by the JavaScript community.

In enterprise projects developed with compiled languages, people often debate whether TDD is really beneficial. With JavaScript, it's nondebatable unless you have unlimited time and budget and are ready to live with unmaintainable JavaScript.

The enterprises that have adopted test-driven development (as well as behavior-driven development) routines make the application development process safer by including test scripts in the continuous integration build process.

Automating unit tests reduces the number of bugs and decreases the amount of time developers need to spend manually testing their code. If automatically launched test scripts (unit, integration, functional, and load testing) don't reveal any issues, you can rest assured that the latest code changes did not break the application logic, and that the application performs according to SLA.

## CHAPTER 8

Upgrading HTTP to WebSocket

This chapter is about upgrading from HTTP to the more responsive HTML5 WebSocket. It begins with a brief overview of the existing legacy web networking, and then you'll learn why and how to use WebSocket.

We're going to show that the WebSocket protocol has literally no overhead compared to HTTP. You might consider using WebSocket to develop the following types of applications:

- Live trading/auctions/sports notifications
- Live collaborative writing
- Controlling medical equipment over the Web
- Chat applications
- Multiplayer online games
- Real-time updates in social streams

For the next version of the Save The Child application, we're going to use WebSocket to implement an online auction communication layer. The goal is to let individuals and businesses purchase handmade arts and crafts made by children. All proceeds will go to Save The Child.

The goal is to let you see the advantages of changing the protocol for client-server communications on the Web. You'll clearly see the advantages of WebSocket over regular HTTP by monitoring network traffic with such tools as Wireshark and Google Chrome Developer Tools.

All the server-side functionality supporting this chapter is written in Java, using the Java API for WebSocket reference implementation (*http://java.net/projects/tyrus*), which is a part of the Java EE 7 specification. We are using the latest release of the GlassFish application server (*http://bit.ly/T7x8GD*). If you don't know Java, just treat this server-side setup as a service that supports the WebSocket protocol. For Java developers interested in diving into the server side, we provide the source code and brief comments as a part of the code samples that come with this book.

We show and compare the server-side data push done with server-sent events and WebSocket. Also, you'll see a brief overview of chosen frameworks such as Portal and Atmosphere that can streamline your WebSocket application development.

Using HTTP for Near Real-Time Applications

The HTTP protocol is the lingua franca of today's web applications, whereby client-server communications are based on the request-response paradigm. On a low level, web browsers establish a TCP/IP connection for each HTTP session. Currently there are three basic options that developers use for browser-server communication: polling, long polling, and streaming. These options are hacks on top of a half-duplex (a one-way street) HTTP protocol to simulate real-time behavior. (By *real-time* we mean the ability to react to some event as it happens.) Let's discuss each of them.

Polling

With *polling*, your client code sends requests to the server based on some preconfigured interval (for example, by using the JavaScript `setInterval()` function). Some of the server's responses will be empty if the requested data is not ready yet, as illustrated in Figure 8-1. For example, if you're running an online auction and send a request to see the updated bids, you won't receive any data back unless someone placed a new bid.

Visualize a child sitting in the back seat of your car and asking every minute, "Have we arrived yet?" And you politely reply, "Not just yet." This is similar to an empty server response. There is no valuable payload for this kid, but she's still receiving some "metadata." HTTP polling can result in receiving verbose HTTP response headers bearing no data load, let alone distracting the driver (think, the server) from performing other responsibilities.

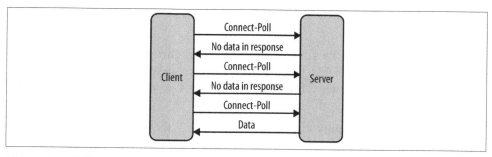

Figure 8-1. Polling

Long Polling

Long polling (see Figure 8-2) begins similarly to polling: the client sends the HTTP request to the server. But in this case, instead of sending an empty response back, the server waits until the data for the client becomes available. If the requested information is not available within the specified time interval, the server sends an empty response to the client, closes, and reestablishes the connection.

We'll give you one more analogy to compare polling and long polling. Imagine a party at the top floor of a building equipped with a smart elevator that goes up every minute and opens the door just in case one of the guests wants to go down to smoke a cigarette. If no one enters the elevator, it goes to the ground level and in 60 seconds goes up again. This is the polling scenario. But if this elevator went up and waited until someone actually decided to go down (or got tired of waiting), we could call it a long polling mode.

From the HTTP specification perspective, it's legitimate: the long polling mode might seem as if we deal with a slow-responding server. That is why this technique also is referred to as *Hanging GET*. If you see an online auction that automatically modifies prices as people bid on items, it looks as if the server pushes the data to you. But the chances are, this functionality was implemented by using long polling, which is not a real server-side data push, but its emulation.

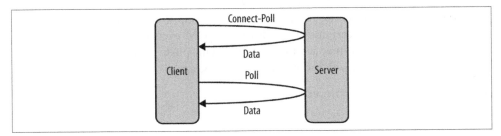

Figure 8-2. Long polling

HTTP Streaming

In HTTP streaming (see Figure 8-3), a client sends a request for data. As soon as the server gets the data ready, it starts streaming (adding more and more data to the response object) without closing the connections. The server pushes the data to the client, pretending that the response never ends. For example, requesting a video from YouTube results in streaming data (frame after frame) without closing the HTTP connection.

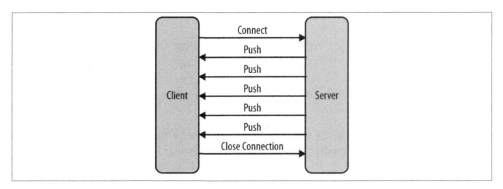

Figure 8-3. HTTP streaming

Polling and streaming can be used as a fallback for legacy browsers that don't support the HTML5 API's server-sent events and WebSocket.

Implementing Server-Sent Events

Before diving into the WebSocket protocol, let's become familiar with the standardized way of implementing server-sent events (SSE) (*http://bit.ly/1iSGbr4*). The World Wide Web Consortium (W3C) has published an API for web browsers to allow them to subscribe to events sent by a server. All modern browsers support the EventSource object, which can handle events arriving in the form of DOM events. This is not a request-response paradigm, but rather a unidirectional data push, from server to browser. Example 8-1 shows how a web browser can subscribe and listen to server-sent events.

Example 8-1. Subscribing to server-sent events

```
var myEventSource = (function() {
    'use strict';
    var eventSource;
    if ( !! window.EventSource) {
        eventSource =
            new EventSource
                ('http://localhost:8080/donate_web/api/donations/events');    ❶
    } else {
        // notify use that her browser doesn't support SSE
    }

    eventSource.addEventListener('open', function() {    ❷
        // Connection was opened.
    }, false);

    eventSource.addEventListener('create', function() {    ❸
        // do something with data
    }, false);
```

```
eventSource.addEventListener('update', function() {    ❹
    // do something with data
}, false);

eventSource.addEventListener('error', function(e) {
    if (e.readyState === EventSource.CLOSED) {
        // Connection was closed.
    }
}, false);

return eventSource;
})();
```

❶ Create a new EventSource object. At this point, the browser will send the GET request to the specified server-side endpoint to register itself on the server.

❷ Add handlers for the open and error events.

❸ Handle messages in create events by processing the e.data content.

❹ Handle messages in update events by processing the e.data content.

The preceding samples create listeners to subscribe specifically to create and update events, but if you'd like to subscribe to any events, you could use the following syntax:

```
eventSource.onmessage(function(e){
    // process the content of e.data here
});
```

SSE is a good technique for the use cases in which the client doesn't need to send the data to the server. A good illustration of such a server might be Facebook's News Feed page. A server can automatically update the client with new data without the client's request.

In the preceding example, the server sends two types of custom events, create and update, to notify subscribed clients about updated donation data so that the active clients can monitor the fundraising process. You can create as many custom events as needed by the application.

The server sends events as text messages that start with data: and end with a pair of newline characters. For example:

```
'data: {"price": "123.45"}/n/n`
```

SSE is still HTTP based, and it requires the server's support of the combination of HTTP 1.1 keep-alive connections and the text/event-stream content type in the HTTP response. The overhead is minimal: instead of hundreds of bytes in request and response headers, the server sends responses only when the data has changed.

Introducing the WebSocket API

> Reducing kilobytes of data to 2 bytes is more than "a little more byte efficient," and reducing latency from 150 ms (TCP round trip to set up the connection plus a packet for the message) to 50 ms (just the packet for the message) is far more than marginal. In fact, these two factors alone are enough to make WebSocket seriously interesting to Google.
>
> — Ian Hickson
> *HTML spec editor at Google (http://bit.ly/1oGOzfN)*

WebSocket is a bidirectional, full-duplex, frame-based protocol. According to RFC 6455 (*http://bit.ly/1uDjE1n*)—the Internet Engineering Task Force (IETF) standard document—the goal of WebSocket technology is to provide a mechanism for web applications that need two-way communication with servers. This technology doesn't rely on HTTP hacks or on opening multiple connections by using XMLHttpRequest or <iframe> and long polling. The idea behind WebSocket is not overly complicated:

- Establish a socket connection between the client and the server using HTTP for the initial handshake.
- Switch the communication protocol from HTTP to a socket-based protocol.
- Send messages in both directions simultaneously (a.k.a., full-duplex mode).
- Send messages independently. This is not a request-response model because both the server and the client can initiate the data transmission that enables the real server-side push.
- Both the server and the client can initiate disconnects, too.

You will get a better understanding of each of the preceding statements after reading this section.

The WebSocket protocol defines two new URI schemes (*http://bit.ly/1vnFXZf*), ws and wss, for unencrypted and encrypted connections, respectively. The ws (WebSocket) URI scheme is similar to the HTTP URI scheme and identifies that a WebSocket connection will be established by using TCP/IP without encryption. The wss (WebSocket Secure) URI scheme identifies that the traffic over that connection will be protected via Transport Layer Security (TLS). The TLS connection provides such benefits over TCP connection, as data confidentiality, integrity, and endpoint authentication. Apart from the scheme name, WebSocket URI schemes use generic URI syntax.

The WebSocket Interface

The W3C expert group uses Interface Description Language (*http://bit.ly/1yKFKDT*) to describe what the WebSocket interface should look like. Example 8-2 shows how it is defined.

Example 8-2. The WebSocket interface

```
[Constructor(DOMString url, optional (DOMString or DOMString[]) protocols)]  ❶
interface WebSocket : EventTarget {
  readonly attribute DOMString url;

  const unsigned short CONNECTING = 0;            ❷
  const unsigned short OPEN = 1;
  const unsigned short CLOSING = 2;
  const unsigned short CLOSED = 3;
  readonly attribute unsigned short readyState;
  readonly attribute unsigned long bufferedAmount;

  // networking
  [TreatNonCallableAsNull] attribute Function? onopen;    ❸
  [TreatNonCallableAsNull] attribute Function? onerror;
  [TreatNonCallableAsNull] attribute Function? onclose;
  readonly attribute DOMString extensions;
  readonly attribute DOMString protocol;               ❹
  void close([Clamp] optional unsigned short code, optional DOMString reason);

  // messaging
  [TreatNonCallableAsNull] attribute Function? onmessage;
          attribute DOMString binaryType;
  void send(DOMString data);                ❺
  void send(ArrayBufferView data);
  void send(Blob data);
};
```

❶ The constructor requires an endpoint URI and optional subprotocol names. A subprotocol is an application-level protocol layered over the WebSocket protocol. The client-side application can explicitly indicate which subprotocols are acceptable for the conversation between the client and server. That string will be sent to the server with the initial handshake in the `Sec-WebSocket-Protocol` GET request header field. If the server supports one of the requested protocols, it selects at most one and echoes that value in the same header parameter `Sec-WebSocket-Protocol` in the handshake's response. The server thereby indicates that it has selected that protocol. It could be a custom protocol or one of the standard application-level protocols (see "Creating the Save The Child Auction Protocol" on page 330). For example, it's possible to transfer the SOAP or XMPP messages over the WebSocket connection. We discuss the handshake in "WebSocket handshake" on page 303.

❷ At any given time, the WebSocket can be in one of four states.

❸ These are the callback functions of the WebSocket object that will be invoked by the browser after the appropriate network event is dispatched.

❹   This property contains the name of the subprotocol used for the conversation. After a successful handshake, this property is populated by the browser with the value from the server's response parameter `Sec-WebSocket-Protocol`, as described in **❶**.

❺   The WebSocket object can send text or binary data to the server by using one of the overloaded `send()` methods.

The Client-Side API

Now that we have introduced the WebSocket interface, take a look at the code in Example 8-3, illustrating how the client's JavaScript can use it.

Example 8-3. Using WebSocket in a JavaScript client

```
var ws;
(function(ws) {
    "use strict";
    if (window.WebSocket) {               ❶
        console.log("WebSocket object is supported in your browser");
        ws = new WebSocket("ws://www.websocket.org/echo");    ❷
        ws.onopen = function() {
            console.log("onopen");
        };        ❸
        ws.onmessage = function(e) {
            console.log("echo from server : " + e.data);      ❹
        };

        ws.onclose = function() {    ❺
            console.log("onclose");
        };
        ws.onerror = function() {
            console.log("onerror");      ❻
        };

    } else {
        console.log("WebSocket object is not supported in your browser");
    }
})(ws);
```

❶   Not all web browsers support WebSocket natively as of yet. Check whether the `WebSocket` object is supported by the user's browser.

❷   Instantiate the new `WebSocket` object by passing an endpoint URI as a constructor parameter.

❸   Set the event handlers for `open`, `message`, and `close` events.

❹ MessageEvent is dispatched when the data is received from the server. This message will be delivered to the function assigned to the WebSocket object's onmessage property. The e.data property of the message event will contain the received message.

❺ Handle the closing connection (more details in "Closing the connection" on page 307).

❻ Handle errors.

WebSocket handshake

Any network communications that use the WebSocket protocol start with an opening handshake. This handshake upgrades the connection from HTTP to the WebSocket protocol. It's an upgrade of HTTP to message-based communications. We discuss messages (a.k.a. frames) later in this chapter.

Why upgrade from HTTP instead of starting with TCP as a protocol in the first place? The reason is that WebSocket operates on the same ports (80 and 443) as do HTTP and HTTPS. It's an important advantage that the browser's requests are routed through the same ports, because arbitrary socket connections may not be allowed by the enterprise firewalls for security reasons. Also, many corporate networks allow only certain outgoing ports. And HTTP/HTTPS ports are usually included in so called *white lists*.

 High Performance Browser Networking by Ilya Grigorik (O'Reilly) provides more information about TCP and HTTP.

The protocol upgrade is initiated by a client request, which also transmits a special key with the request. The server processes this request and sends back a confirmation for the upgrade. This ensures that a WebSocket connection can be established only with an endpoint that supports WebSocket. Here is what the handshake can look like in the client's request:

```
GET HTTP/1.1
Upgrade: websocket
Connection: Upgrade
Host: echo.websocket.org
Origin: http://www.websocket.org
Sec-WebSocket-Key: i9ri`AfOgSsKwUlmLjIkGA==
Sec-WebSocket-Version: 13
Sec-WebSocket-Protocol: chat
```

This client sends the GET request for the protocol upgrade. Sec-WebSocket-Key is just a set of random bytes. The server takes these bytes and appends to this key a special

globally unique identifier (GUID) string `258EAFA5-E914-47DA-95CA-C5AB0DC85B11`.
Then, it creates the Secure Hash Algorithm `SHA1` hash from it and performs *Base64*
encoding. The resulting string of bytes needs to be used by both the server and the client,
and this string won't be used by network endpoints that do not understand the Web-
Socket protocol. Then, this value is copied in the `Sec-WebSocket-Accept` header field.
The server computes the value and sends the response back, confirming the protocol
upgrade:

```
HTTP/1.1 101 Web Socket Protocol Handshake
Upgrade: WebSocket
Connection: Upgrade
Sec-WebSocket-Accept: Qz9Mp4/YtIjPccdpbvFEm17G8bs=
Sec-WebSocket-Protocol: chat
Access-Control-Allow-Origin: http://www.websocket.org
```

The WebSocket protocol uses the `400 Bad Request` HTTP error code to signal an
unsuccessful upgrade. The handshake can also include a subprotocol request and the
WebSocket version information, but you can't include other arbitrary headers. We can't
transmit the authorization information. There are two ways around this. You can either
transmit the authorization information as the first request (for example, the unique
`clientId` can be passed as part of the HTTP request header or HTML wrapper) or put
it into the URL as a query parameter during the initial handshake. Consider the following example:

```
var clientId = "Mary1989";                              ❶
ws = new WebSocket("ws://www.websocket.org/echo/"+clientID);  ❷
```

❶   The `clientId` value, which can be obtained from a Lightweight Directory Access
     Protocol (LDAP) server.

❷   The client connects to the WebSocket endpoint with an extra URI parameter
     that will be stored on the server for future interactions.

Because the WebSocket protocol creates a bidirectional (socket-to-socket) connection,
the server has access to the conversation session associated with such a connection. This
session can be associated with `clientId` and be stored on the server.

> A client can have as many WebSocket connections with the server as
> needed. But servers can refuse to accept connections from hosts/IP
> addresses with an excessive number of existing connections or can
> disconnect from resource-hogging connections in case of high data
> load.

WebSocket frame anatomy

The WebSocket handshake is the first step in switching to the message framing protocol,
which will be layered over TCP. In this section, we're going to explore how WebSocket

data transfer works. WebSocket is not a stream-based protocol like TCP—it's message based. With TCP, a program sends a stream of bytes, which has to have a specific indication that the data transfer ends. The WebSocket specification simplifies this by putting a frame around every chunk of data, and the size of the frame is known. JavaScript can easily handle these frames on the client because each frame arrives packaged in the event object. But the server side has to work a little harder because it needs to wrap each piece of data into a frame before sending it to the client. A frame can look like this:

```
 +-+-+-+-+-------+-+-------------+-------------------------------+
 0                   1                   2                   3
 0 1 2 3 4 5 6 7 8 9 0 1 2 3 4 5 6 7 8 9 0 1 2 3 4 5 6 7 8 9 0 1
 +-+-+-+-+-------+-+-------------+-------------------------------+
 |F|R|R|R| opcode|M| Payload len |    Extended payload length    |
 |I|S|S|S|  (4)  |A|     (7)     |             (16/64)           |
 |N|V|V|V|       |S|             |   (if payload len==126/127)   |
 | |1|2|3|       |K|             |                               |
 +-+-+-+-+-------+-+-------------+ - - - - - - - - - - - - - - - +
 |     Extended payload length continued, if payload len == 127  |
 + - - - - - - - - - - - - - - - +-------------------------------+
 |                               |Masking-key, if MASK set to 1  |
 +-------------------------------+-------------------------------+
 | Masking-key (continued)       |          Payload Data         |
 +-------------------------------- - - - - - - - - - - - - - - - +
 :                     Payload Data continued ...                :
 + - - - - - - - - - - - - - - - - - - - - - - - - - - - - - - - +
 |                     Payload Data continued ...                |
 +---------------------------------------------------------------+
```

The parts of the frame are as follows:

FIN *(1 bit)*

This bit indicates whether this frame is the final one in the message payload. If a message has under 127 bytes, it fits into a single frame and this bit will always be set.

RSV1, RSV2, RSV3 *(1 bit each)*

These bits are reserved for future protocol changes and improvements. They must contain zeros because they are not being used at this time.

opcode *(4 bits)*

The frame type is defined by using opcode. Here are the most-used opcodes:

0x00

This frame continues the payload.

0x01

This frame includes UTF-8 text data.

0x02

This frame includes the binary data.

`0x08`
This frame terminates the connection.

`0x09`
This frame is a ping.

`0xA`
This frame is a pong.

`mask` *(1 bit)*
This indicates whether the frame is masked.

 The client must mask all the frames being sent to the server. The server must close the connection upon receiving a frame that is not masked. The server must not mask any frames that it sends to the client. The client must close a connection if it detects a masked frame. In case of an error, the client or server can send the `Close` frame containing the status code 1002 (the protocol error). All these actions are done automatically by web browsers and web servers that implements WebSocket specification (*http://bit.ly/1uDjE1n*).

`payload_len` *(7 bits, 7 + 16 bits, or 7 + 64 bits)*
The length of the payload. WebSocket frames come in the following length brackets:

- 0–125 indicate the length of the payload.
- 126 means that the following 2 bytes indicate the length.
- 127 means the next 8 bytes indicate the length.

`masking-key` *(32 bits)*
This key is used to *XOR* the payload.

`payload data`
This indicates the actual data. The length of the block is defined in the `payload_len` field.

The heartbeats

A properly designed distributed application has to have a way to ensure that each tier of the system is operational even if there is no active data exchange between the client and the server. This can be done by implementing so-called *heartbeats*—small messages that simply ask the other party, "Are you there?" For example, proxy servers and content-filtering hardware can terminate idle connections, or the server could simply go down. If a client doesn't send any requests, say, for 20 seconds, but the server went down, the client will know about it only when it does the next `send()`. Heartbeats will keep the connection alive to ensure that it won't appear to be idling. In WebSocket jargon, heartbeats are implemented with *ping and pong* frames. The browser sends the *ping* opcode `0x9` at any time to ask the other side to *pong* back (the opcode `0xA`).

A web browser can ping the server when required, but a pong can be sent at the server's discretion. If the endpoint receives a ping frame before responding to the previous one, the endpoint can elect to send just one pong frame for the most recently processed ping. The ping frame may contain the application data (up to 125 bytes), and the pong must have identical data in its message body.

There is no JavaScript API to send pings or receive pong frames (*http://bit.ly/1uDjLtE*). Pings and pongs may or may not be supported by the user's browser. There is also no API (*http://bit.ly/1soFv0D*) to enable, configure, or detect whether the browser supports pings and pongs.

Data frames

Because the WebSocket protocol allows data to be fragmented into multiple frames, the first frame that transmits data will be prepended with one of the following opcodes indicating the type of data being transmitted:

- The opcode `0x01` indicates UTF-8–encoded text data.
- The opcode `0x02` indicates binary data.

When your application transmits JSON over the wire, the opcode is set to `0x01`. When your code emits binary data, it will be represented in a browser-specific `Blob` object or an `ArrayBuffer` object and sent wrapped into a frame with the opcode `0x02`. The following example shows how the WebSocket message listener checks the data type of the incoming message:

 You must choose the type for the incoming binary data on the client by using `webSocket.binaryType = "blob"` or `webSocket.bina ryType = "arraybuffer"` before reading the data. It's a good idea to check the type of the incoming data because the opcodes are not exposed to the client.

```
webSocket.onmessage = function(messageEvent) {
    if (typeof messageEvent.data === "string"){
        console.log("received text data from the server: " + messageEvent.data);
    } else if (messageEvent.data instanceof Blob){
        console.log("Blob data received")
    }
};
```

Closing the connection

The connection is terminated by sending a frame with the close opcode `0x08`.

There is the pattern to exchange close opcodes first and then let the server shut down. The client is supposed to give the server time to close the connection before attempting to do that on its own. The close event can also signal why it has terminated the connection.

A `CloseEvent` is sent to clients using WebSocket when the connection is closed. This is delivered to the listener indicated by the WebSocket object's `onclose` handler. `CloseEvent` has three properties—`code`, `reason`, and `wasClean`:

`code`
> This property represents the close code provided by the server.

`reason`
> A string indicating the reason why the server closed the connection.

`wasClean`
> This property indicates whether the connection was cleanly closed.

The following example illustrates how to handle the connection closing:

```
webSocket.onclose = function(closeEvent) {
    console.log("reason " + closeEvent.reason + "code " + closeEvent.code);
};
```

Using WebSocket Frameworks

Working with the vanilla WebSocket API requires you to do some additional "housekeeping" coding on your own. For example, if the client's browser doesn't support WebSocket natively, you need to make sure that your code falls back to the legacy HTTP. The good news is that there are frameworks that can help you with this task. Such frameworks lower the development time, allowing you to do more with less code. In this section, we include brief reviews of two frameworks that can streamline your web application development with WebSocket.

These frameworks try to utilize the best supported transport by the current web browser and server while sparing the developer from knowing the internals of the used mechanism. The developer can concentrate on programming the application logic, making calls to the framework API when the data transfer is needed. The rest will be done by the framework.

The Portal

The Portal (*http://bit.ly/1q9xdX0*) is a server-agnostic JavaScript library. It aims to utilize a WebSocket protocol and provides a unified API for various transports (long polling, HTTP streaming, WebSocket). Currently, after you've decided to use WebSocket for your next project, you need to remember those users who still use earlier browsers such as Internet Explorer 9 or older, which don't natively support WebSocket. In this case, your application should gracefully fall back to the best available networking alternative. Manually writing code to support all possible browsers and versions requires lots of time, especially for testing and maintaining the code for different platforms. The Portal library could help, as illustrated in Example 8-4.

Example 8-4. Simple asynchronous web application client with Portal

```
portal.defaults.transports = ["ws", "sse", "stream", "longpoll"];       ❶

portal.open("child-auction/auction").on({       ❷
    connecting: function() {
        console.log("The connection has been tried by '"
                                    + this.data("transport") + "'");
    },
    open: function() {                                 ❸
        console.log("The connection has been opened");
    },
    close: function(reason) {
        console.log("The connection has been closed due to '" + reason + "'");
    },
    message: function(data) {
        handleIncommingData(data);
    },
    waiting: function(delay, attempts) {
        console.log("The socket will try to reconnect after " + delay + " ms");
        console.log("The total number of reconnection attempts is " + attempts);
    }
});
```

❶ The Portal framework supports different transports and can fall back from a WebSocket connection to streaming or long polling. The server also has to support a fall-back strategy, but no additional code is required on the client side.

❷ Connecting to the WebSocket endpoint.

❸ The Portal API is event-based, similar to the W3C WebSocket API.

The Portal framework generalizes client-side programming. When defining an array of transports, you don't have to worry about how to handle messages sent by a server with a different transport. The Portal doesn't depend on any JavaScript library.

Atmosphere

A web application that has to be deployed on several different servers (for example, WebSphere, JBoss, and WebLogic) might need to support different WebSocket APIs. At the time of this writing, a plethora of implementations of server-side libraries support WebSocket, and each uses its own proprietary API. The Java EE 7 specification intends to change the situation. But Atmosphere is a framework that allows you to write portable web applications today.

Atmosphere (*http://bit.ly/1sRd2AQ*) is a *portable* WebSocket framework supporting Java, Groovy, and Scala. The Atmosphere framework contains both client and server components for building asynchronous web applications. Atmosphere transparently supports WebSocket, server-side events, long polling, HTTP streaming, and JSONP.

The client-side component Atmosphere.js (*http://bit.ly/1m2j4Jw*) uses the Portal framework internally and simplifies the development of web applications that require a fallback from the WebSocket protocol to long polling or HTTP streaming. Atmosphere hides the complexity of the asynchronous APIs, which differ from server to server, and makes your application portable among them. Treat Atmosphere as a compatibility layer that allows you to select the best available transport for all major Java application servers.

The Atmosphere framework supports a wide range of Java-based server-side technologies via a set of extensions and plug-ins (*http://bit.ly/1ilP7EX*). Atmosphere supports (*http://bit.ly/1piiqsT*) the Java API for WebSocket, so you can have the best of two worlds —the standard API and application portability.

 WebSocket can be used not only for the Web, but in any applications that use networking. If you're developing native iOS or OS X applications, check the SocketRocket (*http://bit.ly/1q9xmcZ*) library developed by the Square engineering team (*http://corner.square up.com/*).

Square uses SocketRocket in its mobile payments application. If you're developing native Android applications and want to use WebSocket protocol goodies in Android-powered devices, check the AsyncHttpClient (*http://bit.ly/UbSPq1*) framework.

Choosing the Format for Application-Level Messages

Although WebSocket is a great solution for real-time data transmission over the Web, it has a downside, too: the WebSocket specification defines only a protocol for transporting frames, but it doesn't include an application-level protocol. Developers need to invent the application-specific text or binary protocols. For example, the auction bid has to be presented in a form agreed upon by all application modules. Let's discuss our options from a protocol-modeling perspective.

Selecting a message format for your application's data communications is important. The most common text formats are CSV, XML, and JSON. They are easy to generate and parse, and are widely supported by many frameworks in most development platforms. Although XML and JSON allow you to represent data in a hierarchical form that is easily readable by humans, they create a lot of overhead by wrapping each data element into additional text identifiers. Sending this additional textual information requires extra bandwidth and might need additional string-to-type conversion on both the client and server's application code. Let's discuss the pros and cons of these message formats.

CSV

CSV stands for comma-separated values, although the delimiter can be any character; you're not restricted to only a comma. This depends on the parser design and implementation. Another popular type of delimiter is | (a pipe).

The pros of this format are as follows:

- This format is very compact. The overhead of the separator symbol is minimal.
- It's simple to create and parse. The CSV message can be turned into an array of values by using the standard JavaScript `String.split()`.

These are the cons of using CSV:

- It's not suitable for storing complex data structures and hierarchies. In the case of our auction application, we need to transfer the client auction items' attributes for each auction. We can't simply use `String.split()` and have to design and implement a more complex parser.

XML

XML nicely represents any hierarchal data structures.

These are its pros:

- It's a human-readable format.
- Most browsers have built-in XML readers and parsers.
- XML data can be validated against XSD or DTD schema.

  An XML schema is a useful language feature because it defines the structure, content, and semantics of an XML document. Because of its human-readability, the XML schema can be used used by people who are not software developers and can be used to integrate systems written in different programming languages.

Its cons are as follows:

- XML is very verbose. To send the name of a customer, you'd need something like this: `<cust_name>Mary</cust_name>`.
- The XML validation on the client is a complex task. As of now, there are no platform-independent solutions or an API to perform validation programmatically based on XSD or DTD.

XML in a Nutshell by Elliotte Rusty Harold and W. Scott Means (O'Reilly) is a well-written book describing the full spectrum of XML features and tools.

JSON

As explained in Chapter 2, *JSON* stands for JavaScript Object Notation, and it's a way of representing structured data, which can be encoded and decoded by all web browsers. JSON is widely accepted by the web community as a popular way to serialize data. As stated earlier, it provides a more compact way than XML to represent data, and all modern web browsers understand and can parse JSON data.

Google Protocol Buffers

A Google *protocol buffer* (or protobuf) is a language and platform-neutral extensible mechanism for structured data serialization. After you define how you want your data to be structured, you can use special generated source code to easily write and read your structured data to and from a variety of data streams. Developers can use the same schemas across diverse environments (*http://bit.ly/1r5z9lc*).

A developer needs to specify how the serializable information has to be structured by defining the protocol buffer message types in *.proto* files. Each protocol buffer message is a small, logical record of information containing a series of name/value pairs. This protocol buffer message file is language agnostic. The `protoc` utility compiles *proto* files and produces language-specific artifacts (for example *.java* and *.js* files).

For example, you can create a protocol buffer *proto* file for Save The Child to represent the information about donors, as shown in Example 8-5.

Example 8-5. Protocol buffer for donation message (donation.proto)

```
package savesickchild;                                    ❶

option java_package = "org.savesickchild.web.donation";   ❷

message Donor{                                            ❸
    required string fullname = 1;
    required string email = 2;                            ❹
    required string address = 3;
    required string city = 4;
    required string state = 5;
    required int32 zip = 6;
    required string country = 7;

    message Donation{                                     ❺
        required Donor donor = 1;                         ❻
```

```
        required double amount = 2;
        optional bool receipt_needed = 3;
    }
}
```

❶ The protobuf supports packages to prevent naming conflicts among messages
    from different projects.

❷ Here we're using a Java-specific protobuf option to define the package in which
    the generated code will reside.

❸ Start defining our custom message with the message keyword.

❹ Each message field can be required, optional, or repeated. The required and
    optional modifiers are self-explanatory. During the serialization-deserization
    process, the protobuf framework checks the message for the existence of fields,
    and if a required property is missing, will throw a runtime exception. The re
    peated modifier is used to create dynamically sized arrays.

❺ The protobuf supports nested messages.

❻ Many standard field types are available in protobuf: string, int32, float, dou
    ble, and bool. You can also define a custom type and use it as a field type.

After creating the *donation.proto* file, you can use the protoc compiler to generate Java
classes according to this file's definitions:

```
protoc -I=. --java_out=src donation.proto          # ❶

.
├── donation.proto
└── src
    └── org
        └── savesickchild
            └── web
                └── donation
                    └── Donation.java              # ❷
```

❶ The Java code will be generated in the *src* directory.

❷ All required code for serialization-deserilization of the Donation message will
    be included in *Donation.java*. We're not going to publish the generated code
    here, but you can generate this code by yourself from the previous message
    declaration.

Check the availability of the protobuf compiler for your preferred language at the protobuf wiki page (*http://bit.ly/1r8m3Rx*). To become familiar with protobuf technology,
check the documentation (*http://bit.ly/1kOjQVS*) and tutorials (*http://bit.ly/1yjEVlk*).

Here are some protobuf pros:

- The message is encoded into a compact and optimized binary format. You can find details of the encoding format at the Protocol Buffers documentation website (*http://bit.ly/UbTSpV*).
- Google supports protocol buffers for a wide range of programming languages (Java, C++, Python). The developer's community (*http://bit.ly/1r8m3Rx*) supports it, too.
- The use of protocol buffers is well documented.

The following are some of the cons:

- The binary format is not human readable.
- Although protobuf is compact, especially when a lot of numeric values are transferred by an encoding algorithm (*http://bit.ly/UbTSpV*), the JSON is natively supported by the JavaScript and doesn't require any additional parser implementation.
- Protobuf requires web browsers to support binary format, but not all of them do just yet. You can find which browsers support raw binary data at Can I Use… (*http://caniuse.com/#search=binary*).

Using WebSocket with Proxies

The WebSocket protocol itself is unaware of intermediaries such as proxy servers, firewalls, and content filters. Proxy servers are commonly used for content caching, security, and enterprise content filtering.

HTTP has always supported protocol upgrades, but many proxy servers seem to have ignored that part of the specification. Until WebSocket came around, the `Upgrade` attribute was not used. The problem with web applications that use a long-lived connection like WebSocket is that the proxy servers might choose to close streaming or idle WebSocket connections because they appear to be trying to connect to an unresponsive HTTP server. Additionally, proxy servers might buffer unencrypted HTTP responses, assuming that the browser needs to receive the HTTP response in its entirety.

If you want more details on how a WebSocket-enabled application has to deal with proxies, check out the comprehensive research paper by Google's Peter Lubbers, WebSocket and Proxy Servers (*http://bit.ly/TJkga3*).

The authors of this book use NGINX (*http://nginx.com*), a hugely popular load balancer and proxy and HTTP server to serve static resources (for example, images and text files), balance the load between Java servers, and perform SSL offloading (turning the web browser's HTTPS requests into HTTP). NGINX uses a small number threads to support thousands of concurrent users, as opposed to traditional web servers that use one worker thread per connection. Recently, NGINX started supporting the WebSocket protocol.

Adding an Auction to Save The Child

We gave you just enough theory to whet your appetite for implementing WebSocket in our Save The Child application. The goal is to create an auction so that people can bid and purchase various goods and have the proceeds go to Save The Child. Auctions require real-time communications: everyone interested in the particular auction item must be immediately notified of being overbid or of winning. So we'll use WebSocket as a means for bidding and providing notifications of the changes in the auction.

To start the auction, the user has to select the Auction option under the menu Way To Give (see Figure 8-4). We realize that only a small number of users will decide to participate in the auction, which from an architectural point of view means that the code supporting the auction should be loaded *on demand* only if the user chooses to visit the auction. This is why we need to write this code as a loadable module, and you will get a practical example of how a web application can be modularized.

In this chapter, we continue to use RequireJS (see Chapter 6) as a framework for modularization. Using RequireJS, we're going to lazy-load some modules if and only if they are requested by the user.

This book is about development of the user interface and client side of web applications, so we're not going to cover all the details of server-side implementation but will make our server-side code available for download. We'll keep our server up and running so that you can test the UI by visiting *http://savesickchild.org:8080/websocket-auction/*, but our main goal in this section is to show you how you can exchange auction data with the server and process it on the client side by using WebSocket. We'll use the Java application server GlassFish 4, which is a reference implementation of the Java EE 7 specification.

The authors of this book are Java developers and we have recorded a screencast (see readme.asciidoc (*http://bit.ly/1lDlWwh*)) highlighting the WebSocket server API. If you are not a Java developer, you might want to learn on your own which WebSocket servers exist for your favorite programming language or platform.

Chapter 6 demonstrates how a web application can be sliced into several modules by using the RequireJS framework. We'll use that project as a base and create a new one, *project-16-websocket-auction*, adding to it the new modules supporting the auction. Example 8-6 shows the code of the WayToGive module.

Example 8-6. WayToGive module (js/modules/way-to-give.js)

```
define([], function() {
    var WayToGive;
    console.log("way-to-give module is loaded");
    WayToGive = function() {
        return {
            render: function() {                                  ❶
                // rendering code is omitted
                console.log("way-to-give module is rendered");
                rendered = true;
                return
            },
            startAuction: function(){                             ❷

            },
            rendered: false                                       ❸
        };
    };
    return WayToGive;
});
```

❶ This function lazy-loads the auction application content and renders it to the top main section of the web page.

❷ The function startAuction() starts the auction.

❸ The module stores the rendering state in the property rendered.

After the application starts, RequireJS loads only the essential modules, login and donation, as shown in Figure 8-4.

In the Google Chrome Developer Tools console, you can see that the login and dona tion modules are reporting about successful loading. Figure 8-5 confirms that these modules perform fine; clicking the Donate Now button reveals the form, and clicking the Login button makes the ID and Password fields visible.

Figure 8-4. Initially only two modules are loaded

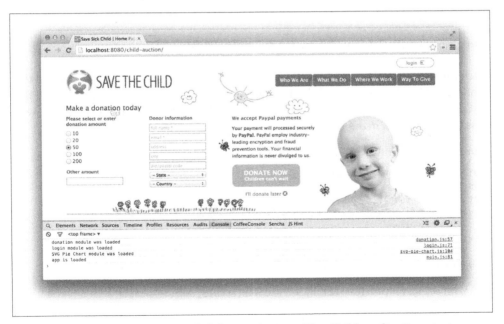

Figure 8-5. Two modules are loaded during the Save The Child application startup

Now click the Way To Give menu and keep an eye on the Developer Tools console (see Figure 8-6). You will see the WayToGive module reporting about its loading and rendering.

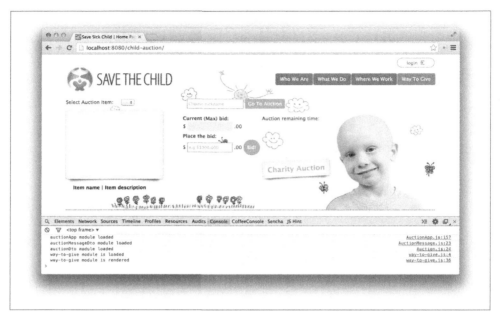

Figure 8-6. The auction controls are loaded and rendered

When the user clicks Way To Give, the RequireJS framework has to load the code of the WebSocket-based auction module. Example 8-7 presents the code snippet from the JavaScript file *app.js*, the entry point of our Save The Child application. This is how it loads the module *on demand* (see Chapter 6 for a RequireJS refresher).

Example 8-7. Loading the Way to Give module

```
require([], function() {     ❶
  'use strict';
  return (function() {
    var lazyLoadingEventHandlerFactory, wayToGiveHandleClick, wayToGiveModule,
        way_to_give;
    way_to_give = document.getElementById('way-to-give');

    wayToGiveModule = null;    ❷

    lazyLoadingEventHandlerFactory = function(module, modulePath) {
      var clickEventHandler;
      clickEventHandler = function(event) {
        console.log(event.target);
        if (module === 'loading') {    ❸
```

```
          return;
        }
        if (module !== null) {
          return module.startAuction();          ❹
        } else {
          module = 'loading';          ❺
          return require([modulePath], function(ModuleObject) {          ❻
            module = new ModuleObject();
            return module.render();          ❼
          });
        }
      };
      return clickEventHandler;
    };
    wayToGiveHandleClick = lazyLoadingEventHandlerFactory(wayToGiveModule,
                                              'modules/way-to-give');

    way_to_give.addEventListener('click', wayToGiveHandleClick, false);          ❽
  })();
});
```

❶ This anonymous function will be lazy-loaded only if the user clicks the Way To Give menu.

❷ The variable wayToGiveModule has a value of null until loaded.

❸ If the user keeps clicking the menu while the way-to-give module is still being loaded, simply ignore these clicks.

❹ If the module has been loaded and the UI has been rendered, start the auction application.

❺ Set an intermediary value to the way-to-give module so that subsequent requests don't try to launch the module more than once.

❻ Load the module asynchronously and instantiate it.

❼ Render the UI component to the screen for the first time.

❽ Register the click event listener for the Way To Give menu.

After the UI elements have rendered, the client can connect to the WebSocket server and request the list of all available auction items, as shown in Example 8-8.

Example 8-8. Connecting to the WebSocket server

```
if (window.WebSocket) {
  webSocket = new WebSocket("ws://localhost:8080/child-auction/auction");
  webSocket.onopen = function() {
    console.log("connection open...");          ❶
    getAuctionsList();
  };
  webSocket.onclose = function(closeEvent) {
    // notify user that connection was closed
```

```
      console.log("close code " + closeEvent.code);
    };
    webSocket.onmessage = function(messageEvent) {
      console.log("data from server: " + messageEvent.data);
      if (typeof messageEvent.data === "string") {
        handleMessage(messageEvent.data);
      }
    };
    webSocket.onerror = function() {
      // notify user about connection error
      console.log("websocket error");
    };
  }
```

❶ After establishing the connection, the code requests the list of available auctions. We'll see details of getAuctionsList() method in the next snippet:

```
var getAuctionsList = function() {
    'use strict';
    var auctionListMessage = {
        type: 'AUCTIONS_LIST',
        data: 'gime',
        auctionId: '-1'
    };          ❶
    if (webSocket.readyState === 1) {    ❷
        webSocket.send(JSON.stringify(auctionListMessage));
    } else {
        console.log('offline');
    }
};
```

❶ Form the request message. You can find the details of the message format in "Creating the Save The Child Auction Protocol" on page 330.

❷ Check the WebSocket object state. If WebSocket is open (readyState===1), the application can send a message. If not, this code just simply logs the "offline" mesage on the console. In the real world, you should always display this message on the user's UI. Also, if your users work on unstable networks such as cellular or 3G, you definitely don't want to lose any bits of data. It's a good idea to use the local storage API (see Chapter 1) to persist the data locally until the application gets back online and resubmits the data.

The user can select the auction lot from the combo box and see its images. Figure 8-7 shows what's displayed on the console, while Figures 8-8 and 8-9 show the content of the Network tab for both images.

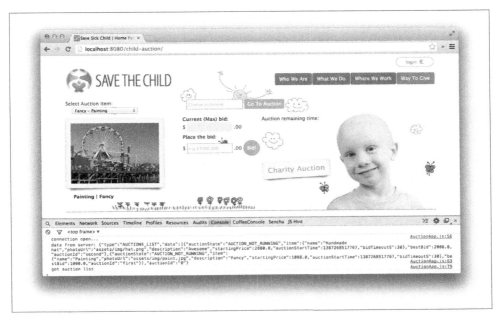

Figure 8-7. The console logs incoming messages containing a list of auction items

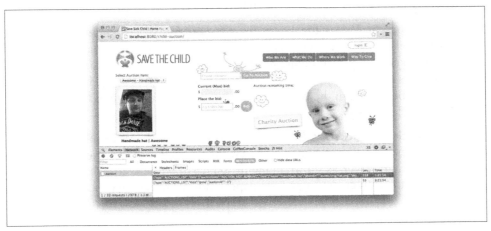

Figure 8-8. By using the Network feature of DevTools, we can monitor WebSocket frames

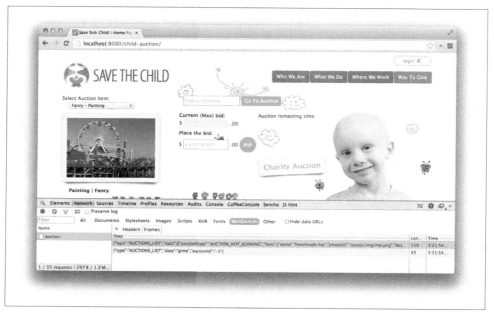

Figure 8-9. The buyer can choose another item on which to bid

Monitoring WebSocket Traffic by Using Chrome Developer Tools

Let's review the practical use of the theory described in "WebSocket handshake" on page 303. With the help of Chrome Developer Tools, you can monitor information about the initial handshake, as shown in Figure 8-10. Monitoring WebSocket traffic in Chrome Developer Tools is, in some ways, not that different from monitoring HTTP requests. The traffic can be viewed in the Network tab after selecting the path of the `WebSocket` endpoint in the left panel.

You can also click WebSockets at the lower right to show only the WebSocket endpoints. Click the Frames tab in the right panel to view the actual frames being exchanged between the client and server, as shown in Figure 8-11. The white-colored rows represent incoming data; those in green (or gray on paper) indicate outgoing data.

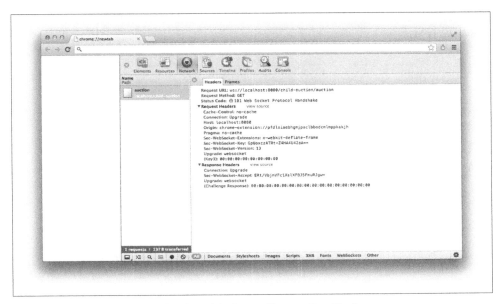

Figure 8-10. Initial WebSocket handshake in Chrome DevTools

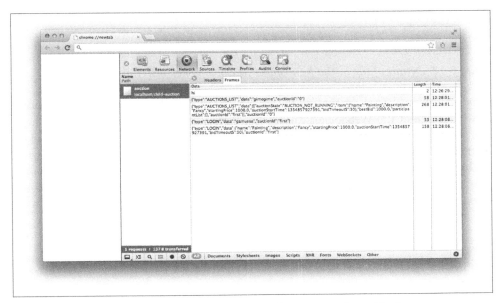

Figure 8-11. Monitoring WebSocket frames in Chrome Developer Tools

For more details, you can navigate Google Chrome to the secret URL *chrome://net-internals*, which provides a lot of useful information (see Figures 8-12 and 8-13). You can find documentation about net-internals in Chromium Design Documents (*http://bit.ly/1ilSHyM*).

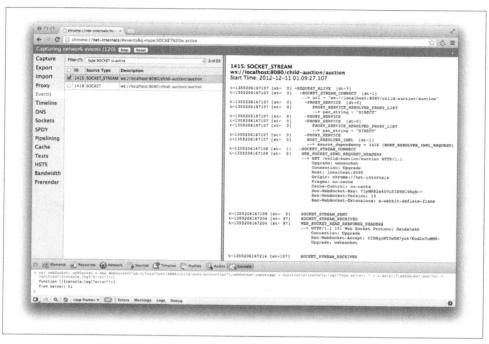

Figure 8-12. Details of the initial handshake in Chrome net-internals

Google Developer Tools show just the length of the data. But *chrome://net-internals* shows the size of the WebSocket frame, too. Figure 8-14 compares the views of net-internals and Developer Tools. As you learned earlier in this chapter, the total size of the frame is slightly different from the size of the payload. There are a few more bytes for the frame header. Moreover, all outgoing messages will be masked by the browser (see "WebSocket frame anatomy" on page 304). This frame's mask is going to be transferred to the server as a part of the frame itself, which creates an additional 32 bits (4 bytes) of overhead.

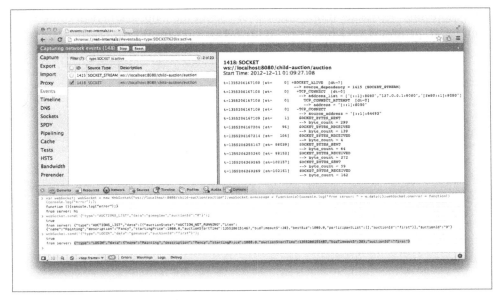

Figure 8-13. Details of the socket connection

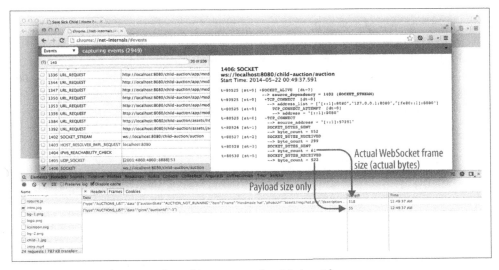

Figure 8-14. Developer Tools and net-internals, side by side

Sniffing WebSocket Frames by Using Wireshark

Wireshark is a powerful and comprehensive monitoring tool for analyzing network traffic. You can download it from Wireshark's website (*http://www.wireshark.org*). To begin capturing WebSocket traffic on *localhost*, select the loopback network interface from the left panel and click Start (see Figure 8-15).

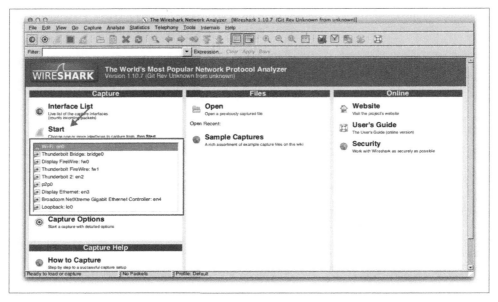

Figure 8-15. The Wireshark application main view

Wireshark captures all network activity. You can set up a filter to see only the data in which you are interested. We want to capture HTTP and TCP traffic on port 8080 because our WebSocket server (Oracle's GlassFish) runs on this port (see Figure 8-16). Enter http && (tcp.dstport==8080) in the filter text box and click Apply.

Figure 8-16. Filter setup

Now Wireshark is ready to sniff out the traffic of our application. You can start the auction session and place bids. After you're done with the auction, you can return to the Wireshark window and analyze the results. You can see the initial handshake (GET request in Figure 8-17 and the Upgrade response in Figure 8-18).

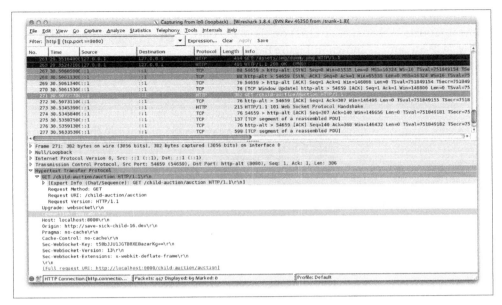

Figure 8-17. The GET request for protocol upgrade

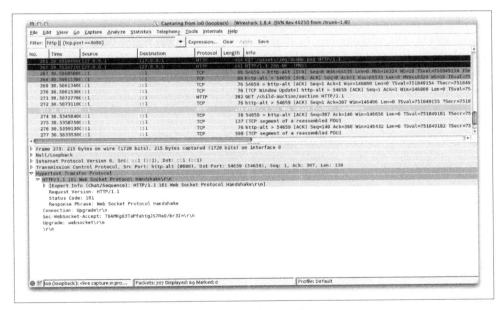

Figure 8-18. The GET response with protocol upgrade

After the successful connection upgrade, Wireshark captures the http-alt stream (this is how it reports WebSocket's traffic) on the 8080 port. Right-click this row and select Follow TCP Stream, as shown in Figure 8-19.

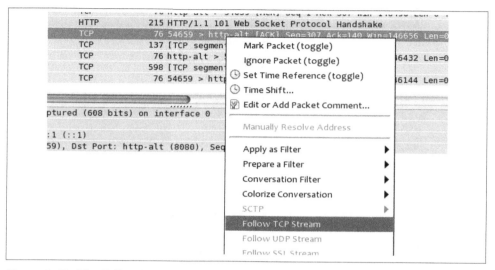

Figure 8-19. The Follow TCP Stream menu

On the next screen, you can see the details of the WebSocket frame (see Figure 8-20). We took this screenshot right after the auction application started. You can see the data with the list of available auctions. The outgoing data appears in red, and the incoming data is shown in blue.

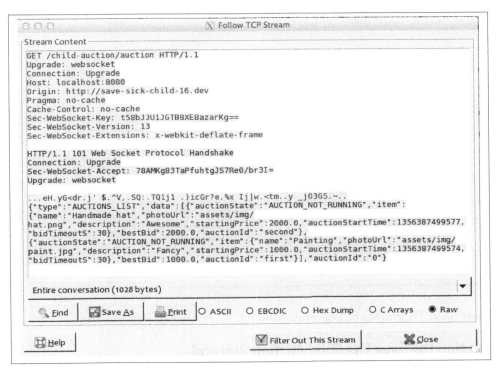

The content of the Follow TCP Stream window shows:

```
GET /child-auction/auction HTTP/1.1
Upgrade: websocket
Connection: Upgrade
Host: localhost:8080
Origin: http://save-sick-child-16.dev
Pragma: no-cache
Cache-Control: no-cache
Sec-WebSocket-Key: t58bJJU1JGTB8XEBazarKg==
Sec-WebSocket-Version: 13
Sec-WebSocket-Extensions: x-webkit-deflate-frame

HTTP/1.1 101 Web Socket Protocol Handshake
Connection: Upgrade
Sec-WebSocket-Accept: 78AMKg83TaPfuhtgJS7Re0/br3I=
Upgrade: websocket

...eH.yG<dr.j' $.^V,.SQ:.TQ1j1 .)icGr?e.%x Ij|w.<tm..y _j03G5.~..
{"type":"AUCTIONS_LIST","data":[{"auctionState":"AUCTION_NOT_RUNNING","item":
{"name":"Handmade hat","photoUrl":"assets/img/
hat.png","description":"Awesome","startingPrice":2000.0,"auctionStartTime":1356387499577,
"bidTimeoutS":30},"bestBid":2000.0,"auctionId":"second"},
{"auctionState":"AUCTION_NOT_RUNNING","item":{"name":"Painting","photoUrl":"assets/img/
paint.jpg","description":"Fancy","startingPrice":1000.0,"auctionStartTime":1356387499574,
"bidTimeoutS":30},"bestBid":1000.0,"auctionId":"first"}],"auctionId":"0"}
```

Figure 8-20. A WebSocket frame

The screenshot shown in Figure 8-21 was taken after the auction closed. You can see all the data sent over the WebSocket connection.

Figure 8-21. The entire auction conversation

Creating the Save The Child Auction Protocol

Because WebSocket is just a transport protocol, we need to come up with an application-level protocol indicating how auction messages should be formatted in the client-server interaction. This is how we decided to do it:

1. The client's code connects to the WebSocket endpoint on the server.

2. The client's code sends the AUCTION_LIST message to retrieve the list of currently running auctions:

    ```
    {
        "type": "AUCTIONS_LIST",    ❶
        "data": "empty",            ❷
        "auctionId": "-1"           ❸
    }
    ```

   ❶ The type of the message is AUCTION_LIST.

   ❷ This message doesn't send any data.

   ❸ This message doesn't request any specific auction ID, so we just send -1.

   Let's review the JSON object that will arrive from the server as the auction's response:

    ```
    {
        "type": "AUCTIONS_LIST",    ❶
        "data": [                   ❷
    ```

```
{
    "auctionState": "AUCTION_NOT_RUNNING",
    "item": {                              ❸
        "name": "Painting",
        "description": "Fancy",
        "startingPrice": 1000.0,
        "auctionStartTime": 6000,
        "bidTimeoutS": 30
    },
    "bestBid": 1000.0,
    "participantList": [],
    "auctionId": "first"      ❹
},
{
    "auctionState": "AUCTION_RUNNING",
    "item": {
        "name": "Handmade hat",
        "description": "Awesome",
        "startingPrice": 2000.0,
        "auctionStartTime": 6000,
        "bidTimeoutS": 30
    },
    "bestBid": 2000.0,
    "participantList": [],
    "auctionId": "second"
}
    ],
    "auctionId": "0"
}
```

❶   The message type is AUCTION_LIST.

❷   The data property of the response object contains the list of all running auctions. An auction can be in one of three states: *not running, running,* or *finished.*

❸   The item property of the response object is a nested object that represents the auction item.

❹   The auctionId property contains a unique identifier of the selected auction.

3. The user picks the auction from the list, enters a desired nickname, and joins the auction. The client-side application sends the following login message:

```
{
    "type": "LOGIN", ❶
    "data": "gamussa", ❷
    "auctionId": "second" ❸
}
```

❶   The message type is LOGIN.

❷   The data property of the request contains the user's nickname.

❸ The `auctionId` property helps the server-side code to route the message to the correct auction.

 As soon as the handshake completes successfully, the server-side code that implements the WebSocket protocol exposes the WebSocket `Session` object. This object encapsulates the conversation between the WebSocket endpoint (server side) and remote endpoint (browser). Check the documentation for your server-side framework for details about how it handles and exposes the remote endpoints in the API.

4. Each time a user enters a bid price, the client's code sends the following `BID` message:

```
{
    "type": "BID",
    "data": "1100.0",
    "auctionId": "second"
}
```

This is the outgoing message. When user clicks the Bid! button, the value from the Bid text box is wrapped into the `BID` message. On the server, when the new higher `BID` message arrives, the message `PRICE_UPDATE` has to be broadcast to all active clients.

5. The `PRICE_UPDATE` message looks like this:

```
{
    "type": "PRICE_UPDATE", ❶
    "data": "1300.0", ❷
    "auctionId": "second"
}
```

❶ If an auction participant outbids others, the rest of the participants will receive an update.

❷ Such an update will contain the current highest bid.

6. The `RESULT` message looks like this:

```
{
    "type": "RESULT",
    "data": "Congrats! You\u0027ve won Painting for $1300.0",
    "auctionId": "first"
}
```

After the auction ends, the server broadcasts the message with the final auction results. If the wining user is online and connected to the auction server, that user will receive a message with congratulations. Other participants will get the "Sorry, you didn't win" notification.

This is pretty much it. The amount of code needed to implement the client's side of the auction is minimal. After the connection and upgrade are done, most of the processing is done in the message handler of the WebSocket object's onmessage.

Summary

After reading this chapter, you should see the benefits of using the WebSocket protocol in web applications. In many cases, WebSocket is an ultimate means for improving application performance, by reducing network latency and removing the overhead of the HTTP headers. You learned how to integrate WebSocket-based functionality into the existing HTTP-based application Save The Child. There is no need to make communication of the web application over WebSocket. Use this powerful protocol when it improves the performance and responsiveness of your application.

As a side benefit, you've learned how to use the network monitoring capabilities of Google Chrome Developer Tools and Wireshark by sniffing the WebSocket traffic. You can't underestimate the importance of monitoring tools, which are the best friends of web developers.

## CHAPTER 9

Introduction to Web Application Security

Every newly deployed web application creates a new security hole and potential access of your organization's data. Hackers gain access to data by sneaking through ports that are supposedly hidden behind firewalls. There is no way to guarantee that your web application is 100 percent secure. If it has never been attacked by hackers, most likely it's too small and is of no interest to them.

This chapter provides a brief overview of major security vulnerabilities of which web application developers need to be aware. We also cover delegated authorization with OAuth, and possible authentication and authorization scenarios for our Save The Child application.

There are plenty of books and online articles that cover security, and enterprises usually have dedicated teams handling security for the entire organization. Dealing with security threats is their bread and butter, and this chapter won't have revelations for security professionals. But a typical enterprise application developer just knows that each person in the organization has an account in some kind of a naming server that stores IDs, passwords, and roles, which takes care of authentication and authorization flows. Application developers should find useful information in this chapter.

If an enterprise developer needs access to an internal application, opening the issue with the technical support team grants the required access privileges. But software developers should have at least a broad understanding of what makes a web application more or less secure, and which threats web applications face—this is what this chapter is about. To implement any of the security mechanisms mentioned in this chapter, you'll need to do additional research.

A good starting point for establishing security processes for your enterprise project is Microsoft's Security Development Lifecycle (*http://bit.ly/1nYsK6v*) website. It contains documents describing the software development process that helps developers build more secure software and address security compliance requirements while reducing development costs.

HTTP versus HTTPS

Imagine a popular nightclub with a tall fence and two entry doors. People are waiting in lines to get in. Door number 80 is not guarded in any way: a college student checks tickets but lets people in whether or not they have a ticket. The other door has the number 443 on it, and it's protected by an armed bully letting only qualified people in. The chances of unwanted people getting into the club through door 443 are pretty slim (unless the bully is corrupt), which is not the case with door 80—once in a while, people who have no right to be there get inside.

On a similar note, your organization has created *network security* with a firewall (the fence) with only two ports (the doors) open: 80 for HTTP requests and 443 for HTTPS. One door is not secure; the other one is.

Don't assume that your web application is secure if it's deployed behind a firewall. As long as there are open ports that allow external users to access your web application, you need to invest in the *application security*, too.

The letter *s* in *HTTPS* stands for *secure*. Technically, HTTPS creates a secure channel over an insecure Internet connection. In the past, only web pages that dealt with logins, payments, or other sensitive data would use URLs starting with *https*. Today, more and more web pages use HTTPS, and rightly so, because it forces web browsers to use Secure Sockets Layer (SSL) or its successor, Transport Layer Security (TLS) protocol, for encrypting all the data (including request and response headers) that travel between connected Internet resources. *High Performance Browser Networking* contains a chapter (*http://bit.ly/1z23t2z*) with detailed coverage of the TLS protocol.

Organizations that run web servers create a public-key certificate that has to be signed by a trusted certificate authority (otherwise, browsers will display invalid certificate warnings). The authority certifies that the holder of the certificate is a valid operator of this web server. SSL/TLS layers authenticate the servers by using these certificates to ensure that the browser's request is being processed by the proper server and not by some hacker's site.

When a client connects to a server via HTTPS, that client offers to the server a list of supported ciphers (authentication-encryption-decryption algorithms). The server replies with a cipher they both support.

 The annual Black Hat (*http://www.blackhat.com*) computer security conference is dedicated to information security. This conference is attended by both hackers and security professionals.

If HTTPS is clearly more secure than HTTP, why doesn't every website use only HTTPS communication? Because HTTPS encrypts all messages that travel between the client's browser and the server, its communications are slower and need more CPU power compared to HTTP-based data exchanges. But this slowness isn't noticeable in most web applications (unless thousands of concurrent users hit the web server), whereas the benefits of using HTTPS are huge.

When entering any sensitive or private information in someone's web application, always pay attention to the URL to make sure that it uses HTTPS.

As a web developer, you should always use HTTPS to prevent an attacker from stealing the user's session ID. The fact that the National Security Agency has broken the SSL encryption algorithm is not a reason for your application to not use HTTPS.

Authentication and Passwords

Authentication is the ability to confirm that a user is who he claims to be. The fact that the user has provided a valid ID and password combination proves only that he is known to the web application. That's all.

Specifying the correct user ID/password combination might not be enough for some web applications. Banks often ask for additional information (for example, "What's your pet's name?" or "What's your favorite movie?").

Large corporations often use RSA SecurID (a.k.a. RSA hard token), which is a physical device with a randomly generated combination of digits. This combination changes every minute or so and has to be entered as a part of the authentication process. In addition to physical devices, programs (soft tokens) can perform user authentication in a similar way. Many financial institutions, social networks, and large web portals support two-factor verification: in addition to asking for a user ID and password, they send you an email, voice mail, or text message with a code that you'll need to use after entering the right ID/password combination.

To make the authentication process more secure, some systems check the biometrics of the user. For example, in the United States, the Global Entry system is implemented in many international airports. People who successfully pass a special background check are entered into the system deployed at passport-control checkpoints. These applications, deployed in a special kiosks, scan users' passports and check the face topography and fingerprints. The process takes only a few seconds, and the *authenticated* person can pass the border without waiting in long lines.

Biometric devices have become more common these days, and fingerprint scanners that can be connected to a user's computer are very inexpensive. Apple's iPhone 5S unlocks based on the fingerprint of its owner—no need to enter a passcode. In some places, you can enter a gym only after your fingerprints have been scanned and matched. The National Institute of Standards and Technology hosts a discussion about using biometric web services, and you can participate by sending an email to *bws-request@nist.gov* with *subscribe* as the subject.

Basic and Digest Authentication

HTTP defines two types of authentication: Basic (*http://bit.ly/1k5Nmam*) and Digest (*http://bit.ly/1ohMIuu*). All modern web browsers support them, but basic authentication uses Base64 encoding and no encryption, which means it should be used only with HTTPS.

A web server administrator can configure certain resources to require basic user authentication. If a web browser requests a protected resource but the user didn't log in to the site, the web server (not your application) sends the HTTP response containing HTTP status code 401 (*Unauthorized* and *WWW-Authenticate: Basic*). The browser pops up the login dialog box. The user enters the ID/password, which is turned into an encoded *userID:password* string and sent to the server as a part of HTTP header. Basic authentication provides no confidentiality because it doesn't encrypt the transmitted credentials. Cookies are not used here.

With digest authentication, the server also responds with 401 (*WWW-Authenticate: Digest*). However, it sends along additional data that allows the web browser to apply a hash function to the password. Then, the browser sends an encrypted password to the server. Digest authentication is more secure than the basic one, but it's still less secure than authentication that uses public keys or the Kerberos authentication protocol.

 The HTTP status code 403 (*Forbidden*) differs from 401. Whereas 401 means that the user needs to log in to access the resource, 403 means that the user is authenticated, but his security level is not high enough to see the data. For example, not every user role is authorized to see a web page that displays salary reports.

In application security, the term *man-in-the-middle attack* refers to an attacker intercepting and modifying data transmitted between two parties (usually the client and the server). Digest authentication protects the web application from losing the clear-text password to an attacker, but doesn't prevent man-in-the-middle attacks.

Whereas digest authentication encrypts only the user ID and password, using HTTPS encrypts everything that goes between the web browser and the server.

Single Sign-on

Often, an enterprise user has to work with more than one corporate web application, and maintaining, remembering, and supporting multiple passwords should be avoided. Many enterprises implement internally a single sign-on (SSO) mechanism to eliminate the need for a user to enter login credentials more than once, even if that user works with multiple applications. Accordingly, signing out from one of these applications terminates the user's access to all of them. SSO solutions make authentication totally transparent to your application.

With SSO, when the user logs on to your application, the logon request is intercepted and handled by preconfigured SSO software (for example, Oracle Enterprise Single Sign-On, CA SiteMinder, IBM Security Access Manager for Enterprise SSO, or Evidian Enterprise SSO). The SSO infrastructure verifies a user's credentials by making a call to a corporate Lightweight Directory Access Protocol (LDAP) server and creates a user's session. Usually a web server is configured with some web agent that will add the user's credentials to the HTTP header, which your application can fetch.

Future access to the protected web application is handled automatically by the SSO server, without even displaying a logon window, as long as the user's session is active. SSO servers also log all login attempts in a central place, which can be important in meeting enterprise regulatory requirements (for example, Sarbanes-Oxley in the financial industry or medical confidentiality in the insurance business).

In the consumer-oriented Internet space, single (or reduced) sign-on solutions have become more and more popular. For example, some web applications allow you to reuse your Twitter or Facebook credentials (provided that you've logged in to one of these applications) without the need to go through additional authentication procedures. Basically, your application can delegate authentication procedures to Facebook, Twitter, Google, and other authorization services, which we'll discuss later in "OAuth-Based Authentication and Authorization" on page 342.

Back in 2010, Facebook introduced its SSO solution (*http://on.fb.me/1lrYTAw*) that still helps millions of people log in to other applications. This is especially important in the mobile world, where users' typing should be minimized. Instead of asking a user to enter credentials, your application can provide a Login with Facebook button.

Facebook has published a JavaScript API with which you can implement Facebook Login in your web applications (it also offers native APIs for iOS and Android apps).

For more details, read the online documentation on the FaceBook Login API (*http://bit.ly/1lE6QlY*).

Besides Facebook, other popular social networks offer authentication across applications:

- If you want your application to have a Login with Twitter button, refer to the Sign in with Twitter API documentation (*http://bit.ly/1eon8lS*).

- LinkedIn is a popular social network for professionals. It also offers an API for creating a Sign In with LinkedIn button. For details, visit the LinkedIn online documentation (*http://linkd.in/1oGVXaT*) for developers.

- Google also offers the OAuth-based authentication API. Details about its client library for JavaScript are published online (*http://bit.ly/1lE72S0*). To implement SAML-based SSO with Google, visit this web page (*http://bit.ly/1lDmN00*).

- Mozilla offers a new way to sign in with any of your existing email addresses by using Persona (*http://mzl.la/1uDllM7*).

- Several large organizations (for example, Google, Yahoo!, Microsoft, and Facebook) either issue or accept OpenID (*http://openid.net*), which makes it possible for users to sign in to more than 50,000 websites.

Typically, large enterprises don't want users to use logins from social networks. But some organizations have started integrating their applications with social networks. Especially now, with the spread of mobile devices, users might need to be authenticated and authorized while being outside the enterprise perimeter. We discuss this in more detail in "OAuth-Based Authentication and Authorization" on page 342.

Save The Child and SSO

Does our Save The Child application have a use for SSO? Certainly. In this book, we're concerned mostly about developing a UI for the consumer-facing part of this application. But there is also a back-office team that is involved with content management and that produces information for the consumer.

For example, the employees of our charity organization create fundraising campaigns in different cities. If an employee of this firm logged in to his desktop, our Save The Child web application shouldn't ask him to log in. SSO can be a solution here.

Handling Passwords

It might sound obvious, but we'll still remind you that the web client should never send passwords in clear text. You should always use a Secure Hash Algorithm (*http://bit.ly/1mdvAaS*) (SHA). Longer passwords are more secure, because if an attacker tries to guess the password by using dictionaries to generate every possible combination of characters (a *brute-force attack* (*http://bit.ly/1l3kzHE*)), it will take a lot more time with long passwords. Periodically changing passwords makes the hacker's work more difficult, too. Typically, after successful authentication, the server creates and sends to the web client the session ID, which is stored as a cookie on the client's computer. Then, on each subsequent request to the server, the web browser places the session ID in the HTTP request object and sends it along with each request. Technically, the user's identity is always known at the server side, so the server-side code can re-authenticate the user more than once (without the user even knowing it), whenever the web client requests the protected resource.

Salted hashes increase security by adding *salt*—randomly generated data that's concatenated with the password and then processed by a hash function.

Have you ever wondered why automated teller machines (ATMs) often ask you to enter your PIN more than once? Say you've deposited a check and then want to see the balance on your account. After the check deposit is completed, your ATM session is invalidated to protect careless users who might rush out from the bank in a hurry as soon as the transaction is finished. This prevents the next person at the ATM from requesting a cash withdrawal from your bank account.

On the same note, if a web application's session is idling for more than the allowed time interval, the session should be automatically invalidated. For example, if a trader in a brokerage house stops interacting with a web trading application for some time, invalidate the session programmatically to prevent someone else from buying financial products on his behalf when he steps out for a coffee.

Authorization

Authorization is a way to determine which operations the user can perform and what data he can access. For example, the owner of a company can perform money withdrawals and transfers from an online business bank account, whereas the company accountant is provided with read-only access.

Similar to authentication, the user's authorization can be checked more than once during that user's session. As a matter of fact, authorization can even change during a session (for example, a financial application can allow trades only during business hours of the stock exchange).

Users of an application are grouped by roles, and each role comes with a set of privileges. A user can be given a privilege to read and modify certain data, whereas other data can be hidden. In the relational DBMS realm, the term *row-level security* means that the same query can produce different results for different users. Such security policies are implemented at the data-source level.

A simple use case for which row-level security is really useful is a salary report. Whereas the employee can see only his salary report, the head of department can see the data of all subordinates.

Authorization is usually linked to a user's session. HTTP is a stateless protocol, so if a user retrieves a web page from a web server, and then goes to another web page, this second page does not know what has been shown or selected on the first one. In an online store, for example, a user adds an item to a shopping cart and moves to another page to continue shopping. To preserve the data reused in more than one web page (for example, the content of the shopping cart), the server-side code must implement *session-tracking*. The session information can be passed all the way down to the database level when need be.

 Session tracking is usually controlled on the server side. To become familiar with session tracking options in greater detail, consult the product documentation for the server or technology being used with your web application. For example, if you use Java, you can read Oracle's documentation for its WebLogic server (*http://bit.ly/ T7Ba1U*) that describes options for session management.

OAuth-Based Authentication and Authorization

To put it simply, OAuth is a mechanism for delegated authorization. OpenID Connect is an OAuth-based mechanism for authentication.

Most likely, you have come across web applications that enable you to share your actions via social networks. For example, if you just made a donation, you might want to share this information via social networks.

If our charity application needs to access a user's Facebook account for authentication, the charity app could ask for the user's Facebook ID and password. This wouldn't be the correct approach, however, because the charity application would get the user's Facebook ID/password in clear text, along with full access to the user's Facebook account. The charity app needs only to authenticate the Facebook user. Hence, there is a need for a mechanism that gives *limited access* to Facebook.

OAuth (*http://oauth.net/*) has become one of the mechanisms for providing limited access to an authorizing facility. OAuth is "An open protocol to allow secure authorization in a simple and standard method from web, mobile and desktop applications." Its current draft specification (*http://bit.ly/rfc-6749*) provides the following definition:

> The OAuth 2.0 authorization framework enables a third-party application to obtain limited access to an HTTP service, either on behalf of a resource owner by orchestrating an approval interaction between the resource owner and the HTTP service, or by allowing the third-party application to obtain access on its own behalf.

"OAuth Study Notes" (*http://bit.ly/1nuEEJC*) includes the following:

> Many luxury cars come with a valet key. It is a special key you give the parking attendant and unlike your regular key, will only allow the car to be driven a short distance while blocking access to the trunk.

This is a good example of limited access to a resource in a real life. The OAuth 2.0 authorization server gives the requesting application an *access token* (think, valet key) so it can access, say, the charity application.

OAuth allows users to give limited access to third-party applications without giving away their passwords. The access permission is given to the user in the form of an access token with limited privileges and for a limited time. Coming back to our example of communication between the charity app and Facebook (unless we have our own enterprise authentication server), the former would gain limited access to the user's Facebook account (just the valet key, not the master key).

OAuth has become a standard protocol for developing applications that require authorization. With OAuth, application developers won't need to use proprietary protocols if they need to add an ability to identify a user via multiple authorization servers.

Federated Identity with OpenID Connect and JSON Web Tokens

Wikipedia defines *federated identity* (*http://bit.ly/1m2k806*) as a means of linking a person's electronic identity and attributes, stored across multiple distinct identity management systems. This is similar to enterprise SSO, but the effect of federated identity is broader because the authentication token with information about a user's identity can be passed across multiple departments or organizations and software systems.

Microsoft's "A Guide to Claims-Based Identity and Access Control" (*http://bit.ly/1r8sgNa*) includes a section on federated identity for web applications (*http://bit.ly/1r8sfsw*) with greater details on this subject.

In the past, the markup language SAML (*http://bit.ly/1pJ5FJv*) was the most popular open-standard data format for exchanging authentication and authorization data. OpenID Connect (*http://openid.net/connect*) is a newer open standard. It's a layer on top of OAuth 2.0 that simply verifies the identity of a user. OpenID providers (*http://openid.net/get-an-openid/*) that can confirm a user's identity include such companies as Google, Yahoo!, IBM, Verisign, and more. Typically, OpenID Connect uses JSON Web Token (JWT) (*http://bit.ly/T7BMED*), which should eventually replace popular XML-based SAML tokens. JWT is a Base64 encoded and signed JSON data structure. Although the OAuth 2.0 spec doesn't mandate using JWT, it became a de facto standard token format.

To have a better understanding of how JWTs are encoded, visit the Federation Lab (*http://openidtest.uninett.no/jwt*), which is a website with a set of tools for testing and verifying various identity protocols. In particular, you can enter a JWT in clear text, select a secret signature, and encode the token by using the HS256 algorithm, as shown in Figure 9-1.

Figure 9-1. Encoding a JSON Web Token

Using the Facebook API

Facebook is one of the authorization servers that offer an OAuth-based authentication and authorization API. The online document "Quickstart: Facebook SDK for Java-Script" (*http://bit.ly/1jzg4jx*) is a good starting point.

Before using the SDK, you need to register your application with Facebook by creating a client ID and obtaining the client secret (the password). Then, use the JavaScript SDK code (provided by Facebook) in your web application. Include the newly created app ID there. During this registration stage, you'll need to specify the URI where the user should be redirected in case of successful login. Then, add a JavaScript code to support the required Facebook API (for example, for Login) to your application. You can find sample JavaScript code that uses the Facebook Login API in this guide (*http://bit.ly/ 1qecvV1*).

The Facebook Login API communicates with your application by sending events as soon as the login status changes. Facebook will send the authorization token to your application's code. As we mentioned earlier, the authorization token is a secure encoded string that identifies the user and the app, contains information about permissions, and has an expiration time. Your application's JavaScript code makes calls to the Facebook SDK API, and each of these calls will include the token as a parameter or inside the HTTP request header.

OAuth 2.0 Main Actors

Any communication with OAuth 2.0 servers are made through HTTPS connections. The following are the main actors of the OAuth flows:

- The user who owns the account with some of the resource servers (for example, an account at Facebook or Google) is called the *resource owner*.

- The application that tries to authenticate the resource owner is called the *client application*. This is an application that offers buttons such as Login with Facebook, Login with Twitter, and the like.

- The *resource server* is a place where the resource owner stores his data (for example, Facebook or Google).

- The *authorization server* checks the credentials of the resource owner and returns an authorization token with limited information about the user. This server can be the same as the resource server but is not necessarily the same one. Facebook, Google, Windows Live, Twitter, and GitHub are examples of authorization servers. For the current list of OAuth 2.0 implementations, visit oauth.net/2.

To implement OAuth in your client application, you need to pick a resource/authorization server and study its API documentation. Keep in mind that OAuth defines two types of clients: public and confidential. Public clients use embedded passwords while communicating with the authorization server. If you're going to keep the password inside your JavaScript code, it won't be safe. To be considered a confidential client, a web application should store its password on the server side.

OAuth has provisions for creating authorization tokens for browser-only applications, for mobile applications, and for server-to-server communications.

Save The Child and OAuth

We can distinguish two major scenarios of a third-party application working with an OAuth server. In one scenario, OAuth authorization servers are publicly available. In the other scenario, the servers are privately owned by the enterprise. Let's consider these scenarios in the context of our charity nonprofit organization.

Public authorization servers

A Facebook account owner works with *the client* (the Save The Child application). The client uses an external *authorization server* (Facebook) to request authorization of the user's work with the charity application. The client has to be registered (has an assigned client ID, secret, and redirect URL) with the authorization server to be able to participate in this OAuth flow. The authorization server returns a token offering limited access (for example, to Facebook's account) to the Save The Child application. Figure 9-2 shows Save The Child using Facebook for authentication and authorization.

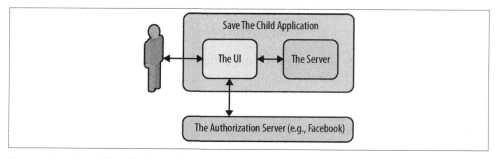

Figure 9-2. Save The Child and OAuth

While the client application tries to get authorization from the authorization server, it can open a so-called *consent window* that warns the user that the Save The Child application is trying to access certain information from the user's Facebook or Google account. In this scenario, the user still has a chance to deny such access. It's a good idea to display a message that the user's password (to Facebook or Google) will not be given to the client application.

Your application should request only minimum access to the user's resource server. For example, if the Save The Child application just needs to offer an easy authentication method for all Facebook users, don't request write access to the user's Facebook account. On the other hand, if a child was cured as a result of the involvement of our charity application, and he wants to share the good news with his Facebook friends, the Save The Child application needs write permission to the user's Facebook account.

The UI code of the Save The Child application doesn't have to know how to parse the token returned by the authorization server. It can simply pass it to Save The Child's server software (for example, via the HTTP request header). The server has to know how to read and decipher the information from the token. The client application sends to the authorization server only the client ID, and not the *client secret* needed for deciphering the user's information from the token.

Private authorization servers

The OAuth authorization server is configured inside the enterprise. However, the server can attend to not only internal employees, but also external partners. Suppose that one of the upcoming charity events is a marathon to fight cancer. To prepare this marathon, our charity organization needs the help of a partner company named Global Marathon Suppliers, which will take care of the logistics (providing banners, water, food, rain ponchos, blankets, branded tents, and so forth).

It would be nice if our supplier could have up-to-date information about the number of participants in this event. If our charity firm sets them up with access to our internal authorization server, the employees of Global Marathon Suppliers can have limited access to the marathon participants. On the other hand, if the suppliers open limited access to their data, this could increase the productivity of the charity company employees. This is a practical and cost-saving setup.

 The authors of this book have helped the Leukemia and Lymphoma Society (LLS) (*http://www.lls.org*) develop both front- and backend software. LLS ran a number of successful marathons as well as many other campaigns for charity causes. We also use an OAuth solution from Intuit QuickBooks (*http://bit.ly/1lVNwVX*) in billing workflows for our insurance industry software product at SuranceBay (*http://www.surancebay.com*). Our partner companies get limited access to our billing systems, and our software can access theirs.

Top Security Risks

The Open Web Application Security Project (OWASP) (*https://www.owasp.org*) is an open source project focused on improving security of web applications by providing a collection of guides and tools. OWASP publishes and maintains a list of the top 10 security risks (*http://bit.ly/1lE9VSQ*). Figure 9-3 shows how this list looked in 2013.

On this website, you can drill down into each list item to see the selected security vulnerabilities and recommendations on how to prevent them. You can also download this list as a PDF document (*http://bit.ly/1r5Bi0m*). Let's review a couple of the top-10 security threats: *injection* and *cross-site scripting*.

Injection

If a bad guy can *inject* a piece of code that will run inside your web application, that code could steal or damage data from the application. In the world of compiled libraries and executables, injecting malicious code is a rather difficult task. But if an application

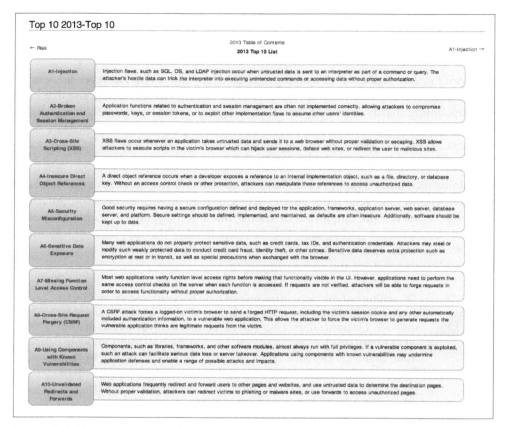

Figure 9-3. Top 10 security risks, circa 2013

uses interpreted languages (for example, JavaScript or clear-text SQL), the task of injecting malicious code becomes a lot easier than you might think. Let's look at a typical example of SQL injection.

Suppose that your application can search for data based on keywords a user enters into a text input field. For example, to find all donors in the city of New York, a user enters the following:

```
"New York"; delete from donors;
```

If the server-side code of your application simply attaches the entered text to the SQL statement, this could result in execution of the following command:

```
Select * from donors where city="New York"; delete from donors;
```

This command doesn't require any additional comments, does it? Is there a way to prevent users of your web application from entering something like this? The first thing that comes to mind is to not allow the user to enter the city, but force her to select it from a list. But such a list of possible values might be huge. Besides, the hacker can modify the HTTP request after the browser sends it to the server.

 Always use precompiled SQL statements that use parameters to pass the user's input into the database query (for example, `PreparedStatement` in Java).

The importance of server-side validation shouldn't be underestimated. In some scenarios, you can come up with a regular expression that checks for matching patterns in data received from clients. In other cases, you can write a regular expression that invalidates data if it contains SQL (or other) keywords that lead to modifications of data on the server.

 Always minimize the interval between validating and using the data.

In an ideal world, client-side code should not even send nonvalidated data to the server. But in the real-world, you'll end up duplicating some of the validation code in both the client and the server.

Cross-Site Scripting

Cross-site scripting (XSS) occurs when an attacker injects malicious code into a browser-side script of your web application. The user is accessing a trusted website, but gets an injection from a malicious server that reaches the user via the trusted server (hence, *cross-site*). Single-page Ajax-based applications make lots of under-the-hood requests to servers, which increases the attack surface compared to traditional legacy websites that download web pages a lot less frequently. XSS can happen in three ways:

Reflected (a.k.a. phishing)
> The web page contains a link that seems valid, but when the user clicks it, the user's browser receives and executes the script created by the attacker.

Stored
> The external attacker manages to store a malicious script on a server that hosts someone's web application, so every user gets the script as a part of that web page,

and their web browser executes it. For example, if a user's forum allows posting texts that include JavaScript code, malicious code typed by a "bad guy" can be saved in the server's database and executed by users' browsers visiting this forum afterward.

Local

No server is involved. Web page A opens web page B with malicious code, which in turn modifies the code of page A. If your application uses a hash tag (#) in URLs (for example, *http://savesickchild.org#something*), make sure that before processing, this *something* doesn't contain anything like `javascript:somecode`, which might have been attached to the URL by an attacker.

The World Wide Web Consortium (W3C) has published a draft of the Content Security Policy (*http://bit.ly/1iMQXiD*) document, "a mechanism web applications can use to mitigate a broad class of content injection vulnerabilities, such as cross-site scripting."

STRIDE—Classification of Security Threats

Microsoft has published a classification (*http://bit.ly/1mzDuFP*) that divides security threats into six categories (hence six letters in the acronym STRIDE):

Spoofing

An attacker pretends to be a legitimate user of an application (for example, a banking system). This can be implemented by using XSS.

Tampering

Modifying data that was not supposed to be modified (for example, via SQL injection).

Repudiation

The user denies sending data (for example, making an online transaction such as a purchase or sale) by modifying the application's logfiles.

Information disclosure

An attacker gains access to classified information.

Denial of service (a.k.a. DoS)

A server is made unavailable to legitimate users, which often is implemented by generating a large number of simultaneous requests to saturate the server.

Elevation of privilege

Gaining an elevated level of access to data (for example, by obtaining administrative rights).

While we were working on a section of this book describing Apple's developer certificates (Chapter 14), its website was hacked, and was not available for about two weeks.

One of the OWASP guides is titled Web Application Penetration Testing (*http://bit.ly/1iMRhxQ*). In about 350 pages, it explains the methodology of testing a web application for each vulnerability. OWASP defines *penetration test* as a method of evaluating the security of a computer system by simulating an attack. Hundreds of security experts from around the world have contributed to this guide. Running penetration tests should become part of your development process, and the sooner you start running them, the better.

For example, the Payment Card Industry published a Data Security Standard, which includes a Requirement 11.3 (*http://bit.ly/TJkRsh*) of penetration testing.

Regulatory Compliance and Enterprise Security

So far in this chapter, we've been discussing security vulnerabilities from a technical perspective. But another aspect can't be ignored: the regulatory compliance of the business you automate.

During the last four years, the authors of this book have developed, deployed, supported, and marketed software that automates certain workflows for insurance agents. We serve several hundred insurance agencies and more than 100,000 agents. In this section, we'll share our real-world experience of dealing with security while running our company, which sells software as a service. In addition to developing the application, we had to set up data centers and take care of security issues, too.

Our customers are insurance agencies and carriers. We charge for our services, and our customers pay by using credit cards via our application. This opens up a totally different category of security concerns:

- Where are the credit card numbers stored?
- What if they are stolen?
- How secure is the payment portion of the application?
- How is the card holder's data protected?
- Is there a firewall protecting each customer's data?
- How is the data encrypted?

One of the first questions our prospective customers ask is whether our application is *PCI compliant*. They won't work with us until they review the *application-level security* implemented in our system. As per the PCI Compliance Guide (*http://bit.ly/ 1r5C4dB*), "The Payment Card Industry Data Security Standard is used by all card brands to assure the security of the data gathered while an employee is making a transaction at a bank or participating vendor."

If your application stores PCI data, authenticating via Facebook, Google, or a similar OAuth service isn't an option. Users are required to authenticate themselves by entering long passwords containing combinations of letters, numbers, and special characters.

Even if you are not dealing with credit card information, there are other areas where application data must be protected. Take a human resources application—Social Security numbers (unique IDs of United States citizens) of employees must be encrypted.

Some of our prospective customers send us a questionnaire to establish whether our security measures are compliant with their requirements. In some cases, this document can include as many as 300 questions.

You might want to implement different levels of security depending on which type of device is being used to access your application—a public computer, an internal corporate computer, an iPad, or an Android tablet. If a desktop user forgets his password, you could implement a recovery mechanism that sends an email to that user and expects to receive a certain response from him. If the user has a smartphone, the application could send a text message to that device.

If the user's record contains both his email and cell phone number, the application should ask where to send the password recovery instructions. If a mobile device runs a hybrid or native version of the application, the user could be automatically switched to a messaging app of the device so that he can read the text message while the main application remains at the view where authentication is required.

In enterprise web applications, more than one layer of security must be implemented: at the communication protocol level, at the session level, and at the application level. The HTTP server NGINX (*http://nginx.com*), besides being a high-performance proxy server and load balancer, can serve as a security layer, too. Your web application can offload authentication tasks and validation of SSL certificates to NGINX.

Most enterprise web applications are deployed on a cluster of servers, which adds another task to your project plan: how to manage sessions in a cluster. The user's session has to be shared among all servers in a cluster. High-end application servers might implement this feature out of the box. For example, an IBM WebSphere server has an option to tightly integrate HTTP sessions with its application security module. Another example is Terracotta clusters, which utilize Terracotta Web Sessions to allow sessions to survive node hops and failures. But small or mid-sized applications might require custom solutions for distributed sessions.

Minimize the amount of data stored in a user's session, to simplify session replication. Store the data in an application cache that can be replicated quickly and efficiently by using open source or commercial products (for example, JGroups or Terracotta).

Here's another topic to consider: multiple data centers, with each one running a cluster of servers. To speed up the disaster recovery process, your web application has to be deployed in more than one data center, located in different geographical regions. User authentication must work even if one of the data centers becomes nonoperational.

An external computer (for example, a NGINX server) can perform token-based authentication, but inside the system, the token is used only when access to protected resources is required. For example, when the application needs to process a payment, it doesn't need to know any credit card details; it just uses the token to authorize the transaction of the previously authenticated user.

This grab bag of security considerations mentioned in this section is not a complete list of security-related issues to which your IT organization needs to attend. If you work for a large enterprise on intranet applications, these security issues might not sound overly important. But as soon as your web application starts serving external Internet users, someone has to worry about potential security holes that were not in the picture for internal applications. Our message to you is simple: Take security very seriously if you are planning to develop, deploy, and run a production-grade enterprise web application.

Summary

Every enterprise web application has to run in a secure environment. The mere fact that the application runs inside a firewall doesn't make it secure. First, if you're opening at least one port to the outside world, malicious code can sneak in. Second, an "angry employee" or just a "curious programmer" inside the organization could inject unwanted code.

Proper validation of received data is very important. Ideally, use *white list* validation to compare user input against a list of allowed values. Otherwise, use *black list* validation to compare against keywords that are not allowed in data entered by users.

There is no way to guarantee that your application is 100 percent protected from security breaches. But you should ensure that your application runs in an environment with the latest available patches for known security vulnerabilities. For example, if your application includes components written in the Java programming language, install critical security patches (*http://bit.ly/Uc1Gbg*) as soon as they become available.

With the proliferation of clouds, social networks, and sites that offer free or cheap storage, people lose control over security, hoping that Amazon, Google, or Dropbox will take care of it. Besides software solutions, software-as-a-service providers deploy specialized hardware—security appliances that serve as firewalls, perform content filtering, and virus and intrusion detection. Interestingly enough, hardware security appliances are also vulnerable.

In any case, end users upload their personal files without thinking twice. Enterprises are more cautious and prefer private clouds installed on their own servers, where they administer and protect data themselves. Users who access the Internet from their mobile devices have little or no control over how secure their devices are. So the person in charge of the web application has to make sure that it's as secure as possible.

## PART III

Responsive Web Design and Mobile Devices

BYOD stands for *bring your own device*. It has become a new trend as a result of the increasing number of enterprises that started allowing their employees to access corporate applications from personal tablets or smartphones.

CYOD stands for *choose your own device*. In this paradigm, corporations let their employees choose from a set of devices that belong to the enterprise. CYOD is about selecting a strategy that organizations should employ while approving new devices.

Developers of new web applications should always think of the users who will try to run the application on a mobile device. This part of the book is about various strategies for developing web applications that look and perform well on both desktop computers and smaller screens.

Today, most enterprise applications are still being developed for desktop computers. The situation is changing, but it's a slow process. If five years ago it was close to impossible to get permission to bring your own computer to work and use it for work-related activities, the situation is entirely different now with BYOD and CYOD.

Sales people want to use tablets while dealing with prospective clients. Business analysts want to be able to run familiar web applications on their smartphones. Enterprises want to offer external access access to valuable data from a variety of devices.

In Chapter 10 we explain *responsive web design* (RWD) and how you can build an HTML5 application that has a single code base for desktops, tablets, and smartphones. We'll apply responsive design principles and redesign our Save The Child application to have a fluid layout (*http://bit.ly/1jLsDZe*) so that it will remain usable on smaller screens, too.

Another approach is to have separate versions of the application for desktops and mobile devices. Chapter 11 and Chapter 12 demonstrate how to create dedicated mobile versions of web applications with the jQuery Mobile library and Sencha Touch framework, respectively. And the Save The Child application is rewritten in each of these chapters.

But if using RWD allows you to have a single code base for all devices, you might be wondering, why not just build every web application this way? RWD works fine for sites that mainly publish information. But if users are expected not just to read, but also to input data on small-screen devices, the UI and the navigation might need to be custom designed to include only partial functionality while each page view provides the best user experience. Besides, with responsive design, the code and CSS for all devices is loaded to a user's smartphone, making the application unnecessarily large and slow when the connection speed is not great.

With small screens, you have to rethink carefully about which widgets are must-haves and what functionality is crucial to the business for which you're creating a web application. If it's a restaurant, you need to provide an easy way to find the menu, phone, address, and directions to your location. If it's a site to collect donations, like Save The Child, the design should provide an easy way to donate, while the rest of the information should be hidden by simple navigational menus.

On rare occasions, an enterprise application is created solely for mobile platforms. More often, the task is to migrate an existing application to a mobile platform or develop separate versions of the same application for desktops and mobile devices. If a decision is made to develop native mobile applications, the choice of programming languages is dictated by the mobile hardware.

If it's a web application, using the same library or framework for desktop and mobile platforms can shorten the development cycle. That's why we decided to cover such pairs in this book, namely:

- jQuery and jQuery Mobile
- Ext JS and Sencha Touch

But even though each of these pairs shares the same code for core components, do not expect to be able to kill two birds with one stone. You are still going to use different versions of the code—for example, jQuery 2.0 and jQuery Mobile 1.3.1. This means that you might have to deal with separate bugs that sneaked into the desktop and mobile version of the frameworks.

What's better: jQuery Mobile or Sencha Touch? There is no general answer to this question. It all depends on the application you're building. If you need a simple mobile application for displaying various information (a publishing type of application), jQuery Mobile will do the job with the least effort. If you are building an application that requires some serious data processing, Sencha Touch is a better choice. Of course, lots of other frameworks and libraries are available that can help you develop a mobile web application. Do your homework and pick the one that best fits your needs.

There's a website (*http://bit.ly/1pKhBt1*) that compares mobile frameworks. It even has a little wizard application with which you can pick a framework that meets your needs and is supported on required devices. Figure III.1 is a fragment snapshot from this site. As you can see, jQuery Mobile supports the largest number of platforms.

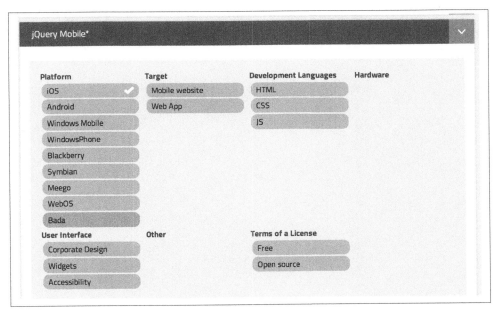

Figure III.1. Platforms supported by jQuery Mobile

 A framework called Zepto (*http://zeptojs.com*) is a minimalist JavaScript library with an API compatible to jQuery. Zepto supports both desktop and mobile browsers.

Finally, in Chapter 13 we talk about yet another approach for developing HTML5 applications for mobile devices: *hybrid* applications. These applications are written in JavaScript but are packaged as native apps. You'll learn how Adobe's PhoneGap can package an HTML5 application to be accepted in online stores where native applications are being offered. To illustrate accessing hardware features of a mobile device, we show you how to access the device's camera; this can be a useful feature for the Save The Child application.

## CHAPTER 10

Responsive Design: One Site Fits All

Up until now, we've been writing and rewriting the desktop version of the Save The Child application. Will it look good on the small screen of a mobile device? Beginning with this chapter, we'll deal with mobile devices, too.

Let's discuss different approaches to developing a web application that can work on both desktop and mobile devices. There are three choices:

Seperate versions of native applications

> In addition to your web application that works on desktops, develop a separate version of the native application for multiple mobile devices. Development of native mobile applications is not covered in this book.

Single HTML applications with multiple UIs

> Develop a single HTML5 web application, but create various UI layouts that will be applied automatically, based on the screen size of the user's device.

Hybrid applications

> In addition to your web application that works on desktops, develop a *hybrid application*. This web application on steroids works inside the mobile browser but is packaged as a native app and can invoke the native API of the mobile device, too. Chapter 13 is dedicated to hybrid applications.

This chapter focuses the second approach, called *responsive web design* (RWD). This term was coined by Ethan Marcotte in his article, "Responsive Web Design." (*http://bit.ly/1soL4vY*) The concept that underlies RWD is that the design of the web page changes, responding (reacting) to the display size of the user's device. We'll modify the design of the Save The Child site to introduce different layouts for the desktop, tablet, and smartphones. By the end of this chapter, the Save The Child site will automatically change its layout (without losing functionality) based on the screen size of the user's device.

One or Two Versions of Code?

Run any version of our Save The Child application from the first chapters on your desktop and start dragging the right border of the browser's window to make it narrower. At some point, you'll see only part of the content; those layouts were not meant to be responsive. The application defines fixed sizes for page sections, which don't change even if the display area shrinks.

Enter **http://savesickchild.org** in your mobile phone's browser. Select the version titled HTML/AJAX. You'll see either partial content on the page or the entire page with illegible small fonts as in Figure 10-1. This design of the Save The Child application doesn't look good on all devices.

Figure 10-1. Nonresponsive version of the app on iPhone 5

Now try the version titled Responsive Design; this looks more usable on a small screen. Of course, this begs the question: how many versions of the UI do we need to create? People responsible for developing web applications that can run on both desktop and mobile platforms usually begin by making an important decision: HTML5 or native? But even if a decision is made in favor of the web platform, the next question is whether desktop and mobile clients will use the same code.

If a decision is made to go with separate versions of the web application, the web server can be configured to perform redirection to the appropriate code depending on the type of device the user has. Web servers can do it based on the value of the User-Agent attribute of the HTTP request header. For example, mobile web browsers trying to access the BBC (*http://www.bbc.com/*) (or any other web page) report their User-Agent to the server differently from desktop computers; hence, they receive different content delivered from a different URL. Figures 10-2 and 10-3 show snapshots of the BBC main page that were taken at the same time. Figure 10-2 shows how the page looks on a desktop computer, whereas Figure 10-3 was taken on an iPhone.

 The Safari browser has a Develop menu, where you can select various User Agents to see how the current web page will look on different web browsers. You can also copy and paste a User Agent string from the site the User Agent string website (*http://bit.ly/1pbrL8i*) to see how a web page will look in hundreds of devices if the website is user-agent driven.

The page layout shown in Figure 10-2 delivers more content because that content can be allocated nicely on a large desktop monitor or a tablet. But the mobile version shown in Figure 10-3 substantially limits what's delivered to the client—not only because the screen is small, but because the user might be accessing the page over a slower network.

Have you ever tried to share the link of a website specifically designed for smartphones? It's so easy! Just press the button and enter the email of the person with whom you want to share the site. Many mobile websites shared this way won't look pretty on the large screen. It might just show a wider version of what you see on your mobile screen.

Maintaining two versions of the application code requires more effort than maintaining one: you need to have two sets of HTML, CSS, JavaScript, and images. Besides, most likely your web application will use a third-party JavaScript framework. At some point, you might run into a bug and will need to upgrade the mobile version to use the latest version of, say, the jQuery framework. But the desktop version works just fine. If you have two separate versions of the application, you'll have to either upgrade jQuery and thoroughly test both mobile and desktop versions of Save The Child, or live with two versions of the framework.

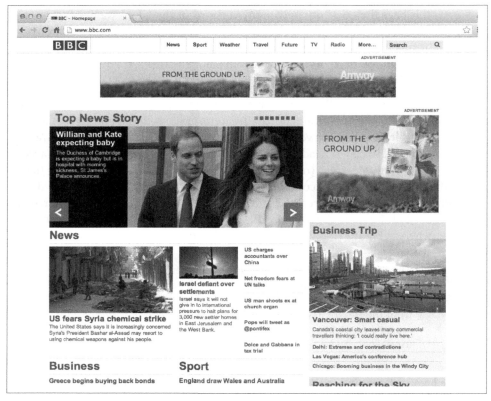

Figure 10-2. The desktop version of bbc.com

Responsive design makes it possible for you to create one version of the web application, which includes multiple sections of CSS controlling page layouts for different screen sizes. In this chapter, we'll create yet another version of the Save The Child application that will render its UI differently on desktop and mobile devices. All these versions, will share the same HTML and JavaScript code, but will include several screen layouts using *CSS media queries*.

Many websites have been built using responsive design. The list that follows presents several examples. Take a few moments to look at them, first from a desktop computer and then from a smartphone (or just lower the width of the desktop browser window), to experience fluid responsive design:

- Boston Globe (*http://bostonglobe.com*)

- Mashable (*http://mashable.com*)

- Cafe Evoke (*http://cafeevoke.com*)

Figure 10-3. The mobile version of bbc.com

- Fork CMS (*http://www.fork-cms.com*)
- A lot more examples (*http://mediaqueri.es*)

Note that each of these web pages displays content on the desktop in three layouts (often in three, four, six, or twelve imaginary columns). As you make the window narrower, the layout automatically switches to a tablet or a large smartphone mode (usually a two-column layout), and then to the phone mode layout (the one-column layout).

This sounds like a great solution, but if you put all your media queries in the same CSS files, your users will be downloading unnecessary bytes—the entire CSS file that includes all versions of screen layouts. This is not the case in the BBC example, which has different versions of the code that load only what's necessary for a particular device category.

You can have several CSS files for different devices. Include these files by using the media attributes. But web browsers were not designed to selectively download only those CSS files that are needed. For example, the following HTML loads both CSS files (without blocking rendering (*http://bit.ly/1pKhJbZ*)) on any user's device:

```
<link media="only screen and (max-width: 480px)"
      href="css/smartphone.css"rel="stylesheet">

<link media="only screen and (max-width: 768px)"
      href="css/tablet.css"rel="stylesheet">
```

Using the `Window.matchMedia` attribute can make it possible for you to conditionally load (*http://bit.ly/1lzY8uQ*) CSS in JavaScript. The JavaScript utility eCSSential (*http://bit.ly/1pyAL33*) can help web browsers download CSS faster.

Consider combining responsive design on the client with some device-specific component (a.k.a. RESS (*http://bit.ly/1nR1yH2*)) optimization on the server.

Although responsive design allows you to rearrange content based on the screen size, it might not be a good idea to show the same amount of content on desktops and smartphones. Making a web application look good on mobile devices must involve not only web designers and developers, but also people who are responsible for content management.

Now comes the million-dollar questions: Do we need to create 2 versions of the web application or 22? Why not 222? How many different mobile devices are there today, and how many will there be tomorrow?

How Many User Agents Are There

The HTTP header's `User-Agent` attribute contains information about the user agent originating the request. Should you decide to create several versions of the UI based on the value in the `User-Agent` field, you can refer to the website (*http://useragent string.com*). It lists not two, but hundreds of strings representing possible content of the `User-Agent` attribute for a variety of desktop and mobile devices. For example, Figure 10-4 shows how the `User-Agent` string from iPhone 5 is reported and explained by User Agent String (*http://useragentstring.com*). But this information might become unreliable after iOS upgrades.

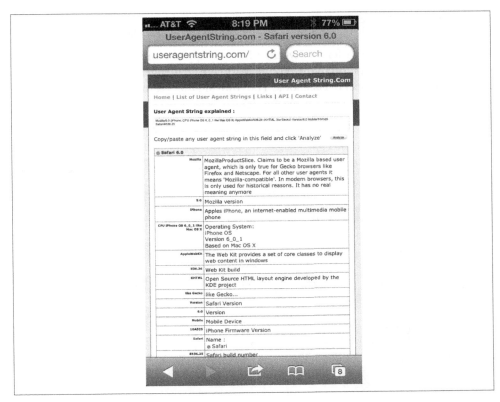

Figure 10-4. The User-Agent string from iPhone 5

There is an easier way to detect on the server that the request came from a mobile device. *Wireless Universal Resource File* (WURF) (*http://wurfl.sourceforge.net*) is a database of thousands of supported devices and their properties. Such Internet giants as Facebook and Google rely on this service, and your application could, too, if need be. WURF offers APIs from several programming languages to detect specific capabilities of user devices. For example, the following code snippet is how you could access the WURF data from a Java servlet:

```java
protected void processRequest(HttpServletRequest request,
                              HttpServletResponse response)
        throws ServletException, IOException {

    WURFLHolder wurfl = (WURFLHolder)getServletContext()
    .getAttribute(WURFLHolder.class.getName());

    WURFLManager manager = wurfl.getWURFLManager();

    Device device = manager.getDeviceForRequest(request);
```

```
log.debug("Device: " + device.getId());
log.debug("Capability: " + device.getCapability("preferred_markup"));
```

It's impossible to create different layouts of a web application for thousands of user agents. Market fragmentation in the mobile world is a challenge. People are using 2,500 different devices to connect to Facebook. The Android market in particular is extremely fragmented. Figure 10-5 is taken from the report, "Android Fragmentation Visualized" (July 2013) (*http://bit.ly/1qegG3h*) by Open Signal.

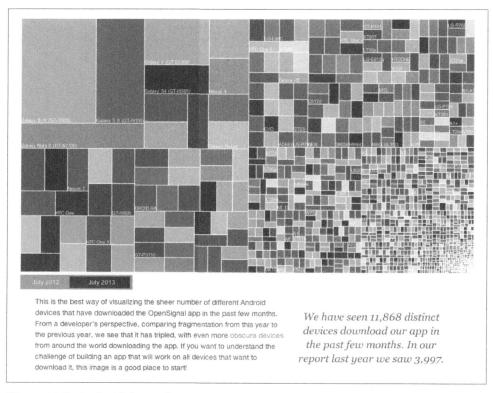

Figure 10-5. Android device fragmentation

Of course, device fragmentation doesn't equal Android OS version fragmentation, but this situation is similar to the challenge that Microsoft has always faced—making sure that Windows works fine on thousands of types of hardware. It's not an easy job to do. In this regard, Apple is in a much better position because it is the only hardware and software vendor of all devices running iOS.

It's great for consumers that Android can be used on thousands of devices, but what about us, the developers? Grouping devices by screen sizes might be a more practical approach for lowering the number of UI layouts supported by your application. Responsive design is a collection of techniques based upon these main pillars:

- CSS media queries
- Fluid grids or fluid layouts
- Fluid media

 Typography can be also considered one of the pillars of responsive design. This subject belongs to publications written for web designers and will not be covered in this book. Oliver Reichenstein's article "Responsive Typography: The Basics" (*http://bit.ly/1iaG8GQ*) is a good introduction to this topic.

A media query (*http://bit.ly/css-mq*) is a CSS element. It consists of a media type (for example, `@media (min-width: 700px) and (orientation: landscape)`) followed by the styles applicable to this media. Using media queries, you can rearrange sections (`<div>`, `<section>`, `<article>`, and so forth) of the page based on the screen size. Fluid grids make it possible for you to properly align and scale the content of these sections. Fluid media is about resizing images or videos.

Data grid components are often included in enterprise applications. Fluid grids are designed by using relative positioning and can scale based on screen sizes. Fluid media is about creating videos and images that react to screen sizes. We'll talk about the aforementioned pillars in greater detail later in this chapter. But before going into technical details, let's get back to creating mockups, as we did in Chapter 1, to see how the UI should look on different devices.

Back to Mockups

Recall Jerry, our web designer who we introduced in Chapter 1. Well, he has come up with another set of Balsamiq mockups for the Save The Child application. This time he has four versions: desktop, tablet, large smartphone, and small smartphone. As a matter of fact, Jerry has provided more mockups to accommodate the user holding both smartphones and tablets either in portrait or landscape mode. Figure 10-6 shows the desktop mockup.

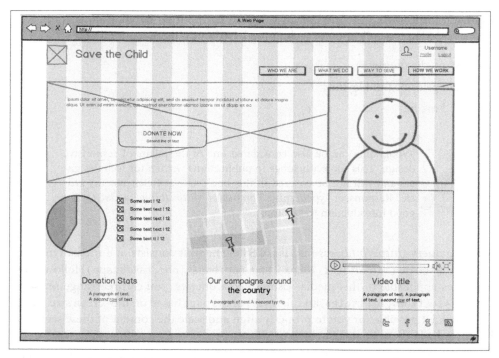

Figure 10-6. The desktop layout

Jerry gives us several versions of the images—with and without the grid background. The use of the grid is explained later, in "Fluid Grids" on page 381. Figure 10-7 depicts the rendering on tablet devices with a screen that is less than 768 pixels wide in portrait mode.

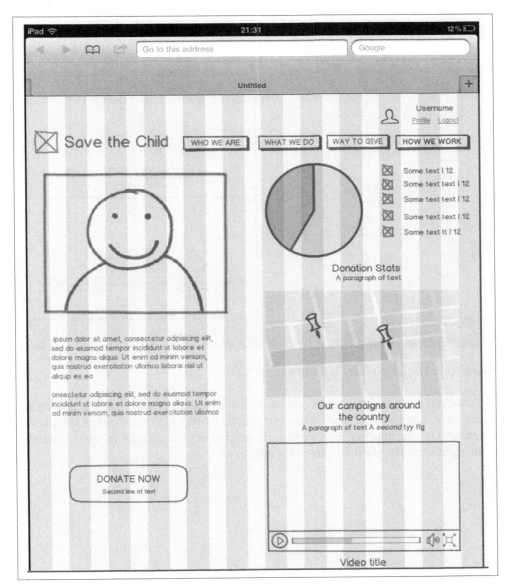

Figure 10-7. The tablet layout (portrait)

Next comes the mockup for large smartphones having a width of up to 640 pixels. Figure 10-8 shows two images of the screen next to each other (a user would need to scroll to see the second image).

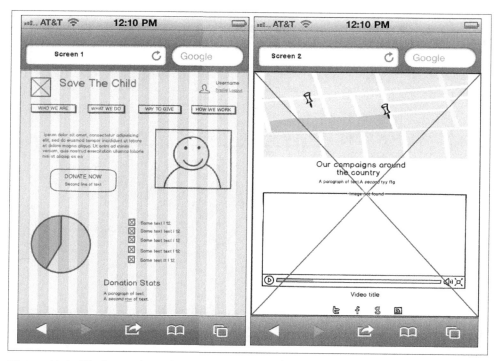

Figure 10-8. The large phone layout (portrait)

The mockup for smaller phones with a width of less than 480 pixels is shown in Figure 10-9. The mockup looks wide, but it actually shows three views of the phone screen next to one another. The user would need to scroll vertically to see the middle or the right view. iPhone 3 falls into this category.

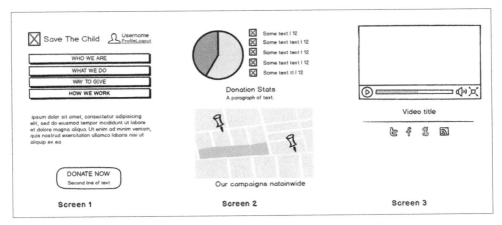

Figure 10-9. The small phone layout (portrait)

If need be, you can ask Jerry to create mockups for real devices with a width less than 320 pixels, but we won't even try it here. Now we need to translate these mockups into working code. The first subject to learn is CSS media queries.

CSS Media Queries

First, let's see the CSS media queries in action, and then we'll explain how this magic is done. Run the project titled *Responsive_basic_media_queries*, and it will look like Figure 10-10. This is a version for desktops (or some tablets in landscape mode). The section chart, map, and video divide the window into three imaginary columns.

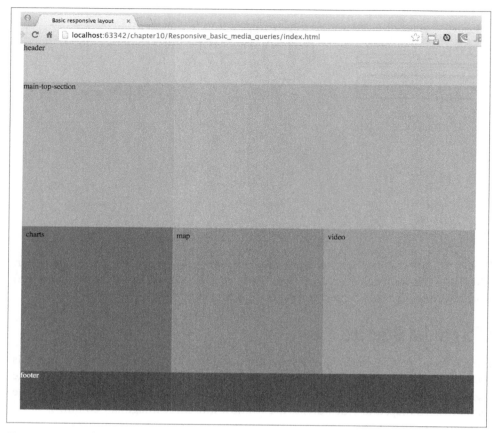

Figure 10-10. The desktop layout implemented

Drag the right border of your desktop web browser's window to the left to make it narrower. After reaching a certain *breakpoint width* (in our project it's 768 pixels), you'll see how the `<div>`s reallocate themselves into the two-column window shown in Figure 10-11.

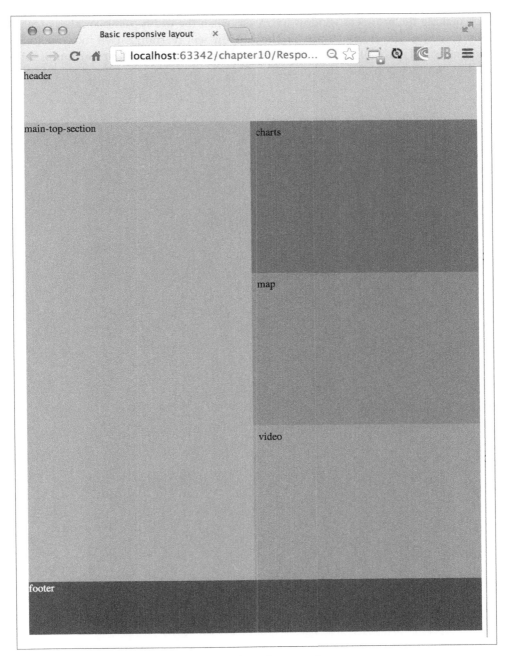

Figure 10-11. The tablet layout (portrait) implemented

Keep making the browser's window narrower; when the width passes another break-point (becomes less than 640 pixels), the window will rearrange itself into one long column, as in Figure 10-12. Users will have to scroll to see the lower portion of this window, but they don't lose any content.

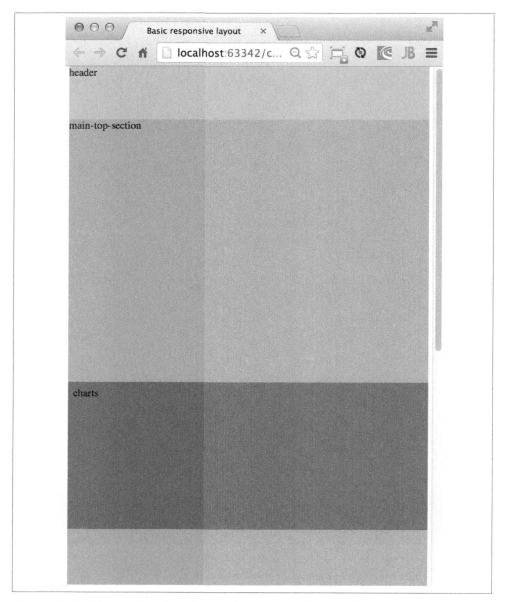

Figure 10-12. The smaller phone layout (portrait) implemented

The W3C recommendation "Media Queries" (*http://bit.ly/Uc4RQa*) was introduced in CSS2 and HTML 4. The idea was to provide different stylesheets for different media. For example, you can specify different stylesheets in HTML by using the `media` attribute for screens that are less than 640 pixels in width:

```
<link rel="stylesheet" href="assets/css/style.css" media="screen">

<link rel="stylesheet" href="assets/css/style_small.css"
                       media="only screen and (max-width: 640px)">
```

You might have several of these `<link>` tags for different screen widths. But all of them will be loaded, regardless of the actual size of the user's display area. Modern browsers might preclude loading CSS files that don't match the current display size.

The other choice is to specify a section in a CSS file by using one or more `@media` rules. For example, the following style will be applied to the HTML element with the `id=main-top-section` if the width of the display area (screen) is less than 640 pixels. `screen` is not the only media type that you can use with media queries. For example, you can use `print` for printed documents or `tv` for TV devices. For an up-to-date list of media types, see the document W3C Recommendation "Media Queries" (*http://bit.ly/Uc4RQa*).

```
@media only screen and (max-width: 640px) {

    #main-top-section {
                width: 100%;
                float: none;
    }
}
```

Two fragments of the CSS file *styles.css* from the project *Responsive_basic_media_queries* are shown next. The first one begins by defining styles for windows having a width of 1280 pixels (we use 1140 pixels to leave some space for padding and the browser's chrome). Example 10-1 presents the first fragment.

Example 10-1. CSS for the devices with a width less than 1280 pixels

```
/* The main container width should be 90% of viewport width */
/* but not wider than 1140px */
#main-container {
        width: 90%;
        max-width: 1140px;            ❶
        margin: 0 auto;
}

/* Background color of all elements was set just as an example */
header {
        background: #ccc;
        width: 100%;
        height: 80px;
}
```

```
#main-top-section {
        background: #bbb;
        width: 100%;
        height: 300px;
        position: relative;
}

#main-bottom-section {
        width: 100%;
}

#video-container, #map-container, #charts-container {
        width: 33.333%;                      ❷
        padding-bottom: 33.333%;
        float: left;                         ❸
        position: relative;
}

#video, #map, #charts {
        background: #aaa;
        width: 100%;
        height: 100%;
        position: absolute;
        padding: 0.5em;
}

#map {
        background: #999;
}

#charts {
        background: #7d7d7d;
}

footer {
        background: #555;
        width: 100%;
        height: 80px;
        color: #fff;
}
```

❶   Set the maximum width of the window on a desktop to 1140 pixels. It's safe to assume that any modern monitor supports the resolution of 1280 pixels in width (minus about 10 percent for padding and chrome).

❷   Allocate one-third of the width for video, charts, and maps each.

❸   `float: left;` instructs the browser to render <div> starting from the left and adding the next one to the right.

This CSS mandates changing page layouts if the screen size is at or is smaller than 768 or 640 pixels. Based on your web designer's recommendations, you can specify as many breakout sizes as needed. Suppose that in the future everyone's monitor is at least 1900 pixels wide; you could provide a layout that would use five imaginary columns. This would be a good idea for online newspapers or magazines, but Save The Child is not a publication, so we'll keep its maximum width within 1140 pixels. Or you might decide to make a version of Save The Child available for LCDs that are only 320 pixels wide; create a new media query section in your CSS and apply fluid grids to make the content readable. Example 10-2 shows the second fragment of the CSS file that defines media queries.

Example 10-2. Two media queries for a viewport with a width of 768 pixels and 640 pixels

```
/* media queries */

@media only screen and (max-width: 768px) {        ❶
        #main-container {
                width: 98%
        }

        #main {
                background: #bbb;
        }

        #main-top-section, #main-bottom-section {
                width: 50%;                         ❷
                float: left;                        ❸
        }

        #main-top-section {
                height: 100%;
        }

        #video-container, #map-container, #charts-container {
                float: none;                        ❹
                width: 100%;
                padding-bottom: 70%;
        }

}

@media only screen and (max-width: 640px) {        ❺

        #main-top-section, #main-bottom-section {
                width: 100%;                        ❻
                float: none;
        }

        #main-top-section {
```

```
        height: 400px;
    }

    #video, #map, #charts {
        height: 60%;
    }
}
```

❶ This media query controls layouts for devices with viewports having a maximum width of 768 pixels.

❷ Split the width fifty-fifty between the HTML elements with the IDs `main-top-section` and `main-bottom-section`.

❸ Allocate `main-top-section` and `main-bottom-section` next to each other (`float: left;`), as in Figure 10-11. To better understand how the CSS `float` property works, visualize a book page that has a small image on the left with the text floating on the right (a text wrap). This is what `float: left;` can do on a web page.

❹ Turn the floating off so the charts, maps, and video containers will start one under another, as in Figure 10-11.

❺ The media query controlling layouts for devices with viewports with a maximum width of 640 pixels starts here.

❻ Let the containers `main-top-section` and `main-bottom-section` take the entire width and be displayed one under another (`float: none;`), as in Figure 10-12.

 Internet Explorer 8 and older don't natively support media queries. Consider using Modernizr to detect support of this feature, and load the Media Queries Polyfill (*http://bit.ly/1sCa9ns*), if needed.

The Viewport Concept

Mobile browsers use the concept of a *viewport*, which is a virtual window that renders the web page content. This virtual window can be wider than the actual width of the display of the user's mobile device. For example, by default iOS Safari and Opera Mobile render the page to the width of 980 pixels, and then shrink it down to the actual width (320 pixels on old iPhones and 640 pixels on iPhone 4 and 5). That's why your iPhone renders the entire web page of, say, *The New York Times* (yes, the fonts are tiny), and not just its upper-left section.

By using the meta tag `viewport`, your web page overrides this default and renders itself according to the actual device size. All code samples in this chapter include the `view` port meta tag in *index.html*. All mobile browsers support it even though it's not a part of the HTML standard yet. Desktop browsers ignore the tag `viewport`.

```
<meta name="viewport" content="width=device-width, initial-scale=1.0">
```

This meta tag tells the browser that the width of the virtual viewport should be the same as the width of the display. This setting will produce good results if your responsive web design includes a version of the page layout optimized for the width of the current user's device. But if you are rendering a page with a fixed width, which is narrower than the default width of the display (for example, 500 pixels), setting the attribute `con tent="width=500"` would instruct the mobile web browser to scale the page to occupy the entire display real estate. In other words, setting a fixed width is like saying, "Dear mobile browser, I don't have a special layout for this device width—do the best you can and scale the content."

Setting the initial scaling to 1.0 ensures that the page will render as close to the physical device size as possible. If you don't want to allow the user to scale the web page, add the attribute `user-scalable=no` to the meta tag `viewport`.

 If you set the initial scale to 1.0 but apply it to a web page that was not built using responsive design principles, users will need to zoom or pan to see the entire page.

For details about configuring the viewport, refer to Apple's (*http://bit.ly/1o0j5xQ*) or Opera's (*http://bit.ly/1nCwqZZ*) documentation.

An important concept to take away from this example is to switch from pixels to percentages when specifying width. In the next examples, you'll see how to switch from using the rigid `px` to more flexible `em` units. In addition, with the CSS `float` property, you can control relative (not absolute) positioning of your page components. There are also such CSS units of measure as `vw` and `vh`, which represent percentages of the viewport width and height, respectively. But the best practice here is to use `rem` units (*http://bit.ly/1pKgV6T*). The app can set the font size on `BODY` and then specify everything in relative-ems that scale only from that number. `ems` cascade their scale down from their parent, meaning lots of extra math for the developer and the browser to do.

Install an add-on for Google Chrome called Window Resizer (*http://bit.ly/TeO5Pj*). It adds an icon to the toolbar for easy switching between the browser screen sizes. This way, you can quickly test how your web page looks in different viewports. Another handy add-on for Chrome called Responsive Inspector (*http://bit.ly/1l7yPdA*) allows you to see the various media queries for a page and automatically resize to them.

Google Chrome Developer Tools offers you a way to test a web page on various emulators of mobile devices. You just need to select the "Show Emulation view in console drawer" in Settings, and then you'll see the Emulation tab under the Elements menu (press the Esc key if it's not shown).

How Many Breakpoints?

How many media queries is too many? It all depends on the web page you're designing. In the sample CSS shown previously, we used the breakpoint of 768 pixels to represent the width of a tablet in portrait mode, and this is fine for the iPad. But several tablets (for example, the 10.1-inch Samsung Galaxy) have 800-pixel-wide viewports, whereas Microsoft Surface Pro is 1080 pixels wide.

There is no general rule as to how many breakpoints are needed for a typical web page. Let the content of your page (and where it breaks) dictate where you add breakpoints. Just create a simple Lorem Ipsum prototype of your website and start changing its size. At a certain point (viewport size), your design begins to break. This is where you need to put your breakpoint and define a media query for it. It is recommended to start by designing for the smallest viewports (the Mobile First principle). As the viewport width increases, you might decide to render more content, and hence define a new breakpoint. Technically, this means that the content of your CSS should default to the smaller viewports and only if the screen is larger, apply media queries. This approach will reduce the CSS handling by the browser of the mobile device (no need to switch from large to smaller layouts).

Use Google Chrome Developer Tools to find out the current width of the viewport. Just type in the console `window.innerWidth` and you'll see the width in pixels.

Don't try to create a pixel-perfect layout by using responsive design. Use common sense, and remember, the more media queries you provide, the larger your CSS file will become. But in a mobile world, you should try to create web applications that are as small as possible.

 Be prepared to see inconsistencies among desktop browsers in measuring the width of the viewport. Our tests showed that WebKit-based browsers add about 15 pixels to the width, supposedly accounting for the width of the scrollbar. So if your media query has to change the layout at 768 pixels, it will change it at about 783 pixels. Do more testing on different viewports and adjust your CSS as needed.

Fluid Grids

Fluid grids are a very important technique in responsive design. Grids have been used by web designers for ages: a web page is divided by a number of imaginary rows and columns. But the fluid grid, as its name indicates, is flexible and can scale based on screen sizes.

Moving Away from Absolute Sizing

When a browser displays text, it uses a default font size unless that size is overruled by the `font-size` property. Typically, the default font size is 16 pixels. But instead of using an absolute font size, you can use a relative one by using em units. The default browser's font size can be represented as 1 em. Because the font size happens to be 16 pixels, 1 em equals 16 pixels.

Absolute sizes are enemies of responsive-design websites, and specifying sizes in em units gives you the freedom to create web pages with relatively flexible and fluid content. The size can be calculated based on a formula offered by Ethan Marcotte in his article on fluid grids (*http://bit.ly/1jLswNi*): `target/context=result`, which in the case of fonts becomes `size-in-pixels/16 = size-in-em`.

For example, instead of specifying the size as 24 pixels, you can set it to 1.5 em: 24/16. In your CSS file, you can write something like `padding-bottom: 1.5em`. This might not seem a big deal, but it is, because if everything is done in relative sizing, your page will look good and proportional regardless of the screen size and regardless of how big or small 24 pixels might look on a particular screen.

If we are talking about using em units to represent font sizes, the font becomes *the context*. But what if you want to represent the width of an arbitrary HTML component in a browser's window or any other container? Then the width of your component becomes the `target`, and the total width of the container becomes the `context`. We can still use the previous formula, but we will multiply the result by 100 percent. This way, the width of an HTML component will be represented not in em units, but in a percentage relative to the total width of the container.

Let's say the total width of the browser's window is 768 pixels, and we want to create a panel on the left that's 120 pixels wide. Instead of specifying this width in pixels, we'll use the formula and turn it into a percentage. We want to calculate the target's width as a percent of the available context (100 percent):

120 / 768 * 100% = 15.625%

This approach makes the page design *fluid*. If someone decides to open this page on a 480-pixel-wide screen, the panel will still take 15.625 percent of the screen rather than demanding 120 pixels, which would look substantially wider on a smaller viewport.

Window as a Grid

While designing your page, you can overlay any HTML container or the entire web page real estate with an imaginary grid containing any number of columns. Make it flexible, though; the width of each column has to be specified in percentages.

Adobe Dreamweaver CS6 (*http://adobe.ly/1jLsxAG*) automates the creation of media queries and introduces the Fluid Grid layout (see Figure 10-13). It also allows you to quickly see how your design will look on a tablet or phone (you can pick screen size, too) with a click of the corresponding status bar button.

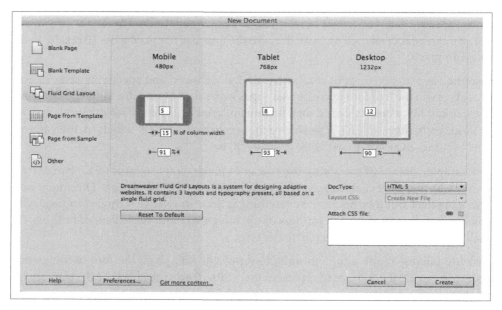

Figure 10-13. Creating a Fluid Grid layout in Dreamweaver

Adobe's Creative Cloud includes a tool called Edge Reflow (*http://adobe.ly/UGyysM*), which helps designers create responsive web pages.

Web designers use different approaches when styling with fluid grids. When you design a new page using Dreamweaver's Fluid Grid layout, it suggests that you allocate a different number of columns for desktop, tablet, and mobile layouts. For example, its default layout is to allocate 12 columns for desktops, 8 for tablets, and 5 for phones, which is a perfectly solid approach. But our web designer, Jerry, prefers using 12 columns for all screen sizes and then playing with the width percentages for different layouts. You'll see how he does it in the project Responsive Donation later in this chapter.

Now imagine that you'll overlay the entire window with an invisible grid containing 12 equally sized columns. Each column will occupy 8.333 percent of the total width. Now, if you need to allocate to an HTML component about 40 percent of the total width, you could do this by allocating 5 grid columns (8.333% x 5 = 41.665%). Accordingly, your CSS file can contain 12 classes that you can use in your page, as shown in Example 10-3.

Example 10-3. Twelve sample classes to support fluid grids

```
.one-column {
        width: 8.333%;
}

.two-column {
        width: 16.666%;
}

.three-column {
        width: 24.999%;
}

.four-column {
        width: 33.332%;
}

.five-column {
        width: 41.665%;
}

.six-column {
        width: 49.998%;
}

.seven-column {
        width: 58.331%;
}
```

```
.eight-column {
        width: 66.664%;
}

.nine-column {
        width: 74.997%;
}

.ten-column {
        width: 83.33%;
}

.eleven-column {
        width: 91.663%;
}

.twelve-column {
        width: 100%;
        float: left;
}
```

Now let's see the fluid grid in action. Run the project Responsive Fluid Grid, and you'll see a web page that looks similar to Figure 10-14. This example changes the grid layout if the viewport width is less than one of the following width breakpoints: 768 pixels, 640 pixels, and 480 pixels. In this context, the term *breakpoints* has nothing to do with debugging; we just want the content of the web page to be rearranged when the width of the viewport passes one of these values.

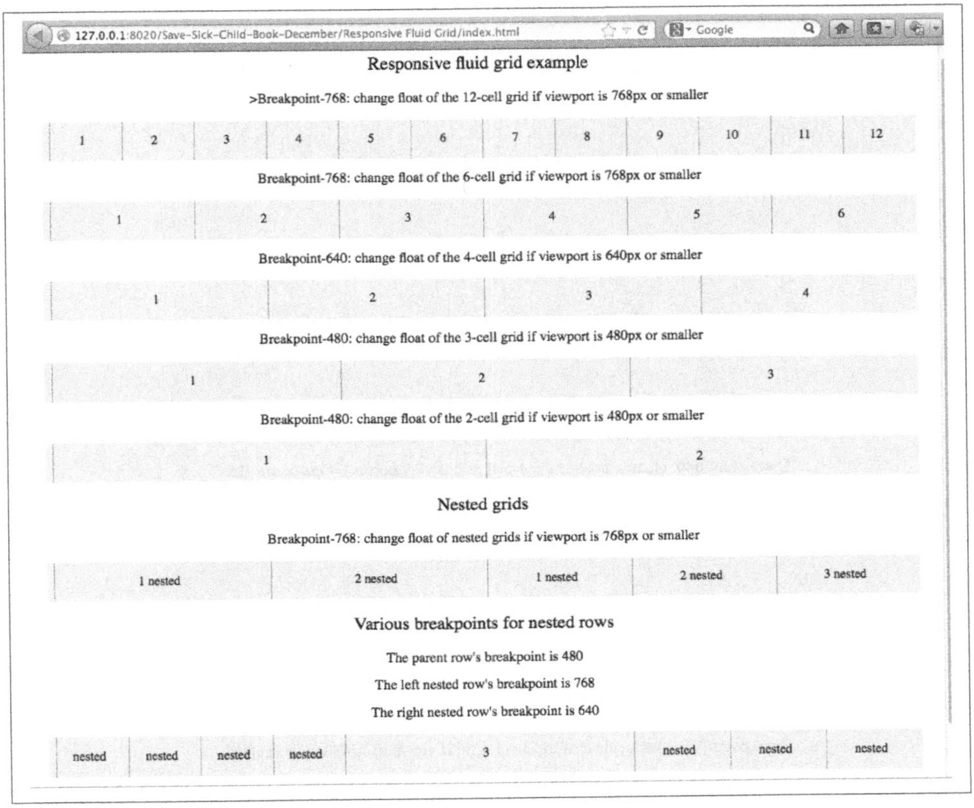
127.0.0.1:8020/Save-Sick-Child-Book-December/Responsive Fluid Grid/index.html
Google
Responsive fluid grid example
>Breakpoint-768: change float of the 12-cell grid if viewport is 768px or smaller
1 2 3 4 5 6 7 8 9 10 11 12
Breakpoint-768: change float of the 6-cell grid if viewport is 768px or smaller
1 2 3 4 5 6
Breakpoint-640: change float of the 4-cell grid if viewport is 640px or smaller
1 2 3 4
Breakpoint-480: change float of the 3-cell grid if viewport is 480px or smaller
1 2 3
Breakpoint-480: change float of the 2-cell grid if viewport is 480px or smaller
1 2
Nested grids
Breakpoint-768: change float of nested grids if viewport is 768px or smaller
1 nested 2 nested 1 nested 2 nested 3 nested
Various breakpoints for nested rows
The parent row's breakpoint is 480
The left nested row's breakpoint is 768
The right nested row's breakpoint is 640
nested nested nested nested 3 nested nested nested

Figure 10-14. Fluid grid on the wide screen

If you narrow the width of the browser's window, you'll see how the grid cells begin to squeeze, but the layout remains the same until the window size becomes smaller than one of the predefined breakpoints. Then, another media query kicks in and the layout changes. For example, Figure 10-15 shows a fragment of the web page when the width of the browser's window narrows to less than 640 pixels. The 12-, 6-, and 4-cell grids display all the cells vertically, one below another. Only the 480-pixel grids still have enough room to display their cells horizontally. But if you keep squeezing the window, all the grids will display their content in one column, as long as the viewport width remains less than 480 pixels.

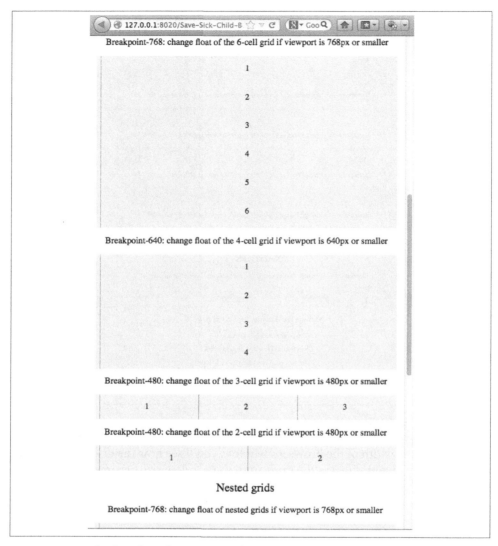

Figure 10-15. Fluid grid on the viewport narrower than 640 pixels

The fragment of *index.html* from the Responsive Fluid Grid project goes next. For brevity, we've replaced some repetitive markup with the comment "A fragment removed for brevity." This code fragment (see Example 10-4) includes the 12-, 6-, and 4-column grids shown at the top of Figure 10-14.

Example 10-4. A sample HTML page that uses fluid grid styling

```
<head>
        <meta charset="utf-8">
```

```html
    <title>Responsive fluid grid</title>
    <meta name="description" content="Responsive fluid grid example">
    <meta name="viewport" content="width=device-width,initial-scale=1">

    <link rel="stylesheet" href="css/style.css">
  </head>

  <body>
    <div id="wrapper-container">

      <h1 class="temp-heading">Responsive fluid grid example</h1>
      <h4 class="temp-heading">Breakpoint-768: change float of HTML elements
                               if viewport is 768px or smaller</h4>
      <div class="row breakpoint-768">
          <div class="one-column cell">
                      1
          </div>
          <div class="one-column cell">
                      2
          </div>
          <div class="one-column cell">
                      3
          </div>

        <!-- A fragment removed for brevity -->

          <div class="one-column cell last-cell" >
                      12
          </div>
      </div>

      <h4 class="temp-heading">Breakpoint-768: change float of the 12-cell grid
                               if viewport is 768px or smaller</h4>

      <div class="row breakpoint-768">
          <div class="two-column cell">
                      1
          </div>
          <div class="two-column cell">
                      2
          </div>

          <!-- A fragment removed for brevity -->

          <div class="two-column cell">
                      6
          </div>
      </div>

      <h4 class="temp-heading">Breakpoint-768: change float of the 6-cell grid
                               if viewport is 768px or smaller</h4>
```

```
<div class="row breakpoint-640">
        <div class="three-column cell">
                1
        </div>
        <div class="three-column cell">
                2
        </div>
        <div class="three-column cell">
                3
        </div>
        <div class="three-column cell">
                4
        </div>
</div>
```

Note that some of the HTML elements are styled with more than one class selector (for example, class="one-column cell"). The entire content of the file *styles.css* from the Responsive Fluid Grids project is shown in Example 10-5, and you can find the declarations of the class selectors one-column and cell there.

Example 10-5. The styles.css file from the Responsive Fluid Grids project

```
* {
        margin: 0;
        padding: 0;
        border: 0;
        font-size: 100%;
        font: inherit;
        vertical-align: baseline;
        -webkit-box-sizing:border-box;
        -moz-box-sizing: border-box;
        box-sizing: border-box;
}

article, aside, details, figcaption, figure, footer, header, hgroup, menu, nav,
                                                        section {
        display: block;
}

ul li {
        list-style: none;
}

.row:before, .row:after, .clearfix:before, .clearfix:after {
        content: "";
        display: table;
}

.row:after, .clearfix:after {
        clear: both;
}
```

```
/* Start of fluid grid styles */

.row {                          ❶
        padding: 0 0 0 0.5em;
        background: #eee;
}

.breakpoint-480 .cell, .breakpoint-640 .cell, .breakpoint-768 .cell,
                       .breakpoint-960 .cell, .no-breakpoint .cell { ❷
        float: left;
        padding: 0 0.5em 0 0;
}

.one-column {
        width: 8.333%;      ❸
}

.two-column {
        width: 16.666%;      ❹
}

.three-column {
        width: 24.999%;      ❺
}

.four-column {
        width: 33.332%;
}

.five-column {
        width: 41.665%;
}

.six-column {
        width: 49.998%;
}

.seven-column {
        width: 58.331%;
}

.eight-column {
        width: 66.664%;
}

.nine-column {
        width: 74.997%;
}

.ten-column {
        width: 83.33%;
}
```

```
.eleven-column {
        width: 91.663%;
}

.twelve-column {
        width: 100%;
        float: left;
}

.right {
        float: right;
}

.row.nested {
        padding: 0;
        margin-right: -0.5em
}
```

❶ Styling grid rows, which are containers for cells.

❷ Defining common class selectors (floating and padding) for the cells located in the viewports of any width. Please note the property float: left; (it will change in the media queries section).

❸ Dividing 100 percent of the container's width by 12 columns results in allocating 8.333 percent of width per column. Each cell in the 12-column table in our HTML has the one-column class selector.

❹ Check the HTML for the 6-column grid. Each cell is styled as two-column and will occupy 16.666 percent of the container's width.

❺ The HTML for the 4-column grid uses the three-column style for each cell that will use 24.999 percent of the container's width.

Example 10-6 shows the section with media queries in this file (the following is just another fragment of the same CSS file).

Example 10-6. Media queries section from the CSS file

```
/* -------------- Media queries ------------- */

@media only screen and (max-width: 768px) {
        .breakpoint-768 .cell {
                float: none;                           ❶
                width: 100%;
                padding-bottom: 0.5em;
        }
}

@media only screen and (max-width: 640px) {
        .breakpoint-640 .cell {                        ❷
```

```css
                float: none;
                width: 100%;
                padding-bottom: 0.5em
        }
}

@media only screen and (max-width: 480px) {
        .breakpoint-480 .cell {
                float: none;
                width: 100%;
                padding-bottom: 0.5em
        }
}

/*End of fluid grid styles*/

#wrapper-container {
        width: 95%;
        max-width: 1140px;
        margin: 0 auto;
}

/* --- .cell visualisation --- */
.cell {
        min-height: 50px;
        text-align:center;
        border-left: 1px solid #aaa;
        vertical-align: middle;
        line-height: 50px;
}
.cell .cell:first-child{
        border-left:none;
}
/* --- .cell visualisation end --- */

h1.temp-heading, h2.temp-heading, h4.temp-heading {
        font-size: 1.4em;
        margin: 1em 0;
        text-align: center
}
h4.temp-heading {
        font-size: 1.1em;
}

p.temp-project-description {
        margin: 2em 0;
}
```

❶ This media query turns off floating (`float:none`) if the viewport is 768 pixels or less. This reallocates the cells vertically. The `width:100%` forces the cell to occupy the entire width of the container as opposed to, say, 8.333 percent in the 12-column grid.

❷ The media query for 640 pixels won't kick in until the viewport width narrows to that size. If you resize the browser window such that it is less than 768 pixels but wider than 640 pixels, note that the 4-column grid (styled as `breakpoint-640`) has not changed its layout just yet.

 At times, you might need to use a mix of fluid and fixed layouts. For example, you might need to include an image of a fixed size on your fluid web page. In these cases, you can use a fixed width on some elements, and if needed, consider using CSS tables (not to be confused with HTML tables). CSS tables are supported (*http://caniuse.com/css-table*) by all current browsers.

Spend some time analyzing the content of *index.html* and *styles.css* from the Responsive Fluid Grid project. Try to modify the values in CSS and see how your changes affect the behavior of the fluid grid. In the next section, we'll apply these techniques to our Save The Child application.

Responsive CSS: The Good News

We have explained how the fluid grid works under the hood, but calculating percentages is not the most exciting job for software developers. The good news is that several responsive frameworks offer CSS, typography, and some JavaScript to jump-start UI development of a web application. They'll spare you from most of the mundane work with cascading style sheets. Here are some of them:

- Consider using Twitter's framework called Bootstrap (*http://twbs.github.io/bootstrap*), which has lots of greatly styled components (*http://bit.ly/1piyvie*) and also supports a fluid grid system.

- The Foundation 4 (*http://foundation.zurb.com*) framework promotes Mobile First design and includes a flexible grid.

- The Skeleton (*http://www.getskeleton.com*) is a collection of CSS files, which includes a scalable grid.

- Semantic-UI (*http://semantic-ui.com*) is a collection of styled UI components, which includes a responsive grid (*http://bit.ly/1pJa675*), too.

People who work with CSS a lot use an authoring framework called Compass (*http://compass-style.org*) with the CSS extension SASS (*http://sass-lang.com*) or the CSS preprocessor LESS (*http://lesscss.org/*). These systems compile to CSS, allowing code to include variables for tracking and calculating numbers such as column width and more. You can now modularize your CSS as well as your code. In Chapter 12 we use a SASS theme that comes with the Sencha Touch framework.

Making Save The Child Responsive

First, run any previous version of the Save The Child application to make sure it is not responsive. Just make the browser window narrower, and note how some of the page content on the right is cut off. We'll gradually make the page responsive: the first version will make the header responsive, then the donation section, and, finally, the entire page will become fluid. In a web browser, open *index.html* from the project Responsive Header. You'll see a page similar to Figure 10-16.

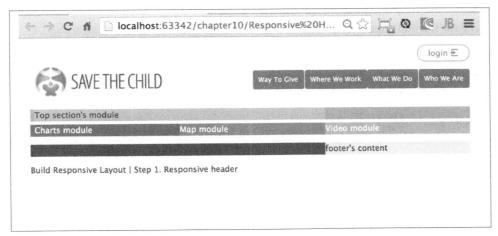

Figure 10-16. Responsive Header (width 580 pixels+)

Example 10-7 is the fragment from *index.html* that displays the logo image and the header's menus.

Example 10-7. An HTML fragment for the logo and the menus

```
<div id="wrapper-container">
  <header class="row breakpoint-640">
      <h1 id="logo" class="four-column cell">
          <img src="assets/img/logo.png" alt="Save The Child logo"/></h1>
      <nav class="eight-column cell">
```

```
        <ul>
                <li>
                        <a href="javascript:void(0)">Who We Are</a>
                </li>
                <li>
                        <a href="javascript:void(0)">What We Do</a>
                </li>
                <li>
                        <a href="javascript:void(0)">Where We Work</a>
                </li>
                <li>
                        <a href="javascript:void(0)">Way To Give</a>
                </li>
        </ul>
</nav>
```

Initially, this code uses the `four-column` style (`width: 33.332%;` of the container) for the logo and `eight-column` (66.664%) for the <nav> element. When the size of the viewport changes, the appropriate media query takes effect. Note the `breakpoint-640` class selector in the <header> tag. Jerry, our web designer, decides that 640 pixels is not enough to display the logo and the four links from the <nav> section in one row. Besides, he wants to fine-tune the width of other elements, too. Example 10-8 shows the media query for the 640-pixel viewport.

Example 10-8. Media query for the 640-pixel viewport

```
@media only screen and (max-width: 640px) {
        .breakpoint-640 .cell {
                float: none;
                width: 100%;
                padding-bottom: 0.5em
        }

        header {
                margin-top: 1em;
        }
        #login {
                top: 1em;
        }
        #logo.four-column {
                width: 40%;
        }
        nav {
                width: 100%;
                margin-top: 0.8em
        }
        nav ul li {
                width: 24.5%;
                margin-left: 0.5%
        }
        nav li a {
```

```
                    text-align: center;
                    font-size: 0.6em;
            }
            #login-link-text {
                    display: none;
            }
            a#login-submit {
                    padding: 0.2em 0.5em
            }
            #login input {
                    width: 9em;
            }
    }
}
```

As you can see, if the cell has to be styled inside breakdown-640, the float is turned off (float: none;) and each of the navigation items has to occupy 100 percent of the container's width. The logo, login, and nav elements will change, too. There is no exact science here; Jerry figured out all these values empirically.

Slowly change the width of the viewport, and you'll see how the layout responds. The *styles.css* of this project has media queries for different viewport sizes. For example, when the page width is less than 580 pixels but more than 480 pixels, it looks like Figure 10-17.

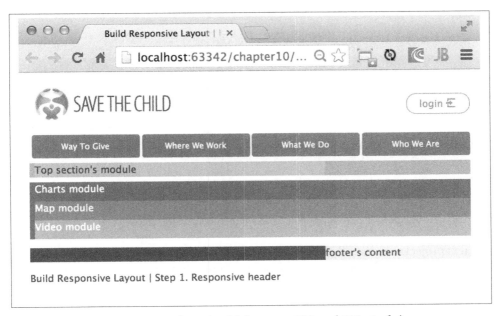

Figure 10-17. Responsive Header 2 (width between 480 and 580 pixels)

When the width of the viewport narrows to less than 480 pixels, the header's content is rearranged and looks like Figure 10-18. Again, we are not tying the design to a specific device; rather, we're focusing on a viewport width. The iPhone 4 will render this page using the layout shown in Figure 10-18, but iPhone 5 will use the layout in Figure 10-17. You can't go by a device type.

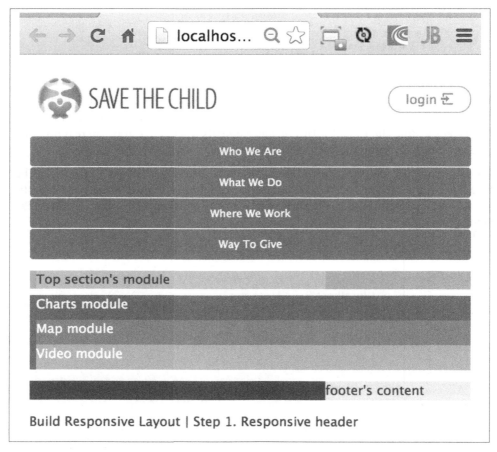

Figure 10-18. Responsive Header (viewport's width below 480 pixels)

The next project to try is called Responsive Donation. This version makes the donation section fluid. The donation section contains the Lorem Ipsum text and the form, which is revealed when the user clicks the Donate Now button. First, let's look at the HTML. The *index.html* file contains the fragment shown in Example 10-9 (some of the content that's irrelevant for layout was removed for better readability).

Example 10-9. The Donate section's HTML

```
<div id="main-content" role="main">
 <section id="main-top-section" class="row breakpoint-480">
  <div id="donation-address" class="seven-column cell">
      <p class="donation-address">
             Lorem ipsum dolor sit amet                </p>
      <button class="donate-button" id="donate-button">
             <span class="donate-button-header">Donate Now</span>
      </button>

 </div>
 <div id="donate-form-container">
      <h3>Make a donation today</h3>
      <form name="_xclick" action="https://www.paypal.com/cgi-bin/webscr"
                           method="post">

    <div class="row nested breakpoint-960">
          <div class="six-column cell">
            <div class="row nested">
            <div id="donation-amount" class="five-column left">
              <label class="donation-heading">Donation amount</label>
              <input type="radio" name="amount" id="d10" value="10"/>
              <label for="d10">10</label>
            </div>
            <div id="donor-info" class="five-column left">
```

The donation section is located in the `main-top-section` of the page. Jerry wants to keep the image of the boy visible for as long as possible in the narrower viewports. The top section of Save The Child has two backgrounds: the flowers (*bg-2.png*) and the boy (*child-1.png*). This is how they are specified in *style.css*:

```
#main-top-section {
       background: url(../img/child-1.png) no-repeat right bottom,
                   url(../img/bg-2.png) no-repeat 20% bottom;
}
```

If the viewport is wide enough, both backgrounds will appear. What's wide enough? Jerry figures it out after experimenting. The `seven-column` style allocates more than half (58.331%) of the viewport width for the `donation-address` section and the `six-column` style allocates 49.998% for for the donation form. For example, Figure 10-19 shows how the donation section will look when the viewport width is 570 pixels.

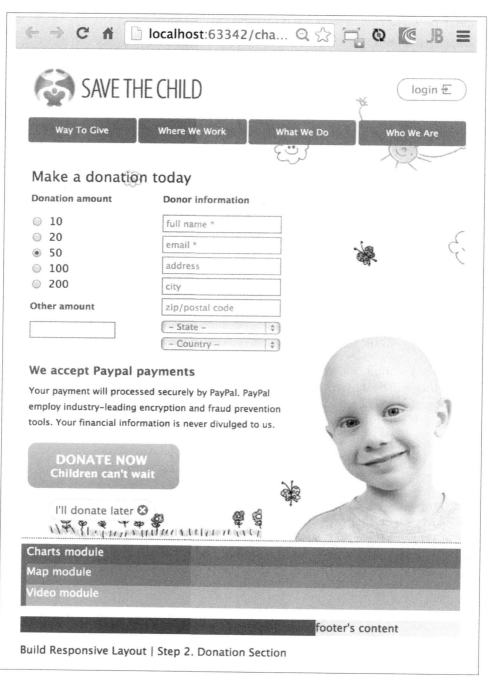

Figure 10-19. Responsive Donate section: 570 pixels

But when the width narrows to less than 480 pixels, there is no room for two background images, and only the flowers will remain on the page background. Example 10-10 presents the media query for a 480-pixel viewport. Note that the background in the main top section has only one image now: *bg2.png*. Floating is off to show the navigation menu vertically, as is depicted in Figure 10-20.

Example 10-10. Media query for the 480-pixel viewport

```
@media only screen and (max-width: 480px) {
        .breakpoint-480 .cell {
                float: none;
                width: 100%;
                padding-bottom: 0.5em
        }
        #logo {
                padding-bottom: 11em
        }
        nav ul li {
                float: none;
                width: 100%;
                margin-left: 0;
                margin-bottom: 0.5%;
        }
        #main-top-section {
                background: url(../img/bg-2.png) no-repeat 20% bottom;
        }
        .donate-button {
                width: 14em;
                margin-left: auto;
                margin-right: auto;
        }
        .donate-button-header {
                font-size: 1.1em;
        }
        .donate-2nd-line {
                font-size: 0.9em;
        }
        #donate-later-link {
                display: block;
                width: 11em;
                margin-left: auto;
                margin-right: auto;
        }
        #make-payment p {
                width: 100%;
        }
        #donation-amount.five-column {
                width: 50%
        }
        #donor-info.six-column {
                width: 50%
        }
```

```
#donate-form-container select, input[type=text], input[type=email] {
        width: 90%;
    }
}
```

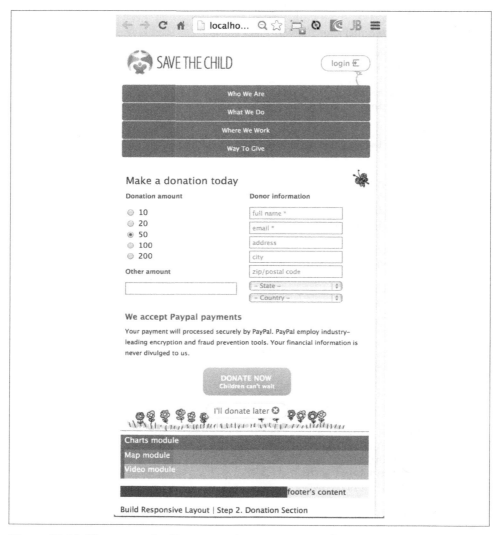

Figure 10-20. The responsive Donate section on a 480-pixel viewport

The project Responsive Final includes the charts, maps, and video. Each of these sections uses the four-column style, which is defined in *styles.css* as 33.332% of the container's width (see Example 10-11).

Example 10-11. Charts, maps, and video section styled as a four-column grid

```
<section id="main-bottom-section" class="row breakpoint-768">

  <div id="charts-container" class="four-column cell">
      <svg id="svg-container"  xmlns="http://www.w3.org/2000/svg">

      </svg>
      <h3>Donation Stats</h3>
      <h5>Lorem ipsum dolor sit amet, consect.</h5>
  </div>
  <div id="map-container" class="four-column cell">
      <div id="location-map"></div>
      <div id="location-ui"></div>
  </div>
  <div id="video-container" class="four-column cell last">
      <div id="video-wrapper">
        <video id="movie" controls="controls"
              poster="assets/media/intro.jpg" preload="metadata">
              <source src="assets/media/intro.mp4" type="video/mp4">
              <source src="assets/media/intro.webm" type="video/webm">
              <p>Sorry, your browser doesn't support the video element</p>
        </video>
      </div>
      <h3>Video header goes here</h3>
      <h5><a href="javascript:void(0);">More video link</a></h5>
  </div>
</section>
```

The ID of this section is still main-bottom-section, and it's shown at the bottom of the page on wide viewports. Now take another look at Figure 10-11. Jerry wants to display these three sections on the righthand side for tablets in portrait mode, as shown in Figure 10-21.

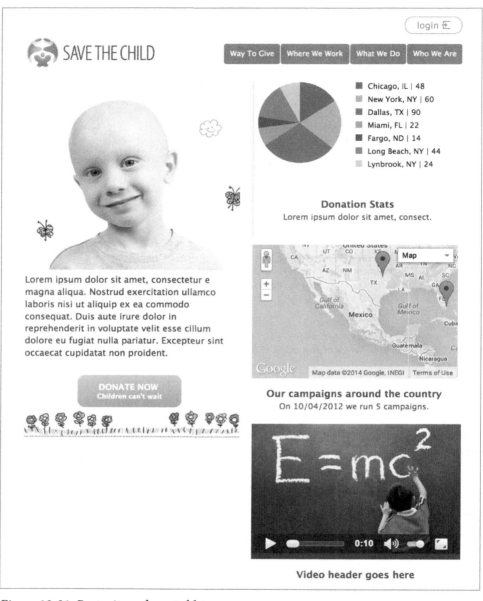

Figure 10-21. Portrait mode on tablets

Example 10-12 shows the relevant code from *style.css*. The top and bottom sections get about half of the width each, and floating is turned off so that the browser distributes charts, maps, and video vertically.

Example 10-12. Media query for tablets in portrait mode

```
@media only screen and (max-width: 768px) {
        .breakpoint-768 .cell {
                float: none;
                width: 100%;
                padding-bottom: 0.5em;
        }

        #main-bottom-section, #main-top-section {
                width: 49%;
        }
}
```

We've explained the use of media queries for applying different styles to the UI based on screen resolutions. But there is a twist. What device comes to mind if you hear about a screen with a resolution of 1920 x 1080 pixels? Most likely you got it wrong unless your answer was the smartphone Galaxy S4 or Sony Xperia Z. The resolution is high, but the screen size is 5 inches. What media query are you going to apply for such a device? Even with this high resolution, you should not apply the desktop's CSS to a mobile device. The CSS media query *device-pixel-ratio* (*http://bit.ly/1quszCd*) can help you distinguish high-resolution small devices from desktops.

Fluid Media

If your responsive web page contains images or videos, you want to make them fluid, too; they should react to the current size of the containers they are in. Our page has a chart image and a video. Both of them are made flexible, but we use different techniques.

If you keep narrowing the viewport, the Responsive Final project will show a layout similar to Figure 10-12. While reading the code of this project, visit the *main.js* file. There is some work done in the JavaScript, too, which listens to the resize event for the charts container:

```
window.addEventListener("resize", windowResizeHandler);
function windowResizeHandler() {
        drawPieChart(document.getElementById('svg-container'),
                        donorsDataCache, labelsDataCache);
}
```

Whenever the size changes, it invokes the function `drawPieChart()` that recalculates the width of the SVG container (it uses the `clientWidth` property of the `HTMLElement`) and redraws the chart accordingly.

Consider storing images in the WebP format (*http://bit.ly/1q5n5jz*), which is a lossless format. WebP images are about 25 percent smaller than PNG or JPEG images. Your application needs to check first whether the user's web browser supports WebP format; otherwise, images in more traditional formats should be rendered. The other choice is to use Thumbor imaging service (*http://thumborize.me*), which can automatically serve WebP images to browsers that support this format.

The video is flexible, too, and it's done a lot simpler. We do not specify the fixed size of the video. Instead, we use the CSS property `width`, instructing the browser to allocate 100 percent of the available container's width. The height of the video must be automatically calculated to keep the proportional size:

```
video {
        width: 100% !important;
        height: auto !important;
}
```

The `!important` part disables regular cascading rules and ensures that these values will be applied, overriding more specific width or height declarations, if any. If you prefer to not always use the entire width of the container for the video, you can use `max-width: 100%;`, which will display the video that fits in the container at its original size. If a video is larger than the container, the browser will resize it to fit inside the container.

Even though the landing page of your web application simply includes links to the required images, the rest of the images should be loaded from the server by making Ajax requests, passing parameters to it regarding the viewport size. This way, the server's software can either resize images dynamically and include them as Base64-encoded strings or use precreated, properly sized images depending on the viewport dimensions.

Although using Base64 encoding increases the total size of the image in bytes, it makes it possible for you to group multiple images to minimize the number of network calls the browser needs to make to retrieve these images separately. The other way to combine multiple images into one is via CSS sprites.

Regardless of the width and height of the image, use tools to reduce image sizes in bytes. These tools include TinyPNG (*http://tinypng.org*) and Smush.it (*http://www.smush it.com/ysmush.it*). If you use *lossy* tools, some of the image data will be lost during compression, but in many cases the difference between the original and compressed image is invisible.

Sencha.io SRC (*http://bit.ly/1kOsNyq*) is a proxy server that allows you to dynamically resize images for various mobile screen sizes.

Besides making images responsive, keep in mind that some people have mobile devices with high-resolution Retina displays. The problem is that to make an image look good on such displays, it has to be large, which increases its loading time. There is no common recipe for properly optimizing the image size; plan to spend extra time just preparing the images for your application.

There is a living W3C document, titled "An HTML extension for adaptive images," (*http://picture.responsiveimages.org*) that provides developers with a means to declare multiple sources for an image. The proposed HTML element <picture> allows you to specify different images for different media (see demos (*http://responsiveimages.org/demos*)). For example:

```
<picture width="500" height="500">
    <source media="(min-width: 45em)" src="large.jpg">
    <source media="(min-width: 18em)" src="med.jpg">
    <source src="small.jpg">
    <img src="small.jpg" alt="">
</picture>
```

Another technique is to use a content delivery network (CDN) that caches and serves images of different sizes for different user agents. The very first time that a request is made from a device with an unknown user engine, this first "unlucky" user will get an image with a low resolution, and then the application makes an Ajax call, passing the exact screen parameters for this device. The CDN server resizes the original high-resolution image for this particular user agent, and caches it, so any other users having the same device will get a perfectly sized image from the get-go.

Imager.js (*http://bit.ly/1lPiwTE*) is an alternative solution to handling responsive image loading, created by developers at BBC News. Imager loads the most suitably sized image and does it once.

Summary

RWD is not a silver bullet that allows using a single code base for all desktop and mobile versions of your HTML5 web application. RWD can be the right approach for developing websites that mainly publish information. It's not likely that you can create a complex single-code-base web application that works well on Android, iPhone, and desktop browsers.

Responsive design can result in unnecessary CSS code being loaded to the user's device. This consideration is especially important for mobile devices operating on 3G or slower networks (unless you find a way to lazy-load them).

Responsive design can still can be a practical business solution when the form factor is relatively low (which enterprises can mandate)—for example, if your target group of users operates specific models of iOS and Android devices.

If you take any JavaScript framework that works on both desktop and mobile devices, you'll get two sets of controls and will have to maintain two different source code repositories. Not using mobile JavaScript frameworks limits the number of user-friendly UI controls. Besides, frameworks spare you from dealing with browsers' incompatibilities.

In this chapter, you saw how the Save The Child application was built with responsive design principles. Our application has several areas (`<div>`s), and one of them included a donation form. (We could have added a responsive `<div>` for the online auction, too.) On the wide screen, we displayed three of these `<div>`s horizontally and two underneath. On the narrow screen, each of these sections could be scaled down and displayed one under another.

But using responsive design for styling the application to run on tablets or mobile devices will require Jerry-the-designer to work in tandem with a user experience specialist so that the UI will have larger controls and fonts while minimizing the need for manual data entry. And don't forget that half of a mobile screen could be covered by a virtual keyboard. If you ignore this, the user will look at your application's UI via a keyhole, and even our fluid `<div>` sections might not fit.

In Chapters 11 and 12, we work on yet two more versions of the Save The Child application. First, we'll use the jQuery Mobile framework and then Sencha Touch.

jQuery Mobile

According to jquerymobile.com, *jQuery Mobile is an HTML5-based user interface system designed to make responsive websites and apps that are accessible on all smartphone, tablet, and desktop devices.* But jQuery Mobile was mainly created for developing web applications for smaller screens.

To start learning jQuery Mobile, you need to know HTML, JavaScript, CSS, and jQuery. In some publications, you might see statements extolling how you can start using jQuery Mobile knowing only HTML. This is true until you run into the first unexpected behavior of your code, which you'll inevitably encounter in one of the web browsers. (Take the statements about being a cross-browser framework with a grain of salt, too.) After that, you need to add some event listeners and scripts, and start debugging.

Obtaining jQuery Mobile

The jQuery Mobile website (*http://jquerymobile.com*) has all you need to start using this library. You can find lots of learning materials in the Demos section: tutorials, an API reference, and samples. The Download section contains links for the library itself.

There are two ways of including jQuery Mobile in the source code of your application: either download and uncompress the ZIP file in your local directory and specify this location in the source code of your application, or include the URLs of the content delivery network (CDN)–hosted files. Visit the jQuery Mobile Download (*http://jquerymobile.com/download*) page for the up-to-date URLs.

In our code samples, we'll be adding the following code snippets, which in Gzipped format will make our application only 90 KB larger:

```
<link rel="stylesheet"
      href="http://code.jquery.com/mobile/1.3.1/jquery.mobile-1.3.1.min.css" />
<script src="http://code.jquery.com/jquery-1.9.1.min.js"></script>
```

```
<script src="http://code.jquery.com/mobile/1.3.1/jquery.mobile-1.3.1.min.js">
  </script>
```

Organizing the Code

The UI of a jQuery Mobile application consists of a set of HTML documents, and certain attributes are added to the regular HTML components. Your web application will consist of *pages*, and the user's mobile device will show one page at a time. After the mockup of your application is ready (see "Prototyping the Mobile Version" on page 425), you know how many pages your application will have and how to navigate among them. Let's see how to define the content of each page in jQuery Mobile.

The HTML5 specification includes an important feature: you can add to any HTML tag any number of custom nonvisible attributes (*http://bit.ly/9Udecy*), as long as they start with `data-` and have at least one character after the hyphen. In jQuery Mobile, this feature is being used in a very smart way. For example, you can add an attribute `data-role` to the HTML tag `<div>` to specify that it's a page with the ID `Stats`:

```
<div data-role="page" id="Stats">
```

The UI of your application will consist of multiple pages, but what's important is that jQuery Mobile will show *one page at a time*. Let's say your application consists of two pages (Stats and Donate); the HTML may be structured as follows:

```
<body>
<!--  Page 1    -->
        <div data-role="page" id="Donate">
               ...
        </div>

   <!--  Page 2    -->
        <div data-role="page" id="Stats">
               ...
        </div>
</body>
```

When this application starts, the user will see only the content of the page Donate because it is included in the code first. We'll talk about defining navigation a bit later.

 The preceding code fragment is an example of a *multipage template*, a single HTML document containing multiple pages. An alternative way of organizing the code is to have the content of each page in a separate file, or a *single-page template*, and you'll see an example later in this chapter.

Let's say you want a page to be divided into the header, content, and the footer. You can then specify the corresponding roles to each of these sections:

```
<body>
<!-- Page 1    -->
        <div data-role="page" id="Donate">

          <div data-role="header" >...</div>
          <div data-role="content" >...</div>
          <div data-role="footer" >...</div>

        </div>

<!-- Page 2    -->
        <div data-role="page" id="Stats">
              ...
        </div>
    </body>
```

It's not a must to split the page with the data roles header, content, and footer. But if you do, the code will be better structured, and additional styling can be applied in the CSS based on these attributes.

 It would be a good idea to replace the three <div> tags on the Donate page with the HTML5 tags <header>, <article>, and <footer>. However, during this learning stage, this could have confused you, because it's easy to mix up the HTML5 <header> and jQuery Mobile data role header. (The footer line might have looked confusing, too.)

Let's say you want to add navigation controls to the header of the page. You can add to the header a container with data-role="navbar". In Example 11-1, we'll use the menus from the Save The Child application.

Example 11-1. Adding a navigation bar

```
<!DOCTYPE html>
<html>
 <head>
  <meta charset="utf-8">
  <meta name="viewport" content="width=device-width, initial-scale=1">
   <link rel="stylesheet"
        href="http://code.jquery.com/mobile/1.3.1/jquery.mobile-1.3.1.min.css"/>
 </head>
 <body>

  <div data-role="page">
   <div data-role="header">
      <h1>Donate</h1>
      <div data-role="navbar">
        <ul>
            <li>
                <a href="#Who-We-Are">Who We Are</a>
```

```
                </li>
                <li>
                        <a href="#What-We-Do">What We Do</a>
                </li>
                <li>
                        <a href="#Where-We-Work">Where We Work</a>
                </li>
                <li>
                        <a href="#Way-To-Give">Way To Give</a>
                </li>
            </ul>
        </div>
    </div> <!-- header -->

    <div data-role="content" >
        The content goes here
    </div>

    <div data-role="footer" >
      The footer goes here
    </div>

    <script src="http://code.jquery.com/jquery-1.9.1.min.js"></script>
    <script src="http://code.jquery.com/mobile/1.3.1/jquery.mobile-1.3.1.min.js">
    </script>
  </body>
</html>
```

We'll explain the meaning of the HTML anchor tags in the section "Adding Page Navigation" on page 414. For now, note the `<viewport>` tag in the preceding example. It instructs the browser of the mobile device to render the content to a virtual window that has to have the same width as that of the device's screen. Otherwise, the mobile browser might assume that it's a website for desktop browsers and will minimize the content, requiring the user to zoom out. Read more about it in the sidebar "The Viewport Concept" on page 378 in Chapter 10.

 You can find a list of all available jQuery Mobile `data-` attributes in the Data attribute reference (*http://bit.ly/1lJd2Oq*) from the online documentation.

The preceding code sample is a complete HTML document that you can test in your browser. If you use desktop web browser, the web page will look like Figure 11-1.

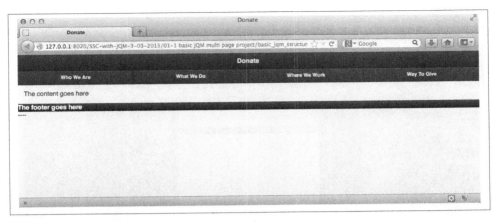

Figure 11-1. Viewing the document in Firefox

Seeing How It Looks on Mobile Devices

Any mobile web developer wants to see how his web application will look on mobile devices. There two major ways of doing this: either test it on a real device or use a software emulator or simulator. Let's talk about the emulators; there are plenty available.

For example, you can use one of the handy tools such as the Apache Ripple emulator. This Chrome browser extension adds a green icon on the right side of the browser's toolbar; click it to enable Ripple to run in its Web Mobile default mode. Next, select the mobile device from the drop-down on the left, and then copy and paste the URL of your HTML document into the Chrome browser's address bar. Figure 11-2 shows how our web page would be rendered on the mobile phone Nokia 97/5800.

 Some emulators target a specific platform. For example, you can consider Android Emulator (*http://bit.ly/1iHi09s*) or use the iOS simulator that comes with Apple's Xcode IDE. Chrome Developer Tools has an emulator panel (*http://bit.ly/1nkbgBb*), too. For Nokia emulators, browse its developer's forum (*http://nokia.ly/1qelhm8*). BlackBerry simulators are here (*http://bit.ly/1soOrTB*). Microsoft also offers an emulator (*http://bit.ly/1nhbjwn*) for its phones. You can find a more detailed list of various emulators and simulators in *Programming the Mobile Web* by Maximiliano Firtman (O'Reilly).

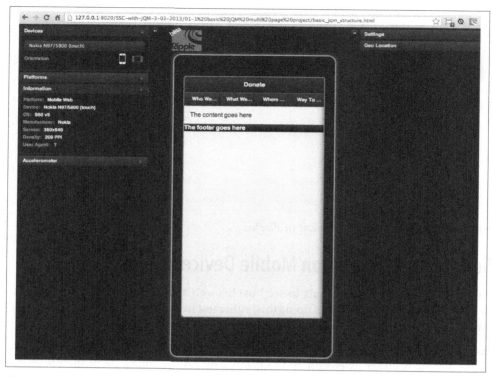

Figure 11-2. Viewing the document in the Ripple emulator

Using emulators really helps in development. Ripple emulates not only the screen resolutions, but some of the hardware features, as well (simulators usually simulate only
the software). For example, you can test an accelerometer by using the corresponding
menu item under Devices (at the upper left in Figure 11-2) or Geo Location under
Settings (at the upper right in Figure 11-2). But keep in mind that emulators run in your
desktop browser, which might render the UI in not exactly the same way as a mobile
browser running on the user's mobile phone. For example, the fonts might look a little
different. Hence, testing your application on a real device is highly recommended even
though it's impossible to test your web application on the thousands of different devices
people use.

If you can afford it, hire real mobile users carrying different devices. You can do this
through the Mob4Hire (*http://www.mob4hire.com*) testing as a service (TaaS) website.
The good news is that creators of jQuery Mobile use about 70 physical devices (*http://
bit.ly/1nhbsj6*) for testing of their UI components, but still, you might want to see how
your application looks and feels on a variety of devices.

If you want to see how your application looks on a real device that you own, the easiest
way is to deploy your application on a web server with a static IP address or a dedicated

domain name. After the code is modified, you need to transfer the code to that remote server and enter its URL in the address bar of your mobile device browser.

If you're developing for iOS on a Mac OS X computer, the procedure is even easier if both devices are on the same WiFi network. Connect your iOS device to your Mac computer via the USB input. In System Preferences, click Networks and select your WiFi connection on the left. You'll see the IP address of your computer on the right (for example, 192.168.0.1). If your application is deployed under the local web server, you can reach it from your iOS device by entering in its browser address bar the URL of your application using the IP address of your computer (for example, *http://192.168.0.1/ myApp/index.html*). For details, read my blog post, "Hack: iPhone, USB, Macbook, Web Server." (*http://bit.ly/Uc8RA3*)

 If your mobile application behaves differently than on a real device, see if there is an option for remote debugging on the device for your platform. For example, in this document (*http://bit.ly/1lDu2VI*), Google explains how to do remote debugging in a Chrome browser running on Android devices. The web browser Safari 7 supports remote debugging on iOS devices (details here (*http://bit.ly/ 1soOK0G*)).

Styling in jQuery Mobile

You might not like the design of the navigation bar shown in Figure 11-1, but it has some style applied to it. Where are the white letters on the black background coming from? They're styled this way because we've included `data-role="navbar"` in the code. This is the power of the custom `data-` attributes in action. The creators of jQuery Mobile included in their CSS predefined styling for `data-` attributes, including the inner buttons of the `navbar`.

What if you don't like this default styling? Create your own CSS, but first see whether you like some of the off-the-shelf themes offered by jQuery Mobile. You can have up to 26 prestyled sets of toolbars, content, and button colors called *swatches*. In the code, you'll refer to them as themes lettered from A to Z. Adding `data-theme="a"` to `<div data-role="page">` will change the look of the entire page. But you can use the `data-theme` attribute with any HTML element, not necessarily the entire page or other container.

By default, the header and the footer use swatch A, and the content area uses swatch C. To change the entire color scheme of Figure 11-2 to swatch A (the background of the content area will become dark gray), use the following line:

```
<div data-role="page" data-theme="a">
```

jQuery Mobile has a tool, ThemeRoller (*http://jquerymobile.com/themeroller*), that you can use to create a unique combination of colors, fonts, backgrounds, and shadows and assign it to one of the letters of the alphabet (see Figure 11-3).

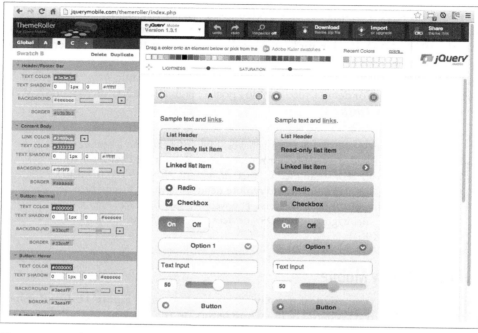

Figure 11-3. ThemeRoller

You can learn about creating custom themes with ThemeRoller by visiting this URL (*http://learn.jquery.com/jquery-mobile/theme-roller/*).

Adding Page Navigation

In jQuery Mobile, page navigation is defined by using the HTML anchor tag `<a href="">`, where the `href` attribute can point at either a page defined as a section in the same HTML document or a page defined in a separate HTML document. Accordingly, you can say that we're using either a *multipage template* or a *single-page template*.

Multipage template

With a multipage template (see Example 11-2) each page is a `<div>` (or other HTML container) with an ID. The `href` attribute responsible for navigation includes a hash character (#) followed by the corresponding ID.

Example 11-2. Organizing code with a multipage template

```
<body>
<!--  Page 1    -->
        <div data-role="page" id="Donate" data-theme="e">
                <h1>Donate</h1>

                <a href="#Stats">Show Stats</a>
        </div>

    <!--  Page 2    -->
        <div data-role="page" id="Stats">
                <h1>Statistics<h1>
        </div>
</body>
```

If you use a multipage document, the ID of the page with a hash character will be added to the URL. For example, if the name of the preceding document is *navigation1.html*, when the Statistics page is open, the browser's URL will look like this:

http://127.0.0.1/navigation1.html#Stats

Let's say that the only way to navigate from the Statistics page is to go back to the Donate page. Now we'll turn the preceding code fragment into a working two-page document with Back-button support. Both pages in the HTML document in Example 11-3 have a designated area with `data-role="header"`, and the Stats page has yet another custom property, `data-add-back-btn="true"`. This is all it takes to ensure that the Back button displays at the left side of the page header, and that when the user *taps* on it, the application navigates to the Donate page.

Example 11-3. The Donate and Stats page

```
<!DOCTYPE html>
<html>
 <head>
        <meta charset="utf-8">
        <meta name="viewport" content="width=device-width, initial-scale=1">
  <link rel="stylesheet"
        href="http://code.jquery.com/mobile/1.3.1/jquery.mobile-1.3.1.min.css"/>
 </head>
<body>
    <!--  Page 1    -->
        <div data-role="page" id="Donate">
                <div data-role="header" >
                  <h1>Donate</h1>
        </div>
                <a href="#Stats">Show Stats</a>
        </div>

        <!--  Page 2    -->
        <div data-role="page" id="Stats" data-add-back-btn="true">
```

```
            <div data-role="header" >
              <h1>Statistics</h1>
              </div>
              Statistics will go here

        </div>

    <script src="http://code.jquery.com/jquery-1.9.1.min.js"></script>
    <script src="http://code.jquery.com/mobile/1.3.1/jquery.mobile-1.3.1.min.js">
    </script>

    </body>
</html>
```

Figure 11-4 shows a snapshot of the Ripple emulator after the user clicks the link on the Donate page. The Statistics page now includes the fully functional Back button.

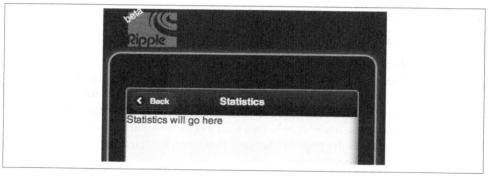

Figure 11-4. The Statistics page with the Back button

 The attribute `data-add-back-btn` works the same way in both the multipage and single-page cases. The Back button appears only if the current page is not the first one and there is a previous page to navigate to.

Single-page template

Now let's rearrange the code in Example 11-3 by using a single-page template. We'll create a folder of pages, which can contain multiple HTML files—one per page. In our case, we'll create one file, *stats.html*, to represent the Statistics page. Accordingly, we'll remove the section marked as Page 2 from the *main.html* file. The *stats.html* file is shown in Example 11-4.

Example 11-4. The HTML code of the Statistics web page

```html
<!DOCTYPE html>
<html>
    <head>
        <meta charset="utf-8">
    </head>
    <body>
        <div data-role="page" data-add-back-btn="true">
            <div data-role="header">
                <h1>Statistics</h1>
    </div>

    <div data-role="content">
      Statistics data will go here
    </div>
  </body>
</html>
```

The main HTML file contains only one home page, which is the Donate page in this example. The anchor tag simply refers to the URL of *stats.html*; there is no need to use hash characters or section IDs any longer. In this case, jQuery Mobile loads *stats.html* by using an internal Ajax request. Example 11-5 shows the main page.

Example 11-5. The HTML of the main page

```html
<!DOCTYPE html>
<html>
<head>
        <meta charset="utf-8">
        <meta name="viewport" content="width=device-width, initial-scale=1">
    <link rel="stylesheet"
        href="http://code.jquery.com/mobile/1.3.1/jquery.mobile-1.3.1.min.css" />
</head>
<body>
    <!-- Main page  -->
            <div data-role="page" id="Donate">
                    <div data-role="header">
                        <h1>Donate</h1>
            </div>

    <!-- A Link to the second page  -->
                    <a href="pages/stats.html">Show Stats</a>
            </div>

  <script src="http://code.jquery.com/jquery-1.9.1.min.js"></script>
  <script src="http://code.jquery.com/mobile/1.3.1/jquery.mobile-1.3.1.min.js">
  </script>

  </body>
</html>
```

Running this version of our simple two-page application produces the same results. The second page looks exactly like Figure 11-4.

If you use single-page documents, the name of the file with the page will be added to the URL. For example, when the Statistics page is open, the browser's URL will look like this:

http://127.0.0.1/pages/stats.html

Multipage or single-page template

So which template style should you use? Both have their pros and cons. If the code base of your application is large, use a single-page template. The code will be split into multiple pages, will be easier to read, and will give you a feeling of being modular without implementing any additional libraries for cutting the application into pieces. The home page of the application loads quicker because you don't need to load the entire code base.

This all sounds good, but be aware that with single-page templates, whenever you navigate from one page to another, your mobile device makes a new request to the server. The user will see the wait cursor until the page arrives at the device. Even if the size of each page is small, additional requests to the server are costlier with mobile devices because they need another second just to re-establish a radio link to the cell tower. After communication with the server is done, the phone lowers its power consumption. However, a new request to the server for loading the page starts increasing power consumption again. Hence, using the multipage template might provide smoother navigation.

On the other hand, there is a way to prefetch pages (*http://bit.ly/1nYvi4y*) into the DOM even in single-page mode such that the number of server requests is minimized. You can do this either with the HTML attribute `data-prefetch="true"` or programmatically by using `$.mobile.loadPage()`. You can also ask the browser to cache previously visited pages with `$.mobile.page.prototype.options.domCache = true;`.

So what's the verdict? Test your application in both single-page and multipage modes and see what works best.

Progressive Enhancement

Web developers use a technique called *progressive enhancement*, especially in the mobile field. The idea is simple: first make sure that the basic functionality works in any browser, and then apply the bells and whistles to make the application as fancy as possible by using CSS or framework-specific enhancements.

But what if you decide to go the opposite route and take a nice-looking UI and remove its awesomeness? For instance, delete the `<script>` and `<link>` tags from Example 11-5 and open it in a web browser. We are testing a situation in which, for whatever reason, we need to remove jQuery Mobile from our code base. The code still works! You'll see the first page, and clicking the link opens the second page. You'll lose the styling and that nice-looking Back button, but you can still use the browser's Back button. The web browser ignores the custom `data-` attributes without breaking anything.

This wouldn't be the case if we were using the multipage template, where each page is a `<div>` or an `<article>` in the same HTML file. With a multipage template, the web browser would open all pages at once—one below another.

Here's another example. With jQuery Mobile, you can create a button in many ways. There are multiple examples in the Buttons section (*http://bit.ly/1kOuWKr*) of the product documentation. The following code produces five buttons, which will look the same but have different labels:

```
<a href="http://cnn.com" data-role="button">Anchor</a>
<form action="http://cnn.com">
    <button>Click me</button>
    <input type="button" value="Input">
    <input type="submit" value="Submit">
    <input type="reset" value="Reset">
</form>
```

If you choose to use the anchor link with `data-role="button"` and then remove the `<script>` tag that includes the code of the jQuery Mobile library, the anchor tag will still work as a standard HTML link. It won't look like a button, but it will function as expected.

When you're making a decision about using any particular framework or library, ask yourself this question: "How easy is it to remove the framework from the application code if it doesn't deliver as expected?" On several occasions, the authors of this book have been invited to help with projects in which the first task was to remove an erroneously selected framework from the application code. Such "surgery" usually lasts at least two weeks. jQuery Mobile is not overly intrusive and is easily removed.

Adding Persistent Toolbars

One of the ways to arrange navigation is to add persistent toolbars that never go away while your application is running. You can add such a toolbar in the footer or header area or in both. We'll create a simple example illustrating this technique by adding a `navbar` to the footer area of the application. Suppose that your application has a starting page and four other pages that can be selected by the user. Figure 11-5 shows the initial view of the application.

Figure 11-5. Four pages in the footer

If the user taps one of the four pages in the footer, the program replaces the starting page with the selected one, and the title of the selected page in the footer becomes highlighted. If you're reading the electronic version of this book, you'll see in Figure 11-6 that the rectangular area for Page #2 in the footer has a blue background. In the printed version, the different background colors might not be so obvious, but you have to trust us on this or run the code sample on your own. Besides, we'll be highlighting the selected page in a similar way while working on the prototype of the Save The Child application, as per the mockups shown in "Prototyping the Mobile Version" on page 425.

Figure 11-6. Page 2 is selected

In jQuery Mobile, implementing persistent toolbars is simple. The content of each page has to be located in a separate file, and each page has to have a footer and header with *the same* data_id. Example 11-6 presents the code of the file *page2.html*, but *page1*, *page3*, and *page4* look similar; check them out in the source code that comes with this book.

Example 11-6. The file page2.html

```
<!DOCTYPE html>
<html>
  <head>
    <meta charset="utf-8">
  </head>
  <body>
    <div data-role="page" data-add-back-btn="true">
      <div data-role="header" data-position="fixed"
           data-tap-toggle="false" data-id="persistent-header"> ❶
        <h1>Page #2</h1>
```

```
    </div><!-- /header -->
    <div data-role="content" >
      <p>
        <b>Page #2</b> content
      </p>
    </div><!-- /content -->
    <div data-role="footer" data-position="fixed"
       data-tap-toggle="false" data-id="persistent-footer"> ❷
       <div data-role="navbar">
         <ul>
           <li>
             <a href="page-1.html" data-transition="slideup">Page #1</a>   ❸
           </li>
           <li>
             <a href="#" class="ui-state-persist">Page #2</a> ❹
           </li>
           <li>
             <a href="page-3.html" data-transition="slideup">Page #3</a>
           </li>
           <li>
             <a href="page-4.html" data-transition="slideup">Page #4</a>
           </li>
         </ul>
       </div><!-- /navbar -->
     </div><!-- /footer -->
   </div><!-- /page -->
 </body>
</html>
```

❶ To prevent the toolbar from being scrolled away from the screen, we use `data-position="fixed"`. The attribute `data-tap-toggle="false"` disables the ability to remove the toolbar from view by tapping on the screen.

❷ The footers of *page1*, *page2*, *page3*, and *page4* have the same `data-id="persistent-footer"`.

❸ While replacing the current page with another one, apply the `data-transition="slideup"` transition effect so that the page appears by sliding from the bottom up. Note that the anchor tags are automatically styled as buttons just because they are placed in the `navbar` container.

❹ Because page 2 is already shown on the screen, tapping the Page #2 button in the navigation bar should not change the page; hence, `href="#"`. The `class="ui-state-persist"` makes the framework to restore the active state each time, when the page existing in the DOM is shown. The file *page3.html* has a similar anchor for the Page #3 button, and so on.

Example 11-7 presents the code of the main page *index.html*. This code also defines the header, content, and footer areas.

Example 11-7. The main page with header, content, and footer sections

```html
<!DOCTYPE html>
<html>
  <head>
    <meta charset="utf-8">
    <meta name="viewport" content="width=device-width,initial-scale=1,
        user-scalable=no,maximum-scale=1">
    <title>Single-page template - start page</title>
    <link rel="stylesheet"
        href="http://code.jquery.com/mobile/1.3.1/jquery.mobile-1.3.1.min.css" />
  </head>
  <body>

    <div data-role="page">
      <div data-role="header" data-position="fixed"
          data-tap-toggle="false" data-id="persistent-header">
        <h1>Start page</h1>
      </div>

      <div data-role="content" >
        <p>
          Single Page template. Start page content.
        </p>
      </div>

      <div data-role="footer" data-position="fixed"
          data-tap-toggle="false" data-id="persistent-footer">
        <div data-role="navbar">
          <ul>
            <li>
              <a href="pages/page-1.html" data-transition="slideup">Page #1</a>
            </li>
            <li>
              <a href="pages/page-2.html" data-transition="slideup">Page #2</a>
            </li>
            <li>
              <a href="pages/page-3.html" data-transition="slideup">Page #3</a>
            </li>
            <li>
              <a href="pages/page-4.html" data-transition="slideup">Page #4</a>
            </li>
          </ul>
        </div><!-- /navbar -->
      </div><!-- /footer -->
    </div><!-- /page -->

    <script src="http://code.jquery.com/jquery-1.9.1.min.js"></script>
    <script src="http://code.jquery.com/mobile/1.3.1/jquery.mobile-1.3.1.min.js">
    </script>
  </body>
</html>
```

To avoid repeating the same footer in each HTML page, you can write a JavaScript function that appends the footer to each page on the pagecreate event. You can also consider using HTML templating (*http://bit.ly/1uDqB2s*) to declare HTML fragments that are parsed on page load, but can be instantiated later, during runtime. In particular, we can recommend Handlebars (*http://handlebarsjs.com*), which lets you build semantic templates easily.

Programmatic navigation

The preceding code samples illustrated page navigation as a response to the user's action. Sometimes, you need to change pages programmatically as a result of certain events, and the method `$.mobile.changePage()` (*http://bit.ly/1nkcXP1*) can do this.

This method requires at least one parameter—the string defining the change-to-page. For example:

```
$.mobile.changePage("pages/stats.html");
```

But you can also invoke this method with a second parameter, which is an object. You can specify such parameters as `data` (the data to send with the Ajax page request), `changeHash` (a boolean to control if the hash in the URL should be updated), and others. Example 11-8 changes the page by using a post request (`type: "post"`), and the page should replace the current page in the browser's history (`changeHash: false`).

Example 11-8. Changing page with Ajax post request

```
$.mobile.changePage("pages/stats.html", {
        type: "post",
        changeHash: false
});
```

Using jQuery Mobile for Save The Child

After the brief introduction to the jQuery Mobile library, we (and you) are eager to start hands-on coding. The mobile version of Save The Child won't show all the features of this application. It will be sliced into a set of screens (pages), and the user will see one page at a time.

You can test the working jQuery Mobile version of our sample application at link:http://savesickchild.org:8080/ssc-jquery-mobile.

Prototyping the Mobile Version

It's time to go back to Jerry, our web designer, and his favorite prototyping tool, Balsamiq Mockups (to which you were introduced in Chapter 1). Designs and layouts for each screen of the mobile version are shown in this section as images taken from the Balsamiq tool. This is not a complete set of images because it doesn't include layouts for tablets. In this book, we test only mobile devices with screen sizes of 640 x 960 and 320 x 480 pixels.

Figure 11-7 shows two versions of the starting page mockup in portrait mode. Figure 11-8 shows two versions of the About page mockups in portrait mode.

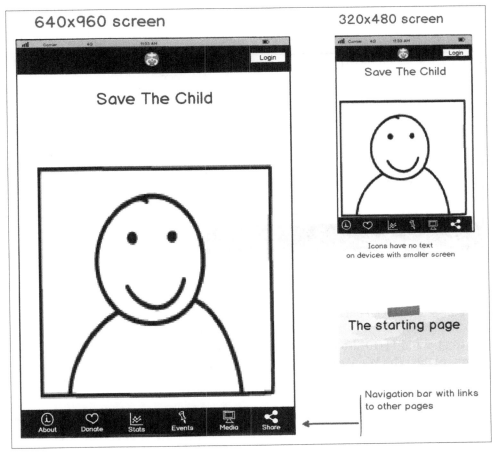

Figure 11-7. The Starting page (portrait)

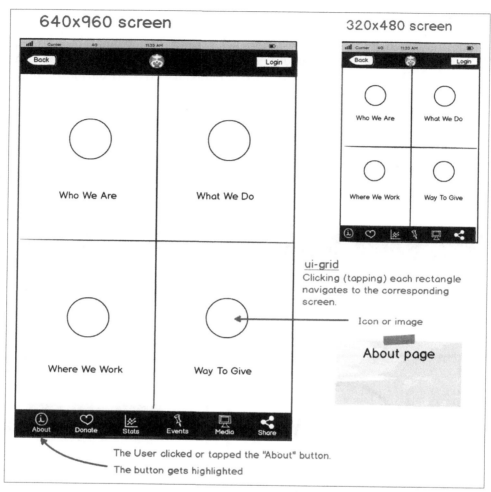

Figure 11-8. The About page (portrait)

Figures 11-9 and 11-10 also show mockups in portrait mode; Figure 11-9 displays two versions of the Who We Are page, and Figure 11-10 depicts two versions of the Donate page.

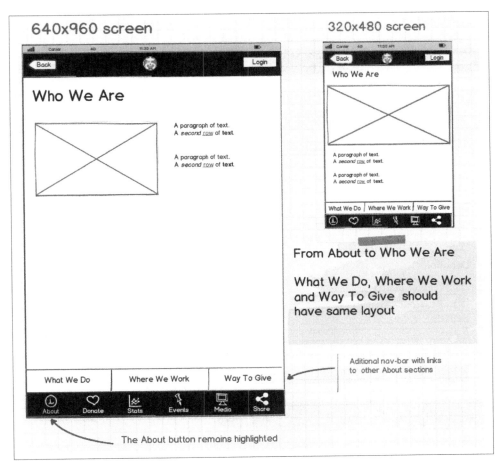

Figure 11-9. The Who We Are section of the About page (portrait)

Figure 11-10 illustrates a term *Above the Fold* used by web designers. This term originated in the newspaper business. It refers to the upper half of the first page of a broadsheet newspaper that has been folded for display and sale at a newstand. This is the section that is visible to passersby and therefore contains the most important headlines —something that a potential buyer would notice immediately. In web design, *Above the Fold* refers to the content on a web page that a user can see without needing to scroll. However, whereas newspaper readers know that there is more to see below the fold, when it comes to web pages, you need to keep in mind that visitors to your web page might not be aware that the scrolling could reveal more information. As it relates to our Save The Child web application, a user with a 320 × 480 screen might not immediately understand that to see the Donate button, she needs to scroll.

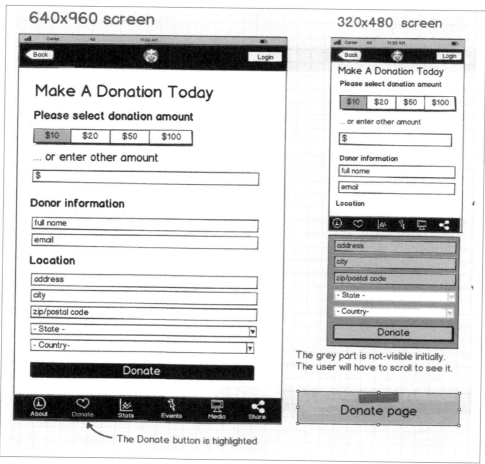

Figure 11-10. The Donate page (portrait)

In general, it's a good idea to minimize the number of form fields that the user must manually fill out. Invest in analyzing the forms used in your application. See if you can design the form smarter; for example, autopopulate some of the fields and show/hide fields based on user input.

 If you have a long form that has to be shown on a small screen, split it into several `<div data-role="page">` sections, all located inside the `<form>` tag. Arrange the navigation between these sections as it was done for multipage documents in the previous section, "Adding Page Navigation" on page 414.

The following images show more of Jerry's mockups. Figure 11-11 shows two versions of the Statistics page in portrait mode. Note the highlighted Stats button indicating the active page.

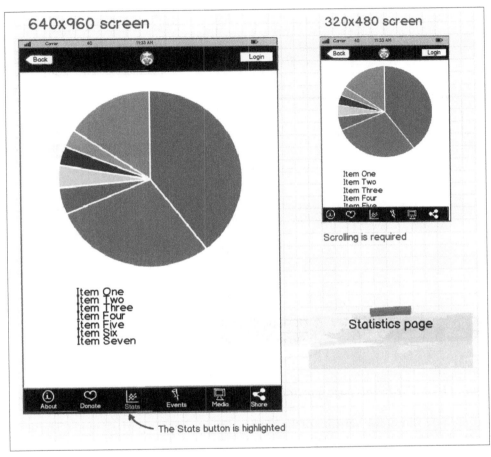

Figure 11-11. The Statistics page (portrait)

Figure 11-12 shows two versions of the Events page mockups in portrait mode. Note the highlighted Events button indicating the active page.

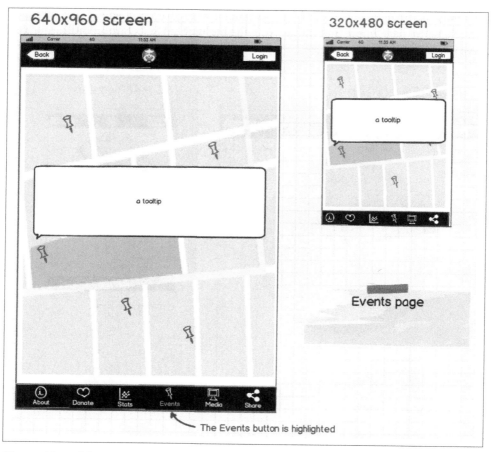

Figure 11-12. The Events page (portrait)

Figure 11-13 shows two versions of the Media page mockups in portrait mode. The user has to click the video title to play it.

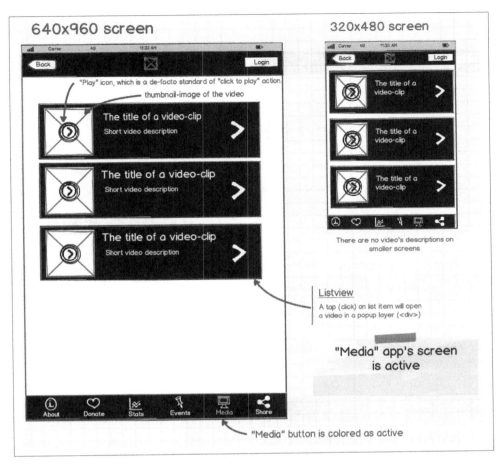

Figure 11-13. The Media page (portrait)

Figure 11-14 shows two versions of the Share page mockups in portrait mode. Jerry decided to divide the viewport into four areas. Each rectangle is a link to the corresponding page.

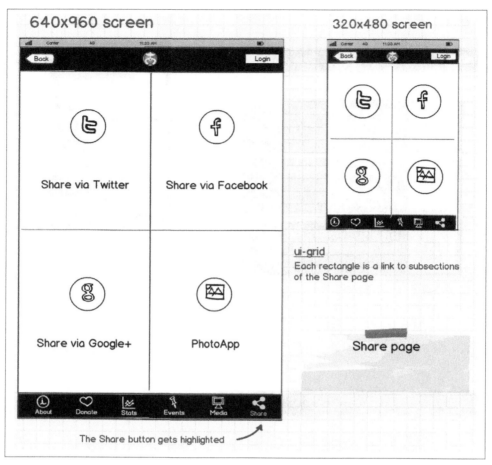

Figure 11-14. The Share page (portrait)

Figure 11-15 shows two versions of the Share Photo page mockups in portrait mode. Note the additional navigation bar at the bottom.

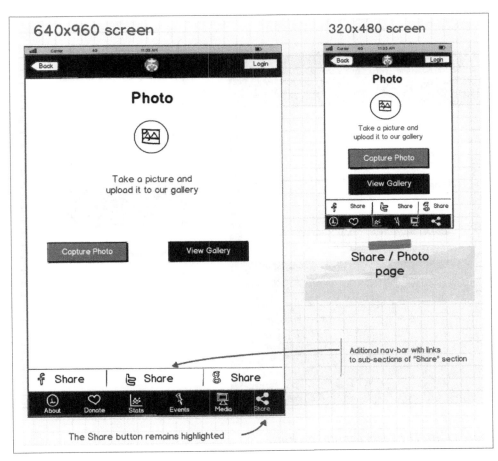

Figure 11-15. The Share/Photo page (portrait)

Figure 11-16 shows two versions of the Login page mockups in portrait mode. The Login panel is implemented as a pop-up window.

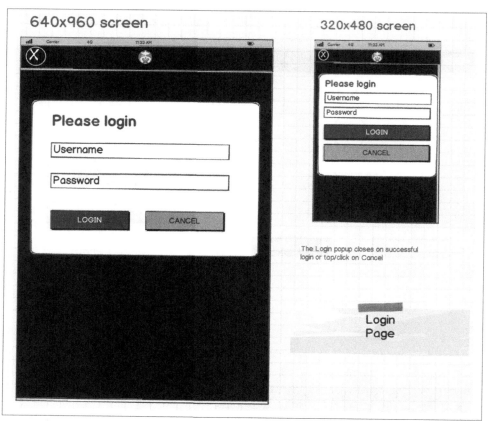

Figure 11-16. The Login pop-up (portrait)

Figure 11-17 shows two versions of the Login page mockups in portrait mode after the Login pop-up is closed.

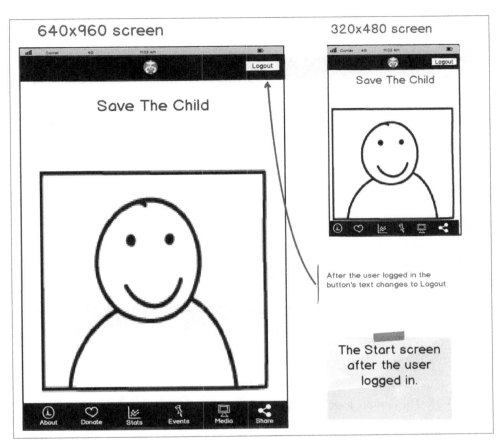

Figure 11-17. After the user logs in

This prototype will be used for developing both jQuery Mobile and Sencha Touch versions of our Save The Child application. We've also included the design for the page that will integrate with the device's camera (see Figure 11-15); this functionality is implemented in Chapter 13.

All of these images show UI layouts when the mobile device is in portrait mode, but you should ask your web designer to prepare mockups for landscape mode, too. Figures 11-18, 11-19, 11-20, and 11-21 show snapshots in landscape mode that Jerry also prepared prepared for us.

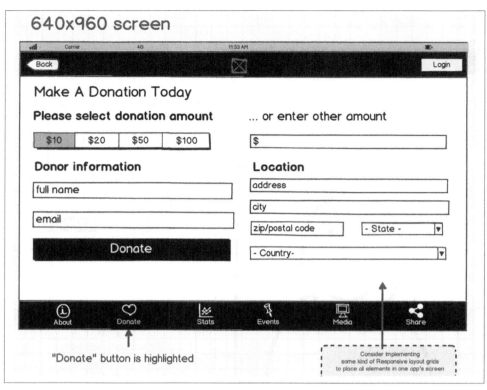

Figure 11-18. The Donate page (landscape, 640 x 960)

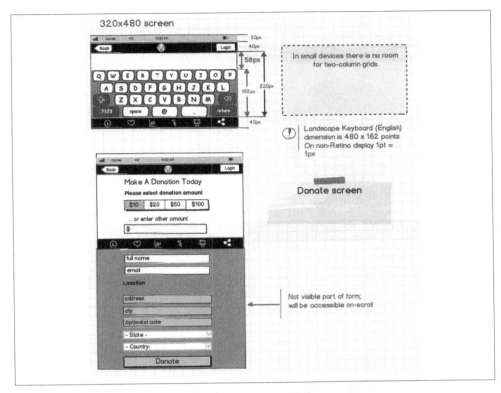

Figure 11-19. The Donate page (landscape, 320 x 480)

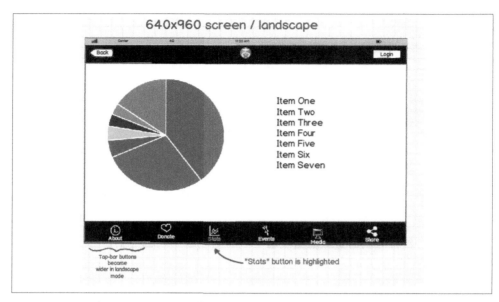

Figure 11-20. The Statistics page (landscape, 640 x 960)

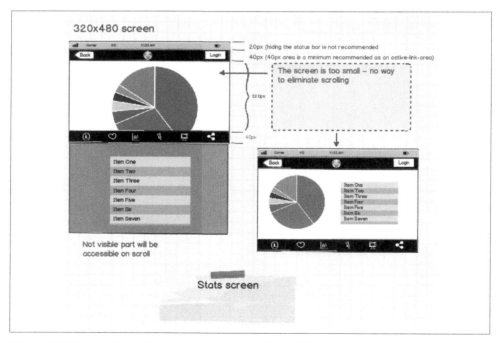

Figure 11-21. The Statistics page (landscape, 320 x 480)

If you want to add a link that will offer to dial a phone number, use the `tel:` scheme (for example, `<a href="tel:+12125551212">Call us</a>`). If you want the phone to look like a button, add the attribute `data-role="button"` to the anchor tag.

Project Structure and Navigation

This time the Save The Child project structure will look like Figure 11-22. We are using the singe-page template here. The *index.html* file is the home page of our application. All other pages are located in the *pages* folder. The JavaScript code is in the folder *js*, and fonts, images, and CSS files are in the folder *assets*. We'll use the same JSON files as in the previous versions of this application, which are located in the folder *data*.

Let's start implementing navigation based on the techniques described earlier, in the section "Adding Persistent Toolbars" on page 419. The source code of *index.html* is shown in Example 11-9. Note that we moved the `<script>` tags with jQuery Mobile code from the `<body>` section to the `<head>` section to avoid a pop-up of a nonstyled page on the initial load of the application.

Example 11-9. The file index.html

```
<!DOCTYPE html>
<html>
  <head>
    <meta charset="utf-8">
    <meta name="viewport" content="width=device-width,initial-scale=1,
      user-scalable=no,maximum-scale=1">
❶
    <meta name="apple-mobile-web-app-capable" content="yes">
    <meta name="apple-mobile-web-app-status-bar-style" content="black">

    <title>Save The Child</title>

    <link rel="stylesheet"
        href="http://code.jquery.com/mobile/1.3.1/jquery.mobile-1.3.1.min.css" />
    <script src="http://code.jquery.com/jquery-1.9.1.min.js"></script>
    <script src="http://code.jquery.com/mobile/1.3.1/jquery.mobile-1.3.1.min.js">
    </script>

    ❷
    <link rel="stylesheet" href="assets/css/jqm-icon-pack-3.0.0-fa.css" />

    <link rel="stylesheet" href="assets/css/app-styles.css" /> ❸
  </head>
  <body>

    <div data-role="page">
❹
```

```
  <div data-role="header" data-position="fixed" data-tap-toggle="false"
  data-id="persistent-header">
    <a href="pages/login.html" data-icon="chevron-down" data-iconpos="right"
    class="ui-btn-right login-btn" data-rel="dialog">Login</a>
    <h1><img class="header-logo" src="assets/img/logo-20x20.png"
                             alt="Save The Child Logo"/> </h1>
  </div>
```
❺
```
  <div data-role="content" >
    <h2>Save The Child</h2>
    <p>
      <b>Start page</b> content.
    </p>
  </div>
```
❻
```
  <div data-role="footer" data-position="fixed" data-tap-toggle="false"
  data-id="persistent-footer">
    <div data-role="navbar" class="ssc-navbar">
      <ul>
        <li>
          <a href="pages/about.html" data-iconshadow="false"
          data-icon="info-sign"
          data-transition="slideup">About</a> ❼
        </li>
        <li>
          <a href="pages/donate.html" data-iconshadow="false"
          data-icon="heart" data-transition="slideup">Donate</a>
        </li>
        <li>
          <a href="pages/stats.html" data-iconshadow="false"
          data-icon="bar-chart" data-transition="slideup">Stats</a>
        </li>
        <li>
          <a href="pages/events.html" data-iconshadow="false"
          data-icon="map-marker" data-transition="slideup">Events</a>
        </li>
        <li>
          <a href="pages/media.html" data-iconshadow="false"
          data-icon="film" data-transition="slideup">Media</a>
        </li>
        <li>
          <a href="pages/share.html" data-iconshadow="false"
          data-icon="share" data-transition="slideup">Share</a>
        </li>
      </ul>
    </div><!-- /navbar -->
  </div><!-- /footer -->
</div><!-- /page -->
<script src="js/app-main.js"></script>
</body>
</html>
```

---

❶ The meta tags to request the full-screen mode and a black status bar on iOS devices. The main goal is to remove the browser's address bar. Some developers suggest JavaScript tricks such as `window.scrollTo(0,1);` (Google it for details). But we are not aware of a reliable solution for a guaranteed full-screen mode in web applications on all devices.

❷ This project uses jQuery Mobile Icon Pack—an extension of standard jQuery Mobile icons.

❸ Our CSS will override some of the jQuery Mobile classes and add new styles specific to our application.

❹ The header shows a Login button and the application logo.

❺ The content of the main page should go here.

❻ All the navigation buttons are located in the footer.

❼ jQuery Mobile includes icons that you can use by specifying their names in the `data-icon` attribute (more details are provided in the upcoming sidebar "Icon Fonts" on page 441). The icon position is controlled by the attribute `data-iconpos`. If you don't want to show text, use `data-iconpos="notext"`.

Icon Fonts

In this application, we use icon fonts (*http://bit.ly/1izPrzY*) for display on the navigation bar. The main advantage over using images for icons is that icon fonts are maintenance free. You don't need to resize and redraw icons. A disadvantage of using icon fonts is that they are single-colored, but for the navigation bar buttons, having multicolored images is not important.

In Example 11-9, we use the jQuery Mobile Icon Pack that's available on GitHub (*http://bit.ly/T7Jajk*). It's an adaptation of the Twitter Bootstrap's Font Awesome for jQuery Mobile. If you need fancier images for your mobile application, consider using Glyphish icons (*http://www.glyphish.com*).

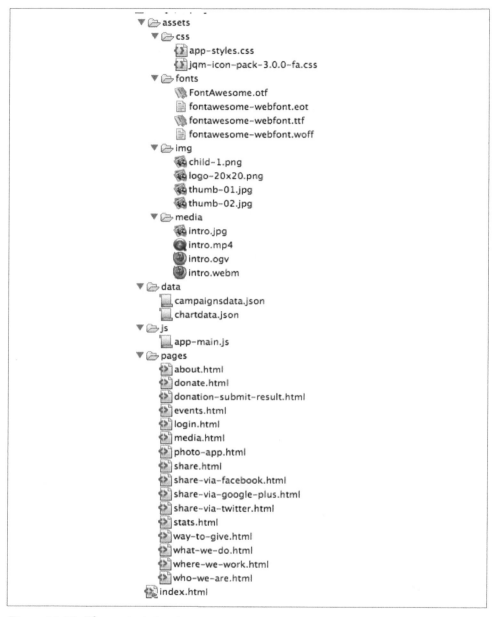

```
▼ 🗁 assets
  ▼ 🗁 css
      📄 app-styles.css
      📄 jqm-icon-pack-3.0.0-fa.css
  ▼ 🗁 fonts
      📄 FontAwesome.otf
      📄 fontawesome-webfont.eot
      📄 fontawesome-webfont.ttf
      📄 fontawesome-webfont.woff
  ▼ 🗁 img
      🖼 child-1.png
      🖼 logo-20x20.png
      🖼 thumb-01.jpg
      🖼 thumb-02.jpg
  ▼ 🗁 media
      🖼 intro.jpg
      🖼 intro.mp4
      🖼 intro.ogv
      🖼 intro.webm
▼ 🗁 data
    📄 campaignsdata.json
    📄 chartdata.json
▼ 🗁 js
    📄 app-main.js
▼ 🗁 pages
    📄 about.html
    📄 donate.html
    📄 donation-submit-result.html
    📄 events.html
    📄 login.html
    📄 media.html
    📄 photo-app.html
    📄 share.html
    📄 share-via-facebook.html
    📄 share-via-google-plus.html
    📄 share-via-twitter.html
    📄 stats.html
    📄 way-to-give.html
    📄 what-we-do.html
    📄 where-we-work.html
    📄 who-we-are.html
  📄 index.html
```

Figure 11-22. The project structure

Figure 11-23 shows how the landing page of the Save The Child application looks in the Ripple emulator. Run it and click each button in the navigation bar.

Figure 11-23. The first take on the Save The Child home page

The content of our custom CSS file *app-styles.css* comes next, which you can see in Example 11-10.

Example 11-10. The file app-styles.css

```
/* First, we want to stop jQuery Mobile from using its standard images */
/* for icons. */

.ui-icon-arrow-l, .ui-icon-alert, .ui-icon-checkbox-off,
.ui-icon-dollar, .ui-icon-wrench,
.ui-icon-plus, .ui-icon-minus, .ui-icon-delete, .ui-icon-arrow-r,
.ui-icon-arrow-u, .ui-icon-arrow-d, .ui-icon-check, .ui-icon-gear,
.ui-icon-refresh, .ui-icon-forward, .ui-icon-back, .ui-icon-grid, .ui-icon-star,
.ui-icon-info, .ui-icon-home, .ui-icon-search, .ui-icon-searchfield:after,
.ui-icon-checkbox-on, .ui-icon-radio-off, .ui-icon-radio-on,
.ui-icon-email, .ui-icon-page, .ui-icon-question, .ui-icon-foursquare,
.ui-icon-euro, .ui-icon-pound, .ui-icon-apple, .ui-icon-chat,
.ui-icon-trash, .ui-icon-mappin, .ui-icon-direction, .ui-icon-heart,
```

```css
.ui-icon-play, .ui-icon-pause, .ui-icon-stop, .ui-icon-person,
.ui-icon-music, .ui-icon-wifi, .ui-icon-phone, .ui-icon-power,
.ui-icon-lightning, .ui-icon-drink, .ui-icon-android {
  background-image: none !important;
}

/* Override the jQuery Mobile CSS class selectors with the icon fonts. */
/* Whenever you create custom icon, jQuery Mobile expects to find a */
/* class with the name starting with `.ui-icon-` and ending with the */
/* name of the icon, like `.ui-icon-donatebtn` . But in HTML attributes */
/* you'll be using it without this prefix, e.g. `data-icon="donatebtn"`. */

.ui-icon-arrow-l:before {
  content: "\f053";
  margin-top: 2px
}
.ui-icon-delete:before {
  content: "\f00d";
  margin-left: 3px;
  margin-top: -2px
}
.ui-icon-arrow-r:before {
  content: "\f054";
  padding-left: 2px;
}
.ui-icon-arrow-d:before {
  content: "\f078";
}
.ui-icon-home:before {
  content: "\f015";
}

.header-logo {
  vertical-align: middle;
  padding-right: 0.3em;
  margin-top: -2px;
}

/* Create some custom styles for the Save The Child application. */

.ssc-navbar .ui-btn-text {
  font-size: 0.9em
}

/* overwide, customize icons css */
.ssc-navbar .ui-icon {
  background: none !important;
  margin-top:2px !important;
}
/* jQM allows not more than 5 items per line in navbar.
We need 6. Hence we should override the default CSS rule.
Each block will occupy 1/6 of the width: 16.66%
```

```
*/
.ssc-navbar .ui-block-a {
  width:16.66% !important;
}
.ssc-navbar .ui-block-b {
  width:16.66% !important;
}

.ssc-grid-nav {
  display: block;
  text-align: center;
  border-top: 1px solid #c0c0c0;
  text-decoration:none;
  color: #555 !important;
  overflow: hidden;
  box-sizing: border-box
}
.ssc-grid-nav:nth-child(odd) {
  border-right: 1px solid #c0c0c0;
}
.ssc-grid-item-icon {
  display:block;
  font-size: 2em;
  padding-bottom: 0.5em
}
```

Selected Code Fragments

All the code that implements Save The Child with jQuery Mobile is available to download from GitHub (*http://bit.ly/T2Vgda*), and we're not going to include all program listings here. But we will show and comment selected code fragments that illustrate various features of jQuery Mobile.

Grid layouts

While testing this initial version of the Save The Child application, note that the content of the About and Share pages is implemented as in the mock ups shown in Figures 11-8 and 11-14, which look like grids. jQuery Mobile has several predefined layouts with which you can show the content as rows and columns. Keep in mind that on small devices, you should avoid displaying grids with multiple rows and columns because the data there will be hardly visible. But in our case, the grid will contain just four large cells. Next, Example 11-11 presents the source code of *share.html*, followed by brief comments (the code for *about.html* looks similar).

Example 11-11. The share.html page

```
<!DOCTYPE html>
<html>
  <head>
    <meta charset="utf-8">
```

```
</head>
<body>

  <div data-role="page" data-add-back-btn="true" id="Share">
    <div class="ssc-grid-header" data-role="header" data-position="fixed"
    data-tap-toggle="false" data-id="persistent-header">
      <a href="login.html" data-icon="chevron-down" data-iconpos="right"
      class="ui-btn-right login-btn" data-rel="dialog">Login</a>
      <h1><img class="header-logo" src="../assets/img/logo-20x20.png"
      alt="Save The Child Logo"/></h1>
    </div>

    <div data-role="content" style="padding:0">
      <div class="ui-grid-a">                          ❶

        <div class="ui-block-a">                       ❷
          <a href="#" class="ssc-grid-nav">
          <span class="ssc-grid-item-icon ui-icon-twitter"></span>
          <br/>
          Share via Twitter</a>
        </div>
        <div class="ui-block-b">
          <a href="#" class="ssc-grid-nav">
          <span class="ssc-grid-item-icon ui-icon-facebook"></span>
          <br/>
          Share via Facebook</a>
        </div>
        <div class="ui-block-a">
          <a href="#" class="ssc-grid-nav">
          <span class="ssc-grid-item-icon ui-icon-google-plus"></span>
          <br/>
          Share via Google+</a>
        </div>
        <div class="ui-block-b">
          <a href="#" class="ssc-grid-nav">
          <span class="ssc-grid-item-icon ui-icon-camera"></span>
          <br/>
          Photo App</a>
        </div>
      </div>
    </div>

    <div class="ssc-grid-footer" data-role="footer" data-position="fixed"
    data-tap-toggle="false" data-id="persistent-footer">
      <div data-role="navbar" class="ssc-navbar">
        <ul>
          <li>
            <a href="about.html" data-iconshadow="false" data-icon="info-sign"
            data-transition="slideup">About</a>
          </li>
          <li>
            <a href="donate.html" data-iconshadow="false" data-icon="heart"
```

```
              data-transition="slideup">Donate</a>
          </li>
          <li>
            <a href="stats.html" data-iconshadow="false" data-icon="bar-chart"
            data-transition="slideup">Stats</a>
          </li>
          <li>
            <a href="events.html" data-iconshadow="false" data-icon="map-marker"
            data-transition="slideup">Events</a>
          </li>
          <li>
            <a href="media.html" data-iconshadow="false" data-icon="film"
            data-transition="slideup">Media</a>
          </li>
          <li>
            <a href="#" data-iconshadow="false" data-icon="share"
              class="ui-state-persist">Share</a>
          </li>
        </ul>
      </div><!-- /navbar -->
    </div><!-- /footer -->
  </div><!-- /page  -->
 </body>
</html>
```

❶   The grid in Figure 11-8 is implemented using a jQuery Mobile multicolumn layout with ui-grid classes (explained in ❷).

❷   Each of the cells in the grid is styled as the ui-block-a for the first grid row and ui-block-b for the second one. Hence, Share via Twitter is in the left cell, and Share via Facebook is on the right.

There are four preset configurations (*http://bit.ly/1nhhbWi*) for grids containing two, three, four, and five columns called ui-grid-a, ui-grid-b, ui-grid-c, and ui-grid-d, respectively. The Statistics and About pages are split into four sections, which can be laid out in two columns with ui-grid-a. With this two-column layout, each column is allocated 50 percent of the width; with a three-column layout, each column gets about 33 percent, and so forth.

Each of the cells is laid out with a class that's named ui-block- followed by the corresponding letter (for example, ui-block-c for the cells located in the third column). Figure 11-24 is a fragment from the jQuery Mobile documentation, and it serves as a good illustration of the grid presets.

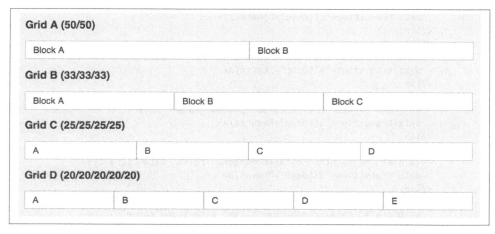

Figure 11-24. Preset grid layouts

The class .ui-responsive allows you to set breakpoints to grids that are less than 35 em (560 pixels) wide.

Control groups

Thee Donation page contains a section in which the user can select one of the donation amounts. This is a good example of a set of UI controls that belong to the same group. In the desktop version of the application, we've been using radio buttons grouped by the same name attribute (<input type="radio" name = "amount"). Revisit Chapter 3 to find the complete code in Example 3-5.

jQuery Mobile utilizes the concept of control groups (*http://bit.ly/Twj2i6*), which are handy for grouping and styling components. The code looks very similar, but now it's wrapped in the <fieldset> container with data-role="controlgroup", as shown in Example 11-12.

Example 11-12. Grouping components by using <fieldset>

```
<div class="donation-form-section">
  <label class="donation-heading">Please select donation amount</label>

  <fieldset data-role="controlgroup" data-type="horizontal" id="radio-container">

    <input type="radio" name="amount" id="d10" value="10"/>
    <label for="d10">$10</label>
    <input type="radio" name="amount" id="d20" value="20" />
    <label for="d20">$20</label>
    <input type="radio" name="amount" id="d50" checked="checked" value="50" />
    <label for="d50">$50</label>
    <input type="radio" name="amount" id="d100" value="100" />
    <label for="d100">$100</label>
```

```
</fieldset>
<label class="donation-heading">...or enter other amount</label>

<input id="customAmount" name="amount"  value="" type="text"
  autocomplete="off" placeholder="$"/>
```

jQuery Mobile renders this code as shown in Figure 11-25. The buttons are laid out horizontally because of the attribute `data-type="horizontal"`. If you don't like the default styling of the radio button input fields, feel free to specify the appropriate `data-theme` either for the entire group or for each input field.

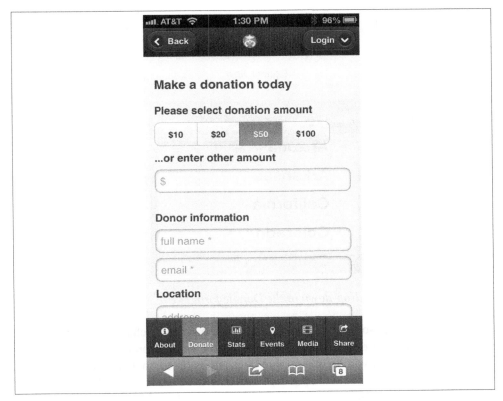

Figure 11-25. A control group for donation amount

Drop-downs and collapsibles

Having the ability to use a minimum amount of screen real estate is especially important in mobile applications. Controls can drop down or pop up a list of information when the user taps a smaller component. Controls that we know as combo boxes or drop-downs in desktop applications look different on mobile devices. The good news is that you don't need to do any special coding to display a fancy-looking drop-down on the iPhone shown in Figure 11-26. Just use the HTML tag `<select>`, and the mobile browser will render it with a native look on the user's device.

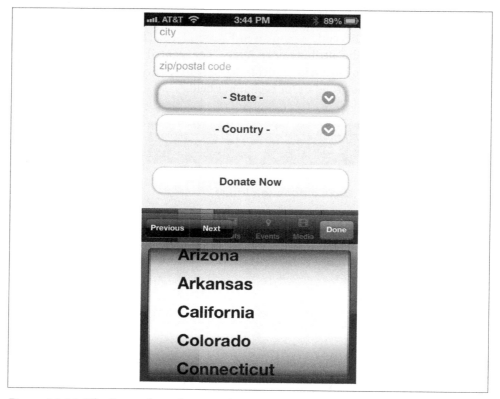

Figure 11-26. The States drop-down in the Donate form

The bad news is that sometimes you don't want the default behavior offered by the `<select>` element. For example, you might want to create a menu that shows a list of items. First, we'll show you how to do that by using a pop-up that contains a list view. Example 11-13 is taken from the jQuery Mobile documentation, which suggests implementing a listview inside a pop-up (*http://bit.ly/1iaKxK1*).

Example 11-13. Using <ul> inside the pop-up

```
<a href="#popupMenu" data-rel="popup" data-role="button"
   data-transition="pop">Select Donation Amount</a>

 <div data-role="popup" id="popupMenu" >
   <ul data-role="listview" data-inset="true" style="min-width:210px;">
      <li data-role="divider">Choose the amount</li>
```

```
        <li><a href="#">$10</a></li>
        <li><a href="#">$20</a></li>
        <li><a href="#">$50</a></li>
        <li><a href="#">$100</a></li>
    </ul>
</div>
```

Initially, the screen will look like Figure 11-27, which shows an anchor styled as a button.

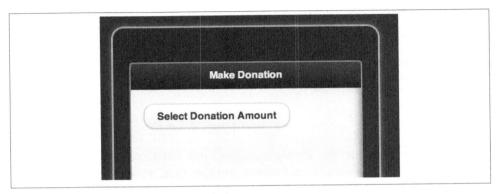

Figure 11-27. The Select Donation Amount button before being tapped

After the user taps Select Donation Amount, the menu pops up, as shown in Figure 11-28.

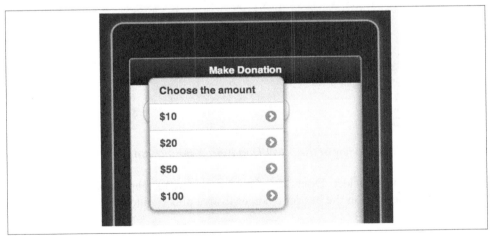

Figure 11-28. After tapping Select Donation Amount

Example 11-14 demonstrates another way of creating drop-downs by using collapsibles (*http://bit.ly/1oHhrEL*). If the data role of a container is set to be collapsible, the content of the container won't be initially shown. It will be collapsed, showing only its header with a default icon (the plus sign) until the user taps it.

Example 11-14. Using a collapsible container

```
<div data-role="collapsible" data-theme="b"
                         data-content-theme="c">
   <h2>Select Donation Amount</h2>

   <ul data-role="listview">
       <li><a href="#">$10</a></li>
       <li><a href="#">$20</a></li>
       <li><a href="#">$50</a></li>
       <li><a href="#">$100</a></li>

   </ul>
</div>
```

If you test this code in the Ripple emulator, the initial screen will look like Figure 11-29; it's a <div> with the data-role=collapsible. This code sample also illustrates using different themes for the collapsed and expanded versions of this <div>. If you are reading the electronic version of this book on a color display, the collapsed version will have the blue background: data-theme="b".

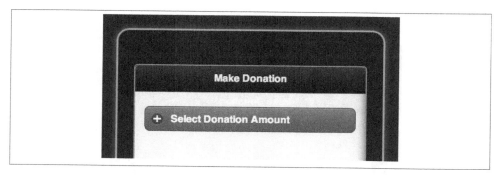

Figure 11-29. Collapsed view of the Select Donation Amount container

After the user taps Select Donation Amount, a menu pops up, as shown in Figure 11-30. The icon on the header changes from a plus sign to a minus sign.

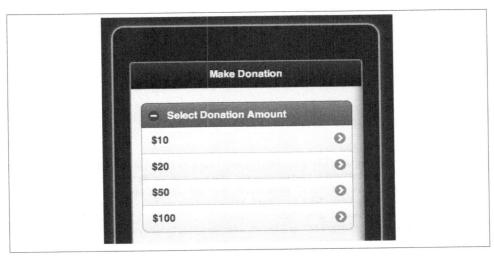

Figure 11-30. Expanded view of the Select Donation Amount container

List views

In the previous section, you saw how easy it is to create a nice-looking list (Figure 11-30) by using `data-role="listview"`. jQuery Mobile offers many ways of arranging items in lists, and we encourage you to pay a visit to the Listviews (*http://bit.ly/1z24Pu3*) section of the online documentation.

Each list item can contain any HTML element. The media page of the Save The Child application uses `listview` to arrange videos in the list. Example 11-15 is a code fragment from *media.html*.

Example 11-15. The listview element with videos

```
<div data-role="header"> ...   </div>

iv data-role="content" >
<ul data-role="listview" data-theme="a" data-inset="true" id="video-list">
  <li data-icon="chevron-right">
    <a href="#popupHtmlVideo" data-rel="popup" id="video-1">
    <img src="../assets/img/thumb-01.jpg" class="ui-liicon"
    alt=""/> <h3>The title of a video-clip</h3>
    <p>
      Video description goes here. Lorem ipsum dolor sit amet,
      consectetuer adipiscing elit.
    </p> </a>
  </li>
  <li data-icon="chevron-right">
    <a href="#ytVideo" data-rel="popup"> <img src="../assets/img/thumb-02.jpg"
                        class="ui-liicon"
    alt=""/> <h3>The title of a video-clip</h3>
    <p>
```

```
         Video description goes here. Lorem ipsum dolor sit amet, consectetuer
         adipiscing elit.
      </p> </a>
   </li>
</ul>

</div>

<div data-role="footer"> ...  </div>

<!-- html5 video in a popup -->
    <div data-role="popup" id="popupHtmlVideo" data-transition="slidedown"
    data-theme="a" data-position-to="window" data-corners="false">
     <a href="#" data-rel="back" data-role="button" data-theme="a"
             data-icon="delete" data-iconpos="notext"
             class="ui-btn-right">Close</a>
      <video controls="controls" poster="../assets/media/intro.jpg"
             preload="metadata">
       <source src="../assets/media/intro.mp4" type="video/mp4">
       <source src="../assets/media/intro.webm" type="video/webm">
       <p>Sorry, your browser doesn't support the video element</p>
      </video>
    </div>

<!-- YouTube video in a popup -->
    <div data-role="popup" id="ytVideo" data-transition="slidedown"
    data-theme="a" data-position-to="window" data-corners="false">
     <a href="#" data-rel="back" data-role="button" data-theme="a"
      data-icon="delete" data-iconpos="notext" class="ui-btn-right">Close</a>
      <iframe id="ytplayer"
      src="http://www.youtube.com/embed/VGZcer0hCuo?wmode=transparent&hd=
        1&vq=hd720" frameborder="0" width="480" height="270" allowfullscreen>
      </iframe>
    </div>
  </div>
```

This code uses an unordered HTML list, <ul>. Each list item <li> contains three HTML
elements: <a>, <p>, and <span>. The anchor contains a link to the corresponding video
to show in a pop-up. The content of each pop-up is located in <div data-
role="popup">. The data-rel="popup" in the anchor means that the resource from
href has to be opened as a pop-up when the user taps this link.

The <div id="popupHtmlVideo"> illustrates how to include a video by using the
HTML5 <video> tag, and <div id="ytVideo"> shows how to embed a YouTube video.
Both of these <div> elements are placed below the footer, and jQuery Mobile won't show
them until the user taps the links.

Note that the jQuery Mobile `listview` (shown in Figure 11-31) is styled in a way that each list item looks like a large rectangle, and the user can tap a list item with a finger without being afraid of touching neighboring controls. There is no such problem with desktop applications because the mouse pointer is much more precise than a finger or even a stylus.

Figure 11-31. Using listview in media.html

 The `<video>` tag has the attribute `autoplay`. But because some mobile users are charged by their phone companies based on their data usage, the application should not automatically start playing video until the user explicitly taps the Play button. There is no such restriction in desktop browsers.

jQuery Mobile Events

jQuery Mobile events can be grouped by their use. Some events deal with the page life cycle. For a detailed description of events, read the Events section (*http://bit.ly/1pEgiOO*) in the online documentation. We'll just briefly mention some of the events available in jQuery Mobile.

You should be using `$(document).on("pageinit")` and not `$(document).ready()`. The former is triggered even for pages loaded as result of Ajax calls, whereas the latter is not. Prior to `pageinit`, two more events are dispatched: `pagebeforecreate` and `pagecreate`. After these two, widget enhancement takes place.

The `pagebeforeshow` and `pageshow` events occur right before or after the to-page is displayed. Accordingly, `pagebeforehide` and `pagehide` are dispatched on the from-page. The `pagechange` event is dispatched when the page is being changed as the result of programmatic invocation of the `changePage()` method.

If you are loading an external page (for example, a user clicks the link `<a href="externalpage.html">Load External</a>`), expect two events: `pagebeforeload` and `pageload` (or `pageloadfailed`).

Touch events are another group of events that are dispatched when the user touches the screen. Depending on how the user touches the screen, your application may receive `tap`, `taphold`, `swipe`, `swipeleft`, and `swiperight` events. The tap event handlers may or may not work reliably on iOS devices.

The `touchend` event may be more reliable. Create a combined event handler for `click` and `touchend` events and your code will work on both desktop and mobile devices. For example:

```
$('#radio-container .ui-radio').on('touchend click', function() {
  // the event handler code goes here
}
```

Orientation events are important if your code needs to intercept the moments when a mobile device changes orientation. This is when jQuery Mobile fires the `orientation change` event. The event object will have the property `orientation`, which will have a value of either `portrait` or `landscape`.

There is one event that you can use to set configuration options for jQuery Mobile itself. The name of this event is `mobileinit`, and you should call the script to apply overrides after the jQuery Core but before jQuery Mobile scripts are loaded. You can find more details in the online documentation (*http://bit.ly/1nWDErS*).

Adding JavaScript

So far we have been able to get by with HTML and CSS only; the jQuery Mobile library is doing its magic, which is helpful for the most part. But we still need a place for JavaScript. The Save The Child application has several hundred lines of JavaScript code, and we need to find it a new home. You'll find pretty much the same code that we used in previous chapters to deal with logins, donations, maps, and stats. It's located in the *jquerymobile* sample project in the file *js/app-main.js*.

You might also need to write some scripts specific to jQuery Mobile workflows, because in some cases, you might want to override certain behaviors of the library. In these cases, you need to write JavaScript functions to serve as event handlers. For example, jQuery Mobile restricts you from putting more than five buttons on the navbar. But we need six. As you can see in Example 11-16, the footer contains the attribute data-role="navbar", which has the unordered list ul with six <li> items (not shown in the code for brevity).

Example 11-16. The footer with navbar

```
<div data-role="footer" data-position="fixed" data-tap-toggle="false"
                       data-id="persistent-footer">
  <div data-role="navbar" class="ssc-navbar">
    <ul>
      ...
    </ul>
  </div>
</div><
```

Run the application with six buttons in navbar, and get ready for a surprise. You'll see a footer with a two-column and three-row grid, as shown in Figure 11-32, which is a screenshot of a Ripple emulator with an open Chrome Developer Tools panel while inspecting the navbar element in the footer.

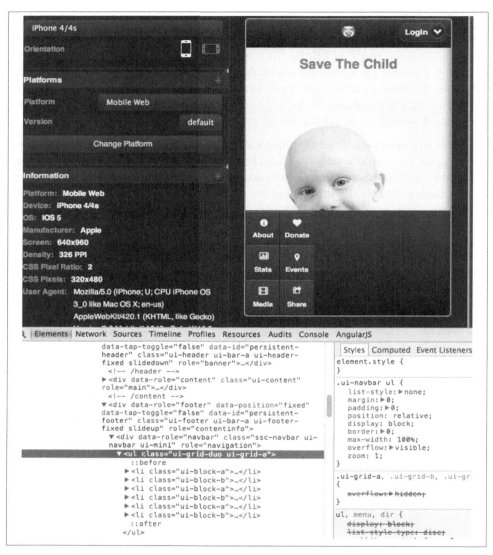

Figure 11-32. Using listview in media.html

Take a look at the styling of the `navbar`. Our original `<ul>` HTML element didn't include the class `ui-grid-a`. jQuery Mobile couldn't find the predefined layout for a six-button navigational bar and "decided" to deploy `ui-grid-a`, which is a two-column grid (see "Grid layouts" on page 445).

The CSS file *app-styles.css* (see "Project Structure and Navigation" on page 439) has a provision for giving 16.6 percent of the width for each of six buttons, but we need to programmatically remove `ui-grid-a`, which jQuery Mobile injected into our code. We'll do it in JavaScript in the handler for the `pagebeforeshow` event. The next code snippet from *app-main.js* finds the `ul` element that includes `ssc-navbar` as one of the styles and removes the class `ui-grid-a` from this unordered list:

```
$(document).on('pagebeforeshow', function() {
    $(".ssc-navbar > ul").removeClass("ui-grid-a");
```

Now the 16.6 percent of the width will take effect and properly position all six buttons in a row. This is an example of overriding unwanted behavior by using JavaScript. The rest of the code contains familiar functionality from previous sections. We won't repeat it here, but we will show you some of the code sections that are worth commenting (see Example 11-17).

Example 11-17. Handling navigation in app-main.js

```
$(document).on('pagebeforeshow', function() {

  $(".ssc-navbar > ul").removeClass("ui-grid-a");

  if ( typeof (Storage) != "undefined") {
    var loginVal = localStorage.sscLogin;              ❶

    if (loginVal == "logged") {
      $('.login-btn').css('display', 'none');
      $('.logout-btn').css('display', 'block');
    } else {
      $('.login-btn').css('display', 'block');
    }
  } else {
    console.log('No web storage support...');
  }
});

  function logIn(event) {
    event.preventDefault();

    var userNameValue = $('#username').val();
    var userNameValueLength = userNameValue.length;
    var userPasswordValue = $('#password').val();
    var userPasswordLength = userPasswordValue.length;

    //check credential
    if (userNameValueLength == 0 || userPasswordLength == 0) {
      if (userNameValueLength == 0) {
        $('#error-message').text('Username is empty');
      }
      if (userPasswordLength == 0) {
        $('#error-message').text('Password is empty');
      }
      if (userNameValueLength == 0 && userPasswordLength == 0) {
```

```
            $('#error-message').text('Username and Password are empty');
        }
        $('#login-submit').parent().removeClass('ui-btn-active');
        $('[type="submit"]').button('refresh');
    } else if (userNameValue != 'admin' || userPasswordValue != '1234') {
        $('#error-message').text('Username or password is invalid');
    } else if (userNameValue == 'admin' && userPasswordValue == '1234') {
        $('.login-btn').css('display', 'none');
        $('.logout-btn').css('display', 'block');

        localStorage.sscLogin = "logged";          ❷
        history.back();
    }

}

$('#login-submit').on('click', logIn);

...

$(document).on('pageshow', "#Donate", function() {   ❸
    ...
}

$(document).on("pageshow", "#Stats", function() {   ❹
    ...
}

$(document).on("pageshow", "#Events", function() {   ❺

}
```

❶ The Login button is located on the header of each page, and it turns into the Logout button when the user logs in. When the user moves from page to page, the old pages are removed from the DOM. To make sure that the login status is properly set, we check that the variable sscLogin in the local storage has the value logged (see ❷).

❷ When the user logs in, the program saves the word logged in local storage and closes the Login pop-up by calling history.back().

❸ The Donate form code is located in this function. No Ajax calls are made in this version of the Save The Child application.

❹ The SVG charts are created in this function.

❺ The geolocation code that uses the Google Maps API goes here.

While experimenting with the Save The Child application, we created one more version that uses the multipage template, just to get a feeling of how smooth transitioning between pages will be if the entire code base is loaded upfront. Of course, the wait cursor that would otherwise appear between the pages is gone, but the code itself becomes less manageable.

 The Ripple emulator described earlier in this chapter makes it possible for you to test the look and feel of the jQuery Mobile version of the Save The Child application on various iOS and Android devices. But again, nothing beats testing on real devices.

Summary

In this chapter, you became familiar with a simple-to-use mobile framework. We've been using its version 1.3.1, which is pretty stable, but it's not a mature library just yet. You can still run into situations when a feature advertised in the product documentation doesn't work (for example, page prefetching breaks images (*http://bit.ly/1soS4ZX*)). So be prepared to study the code of this library and to fix the critical features on your own. But there is a group of people who are actively working on bug fixing and improving jQuery Mobile, and using it in production is pretty safe.

By now you should have a pretty good understanding of how to begin creating a user interface with jQuery Mobile and where to find more information. Find some time to read the entire online documentation (*http://api.jquerymobile.com*) for jQuery Mobile. The learning curve is not steep, but there is a lot to read if you want to become productive with jQuery Mobile.

## CHAPTER 12

Sencha Touch

The Sencha Touch framework is a little brother of Ext JS. They both have the same creator, Sencha (*http://www.sencha.com*), and they both are built on the same set of core classes. But Sencha Touch is created for developing mobile web applications, whereas Ext JS is for desktop web applications.

Enterprise IT managers need to be aware of another important difference: Ext JS offers free licenses only for open source projects, but Sencha Touch licenses (*http://bit.ly/1uDs3lm*) are free unless you decide to purchase this framework bundled with developer tools.

This chapter is structured similarly to Chapter 11, which describes jQuery Mobile—minimum theory followed by the code. A fundamental difference, though, is that whereas Chapter 11 has almost no JavaScript, this chapter has almost no HTML.

We'll try to minimize repeating the information you can find in Sencha Touch Learning Center (*http://bit.ly/SUH5qs*) and extensive product documentation, which has multiple well-written Guides (*http://bit.ly/1oHj7Ov*) on various topics. This chapter begins with a brief overview of the features of Sencha Touch followed by a code review of yet another version of the Save The Child application. In this chapter, we are going to use Sencha Touch 2.3.1, which is the latest version at the time of this writing. It supports iOS, Android, BlackBerry, and Windows Phone.

If you haven't read Chapter 4 on Ext JS, please do it now. Both of these frameworks are built on the same foundation, and we assume that you are familiar with such concepts as MVC architecture and xtype, SASS, and other terms that are explained in that chapter. For the most part, Ext JS and Sencha Touch non-UI classes are compatible, but there are some differences that might prevent you from attaining 100 percent code reuse between these frameworks (for example, see the section "Stores and Models" on page 511). Future releases of Sencha should come up with some standard solutions to remove the differences in class systems of both frameworks.

Introducing Sencha Touch

Let's begin by downloading Sencha Touch (*http://bit.ly/1mMXHwG*). If you want to get a free commercial license, just specify your email address; you'll receive the download link in the email. The Sencha Touch framework comes as a ZIP file, which you can unzip in any directory. Later, you'll copy the framework's code either into your project directory or in the document root of your web server.

 A commercial license of Sencha Touch doesn't include charts (you need to get either Sencha Complete or Sencha Touch Bundle for chart support). Therefore, we'll use the General Public License (GPL) of Sencha Touch for the open source Save The Child project, and our users will see the little watermark, "Powered by Sencha Touch GPLv3," as shown in Figure 12-1.

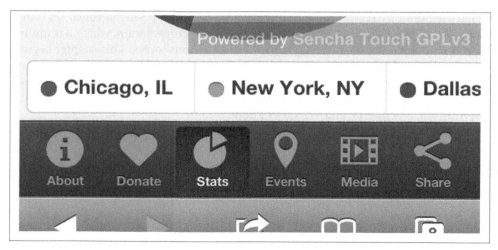

Figure 12-1. The GPL watermark

After downloading Sencha Touch, unzip it into the directory */Library/touch-2.3.1*. The code-generation process copies this framework into our application directory.

Performing Code Generation and Distribution

If you haven't downloaded and installed the Sencha CMD tool, do it now as described in "Generating Applications with the Sencha CMD Tool" on page 129. This time we'll use Sencha CMD to generate a mobile version of Hello World. After opening a terminal or command window, enter the following command, specifying the absolute path to your Ext JS SDK directory and to the output folder, where the generated project should reside:

sencha -sdk /Library/touch-2.3.1 generate app HelloWorld /Users/yfain11/hellotouch

After the code generation is complete, you'll see the folder *hello* with the structure shown in Figure 12-2. It follows the Model-View-Controller (MVC) pattern discussed in Chapter 4.

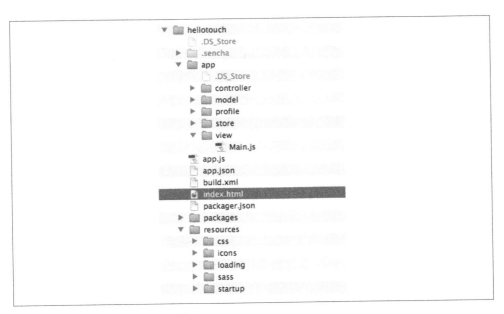

Figure 12-2. A CMD-generated project

To test your newly generated application, make sure that the directory *hellotouch* is deployed on a web server (simply opening *index.html* in a web browser won't work). You can either install any web server or just follow the instructions in "Developing Save The Child with Ext JS" on page 150 in Chapter 4. In the same chapter, you can find the command to start the Jetty web server embedded in the Sencha CMD tool.

Here, we are going to use the internal web server that comes with the WebStorm IDE. It runs on port 63342, and if your project's name is *helloworld*, the URL to test it is *http://localhost:63342/helloworld*.

To debug your code inside WebStorm, choose Run→Edit Configurations, click the plus sign in the upper-left corner, and then in the JavaScript Debug→Remote panel, enter the URL *http://localhost:63342*, followed by the name of your project (for example, *ssctouch*) and name your new debug configuration. After that, you'll be able to debug your code in your Chrome web browser (it will ask you to install the JetBrains IDE Support extension on the first run).

Mac OS X users can install the small application Anvil (*http://anvilformac.com*), which can easily serve static content of any directory as a web server with a URL that ends with *.dev*.

Figure 12-3 shows how the generated Hello World application will look in a Chrome browser. It'll consist of two pages controlled by the buttons in the footer toolbar.

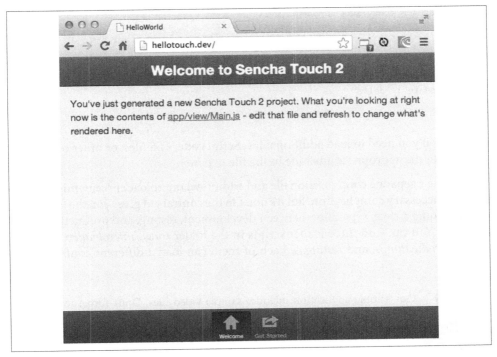

Figure 12-3. Running CMD-generated Hello World

Microloader and configurations

The main application entry is the JavaScript file *app.js*. But if in Ext JS, this file was directly referenced in *index.html*, Sencha Touch applications generated by the CMD tool use a separate microloader script, which starts with loading the file *app.json* that contains the names of the resources needed for your application, including *app.js*. The only script included in the generated *index.html* is this one:

```
<script id="microloader" type="text/javascript"
        src="touch/microloader/development.js"></script>
```

This script uses one of the scripts located in the *microloader* folder, which gets the object names to be loaded from the configuration file *app.json*. This file contains a JSON object with various attributes such as js, css, resources, and others. So if your application needs to load the scripts *sencha-touch.js* and *app.js*, they should be located in the js array. Example 12-1 illustrates what the js attribute of *app.json* contains after the initial code generation by Sencha CMD.

Example 12-1. The js attribute of app.json

```
"js": [
    {
```

```
        "path": "touch/sencha-touch.js",
        "x-bootstrap": true
    },
    {
        "path": "app.js",
        "bundle": true,
        "update": "delta"
    }
]
```

Eventually, if you need to load additional JavaScript code, CSS files, or other resources, add them to the appropriate attribute in the file *app.json*.

Introducing a separate configuration file and additional microloader script might seem like an unnecessary complication, but it's not. On the contrary, it gives you the flexibility of maintaining a clean separation between development, testing, and production environments. You can find three loader scripts in the folder *touch/microloader*: *development.js*, *production.js*, and *testing.js*. Each of them can load a different configuration file.

 Our sample application includes sample video files. Don't forget to include the *resources/media* folder in the `resources` section of *app.json*.

If you open the source code of the production loader, you'll see that it uses an application cache to save files locally on the device (see "Application Cache API" on page 567 for a refresher), so the user can start the application even without having an Internet connection.

The production microloader of Sencha Touch offers a smarter solution for minimizing unnecessary loading of cached JavaScript and CSS files than the HTML5 application cache. The standard HTML5 mechanism doesn't know which resources have changed and reloads all cacheable files. CMD-generated production builds for Sencha Touch keep track of changes and create deltas, so the mobile device will download only those resources that have been actually changed. To create a production build, open a terminal or a command window, change to your application directory, and run the following command:

```
sencha app build production
```

See "Deploying Your Application" (*http://bit.ly/1ocA8Pn*) for more details on Sencha CMD builds. When we start building our Save The Child application, you'll see how to prompt the user that the application code has been updated. Refer to the online documentation (*http://bit.ly/1gp2l2H*) on using Sencha CMD with Sencha Touch for details.

Code Distribution and Modularization

The ability of Sencha Touch to monitor modified pieces of code helps with deployment; just change *SomeFile.js* on the server and it will be automatically downloaded and saved on the user's mobile device. This can have an effect on the application modularization decisions you make.

Reducing the startup latency and implementing lazy loading of certain parts of the application are the main reasons for modularizing web applications. The other reason for modularization is an ability to redeploy certain portions of the code versus the entire application if the code modifications are limited in scope.

So, should we load the entire code base from local storage (it's a lot faster than getting the code from remote servers) or still use loaders to bring up the portion of the code (a.k.a. modules) on an as-needed basis? There is no standard answer to this question— every application is different.

If your application is not too large and the mobile device has enough memory, loading the entire code of the application from local storage can lower the need for modularization. For larger applications, consider the Workspaces (*http://bit.ly/1k181ef*) feature of Sencha CMD, with which you can create some common code to be shared by several scripts.

The code of Hello World

Similar to Ext JS, the starting point of the Hello World application is the *app.js* script, which is shown in Example 12-2.

Example 12-2. The app.js file of the Sencha Touch version of Save The Child

```
Ext.Loader.setPath({
    'Ext': 'touch/src',          ❶
    'HelloWorld': 'app'
});

Ext.application({
    name: 'HelloWorld',

    requires: [
        'Ext.MessageBox'
    ],

    views: [
        'Main'
    ],

    icon: {
        '57': 'resources/icons/Icon.png',
```

```
            '72': 'resources/icons/Icon~ipad.png',
            '114': 'resources/icons/Icon@2x.png',
            '144': 'resources/icons/Icon~ipad@2x.png'
    },

    isIconPrecomposed: true,

    startupImage: {
            '320x460': 'resources/startup/320x460.jpg',
            '640x920': 'resources/startup/640x920.png',
            '768x1004': 'resources/startup/768x1004.png',
            '748x1024': 'resources/startup/748x1024.png',
            '1536x2008': 'resources/startup/1536x2008.png',
            '1496x2048': 'resources/startup/1496x2048.png'
    },

    launch: function() {
        // Destroy the #appLoadingIndicator element
        Ext.fly('appLoadingIndicator').destroy();

        // Initialize the main view
        Ext.Viewport.add(Ext.create('HelloWorld.view.Main'));
    },

    onUpdated: function() {                     ❷
        Ext.Msg.confirm(
            "Application Update",
            "This application has just successfully
             been updated to the latest version. Reload now?",
            function(buttonId) {
                if (buttonId === 'yes') {
                    window.location.reload();
                }
            }
        );
    }
});
```

❶   This code instructs the loader that any class that starts with *Ext* can be found in
     the directory *touch/src* or its subdirectories. The classes with names that begin
     with *HelloWorld* are under the *app* directory.

❷   This is an interception of the event that's triggered if the code on the server is
     updated. The user is warned that the new version of the application has been
     downloaded. You can see more on this in the comments to *app.js* in the section
     "Using Sencha Touch for Save The Child" on page 479.

The code of the generated main view of this application (*Main.js*) is shown next. It
extends the class Ext.tab.Panel so that each page of the application is one tab in this
panel. Figure 12-4 is a snapshot of a collapsed version of *Main.js* taken from the Web-

Storm IDE (*http://bit.ly/1lJdQmx*) from JetBrains, which is our IDE of choice in this chapter.

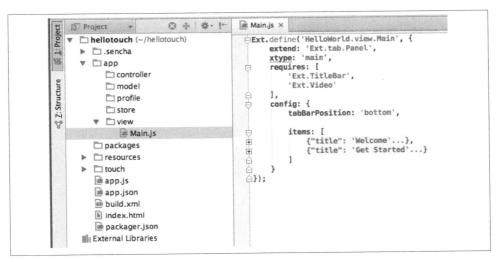

Figure 12-4. Collapsed version of Main.js from Hello World

As you can see from this figure, the `items[]` array includes two objects, Welcome and Get Started, and each of them represents a tab (screen) on the panel. Example 12-3 shows the code of the Welcome and Get Started screens.

Example 12-3. Code of the Welcome and Get Started screens

```
Ext.define('HelloWorld.view.Main', {
  extend: 'Ext.tab.Panel',
  xtype: 'main',
  requires: [
      'Ext.TitleBar',
      'Ext.Video'
  ],
  config: {
    tabBarPosition: 'bottom',            ❶

    items: [
        {                                ❷
            title: 'Welcome',
            iconCls: 'home',

            styleHtmlContent: true,
            scrollable: true,

            items: {
                docked: 'top',
                xtype: 'titlebar',
```

```
                    title: 'Welcome to Sencha Touch 2'
                },

                html: [
                    "You've just generated a new Sencha Touch 2 project."
                    "What you're looking at right now is the ",
                    "contents of <a target='_blank' href=\"app/view/Main.js\">"
                    "app/view/Main.js</a> - edit that file ",
                    "and refresh to change what's rendered here."
                ].join("")
            },
            {                               ❸
                title: 'Get Started',
                iconCls: 'action',

                items: [
                    {
                        docked: 'top',
                        xtype: 'titlebar',
                        title: 'Getting Started'
                    },
                    {
                        xtype: 'video',
                        url: 'http://av.vimeo.com/64284/137/87347327.mp4?token=
                        1330978144_f9b698fea38cd408d52a2
                        393240c896c',
                        posterUrl:
                            'http://b.vimeocdn.com/ts/261/062/261062119_640.jpg'
                    }
                ]
            }
        ]
    }
});
```

❶   The tab bar has to be located at the bottom of the screen.

❷   The first tab is a Welcome screen.

❸   The second tab is the Getting Started screen. It has xtype: video, which means
     it's ready for playing video located at the specified url.

This application has no controllers, models, or stores. But it does include the default
theme from the SASS stylesheet *resources/sass/app.scss*, which was compiled by the
Sencha CMD generation process into the file *resources/css/app.css*.

Constructing the UI

Sencha Touch has UI components specifically designed for mobile devices. These components include lists, forms, toolbars, buttons, charts, audio, video, carousels, and more.
The quickest way to become familiar with them is by browsing the Kitchen Sink (*http://*

---

bit.ly/1pPBw87) website, where you can find examples of how UI components look and see the source code.

Containers

In general, the process of implementing a mobile application with Sencha Touch consists of selecting appropriate containers and arranging navigation among them. Each screen that a user sees is a container. Often, it will include a toolbar *docked* at the top or bottom of the container.

Containers can be nested; they are needed for better grouping of UI components on the screen. The lightest container is `Ext.Container`. It inherits all the functionality from its ancestor `Ext.Component`, plus it can contain other components. When you review the code of the Save The Child application, note that the main view `SSC.view.Main` from *Main.js* extends `Ext.Container`. The hierarchy of Sencha Touch containers is shown in Figure 12-5.

```
ALTERNATE NAMES
  Ext.lib.Container

HIERARCHY
  Ext.Base
   Ext.Evented
     Ext.AbstractComponent
       Ext.Component
         Ext.Container

INHERITED MIXINS
  Ext.mixin.Observable
  Ext.mixin.Traversable

REQUIRES
  Ext.ItemCollection
  Ext.Mask
  Ext.behavior.Scrollable
  Ext.layout.*

SUBCLASSES
  Ext.Map
  Ext.Panel
  Ext.SegmentedButton
  Ext.TitleBar
  Ext.Toolbar
  Ext.carousel.Carousel
  Ext.dataview.DataView
  Ext.dataview.NestedList
  Ext.dataview.component.Container
  Ext.dataview.component.DataItem
  Ext.draw.Component
  Ext.form.FieldSet
  Ext.navigation.View
  Ext.slider.Slider
  Ext.tab.Panel
  Ext.viewport.Default
```

Figure 12-5. Sencha Touch containers hierarchy

The FieldSet is also a pretty light container; it simply adds a title to a group of fields that belong together. You'll see several code samples in this chapter with xtype: 'field set' (for example, Login or Donate screens).

If your containers display forms with such inputs as text field, text area, password, and numbers, the virtual keyboard will automatically show up, occupying half of the user's screen. On some platforms, virtual keyboards adapt to the type of input field—for example, if the field has `xtype: 'emailfield'`, the keyboard will be modified for easier input of emails. Figure 12-6 is a snapshot taken from the Donate screen of the Save The Child application as the user taps inside the Email field. Note the key with the "at" sign (@) on the main keyboard, which wouldn't be shown for nonemail inputs.

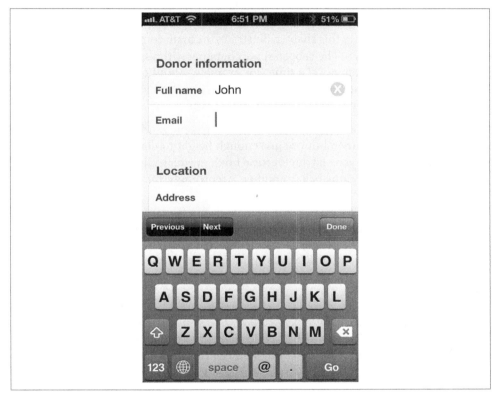

Figure 12-6. The iPhone virtual keyboard for entering emails

If the field is for entering a URL (`xtype: 'urlfield'`), expect to see a virtual keyboard with a button labeled *.com*. If the input field has `xtype: 'numberfield'`, the user might see a numeric keyboard when the focus is in this field.

 If you need to detect the environment on the user's mobile device, use `Ext.os.` to detect the operating system, `Ext.browser` to detect the browser, and `Ext.feature` to detect supported features.

Layouts

Besides grouping components, containers allow you to assign a Layout to control its children arrangements. In desktop applications, physical screens are larger, and often you can place multiple containers on the same screen at the same time. In the mobile world, you don't have that luxury, and typically you'll be showing just one container at a time. Not all layouts (*http://bit.ly/UcgLt8*) are practical to use on smaller screens, which is why not all Ext JS layouts are supported in Sencha Touch.

Figure 12-10, shown later in this chapter, illustrates the main container that shows either the tabpanel or loginform. The tabpanel is a container with a special layout that shows only one of its child containers at a time (for example, About or Donate). You can see all these components in action at *savesickchild.org*—just run the Sencha Touch version of our Save The Child application and view the sources.

By default, a container's layout is auto, which instructs the rendering engine to use the entire width of the container, but use just enough height to display the children. This behavior is similar to the vbox layout (vertical box), in which all components are added to the container vertically, one below another. Accordingly, the hbox arranges all components horizontally, one next to the other.

 If you want to control how much vertical or horizontal screen space is given to each component, use the flex property as described in "Setting proportional layouts by using the flex property" on page 149.

The fit (*http://docs.sencha.com/touch/2.3.0/#!/guide/layouts-section-fit-layout*) layout fills the entire container's space with its child element. If you have more than one child element in the container, the first one will fill the entire space and the other one will be ignored.

The card (*http://bit.ly/1mdxyIg*) layout can accommodate multiple children while displaying only one at a time. The container's method setActiveItem() allows you to programmatically select the "card" to be on top of the deck. With a card layout, all containers are preloaded to the device, but if you want to create new containers at runtime, you can use the method setActiveItem(), passing a config object that describes the new container.

You can find examples of card and fit layouts in the code of *Main.js* of the Save The Child application. Figure 12-11 shows the card layout, but if you expand the tabpanel container, each tab has the fit layout.

The classes TabPanel and Carousel represent two implementations of containers that use the card layout.

Events

Events can be initiated either by the browser or by the user. "Working with Events" on page 147 covers general rules of dealing with events in the Ext JS framework. Many system events are dispatched during UI component rendering. The online documentation (*http://bit.ly/1vTI2yd*) lists every event that can be dispatched on Sencha classes. Look for the Events section on the top toolbar in the online documentation. Figure 12-7 is a snapshot from online documentation for the class `Ext.Container`, which has 32 events.

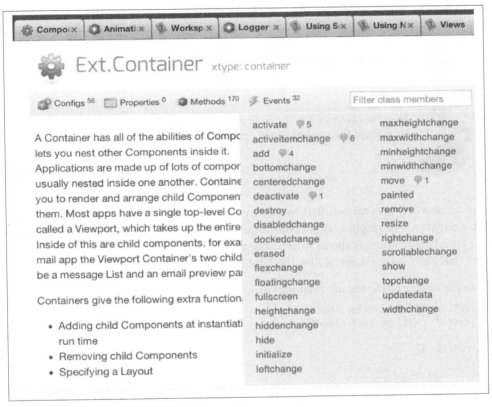

Figure 12-7. Events in the Sencha online documentation

Sencha Touch knows how to handle various mobile-specific events. Check out the documentation for the class `Ext.dom.Element` (*http://bit.ly/UciVsM*): you'll find such events as `touchstart`, `touchend`, `tap`, `doubletap`, `swipe`, `pinch`, `longpress`, `rotate`, and others.

You can add event listeners by using techniques. One of them is defining the `listen ers` (*http://bit.ly/1ohO6gS*) `config` property during object instantiation. This property is declared in the `Ext.Container` object and makes it possible for you to define more than one listener at a time. You should use it while calling the `Ext.create()` method:

```
Ext.create('Ext.button.Button', {
    listeners: {
        tap: function() { // handle event here }
    }
}
```

If you need to handle an event only once, you can use the option `single: true`, which will automatically remove the listener after the first handling of the event. For example:

```
listeners: {
  tap: function() { // handle event here },
  single: true
}
```

 Read the comments to the code of `SSC.view.CampaignsMap` in Chapter 4 about the right place for declaring listeners.

You can also define event handlers by using yet another `config` property, `control` from `Ext.Container`. Example 12-4 is a code fragment from the Login controller of the Save The Child application. It shows how to assign the `tap` event handler functions `showLo ginView()` and `cancelLogin()` for the Login and Cancel buttons.

Example 12-4. Registering tap event handlers

```
Ext.define('SSC.controller.Login', {
    extend: 'Ext.app.Controller',

    config: {

        control: {
            loginButton: {
                tap: 'showLoginView'
            },
            cancelButton: {
                tap: 'cancelLogin'
            }
        }
    },
    showLoginView: function () {
      // code of this function is removed for brevity
    },
```

```
    cancelLogin: function () {
      // code of this function is removed for brevity
    }
});
```

With the proliferation of touch screens, Sencha has introduced the tap gesture, which is semantically equivalent to the click event.

Read more about the role of controllers in event handling in the section "Controller" on page 490. Online documentation includes the Event Guide (*http://bit.ly/1nYwaWT*), which describes the process of handling events in detail.

If you want to fire custom events, use the method fireEvent(), providing the name of your event. The procedure for defining the listeners for custom events remains the same.

Bring Your Own Device (BYOD) is becoming more and more popular in enterprises. Sencha offers a product called Sencha Space, which is a secure and managed environment for deploying enterprise HTML5 applications that can be run on a variety of devices that employees bring to the workplace. Sencha Space promises a clear separation between work-related applications and personal data. It uses a secure database and secure file API and facilitates app-to-app communication. For more details, visit the Sencha Space web page (*http://bit.ly/1qJRAJX*).

Using Sencha Touch for Save The Child

The Sencha Touch version of the Save The Child application is based on the mockup presented in "Prototyping the Mobile Version" on page 425 with some minor changes. This time, the home page of the application will be a slightly different version of the About page shown in Figure 12-8.

Building the Application

The materials presented in this chapter were tested with the Sencha Touch 2.3.1 framework, which was current at the time of this writing, and you can use the source code of the Save The Child application that comes with the book. It's packaged with Sencha

2.3.1. We've also deployed this application at link:http://savesickchild.org:8080/ssc-touch-prod.

If you need to use a newer version of Sencha Touch, just download and unzip it to the directory of your choice (in our case, we use */Library/touch-2.3.1*). Download the book code and remove the content of the *touch* directory from *Lesson12/ssc-mobile*. After that, cd to this directory and copy a newer version of Sencha Touch there. For example, on Mac OS we did it as follows:

```
cd ssc-mobile
cp -r /Library/touch-2.3.1/ touch
```

Then, run the Sencha CMD (version 4 or above) command to make a production build of the application and start the embedded web server:

```
sencha app build
sencha web start
```

Finally, open this application at *http://localhost:1841* in one of the emulators or just on your desktop browser. You'll see the starting page that looks like Figure 12-8.

Figure 12-8. The Starting/About page

We'll review the code of this application next.

The Application Object

The code of the *app.js* in the Save The Child project is shown in Example 12-5 (we removed the default startup images and icons for brevity). For the most part, it has the same structure as the Ext JS applications.

Example 12-5. The app.js file of Save The Child

```
Ext.application({
    name: 'SSC',

    requires: [
        'Ext.MessageBox'
    ],

    views: [
        'About',
        'CampaignsMap',
        'DonateForm',
        'DonorsChart',
        'LoginForm',
        'LoginToolbar',
        'Main',
        'Media',
        'Share',
        'ShareTile'
    ],

    stores: [
        'Campaigns',
        'Countries',
        'Donors',
        'States',
        'Videos'
    ],

    controllers: [
        'Login'
    ],

    launch: function() {
        // Destroy the #appLoadingIndicator element
        Ext.fly('appLoadingIndicator').destroy();

        // Initialize the main view
        Ext.Viewport.add(Ext.create('SSC.view.Main'));
    },

    onUpdated: function() {
        Ext.Msg.confirm(
```

```
            "Application Update",
            "This application has just successfully been updated to the latest "
            "version. Reload now?",
            function(buttonId) {
                if (buttonId === 'yes') {
                    window.location.reload();
                }
            }
        );
    }
});
```

 Compare this application object with that of Ext JS, shown in "Best Practice: MVC" on page 139. They are similar.

The application loads all the dependencies listed in *app.js* and instantiates models and stores. The views that require data from the store will either mention the store name (for example, store: 'Videos') or will use the get method from the class StoreMgr (for example, Ext.StoreMgr.get('Campaigns');). After this is done, the launch function is called—and this is where the main view is created.

In this version of the Save The Child application, we have only one controller, Login, that doesn't use any stores, but the mechanism of pointing controllers to the appropriate store instances is the same as for views. The application instantiates all controllers automatically. Accordingly, all controllers live in the context of the Application (*http://bit.ly/1nhoj4W*) object.

We don't use explicitly defined models here. All the data is hardcoded in the stores in the data attributes.

You'll see the code of the views a bit later, but we want to draw your attention to the onUpdated() event handler. In the earlier section "Microloader and configurations" on page 467, we mentioned that production builds of Sencha Touch applications watch the locally cached JavaScript and CSS files listed in the JS and CSS sections of the configuration file *app.json* and compare them with their peers on the server. They also watch all the files listed in the appCache section of *app.json*. If any of these files change, the onUpdated event handler is invoked. For illustration purposes, we decided to intercept this event. Figure 12-9 shows how the update prompt looks on iPhone 5.

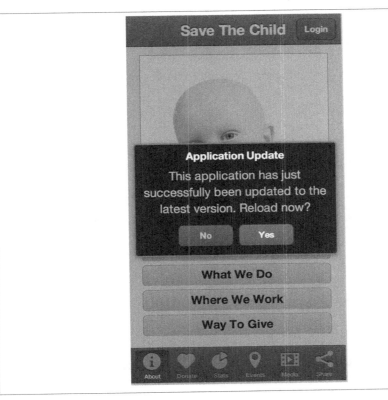

Figure 12-9. The code on the server has changed

At this point, the user can either choose to work with the previous version of the application or reload the new one.

Our *index.html* file includes one more script (besides the microloader script) that support the Google Maps API:

```
<script type="text/javascript"
        src="http://maps.google.com/maps/api/js?sensor=true"></script>
```

 If you want your program documentation to look as good as Sencha's, use the JSDuck tool (*https://github.com/senchalabs/jsduck*).

The Main View

The code of the UI landing page of this application is located in the *views* folder in the file *Main.js*. First, take a look at the screenshot from WebStorm in Figure 12-10; note that it shows only two objects on the top level: the container and a login form.

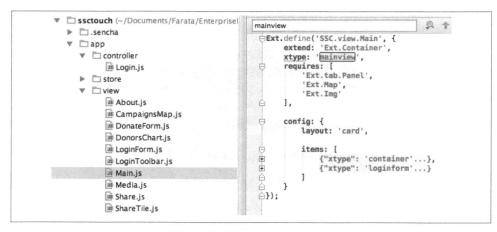

Figure 12-10. Main.js in a collapsed form

The `card` layout means that the user will see either the content of that container or the login form—one at a time. Let's open the container. It has an array of children, which are our application pages. Figure 12-11 shows the titles of the children.

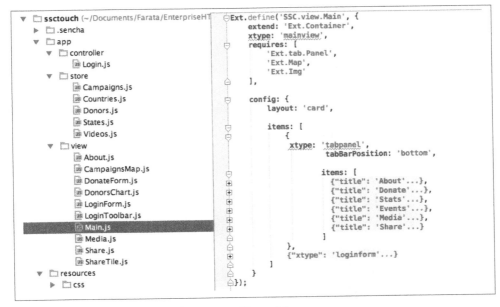

Figure 12-11. TabPanel's children in a collapsed form

The entire code of *Main.js* is shown in Example 12-6.

Example 12-6. The complete version of Main.js

```
Ext.define('SSC.view.Main', {
 extend: 'Ext.Container',
 xtype: 'mainview',                              ❶
 requires: [
     'Ext.tab.Panel',
     'Ext.Map',
     'Ext.Img'
 ],

 config: {
    layout: 'card',

    items: [
      {
       xtype: 'tabpanel',                         ❷
               tabBarPosition: 'bottom',

           items: [
             {
                     title: 'About',
                     iconCls: 'info',             ❸
                     layout: 'fit',               ❹
                     items: [
```

```
                    {xtype: 'aboutview'
                    }
                ]
        },
        {
            title: 'Donate',
            iconCls: 'love',
            layout: 'fit',
            items: [
                {xtype: 'logintoolbar',    ❺
                 title: 'Donate'
                },
                {xtype: 'donateform'
                }
            ]
        },
        {
            title: 'Stats',
            iconCls: 'pie',
            layout: 'fit',
            items: [
                {xtype: 'logintoolbar',
                 title: 'Stats'
                },
                {xtype: 'donorschart'
                }
            ]
        },
        {
            title: 'Events',
            iconCls: 'pin',
            layout: 'fit',
            items: [
                {xtype: 'logintoolbar',
                 title: 'Events'
                },
                {xtype: 'campaignsmap'
                }
            ]
        },
        {
            title: 'Media',
            iconCls: 'media',
            layout: 'fit',
            items: [
                {xtype: 'mediaview'
                }
            ]
        },
        {
            title: 'Share',
            iconCls: 'share',
```

```
                 layout: 'fit',
                 items: [
                     {xtype: 'logintoolbar',
                         title: 'Share'
                     },
                     {xtype: 'shareview'
                     }
                 ]
             }
         ]
     },

     {xtype: 'loginform',
         showAnimation: {
             type: 'slide',
             direction: 'up',
             duration: 200
         }
     }
   ]
 }
});
```

❶   We've assigned the `xtype: 'mainview'` to the main view so that the Login
     controller can refer to it.

❷   Note that the `tabpanel` doesn't explicitly specify any layout; it uses `card` by
     default.

❸   Each tab has a corresponding button on the toolbar. It shows the text from the
     `title` attribute and the icon specified in the class `iconCls`.

❹   Each view has the `fit` layout (*http://bit.ly/1h8ANPP*), which forces the content
     to expand to fill the layout's container.

❺   Each view has a Login button on the toolbar. It's implemented in *LoginToolbar.js*,
     shown later in this chapter.

Sencha Touch can render icons by using icon fonts from the Pictos library (*http://
pictos.cc/*) located in the folder *resources/sass/stylesheets/fonts*. We've used icon fonts in
the jQuery Mobile version of our application, and in this version we'll also use fonts,
which consume much less memory than images. Example 12-7 presents the content of
our *app.scss* file, which includes several font icons used in the Save The Child application.

Example 12-7. The application styles are located in app.scss

```
@import 'sencha-touch/default';
@import 'sencha-touch/default/all';

@include icon-font('IcoMoon', inline-font-files('icomoon/icomoon.woff', woff,
'icomoon/icomoon.ttf', truetype,'icomoon/icomoon.svg', svg));
```

```scss
@include icon('info',  '!', 'IcoMoon');
@include icon('love',  '"', 'IcoMoon');
@include icon('pie',   '#', 'IcoMoon');
@include icon('pin',   '$', 'IcoMoon');
@include icon('media', '%', 'IcoMoon');
@include icon('share', '&', 'IcoMoon');

.child-img {
  border: 1px solid #999;
}

// Reduce size of the icons to fit 6 buttons in the tabbar; add Share tab
.x-tabbar.x-docked-bottom .x-tab {
  min-width: 2.8em;

  .x-button-icon:before {
    font-size: 1.4em;
  }
}

// Share icons
.icon-twitter, .icon-facebook, .icon-google-plus, .icon-camera {
  font-family: 'icomoon';
  speak: none;
  font-style: normal;
  font-weight: normal;
  font-variant: normal;
  text-transform: none;
  line-height: 1;
  -webkit-font-smoothing: antialiased;
}
.icon-twitter:before {
  content: "\27";
}
.icon-facebook:before {
  content: "\28";
}
.icon-google-plus:before {
  content: "\29";
}
.icon-camera:before {
  content: "\2a";
}

// Share tiles
.share-tile {
  top: 25%;
  width: 100%;
  position: absolute;
  text-align: center;
  border-width: 0 1px 1px 0;
```

```scss
  p:nth-child(1) {
    font-size:4em;
  }

  p:nth-child(2) {
    margin-top: 1.5em;
    font-size: 0.9em;
  }
}

$sharetile-border: #666 solid;

.sharetile-twitter {
  border: $sharetile-border;
  border-width: 0 1px 1px 0;
}

.sharetile-facebook {
  border: $sharetile-border;
  border-width: 0 0 1px;
}

.sharetile-gplus {
  border: $sharetile-border;
  border-width: 0 1px 0 0;
}

// Media
.x-videos {
  .x-list-item > .x-innerhtml {
    font-weight: bold;
    line-height: 18px;
    min-height: 88px;

    > span {
      display: block;
      font-size: 14px;
      font-weight: normal;
    }
  }

  .preview {
    float: left;
    height: 64px;
    width: 64px;
    margin-right: 10px;
    background-size: cover;
    background-position: center center;
    background: #eee;
    @include border-radius(3px);
    -webkit-box-shadow: inset 0 0 2px rgba(0,0,0,.6);
  }
```

```
  .x-item-pressed,
  .x-item-selected {
    border-top-color: #D1D1D1 !important;
  }
}
```

The first two lines of *app.scss* import the icons from the default theme. We've added several more. Note that we had to reduce the size of the icons to fit six buttons in the application's toolbar. All the @include statements use the SASS mixin icon().

If you need more icons, use the IcoMoon application (*http://icomoon.io/app*). Pick an icon there and click the Font button to generate a custom font (see Figure 12-12). Download and copy the generated fonts into your *resources/sass/stylesheets/fonts* directory and add them to *app.scss* by using the @include icon-font directive. The downloaded ZIP file will contain the fonts as well as the *index.html* file that will show you the class name and the code of the generated font icon(s).

Figure 12-12. Generating Twitter icon font with IcoMoon

When you compile the SASS with compass (*http://bit.ly/1pEgCNi*) (or build the application by using Sencha CMD), the SASS styles are converted into a standard CSS file, *resources/css/app.css*.

Controller

Now let's review the code of the Login page controller, which reacts to the user's actions performed in the view LoginForm. The name of the controller's file is *Login.js*. It's located in the folder *controller*, and Example 12-8 presents the code.

Example 12-8. The Login controller

```
Ext.define('SSC.controller.Login', {
    extend: 'Ext.app.Controller',

    config: {
        refs: {
            mainView: 'mainview',                    ❶
            loginForm: 'loginform',                   ❷
            loginButton: 'button[action=login]',      ❸
            cancelButton: 'loginform button[action=cancel]'
        },

        control: {                                    ❹
            loginButton: {
                tap: 'showLoginView'
            },
            cancelButton: {
                tap: 'cancelLogin'
            }
        }
    },

    showLoginView: function () {
        this.getMainView().setActiveItem(1);   ❺
    },

    cancelLogin: function () {
        this.getMainView().setActiveItem(0);   ❻
    }

});
```

❶ Including `mainView: 'mainview'` in the refs attribute forces Sencha Touch to generate the getter function `getMainView()`, providing access to the main view if need be.

❷ This controller uses components from the LoginForm view (its code comes a bit later).

❸ The `loginButton` is the one that has `action=login`. The `cancelButton` is the one that's located inside the `loginform` and has `action=cancel`.

❹ Defining the event handlers for tap events for the buttons Login and Cancel from the LoginForm view.

❺ The main view has two children (see Figure 12-10). When the user taps the Login button, show the second child: `setActiveItem(1)`.

❻ When the user clicks the Cancel button, show the main container: the first child of the main view, `setActiveItem(0)`.

Controllers are automatically instantiated by the `Application` object. If you want a controller's code to be executed even before the application `launch` function is called, put it in the `init` function. If you want code to be executed right after the application is launched, put it in the controller's `launch` function.

For illustration purposes, we'll show you a shorter (but not necessarily better) version of *Login.js*. The preceding code defines a reference to the login form and button selectors in the `refs` section. Sencha Touch will find the references and generate the getter for these buttons. But in this particular example, we are using these buttons only to assign them the event handlers. Hence, we can make the `refs` section slimmer and use the selectors right inside the `control` section, as shown in Example 12-9.

Example 12-9. Making the ref section slimmer in Login controller

```
Ext.define('SSC.controller.Login', {
    extend: 'Ext.app.Controller',

    config: {
        refs: {
            mainView: 'mainview',
        },

        control: {
            'button[action=login]': {
                tap: 'showLoginView'
            },
            'loginform button[action=cancel]': {
                tap: 'cancelLogin'
            }
        }
    },

    showLoginView: function () {
        this.getMainView().setActiveItem(1);
    },

    cancelLogin: function () {
        this.getMainView().setActiveItem(0);
    }
});
```

This version of *Login.js* is shorter, but the first one is more generic. In both versions, the button selectors are the shortcuts for the `ComponentQuery` (*http://bit.ly/VzPvpq*) class, which is a singleton that is used to search for components.

With the Model-View-Controller (MVC) pattern, the event-processing logic is often located in controller classes. By using `refs` and `ComponentQuery` selectors, you can reach event-generating objects located in different classes. For example, if the user taps a button in a view, the controller's code includes the `tap` event handler, where it triggers an event on a store class to initiate the data retrieval.

But if the `control` config is defined not in the controller, but in a component, the scope where `ComponentQuery` operates is limited to the component itself. You'll see an example of using the `control` config inside *DonateForm.js*, later in this chapter.

Other Views in Save The Child

Let's do a brief code review of the other Save The Child views.

LoginForm

Figure 12-13 is a snapshot of the Login view taken from an iPhone 5, which was the only mobile device on which we've tested this application.

Figure 12-13. The Login form view

Example 12-10 shows the code of the LoginForm view; it's self-explanatory. The `ui: 'decline'` is the `Ext.Button` style (*http://bit.ly/1jCAcS7*) that causes the Cancel button to have a red background.

Example 12-10. The LoginForm view

```
Ext.define('SSC.view.LoginForm', {
    extend: 'Ext.form.Panel',
    xtype: 'loginform',
    requires: [
        'Ext.field.Password'
    ],

    config: {
        items: [
            {   xtype: 'toolbar',
                title: 'Login',

                items: [
                    {   xtype: 'button',
                        text: 'Cancel',
                        ui: 'decline',
                        action: 'cancel'
                    }
                ]
            },
            {   xtype: 'fieldset',
                title: 'Please enter your credentials',

                defaults: {
                    labelWidth: '35%'
                },

                items: [
                    {   xtype: 'textfield',
                        label: 'Username'
                    },
                    {   xtype: 'passwordfield',
                        label: 'Password'
                    }
                ]
            },
            {   xtype: 'button',
                text: 'Login',
                ui: 'confirm',
                margin: '0 10'
            }
        ]
    }
});
```

One of the reviewers of this book reported that the text fields from this Login form do not display on his Android Nexus 4 smartphone. This can happen, and it illustrates why real-world applications should be tested on a variety of mobile devices. If you run into a similar situation while developing your application with Sencha Touch, use platform-specific themes (*http://bit.ly/1lWfTTW*), which are automatically loaded based on the detected user's platform (see the `platformConfig` object (*http://bit.ly/1uDtGzq*)). Sencha Touch offers a number of out-of-the-box schemes (*http://bit.ly/1vTNkJV*) and theme switching capabilities (*https://vimeo.com/66191847*).

The Login form displays when the user clicks the Login button that is displayed on each other page in the toolbar. For example, Figure 12-14 shows the top portion of the Donate view.

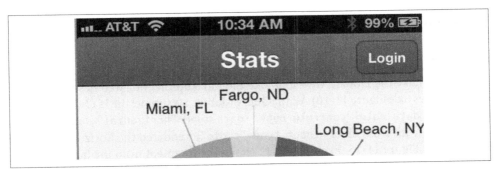

Figure 12-14. The Login toolbar

The Login button is added as `xtype: 'logintoolbar'` to the top of each view in *Main.js*. It's implemented in *LoginToolbar.js*, shown in Example 12-11.

Example 12-11. The LoginToolbar.js

```
Ext.define('SSC.view.LoginToolbar', {
  extend: 'Ext.Toolbar',
  xtype: 'logintoolbar',

  config: {
    title: 'Save The Child',
    docked: 'top',                    ❶

    items: [
      {
        xtype: 'spacer'               ❷
      },
      {
        xtype: 'button',
```

```
                action: 'login',
                text: 'Login'
            }
        ]
    }
});
```

❶   The Login toolbar has to be located at the top of the screen.

❷   Adding the Ext.Spacer component to occupy all the space before the Login
     button. By default, the spacer has a flex value of 1, which means it takes all the
     space in this situation. You can read more about it in "Setting proportional
     layouts by using the flex property" on page 149.

> If you add the Save The Child application as an icon to the home
> screen on iOS devices, the browser's address bar will not be displayed.

DonateForm

We want to make the Donate view look like the mockup that our web designer, Jerry,
supplied for us (see Figure 11-10). With jQuery Mobile, it's simple: the HTML container
`<fieldset data-role="controlgroup" data-type="horizontal" id="radio-
container">` with a bunch of `<input type="radio">` rendered the horizontal button
bar shown in Figure 11-25. Example 12-12 shows the fragment from the initial Sencha
Touch version of *DonateForm.js*.

Example 12-12. The fragment of the initial version of DonateForm.js

```
config: {
  title: 'DonateForm',

  items: [
      { xtype: 'fieldset',
        title: 'Please select donation amount',

        defaults: {
            name: 'amount',
            xtype: 'radiofield'
        },

        items: [
            { label: '$10',
              value: 10
            },
            { label: '$20',
              value: 20
```

```
        },
        { label: '$50',
          value: 50
        },
        { label: '$100',
            value: 100
        }
    ]
},
{ xtype: 'fieldset',
  title: '... or enter other amount',

    items: [
        { xtype: 'numberfield',
          label: 'Amount',
          name: 'amount'
        }
    ]
}
```

It's also a `fieldset` with several radio buttons, `xtype: 'radiofield'`. But the result is not what we expected. These four radio buttons occupy half of the screen, which looks like Figure 12-15.

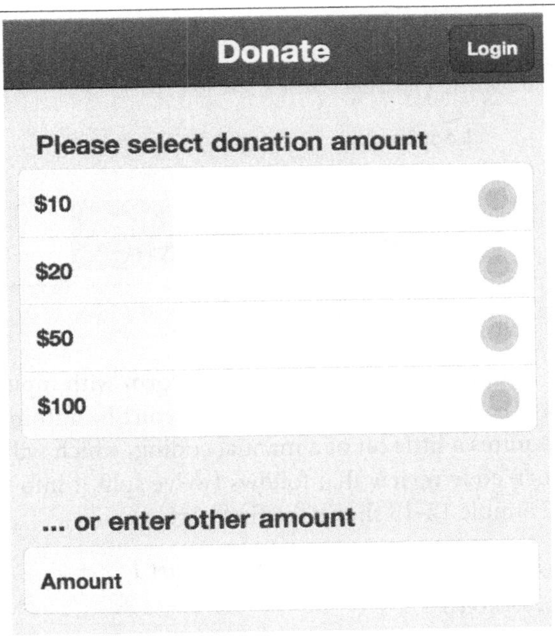

Figure 12-15. Rendering of xtype radio field

After doing some research, we discovered that Sencha Touch has a UI component called Ext.SegmentedButton (*http://bit.ly/1qHmHYE*) with which you can create a horizontal bar with toggle buttons, which is exactly what is needed from the rendering perspective. The resulting Donate screen is shown in Figure 12-16.

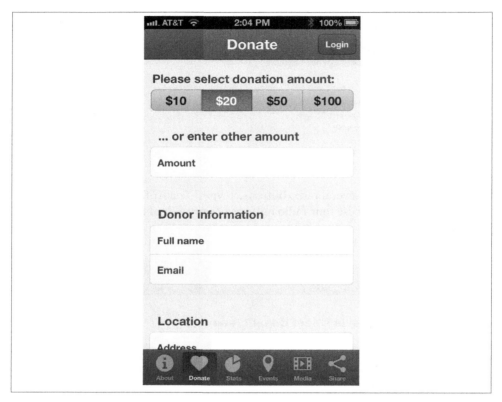

Figure 12-16. Donation form with SegmentedButton

This looks nice, but as opposed to a regular HTML form with inputs, the Segmented Button is not an HTML <input> field and its value won't be automatically submitted to the server. This requires a little bit of a manual coding, which will be explained as a part of the DonateForm code review that follows (we've split it into two fragments for better readability). Example 12-13 shows the first part.

Example 12-13. The final version of DonateForm.js, part 1

```
Ext.define('SSC.view.DonateForm', {
 extend: 'Ext.form.Panel',
 xtype: 'donateform',
 requires: [
    'Ext.form.FieldSet',
```

```
        'Ext.field.Select',
        'Ext.field.Number',
        'Ext.field.Radio',
        'Ext.field.Email',
        'Ext.field.Hidden',
        'Ext.SegmentedButton',
        'Ext.Label'
    ],

    config: {
        title: 'DonateForm',

        control: {                                    ❶
            'segmentedbutton': {
                toggle: 'onAmountButtonChange'
            },
            'numberfield[name=amount]': {
                change: 'onAmountFieldChange'
            }
        },

        items: [
            { xtype: 'label',
              cls: 'x-form-fieldset-title',          ❷
              html: 'Please select donation amount:'
            },
            { xtype: 'segmentedbutton',               ❸
              margin: '0 10',

              defaults: {
                  flex: 1
              },

              items: [
                  { text: '$10',
                    data: {
                        value: 10                     ❹
                    }
                  },
                  { text: '$20',
                    data: {
                        value: 20
                    }
                  },
                  { text: '$50',
                    data: {
                        value: 50
                    }
                  },
                  { text: '$100',
                    data: {
                        value: 100
```

```
            }
          }
        ]
      },
      { xtype: 'hiddenfield',              ❺
        name: 'amount'
      },
```

❶ Define event listeners for the segmentedbutton and the field for entering another
amount. When the control section is used not in a controller, but in a component,
it's scoped to the object in which it was defined. Hence the ComponentQuery will
be looking for segmentedbutton and numberfield[name=amount] only within
the DonateForm instance. If these event handlers were defined in the controller,
the scope would be global.

❷ Borrow the class that Sencha Touch uses for all fieldset containers, so our title
looks the same.

❸ The segmentedbutton is defined here. By default, its config property is allow
Toggle=true, which allows only one button to be pressed at a time.

❹ The segmentedbutton has no property to store the value of each button. But any
sublcass of Ext.Component has the property data. We are extending the data
property to store the button's value. It will be available in the event handler in
button.getData().value.

❺ Because the buttons in the segmentedbutton are not input fields, we define a
hidden field to remember the currently selected amount.

Example 12-14 presents the second half of SSC.view.DonateForm.

Example 12-14. The final version of DonateForm.js, part 2

```
      { xtype: 'fieldset',
        title: '... or enter other amount',

          items: [
              { xtype: 'numberfield',       ❶
                label: 'Amount',
                name: 'amount'
              }
          ]
      },
      {
        xtype: 'fieldset',
        title: 'Donor information',

        items: [
          { name: 'fullName',
            xtype: 'textfield',
```

```
                label: 'Full name'
            },
            { name: 'email',
              xtype: 'emailfield',
              label: 'Email'
            }
        ]
    },
    {
        xtype: 'fieldset',
        title: 'Location',

        items: [
            { name: 'address',
              xtype: 'textfield',
              label: 'Address'
            },
            { name: 'city',
              xtype: 'textfield',
              label: 'City'
            },
            { name: 'zip',
              xtype: 'textfield',
              label: 'Zip'
            },
            { name: 'state',
              xtype: 'selectfield',
              autoSelect: false,
              label: 'State',
              store: 'States',
              valueField: 'id',
              displayField: 'name'
            },
            { name: 'country',
              xtype: 'selectfield',
              autoSelect: false,
              label: 'Country',
              store: 'Countries',
              valueField: 'id',
              displayField: 'name'
            }
        ]
    },
    {
        xtype: 'button',
        text: 'Donate',
        ui: 'confirm',
        margin: '0 10 20'
    }
  ]
},
```

```
onAmountButtonChange: function (segButton,
                                button, isPressed) { ❷

  if (isPressed) {                              ❸
      this.clearAmountField();
      this.updateHiddenAmountField(button.getData().value);
      button.setUi('confirm');                  ❹
  }
  else {
      button.setUi('normal');
  }
},

onAmountFieldChange: function () {              ❺

  this.depressAmountButtons();
  this.clearHiddenAmountField();
},

clearAmountField: function () {
  var amountField = this.down('numberfield[name=amount]');

  amountField.suspendEvents();                  ❻
  amountField.setValue(null);
  amountField.resumeEvents(true);               ❼
},

updateHiddenAmountField: function (value) {
  this.down('hiddenfield[name=amount]').setValue(value);
},

depressAmountButtons: function () {
  this.down('segmentedbutton').setPressedButtons([]);
},

clearHiddenAmountField: function () {
  this.updateHiddenAmountField(null);
}
});
```

❶ This numberfield stores the *other amount*, if entered. Note that it has the same
    name amount as the hidden field. The methods clearAmountField() and clear
    HiddenAmountField() ensure that only one of the amounts has a value.

❷ When the toggle event is fired, it comes with an object that contains a reference
    to the button that was toggled, and whether the button becomes pressed as the
    result of this event.

❸ The toggle event is dispatched twice: once for the button that is pressed, and again for the button that was pressed before. If the button is clicked (is Pressed=true), clean the previously selected amount and store a new one in the hidden field.

❹ Change the style of the button to make it visibly highlighted. We use the predefined confirm style (see the Kitchen Sink (*http://bit.ly/1ohOj3B*) application for other button styles).

❺ When the *other amount* field loses focus, this event handler is invoked. The code cleans up the hidden field and removes the pressed state from all buttons.

❻ Temporarily suspend dispatching events while setting the value of the amount numberfield to null. Otherwise, setting to null would cause unnecessary dispatching of the change event.

❼ Resume event dispatching. The true argument is for discarding all the queued events.

Previous versions of the Save The Child application illustrated how to submit the Donate form to the server for further processing. The Sencha Touch version of this application doesn't include this code. If you'd like to experiment with this, just create a new controller class that extends Ext.app.Controller and define an event handler for the Donate Now button (see the Login controller as an example).

On the tap event, invoke donateform.submit(), specifying the URL of the server that knows how to process this form. You can find details on submitting and populating forms in the online documentation for Ext.form.Panel (*http://bit.ly/1piOm01*)—the ancestor of the "DonateForm".

 If you want to use Ajax-based form submission, use submit(). Otherwise, use the method standardSubmit(), which performs a standard HTML form submission.

Charts

The charting support is just great in Sencha Touch (and similar to Ext JS). It's JavaScript based, and the charts are live and can get the data from the stores and model. Figure 12-17 shows how the chart looks on an iPhone when the user selects the Stats page.

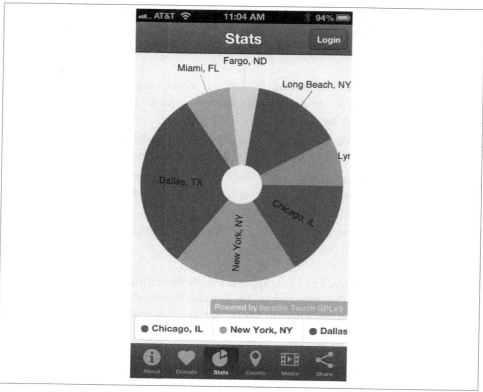

Figure 12-17. Donor's statistics chart

The code that supports the UI part of the chart is located in the view DonorsChart that's shown in Example 12-15. It uses the classes located in the Sencha Touch framework in the folder *src/chart*.

Example 12-15. The view DonorsChart.js

```
Ext.define('SSC.view.DonorsChart', {
    extend: 'Ext.chart.PolarChart',          ❶
    xtype: 'donorschart',

    requires: [
        'Ext.chart.series.Pie',
        'Ext.chart.interactions.Rotate'      ❷
    ],

    config: {
        store: 'Donors',
        animate: true,                        ❸
        interactions: ['rotate'],
```

```
            legend: {                        ❹
                inline: false,
                docked: 'left',
                position: 'bottom'
            },

            series: [
                {
                    type: 'pie',
                    donut: 20,
                    xField: 'donors',
                    labelField: 'location',
                    showInLegend: true,
                    colors: ["#115fa6", "#94ae0a", "#a61120", "#ff8809",
                      "#ffd13e", "#a61187", "#24ad9a", "#7c7474", "#a66111"]
                }
            ]
        }
    }
});
```

❶ Create a chart that uses polar coordinates.

❷ The Rotate class allows the user to rotate (with a finger) a polar chart around its central point.

❸ The data shown on the chart comes from the store named Donors, which is shown in the section "Stores and Models" on page 511.

❹ The legend is a bar at the bottom of the screen. The user can horizontally scroll it with a finger.

Media

The Media page of our application displays the list of available videos. When the user taps one of them, a new page opens on which the user must tap the Play button. We use the Ext.dataview.List (*http://docs.sencha.com/touch/2.3.1/#!/api/Ext.dataview.List*) component to display video titles from the Videos store.

The Media view extends Ext.NavigationView, which is a container with the card layout that also allows pushing a new view into this container. We use it to create a view for the selected video from the list. The code of the Media view is shown in Example 12-16.

Example 12-16. The view Media.js

```
Ext.define('SSC.view.Media', {
    extend: 'Ext.NavigationView',
    xtype: 'mediaview',
    requires: [
        'Ext.Video'                          ❶
    ],
```

```
    config: {
        control: {
            'list': {
                itemtap: 'showVideo'        ❷
            }
        },

        useTitleForBackButtonText: true,    ❸
        navigationBar: {
            items: [
                {   xtype: 'button',
                    action: 'login',
                    text: 'Login',
                    align: 'right'
                }
            ]
        },

        items: [
            {   title: 'Media',
                xtype: 'list',
                store: 'Videos',
                cls: 'x-videos',
                variableHeights: true,
                itemTpl: [                      ❹
                    '<div class="preview"
                    style="background-image:url(resources/media/{thumbnail});">
                    </div>',
                    '{title}',
                    '<span>{description}</span>'
                ]
            }
        ]
    },

    showVideo: function (view, index, target, model) {

        this.push(Ext.create('Ext.Video', {        ❺
            title: model.get('title'),
            url: 'resources/media/' + model.get('url'),
            posterUrl: 'resources/media/' + model.get('thumbnail')
        }));
    }
});
```

❶ Sencha Touch offers Ext.Video a wrapper for the HTML5 <video> tag. In
    Chapter 4, we used the HTML5 tag <video> directly.

❷ Define the event listener for the itemtap event, which fires whenever the list
    item is tapped.

❸ When the video player's view is pushed to the Media page, we want its Back button to display the previous view's title, which is Media. It's a config property in NavigationView.

❹ The list with descriptions of videos is populated from the store Videos by using the list's config property itemTpl. This is an HTML template for rendering each item. We decided to use the <div> showing the content of the store's properties title, description with a background image from the property thumbnail, and the video located at the specified url. The source code of the store Videos is included in the section "Stores and Models" on page 511.

❺ Create a video player and push it into NavigationView. When the itemtap event is fired, it passes several values to the function handler. We just use the model that corresponds to the tapped list item. For all available config properties, refer to the Ext.Video documentation (http://bit.ly/1rPwM3w).

A template [Ext.Template] represents an HTML fragment. The values in square braces are passed to the template from the outside. In the preceding example, the values are coming from the store Vid eos. The class Ext.XTemlate (http://bit.ly/ext-docs) offers advanced templating—for example, auto-filling HTML with the data from an array, which is used here.

Maps

Integration with Google Maps is a pretty straightforward task in Sencha Touch, which comes with Ext.Map (http://docs.sencha.com/touch/2.3.1/#!/api/Ext.Map), a wrapper class for the Google Maps API. Our view CampainsMap is a subclass of Ext.Map. Note that we've imported the Google Maps API in the file index.html as follows:

```
<script type="text/javascript"
        src="http://maps.google.com/maps/api/js?sensor=true"></script>
```

Figure 12-18 shows the iPhone's screen when the Events button is tapped.

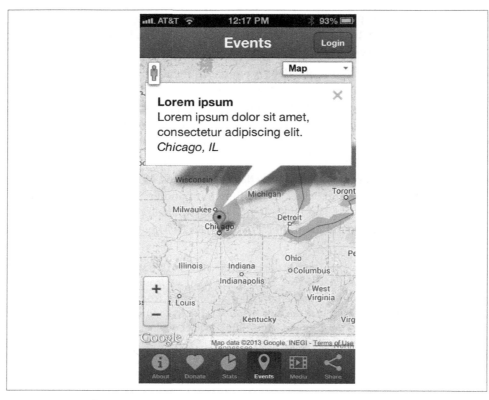

Figure 12-18. The Events page

Of course, some additional styling is needed before offering this view in a production environment, but the *CampaignsMap.js* that supports this screen (see Example 12-17) is only 90 lines of code!

Example 12-17. The view CampaignsMap.js

```
Ext.define('SSC.view.CampaignsMap', {
  extend: 'Ext.Map',
  xtype: 'campaignsmap',

  config: {                                        ❶
    listeners: {
      maprender: function () {                      ❷

        if (navigator && navigator.onLine) {
          try {
            this.initMap();
            this.addCampaignsOnTheMap(this.getMap());
          } catch (e) {
            this.displayGoogleMapError();
```

```
            }
        } else {
            this.displayGoogleMapError();
        }
    }
    }
},

initMap: function () {

    // latitude = 39.8097343 longitude = -98.55561990000001
    // Lebanon, KS 66952, USA Geographic center
    // of the contiguous United States
    // the center point of the map

    var latMapCenter = 39.8097343,
        lonMapCenter = -98.55561990000001;

    var mapOptions = {
        zoom     : 3,
        center   : new google.maps.LatLng(latMapCenter, lonMapCenter),
        mapTypeId: google.maps.MapTypeId.ROADMAP,
        mapTypeControlOptions: {
            style   : google.maps.MapTypeControlStyle.DROPDOWN_MENU,
            position: google.maps.ControlPosition.TOP_RIGHT
        }
    };

    this.setMapOptions(mapOptions);
},

addCampaignsOnTheMap: function (map) {
    var marker,
        infowindow = new google.maps.InfoWindow(),
        geocoder   = new google.maps.Geocoder(),
        campaigns  = Ext.StoreMgr.get('Campaigns');

    campaigns.each(function (campaign) {
        var title       = campaign.get('title'),
            location    = campaign.get('location'),
            description = campaign.get('description');

        geocoder.geocode({
            address: location,
            country: 'USA'
        }, function(results, status) {
            if (status == google.maps.GeocoderStatus.OK) {

                // getting coordinates
                var lat = results[0].geometry.location.lat(),
                    lon = results[0].geometry.location.lng();
```

```
// create marker
marker = new google.maps.Marker({
    position: new google.maps.LatLng(lat, lon),
    map      : map,
    title    : location
});

// adding click event to the marker to show info-bubble
// with data from json
google.maps.event.addListener(marker, 'click', (function(marker)
    {
    return function () {
        var content = Ext.String.format(
            '<p class="infowindow"><b>{0}</b><br/>{1}
            <br/><i>{2}</i></p>',
            title, description, location);

            infowindow.setContent(content);
            infowindow.open(map, marker);
        };
    })(marker));
} else {
    console.error('Error getting location data for address: ' +
                                        location);
    }
    });
    });
},

displayGoogleMapError: function () {
    console.log("Sorry, Google Map service isn't available");
    }
});
```

❶ We use just the listeners config here, but Ext.Map has 60 of them. For example, if we wanted the mobile device to identify its current location and put it in the center of the map, we'd add useCurrentLocation: true.

❷ This event is fired when the map is initially rendered. We are reusing the same code as in previous chapters for initializing the map (showing the central point of the United States) and adding the campaign information. The code of the store Campaigns is shown in the section "Stores and Models" on page 511.

Sencha Touch is a framework for mobile devices, which can be on the move. Ext.util.Geolocation (*http://bit.ly/1z25rQk*) is a handy class for applications that require knowing the current position of the mobile device. When your program instantiates Geolocation, it starts tracking the location of the device by firing the locatio nupdate event periodically (you can turn auto updates off). Example 12-18 shows how to get the current latitude of the mobile device.

Example 12-18. Getting the current latitude of the device

```
var geo = Ext.create('Ext.util.Geolocation', {
  listeners: {
    locationupdate: function(geo) {
      console.log('New latitude: ' + geo.getLatitude());
    }
  }
});

geo.updateLocation();  // start the location updates
```

Stores and Models

In the Sencha Touch version of the Save The Child application, all the data is hard-coded. All store classes are located in the *store* directory (see Figure 12-11), and each of them has the data property. Example 12-19 presents the code of *Videos.js*.

Example 12-19. The store Video.js

```
Ext.define('SSC.store.Videos', {
  extend: 'Ext.data.Store',

  config: {
    fields: [
      { name: 'title',       type: 'string' },
      { name: 'description', type: 'string' },
      { name: 'url',         type: 'string' },
      { name: 'thumbnail',   type: 'string' }
    ],

    data: [
      { title: 'The title of a video-clip 1', description: 'Short video
      description 1', url: 'intro.mp4', thumbnail: 'intro.jpg' },

      { title: 'The title of a video-clip 2', description: 'Short video
      description 2', url: 'intro.mp4', thumbnail: 'intro.jpg' },

      { title: 'The title of a video-clip 3', description: 'Short video
      description 3', url: 'intro.mp4', thumbnail: 'intro.jpg' }
    ]
  }
});
```

There is a compatibility issue between Ext JS and Sencha Touch 2 stores and models. For example, in the preceding code, fields and data are wrapped inside the config object, whereas in the Ext JS store they are not. Until Sencha offers a generic solution to resolve these compatibility issues, you have to come up with your own if you want to reuse the same stores.

The code of the Donors store supports the charts on the Stats page. It's self-explanatory, as you can see in Example 12-20.

Example 12-20. The store Donors.js

```
Ext.define('SSC.store.Donors', {
  extend: 'Ext.data.Store',

  config: {
    fields: [
        { name: 'donors',   type: 'int' },
        { name: 'location', type: 'string' }
    ],

    data: [
        { donors: 48, location: 'Chicago, IL' },
        { donors: 60, location: 'New York, NY' },
        { donors: 90, location: 'Dallas, TX' },
        { donors: 22, location: 'Miami, FL' },
        { donors: 14, location: 'Fargo, ND' },
        { donors: 44, location: 'Long Beach, NY' },
        { donors: 24, location: 'Lynbrook, NY' }
    ]
  }
});
```

The Campaigns store is used to display the markers on the map, where charity campaigns are active. Tapping the marker will show the description of the selected campaign, as shown in Figure 12-18 (we tapped the Chicago marker). Example 12-21 presents the code of the store *Campaigns.js*.

Example 12-21. The store Campaigns.js

```
Ext.define('SSC.store.Campaigns', {
    extend: 'Ext.data.Store',

    config: {
        fields: [
            { name: 'title',       type: 'string' },
            { name: 'description', type: 'string' },
            { name: 'location',    type: 'string' }
        ],

        data: [
            {
                title: 'Mothers of Asthmatics',
                description: 'Mothers of Asthmatics - nationwide Asthma network',
                location: 'Chicago, IL'
            },
            {
                title: 'Lawyers for Children',
                description: 'Lawyers offering free services for the children',
```

```
                    location: 'New York, NY'
                },
                {
                    title: 'Sed tincidunt magna',
                    description: 'Donec ac ligula sit amet libero vehicula laoreet',
                    location: 'Dallas, TX'
                },
                {
                    title: 'Friends of Blind Kids',
                    description: 'Semi-annual charity events for blind kids',
                    location: 'Miami, FL'
                },
                {
                    title: 'Place Called Home',
                    description: 'Adoption of the children',
                    location: 'Fargo, ND'
                }
            ]
        }

});
```

Working with Landscape Mode

Handling landscape mode with Sencha Touch is done differently depending on how you deploy your application. If you decide to package this app as a native one (*http://bit.ly/1iMTCJd*), landscape mode will be supported. Sencha CMD will generate the file *packager.json*, which will include a section dealing with orientation:

```
"orientations": [
    "portrait",
    "landscapeLeft",
    "landscapeRight",
    "portraitUpsideDown"
]
```

If you're not planning to package your app as a native one, you'll need to do some manual coding by processing the `orientationchange` event. For example:

```
Ext.Viewport.on('orientationchange', function() {
    // write the code to handle the landscape code here
});
```

This concludes the review of the Sencha Touch version of our sample application, which consists of six nice-looking screens. The amount of manual coding to achieve this is minimal. In the real world, you'd need to add business logic to this application, which comes down to inserting the JavaScript code into well-structured layers. The code to communicate with the server goes to the stores, the data is placed in the models, the UI remains in the views, and the main glue of your application is controllers. Sencha Touch does a good job for us, wouldn't you agree?

Comparing jQuery Mobile and Sencha Touch

In Chapter 11 and this chapter, you've learned about two different ways of developing a mobile application. So, what's better, jQuery Mobile or Sencha Touch? There is no correct answer to this question, and you will have to make a decision on your own. But here's a quick summary of pros and cons for each library or framework.

Use jQuery Mobile if the following are true:

- You are afraid of being locked into any one vendor. The effort to replace jQuery Mobile in your application with another framework (if you decide to do so) is a magnitude lower than switching from Sencha Touch to something else.
- You need your application to work on most mobile platforms.
- You prefer declarative UI and hate debugging JavaScript.

Use Sencha Touch if the following are true:

- You like to have a rich library of precreated UIs.
- Your application needs smooth animation. Sencha Touch performs automatic throttling based on the actual frames-per-second supported on the device.
- Splitting the application code into cleanly defined architectural layers (model-view-controller-service) is important.
- You believe that using code generators adds value to your project.
- You want to be able to customize and extend components to fit your application's needs perfectly. Yes, you'll be writing JavaScript, but it still may be simpler than trying to figure out the enhancements done to an HTML component by jQuery Mobile under the hood.
- You want to minimize the effort required to package your application as a native one.
- You want your application to look as close to the native ones as possible.
- You prefer to use software that is covered by the commercial support offered by a vendor.

While considering support options, do not just assume that paid support translates into better quality. This is not to say that Sencha won't offer you quality support, but in many cases, having a large community of developers will lead to a faster solution to a problem than dealing with one assigned support engineer. Having said this, we'd like you to know that the Sencha forum (*http://www.sencha.com/forum*) has about half a million registered users who are actively discussing problems and offering solutions to one another.

Even if you are a developer's manager, you don't have to make the framework choice on your own. Bring your team into a conference room, order pizza, and listen to what *your team members* have to say about these two frameworks, or any other, being considered. We have offered you information about two of many frameworks, but the final call is yours.

## CHAPTER 13

Hybrid Mobile Applications

The word hybrid (*http://bit.ly/1iukzBj*) means something of mixed origin or composition. In the realm of mobile web applications, such a mix consists of the code written in HTML5, which accesses the APIs written in native languages. If an organization doesn't want or can't hire separate teams of software developers (for example, Objective-C developers for iPhone, Java for Android, C# for Windows Phone), there is a way to have one team of developers with HTML/JavaScript skills who can develop applications by having the same code deployed on various mobile devices packaged as native applications. Let's do a quick comparison of native, web, and hybrid mobile applications.

Native Applications

We call a mobile application *native* if it was written not in HTML/JavaScript, but in a programming language recommended for devices of this mobile platform. The manufacturer of mobile devices releases an SDK and describes a process for creating native applications. This SDK provides an API for accessing all components (both hardware and software) of the mobile device, such as phone, contact list, camera, microphone, and others. Such SDKs include UI components that have a *native look and feel*, so applications developed by third parties look the same as those developed by the respective device manufacturer.

Native applications can seamlessly communicate with one another. They can use all available hardware and software components of the device to create convenient workflows to which people quickly become accustomed. For example, a person can take a picture with her mobile phone, which can figure out the current geographical location and allow her to share the photo with other people from her Contacts list. To support such functionality, a native application has to access the camera of the mobile device, use GPS to discover the device coordinates, and access the Contacts application.

If you are in the business of writing mobile flight simulators or games that heavily rely on graphics (not a Sudoku type of game), select a programming language that can use the device hardware (for example, graphic accelerators) to its fullest and works as fast as possible on this device. Faster applications use less battery power, too.

For native applications, a device manufacturer usually offers an *application store*, which serves as an online marketplace where people can shop for applications. Apple has the *App Store* for iOS and Mac OS X applications. Google has *Google Play* market for Android applications. *BlackBerry World* is a store where you can find applications for mobile devices manufactured by RIM. Microsoft has its store, too.

Other application stores are available, and having a one-stop shop is a great way to distribute consumer-oriented applications. For enterprise applications, having a public distribution channel might be less important, but enterprises still need a way to publish mobile applications for private use. Apple has the iOS Developer Enterprise Program (*http://bit.ly/1ohOyvm*). For Android applications, there is a Google Play Private Channel (*http://bit.ly/1rPx8ai*) for internal distribution channels. Microsoft has its process (*http://bit.ly/1mzH9mW*) for business applications, as well.

 The HTML5 stack is not the only way to develop hybrid applications using the same language for different mobile platforms. With Xamarin (*http://xamarin.com*), you can develop applications in C# for iOS, Android, and Windows Phone.

Native versus Web Applications

Both web and native applications have their pros and cons. The latter are usually faster than web applications. Let's go through some of the examples of native mobile business applications that exist today.

Bank of America, Chase, and other major banks have native mobile applications that you can use to deposit a check by taking a photo of its front and back sides and entering the amount. At the time of this writing, these applications support iPhones, Android, Windows phones, and iPads.

Native applications implementing Near-Field Communication (NFC) technology makes it possible for two NFC-enabled devices to communicate with each other at close distances by using radio frequencies. NFC can be used for payments (no need to enter passwords) and data sharing (contacts, photos, and so forth). Proliferation of NFC in banking will seriously hurt the credit card industry. A number of smartphones already support NFC technology (*http://bit.ly/1pJkDiG*). Add one of the existing fingerprint biometric solutions, and your mobile phone becomes your wallet.

Although native applications have full access to all APIs of the mobile device (for example, contacts, camera, and microphone), they have drawbacks, too. For instance, if you want to publish your application at Apple's App Store, you have to submit your application in advance and wait for its approval. And later, if users run into a crucial bug in your application, even if you fixed it the same day, you can't put a new version in production until it goes through the approval process again. Besides this inconvenience, there can be other roadblocks. For instance, back in 2011, the *Financial Times* (FT) decided to stop using its native iOS application because Apple wouldn't agree to share the data about FT subscribers with FT—the owner of this application.

Mobile web applications don't require any third-party involvement for distribution. An enterprise can make them available at any time by simple adding a Download button on the corporate website. It's good to have the ability to quickly publish the latest versions of web applications on your own servers without having to ask for permission. On the other hand, maintaining a presence on one of the popular app stores is a good channel for getting new customers.

The publisher of *New York* magazine is heavily investing in its native application for iPad, but the newer version of its web application is as engaging as its native peer. If you want your application to be discoverable and visible by search engines, develop it as a web application, not a native one.

Hybrid Applications

Hybrid applications promise you the best of both worlds. You can develop a web application in HTML/JavaScript, but access the native API of the mobile device via third-party solutions such as PhoneGap (*http://phonegap.com*) from Adobe or Titanium (*http://bit.ly/1ls1qKV*) from Appcelerator. Let's see what tools are available for creating hybrids.

Cordova and PhoneGap

Cordova (*http://cordova.apache.org*) is a library (and a build tool) that serves as a bridge between JavaScript and a native API. Cordova started from code donated by Adobe to the Apache Software Foundation. Cordova is an open source platform created for building mobile applications with HTML5, but packaged as native ones. PhoneGap is a brand owned by Adobe. Besides the Cordova library, it offers developers a remote server, on which they can package their applications for various mobile platforms. If the role of the Cordova library in the PhoneGap product is not clear to you, think of a similar situation in which the same software library is used in different products. For example, the rendering engine WebKit is used in Chrome and Safari browsers.

Cordova can be used without PhoneGap. For example, Facebook and Salesforce use Cordova in their mobile SDK.

Figure 13-1 illustrates the interaction of PhoneGap, Cordova, and a web application.

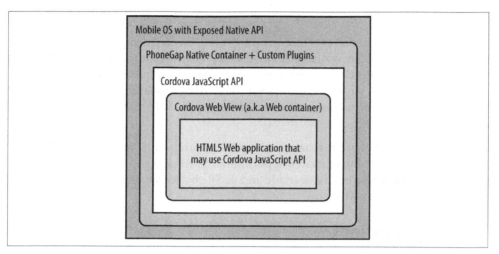

Figure 13-1. PhoneGap, Cordova, and a web application

PhoneGap includes APIs, a code generator, and a workflow for creating *native application containers* for web applications written in HTML5 (with or without JavaScript frameworks). PhoneGap also facilitates making JavaScript calls to access native APIs offered by the mobile OS.

PhoneGap Build (*https://build.phonegap.com*) is a cloud service to which you can upload your HTML/JavaScript/CSS code to be packaged for multiple mobile platforms. PhoneGap Build creates several native applications—one per mobile platform. Each application is a wrapper with an embedded chrome-less web browser (a.k.a. web view) that looks native to the mobile OS, and has access to various native APIs. Refer to the PhoneGap documentation (*http://bit.ly/1mzHjuz*) to see what APIs are supported on each mobile platform. The native wrapper serves as a messaging bus between the external native API and HTML-based applications running inside the web view.

For iOS applications, the PhoneGap Build server creates an *.ipa* file; for deployment on Android devices, it generates an *.apk* file, and so on. After that, if you want to submit your application to a public or private application store, follow the procedure that exists for native applications for the selected store. The PhoneGap Build service can package your application for iOS, Android, Windows Phone, BlackBerry, and other platforms.

PhoneGap applications can run slower compared to HTML-based applications running in a mobile web browser. This is because there is yet another middleman: a web view. In Android SDK, the WebView control is used to embed an HTML5 application into a native shell, and the iOS SDK has the UIWebView control for the same purpose. Both of these controls perform slower than their respective mobile web browsers.

 To compare performance of an application that runs in a mobile browser versus a WebView or UIWebView control, use Google's V8 Benchmark Suite (*http://bit.ly/V2hgGA*) or SunSpider benchmark utility (*http://bit.ly/1lJfu7J*).

The UI components of the HTML5 framework of your choice might not look native enough. But the main selling point is that with PhoneGap (and Cordova), you can take advantage of existing HTML/JavaScript developers' skills for all major mobile platforms, and their bridge to native APIs is easy to learn.

Titanium

Titanium offers its own set of tools and a more extensive API. It has no relation to Cordova or PhoneGap. You'd be writing code in JavaScript (no HTML or CSS) and would need to learn lots of APIs. The compiled and deployed application is JavaScript code embedded inside Java or Objective-C code, plus the JavaScript interpreter, plus the platform-specific Titanium API. An important difference between PhoneGap and Titanium is that the latter doesn't use a web view container for rendering. The business logic written in JavaScript is executed by an embedded interpreter, and the final UI components are delivered by native application to iOS or Android components from Titanium.

Titanium UI components can be extended to use native OS interface abilities to their fullest. Some components are cross-platform; Titanium has a compatibility layer, whereas others are platform-specific. But if you want to learn platform-specific components, you might rather invest time in learning to develop the entire application in the native language and APIs. Besides, as new platforms are introduced, you'll depend on the willingness of Titanium developers to create a new set of components in a timely fashion.

Don't expect top performance from the old Rhino JavaScript engine, which is used by Titanium for Android and BlackBerry applications. Oracle has a new JavaScript engine called Nashorn, but it's available only for Java 8, which doesn't run on Android and won't for the foreseeable future. Nashorn is as fast as Google's V8 (*http://bit.ly/V2hlKC*), but Rhino is slower. Does this mean that Titanium applications on Android and BlackBerry will always run slower? This seems to be the case, unless Oracle and Google find a way to stop their quarrels about Java.

The learning curve of the Titanium API is steeper (it has over 5,000 APIs) than with PhoneGap. At the time of this writing, Titanium supports iOS, Android, and older versions of BlackBerry devices. It plans to support Windows Phone by the end of 2014.

 PhoneGap and Titanium are not the only solutions that allow building hybrid applications using HTML5. The framework Kendo UI Mobile (*http://www.kendoui.com/mobile.aspx*) can build hybrid applications for iOS, Android, BlackBerry, and Windows Phone 8. The Mobile Conduit API (*http://bit.ly/1uDu7tF*) allows you to build cross-platform mobile applications with HTML5. Convertigo Mobilizer (*http://www.convertigo.com*) is a cross-platform enterprise mashup environment that incorporates PhoneGap and Sencha Touch for building mobile applications. IBM Worklight (*http://ibm.co/1piOUmG*) offers a client/server/cloud to enterprises so they can develop, test, run, and manage HTML5, hybrid, and native mobile applications.

The Bottom Line

If a particular enterprise application is intended only for internal use by people carrying a limited variety of mobile devices, and if making business users productive is your main goal, consider developing native applications, which can be fine-tuned to look and feel as best as a selected platform allows. You can start by developing and deploying your first application for the pilot mobile OS (typically for the latest iOS or Android OS) and then gradually add support for more platforms, budget permitting. If you are planning to develop a web application with a relatively simple UI and have to support a wide variety of unknown consumer devices (for example, you want to enable people to donate from any device), develop an HTML5 web application.

Consider developing a hybrid application for anything in between. In this chapter, we'll show you how to access the camera of a mobile device by using the PhoneGap (*http://phonegap.com*) framework. Such functionality can be quite useful for our Save The Child application because kids who receive donations might want to share their success stories and publish their photos after being cured.

Still, remain open-minded about native versus hybrid discussions. Be prepared that going hybrid might not become your final choice. Picking a platform is a complex, business-specific decision that might change over the life of your application.

Introduction to the PhoneGap Workflows

In this section, you'll go through the entire process of building a PhoneGap application. PhoneGap 3.1 offers two major workflows. Each allows you to build a mobile application, but the main difference is where you build it—either locally or remotely. Here are the options:

- Install all required mobile SDKs and tools for the mobile platforms for which you want to develop (for example, iOS and Android), generate the initial project by using the command-line interface (CLI), write your HTML5 application code, build it locally, and then test the application by using the IDE, simulators, and physical devices.

- Don't install any mobile SDK and tools. Just generate the initial project by using CLI, add the application code, zip up the *www* folder, and upload it to Adobe PhoneGap Build (*https://build.phonegap.com*) server, which will build the application for all supported mobile platforms. Then, download and test the application on physical devices.

The second workflow requires running a trivial installation of PhoneGap and then just letting Adobe's Build PhoneGap server do the build for various mobile platforms. The first workflow is more involved, and we'll illustrate it by showing how to use the local SDKs for iOS deployment.

> For some platforms, PhoneGap supports only local builds (for example, BlackBerry 10, Windows Phone 8), whereas builds for WebOS and Symbian can be done only remotely.

In any case, you need to install the PhoneGap software according to the instructions from the command-line interface (*http://bit.ly/1lIUZDb*) documentation. Begin by installing *Node.js*, which will also install its package manager *npm* used for installing Cordova (and the PhoneGap library). We're developing on Mac OS X, and here's the command that installs PhoneGap:

```
sudo npm install -g phonegap
```

This command installs the JavaScript file *phonegap* in */usr/local/bin* and the Cordova library with supporting files in */usr/local/lib/node_modules/phonegap*. Figure 13-2 shows a snapshot of some of the files and directories that come with PhoneGap. We've highlighted the *create.js* script, which will be used to generate the Hello World and Save The Child projects.

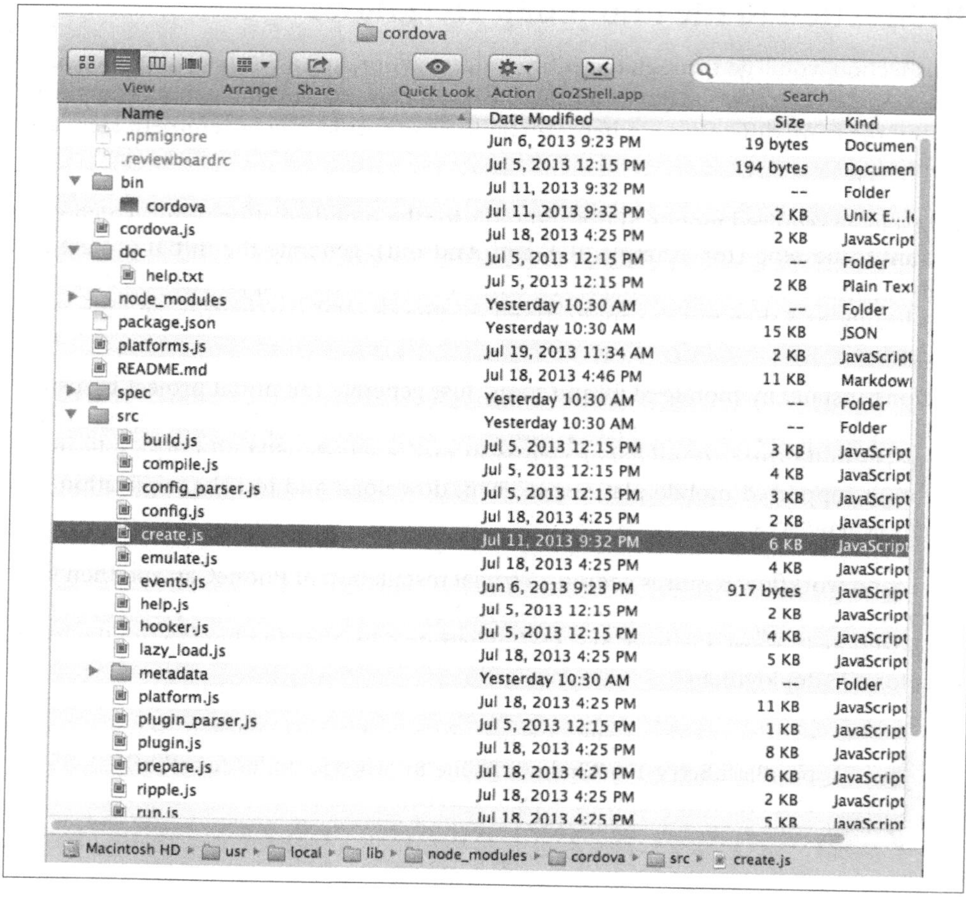

Figure 13-2. PhoneGap 3.1 installed

In this chapter, we'll be developing a sample application for the iOS platform to illustrate the most involved deployment-deployment cycle. It requires the Xcode IDE (*http:// bit.ly/TsGHAi*), which is available at Apple's App Store at no charge. After installing Xcode, open the Preferences menu and install the Command-Line Tools (CLT) from the Downloads panel. By default, Xcode comes with the latest iOS simulator (as of this writing, this is version 6.1).

Creating One More Hello World

The time has come for a PhoneGap version of Hello World. We are going to generate the initial project by using CLI as described in the same document (*http://docs.phone gap.com/en/3.0.0/guide_cli_index.md.html#The%20Command-line%20Interface*) we used for installing PhoneGap in the preceding section. We'll be running the *phonegap* script:

```
phonegap create HelloWorld com.example.hello "Hello World"
```

After generating the Hello World code with the `phonegap create` command (you might need to run it as a superuser with `sudo`), you'll see the files and directories as depicted in Figure 13-3.

 While using the command `phonegap create HelloWorld com.example.hello "Hello World"`, keep in mind that for iOS, you'll need to create a certificate, which has to be valid for application packages located under *com.example*. For more details, see the section "Testing Applications on iOS Devices" on page 529.

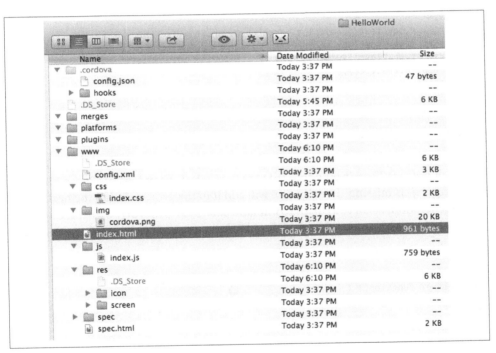

Figure 13-3. The CLI-generated project Hello World

The content of the generated *index.html* is shown in Example 13-1. It includes several meta tags instructing the browser to use the entire screen of the mobile device without allowing scaling with user's gestures. Then it includes a couple of JavaScript files in the `<script>` tags.

Example 13-1. The generated file index.html

```html
<!DOCTYPE html>
<html>
 <head>
     <meta http-equiv="Content-Type" content="text/html; charset=UTF-8" />
     <meta name = "format-detection" content = "telephone=no"/>
     <meta name="viewport" content="user-scalable=no, initial-scale=1,
           maximum-scale=1, minimum-scale=1, width=device-width;" />
     <link rel="stylesheet" type="text/css" href="css/index.css" />
     <title>Hello World</title>
 </head>
 <body>
     <div class="app">
         <h1>Apache Cordova</h1>
         <div id="deviceready">
             <p class="status pending blink">Connecting to Device</p>
             <p class="status complete blink hide">Device is Ready</p>
         </div>
     </div>
     <script type="text/javascript" src="phonegap.js"></script>
     <script type="text/javascript" src="js/index.js"></script>
     <script type="text/javascript">
         app.initialize();
     </script>
 </body>
</html>
```

Figure 13-5 is a screenshot the Hello World application running.

This HTML file includes the code to load the *phonegap.js* library and the initialization code from *index.js.*Then it calls `app.initialize()`. But if you look at Figure 13-3, the file *phonegap.js* is missing. The CLI tool will add it to the project during the next phase of code generation, when you run the command `phonegap platform add` to add specific mobile platforms to your project. Let's look at the code of *index.js* (see Example 13-2).

Example 13-2. The file index.js

```javascript
var app = {
  initialize: function() {                    ❶
     this.bind();
  },

  bind: function() {
    document.addEventListener('deviceready',   ❷
             this.deviceready, false);
  },

  deviceready: function() {

    app.report('deviceready');
  },
```

```
    report: function(id) {                          ❸

        console.log("report:" + id);

        document.querySelector('#' + id + ' .pending').className += ' hide';
        var completeElem = document.querySelector('#' + id + ' .complete');
        completeElem.className = completeElem.className.split('hide').join('');
    }
};
```

❶   This function is called when all scripts are loaded in *index.html*.

❷   The mobile OS sends the `deviceready` event to the PhoneGap application when
     it's ready to invoke native APIs.

❸   The function `report()` is called from the `deviceready` event handler. It hides
     the text `.pending` `<p>` and shows the text `.complete` `<p>` in *index.html*.
     Technically, `split('hide')` followed by `join('')` performs the removal of the
     word *hide*.

It wouldn't be too difficult to prepare such simple HTML and JavaScript files manually,
but we prefer using code generators. They are faster and less error prone.

Neither Cordova nor PhoneGap restrict you from using any HTML5
frameworks of your choice.

Prerequisites for Local Builds

If you are planning to build your application locally, install the supporting files for the
required platforms. For example, you can run the following commands from the command window (switch to the *HelloWorld* directory) to request the builds for iOS, Android, and BlackBerry:

```
phonegap install ios

phonegap install android
```

The first command will run fine, because we have Xcode in-
stalled. The second command will fail until you install the latest
Android SDK as described in the section "Installing More Local
SDKs" on page 530.

After running these commands, the initially empty directory *platforms* is filled with additional subdirectories specific to each platform. Technically, these commands generate separate Hello World projects—one per platform. Each of them will have its own *www* directory with *index.html* and *phonegap.js* that was missing during the initial project generation. Don't make any modifications in these *www* folders, because they will be regenerated each time the *install* or *run* command is run. Make the required modification in the root *www* folder.

Figure 13-4 shows the content of the *ios* folder that was generated as a result of executing the command `phonegap install ios`.

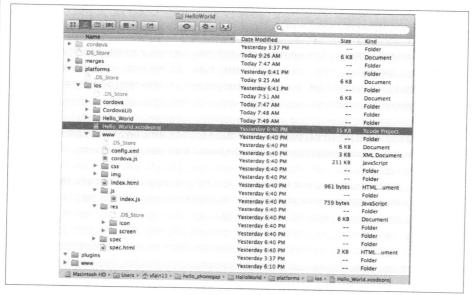

Figure 13-4. CLI-generated project for the iOS platform

Double-click the file *Hello_World.xcodeproj*, and Xcode will open it as a project. In the upper-left corner of the toolbar, click the Run button to compile the project and start it in the iOS simulator (see Figure 13-5). Note the "Device is ready" text from *index.html* (as per *index.css*, this text is blinking and is shown in uppercase).

Figure 13-5. Running Hello World in Xcode

The description of the workflow with the Build PhoneGap server follows.

Testing Applications on iOS Devices

If you want to test your application not in a simulator, but on a physical iOS device, it has to be connected to your Mac computer, enabled for deployment, and recognized by Apple. Details on *provisioning your devices for development* are described in the online iOS Developer Library (*http://bit.ly/1qqTQYV*). If you prefer shorter instructions, here's what worked for us:

1. Open a Keychain Access application on your Mac computer and create a certificate request by choosing Keychain Access→Certificate Assistant→Request a Certificate from Certificate Authority. This creates a file with the name extension *.certSigning-Request*.

2. Log in to Member Center at developer.apple.com (*https://developer.apple.com*) and create a certificate for iOS Development specifying a wildcard (an asterisk) in the Bulk name unless you want to restrict this certificate to be used only with applications that begin with a certain prefix. In this step, you'll need to upload the *.cert-SigningRequest* file created in the previous step.

3. After this certificate is created, download this file (its name ends with *.cer*), and double-click it to open it in your local keychain. Find it in the list of certificates and expand it; it should include the private key.

4. Remain in the Member Center, and create a unique application ID.

5. Finally, in the same Member Center, create a Provisioning Profile.

6. In Xcode, open the menu Window→Organizer, go to the Provisioning profiles window, and refresh it. You should see the newly created provisioning profile marked with a green bullet. A physical file with the name extension *.mobileprovision* corresponds to this profile.

7. Select your iOS device in the active scheme window and run your Hello World or other project on the connected device.

 Read Apple's App Distribution Guide (*http://bit.ly/1k5RLdh*) to learn how to distribute your iOS applications.

Installing More Local SDKs

As we stated earlier, you don't have to install SDKs locally, but if you decide to do so, consult the instructions provided by the respective mobile platform vendor. For example, BlackBerry developers can download the WebWorks SDK at developer.blackberry.com/html5/download (*http://bit.ly/1r5GK38*) as well as a BlackBerry 10 Simulator. If you haven't downloaded the Ripple emulator (for instructions, see Chapter 12), you can get it there, too.

Instructions for installing the Windows Phone SDK are available at the Windows Phone Dev Center (*http://bit.ly/1mdyGf4*).

First, get the Android SDK (*http://developer.android.com/sdk*). We are going to perform a simple installation by pressing the Download the SDK ADT Bundle for Mac button, which will download and install the Eclipse IDE with the ADT plug-in, Android SDK tools, Android Platform tools, and the Android platform. But if you already have the Eclipse IDE and prefer to install and configure the required tooling manually, follow the instructions published on this website in the section Setting Up an Existing IDE.

After downloading the bundle, unzip this file; it will create a folder with two subfolders: *sdk* and *eclipse*. Start Eclipse from the *eclipse* folder, accepting the location of the default workspace. On the top toolbar, click the plus sign (+) and open the perspective DDMS. There you can use an Android emulator while developing Android applications.

Using the Adobe PhoneGap Build Service

Instead of installing multiple SDKs for different platforms, you can use the cloud service Adobe PhoneGap Build (*https://build.phonegap.com/*), which already has installed and configured all supported SDKs and will do a build of your application for different platforms. For our example, we're going to use iOS build.

Visit build.phonegap.com (*https://build.phonegap.com*) and sign in with your Adobe or GitHub ID. If your project resides on GitHub, copy its URL to the text field shown in Figure 13-6. The other way to do a build is to compress your project's *www* directory and upload this ZIP file there.

Starting from PhoneGap 3.0, all code modifications are done in the main *www* folder of your project. During local rebuilds, all the changes are automatically replicated to each installed platform's *www* folder.

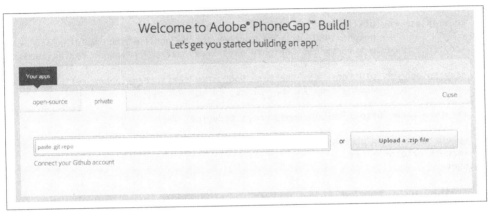

Figure 13-6. Submitting the application to PhoneGap Build server

Before zipping up Hello World's *www* directory, open and modify the file *config.xml*. The generated XML contains entries for every platform. Because we are doing a build for iOS, we remove all the lines that contain the words *android* or *blackberry*, as shown in Example 13-3.

Example 13-3. The file config.xml without Android or BlackBerry options

```
<?xml version='1.0' encoding='utf-8'?>
<widget id="com.example.hello" version="2.0.0"
        xmlns="http://www.w3.org/ns/widgets"
        xmlns:cdv="http://cordova.apache.org/ns/1.0">

    <name>Hello World</name>

    <description>
        A sample Apache Cordova application that responds to the deviceready event.
    </description>

    <author email="callback-dev@incubator.apache.org" href="http://cordova.io">
        Apache Cordova Team
```

```
</author>

<icon height="512" src="res/icon/cordova_512.png" width="512" />
<icon cdv:platform="ios" height="144" src="res/icon/cordova_ios_144.png"
        width="144" />
<cdv:splash cdv:platform="ios" height="748" src="res/screen/ipad_landscape.png"
        width="1024" />
<cdv:splash cdv:platform="ios" height="1004" src="res/screen/ipad_portrait.png"
        width="768" />
<cdv:splash cdv:platform="ios" height="1496" src="res/screen/ipad_retina_landscape.png"
        width="2048" />
<cdv:splash cdv:platform="ios" height="2008" src="res/screen/ipad_retina_portrait.png"
        width="1536" />
<cdv:splash cdv:platform="ios"
        height="320" src="res/screen/iphone_landscape.png" width="480" />
<cdv:splash cdv:platform="ios"
        height="480" src="res/screen/iphone_portrait.png" width="320" />
<cdv:splash cdv:platform="ios" height="640" src="res/screen/iphone_retina_landscape.png"
        width="960" />
<cdv:splash cdv:platform="ios" height="960" src="res/screen/iphone_retina_portrait.png"
        width="640" />

<feature name="http://api.phonegap.com/1.0/device" />

<preference name="phonegap-version" value="3.1.0" />
<access origin="*" />
</widget>
```

Specify the latest *supported* PhoneGap version in the phonegap-version attribute. The online document Using config.xml (*http://bit.ly/1icoiDw*) contains current information about supported versions and other essential properties. Let's change the phonegap-version value to 3.1.0, which is the latest version supported by PhoneGap Build at the time of this writing. You'll see other entries in *config.xml* of the Save The Child application.

Now select all the content inside the *www* folder and compress it into a ZIP file named *helloworld-build.zip*. Open the web browser, go to link:https://build.phonegap.com, click the Upload a ZIP File button, and select your local file *helloworld-build.zip*. When uploading is done, you'll see the next screen, shown in Figure 13-7.

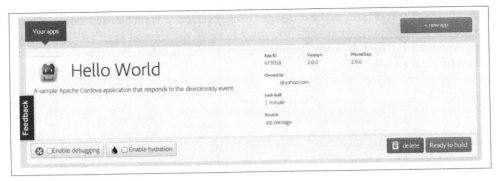

Figure 13-7. After helloworld-build.zip was uploaded

Click the Ready to build button to start the build for all available platforms. If you did everything right, after watching the wait cursor above each icon, all the builds will successfully complete, and you'll see a blue line under each button. Figure 13-8 illustrates a case when the build failed for iOS and BlackBerry platforms (the first and fourth buttons are underlined in red).

 You can create remote builds with the Adobe PhoneGap Build service by using the command line, too (*phonegap remote build*). To learn how, read the section "Build Applications Remotely" in the Phone-Gap CLI Guide (*http://bit.ly/1lIUZDb*).

Fixing the BlackBerry version of the application is not on our agenda. Refer to the Platform Guides (*http://bit.ly/1ynrUHn*) documentation that contains specific information on what has to be done to develop and deploy PhoneGap applications for each platform. We'll just take care of the iOS issue.

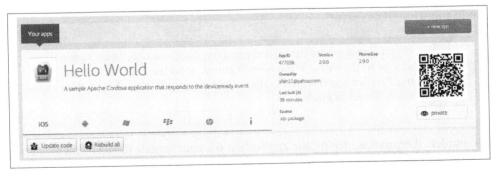

Figure 13-8. Two builds failed

After clicking the iOS button, the message "No key selected" is revealed in a drop-down box. Another error message reads, "You must provide the signing key first." The drop-down also offers an option to add the missing key. Selecting this option reveals the panel shown in Figure 13-9.

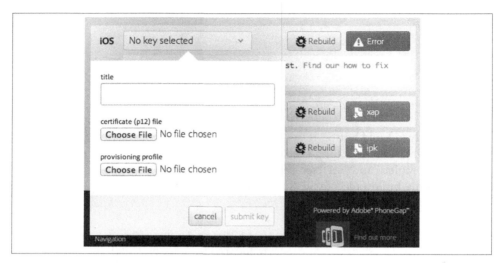

Figure 13-9. Uploading the certificate and profile

The missing key message actually means the PhoneGap server needs the provisioning profile and the certificate discussed in the section "Testing Applications on iOS Devices" on page 529. The certificate has to be in the P12 format, and you can export it into the *.p12* file from the Keychain Access program under Mac OS X. During the export, you'll assign a password to the certificate that will be required by the PhoneGap Build process. After uploading the *.p12* and *.mobileprovision* files to PhoneGap Build and unlocking the little yellow lock, rebuild the Hello World application for iOS, and it should run without any errors.

 If you forgot where the *.mobileprovision* file is located, open Xcode and go to the menu Window→Organize, open the panel Provisioning Profiles under Library, right-click the profile record, and then select Reveal in Finder.

To complete the process, deploy the application on your mobile device, which can be done by one of the following methods:

- Use the QR Code (*http://en.wikipedia.org/wiki/QR_code*) that was generated specifically for our application; it's shown on the right side of Figure 13-8. Just install a

QR Reader program on your device, scan this code, and the Hello World application will be installed on your device.

- Download the application file from link:https://build.phonegap.com to your computer and then copy it onto the mobile device. For example, to get the Android version of Hello World, just click the button displaying the Android logo, and the file *HelloWorld-debug.apk* will download to your computer. Copy this file to your Android device and enjoy the application. For the iOS version, click the button displaying the iOS logo, which will download the file *HelloWorld.ipa* on your Mac computer. Double-click this file in Finder, and it will be placed into the Application section of iTunes. Synchronize the content of iTunes with your iOS device, and Hello World will be installed there.

 Using the PhoneGap Build service is free as long as you're building public applications that have their source code hosted on a publicly accessible repository on GitHub or other hosting service. Our Hello World application is considered private because we submitted it to PhoneGap Build in a ZIP file (note the *private* tab in Figure 13-6). Only one private application at a time can be built for free by using PhoneGap Build. To build multiple private applications, you need to purchase an inexpensive subscription from Adobe. To replace one application with another, click its name, click the Settings button, and then click Delete this app.

Phew! This was the longest description of developing and deploying the Hello World application that we've ever written! We picked deployment on Apple's devices, which is the most complicated process among all mobile platforms. And we didn't even cover the process of submitting the application to the App Store (you'll read more about that in the next section)! But developing and deploying an application that has to run natively on multiple platforms is expected to be more complicated than deploying an HTML5 application in a web browser.

 The Hello World application does not use any API to access the hardware of the mobile device, and it doesn't have to. You can use PhoneGap Build simply to package any HTML5 application as a native one to be submitted to an app store.

Instead of using the JavaScript function `alert()`, you can display messages by using `navigator.notification.alert()`, and Phone-Gap will display them in the native message box of the device. The `Notification` object also supports `confirm()`, `beep()`, and `vibrate()` methods.

Distributing Mobile Applications

Mobile device manufacturers set their own rules for application distribution. Apple has the strictest rules for iOS developers.

Apple runs the iOS Developer Program (*http://bit.ly/1nmiip1*), and if you're an individual who wants to distribute iOS applications via the App Store, it will cost you $99 per year. Higher education institutions that teach iOS development can enroll in this program free of charge. The iOS Developer Enterprise program costs $299 per year. To learn the differences between these programs, and visit Apple's Developer web page (*http://bit.ly/1kRh2Y5*).

Besides being able to deploy applications in the App Store, developers can give their beta-customers an opportunity test applications even before they are accepted in the App Store. Individual developers can share their applications with up to 100 iOS devices identified by UUID (click the serial number of your device in iTunes to see it). This is called *ad hoc distribution*.

For example, after the PhoneGap Build service has built the *.ipa* file for iOS, you can make it available for installation directly on the beta-tester's device by using such services as diawi (*http://www.diawi.com*) or TestFlight (*https://testflightapp.com*). To do so, upload the *.ipa* file and its provisioning profile to one of these services and you'll get the link (a URL) to be given to your testers; the UUID of their devices must be registered with your developer's profile. To do this, log in to your account at link:https://developer.apple.com, select the section Certificates, Identifiers & Profiles, and then go to Devices and add the UUID of the iOS device to the existing list of registered devices.

Owners of the enterprise license can distribute their applications directly from their own websites.

Android developers are not restricted in distributing their application; upload the application's APK package to your corporate website and send the URL to anyone who's interested. For example, the authors of this book are creating software for the insurance industry and are offering downloads of both iOS and Android versions of the application directly from their corporate website, as shown in Figure 13-10.

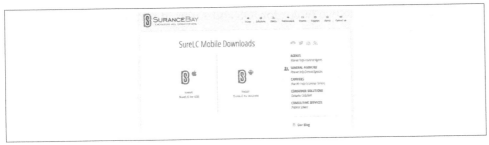

Figure 13-10. Distributing mobile applications at surancebay.com

Even though simulators and emulators can be very handy, nothing is better than testing on real devices. There are several models of iPhones that vary in terms of the CPU power and screen resolution. Ensuring that an application performs well on Android devices is a lot more challenging; this market is really fragmented in both hardware and OS use. Android emulators are not as good as those for iOS. On the other hand, an iOS emulator won't allow you to test integration with a camera. Features of real devices such as an accelerometer or gyroscope simply can't be tested with emulators. The PhoneGap emulator (*http://emulate.phonegap.com*) is based on a Ripple add-on (see Chapter 11), with it, you can subscribe to the deviceready event and emulate responses for your custom plug-ins.

You can use TestFlight (*http://testflightapp.com*) as a way to test, distribute apps, and manage provisioning profiles for iOS. HockeyApp (*http://hockeyapp.net*) is a platform for collecting live crash reports, getting feedback from your users, distributing your betas, recruiting new testers, and analyzing your test coverage.

If you've architected your hybrid application in a modularized fashion as described in Chapter 6, you'll get an additional benefit. If the code of one of the loadable modules changes, but the main application shell remains the same, there is no need to resubmit the new version of the application to the App Store or another marketplace. This can be a serious time-saver, especially on Apple devices, because you eliminate the approval process of each new version of the application.

Save The Child with PhoneGap

To demonstrate how to turn a web application into a hybrid one, we'll take the code of the jQuery Mobile version of the Save The Child application from Chapter 12. Initially, we'll just turn it into a hybrid PhoneGap application as is, without adding any native API calls. After that, we'll add to it the ability to work with a camera by using the

PhoneGap API and create two builds for iOS and Android platforms. In this exercise, we'll use PhoneGap 3.3.

 Usually, PhoneGap is mentioned in the context of building hybrid applications that need to access a native API. But you can use PhoneGap for packaging any HTML5 application as a native one, even if it doesn't use a native API.

Using PhoneGap to Package Any HTML5 Application

Let's go through the process of building and deploying the jQuery Mobile version of Save The Child in its existing form, without changing even one line of code. Here's the step-by-step procedure:

1. Generate a new PhoneGap project by using PhoneGap CLI, as we did with Hello World. This time, we won't add any specific mobile SDKs to the project, though.

2. Copy the existing HTML, CSS, JavaScript, and other resources from the jQuery Mobile Save The Child application into the directory *www* of the newly generated PhoneGap project.

3. Create platforms where we're planning to deploy our application:

   ```
   $ sudo phonegap build ios
   $ sudo phonegap build android
   ```

4. Install the following PhoneGap plug-ins that are necessary for supporting such functionality as Splashscreen, Camera, Inappbrowser, File, and File-transfer:

   ```
   $ sudo phonegap local plugin add https://git-wip-us.apache.org/repos/asf/cord
   ova-plugin-splashscreen.git_
   $ sudo phonegap local plugin add https://git-wip-us.apache.org/repos/asf/cord
   ova-plugin-camera.git_
   $ sudo phonegap local plugin add https://git-wip-us.apache.org/repos/asf/cord
   ova-plugin-inappbrowser.git_
   $ sudo phonegap local plugin add https://git-wip-us.apache.org/repos/asf/cord
   ova-plugin-file.git_
   $ sudo phonegap local plugin add https://git-wip-us.apache.org/repos/asf/cord
   ova-plugin-file-transfer.git_
   ```

5. Test the Save The Child application on the Android, iOS, or other mobile devices.

 If you don't have the SDKs for some of the platforms installed locally (as we did in step 2), you can compress the entire content of the *www* directory into a ZIP file, upload it to a PhoneGap Build server, and generate the packages for several platforms there.

Adding Camera Access to Save The Child

Charity websites help millions of people get better. When this happens, those people want to share their success stories, and maybe publish photos of themselves or their families and friends. These days, everyone uses smartphones and tablets to take pictures, and adding the ability to access the camera of a mobile device and upload photos seems like a useful feature for our Save The Child application.

We'll add camera access to the jQuery Mobile version of our application. Example 13-4 is an extract from the file *app-main.js*.

Our next goal is to use PhoneGap to access the native API of the camera of the mobile device to take photos. After that, the user should be able to upload images to the server.

For starting the device's default camera application and taking photos, PhoneGap offers the function navigator.camera.getPicture(), which takes three arguments: the name of the function handler if the photo has been successfully taken, the handler for the error, and the object with optional parameters describing the image. Details about the camera API are available in the PhoneGap documentation (*http://bit.ly/1nYyaOK*).

Example 13-4. Using the PhoneGap camera API

```
var pictureSource;
var destinationType;
var uploadedImagesPage =
                "http://savesickchid.org/ssc-phonegap/uploaded-images.php";
var photo;

function capturePhoto() {

        navigator.camera.getPicture(
            onPhotoDataSuccess, onCapturePhotoFail,
            {
            quality : 49,
            destinationType: destinationType.FILE_URI
        });
}

function onCapturePhotoFail(message) {
        alert('Capture photo failed: ' + message);
}

function onPhotoDataSuccess(imageURL) {
        var smallImage = $('#smallImage');
        photo = imageURL;
        $('#photoUploader').css('display', 'block');
    $('#ssc-photo-app-description').css('display', 'none');
        smallImage.css('display', 'block');
        smallImage.attr("src", imageURL);
        $('#largeImage').attr("src", imageURL);
```

```
$('#uploadPhotoBtn').removeClass('ui-disabled');
$('#done-msg-holder').css('display', 'none');
```

}

Depending on the options in the third argument of `getPicture()`, the image will be returned as either a Base64-encoded string, or as in our case, the URI of the file where the image is saved. If the photo was taken successfully, the application will make the `#photoUploader` button visible.

This code sample uses `quality:49` for picture quality; you can request the picture quality as a number on a scale of 1 to 100 (the larger number means better quality). Based on our experience, 49 gives a reasonable quality/file size ratio. For a current list of options, refer to the PhoneGap Camera API (*http://bit.ly/1k5SxXz*) documentation.

 For illustration purposes, the preceding code uses the JavaScript `alert()` function to report a failure. For a more robust solution, consider creating a custom way of reporting errors—for example, red borders, modal dialog boxes with images, or status bars.

The `capturePhoto()` function in Example 13-4 should be called when the user taps the button on the application's screen. Hence, we need to register an event listener for this button. Example 13-5 is a fragment of the `onDeviceReady` function that registers all required event listeners.

Example 13-5. Handling events of the button that captures photos

```
function onDeviceReady() {

    pictureSource = navigator.camera.PictureSourceType;
    destinationType = navigator.camera.DestinationType;

      $(document).on("pageshow", "#Photo-app",
        function() {

      $('#capturePhotoBtn').on('touchstart', function(e) {
         $(e.currentTarget).addClass('button-active');
      });

      $('#capturePhotoBtn').on('touchend', function(e) {
         $(e.currentTarget).removeClass('button-active');
         capturePhoto();
      });

      $('#uploadPhotoBtn').on('touchstart', function(e) {
         $(e.currentTarget).addClass('button-active');
      });
```

```
$('#uploadPhotoBtn').on('touchend', function(e) {
        $(e.currentTarget).removeClass('button-active');
        uploadPhoto(photo);
});

$('#viewGallerylBtn').on('touchend', function() {
        window.open(uploadedImagesPage, '_blank', 'location=no');
});
  }
);
```

If the user clicks the Upload Photo button, we use the `FileTransfer` object to send the image to the server-side script *upload.php* for further processing. The code to support file uploading on the client side is shown in Example 13-6.

Example 13-6. Uploading photos in JavaScript

```
function uploadPhoto(imageURI) {

        var uploadOptions = new FileUploadOptions();
        uploadOptions.fileKey = "file";
        uploadOptions.fileName = imageURI.substr(imageURI.lastIndexOf('/') + 1);
        uploadOptions.mimeType = "image/jpeg";

        uploadOptions.chunkedMode = false;

        var fileTransfer = new FileTransfer();
        fileTransfer.upload(imageURI,
                    "http://savesickchild.org/ssc-test/upload.php",
                    onUploadSuccess, onUploadFail, uploadOptions);

        var uploadedPercentage = 0;
        var uploadedPercentageMsg = "Uploading...";

        fileTransfer.onprogress = function(progressEvent) {
                if (progressEvent.lengthComputable) {
                        uploadedPercentage = Math.floor(progressEvent.loaded /
                                    progressEvent.total * 100);
                        uploadedPercentageMsg = uploadedPercentage +
                                        "% uploaded...";
                } else {
                        uploadedPercentageMsg = "Uploading...";
                }
                $.mobile.showPageLoadingMsg("b", uploadedPercentageMsg);
        };
}

function onUploadSuccess(r) {
        $.mobile.hidePageLoadingMsg();

        $('#done-msg-holder').css('display', 'block');
        $('#uploadPhotoBtn').addClass('ui-disabled');
```

```
}

function onUploadFail(error) {
        alert("An error has occurred: Code = " + error.code);
}
```

This sample code uses the PHP script located at link:http://savesickchild.org/ssc-test/
upload.php. You'll see this script in the next section. The "b" in the showPageLoa
dingMsg() function defines the jQuery Mobile theme (*http://bit.ly/1nywMkp*).
Figure 13-11 is a screenshot taken on an iPhone while the Save The Child application
was uploading a photo.

Figure 13-11. Uploading a photo

Providing Sever-Side Support for Photo Images

To support this application on the server side, we've created several PHP scripts. Of
course, you can use the programming language of your choice instead of PHP.

The PHP script *upload.php* shown in Example 13-7 uploads the image into a folder on the server and then creates two versions of this image: a thumbnail and an optimized image. The thumbnail can be used for showing the image's preview in a grid. The optimized image file will have reduced dimensions for showing the image in a mobile browser. This script also moves and saves the thumbnail, optimal, and original files in the corresponding folders on disk.

Example 13-7. The server-side script upload.php

```php
<?php

function resizeAndSave ($new_width, $new_height, $input, $output, $quality) {

        // Get new dimensions
        // assign variables as if they were an array
        list($width_orig, $height_orig) = getimagesize($input);
        $ratio_orig = $width_orig/$height_orig;

        if ($new_width/$new_height > $ratio_orig) {
            $new_width = $new_height*$ratio_orig;
        } else {
            $new_height = $new_width/$ratio_orig;
        }

        //using the GD library
        $original_image = imagecreatefromjpeg($input);

        // Resampling
        $image = imagecreatetruecolor($new_width, $new_height);
        imagecopyresampled($image, $original_image, 0, 0, 0, 0, $new_width,
                    $new_height, $width_orig, $height_orig);

        // Output
        imagejpeg($image, $output, $quality);
        imagedestroy($image);
}

$timestamp = time();
$image_name = $timestamp.'.jpg';
$path_to_original = 'upload/original/'.$image_name;

if(move_uploaded_file($_FILES["file"]["tmp_name"], $path_to_original)) {

        $thumb_width = 200;
        $thumb_height = 200;
        $thumb_output = 'upload/thumbs/'.$image_name;

        $optimum_width = 800;
        $optimum_height = 800;
        $optimum_output = 'upload/optimum/'.$image_name;

        $quality = 90;
```

```
        resizeAndSave ($thumb_width, $thumb_height, $path_to_original,
                        $thumb_output, $quality);
        resizeAndSave ($optimum_width, $optimum_height, $path_to_original,
                        $optimum_output, $quality);
}

?>
```

The script *uploaded-images.php* (see Example 13-8) serves the web page with a list showing thumbnails of uploaded images.

Example 13-8. The server-side script uploaded-images.php

```
<!DOCTYPE html>
<html lang="en">
<head>
  <meta charset="utf-8">
  <meta name="viewport" content="width=device-width,initial-scale=1">
  <title>SSC. Uploaded Images</title>
  <link rel="stylesheet" href="styles.css?<?php echo(time()); ?>">
</head>
<body>
        <ul>
        <?php
            $thumbs_dir = "upload/thumbs/";
            //get all image files with a .jpg and .png extension.
            $thumbs = glob($thumbs_dir."{*.jpg,*.png}", GLOB_BRACE);

            foreach($thumbs as $thumb){
                    $filename = basename($thumb);
                    echo('<li><a href="show-img.php?p='.$filename.'">
                      <img src="'.$thumb.'"></a></li>');
            }
        ?>
        </ul>
</body>
</html>
```

During development, you might often be changing the CSS content. The php echo(time()); in the preceding code is just a trick to prevent the web browser from performing CSS caching during local tests. The newly generated time makes the CSS URL different on each load.

The script *show-img.php* in Example 13-9 shows an optimized single image in the user's browser window.

Example 13-9. The server-side script show-img.php

```
<!DOCTYPE html>
<html lang="en">
<head>
  <meta charset="utf-8">
  <meta name="viewport" content="width=device-width,initial-scale=1">
  <title>The Uploaded Image</title>
  <link rel="stylesheet" href="styles.css?<?php echo(time()); ?>">
</head>
<body>
        <div id="wrapper"><?php $img=$_GET["p"];
                        echo('<img src="upload/optimum/'.$img.'">'); ?></div>
</body>
</html>
```

The complete source code of the PhoneGap version of the Save The Child application with camera support is available for download among the book's code samples.

Summary

Hybrid applications make it possible for you to take an HTML5-based web application, connect it with the native API of the mobile device, and package it as a native application. The selling point of using hybrids is that you can reuse existing HTML5/JavaScript expertise. In the enterprise setup, maintaining bugs in a one-language bug database is a lot easier than if you had multiple versions of the application written in different languages. Maintaining a single set of images, videos, and CSS files is yet another advantage that lowers both time to market and cost of ownership of the application.

Thorough testing of hybrid applications is a must. With the BYOD policies, even enterprise applications must be tested on a variety of mobile devices. The development manager and application owners have to agree on the list of mobile devices on which your application will be deployed first. This has to be done in writing, in the early stages of the project, and be as detailed as possible. Statements such as "The initial version of the application will run on iOS devices" is not good enough, because the difference between an iPhone 3GS and iPhone 5 is huge. The former has 256 MB of RAM, a 600-MHz CPU, and a 480 × 320–pixel screen, whereas the latter boasts 1 GB of RAM, a three-core A6 CPU running at 1.3 GHz, and a 1135 × 640–pixel display.

Hybrid applications not only give developers and users access to the native capabilities of mobile devices, they also give you the ability to distribute your HTML5 application through multiple app stores or marketplaces offered by device manufacturers.

Enterprise managers are always concerned with the availability of paid technical support. A substantial part of this chapter was about using PhoneGap, and Adobe offers various support packages (*http://bit.ly/1uFQQW2*) for purchase.

Make no mistake, though: if you want to create the fastest possible application that looks exactly like other applications on a selected mobile platform, develop it in the native language prescribed by the device manufacturer. Faster applications take less CPU power, which translates to a longer battery life. If you can't hire experts in each mobile OS, going hybrid can be a practical compromise.

## CHAPTER 14

Epilogue

Even though this book is about HTML5, the authors would rather work with compiled languages that produce applications running on virtual machines. Such software platforms are more productive for development and more predictable for deployment.

HTML5 Is Not a Rosy Place

While writing this book, we often argued about the pros and cons of switching to HTML5, and so far we are concerned that the HTML/JavaScript/CSS platform is not overly productive for developing enterprise applications just yet. We live in an era when amateurs feel comfortable creating websites, and HTML with a little JavaScript inserted provides the flexibility and customization that Microsoft Access and Excel provided in the good old PC times.

Until this day, Microsoft Excel remains the most popular application among business users in enterprises. They start Excel locally, and it has local storage that enables work in occasionally connected scenarios. Both the data and the code are physically located close to the user's heart. Microsoft Excel makes it possible for users to have their own little pieces of data and amateurish-but-working code (a.k.a. formulas) very close and personal, right on the desktop. Fine print: until their computer crashes due to viruses or other problems. No need to ask those IT prima donnas for programming favors. Business users prefer not being dependent on connectivity or some mysterious servers being slow or down. The most advanced business users even learn how to operate MS Access databases to further lessen their dependency on the IT labor force.

But there is only so much you can do with primitive tools. Visual Basic was "JavaScript" of the '90s—it had similar problems, but nevertheless had huge followings. Now the same people are doing JavaScript. If we don't break this cycle by adopting a VM common to all browsers, we are doomed to go through generation after generation of underpowered crap.

Recently, one of our clients from Wall Street sent us a list of issues to be fixed in a web application that we were developing by using the Adobe Flex framework (these applications run inside a Flash Player virtual machine). One of the requested fixes was "remove a random blink while a widget moves in the window and snaps to another one." We fixed it. What if that fix had to be implemented in HTML5 and tested in a dozen web browsers? Dealing with a single VM is easier.

You can argue that a browser's plug-in Flash Player (as well as Silverlight or a browser's Java runtime) is going away; it was crashing browsers and had security holes. But the bar for the UI of Flash-based enterprise applications is set pretty high. Business users will ask for features or fixes they are accustomed to in desktop or VM-based applications. We hope that future enterprise web applications developed with support for future HTML 6 or 7 specifications will be able to accommodate user expectations in the UI area. The time will come when HTML widgets won't blink in any of the major browsers.

We wrote this book to help people understand what HTML5 applications are about. But make no mistake: the world of HTML5 is not a peachy place in the future, preached about by educated and compassionate scientists, but rather a nasty past that is catching up and trying to transform into a usable instrument in the web application developer's toolbox.

It's the past and the future. The chances are slim that any particular vendor will win all or even 80 percent of the mobile device market. In competitive business, being able to make an application available to *only* 80% of the market is not good enough, so the chances that any particular native platform will dominate in web development are slim. HTML5 and related technologies will serve as a common denominator for mobile developers.

Check out one of the trading applications named tradeMonster (*https://www.trademon ster.com/trading/mobile-trading.jsp*). It has been developed by using HTML5 and uses the same code base for all mobile devices. The desktop version was built by using the Adobe Flex framework and runs in Flash Player's VM. Yes, they have created native wrappers to offer tradeMonster in Apple's or Google's application stores, but it's still an HTML5 application, nevertheless. Create a paper trading account (no money needed) and test their application. If you like it, consider developing in HTML5.

Enterprise IT managers need a cross-platform development and deployment platform, which HTML5 is promising to become. But take with a grain of salt all the promises of being 100 percent cross-platform made by any HTML5 framework vendor: *"With our HTML5 framework, you won't need to worry about differences in web browsers."* Yeah, right! HTML5 is not a magic bullet, and don't expect it to be. But HTML5 is for real and might become the most practical development platform for your organization today.

Dart: A Promising Language

Unfortunately, developing an application in JavaScript is not overly productive. Some people use CoffeScript or TypeScript to be converted into JavaScript for deployment. We are closely watching the progress of Google's new programming language called Dart (*http://www.dartlang.org*), which is a compiled language with an elegant and terse syntax. Dart is easy to understand for anyone who knows Java or C#. Although the compiled version of Dart code requires Dartium VM, which is currently available only in the Chromium browser, Google created the *dart2js* compiler, which turns your application code into JavaScript in seconds, so it can run in all web browsers today. Google also offers the Dart IDE with debugger and autocomplete features. You can debug Dart code in the Dart Editor while running generated JavaScript in the browser.

Dart's VM can communicate with JavaScript's VM, so if you have a portion of your application written in JavaScript, it can peacefully coexist with the Dart code. You can literally have two buttons on the web page: one written in JavaScript and the other in Dart.

The World Wide Web Consortium (W3C) published a document called "Introduction to Web Components," (*http://bit.ly/1ynGrmq*) which among other things defines recommendations on how to create custom HTML components. The existing implementation of the web UI package includes a number of UI components and facilitates defining new custom HTML elements in a declarative way. Here's an example we borrowed from the Dart website (*http://www.dartlang.org/articles/web-ui/*):

```
<element name="x-click-counter" constructor="CounterComponent" extends="div">
  <template>
    <button on-click="increment()">Click me</button>
    <span>(click count: {{count}})</span>
  </template>
  <script type="application/dart">
    import 'package:web_ui/web_ui.dart';

    class CounterComponent extends WebComponent {
      int count = 0;
      void increment(e) { count++; }
    }
  </script>
</element>
```

This code extends the web UI element div and includes a template, which uses binding. The value of the variable count is bound to <span>, and as soon as a counter increases, the web page immediately reflects its new value without the need to write any other code. The web UI package will be replaced soon with the Polymer Stack (*http://www.polymer-project.org/*) built on top of web components.

Google has ported its popular JavaScript framework AngularJS into AngularDart (*http://bit.ly/1qhydYh*). Farata Systems is working on Pint (*http://bit.ly/1jAOJ0n*), which is an open source library of AngularDart components built on top of Semantic UI (*http://semantic-ui.com/*), a library of rich UI components for developing responsive web applications.

In 2014, the popularity of Dart should increase. In this case, we'll send a new proposal to O'Reilly Media for a book titled *Enterprise Web Development with Dart*.

HTML5 Is in Demand Today

Having said that, we'd like you to know that at the time of this writing, the popular job search engine Indeed.com reports that HTML5 is the #1 job trend (*http://www.indeed.com/jobtrends*)—the fastest growing keyword found in online job postings—ahead of iOS in third place, and Android in fourth place. We'll be happy if our book helps you to master HTML5 and find an interesting and financially rewarding job!

Selected HTML5 APIs

This appendix is a brief review of selected HTML5 APIs. *HTML5* is just a commonly used term for a combination of HTML, JavaScript, CSS, and several new APIs that appeared during the last several years. Five years ago, people were using the term *Web 2.0* to define modern-looking applications. These days, HTML5 is almost a household name, and we'll go along with it. But HTML5 is about the same old development in JavaScript plus the latest advances in HTML and CSS.

This appendix is more of an overview of selected APIs that are included in the HTML5 specification—namely, Web Messaging, Web Storage, Application Cache, IndexedDB, localStorage, Web Workers, and History APIs.

 To understand the code samples included in this appendix, you must be familiar with JavaScript and some monitoring tools such as Chrome Developer Tools. We assume that you are familiar with the materials covered in the bonus online chapter.

Does Your Browser Support HTML5?

The majority of modern web browsers already support the current version of the HTML5 specification (*http://bit.ly/1oEqN0z*), which will become a World Wide Web Consortium (W3C) standard in 2014. The question is whether the users of your web application have a modern browser installed on their device. There are two groups of users who will stick to outdated browsers for some time:

- Less technically savvy people might be afraid of installing any new software on their PCs, especially people of the older generation. *"John, after the last visit of our grandson, our computer works even slower than before. Please don't let him install these new fancy browsers here. I just need my old Internet Explorer, access to Hotmail and Facebook."*

- Business users working for large corporations, where all software installations on their PCs are done by a dedicated technical support team. They say, *"We have 50,000 PCs in our firm. An upgrade from Internet Explorer version 8 to version 9 is a major undertaking. Internal users work with hundreds of web applications on a regular basis. They can install whatever browser they want, but if some of these applications won't work as expected, the users will flood us with support requests we're not qualified to resolve.* Hence, the strategy of using the lowest common denominator browser often wins.

Often web developers need to make both of these groups of users happy. Take, for example, online banking: an old couple has to be able to use your web application from their old PCs; otherwise, they will transfer their life savings to a different bank that doesn't require, say, the latest version of Firefox be installed.

Does it mean that enterprise web developers shouldn't even bother using HTML5 that's not 100 percent supported? Not at all. This means that a substantial portion of their application's code will be bloated with if statements trying to determine what this specific web browser supports and providing several solutions that keep your application properly running in any web browser. This is what makes the job of DHTML developers a lot more difficult than that of, say, Java or .NET developers who know exactly the VM where their code will work. If you don't install the Java Runtime of version 1.6, our application won't work. It's as simple as that. How about asking Java developers to write applications that will work in any runtime released during the past 10 years? No, we're not that nasty.

Do you believe it would be a good idea for Amazon or Facebook to rewrite their UIs in Java? Of course not, unless those companies want to lose most of their customers, who will be scared to death after seeing a message from a 20-step Java installer asking to access the internals of their computer. Each author of this book is a Java developer, and we love using Java—on the server side. But when it comes to the consumer-facing web applications, there are better choices.

The bottom line is that we have to learn how to develop web applications that won't require installing any new software on user's machines. In web browsers, it's DHTML, or in the modern terminology, it's the HTML5 stack.

In the unfortunate event that you need to support both new and old HTML and CSS implementations, you can use HTML5 Boilerplate (*http://html5boilerplate.com*) that is not a framework, but a template for creating a new HTML project that will support HTML5 and CSS3 elements and yet will work even in the hostile environments of the older browsers. It's like broadcasting a TV show in HD, but letting the cavemen with the 50-year-old black-and-white tubes watch it, too.

HTML Boilerplate comes with a simple way to start your project, prepackaged with solutions and workarounds offered by well-known gurus in the industry. Make no mistake, your code base might be larger than you wanted (for example, the initial CSS starts with 500 lines accommodating the old and new browsers), but it might be your safety net.

 Watch this screencast by Paul Irish (*http://bit.ly/1nutL8e*), a co-creator of HTML5 Boilerplate. You can also read the current version of the Getting started with HTML5 Boilerplate (*http://bit.ly/ TPQeSF*) on GitHub.

Handling Differences in Browsers

This appendix is about selected HTML APIs that we find important to understand in web applications. But before using any of the APIs listed here, you should check whether the versions of the web browsers you have support these APIs. The website *http:// caniuse.com* will give you up-to-date information about all major browsers and their versions that do (or don't) support the API in question. For example, to see which browsers support the Web Workers API, visit caniuse.com (*http://caniuse.com/ #search=Worker*).

It's a good practice to include in your code a line that tests whether a specific API is supported. For example, if the following `if` statement returns false, the Web Workers API is not supported and the code should fall back to a single-threaded processing mode:

```
if (window.Worker) {
    // create a Worker instance to execute your
    // script in a separate thread
) else{
        // tough luck, fallback to a single-threaded mode
}
```

Chapter 1 demonstrates the feature-detection tool *Modernizr* with which you can programmatically check whether a particular HTML5 API is supported by the browser being used:

```
if (Modernizr.Worker) {
    // create a Worker instance to execute your
    // script in a separate thread
)
```

HTML5 Web Messaging API

With HTML5 Web Messaging (*http://bit.ly/1z26wIa*), you can arrange for communication between different web pages of the same web application. More officially, it's about "communicating between browsing contexts in HTML documents." Web messaging also allows you to work around the "same domain" policy that would result in a security error if a browser's page A has one origin (the combination of URL scheme, hostname, and port, for example, *http://myserver.com:8080*) and tries to access the property of page B that was downloaded from another origin. But with the Messaging API, windows downloaded from different origins can send messages to each other.

Sending and Receiving Messages

The API is fairly straightforward: if a script in the page WindowA has a reference to WindowB where you want to send a message, invoke the following method:

```
myWindowB.postMesage(someData, targetOrigin);
```

The object referenced by myWindowB will receive an event object with the content of payload someData in the event's property data. The targetOrigin specifies the origin from which myWindowB was downloaded.

Specifying a concrete URI of the destination window in targetOrigin is the right way to do messaging. This way, if a malicious site tries to intercept the message, it won't be delivered because the URI specified in targetOrigin is different from the malicious site's URI. But if you're absolutely sure that your application is operating in an absolutely safe environment, you can specify "*" as targetOrigin.

Accordingly, myWindowB has to define an event handler for processing this external event message. For example:

```
window.addEventListener('message', myEventHandler, false);

function myEventHandler(event){
        console.log(`Received something: ` + event.data);
}
```

Communicating with an iFrame

Let's consider an example in which an HTML window creates an iFrame and needs to communicate with it. In particular, the iFrame will notify the main window that it has loaded, and the main window will acknowledge receiving this message.

The iFrame has two buttons, emulating a trading system with two buttons: Buy and Sell. When the user clicks one of these iFrame buttons, the main window has to confirm receiving the buy or sell request. Figure A-1 is a screenshot from a Chrome browser; the Developer Tools panel shows the output on the console after the iFrame is loaded and the user clicks the Buy and Sell buttons.

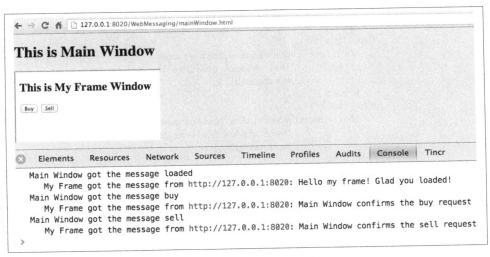

Figure A-1. Message exchange between the window and iFrame

The source code of this example is shown next. It's just two HTML files: *mainWindow.html* and *myFrame.html*. Here's the code of *mainWindow.html*:

```html
<!DOCTYPE html>
<html lang="en">

<head>
    <title>The main Window</title>
</head>

<body bgcolor="cyan">

    <h1>This is Main Window </h1>

    <iframe id="myFrame">
        <p>Some page content goes here</p>
    </iframe>

    <script type="text/javascript">
        var theiFrame;

        function handleMessage(event) {                    ❶
                console.log('Main Window got the message ' +
                                    event.data );

                // Reply to the frame here
                switch (event.data) {                      ❷

                case 'loaded':
                    theiFrame.contentWindow.postMessage(
                                    "Hello my frame! Glad you loaded! ",
```

```
                                        event.origin);   ❸
                    break;
                case 'buy':
                    theiFrame.contentWindow.postMessage(
                                "Main Window confirms the buy request ",
                                event.origin);
                    break;
                case 'sell':
                    theiFrame.contentWindow.postMessage(
                                "Main Window confirms the sell request. ",
                                event.origin);
                    break;
            }
        }

        window.onload == function() {                    ❹
            window.addEventListener('message', handleMessage, false);
            theiFrame == document.getElementById('myFrame');
            theiFrame.src == "myFrame.html";
        }

    </script>

  </body>
</html>
```

❶ This function is an event handler for messages received from the iFrame window.
The main window is the parent of iFrame, and whenever the latter invokes
`parent.postMessage()`, this event handler will be engaged.

❷ Depending on the content of the message payload (`event.data`), respond to the
sender with an acknowledgment. If the payload is `loaded`, this means that the
iFrame has finished loading. If it's buy or `sell`, this means that the corresponding
button in the iFrame has been clicked. As an additional precaution, you can
ensure that `event.origin` has the expected URI before even starting processing
received events.

❸ Although this code shows how a window sends a message to an iFrame, you can
send messages to any other window as long as you have a reference to it. For
example:

```
var myPopupWindow == window.open(...);
myPopupWindow.postMessage("Hello Popup", "*");
```

❹ On loading, the main window starts listening to messages from other windows
and loads the content of the iFrame.

To implement error processing, add a handler for the window.oner
ror property.

The code of *myFrame.html* comes next. This frame contains two buttons, Buy and Sell, but there is no business logic to buy or sell anything. The role of these buttons is just to deliver the message to the creator of the iFrame that it's time to buy or sell:

```
<!DOCTYPE html>
<html lang="en">

<body bgcolor="white">

    <h2> This is My Frame Window </h2>

    <button type="buy" onclick="sendToParent('buy')">Buy</button>
    <button type="sell" onclick="sendToParent('sell')">Sell</button>

  <script type="text/javascript">

        var senderOrigin == null;

        function handleMessageInFrame(event) {
                console.log('   My Frame got the message from ' +
                event.origin +": " + event.data);
                if (senderOrigin === null) senderOrigin == event.origin; ❶
        }

        window.onload == function(){
                window.addEventListener('message', handleMessageInFrame, false);
            parent.postMessage('loaded', "*"); ❷
        };

        function sendToParent(action){
                parent.postMessage(action,  senderOrigin);         ❸
        }

  </script>
 </body>
</html>
```

❶   When the iFrame receives the first message from the parent, store the reference to the sender's origin.

❷   Notify the parent that the iFrame is loaded. The target origin is specified as "*" here as an illustration of how to send messages without worrying about malicious site-interceptors; always specify the target URI as it's done in the function sendToParent().

❸ Send the message to the parent window when the user clicks the Buy or Sell
button.

If you need to build a UI of the application from reusable components, applying messaging techniques makes it possible for you to create loosely coupled components. Suppose that you've created a window for a financial trader. This window receives the data
push from the server, showing the latest stock prices. When a trader likes the price, he
can click the Buy or Sell button to initiate a trade. The order to trade can be implemented
in a separate window, and establishing interwindow communications in a loosely coupled manner is really important.

Applying the Mediator Design Pattern

Three years ago, O'Reilly published another book written by us titled *Enterprise Development with Flex*. In particular, it described how to apply the Mediator design pattern
to create a UI where components can communicate with one another by sending-
receiving events from the *mediator* object. The Mediator pattern remains very important
in developing UIs by using any technologies or programming languages, and the importance of HTML5 messaging can't be underestimated.

Figure A-2 is an illustration from that Enterprise Flex book. The Price panel on the left
gets the data feed about current prices of IBM stock. When the user clicks the Bid or
Ask button, the Price panel just sends the event with the relevant information (for
example, a JSON-formatted string containing the stock symbol, price, buy or sell flag,
or date). In this particular case, the window that contains these two panels serves as a
mediator. In the HTML5 realm, we can say that the Price panel invokes `parent.post`
`Message()` and shoots the message to the mediator (a.k.a. main window).

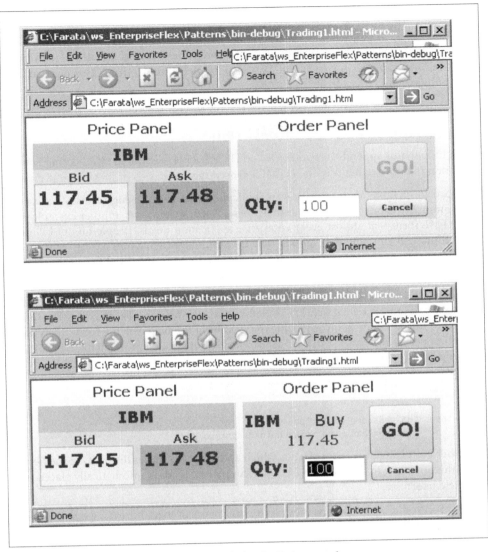

Figure A-2. Before and after the trader clicks the Price panel

The Mediator receives the message and reposts it to its other child—the Order panel— that knows how to place orders to purchase stocks. The main takeaway from this design is that the Price and Order panels do not know about each other and are communicating by sending-receiving messages to/from a mediator. Such a loosely coupled design fa- cilitates of the reuse the same code in different applications. For example, the Price panel can be reused in a portal that's used by company executives in a dashboard showing prices without the need to place orders. Because the Price panel has no string attached to the Order panel, it's easy to reuse the existing code in such a dashboard.

You can find a more advanced example of intercomponent communication techniques using the *Mediator design pattern* in "Loosely Coupled InterModule Communications with Mediator" on page 246.

HTML5 Forms

Even though this appendix is about selected HTML APIs, we should briefly bring your attention to improvements in the HTML5 `<form>` tag, too.

It's hard to imagine an enterprise web application that is not using forms. At a very minimum, the Contact Us form has to be there. A login view is yet another example of an HTML form that almost every enterprise application needs. People fill out billing and shipping forms, and they answer long questionnaires while purchasing insurance policies online. HTML5 includes some very useful additions that simplify working with forms.

We'll start with the prompts. Showing the hints or prompts right inside the input field will save you some screen space. HTML5 has a special attribute, `placeholder`. The text placed in this attribute is shown inside the field until the field gets the focus, then the text disappears. You can see the `placeholder` attribute in action in Chapter 1, in the logging part of our sample application:

```
<input id="username" name="username" type="text"
                     placeholder="username" autofocus/>

<input id="password" name="password"
          type="password" placeholder="password"/>
```

Another useful attribute is `autofocus`, which automatically places the focus in the field with this attribute. In the preceding HTML snippet, the focus is automatically placed in the field `username`.

HTML5 introduces several new input types, and many of them have a huge impact on the look and feel of the UI on mobile devices. The following are brief explanations.

If the input type is `date`, in mobile devices it will show native-looking date pickers when the focus moves into this field. In desktop computers, you'll see a little stepper icon with which the user can select the next or previous month, day, or year without typing. Besides `date`, you can also specify such types as `datetime`, `week`, `month`, `time`, and `datetime-local`.

If the input type is `email`, the main view of the virtual keyboard on your smartphone will include the @ key.

If the input type is `url`, the main virtual keyboard will include the buttons *.com*, *.*, and */*.

The tel type will automatically validate telephone numbers for the right format.

The color type opens a color picker control to select the color. After selection, the hexadecimal representation of the color becomes the value of this input field.

The input type range shows a slider, and you can specify its min and max values.

The number type shows a numeric stepper icon on the right side of the input field.

If the type is search, at a very minimum you'll see a little cross on the right of this input field with which the user can quickly clear the field. On mobile devices, bringing the focus to the search field brings up a virtual keyboard with the Search button. Consider adding the attributes placeholder and autofocus to the search field.

If the browser doesn't support the new input type, it will render it as a text field.

To validate the input values, use the required attribute. It doesn't include any logic, but won't allow submitting the form until the input field marked as required has something in it.

Using the pattern attribute, you can write a regular expression that ensures that the field contains certain symbols or words. For example, adding pattern="http:.+" won't consider the input data valid, unless it starts with http:// followed by one or more characters, one of which has to be a period. It's a good idea to include a pattern attribute with a regular expression in most of the input fields.

If you're not familiar with regular expressions, watch the presentation Demistifying Regular Expressions (*http://bit.ly/1ynI6IN*) by Lea Verou at the O'Reilly Fluent conference; it's a good primer on this topic.

Web Workers API

When you start a web browser or any other application on your computer or other device, you start *a task* or *a process*. *A thread* is a lighter process within another process. Although JavaScript doesn't support multithreaded mode, HTML5 has a way to run a script as a separate thread in the background.

A typical web application has a UI part (HTML) and a processing part (JavaScript). If a user clicks a button, which starts a JavaScript function that runs, say, for a hundred milliseconds, there won't be any noticeable delays in user interaction. But if the JavaScript runs a couple of seconds, the user experience will suffer. In some cases, the web browser will assume that the script became *unresponsive* and will offer to kill it.

Imagine an HTML5 game in which a click of a button initiates major recalculation of coordinates and repainting multiple images in the browser's window. Ideally, we'd like to parallelize the execution of UI interactions and background JavaScript functions as much as possible, so the user won't notice any delays. Another example is a CPU-intensive spellchecker function that finds errors while the user keeps typing. Parsing the JSON object is yet another candidate to be done in the background. Web workers are also good at polling server data.

In other words, use web workers when you want to be able to run multiple parallel *threads of execution* within the same task. On a multiprocessor computer, parallel threads can run on different CPUs. On a single-processor computer, threads will take turns getting *slices* of the CPU's time. Because switching CPU cycles between threads happens fast, the user won't notice tiny delays in each thread's execution, getting a feeling of smooth interaction.

Creating and Communicating with Workers

HTML5 offers a solution (*http://bit.ly/1oEqN0z*) for multithreaded execution of a script with the help of the Worker object. To start a separate thread of execution, you'll need to create an instance of a Worker object, passing it the name of the file with the script to run in a separate thread. For example:

```
var mySpellChecker == new Worker("spellChecker.js");
```

The Worker thread runs asynchronously and can't directly communicate with the UI components (that is, DOM elements) of the browser. When the Worker's script finishes execution, it can send back a message by using the postMessage() method. Accordingly, the script that created the worker thread can listen for the event from the worker and process its responses in the event handler. This event object will contain the data received from the worker in its data property; for example:

```
var mySpellChecker == new Worker("spellChecker.js");
    mySpellChecker.onmessage == function(event){

        // processing the worker's response
        document.getElementById('myEditorArea').textContent == event.data;
    };
```

You can use an alternative and preferred JavaScript function addEventListener() to assign the message handler:

```
var mySpellChecker == new Worker("spellChecker.js");
    mySpellChecker.addEventListener("message", function(event){

        // processing the worker's response
        document.getElementById('myEditorArea').textContent == event.data;
    });
```

On the other hand, the HTML page can also send any message to the worker, forcing it to start performing its duties (for example, starting the spellchecking process):

```
mySpellChecker.postMessage(wordToCheckSpelling);
```

The argument of `postMessage()` can contain any object, and it's being passed by value, not by reference.

Inside the worker, you also need to define an event handler to process the data sent from outside. To continue the previous example, *spellChecker.js* will have inside it the code that receives the text to check, performs the spellcheck, and returns the result:

```
self.onmesage == function(event){

    // The code that performs spellcheck goes here

        var resultOfSpellCheck == checkSpelling(event.data);

    // Send the results back to the window that listens
    // for the messages from this spellchecker

        self.postMessage(resultOfSpellCheck);
};
```

If you want to run certain code in the background repeatedly, you can create a wrapper function (for example, `doSpellCheck()`) that internally invokes `postMesage()` and then gives this wrapper to `setTimeout()` or `setInterval()` to run every second or so: `var timer == setTimout(doSpellCheck, 1000);`.

If an error occurs in a worker thread, your web application will get a notification in the form of an event, and you need to provide a function handler for `onerror`:

```
mySpellChecker.onerror == function(event){
    // The error handling code goes here
};
```

Dedicated and Shared Workers

If a window's script creates a worker thread for its own use, we call it *a dedicated worker*. A window creates an event listener, which gets the messages from the worker. On the other hand, the worker can have a listener, too, to react to the events received from its creator.

A *shared worker* thread can be used by several scripts, as long as they have the same origin. For example, if you want to reuse a spellchecker feature in several views of your web application, you can create a shared worker as follows:

```
var mySpellChecker == new SharedWorker("spellChecker.js");
```

Another use case is funneling all requests from multiple windows to the server through a shared worker. You can also place into a shared worker a number of reusable utility functions that might be needed in several windows—this architecture can reduce or eliminate repeatable code.

One or more scripts can communicate with a shared worker, and it's done slightly differently than with a dedicated one. Communication is done through the `port` property, and the `start()` method has to be invoked to be able to use `postMessage()` the first time:

```
var mySpellChecker == new SharedWorker("spellChecker.js");
    mySpellChecker.port.addEventListener("message", function(event){
        document.getElementById('myEditorArea').textContent == event.data;
    });
    mySpellChecker.port.start()
```

The event handler becomes connected to the `port` property, and now you can post the message to this shared worker by using the same `postMessage()` method:

```
    mySpellChecker.postMessage(wordToCheckSpelling);
```

Each new script that will connect to the shared worker by attaching an event handler to the port results in incrementing the number of active connections that the shared worker maintains. If the script of the shared worker invokes `port.postMessage("Hello scripts!")`, all listeners that are connected to this port will get it.

 If a shared thread is interested in processing the moments when a new script connects to it, add an event listener to the `connect` event in the code of the shared worker.

If a worker needs to stop communicating with the external world, it can call `self.close()`. The external script can kill the worker thread by calling the method `terminate()`; for example:

```
    mySpellChecker.terminate();
```

 Because the script running inside the `Worker` thread doesn't have access to the browser's UI components, you can't debug these scripts by printing messages onto the browser's console with `con sole.log()`. In the bonus online chapter, we used the Firefox browser for development, but now we'll illustrate how to use Chrome Browser Developer Tools, which includes the *Workers* panel (*http://bit.ly/1r5J4qR*) that can be used for debugging code that's launched in worker threads. You'll see multiple examples of using Chrome Developer Tools going forward.

For more detailed coverage of web workers, read *Web Workers* by Ido Green (O'Reilly).

 When the user switches to another page in a browser and the current web page loses focus, you might want to stop running processes that would unnecessarily use CPU cycles. To catch this moment, use the Page Visibility API (*http://mzl.la/1q9FiLm*).

The WebSocket API

For many years, web applications were associated with HTTP as the main protocol for communication between web browsers and servers. HTTP is a request-response–based protocol that adds hundreds of bytes to the application data being sent between browsers and servers. WebSocket is not a request-response, but a bidirectional, full-duplex, socket-based protocol, which adds only a couple of bytes (literally) to the application data. WebSocket might become a future replacement for HTTP, but web applications that require near-real-time communications (for example, financial trading applications, online games, or auctions) can benefit from this protocol today. The authors of this book believe that WebSocket is so important that we dedicated Chapter 8 to this API. In this section, we just introduce this API very briefly.

This is how the WebSocket workflow proceeds:

- A web application tries to establish a socket connection between the client and the server, using HTTP only for the initial handshake.
- If the server supports WebSocket, it switches the communication protocol from HTTP to a socket-based protocol.
- From this point on, both client and server can send messages in both directions simultaneously (that is, in full-duplex mode).
- This is not a request-response model, because both the server and the client can initiate the data transmission that enables the real server-side push.
- Both the server and the client can initiate disconnects, too.

This is a very short description of what the WebSocket API is about. We encourage you to read Chapter 8 and find a use for this great API in one of your projects.

Offline Web Applications

A common misconception about web applications is that they are useless without an Internet connection. Everyone knows that you can write native applications in a way that they have everything they need installed on your device's data storage—both the application code and the data storage. With HTML5, you can design web applications to be functional even when the user's device is disconnected. The offline version of a web application might not offer full functionality, but certain functions can still be available.

Prerequisites for Developing Offline Web Applications

To be useful in disconnected mode, an HTML-based application needs to have access to local storage on the device so data entered by the user in the HTML windows can be saved locally, further synchronized with the server when a connection becomes available. Think of a salesperson of a pharmaceutical company visiting medical offices and trying to sell new pills. What if a connection is not available at a certain point? She can still use her tablet to demonstrate the marketing materials, and more important, collect data about this visit and save it locally. When the Internet connection becomes available again, the web application should support automatic or manual data synchronization so the information about the sales activity is stored in a central database.

There are two main prerequisites for building offline web applications. You need local storage, and you need to ensure that the server sends only raw data to the client, with no HTML markup (see Figure A-3). So all these server-side frameworks that prepare data heavily sprinkled with HTML markup should not be used. For example, the frontend should be developed in HTML/JavaScript/CSS, the backend in your favorite language (Java, .NET, PHP), and the JSON-formatted data should be sent from the server to the client and back.

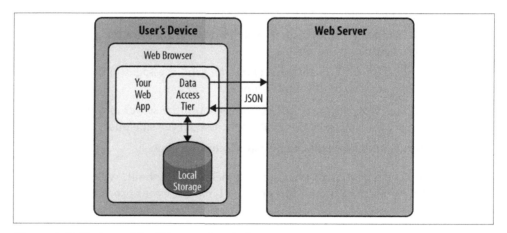

Figure A-3. Design with offline use in mind

The business logic that supports the client's offline functionality should be developed in JavaScript and run in the web browser. Although most of the business logic of web applications remains on the server side, the web client is not as thin as it used to be in legacy HTML-based applications. The client becomes fatter and it can have state.

It's a good idea to create a data layer in your JavaScript code that will be responsible for all data communications. If the Internet connection is available, the data layer will make requests to the server; otherwise, it will get the data from the local storage.

Application Cache API

First, an application's cache is not related to the web browser's cache. Its main reason for existence is to facilitate creating applications that can run even without an Internet connection available. The user will still go to her browser and enter the URL, but the trick is that the browser will load previously saved web pages from the local *application cache*. So even if the user is not online, the application will start anyway.

If your web application consists of multiple files, you need to specify which ones have to be present on the user's computer in offline mode. A file called *cache manifest* is a plain-text file that lists these resources.

Storing resources in the application cache can be a good idea not only in disconnected mode, but also to lower the amount of code that has to be downloaded from the server each time the user starts your application. Here's an example of the file *mycache.manifest*, which includes one CSS file, two JavaScript files, and one image to be stored locally on the user's computer:

```
CACHE MANIFEST
/resources/css/main.css
/js/app.js
/js/customer_form.js
/resources/images/header_image.png
```

The manifest file has to start with the line CACHE MANIFEST and can be optionally divided into sections. The landing page of your web application has to specify an explicit reference to the location of the manifest. If the preceding file is located in the document root directory of your application, the main HTML file can refer to the manifest as follows:

```
<!DOCTYPE html>
<html lang="en" manifest="/mycache.manifest">
...
</html>
```

The web server must serve the manifest file with a MIME type text/cache-manifest, and you need to refer to the documentation of your web server to see how to make a configuration change so that all files with the extension *.manifest* are served as text/cache-manifest.

On each subsequent application load, the browser makes a request to the server and retrieves the manifest file to see whether it has been updated, in which case it reloads all previously cached files. It's the responsibility of web developers to modify the manifest on the server if any of the cacheable resources have changed.

Is Your Application Offline?

Web browsers have a `boolean` property, `window.navigator.onLine`, which should be used to check for a connection to the Internet. The HTML5 specification states that *"The navigator.onLine attribute must return false if the user agent will not contact the network when the user follows links or when a script requests a remote page (or knows that such an attempt would fail), and must return true otherwise."* Unfortunately, major web browsers deal with this property differently, so you need to do a thorough testing to see if it works as expected with the browser you care about.

To intercept changes in the connectivity status, you can also assign event listeners to the `online` and `offline` events. For example:

```
window.addEventListener("offline", function(e) {
    // The code to be used in the offline mode goes here
});

window.addEventListener("online", function(e) {
    // The code to synchronize the data saved in the offline mode
    // (if any) goes here
});
```

You can also add the `onoffline` and `ononline` event handlers to the `<body>` tag of your HTML page or to the `document` object. Again, test the support of these events in your browsers.

What if the browser's support of the offline/online events is still not stable? You'll have to write your own script that will periodically make an Ajax call (see Chapter 2) trying to connect to a remote server that's always up and running—for example, google.com. If this request fails, it's a good indication that your application is disconnected from the Internet.

Options for Storing Data Locally

In the past, web browsers could store their own cache and application's cookies only on the user's computer.

Cookies are small files (up to 4 KB) that a web browser automatically saves locally if the server's `HTTPResponse` includes them. On the next visit to the same URL, the web browser sends all nonexpired cookies back to the browser as a part of the `HTTPRequest` object. Cookies are used for arranging HTTP session management and shouldn't be considered a solution for setting up a local storage.

HTML5 offers a lot more advanced solutions for storing data locally, namely:

Web Storage (http://www.w3.org/TR/webstorage)
Offers local storage for long-term data storage and session storage for storing a single data session.

IndexedDB (http://www.w3.org/TR/IndexedDB)
A NoSQL database that stores key-value pairs.

There is another option worth mentioning: Web SQL Database (*http://bit.ly/1mzIOcc*). The specification was based on the open source SQLite database. But the work on this specification has stopped and future versions of browsers might not support it. That's why we don't discuss Web SQL Database in this book.

By the end of 2013, local and session storage were supported by all modern web browsers. Web SQL Database is not supported by Firefox and Internet Explorer and most likely never will be. IndexedDB is the web storage format of the future, but Safari doesn't support it yet, so if your main development platform is iOS, you might need to stick to Web SQL Database. Consider using a polyfill for indexedDB by using a Web SQL API called IndexedDBShim (*http://bit.ly/1lZrNfP*).

To get the current status of support for HTML5 features, visit can-iuse.com and search for the API you're interested in.

Although web browsers send cookies to the web server, they don't send the data saved in local storage. The saved data is used only on the user's device. Also, the data saved in the local storage never expires. A web application has to programmatically clean up the storage, if need be, which will be illustrated next.

Web Storage Specification APIs

With `window.localStorage` or `window.sessionStorage` (a.k.a. web storage), you can store any objects on the local disk as key-value pairs. Both objects implement the `Stor age` interface. The main difference between the two is that the lifespan of the former is longer. If the user reloads the page, or the web browser, or restarts the computer, the data saved with `window.localStorage` will survive, whereas the data saved via `win dow.sessionStorage` won't.

Another distinction is that the data from `window.localStorage` is available for any page loaded from the same origin as the page that saved the data. With `window.session Storage`, the data is available only to the window or a browser's tab that saved it.

localStorage API

Saving the application state is the main use of local storage. Coming back to the use-case of the pharmaceutical salesperson, in offline mode, you can save the name of the person she talked to in a particular medical office and the notes about the conversation that took place. For example:

```
localStorage.setItem('officeID', 123);
localStorage.setItem('contactPerson', 'Mary Lou');
localStorage.setItem('notes', 'Drop the samples of XYZin on 12/15/2013');
```

Accordingly, to retrieve the saved information, you'd need to use the method `getItem()`:

```
var officeID == localStorage.getItem('officeID');
var contact == localStorage.getItem('contactPerson');
var notes == localStorage.getItem('notes');
```

These code samples are fairly simple because they store single values. In real-life scenarios, we often need to store multiple objects. What if our salesperson visits several medical offices and needs to save information about all these visits in the web store? For each visit, we can create a key-value combination, where a *key* includes the unique ID (for example, office ID), and the *value* is a JavaScript object (for example, Visit) turned into a JSON-formatted string (see Chapter 2 for details) by using `JSON.stringify()`.

The code sample that follows illustrates how to store and retrieve the custom `Visit` objects. Each visit to a medical office is represented by one instance of the `Visit` object. To keep the code simple, we haven't included any HTML components. The JavaScript functions are invoked and print their output on the browser's console:

```
<!doctype html>
<html>
<head>
  <meta charset="utf-8" />
  <title>My Today's Visits</title>
</head>
<body>
```

```
<script>

  // Saving in local storage
  var saveVisitInfo == function (officeVisit) {
        var visitStr=JSON.stringify(officeVisit);              ❶
        window.localStorage.setItem("Visit:"+ visitNo, visitStr);
        window.localStorage.setItem("Visits:total", ++visitNo);

        console.log("saveVisitInfo: Saved in local storage " + visitStr);
  };

// Reading from local storage
  var readVisitInfo == function () {

    var totalVisits == window.localStorage.getItem("Visits:total");
    console.log("readVisitInfo: total visits " + totalVisits);

    for (var i == 0; i < totalVisits; i++) {       ❷

        var visit == JSON.parse(window.localStorage.getItem("Visit:" + i));
        console.log("readVisitInfo: Office " + visit.officeId +
                    " Spoke to " + visit.contactPerson + ": " + visit.notes);
  }
  };

// Removing the visit info from local storage
var removeAllVisitInfo == function (){              ❸
        var totalVisits == window.localStorage.getItem("Visits:total");

        for (i == 0; i < totalVisits; i++) {
            window.localStorage.removeItem("Visit:" + i);
    }

    window.localStorage.removeItem("Visits:total");

    console.log("removeVisits: removed all visit info");
}

    var visitNo == 0;

    // Saving the first visit's info
    var visit == {                                  ❹
        officeId: 123,
        contactPerson: "Mary Lou",
        notes: "Drop the samples of XYZin on 12/15/2013"
    };
    saveVisitInfo(visit);

    // Saving the second visit's info              ❺
    visit == {
        officeId: 987,
        contactPerson: "John Smith",
```

```
            notes: "They don't like XYZin - people die from it"
        };
        saveVisitInfo(visit);

        // Retrieving visit info from local storage
        readVisitInfo();                                    ❻

        // Removing all visit info from local storage
        removeAllVisitInfo();                               ❼

        // Retrieving visit info from local storage - should be no records
        readVisitInfo();                                    ❽

    </script>
  </body>
</html>
```

❶ The function saveVisitInfo() uses a JSON object to turn the visit object into a string with JSON.stringify(). It then saves this string in local storage. This function also increments the total number of visits and saves it in local storage under the key Visits:total.

❷ The function readVisitInfo() gets the total number of visits from local storage and then reads each visit record, re-creating the JavaScript object from the JSON string by using JSON.parse().

❸ The function removeAllVisitInfo() reads the number of visit records, removes each of them, and then removes the Visits:total, too.

❹ Creates and saves the first visit record.

❺ Creates and saves the second visit record.

❻ Reads saved visit info.

❼ Removes saved visit info. To remove the entire content that was saved for a specific origin, call the method localStorage.clear().

❽ Rereads visit info after removal.

Figure A-4 shows the output on the console of Chrome Developer Tools. Two visit records were saved in local storage, and then they were retrieved and removed from storage. Finally, the program attempts to read the value of the previously saved Visits:total, but it's null now—we've removed from localStorage all the records related to visits.

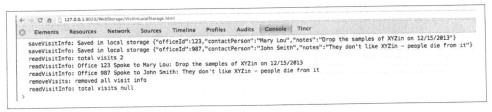

```
saveVisitInfo: Saved in local storage {"officeId":123,"contactPerson":"Mary Lou","notes":"Drop the samples of XYZin on 12/15/2013"}
saveVisitInfo: Saved in local storage {"officeId":987,"contactPerson":"John Smith","notes":"They don't like XYZin - people die from it"}
readVisitInfo: total visits 2
readVisitInfo: Office 123 Spoke to Mary Lou: Drop the samples of XYZin on 12/15/2013
readVisitInfo: Office 987 Spoke to John Smith: They don't like XYZin - people die from it
removeVisits: removed all visit info
readVisitInfo: total visits null
```

Figure A-4. Chrome's console after running the Visits sample

If you are interested in intercepting the moments when the content of local storage gets modified, listen to the DOM `storage` event, which carries the old and new values and the URL of the page whose data is being changed.

Another good example of a use case when `locaStorage` becomes handy is when a user is booking airline tickets by using more than one browser's tab.

sessionStorage API

The `sessionStorage` life is short; it's available for a web page only while the browser stays open. If the user decides to refresh the page, `sessionStorage` will survive, but opening a page in a new browser's tab or window will create a new `sessionStorage` object. Working with session storage is fairly straightforward; for example:

```
sessionStorage.setItem("userID","jsmith");

var userID == sessionStorage.getItem("userID");
```

Chrome Developer Tools includes the tab Resources that allows browsing the local or session storage if a web page uses it. For example, Figure A-5 shows the storage used by *cnn.com*.

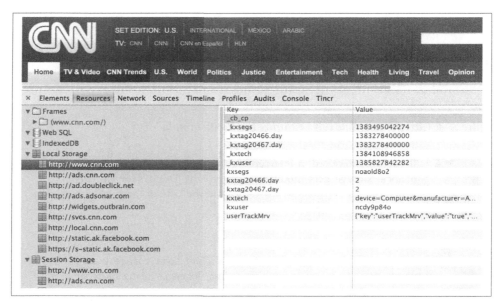

Figure A-5. Browsing local storage in Chrome Developer Tools

localStorage and sessionStorage commonalities

Both `localStorage` and `sessionStorage` are subject to the same-origin policy, meaning that saved data is available only for web pages that come from the same host, from the same port, and via the same protocol.

Both `localStorage` and `sessionStorage` are browser-specific. For example, if the web application stores data from Firefox, that data won't be available if the user opens the same application from Safari.

The APIs from the Web Storage specification are simple to use, but their major drawbacks are that they don't give you a way to structure the stored data, you always have to store strings, and the API is synchronous, which can cause delays in the user interaction when your application accesses the disk.

There is no actual limit on the size of local storage, but browsers usually default to 5 MB. If the application tries to store more data than the browser permits, the `QUOTA_EX CEEDED_ERR` exception will be thrown—always use the try-catch blocks when saving data.

Even if the user's browser allows increasing this setting (for example, via the *about:config* URL in Firefox), access to such data might be slow. Consider using the File API (*http://www.w3.org/TR/FileAPI/*) or IndexedDB, which are introduced in the next section.

Introduction to IndexedDB

Indexed Database API (*http://www.w3.org/TR/IndexedDB*) (a.k.a., IndexedDB) is a solution based on the NoSQL database. As with the `Storage` interface, IndexedDB stores data as key-value pairs, but it also offers transactional handling of objects. IndexedDB creates indexes of the stored objects for fast retrieval. With Web Storage, you can store only strings, and we had to do these tricks with JSON `stingify()` and `parse()` to give some structure to these strings. With IndexedDB, you can directly store and index regular JavaScript objects.

Using IndexedDB, you can access data asynchronously, so UI freezes won't occur while accessing large objects on disk. You make a request to the database and define the event handlers that should process the errors or the result when ready. IndexedDB uses DOM events for all notifications. Success events don't bubble, whereas error events do.

Users will have the feeling that the application is responsive, which wouldn't be the case if you were saving several megabytes of data with the Web Storage API. Similar to Web Storage, access to the IndexedDB databases is regulated by the same-origin policy.

> In the future, web browsers might implement synchronous IndexedDB API (*http://mzl.la/1iSK0fT*) to be used inside web workers.

Because not every browser supports IndexedDB yet, you can use Modernizr (see Chapter 1) to detect whether your browser supports it. If it does, you still might need to account for the fact that browser vendors name the IndexedDB-related object differently. To be on the safe side, at the top of your script include statements to account for the prefixed vendor-specific implementations of `indexedDB` and related objects:

```
var medicalDB == {};   // just an object to store references

medicalDB.indexedDB == window.indexedDB || window.mozIndexedDB
      || window.msIndexedDB || window.webkitIndexedDB ;
if (!window.indexedDB){
    // this browser doesn't support IndexedDB
} else {
    medicalDB.IDBTransaction == window.IDBTransaction ||
                        window.webkitIDBTransaction;
    medicalDB.IDBCursor == window.IDBCursor || window.webkitIDBCursor;
    medicalDB.IDBKeyRange == window.IDBKeyRange || window.webkitIDBKeyRange;
}
```

In this code snippet, the `IDBKeyRange` (*http://mzl.la/TwkJMs*) is an object that allows you to restrict the range for the continuous keys while iterating through the objects. `IDBTransaction` (*http://mzl.la/1iSK4Mq*) is an implementation of transaction support.

IDBCursor (*http://mzl.la/1vnNbMO*) is an object that represents a cursor for traversing over multiple objects in the database.

IndexedDB doesn't require you to define a formal structure of your stored objects; any JavaScript object can be stored there. Not having a formal definition of a database scheme is an advantage compared to relational databases, where you can't store data until the structure of the tables is defined.

Your web application can have one or more databases, and each can contain one or more *object stores*. Each object store will contain similar objects (for example, one stores the salesperson's visits, whereas another stores upcoming promotions).

Every object that you are planning to store in the database has to have one property that plays a role similar to a primary key in a relational database. You have to decide whether you want to maintain the value in this property manually, or use the autoIncrement option, where the values of this property will be assigned automatically. Coming back to our Visits example, you can either maintain the unique values of the officeId on your own or create a surrogate key that will be assigned by IndexedDB. The current generated number to be used as a surrogate keys never decreases, and starts with the value of 1 in each object store.

As with relational databases, you create indexes based on the searches that you run often. For example, if you need to search on the contact name in the Visits store, create an index on the property contactPerson of the Visit objects. Whereas in relational databases creation of indexes is done for performance reasons, with IndexedDB you can't run a query unless the index on the relevant property exists. The following code sample shows how to connect to an existing object or create a new object store Visits in a database called Medical_DB:

```
var request == medicalDB.indexedDB.open('Medical_DB');        ❶

request.onsuccess == function(event) {        ❷
    var myDB == request.result;

};

request.onerror == function (event) {        ❸
    console.log("Can't access Medical_DB: " + event.target.errorCode);
};

request.onupgradeneeded == function(event){ ❹
    event.currentTarget.result.createObjectStore ("Visits",
        {keypath: 'id', autoIncrement: true});
};
```

❶ The browser invokes the method `open()`, asynchronously requesting to establish the connection with the database. It doesn't wait for the completion of this request, and the user can continue working with the web page without any delays or interruptions. The method `open()` returns an instance of the `IDBRequest` (*http://mzl.la/1rPytxR*) object.

❷ When the connection is successfully obtained, the `onsuccess` function handler will be invoked. The result is available through the `IDBRequest.result` property.

❸ Error handling is done here. The event object given to the `onerror` handler will contain the information about the error.

❹ The `onupgradeneeded` handler is the place to create or upgrade the storage to a new version. This is explained next.

 There are several scenarios to consider while deciding whether you need to use the `autoIncrement` property with the store key. Kristof Degrave described in the article "Indexed DB: To provide a key or not to provide a key." (*http://bit.ly/1lJjjEN*)

Object stores and versioning

In the world of traditional DBMS servers, when the database structure has to be modified, the DBA will do this upgrade, the server will be restarted, and the users will work with the *new version* of the database. With IndexedDB, it works differently. Each database has a version, and when the new version of the database (for example, `Medical_DB`) is created, `onupgradeneeded` is dispatched, which is where object store(s) are created. But if you already had object stores in the older version of the database, and they don't need to be changed, there is no need to re-create them.

After successful connection to the database, the version number is available in the `IDBRequest.result.version` property. The starting version of any database is 1.

The method `open()` takes a second parameter: the database version to be used. If you don't specify the version, the latest one will be used. The following line shows how the application's code can request a connection to version 3 of the database `Medical_DB`:

```
var request == indexedDB.open('Medical_DB',3);
```

If the user's computer already has the `Medical_DB` database of one of the earlier versions (1 or 2), the `onupgradeneeded` handler will be invoked. The initial creation of the database is triggered the same way—the absence of the database also falls under the "upgrade is needed" case, and the `onupgradeneeded` handler has to invoke the `createObjectStore()` method. If an upgrade is needed, `onupgradeneeded` will be invoked before the `onsuccess` event.

The following code snippet creates a new or initial version of the object store `Visits`, requesting autogeneration of the surrogate keys named `id`. It also creates indexes to allow searching by office ID, contact name, and notes. Indexes are updated automatically, as soon as the web application makes any changes to the stored data. If you couldn't create indexes, you'd be able to look up objects only by the value of the key.

```
request.onupgradeneeded == function(event){    ❶
    var visitsStore ==
        event.currentTarget.result.createObjectStore ("Visits",
            {keypath='id',
            autoIncrement: true
            });

    visitsStore.createIndex("officeIDindex", "officeID",
                                        {unique: true});
    visitsStore.createIndex("contactsIndex", "contactPerson",
                                        {unique: false});
    visitsStore.createIndex("notesIndex", "notes",
                                        {unique: false});
};
```

Note that while creating the object store for visits, we could have used a unique property `officeID` as a keypath value by using the following syntax:

```
var visitsStore ==
    event.currentTarget.result.createObjectStore ("Visits",
        {keypath='officeID'});
```

The `event.currentTarget.result` (as well as `IDBRequest.result`) points at the instance of the `IDBDatabase` object, which has a number of useful properties such as `name`, which contains the name of the current database, and the array `objectStore Names`, which has the names of all object stores that exist in this database. Its property `version` has the database version number. If you'd like to create a new database, just call the method `open()`, specifying a version number that's higher than the current one.

To remove the existing database, call the method `indexedDB.deleteDatabase()`. To delete the existing object store, invoke `indexedDB.deleteObjectStore()`.

 IndexedDB doesn't offer a secure way of storing data. Anyone who has access to the user's computer can get a hold of the data stored in IndexedDB. Do not store any sensitive data locally. Always use the secure HTTPS protocol with your web application.

Transactions

A *transaction* is a logical unit of work. Executing several database operations in one transaction guarantees that the changes will be committed to the database only if all operations finished successfully. If at least one of the operations fails, the entire transaction will be rolled back (undone). IndexDB supports three transaction modes: `re` `adonly`, `readwrite`, and `versionchange`.

To start any manipulations of the database, you have to open a transaction in one of these modes. The `readonly` transaction (the default one) allows multiple scripts to read from the database concurrently. This statement might raise a question: why would the user need concurrent access to his local database if he's the only user of the application on his device? The reason is that the same application can be opened in more than one tab, or by spawning more than one worker thread that needs to access the local database. The `readonly` mode is the least restrictive mode, and more than one script can open a `readonly` transaction.

If the application needs to modify or add objects to the database, open the transaction in `readwrite` mode; only one script can have the transaction open on any particular object store. But you can have more than one `readwrite` transaction open at the same time on different stores. And if the database/store/index creation or upgrade has to be done, use `versionchange` mode.

When a transaction is created, you should assign listeners to its `complete`, `error`, and `abort` events. If the `complete` event is fired, the transaction is automatically committed; manual commits are not supported. If the `error` event is dispatched, the entire transaction is rolled back. Calling the method `abort()` will fire the `abort` event and will roll back the transaction, too.

Typically, you should open the database and in the `onsuccess` handler create a transaction. Then, open a transaction by calling the method `objectStore()` and perform data manipulations. In the next section, you'll see how to add objects to an object store by using transactions.

Modyfying the object store data

The following code snippet creates a transaction that allows updates of the store `Vis` `its` (you could create a transaction for more than one store) and adds two `visit` objects by invoking the method `add()`:

```
request.onsuccess == function(event) {          ❶
    var myDB == request.result;

  var visitsData == [{                          ❷
        officeId: 123,
        contactPerson: "Mary Lou",
        notes: "Drop the samples of XYZin on 12/15/2013"
    },
    {
        officeId: 987,
        contactPerson: "John Smith",
        notes: "They don't like XYZin - people die from it"
```

```
    }];

    var transaction == myDB.transaction(["Visits"],
                                        "readwrite");   ❸
    transaction.oncomplete == function(event){
        console.log("All visit data have been added);
    }

    transaction.onerror == function(event){
        // transaction rolls back here
        console.log("Error while adding visits");
    }

    var visitsStore == transaction.objectStore("Visits");   ❹

      for (var i in visitsData) {
        visitsStore.add(visitsData[i]);         ❺
      }
```

❶ The database opened successfully.

❷ Create a sample array of `visitsData` to illustrate adding more than one object
to an object store.

❸ Open a transaction for updates and assign listeners for success and failure. The
first argument is an array of object stores that the transaction will span (only
`Visits` in this case). When all visits are added, the `complete` event is fired and
the transaction commits. If adding any visit fails, the `error` event is dispatched
and the transaction rolls back.

❶❹ Get a reference to the object store `visits`.

❺ In a loop, add the data from the array `visitsData` to the object store `Visits`.

 In the preceding code sample, each object that represents a visit has
a property `notes`, which is a string. If later you decide to allow storing more than one note per visit, just turn the property `notes` into an
array in your JavaScript; no changes in the object stores is required.

The method `put()` allows you to update an existing object in a record store. It takes two
parameters: the new object and the key of the existing object to be replaced; for example:

```
    var putRequest == visitsStore.put({officeID: 123, contactName: "Mary Lee"}, 1);
```

To remove all objects from the store, use the method `clear()`. To delete an object, specify
its ID:

```
    var deleteRequest == visitsStore.delete(1);
```

You can browse the data from your IndexedDB database in Chrome Developer Tools under the tab Resources (see Figure A-5).

Retrieving the data

IndexedDB doesn't support SQL. You'll be using cursors to iterate through the object store. First, you open the transaction. Then, you invoke openCursor() on the object store. While opening the cursor, you can specify optional parameters like the range of object keys you'd like to iterate and the direction of the cursor movement: IDBCursor.PREV or IDBCursor.NEXT. If none of the parameters is specified, the cursor will iterate all objects in the store in ascending order. The following code snippet iterates through all Visit objects, printing just contact names:

```
var transaction == myDB.transaction(["visits"], "readonly");
var visitsStore == transaction.objectStore("Visits");

visitsStore.openCursor().onsuccess == function(event){
    var visitsCursor == event.target.result;
    if (visitsCursor){
        console.log("Contact name: " + visitCursor.value.contactPerson);
        visitsCursor.continue();
    }
}
```

If you want to iterate through a limited key range of objects, you can specify the from-to values. The next line creates a cursor for iterating the first five objects from the store:

```
var visitsCursor == visitsStore.openCursor(IDBKeyRange.bound(1, 5));
```

You can also create a cursor on indexes. This makes it possible to work with sorted sets of objects. In one of the earlier examples we created an index on officeID. Now we can get a reference to this index and create a cursor on the specified range of sorted office IDs, as in the following code snippet:

```
var visitsStore == transaction.objectStore("visits");
var officeIdIndex == visitsStore.index("officeID");

officeIdIndex.openCursor().onsuccess == function(event){
    var officeCursor == event.target.result;
    // iterate through objects here
}
```

To limit the range of offices to iterate through, you could open the cursor on the officeIdIndex differently. Suppose that you need to create a filter to iterate the offices with numbers between 123 and 250. This is how you can open such a cursor:

```
officeIdIndex.openCursor(IDBKeyRange.bound(123, 250, false, true);
```

The `false` in the third argument of bound() means that 123 should be included in the range, and the `true` in the fourth parameter excludes the object with officeID=250 from the range. The methods lowerbound() and upperbound() are other variations of the method bound()—consult the online documentation (*http://bit.ly/1nR65dF*) for details.

If you need to fetch just one specific record, restrict the selected range to only one value by using the method only():

```
contactNameIndex.openCursor(IDBKeyRange.only("Mary Lou"));
```

Runninng the sample code

Let's bring together all of the previous code snippets into one runnable HTML file. While doing this, we'll be watching the script execution in the Chrome Developer Tools panel. We'll do it in two steps. The first version of this file will create a database of a newer version than the one that currently exists on the user's device. Here's the code that creates the database Medical_DB with an empty object store Visits:

```
<!doctype html>
<html>
<head>
  <meta charset="utf-8" />
  <title>My Today's Visits With IndexedDB</title>
</head>
<body>
  <script>
    var medicalDB == {};   // just an object to store references
    var myDB;

  medicalDB.indexedDB == window.indexedDB || window.mozIndexedDB
        || window.msIndexedDB || window.webkitIndexedDB ;
  if (!window.indexedDB){
    // this browser doesn't support IndexedDB
  } else {
    medicalDB.IDBTransaction == window.IDBTransaction ||
                            window.webkitIDBTransaction;
    medicalDB.IDBCursor == window.IDBCursor || window.webkitIDBCursor;
    medicalDB.IDBKeyRange == window.IDBKeyRange || window.webkitIDBKeyRange;
  }

  var request == medicalDB.indexedDB.open('Medical_DB', 2);   ❶

      request.onsuccess == function(event) {
          myDB == request.result;
    };

  request.onerror == function (event) {
      console.log("Can't access Medical_DB: " + event.target.errorCode);
    };
```

```
request.onupgradeneeded == function(event){
    event.currentTarget.result.createObjectStore ("Visits",
        {keypath:'id', autoIncrement: true});        ❷
};

    </script>
  </body>
</html>
```

❶   This version of the code is run when the user's computer already had a database
     Medical_DB: initially we invoke open() without the second argument. Running
     the code and specifying 2 as the version causes invocation of the callback onup
     gradeneeded even before onsuccess is called.

❷   Create an empty object store Visits.

Figure A-6 shows a screenshot from the Chrome Developer Tools at the end of processing the success event. Note the Watch Expression section on the right. The name
of the database is Medical_DB, its version number is 2, and the IDBDatabase property
objectStoreNames shows that there is one object store named Visits.

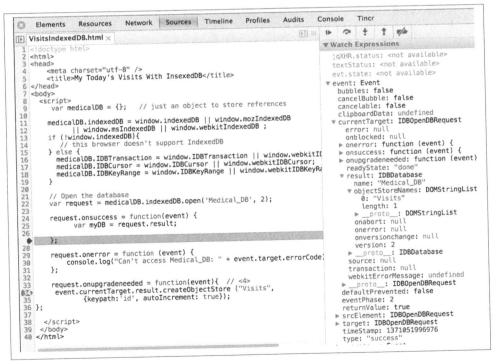

Figure A-6. Chrome's console after running the Visits sample

The next version of our sample HTML file populates the object store `Visits` with some data and then iterates through all the `Visit` objects and displays the values of their properties on the console:

```html
<!doctype html>
<html>
<head>
  <meta charset="utf-8" />
  <title>My Today's Visits With IndexedDB</title>
</head>
<body>
  <script>
    var medicalDB == {};    // just an object to store references
    var myDB;

medicalDB.indexedDB == window.indexedDB || window.mozIndexedDB
      || window.msIndexedDB || window.webkitIndexedDB ;
if (!window.indexedDB){
    // this browser doesn't support IndexedDB
} else {
  medicalDB.IDBTransaction == window.IDBTransaction ||
                          window.webkitIDBTransaction;
  medicalDB.IDBCursor == window.IDBCursor || window.webkitIDBCursor;
  medicalDB.IDBKeyRange == window.IDBKeyRange || window.webkitIDBKeyRange;
}

var request == medicalDB.indexedDB.open('Medical_DB', 2);

  request.onsuccess == function(event) {
      myDB == request.result;

var visitsData == [{
        officeId: 123,
        contactPerson: "Mary Lou",
        notes: "Drop the samples of XYZin on 12/15/2013"
    },
    {
        officeId: 987,
        contactPerson: "John Smith",
        notes: "They don't like XYZin - people die from it"
    }];

  var transaction == myDB.transaction(["Visits"],
                              "readwrite");
  transaction.oncomplete == function(event){
    console.log("All visit data have been added.");

    readAllVisitsData();                      ❶
  }

  transaction.onerror == function(event){
    // transaction rolls back here
```

```
        console.log("Error while adding visits");
      }

      var visitsStore == transaction.objectStore("Visits");

      visitsStore.clear();                              ❷

    for (var i in visitsData) {
       visitsStore.add(visitsData[i]);
    }

    };

  request.onerror == function (event) {
      console.log("Can't access Medical_DB: " + event.target.errorCode);
  };

  request.onupgradeneeded == function(event){
     event.currentTarget.result.createObjectStore ("Visits",
          {keypath:'id', autoIncrement: true});
};

function readAllVisitsData(){
  var readTransaction == myDB.transaction(["Visits"], "readonly");

    readTransaction.onerror == function(event){
        console.log("Error while reading visits");
    }

    var visitsStore == readTransaction.objectStore("Visits");

  visitsStore.openCursor().onsuccess == function(event){   ❸
        var visitsCursor == event.target.result;

        if (visitsCursor){
          console.log("Contact name: " +
                      visitsCursor.value.contactPerson +
                      ", notes: " +
                      visitsCursor.value.notes);
          visitsCursor.continue();                          ❹
      }
    }
  }
  }
   </script>
   </body>
</html>
```

❶ After the data store is populated and the transaction is commited, invoke the
method to read all the objects from the Visits store.

❷ Remove all the objects from the store `Visits` before populating it with the data from the array `VisitsData`.

❸ Open the cursor to iterate through all visits.

❹ Move the cursor's pointer to the next object after printing the contact name and notes in the console.

Figure A-7 shows the screenshot from Chrome Developer Tools when the debugger stops in `readAllVisitsData()`, directly after reading both objects from the `Visits` store. The console output is shown at the bottom. Note the content of `visitsCursor` on the right. The cursor is moving forward (the `next` direction), and the `value` property points at the object at the cursor. The `key` value of the object is 30. It's autogenerated, and on each run of this program, you'll see a new value, because we clean the store and reinsert the objects, which generates the new keys.

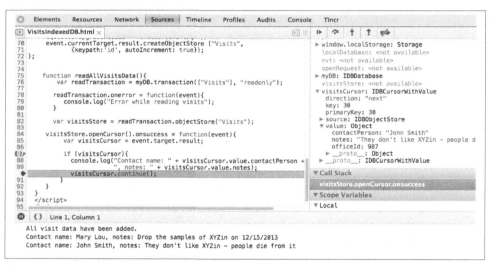

Figure A-7. Chrome's console after reading the first Visit object

This concludes our brief introduction to IndexedDB. Those of you who have experience working with relational databases might find the querying capabilities of IndexedDB rather limited compared to powerful relational databases such as Oracle or MySQL. On the other hand, IndexedDB is quite flexible. With it, you can store and look up any JavaScript objects without worrying about creating a database schema first. At the time of this writing, there are no books dedicated to IndexedDB. For up-to-date information, refer to the IndexedDB online documentation (*http://mzl.la/1x4Sh3l*) at Mozilla Developer Network.

The History API

To put this simply, the History API (*http://bit.ly/1q9FWIS*) is about ensuring that the Back/Forward buttons on the browser toolbar can be controlled programmatically. Each web browser has the `window.history` object. The History API is not new to HTML5. The `history` object has been around for many years, with methods like `back()`, `forward()`, and `go()`. But HTML5 adds new methods, `pushState()` and `replaceState()`, with which you can modify the browser's address bar without reloading the web page.

Imagine a single-page application (SPA) that has a navigational menu to open various views, based on the user's interaction. Because these views represent URLs loaded by making Ajax calls from your code, the web browser still shows the original URL of the home page of your web application.

A perfect user always navigates your application by using the menus and controls you provided, but what if she clicks the Back button of the web browser? If the navigation controls aren't changing the URL in the browser's address bar, the browser obediently will show the web page that the user has visited before, even launching your application, which is most likely not what she intended to do. Using the History API, you can create more fine-grained bookmarks that define a specific state within the web page.

 Not writing any code that would process clicks on the Back and Forward buttons is the easiest way to frustrate your users.

Modifying the Browser's History by Using pushState()

Imagine that you have a customer-management application with the URL *http://myapp.com*. The user clicks the menu item Get Customers, which makes an Ajax call loading the customers. You can programmatically change the URL on the browser's address line to *http://myapp.com/customers* without asking the web browser to make a request to this URL. You do this by invoking the `pushState()` method.

The browser will just remember that the current URL is *http://myapp.com/customers*, while the previous was *http://myapp.com*. So pressing the Back button changes the address back to *http://myapp.com*, and not some unrelated web application. The Forward button will also behave properly, as per the history chain set by your application.

The `pushState()` takes three arguments (the values from the first two might be ignored by some web browsers):

- The application-specific state to be associated with the current view of the web page

- The title of the current view of the web page.
- The suffix to be associated with the current view of the page. It will be added to the address bar of the browser:

```
<head>
        <meta charset="utf-8">
        <title>History API</title>
</head>
<body>
 <div id="main-container">

        <h1>Click on Link and watch the address bar...</h1>

    <button type="button" onclick="whoWeAre()">Who we are</button>  ❶

    <button type="button" onclick="whatWeDo()">What we do</button>

 </div>

 <script>

    function whoWeAre(){
        var locationID== {locID: 123,                               ❷
                        uri: '/whoweare'};

        history.pushState(locationID,'', 'who_we_are' );            ❸
    }

    function whatWeDo(){
        var actionID== {actID: 123,                                 ❹
                        uri: '/whatwedo'};

        history.pushState(actionID,'', 'what_we_do' );              ❺
    }
 </script>
 </body>
</html>
```

❶ On a click of the button, call the event handler function. Call pushState() to modify the browser's history. Other processing, such as making an Ajax request to the server, can be done in whoWeAre(), too.

❷ Prepare the custom state object to be used in server-side requests. The information about *who we are* depends on the location ID.

❸ Call pushState() to remember the customer ID, and add the suffix / who_we_are to serve as a path to the server-side RESTful request. The page title is empty; the History API currently ignores it.

❹ Prepare the custom state object to be used in server-side requests. The information about *what we do* depends on customer ID.

❺ Call `pushState()` to remember the customer ID, and add the suffix /what_we_do to serve as a path to the server-side RESTful request. The page title is empty; the History API currently ignores it.

This preceding sample is a simplified example and would require more code to properly form the server request, but our goal here is just to clearly illustrate the use of the History API.

Figure A-8 depicts the view after the user clicks the Who We Are button. The URL now shows *http://127.0.0.1:8020/HistoryAPI/who_we_are*, but keep in mind that if you try to reload the page while this URL is shown, the browser will give you a Not Found error, and rightly so. There is no resource that represents the URL that ends with *who_we_are*—it's just the name of the view in the browser's history.

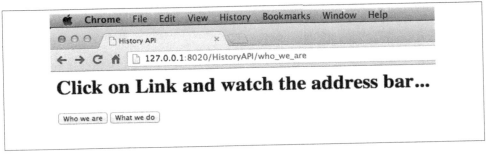

Figure A-8. Testing pushState()

Using `replaceState()`, you can technically change history. We are talking about the browser's history, of course.

Processing the popstate Event

But changing the URL when the user clicks the Back or Forward button is just half of the job to be done. The content of the page has to be refreshed, accordingly. The browser dispatches the event `window.popstate` whenever the browser's navigation history changes either on initial page load, as a result of clicking the Back/Forward buttons, or by invoking `history.back()` or `history.forward()`.

Your code has to include an event handler function that will perform the actions that must be done whenever the application gets into the state represented by the current suffix (for example, make a server request to retrieve the data associated with the state *who_we_are*). The `popstate` event will contain a copy of the history's entry state object. Let's add the following event listener to the `<script>` part of the code sample from the previous section:

```
addEventListener('popstate',function (evt){
  console.log(evt);
});
```

Figure A-9 depicts the view of the Chrome Developer Tools when the debugger stops in the listener of the **popstate** event after the user clicks the Who We Are and then the What We Do buttons, and then the browser's Back button. On the righthand side, you can see that the event object contains the **evt.state** object with the right values of **locID** and **uri**. In real-world scenarios these values could have been used in, say, an Ajax call to the server to re-create the view for the location ID 123.

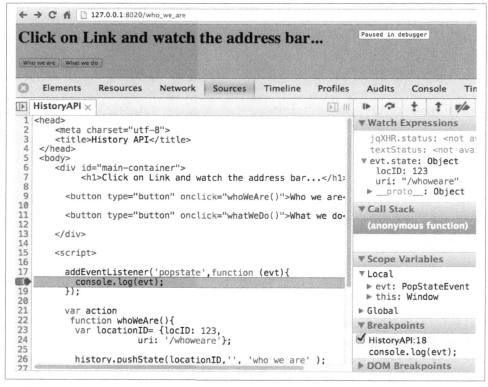

Figure A-9. Monitoring popState with Chrome Developers Tool

If you run into a browser that doesn't support the HTML5 History API, consider using the History.js (*https://github.com/browserstate/ History.js*) library.

Custom Data Attributes

We've included this sidebar in this appendix, even though it's not an API. But we're talking about HTML here and don't want to miss this important feature of the HTML5 specification: you can add to any HTML tag any number of custom nonvisible attributes (*http://bit.ly/9Udecy*) as long as they start with `data-` and have at least one character after the hyphen. For example, this is absolutely legal in HTML5:

```
<ol>
 <li data-phone="212-324-6656">Mary</li>
 <li data-phone="732-303-1234">Anna</li>
 ...
</ol>
```

Behind the scenes, a custom framework can find all elements that have the `data-phone` attribute and generate additional code for processing the provided phone number. If this example doesn't impress you, go to Chapter 10, where you'll learn how to use jQuery Mobile. The creators of this library use these `data-` attributes in a very smart way.

Summary

In this appendix, you were introduced to a number of useful HTML5 APIs. You know how to check whether a particular API is supported by your web browser. But what if you are one of many enterprise developers who must use an Internet Explorer version earlier than 10.0? Google used to offer a nice solution: Google Chrome Frame (*http://www.google.com/chromeframe*), which was a plug-in for Internet Explorer.

Users had to install Chrome Frame on their machines, and web developers just needed to add the following line to their web pages:

```
<meta http-equiv="X-UA-Compatible" content="chrome=1" />
```

After that, the web page rendering would be done by Chrome Frame, whereas your web application would run in Internet Explorer. Unfortunately, Google decided to discontinue supporting the Chrome Frame project as of January 2014. It is recommending to prompt the user of your application to upgrade the web browser, which might not be something users are willing to do. But let's hope for the best.

Running Code Samples and IDE

The code samples used in this book are available on GitHub (*http://bit.ly/1uFXI5u*)—they are grouped by chapters. If a chapter has code samples, look for the directory with the respective name.

Technically, you don't have to use any integrated development environment (IDE) to run code examples (except the CDB example from Chapter 5). Just open the main file in a web browser, and off you go. But using an IDE will make you more productive.

Choosing an IDE

Selecting an IDE that supports JavaScript is a matter of personal preference. Because there is no compilation stage and most of your debugging will be done by using the web browser tools, picking a text editor that supports syntax highlighting is all that most developers need. For example, there is an excellent text editor called Sublime Text 2 (*http://www.sublimetext.com*). Among many programming languages, this editor understands the keywords of HTML, CSS, and JavaScript, and it offers not only syntax highlighting, but also context-sensitive help, and autocomplete.

If you are coming from a Java background, the chances are that you are familiar and comfortable with the Eclipse IDE. In this case, install the Eclipse plug-in VJET (*http://eclipse.org/vjet*) for JavaScript support.

Oracle's IDE NetBeans 7.3 (*http://wiki.netbeans.org/HTML5*) and above support HTML5 and JavaScript development. NetBeans includes a JavaScript debugger that allows your code to connect to the web browser while debugging inside the IDE.

If you prefer Microsoft technologies, they offer excellent JavaScript support in Visual Studio 2012.

Appcelerator offers a free Eclipse-based Aptana Studio 3 IDE (*http://aptana.com*). Aptana Studio comes with an embedded web server so that you can test your JavaScript code without the need to start any additional software.

The authors of this book like and recommend using the WebStorm IDE (*http://www.jetbrains.com/webstorm*) from JetBrains. In addition to smart context-sensitive help, autocomplete, and syntax highlighting, WebStorm offers HTML5 templates, and a code coverage feature that identifies code fragments that haven't been tested.

Running Code Samples in WebStorm

The WebStorm IDE is pretty intuitive to use. If you've never used it before, refer to its Quick Start Guide (*http://www.jetbrains.com/webstorm/quickstart*). When you first start WebStorm, on the Welcome screen, select the option Open Directory. Then, select the directory where you downloaded the samples of a specific book chapter. For example, after opening code samples from Chapter 1, the WebStorm IDE might look as shown in Figure B-1.

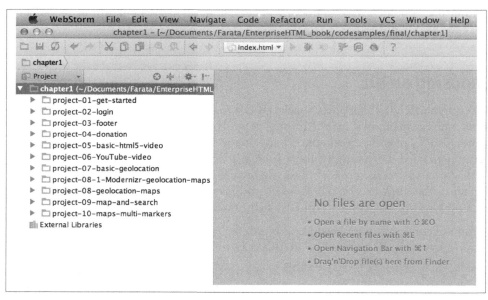

Figure B-1. Code samples from Chapter 1 displayed in WebStorm

If you want to create a new HTML or JavaScript file in WebStorm, just select the appropriate menu option under File→New. For example, selecting the menu File→New→HTML File creates the following file with the basic markup:

```
<!DOCTYPE html>
<html>
  <head>
    <title></title>
  </head>

  <body>

  </body>
</html>
```

WebStorm comes with a simple internal web server (*http://blog.jetbrains.com/webide/ 2013/03/built-in-server-in-webstorm-6/*). Right-click the HTML file that you want to open (for example, *index.html*) and choose Open in Browser. WebStorm's internal server will serve the file to the browser.

For example, if WebStorm opens the directory *chapter1*, as in Figure B-1, you'll see the following URL in your web browser: *http://localhost:63342/chapter1/project-01-get-started*.

 You can configure in WebStorm the port number of the internal web server via Preferences→Debugger→JavaScript→Built-in server port.

Using Two IDEs: WebStorm and Eclipse

Although we prefer using WebStorm for JavaScript development, we have to use Eclipse for some Java-related projects. In such cases, we create a project in WebStorm pointing at the *WebContent* directory of our Eclipse project. This way, we still enjoy very smart context-sensitive help offered by WebStorm, and all code modifications become immediately visible in the Eclipse project.

To open the content of the Eclipse *WebContent* directory in WebStorm, choose File→Open Directory and point it at the *WebContent* directory of your Eclipse project.

Mac users can also do it another way:

1. Create a script to launch WebStorm from the command line. To do this, start WebStorm and choose Tools→Create Launcher Script. Agree with defaults offered by the pop-up window shown in Figure B-2 or select another directory located in the PATH system variable of your computer. This creates a script named *wstorm*, and you'll be able to start WebStorm from a command line.

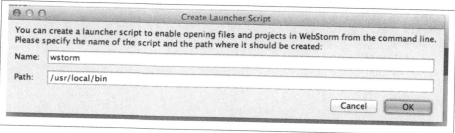

Figure B-2. Creating the launch script for WebStorm

2. Open a terminal window and switch to the directory *WebStorm* of your Eclipse project. Type the command `wstorm .` to open WebStorm with the entire content of your WebContent project. So you'll be doing all JavaScript development in Web-Storm, and the Java-related coding in Eclipse while using the same WebContent directory.

Such a complex setup looks like overkill, but we are talking about enterprise development, for which you might have to jump through some hoops to create a convenient working environment for yourself. Besides, you do it only once.

Index

Symbols

$() constructor, 90
\<canvas\> tag, 73
\<form\> tag, 560
\<link\> tags, 375
\<script\> tag, 219
\<svg\> tag, 73
@media rules, 375

A

AAAR (arrange-act-assert-reset), 260
Above the Fold design, 427
absolute sizing, 381
access tokens, 343
ActiveX controls, 54
ad hoc distribution, 536
Adobe Flex framework, 548
Adobe PhoneGap Build Service, 530
Ajax (Asynchronous JavaScript and XML)
    asynchronous nature of, 98
    benefits/drawbacks of, 59
    development of, 53
    displaying errors, 61
    jQuery shorthand methods, 99
    loading data with XMLHTTPRequest, 67
    steps for data retrieval, 56
    using jQuery with, 97
ajaxSetup(), 98

AngularJS, 124
Apache Benchmark, 257
Apache Ripple emulator, 411
Apache Tomcat, 150
App Store, 517
application cache, 567
application store, 517
application-level security, 336, 352
    (see also security)
arrays
    using, 66
assertions, 259
Asynchronous Module Definition (AMD)
    benefits of, 229
    drawbacks of, 229
    main functions, 227
    writing AMD modules, 238
Atmosphere framework, 309
auction application
    loading modules on demand, 315
    messaging protocol, 330
    traffic monitoring with Chrome, 322
    traffic monitoring with Wireshark, 326
authentication/passwords
    biometric checks, 338
    brute-force attack, 340
    encryption, 340
    re-authentication, 340
    RSA SecurID, 337

We'd like to hear your suggestions for improving our indexes. Send email to index@oreilly.com.

typography, 367

U

unbind(), 97
unit testing, 255
Universal Module Definition (UMD), 230
user acceptance testing (UAT), 254
user interface (UI)
    component life cycle, 146
    containers in Sencha Touch, 473
    data input on mobile devices, 356
    designing (see web design)
    events in Sencha Touch, 477
    multi- and single-page templates, 408
User-Agent attribute, 361

V

V8 JavaScript engine, 188
validation
    of forms using regular expressions, 27
    of forms with jQuery Validator plug-in, 114
    server-side validation, 349
    white list/black list, 353
Validator plug-in, 114
values, in localStorage API, 570
vector graphics images, 23, 73
vendor prefixes, 22
video
    adding HTML5 video element, 30
    adding in Ext JS, 173
    adding YouTube videos, 33
    in Sencha Touch, 505
    responsive display of, 403
VideoPanel.js, 173
viewport concept, 378
VJET plug-in, 593

W

watch task, 192
Web 2.0 (see HTML5)
Web Application Penetration Testing, 351
web applications
    anatomy of, 54
    vs. native, 518
web design
    Balsamiq Mock-ups, 6
    creating first mockups, 7

for enterprise applications, 3, 547
for mobile devices (see mobile devices)
geolocation support
    browser feature detection, 43
    code for, 37
    for desktop applications, 35
    integration with Google Maps, 40
    multiple map markers, 50
    search, 48
Mobile First approach, 4
prototypes
    clickable logos/anchor tags, 18
    CSS styling of, 13, 21
    determining resource size, 52
    donate section, 24
    footer section, 22
    JavaScript code on home page, 18
    JavaScript code placement, 21
    layout, 16
    running code examples in WebStorm, 12
    single-page applications, 12
    user ID/password, 20
video
    adding HTML5 video element, 30
    adding YouTube videos, 33
working with a designer, 4, 7
Web Messaging
    applying Mediator design pattern, 558
    communicating with iFrames, 554
    overview of, 554
    sending/receiving messages, 554
web pages
    bringing external data to (see Ajax; JSON)
    single-page applications (SPA), 12
Web SQL Database, 569
Web Storage, 569
Web Workers
    communicating with, 562
    dedicated and shared, 563
    overview of, 561
WebP format, 404
WebSocket protocol
    advantages of, 295
    application-level message format, 310
    applications based on, 295
    auction application using, 315–333
    client-side API
        connection termination, 307
        data frames, 307

About the Authors

Yakov Fain is a cofounder of the Farata Systems and SuranceBay companies. The first company provides consulting services in the field of enterprise web development and ecommerce, and the second one is a software product company, which develops software for the insurance industry. A leader of the Princeton Java Users Group, he has authored several technical books and dozens of articles on software development. Yakov received the title of Java Champion, which has been presented to only 150 people worldwide. Yakov's video course "Intro to Java" is available for free on YouTube (*http://bit.ly/UFrVHb*). Yakov also holds an MS in applied math. You can reach him at *yfain@faratasystems.com* and follow him on Twitter (*http://twitter.com/yfain*).

Dr. Victor Rasputnis is a cofounder of the Farata Systems and SuranceBay companies. He spends most of his time providing architectural design, implementation management, and mentoring to companies migrating to ecommerce technologies with Hybris. Victor has authored several books and dozens of technical articles. He holds a PhD in computer science. You can reach Victor at *vrasputnis@faratasystems.com*.

Anatole Tartakovsky is a cofounder of the Farata Systems and SuranceBay companies. He spent more than 25 years developing system and business software. In the last 15 years, his focus has been on creating frameworks and business applications for dozens of enterprises ranging from Walmart to Wall Street firms. Anatole has authored a number of books and articles on Ajax, Flex, XML, the Internet, and client-server technologies. He holds an MS in mathematics. You can reach Anatole at *atartakovsky@farata-systems.com*.

Viktor Gamov is a senior software engineer at Farata Systems. He consults financial institutions and startups in design and implementation of web applications with HTML5 and Java. A co-organizer of the Princeton Java Users Group, Viktor is passionate about writing code and about the open source community. He holds an MS in computer science. You can reach Viktor at *viktor.gamov@faratasystems.com* and follow him on Twitter (*http://twitter.com/gamussa*).

Colophon

The animal on the cover of *Enterprise Web Development* is a roseate spoonbill (*Platalea ajaja*), and is a resident breeder in South America, often found east of the Andes, around the coast of Central America, the Caribbean, Mexico, and the Gulf Coast. The roseate spoonbill was found to be a close relative of yellow-billed spoonbills, both descended of the other four spoonbill species.

With a wingspan averaging around 47–52 inches, these spoonbills are often about 28–34 inches long. Immature birds have white, feathery heads with pale pink plumage and a yellow or pinkish bill. Adults have a bare greenish head that turns golden when breeding with a white neck, back, and breast. The rest of their bodies are a deep pink, aside from a grey bill. Similar to the American flamingo, the pink color of the roseate spoonbill is diet-derived, coming mostly from the carotenoid pigment canthaxanthin.

This species feeds by wading through shallow fresh or coastal waters, swinging its bill from side to side. They are gregarious and often feed in groups. Its spoon-shaped bill helps to sift through the mud for crustaceans, aquatic insects, frogs, newts, and very small fish.

They nest in shrubs or trees, and lay from two to five whitish eggs with brown markings. There is not much information available about the roseate spoonbill's predators, however, nestlings are sometimes killed by turkey vultures, bald eagles, raccoons, and fire ants.

The cover image source is unknown. The cover fonts are URW Typewriter and Guardian Sans. The text font is Adobe Minion Pro; the heading font is Adobe Myriad Condensed; and the code font is Dalton Maag's Ubuntu Mono.

Have it your way.

Get even more for your money.

Join the O'Reilly Community, and register the O'Reilly books you own. It's free, and you'll get:

- $4.99 ebook upgrade offer
- 40% upgrade offer on O'Reilly print books
- Membership discounts on books and events
- Free lifetime updates to ebooks and videos
- Multiple ebook formats, DRM FREE
- Participation in the O'Reilly community
- Newsletters
- Account management
- 100% Satisfaction Guarantee

Signing up is easy:

1. Go to: oreilly.com/go/register
2. Create an O'Reilly login.
3. Provide your address.
4. Register your books.

Note: English-language books only

To order books online:
oreilly.com/store

For questions about products or an order:
orders@oreilly.com

To sign up to get topic-specific email announcements and/or news about upcoming books, conferences, special offers, and new technologies:
elists@oreilly.com

For technical questions about book content:
booktech@oreilly.com

To submit new book proposals to our editors:
proposals@oreilly.com

O'Reilly books are available in multiple DRM-free ebook formats. For more information:
oreilly.com/ebooks

O'REILLY®

CPSIA information can be obtained at www.ICGtesting.com
Printed in the USA
BVOW10s0331080714

358081BV00002B/2/P

9 781449 356811